CIB
Study Text

Associateship

Management

First edition 1993
Second edition October 1995

ISBN 0 7517 1043 1 (previous edition 0 7517 1012 1)

British Library Cataloguing-in-Publication Data

A catalogue record for this book
is available from the British Library

Published by
BPP Publishing Limited
Aldine House, Aldine Place
London W12 8AW

Printed in England by
DACOSTA PRINT
35/37 Queensland Road
London N7 7AH
(0171) 700 1000

We are grateful to the Chartered Institute of Bankers the Chartered
Institute of Management Accountants, the Chartered Association of
Certified Accountants, the Institute of Chartered Secretaries and
Administrators, and the Association of Accounting Technicians for
permission to reproduce past examination questions. The suggested
solutions have been prepared by BPP Publishing Limited.

CONTENTS

CONTENTS

PREFACE

The examinations of the Chartered Institute of Bankers are a demanding test of each student's ability to master the wide range of financial, legal and commercial knowledge required of the modern banker. The Institute's rapid response to the pace of change is shown both in the content of the syllabuses and in the style of examination questions set.

BPP's experience in producing study material for the Institute's examinations is unparalleled. Over the years, BPP's Study Texts and Practice & Revision Kits have helped thousands of students to attain the examination success that is a prerequisite of career development. Our material is *comprehensive* - covering the whole syllabus - *on target* - covering only the syllabus - and *up-to-date* at the month of publication.

This Study Text has been written specifically for the Associateship core paper *Management*. The syllabus (reproduced on pages (viii) and (ix)) has been cross-referenced to the text, so you can be assured that coverage is complete. This is followed by details of the examination paper format and analyses of recent past exam papers. There is a brand new study guide, containing useful advice on studying, revising and approaching the exam itself. It also identifies a number of 'hot topics' and highlights problem areas in the syllabus. There is also a study checklist so you can plan and monitor your progress through the syllabus.

The main body of this Study Text takes you through the syllabus in easily managed stages with plenty of opportunity for skill - and exam question - practice. For a brief guide to the structure of the text and how it may most effectively be used, see pages (vi) and (vii).

The October 1995 edition of this Study Text

This Study Text has been improved and updated in the following ways.

(a) There are sections dealing with ethical and technological issues (including Mondex and the Internet) in banking as these have been added to the syllabus.

(b) The most recent Code of Banking Practice is reproduced in full.

(c) More material is provided about cost control and the branch network.

(d) Chapter 15 on organisations now includes a brief description of the McKinsey 7's' framework as a means of approaching the organisation.

(e) There is a description of the principles of business process re-engineering.

(f) More is provided on scalar chains.

(g) There is a general discussion of current relevant environmental issues facing banks.

BPP Publishing
October 1995

For details of other BPP titles relevant to your studies for this examination and for a full list of books in the BPP CIB range, please turn to pages 509 and 510. If you wish to send in your comments on this Study Text, please turn to page 511.

HOW TO USE THIS STUDY TEXT

This Study Text has been designed to help students and lecturers to get to grips as effectively as possible with the content and scope of the Associateship core paper *Management.*

The framework of this Study Text is structured so that many will find it to be the most coherent way of covering the *syllabus.* Syllabus coverage in the text is indicated on pages (viii) and (ix) by chapter references set against each syllabus topic. It is thus easy to trace your path through the syllabus.

As a further guide - and a convenient means of monitoring your progress - we have included a *study checklist* on page (xviii) on which to chart your completion of chapters and their related illustrative questions.

Each chapter of the Study Text is divided into *sections* and contains:

- learning objectives
- an introduction, indicating how the subject area relates to others in the syllabus
- clear, concise topic-by-topic coverage
- examples and exercises to reinforce learning, confirm understanding and stimulate thought
- a 'roundup' of the key points in the chapter
- a test your knowledge quiz
- a recommendation on illustrative questions to try for practice. These are provided in a bank at the end of the text, with full suggested solutions.

Exercises

Exercises are provided throughout the text to enable you to check your progress as you work through the text. These come in a large variety of forms: some test your ability to analyse material you have read, others see whether you have taken in the full significance of a piece of information. Some are meant to be discussed with colleagues, friends or fellow students.

A suggested solution is usually given, but often in an abbreviated form to help you avoid the temptation of merely reading the exercise rather than actively engaging your brain. We think it is preferable on the whole to give the solution immediately after the exercise rather than making you hunt for it at the end of the chapter, losing your place and your concentration. Cover up the solution with a piece of paper if you find the temptation to cheat too great!

Examples can also often be used as exercises, if not the first time you read a passage, then certainly afterwards when you come to revise.

Chapter roundup and Test your knowledge quiz

At the end of each chapter you will find two features. The first is the *Chapter roundup,* which follows the final section of each chapter. It summarises key points and arguments and sets out what you should know or be able to do having studied the chapter. The second feature, in a box, is a quiz that serves a number of purposes.

(a) It is an essential part of the chapter roundup and can be glanced over quickly to remind yourself of key issues covered by the chapter.

(b) It is a quiz pure and simple. Try doing it in your head on the train in the morning to revise what you read the night before.

(c) It is a revision tool. Shortly before your examination sit down with pen and paper and try to answer all the questions fully. Many of the questions are typical of the four- or five-mark-earning opportunities that feature so regularly in examination questions.

HOW TO USE THIS STUDY TEXT

Illustrative questions

Each chapter also has at least one illustrative question, in the bank at the end of the Study Text. Initially you might attempt such questions with reference to the chapter you have just covered. Later in your studies, it would be helpful to attempt some without support from the text. Only when you have attempted each question as fully as possible should you refer to the suggested solution to check and correct your performance.

A number of the illustrative questions are in the style of full exam questions. These questions are provided with mark and time allocations.

Index

Finally, we have included a comprehensive index to help you locate key topics.

A note on pronouns

On occasions in this Study Text, 'he' is used for 'he or she', 'him' for 'him or her' and so forth. Whilst we try to avoid this practice it is sometimes necessary for reasons of style. No prejudice or stereotyping according to sex is intended or assumed.

A note on terminology

Throughout this text, 'banks' should be taken to include 'building societies' unless otherwise stated.

SYLLABUS

Objective

- To provide you with a backcloth against which to judge issues relating to management.

- To enable you to understand the role, functions and methods of management in the context of financial services.

Syllabus	*Chapter in this Text*

1 Self management

Problem solving. Decision making. Project planning and management. Time management. Stress management. Career management.   1, 12, 13

2 Managing other people

2.1 People as individuals
Perceptions. Differences in people. Managing boss/ subordinate relationships: selection; induction; training; coaching and developing; feedback and appraising; career management; motivating; counselling.   2, 3, 4, 5

2.2 Interviewing
Conducting interviews with: customers; staff (re: selection, appraisal, grievance, discipline, counselling, exit)   7, 8

2.3 People in groups
Group dynamics. Communication systems. Team roles. Motivating and controlling groups. Managing and participating in meetings. Consensus decisions.   9

2.4 Organisational issues
Recruitment and selection procedures. Work and job design. Training and career development systems. Equal opportunities. Power. Management of change.   6, 10, 20

3 Management processes, theories, models, skills and techniques

3.1 'The manager'
The functions of management. Management roles and the transition to management.   11

3.2 Managing 'the system'
Forecasting. Planning. Organising. Monitoring and controlling. Feedback.   12, 13

3.3 Managing the people
Choice of management style. Relationship management with: internal customers; external customers; bosses, peers and subordinates; delegation   14

4 Organisations and their systems

4.1 Organisational design and development
Organisational structures. Organisational cultures. Power in organisations. Communication in organisations. Inter-departmental co-operation. The 'internal customer'. Reward systems.   15, 16, 17

4.2 Information systems
Importance of technology. Management information systems. Cost management and budgetary control. Risk analysis and management.   13, 18, 19

4.3 Personnel systems
Design of work. Job evaluation. Discipline procedures. Grievance procedures. Appraisal systems.   5, 7, 20

SYLLABUS

THE EXAMINATION PAPER

Format of the examination paper

Questions in the past have fallen into four broad 'styles':

- Bookwork - ie factual knowledge-based questions (mainly section B).
- World of Banking - ie topics of current interest to bankers (mainly section A).
- Your World - ie topics related directly to your own working life (possibly through use of a scenario, as well as conventional essay questions) (mainly section A).
- Scenario - ie case studies which must be treated as problem-solving exercises (mainly section C).

Time allowed:	Three hours
Examination format:	The paper is divided into three sections; you should answer four questions including at least one from each section.
	Section A consists of three questions on topics of current interest to management and/or the financial services industry.
	Section B consists of two questions on theoretical aspects of management which will relate to the management of any of the following: organisations, systems, people or the individual.
	Section C contains three scenario questions in which you are asked to apply theory to practical situations.
	All questions carry 25 marks.
Calculators:	Calculators may not be used.

Analysis of past papers

An analysis of topics examined so far under the new *Management* syllabus is set out below.

May 1995

Section A
1   Management information systems
2   Stress: sources and cures
3   Induction and early training of a new recruit

Section B
4   Delegation
5   Grievance procedure

Section C
6   Recruitment procedures and pressure to breach them
7   Interview with an angry customer
8   Unexpectedly high staff turnover

October 1994

Section A
1   Stakeholders of financial service firms
2   Total quality and the internal customer
3   Changes in financial services firms

Section B
4   Programmed and unprogrammed decisions
5   Management by objectives. Meetings

Section C
6   Change management
7   Performance appraisal
8   Interpersonal conflict

THE EXAMINATION PAPER

May 1994

Section A
1   Equal opportunities legislation
2   Controlling costs
3   Counselling and career development interview

Section B
4   Job design
5   Training

Section C
6   Leadership problems
7   Motivation of the team
8   Promotion to management

October 1993

Section A
1   Stakeholders
2   Managing risk
3   Increasing complaints

Section B
4   Recruitment process
5   Stress. Management roles

Section C
6   Supervisor with personal problems
7   Power
8   Improving procedures

Analysis of old syllabus papers

An analysis of topics examined in the last four sittings under the old syllabus for *Management in Banking* is set out below. The paper was divided into two parts: Section A containing six compulsory six-mark questions on terminology and underlying theory, and Section B consisting of six questions on the application of IT in financial services from which candidates were required to answer four. Students should not assume that old syllabus examinations are representative of examinations which will be set under the new syllabus.

May 1993

1   Coping with the recession and poor image
2   Organisational risk management
3   Producing a marketing plan
4   Managerial functions
5   Transactional analysis. Expectancy theory
6   Management training and support
7   Dealing with a grievance
8   Marketing objectives and system efficiency

October 1992

1   Customer service programmes
2   Banks and small businesses
3   Banking careers
4   Appraisal interview
5   Organisation culture
6   Time management
7   Disciplinary interview
8   Change management

THE EXAMINATION PAPER

May 1992

1   Formulation and implementation of marketing plans by banks
2   Management information system
3   Reducing the size of the workforce
4   Recruitment
5   Groups. Change management
6   Motivation, job enrichment, job design
7   Conflict between departments. Service departments
8   Managing managers

October 1991

1   Single European market
2   Costs
3   Motivation
4   Risk taking (and IT)
5   Job design. Meetings
6   Project management
7   Teams
8   Sexual harassment

STUDY GUIDE

In the next few pages, we offer some advice and ideas on studying, revising and approaching the examination itself. We then provide a brief review of a couple of 'hot topics', covered in more detail in the body of this Study Text, and identify some problem areas which have caused difficulties in recent sittings of this paper.

Studying

As with examinations, there is no substitute for preparation based on an organised and disciplined study plan. You should devise an approach which will enable you to get right through this Study Text and still leave time for revision of this and any other subjects you are taking at the same time. Many candidates find that about six weeks is the right period of time to leave for revision - enough time to get through the revision material, but not so long that it is no longer fresh in your mind by the time you reach the examination.

This means that you should plan how to get to the last chapter by, say, the end of March for a May sitting or the end of August for an October sitting. This includes not only reading the text, but making notes and attempting the bulk of the illustrative questions in the back of the text.

We offer the following as a starting point for approaching your study.

- Plan time each week to study a part of this Study Text. Make sure that it is 'quality' study time: let everyone know that you are studying and that you should not be disturbed. If you are at home, unplug your telephone or switch the answerphone on; if you are in the office, put your telephone on 'divert'.

- Set a clearly defined objective for each study period. You may simply wish to read through a chapter for the first time or perhaps you want to make notes on a chapter you have already read a couple of times. Don't forget the illustrative questions.

- Review your study plan. Use the study checklist a couple of pages on to see how well you are keeping up. Don't panic if you fall behind, but do think how you will make up for lost time.

- Look for examples of what you have covered in the 'real' world. If you work for a financial organisation, this should be a good starting point. If you do not, then think about your experiences as an individual bank or building society customer or perhaps about your employer's position as a corporate customer of a bank. Keep an eye on the quality press for reports about banks and building societies and their activities: you are bound to find something of relevance to this subject.

Revising

The period which you have earmarked for revision is a very important time. Now it is even more important that you plan time each week for study and that you set clear objectives for each revision session.

- Use time sensibly. How much revision time do you have? Remember that you still need to eat, sleep and fit in some leisure time.

- How will you split the available time between subjects? What are your weaker subjects? You will need to focus on some topics in more detail than others. You will also need to plan your revision around your learning style. By now, you should know whether, for example, early morning, early evening or late evening is best.

- Take regular breaks. Most people find that they can absorb more if they do not attempt to revise for long uninterrupted periods of time. Award yourself a five minute break every hour. Go for a stroll or make a cup of coffee, but do not turn the television on.

- Believe in yourself. Are you cultivating the right attitude of mind? There is absolutely no reason why you should not pass this exam if you adopt the correct approach. Be confident: you have passed exams before and you can pass this one.

The day of the exam

Passing professional examinations is half about having the knowledge, and half about doing yourself full justice in the examination. You must have the right technique.

- Set at least one alarm (or get an alarm call) for a morning exam.

- Having something to eat but beware of eating too much; you may feel sleepy if your system is digesting a large meal.

- Allow plenty of time to get to the exam hall; have your route worked out in advance and listen to news bulletins to check for potential travel problems.

- Don't forget pens, pencils, rulers, erasers and anything else you will need.

- Avoid discussion about the exam with other candidates outside the exam hall.

Tackling the examination paper

First, make sure that you satisfy the examiner's requirements.

- *Read the instructions on the front of the exam paper carefully*. Check that the exam format hasn't changed. It is surprising how often examiners' reports remark on the number of students who attempt too few - or too many - questions, or who attempt the wrong number of questions from different parts of the paper. Make sure that you are planning to answer the right number of questions.

- *Read all the questions on the exam paper before you start writing*. Look at the weighting of marks to each part of the question. If part (a) offers only 4 marks and you can't answer the 12 marks part (b), then don't choose the question.

- *Don't produce irrelevant answers*. Make sure you answer the question set, and not the question you would have preferred to have been set.

- *Produce an answer in the correct format*. The examiner will state in the requirements the format in which the question should be answered, for example in a report or memorandum. If a question asks for a diagram or an example, give one. If a question does not specifically ask for a diagram or example, but it seems appropriate, give one.

Second, observe these simple rules to ensure that your script is pleasing to the examiner.

- *Present a tidy paper*. You are a professional, and it should show in the presentation of your work. Candidates are penalised for poor presentation and so you should make sure that you write legibly, label diagrams clearly and lay out your work professionally. Markers of scripts each have dozens of papers to mark; a badly written scrawl is unlikely to receive the same attention as a neat and well laid out paper.

- *State the obvious*. Many candidates look for complexity which is not required and consequently overlook the obvious. Make basic statements first. Plan your answer and ask yourself whether you have answered the main parts of the question.

- *Use examples*. This will help to demonstrate the examiner that you keep up-to-date with the subject. There are lots of useful examples scattered through this Study Text and you can read about others if you dip into the quality press or take notice of what is happening in your working environment.

- *Answer the question set*. Do not answer the question which you would have liked to see on the paper. The marker may, in passing, be impressed by your knowledge, but you will only pick up marks if your answer is relevant.

Finally, make sure that you give yourself the opportunity to do yourself justice.

- *Select questions carefully*. Read through the paper once, then quickly jot down key points against each question in a second read through. Reject those questions against which you have jotted down very little. Select those where you could latch on to 'what the question is about' - but remember to check carefully that you have got the right end of the stick before putting pen to paper.

- *Plan your attack carefully*. Consider the order in which you are going to tackle questions. It is a good idea to start with your best question to boost your morale and get some easy marks 'in the bag'.

- *Check the time allocation for each question*. Each mark carries with it a time allocation of 1.8 minutes (including time for selecting and reading questions). A 20 mark question should be completed in 36 minutes. When time is up, you must go on to the next question or part. Going even one minute over the time allowed brings you significantly closer to failure.

- *Read the question carefully and plan your answer*. Read through the question again very carefully when you come to answer it. Plan your answer to ensure that you keep to the point. Two minutes of planning plus eight minutes of writing is virtually certain to earn you more marks than ten minutes of writing.

- *Gain the easy marks*. Include the obvious if it answers the question and do not spend unnecessary time producing the perfect answer. As suggested above, there is nothing wrong with stating the obvious.

  Avoid getting bogged down in small parts of questions. If you find a part of a question difficult, get on with the rest of the question. If you are having problems with something, the chances are that everyone else is too.

- *Don't leave the exam early*. Use your spare time checking and rechecking your script.

- *Don't worry if you feel you have performed badly in the exam*. It is more than likely that the other candidates will have found the exam difficult too. Don't forget that there is a competitive element in these exams. As soon as you get up to leave the exam hall, forget that exam and think about the next - or, if it is the last one, celebrate!

- *Don't discuss an exam with other candidates*. This is particularly the case if you still have other exams to sit. Put it out of your mind until the day of the results. Forget about exams and relax!

Hot topics

- Issues of ethics have been included in the syllabus. Ethics is a broad subject, but it is more than mere compliance with the law. Situations where financial service firms have been criticised include the overselling of personal pensions, and the Maxwell affair, or overzealous lending. Management concerns might relate to ethical dilemmas on the one hand, or introducing codes of ethics into organisations on the other.

- In a *Signpost* article in the February 1995 edition of *Banking World*, the examiner indicates some topics which might be examined in Section A.

  o *Complaints.* Customer complaints should be seen as opportunities to learn how to improve the service (especially if complaints arose from poor *systems*).

  o *Human resources.* Downsizing has led to job losses and changed employment practices leading especially to 'flatter' organisations.

  o *Induction.* Recruitment faded in the late 1980s, but staff still need to be taken on, and this poses management problems.

  o *Management information.* Many MISs have been designed for financial reporting. However managers have been wishing to develop suitable MIS which highlight key business indicators and which enable them to judge risk.

  o *Quality.* Banks might copy manufacturers in introducing TQM initiatives. They might apply for quality certification, or might even get involved in business process re-engineering.

  o *Stress and workplace bullying.* Some organisations are liable at law for stress related illnesses which their staff suffer from. Workplace bullying has increased for a number of reasons, including which organisational stresses and problems in boss-subordinate relations. Bullying can give rise to 'constructive dismissal' actions.

Problem areas

The Chief Examiner has, on the basis of a review of past questions which proved unpopular, or were answered badly, identified the following as topics which give problems to students.

- In a February 1995 signpost article in *Banking World*, the examiner commented that 'there was much confusion as to what is meant by internal customer'. In a large organisation, departments do jobs for other departments, which are their internal customers.

- Although MbO is not a significant feature of management life, its principles underlie many management systems and performance related pay.

- In scenario questions candidates should concentrate on the facts of the scenario and not make assumptions which cannot be justified.

An approach to scenario questions

The *Management* exam includes three scenario questions, of which you will have to answer at least one. Students frequently have difficulty in answering scenario questions because:

(a) they do not simply require a *description* of a topic;

(b) they require knowledge and understanding of the *application* of an idea to a particular situation or problem;

(c) they often involve more than one topic and an understanding of the *relationship* of several topics within a given problem.

Scenario questions test your ability to apply your knowledge in a practical way. They also test your approach to problem solving. The systematic approach to problem solving involves several stages in a carefully ordered sequence.

1	Define the problem.
2	Identify the factors likely to be causing the problem.
3	Collect and analyse the relevant facts.
4	Identify the range of alternative courses of action likely to solve the problem.
5	Examine the consequences of taking each action.
6	Select and implement the best course of action.
7	Follow up to ensure your actions have solved the problem.

Not *all* of these stages are required in every answer. Answer the question set. You may be asked to:

(a) analyse the *nature* of a particular problem: ie *what* is actually happening? [stage 1]

(b) analyse the *causes* of a particular problem: ie *why* is it happening? [stage 2]

(c) offer a *range of possible solutions* to a problem: ie what *could* be done? [stage 4]

(d) offer *suggestions* for solution of a problem, giving reasons for your choice of solution: ie what *should* be done? [stages 5-6]

If you are asked to outline the *steps* involved in solving the problem, however, you would include stages 1-7: 'follow-up', in particular, is a vital ingredient in approaching problem-solving.

A simple way for you to look at any scenario is:

Problem: State the *symptoms* in the scenario that indicate that there is a problem, and any 'knock on' effects of these symptoms in causing further problems. Define the problem(s) carefully and precisely. (A 'leadership' or 'productivity' problem may on closer analysis be a problem of failure to delegate, poor planning etc)

Analysis: What are the likely *causes* of the problem? Look at all aspects of the situation:

- The leader
- The other people
- The work
- The circumstances
- The environment

Action: What are you going to do about it? Depending on the situation, you may have to state your intentions to:

- gather more information
- plan remedies (with alternatives, if required)
- implement remedies (noting possible constraints, if there are any)
- set up controls to monitor the situation

STUDY CHECKLIST

This page is designed to help you chart your progress through the Study Text, including the illustrative questions at the back of it. You can tick off each topic as you study and try questions on it. Insert the dates you complete the chapters and questions in the relevant boxes. You will thus ensure that you are on track to complete your study before the exam.

PART A: SELF MANAGEMENT

		Text chapters Date completed	Illustrative questions Question numbers	Date completed
1	Time, stress and career management		1	

PART B: MANAGING OTHER PEOPLE

		Text chapters Date completed	Question numbers	Date completed
2	Recruitment and selection		2	
3	Motivation		3	
4	Reward		4	
5	Appraisal		5	
6	Training and development		6	
7	Discipline, grievance and exit		7	
8	Interpersonal behaviour: interviewing		8	
9	People in groups		9	
10	Managing change		10	

PART C: MANAGEMENT PROCESSES, THEORIES, MODELS, SKILLS AND TECHNIQUES

		Text chapters Date completed	Question numbers	Date completed
11	The manager		11	
12	Decision-making and problem-solving		12	
13	Planning and controlling		13	
14	Management and leadership		14	

PART D: ORGANISATIONS AND THEIR SYSTEMS

		Text chapters Date completed	Question numbers	Date completed
15	The nature of organisations		15	
16	Organisation design and culture		16	
17	Communication and co-ordination		17, 18	
18	Information systems		19	
19	Information technology		20	
20	The design of work		21	

PART E: THE BUSINESS ENVIRONMENT

		Text chapters Date completed	Question numbers	Date completed
21	The organisation and the environment		22	
22	Achieving corporate goals		23	
23	Customers, competition and quality		24	
24	Human resource management		25	

PART A
SELF MANAGEMENT

Chapter 1

TIME, STRESS AND CAREER MANAGEMENT

This chapter covers the following topics.

1. Self management
2. Time management
3. Stress
4. Career management

Introduction

In this chapter we look at some of the ways in which managers in the bank environment can manage themselves and their own work. After all, managers who cannot manage themselves are hardly likely to be able to manage others.

In this chapter we look at how managers can take control of their time at work, and of their careers generally, and we discuss one of the great problems facing managers today - stress - and how it can be managed. We discuss more about the manager's role in Chapter 11.

---

1. SELF-MANAGEMENT

1.1 There are a number of different definitions of management, but one that is most popular, without being too specific, is that management is about 'deciding what to do and getting people to do it'.

1.2 More elaborate theories have been developed, which we explore in Chapter 11. For the time being, let us assume that managers are supposed to do the following.

(a) *Planning*. This involves selecting objectives and ways for achieving them.

(b) *Organising*. This involves establishing a structure of tasks.

(c) *Commanding*. This involves giving instructions to subordinates.

(d) *Co-ordinating*. The individual's activities should be harmonised with those of the organisation.

(e) *Controlling*. This is the task of renewing, measuring and, if necessary, correcting the activities of individuals.

1.3   As you will learn in Chapter 11, there are other definitions of management and descriptions of what managers do which differ quite radically from the list in 1.2 above. However the list offers a useful introduction.

1.4   If management is about 'deciding what to do and getting people to do it' the first person that a manager should 'manage' is himself/herself. After all, few, if any, of the activities mentioned in the list above cannot be applied to the manager personally.

   (a)   *Planning*. Many managers *have* to plan their day, just to ensure, if nothing else, that their meetings do not clash with each other.

   (b)   *Organising*. Managers, especially those who still do some technical work, must identify the tasks they must do and how they fit together - the essence of project management discussed in Chapter 12. Some of these tasks they must do themselves, some they must delegate.

   (c)   *Commanding*. A manager is unlikely to 'command' himself or herself to do anything - although a manager could make a commitment to do an unpleasant task, and not put it off. This is basically a matter of discipline.

   (d)   *Co-ordinating*. Managers have to co-ordinate what they do with the activities of other individuals within the department and with the work of other departments.

   (e)   *Controlling*. Managers should exact the same standards of themselves as they do of their subordinates.

1.5   Self-management is not only necessary for the manager's own personal efficiency and effectiveness, but also for the manager's health - as we shall see in the section on stress.

2.   TIME MANAGEMENT

The use of managerial time

2.1   In the past, the relationship between time and job performance was considered relevant only to manual workers or (through O & M) clerical workers. It is only recently that attention has been given to time management at higher and more 'discretionary' levels of activity.

2.2   A manager's use of his time is affected by a number of factors, such as:

   (a)   the nature of his job;
   (b)   his own personality; and
   (c)   his work environment.

2.3   *The nature of the job*. A manager's job involves regular contact with other people in the organisation. It is important to ensure that the inevitable interruptions which this causes are not allowed to encroach too much upon the manager's time. Keeping a detailed time diary is a common method of highlighting the amount of time taken up by interruptions and may suggest ways of reducing them.

Typical causes of wasted time in a manager's job might be prolonged or unnecessary meetings with colleagues or the preparation of unnecessary paperwork (which could be replaced with a brief oral communication). Managers should be on their guard against this and should consider whether such meetings and paperwork can be dispensed with.

The job may be such that there is a great requirement for the manager to supervise and control his subordinates, which takes time away from his own tasks.

2.4 *The personality of the manager.* A manager whose personality is confident and assertive will be better able to resist interruptions and unnecessarily lengthy contacts than one who is diffident, and finds it difficult to 'say no' to subordinates and colleagues.

A manager may wish to retain control over his work, being a perfectionist and distrustful of his subordinates, and so may fail to delegate, and end up with a lot of routine work on his own 'plate'. The manager may be subject to fluctuating work patterns: some people work best at certain times of the day, in short bursts etc. On the other hand, he may simply be disorganised or lacking in self discipline and be comparatively idle one minute and hectically busy the next.

2.5 *The influence and demands of colleagues.* Colleagues include superiors and subordinates as well as fellow managers.

(a) Although communication skills are important in a manager's job, there is a need to avoid unnecessary and time-wasting communication (eg in prolonged meetings). If subordinates keep referring to the manager for decisions, require close supervision or work best under a consultative style of management, there will be extra demands on the manager's time.

(b) A superior who interferes too much in the manager's job and wants constant reports can be very disruptive. (Tact in warding off such attention can be a valuable attribute.) On the other hand, if the superior delegates too much, the manager's workload may be excessive.

(c) The culture of the organisation or department may require lots of communication, informal relationship-building, Management by Walking Around, an 'Open Door' availability policy etc: this takes time.

2.6 *The work environment.*

(a) The physical surroundings in which a person works may affect his use of time. Even if a manager does not have an office of his own, he should try to appropriate a reasonably quiet area where concentrated work can be carried out without interruptions.

(b) Trips to shared facilities eg the photocopier or to computer terminals should be minimised, particularly if they are housed in distant parts of the building.

(c) Fixed procedures and red tape can be time-consuming. Managers should try to minimise the time they spend on merely complying with laid-down procedures, without cutting corners that might lead to lower quality of output. The culture of the organisation may help by making 'short cuts' acceptable.

2.7 There are two elements to a manager's making effective use of his time:

(a) *job management* - making sure that he is equipped for his job, and that his job is itself conducive to effectiveness; and

(b) *time management* - allocating time to tasks in the most effective manner.

2.8 *Job management* will first of all mean ensuring that the manager knows what his job is, as well as training or coaching him the most efficient way of performing necessary tasks. The manager will then not waste time wondering what to do next, or doing tasks that will not help him (or the organisation) to achieve objectives, or doing tasks that might better be done by someone else.

He ought to be thoroughly knowledgeable about the policies, systems and procedures of the organisation, and about the structure of authority and responsibility (the 'proper channels') as well as about his own area of authority or expertise. If this is not possible, for all eventualities, he should at least know where (or to whom) to go for information or assistance. He will then not have to 'reinvent the wheel' by coming up with fresh solutions to every problem: many will be covered by policy or precedent.

2.9 *Delegation skills* will be an important element in job management. Effective use of opportunities for delegation will involve the following.

(a) Make sure that the manager is not having unnecessary demands made on his time by work inappropriately delegated upwards by subordinates, or downwards by his superiors. Training should be given at all levels on when to delegate and when to refer back decisions;

(b) Training subordinates to do their job properly, making it very clear what is expected of them, giving feedback information etc. so that the manager can delegate with confidence and not feel that he has to stay involved because he doubts his subordinates.

(c) Make best use of staff colleagues' specialist help or advice eg. not indulging in office politics, jealously guarding control, and so having to search for information which could simply be requested of another department.

2.10 *Communication* skills will also be important. You may think that communication is part of the problem, rather than part of the solution, since managers spend so much time in communication tasks which may not seem directly productive. However, skills in interpersonal relations can be used to get to the purpose of conversations, interviews and meetings with less time wasted. They can be used to say 'no', tactfully, when unhelpful interruptions present themselves. Learning to read faster, write more concise reports and sort out essential from non-essential information will also help efficient management of time.

2.11 *Time management* involves applying general management principles to your own time.

(a) *Identifying objectives* and the key tasks which are most relevant to achieving them - sorting out what the manager *must* do, from what he *could* do, and from what he would *like* to do. 'Urgent' is not always the same as 'important'.

(b) *Prioritising and scheduling* - assessing key tasks for relative importance, amount of time required, and any deadlines or time-spans. Routine non-essential tasks should be delegated - or done away with if possible. Routine key tasks should be organised as standard procedures and systems. Non-routine key tasks will have to be carefully scheduled as they arise, according to their urgency and importance; an up-to-date diary with a 'carry forward' system (to check on consequences of decisions, follow-up action etc) will be helpful.

(c) *Planning and control* - avoiding, where possible, disruption by the unexpected. Schedules should be drawn up and regularly checked for 'slippage': priorities will indicate which areas may have to be set aside for more important or urgent interventions. Information and control systems in the organisation should be utilised so that problems can (as far as possible) be anticipated, and sudden decisions can be made on the basis of readily available information.

Exercise

Draw up a realistic time plan for your next week's activities. Identify your most important tasks.

Improving personal time management

2.12 Ways in which managers can improve their own personal organisation thus include:

(a) personal planning, in conjunction with detailed goal-planning or target setting;

(b) willingness to delegate tasks to staff who are competent to perform them;

(c) developing necessary skills in communication, gaining the co-operation of others, assertiveness etc;

(d) cutting down on time-wasting activities, eg unnecessary or lengthy meetings and paperwork, and interruptions.

2.13 Other points for improving efficiency include the following.

(a) *Ensuring that resources are available* for forthcoming work, in sufficient supply and good condition. (Do YOU know when your paper or ink is about to run out *before* it happens?).

(b) *Ensuring that they are to hand* (not buried under irrelevant files, items or litter on a desk, nor 'somewhere else'). *Tidiness* is important for efficiency in the office as well as for the organisation's image: files and pieces of work should be easily locatable at all times (and should in any case never be left lying around, as a breach of security, fire hazard etc). (However, you might have read recently that some behavioural and information scientists regard the 'uncluttered' desk as an ideal filing system. Trivial, or barely used items, get buried. Important items can be identified by their colour and shape, rather than namely an index reference in a filing system.)

(c) *Organising work in batches*, while relevant files are to hand, machines switched on etc to save time spent in turning from one job to another.

(d) *Working to plans, schedules, checklists etc.*

(i)   Do not rely on memory alone for appointments, events and duties.

(ii)   Work on one thing at a time, and finishing each task you start. However, this is almost impossible as it is the nature of managerial work, as evidenced by Mintzberg in an earlier chapter, to be discontinuous.

(iii) Do put off large, difficult or unpleasant tasks simply because they are large, difficult or unpleasant. 'Never do today what you can put off till tomorrow' is *not* a good motto; today's routines will be tomorrow's emergencies, and today's emergencies will *still* be tomorrow's emergencies (and usually won't go away!).

(iv) Learn to anticipate and allow for work coming up; recognise and set reasonable deadlines.

(e)   *Taking advantage of work patterns.* Self-discipline is aided by developing regular hours or days for certain tasks: getting into the habit of dealing with correspondence first thing, filing at the end of the day, (Christmas shopping in October?) etc. If you are able to plan your own schedules, you might also take into account your personal 'patterns' of energy, concentration, alertness etc. Large or complex tasks might be undertaken in the mornings before you get tired, or perhaps late at night with fewer distractions, while Friday afternoon is not usually a good time to start a demanding task in the office.

(f)   *Following up tasks* - seeing them through. Uncompleted work, necessary future action, expected results or feedback etc should be scheduled for the appropriate time and entered in a 'follow-up' file or diary so that you will be reminded to check that the result/action has occurred when it was supposed to, or to give someone a decision as promised etc. *Checklists* are also useful for making sure an operation is completed, marking the stage reached in case it has to be handed over to someone else (because of illness, holiday etc) or temporarily laid aside (because of higher priority interruptions).

3. STRESS

3.1 'Stress' is a term which is often loosely used to describe feelings of tension or exhaustion - usually associated with too much, or overly demanding, work. In fact, stress is the product of demands made on an individual's physical *and mental* energies: monotony, feelings of failure or insecurity etc. are sources of stress, as much as the conventionally-considered factors of 'pressure', 'overwork' etc.

3.2 It is worth remembering, too, that demands on an individual's energies may be *stimulating as well as harmful:* many people, especially those suited to managerial jobs, work well under pressure, and even require some form of stress to bring out their best performance. (Excessive stress, however, can be damaging, and may be called 'strain'.) This is why we talk about stress *management*, not 'elimination': it is a question of keeping stress to 'helpful' proportions and avenues.

Symptoms of stress (strain)

3.3 Harmful stress, or 'strain', can be identified by its effects on the individual and his performance. *Symptoms* usually include the following.

(a) *Nervous tension.* This may manifest itself in various ways: irritability and increased sensitivity, preoccupation with details, a polarised perspective on the issues at hand, sleeplessness, etc. Various physical symptoms - eg skin and digestive disorders - are also believed to be 'stress-related'.

(b) *Withdrawal.* This is essentially a defence mechanism which may manifest itself as unusual quietness and reluctance to communicate, or as physical withdrawal ie absenteeism, poor time-keeping, or even leaving the organisation.

(c) *Low morale:* low confidence, dissatisfaction, expression of frustration or hopelessness etc.

(d) Signs that the individual is *repressing* the problem, trying to deny it. Forced cheerfulness, boisterous playfulness, excessive drinking etc may indicate this. Irritability *outside* work (if noticed by the manager) may point to transference of the problem to the non-work environment.

3.4 It is worth noting that some of these symptoms - drinking, absenteeism etc - may or may not be *correctly* identified with stress: there are many other possible causes of such problems, both at work (eg lack of motivation) and outside (personal problems). The same is true of physical symptoms such as headaches and stomach pains: these are not invariably correlated with personal stress. Arguably some *symptoms* (eg alcoholism) might be causes of stress.

3.5 All these things can adversely affect performance, which is why 'stress management' has become a major workplace issue. Considerable research effort has been directed at:

(a) investigating the causes of stress;
(b) increasing awareness of stress in organisations; and
(c) designing techniques and programmes for stress control.

Causes of stress

3.6 Stress may be caused by all kinds of personal and environmental variables. It is believed to be influenced by *personality*. Most people experience stress of some kind, at some time: there are simply some individuals who 'handle' it better than others, and it is important for organisations to identify those individuals. Pincherle did a study of 2,000 UK managers at a medical centre, and found that physical symptoms of stress were related to age, and to the level of responsibility - especially for other people. But are there *types* of people who are more prone to stress than others?

3.7 People have been divided into two types (first, by Friedman and Rosenheim).

(a) 'Type A' - competitive, 'thrusting', dynamic, impatient, restless, tense, and sensitive to pressure.

(b) 'Type B' - 'laid back', patient, calm, etc.

Type A individuals are the 'get-up-and-go' individuals in the organisation, the self-starters and innovators - but their behaviour has been associated by several research studies with a range of unhealthy symptoms (high blood pressure, cholesterol, smoking and drinking). One national study in America showed that Type A men in their forties had 6.5 times the incidence of coronary heart disease of Type B men!

3.8 Some people seem to *feel* less stress than others. Others, like Type A managers, may feel it acutely, but try to *overcome* it - with consequent risk to health. Personality traits which might affect one's ability to cope with stress, in either fashion, include the following.

(a) *Sensitivity*. Emotionally sensitive individuals are pressured more by conflict and doubt, which insensitive people are more able to shrug off (although in extreme cases, insensitivity may prove such a barrier to satisfactory relationships with others, that another source of stress may be created).

(b) *Flexibility*. Individuals who are seen to give in to pressure tend to invite further pressure from those who seek to influence them: intractable, 'stubborn' individuals may suffer less from this, although, when they *are* subjected to pressure, they tend to 'snap' rather than 'bend', as there is more dissonance involved in their giving way.

(c) *Interpersonal competence*. The effects of stress may be handled better from a basis of strong, supportive relationships with others, and indeed many role problems may be solved by maintaining and fostering relationships and reaching co-operative solutions. The individual who turns his back on others in times of stress, like a wounded animal, is unlikely to find a satisfactory resolution.

(d) *Sense of responsibility*. Some individuals have an 'easy come, easy go' outlook - where their own affairs are concerned, as well as those of others that are affected by their actions. Others have a more acute sense of 'owing' other people something, or of their accountability to others for the consequences of their decisions, actions etc. The burden of perceived *guilt* can be a very painful source of stress.

Role stress

3.9 Several major sources of stress have been identified by 'role theory'. (We will discuss 'roles' in Chapter 8.) A role is a type of behaviour, in relation to others, that the individual displays.

(a) *Role ambiguity* is a situation where an individual is not sure what his role is, or when those around him are not clear what his role is. This may arise for a manager through:

(i) uncertainty about the responsibilities of his job;
(ii) uncertainty about other people's expectations of him;
(iii) lack of clarity about how his performance is evaluated.

(b) *Role conflict* occurs when the individual is called upon to act in several roles at the same time, and they are incompatible - eg the dual roles of a working mother, or a participative manager called upon to administer discipline.

(c) Role *overload* occurs when an individual has too many roles to cope with, and feels out of his depth - eg on moving from a functional to a general management position.

10

(d) Role *underload* occurs when an individual moves into a role or set of roles which he perceives as being below his capacity (ie out of line with his self-concept). Delegation may make a manager feel un-needed and insecure. Monotony may be as stressful as constant change and challenge.

Insecurity

3.10 Other situations in which stress may be particularly acute involve uncertainty, and therefore insecurity, together with a sense of responsibility for their outcome.

(a) A manager may find himself having to initiate change or growth: attempts at innovation may be highly stressful, especially if there is an element of risk. (This may partly be a role problem - if, for example, there is a political conflict in the organisation between the supporters of the status quo and the supporters of change.)

(b) Career change, end or uncertainty. Worrying about 'burn-out' or redundancy or retirement - or even about ability to cope with promotion - can be a source of stress. The pace of change in technology and markets adds to the uncertainties which now attach to the work environment.

Management style

3.11 A recent American report entitled *Working well: managing for health and high performance* pointed out particular management traits that were held responsible by workshop interviewees for causing stress and health problems (eg high blood pressure - hypertension - insomnia, coronary heart disease and alcoholism). These included:

(a) unpredictability, so that staff work under constant threat of an outburst;
(b) destruction of workers' self esteem which makes them feel helpless and insecure;
(c) setting up win/lose situations by turning work relationships into a battle for control;
(d) providing too much, or too little, stimulation.

3.12 In British research, managers are criticised for:

(a) not giving credit where it is due;
(b) failing to communicate policy or involve staff in decisions;
(c) supervising too closely; and
(d) not defining duties clearly enough.

3.13 The most 'harmful' style of management is said to be *leave alone and zap* - where the employee (frequently young and inexperienced) is given a task, left without guidance, and then 'zapped' with a reprimand or punishment when mistakes are discovered. This simply creates a vicious circle of anxiety and guilt.

Sources of stress in banking

3.14 Current factors in the employment environment can be identified as sources of stress.

(a) The current job market may be a source of stress through anxiety and insecurity. No job can be regarded as secure for life in the current climate, an awareness of which is increasingly filtering through to workers outside manufacturing industries which have declined in job terms over some years: employees in banking, insurance, the public sector and other service industries are starting to feel the same pressures.

(b) The pace of change in the market and technological environment of banks is still accelerating. 'Innovation' and 'adaptability' are the catchwords for management. Managers may find themselves having to initiate or implement change, growth, contraction or innovation. There may be an element of risk involved, or the manager may have to make decisions with unpleasant consequences for some of the workforce (eg redundancy).

(c) Bankers suffer from the combination of responsibility (for customers' money, the bank's success etc) and risk (in lending, investment and general management decisions which are affected by uncertainty).

(d) The current trend of automation in the banking world can work *both* ways in regard to the incidence of stress.

    (i) The introduction of technology can be stressful, as a form of change which threatens the individual's self image of competence, experience, skill etc: 'What if I can't cope?' There are various pressures on the individual's perceived job security, arising not only from uncertainty as to whether he will be able to learn new methods - or learn them fast enough - to maintain his performance and position, but also from fears of replacement (ie 'all the people will be made redundant and machines will do the jobs'). Stress arising from monotony and isolation may be caused if the effect of automation is to remove task variety and discretion from the individual.

    (ii) On the other hand, working with technology can offer new 'user' skills and responsibilities in a high status field.

Methods of controlling stress

3.15 Individuals have various methods of coping with stress.

(a) *Withdrawal*.

(b) *Repression*, ie refusal to admit the existence of the problem. Forced cheerfulness, playfulness, excessive drinking or drug abuse may indicate that this is occurring, as may exhibitions of irritability etc. outside work, if the problem has been transferred elsewhere.

(c) *Rationalisation*, ie deciding simply to endure, or come to terms with, the situation, if it is inevitable. Stress can be contained, so that its harmful effects may be alleviated. Nervous tension can be reduced by the creation of opportunities for rest, recreation and generally 'getting things into perspective', ie. areas of stability and non-work stimulation. The organisation may be able to help by offering time, facilities or counselling.

3.16 *Role* stress can be resolved to an extent.

(a) The individual can take unilateral action to redefine his role, the scope of his job, the roles which are most important to him and those which can be downgraded etc. He will then have to force his expectations on the others involved - which may aggravate stress in inter-personal relations.

(b) The individual co-operating with other members of his role set, can try and classify or resolve his role(s) relative to the other demands made on him. This may be a matter of redrafting job-descriptions, boundaries of authority or timetables (eg to make room for conflicting demands).

3.17 Only role *underload* offers no possibility of a co-operative solution, such as those in (b) above. It can only be alleviated by the exercise of 'nuisance' power, or by encroaching on someone else's role (ie job enlargement - but this is rarely a solution that employees feel able to *ask* for and it is more likely to lead to inter-personal conflict, or effort wasted in duplicated tasks).

3.18 Stress related to *insecurity* can also be managed to an extent. The organisation will have to ensure that uncertainty is reduced as far as possible by the availability of relevant information. The management style of superiors will be important in offering accessibility (eg an 'open door' policy) in the event of problems, offering positive reinforcement (boosting self-image etc), establishing trust (confidentiality, support etc) and arranging for counselling and training where necessary.

3.19 Greater *awareness* of the nature and control of stress is also a feature of the modern work environment, through the well-known work of writers such as Dr Cary Cooper, and through educational programmes in the work place. Stress management techniques are increasingly taught and encouraged by organisations, and include:

(a) time off or regular rest breaks;
(b) relaxation techniques (breathing exercises, meditation etc);
(c) biofeedback (awareness of physical 'signals' from the body);
(d) physical exercise and self-expression as a 'safety valve' for tension;
(e) delegation and planning (to avoid work-load related stress);
(f) assertiveness (to control stress related to insecurity in personal relations).

In addition, *job* training can increase the individual's sense of competence and security.

3.20 'Ecological' control is also being brought to bear on the problem of stress, creating conditions in which stress is less likely to be a problem. This may be achieved through job design (eg enrichment); organisation culture built on meaningful work, mutual support, communication and teamwork; 'people programmes' providing social activities, leisure facilities etc.

Stress and workplace bullying

3.21 The sources of stress described above develop from the pace of work and the individual's response to it. Media attention recently has been focused on the worrying issue of workplace bullying.

3.22 Bullying at work, as at school, occurs between:

(a) individuals of the same grade;
(b) people of different grades.

Most worrying is when a boss bullies a subordinate.

3.23 A bullying boss is not simply one who has a bad temper, say, or who expects his or her every word to be obeyed without question. Just because someone has an unpleasant character or an autocratic leadership style, or requires and expects high standards from subordinates, this does not make him/her a bully.

3.24 Rather, bullying occurs when the bully singles out an individual and subjects them to a campaign of persecution or intimidation. As opposed to school, in the work context this is unlikely to be physical, but it might involve the following.

(a) Public insults and humiliating remarks.

(b) Criticisms made by a boss of a person's work performance which are:

(i) unfair in relation to standards expected of others;
(ii) unreasonable in relation to the work done;
(iii) designed to lower self-confidence, rather than improve performance.

(c) A boss who refuses or is incapable of separating personal issues (eg character incompatibility) from work issues is likely to act in a bullying way.

(d) Unreasonable threats made to a person's status and career.

(e) Deliberate sidelining of an individual from decisions over which he or she has a legitimate interest.

(f) Unnecessarily close supervision.

3.25 From a management point of view any workplace bullying is undesirable.

3.26 Where bullying occurs between individuals of the same grade, it is fairly easy, once the matter has been aired, to deal with the problem. The boss can investigate the issue, and if appropriate, the bully can be disciplined in a suitable way. The bully or the bully's victim might be moved to different tasks or departments.

3.27 Where a boss bullies the subordinate the situation is more complex.

(a) A boss *always* has more power than a subordinate, and for this reason, despite fashionable talk of 'partnership' between managers and workers the relationship is inherently unequal.

The boss is responsible for assessing the performance of subordinates, and recommendations for rewards and promotion are in the boss's gift.

(b) There is an understandable reluctance of the subordinate to 'go above the boss's head' to the boss's own superior. The boss's own superior will want evidence and will probably hope that this problem will go away. The boss will always put a more credible case, however dishonest this may be. It will be a case of one person's word against another's.

(c) As a lot of bullying is hidden, and the victim may not be in a position to invoke the firm's grievance procedure. As work places become de-unionised, it is likely that this support will be harder to obtain.

3.28 A bullying boss, it must be said, is acting unprofessionally. Bullying destroys the victim's morale and effectiveness, and it cannot be good for the organisation either. Finally, bullying can be construed as *constructive dismissal* and the firm might find itself liable to suffer the unwelcome publicity and expense of a court case and any compensation.(Constructive dismissal is when the employee resigns having effectively been forced to do so.)

3.29 Bullying by bosses should be seen as a disciplinary issue in the normal way.

3.30 It might be argued that the work environment has made it easy for bullying to occur:

(a) fewer and weaker trade unions;

(b) greater commercial pressure on those in work: British workers put in the longest hours in Europe.

4. CAREER MANAGEMENT

4.1 Many organisations like banks, which depend on internal promotion to fill their senior management posts, have systems for planning the career development of managers. The danger of this might be that the individual sees the *organisation* as taking responsibility for his career and personal development: he ceases to think creatively about his future and to plan *self-development*. This is undesirable because:

(a) the manager is a person as well as an employee of his particular organisation, and has a responsibility to himself as well as his employers;

(b) it is also counterproductive for the organisation, producing a dependent, apathetic individual who may well become unsuited to senior management roles which require self-discipline, self-motivation and entrepreneurship.

4.2 The kinds of reward an individual *wants* from his career in the long term will differ with personality, goals and circumstances. It would be a mistake to think of 'career management' simply as 'getting promoted'.

4.3 Edgar Schein (*Organisational psychology*) studied managers over the first twelve years of their careers, and saw their careers as a process of finding a 'career anchor', which becomes their orientation to work, the source of their self image. The 'anchor' will differ according to the manager's needs, motives, talents and values. Some possible anchors or career focuses are as follows.

(a) *Technical/functional competence:* the career is organised around a set of technical or functional skills, which can often be used in a range of organisations. Accountants or tax specialists may have this career approach - moving from their practices, to banks, to consultancies etc but centred on their own specialism.

(b) *Managerial competence:* the career is built upon the ascent of an organisational ladder of increasingly senior management positions - not necessarily in the same organisation or even type of organisation, although career bankers, say, may have this orientation.

(c) *Creativity:* the purpose of the career is to create new things - products, services, businesses or business units. This is an entrepreneurial orientation: a marketing specialist in the banking context may plan his career this way.

(d) *Security or stability:* the point of the career is to provide stability and security for the individual and his family. Some people do not seek advancement as a form of career structure.

(e) *Autonomy:* the career is organised around the search for an occupation which allows the individual to determine his own work hours and life-style. Writers and consultants, for example, structure their careers this way.

(f) *Service to others:* the purpose of the career is to serve other people. Individuals attracted to nursing, for example, are oriented by service: perhaps elements of this 'anchor' are present in bank staff in customer service roles as well.

Self-development

4.4 The implication is that choice and responsibility for development are basically in the hands of the individual. All training and development - even when it is provided by the organisation - is *self-development:* if a person does not want or is not motivated to learn, acquire skills, change his behaviour etc, he will not do so effectively. No 'programmes' imposed as a result of appraisal procedures and promotion planning will make him do so.

4.5 Braddick *(Management for Bankers)* suggests that there are seven key elements to self-development.

(a) *Clarification of personal goals*, in the short and long term, and periodic reappraisal of goals in the light of life changes (career launch, marriage, children, career 'take off', mid career 'plateau', approaching retirement etc).

(b) *Value system* - 'a reasonably stable standpoint from which [the individual] can take stock and which enables him to develop consistent behaviour'.

(c) *Effective use of time.* Time is a precious resource, and energy must be channelled into priority activities.

(d) *Health.* Business and social life should be managed for personal health and the conservation or stimulation of energy.

(e) *Creative learning opportunities.* 'The self-developer searches out opportunities to learn, creates possibilities, makes sure that others know of his ambitions. He does not wait for others to create chances for him.'

(f) *Personal skills.* Influencing, teamworking and delegating skills are essential to create opportunities for self-development challenges.

(g) *Feedback.* Learn from others what your strengths and limitations are, as a basis for development.

Career advancement

4.6 If an individual *wants* to advance his career by gaining promotion or greater challenge etc in his job, a strategy for doing so will involve the following factors.

(a) *Personal factors*

    (i) Clarify and modify (as appropriate) your career *goals.*

    (ii) Develop legitimate *self-interest.* (Much as organisations hate to think so, individuals must look out for themselves - and their goals will not always be compatible with those of the organisation.)

    (iii) *Analyse* your capacities and motivations and set realistic and attainable *targets* for self development, building on your strengths, minimising your weaknesses.

    (iv) Acquire *skills* and *knowledge* that will open up new opportunities.

    (v) Develop good personal *relationships* which support you through change, and enhance your interpersonal skills.

    (vi) Learn to spot *opportunities* and analyse how they can be exploited.

(b) *Organisational factors*

    (i) Identify opportunities in the *career development structure* of the organisation: is there a succession/promotion plan?

    (ii) If you are a woman, take advantage of special opportunities arising from equal opportunities initiatives in banks.

    (iii) Identify and exploit *training, education* and *development* opportunities offered by the organisation - skill acquisition, experience of other areas, more responsibility etc.

    (iv) Utilise the *performance appraisal* system to gain feedback and plan opportunities.

    (v) Utilise *'mentoring'* or *counselling* by your superiors if it is available and might be helpful in your development/problem solving.

    (vi) Do *high quality work.* Show concern for quality, consistency, familiarity with policies and procedures, mastery of systems, commitment to 'culture' etc.

    (vii) Demonstrate *abilities* highly valued in the organisation - particularly those associated with management positions: ability to motivate others, selling skills, innovative ideas, teamworking, technology tolerance etc.

(viii) Show interest in and awareness of *issues* relevant to the organisation: say, competition and marketing strategy in financial services, 1992, new technology.

(ix) Present the right *impression*: committed, able, hard-working, customer-oriented, team spirit etc.

(c) *Political factors*

(i) Understand where *power* lies in the organisation and who has influence.

(ii) Form strategic *alliances* with powerful individuals. Ideally, find a *sponsor* among the influential people.

(iii) *Avoid* working with incompetent or poorly-regarded managers.

(iv) Get *noticed* - without giving false impressions of your abilities which might rebound later.

(d) *Environmental factors*

(i) Be aware of *opportunities* and *constraints* in the environment: the state of the job market for your skills, discrimination against you on the grounds of sex or race or disability etc.

(ii) Be aware of the affect of environmental *changes* on your organisation: will you still have the job/working conditions you want there?

(iii) Develop your *non-work* abilities and interests to 'round' your personality and keep things in proportion.

4.7 Of course, many of the opportunities will be offered by the organisation. However, individual choices and individual responsibility for identifying and exploiting opportunities are vital.

4.8 In an article on management development in *Banking World* (September 1990), a survey of banks indicates that demographic, competitive and technological changes have forced large employers to 'look hard' at management development programmes, in order to retain and develop managers. 'One of the most important factors is giving managers and potential managers more say in their own careers ... The same attitude lies behind an increasing tendency to let managers identify their own development needs and make them known to the trainers.'

4.9 Distance learning (say, using this study text!) and project-based learning were identified as part of the process of 'giving managers power to control their own development'.

'But while all the bankers we spoke to believe that managers need a greater say in their own career and development they also emphasise the importance of planning by banks for their own requirements. For example, one issue facing banks over the next decade is how to produce good generalist bankers for senior management positions in an age of increasing specialisation.'

The transition from functional to general management

4.10 Perhaps the most traumatic stage of manager's career development is the stage (usually at a senior level) at which he makes the transition from functional management to general management, where the requirement is for broader management skills. An idea of the bridge to be crossed can be given by highlighting some of the differences in the two roles.

	Functional manager	*General manager*
Orientation	● task orientated - focus on the functional tasks in hand	● goal orientated focus on achievement of organisational (and divisional) goals and objectives
Role	● organiser	● facilitator - co-ordinating interdepartmental activities; obtaining and allocating resources
Information	● defined sources ● usually through formal channels	● poorly defined sources ● often acquired by informal contacts
Goals	● short term	● long term

4.11 Recent research has brought to light the difficulties which managers face in changing from one role to another and these are often particularly acute when the change involves moving from a functional to a general management position. In addition to the normal problems of switching jobs, the manager taking up a general management post has to deal with an abrupt change in the skills needed to perform his role effectively.

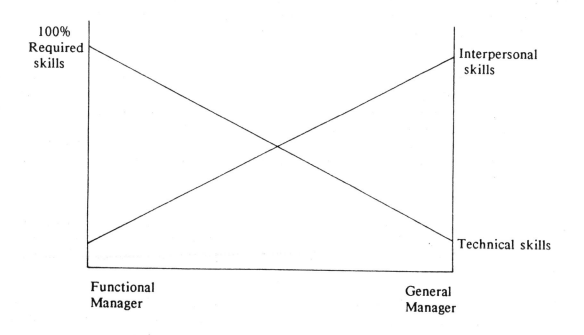

Changing jobs: the transition curve

4.12 The transition from one job to a more senior job is a complex process and the time taken to complete the 'learning curve' varies depending on the degree of perceived change. Since a move from functional to general management is often, and correctly, viewed as a major change, transitions of this sort take longer than average to complete. The diagram below shows a typical transition curve.

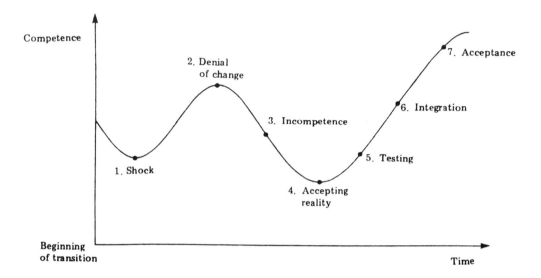

4.13 *Stage 1* is characterised by immobilisation or shock; a sense of feeling overwhelmed. This occurs because the reality of the new job does not match the person's expectations. The individual stops and tries to understand what is happening. Typical attitudes at this stage are 'did I really want this job?' and 'this isn't the job I expected'.

4.14 *Stage 2* is characterised by a denial of change. There is a reversion to previously successful behaviour. This can be useful if it is temporary, but becomes a handicap if it goes on too long and inappropriate behaviour becomes dominant.

4.15 *Stage 3* involves an awareness that change is necessary, and is accompanied by frustration because the individual finds it difficult to cope with the new situation or relationships. A fall in performance level is common but, despite this, the phase is very important in the transition process since, without the realisation of change, people can never develop new attitudes and patterns of behaviour. Organisations which adopt a 'sink or swim' approach to transition actually hinder the process in that this phase is commonly regarded as the start of 'sinking'.

4.16 *Stage 4* is the time when the reality of the new situation is accepted for the first time. Up to this point managers have been concerned with hanging on to past values, attitudes and behaviours. There is now a preparedness and willingness to experiment with change.

4.17 *Stage 5* is concerned with testing new behaviour and approaches. There is a lot of activity and energy as the testing progresses, Mistakes are liable to be made, but the experimentation needs to be encouraged since only by doing this can effective approaches be found.

4.18 *Stage 6* is a reflective period, in which individuals search for meaning in an attempt to understand all the activity, anger and frustration that went before.

4.19 *Stage 7* is the final phase of the transition. Effective new approaches are introduced and the sense of being involved in change disappears. Self-esteem, and performance, rises.

5.   CHAPTER ROUNDUP

5.1

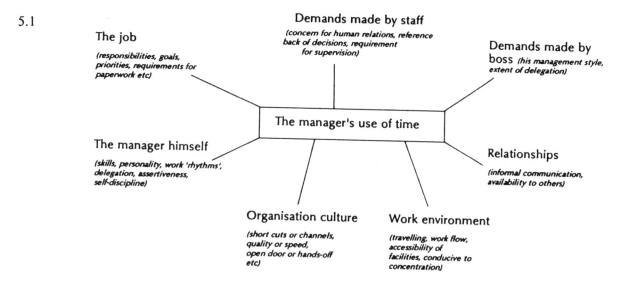

5.2   Stress management tactics include:

Rest
Assertiveness
Planning
Information
Delegation

Relationships
Unwinding
Insensitivity (!)
Negotiating roles

5.3   If you want to 'get to the top' your strategy will be:

Personal
Organisational
Political
Environmental

TEST YOUR KNOWLEDGE

The numbers in brackets refer to paragraphs of this chapter

1   Why is delegation important for time management? What does it involve? (2.5, 2.9)

2   How can managers improve their use of time? (2.11, 2.13)

3   What signs might lead to suspect that you, or others, were suffering from stress? (3.3)

4   List possible causes of stress and ways of managing each cause. (3.6 - 3.20)

5   What is your career 'anchor' or orientation? (4.3 for ideas)

6   What opportunities for self development can you see in your job and bank? Are you seizing them? If not, what holds you back? (4.6(b))

7   What personal and political tactics would you adopt if you wanted to advance your career? (4.6(a) and (b))

8   Describe the transition curve for somebody who has just been promoted to a new job. (4.12 - 4.19)

Now try question 1 at the end of the text

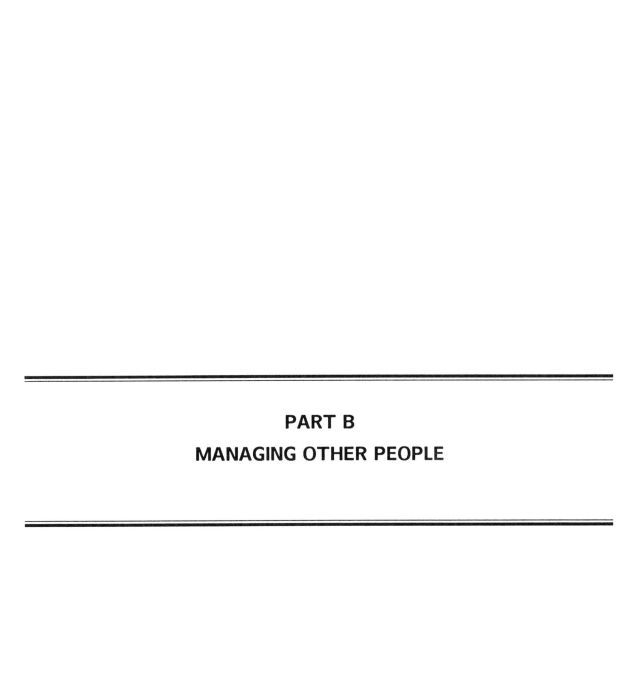

PART B

MANAGING OTHER PEOPLE

Chapter 2

RECRUITMENT AND SELECTION

This chapter covers the following topics.

1. The process recruitment and selection
2. Recruitment
3. Selection
4. Discrimination and equal opportunities

Introduction

The overall aim of the recruitment and selection process in an organisation is to obtain the quantity and quality of employees required, with maximum efficiency (ie. at least cost consistent with fulfilment of the objectives).

---

1. THE PROCESS OF RECRUITMENT AND SELECTION

1.1 This process can be broken down into four main stages.

(a) Identifying the needs of the organisation.

(b) Preparation of job descriptions and specifications, thereby defining the requirements of each job.

(c) The attracting of potential employees, including the evaluation and use of various methods of reaching sources of applicants, inside and outside the organisation.

(d) The selection of candidates.

1.2 Note that there is a distinction between recruitment and selection.

(a) *Recruitment* is the part of the process concerned with finding the applicants: it is a 'positive' action by management, going out into the labour market, communicating opportunities and information, generating interest.

(b) *Selection* is the part of the employee resourcing process which involves choosing between applicants for jobs: it is largely a 'negative' process, eliminating unsuitable applicants.

1.3 If not approached systematically, the process of recruitment and selection can become costly and time-consuming. The organisation needs a very clear plan of what resources it needs, what resources are available, and where and how those resources are to be found.

1.4 A systematic approach will therefore embrace:

    (a) detailed manpower planning;

    (b) job analysis;

    (c) an identification of vacancies;

    (d) evaluation of the sources of labour;

    (e) preparation and publication of information, which will:

        (i) attract the attention and interest of potentially suitable candidates;
        (ii) give a favourable (but accurate) impression of the job and the organisation; and
        (iii) equip those interested to make an attractive and relevant application;

    (f) processing applications, assessing the relative merits of broadly suitable candidates;

    (g) notifying applicants of the results of the selection process;

    (h) preparing employment contracts, induction, training programmes etc.

1.5 A manpower plan is a statement of what human resources the organisation requires to meet its business objectives. We discuss this in Chapter 24.

2. RECRUITMENT

2.1 The administrative activities involved in recruitment include the following.

    (a) Obtain approval or authorisation for engagement (in accordance with the manpower budget).

    (b) Prepare, or update and confirm job description and specification, as appropriate to the job requisition received from the departmental head.

    (c) Select media of advertisement or other notification of the vacancy.

    (d) Prepare advertising copy, and place advertisement.

    (e) Screen replies, at the end of a specified period for application.

    (f) Shortlist candidates for initial interview.

    (g) Advise applicants accordingly.

    (h) Draw up a programme for the selection process which follows.

2.2 The process of recruitment can be formulated as a flowchart, as seen on the following page.

2: RECRUITMENT AND SELECTION

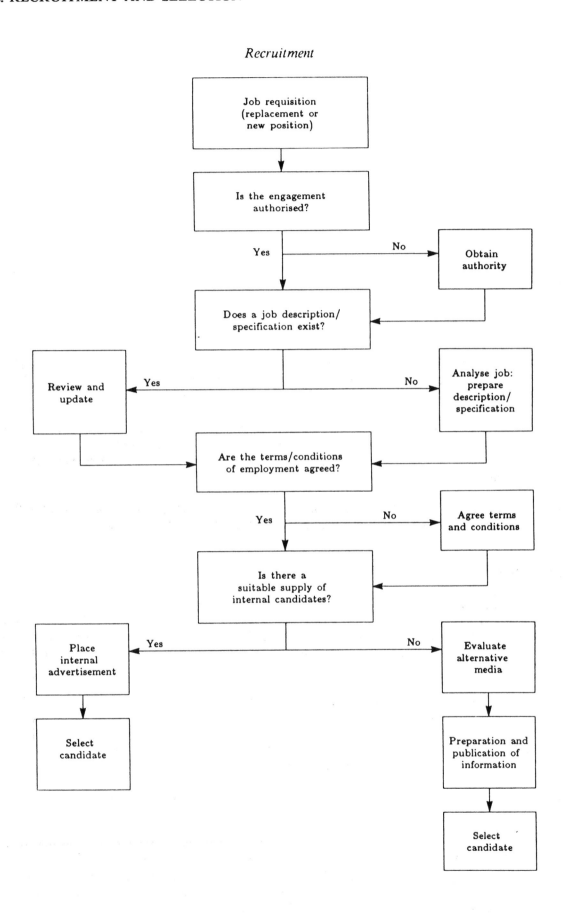

Recruitment

Job analysis

2.3 According to the British Standards Institution, job analysis is 'the determination of the essential characteristics of a job', ie the process of examining a 'job' to identify its component parts and the circumstances in which it is performed. This job appraisal may be used for vocational guidance, personnel selection, training or equipment design.

2.4 The product of the analysis is usually a *job specification* - a detailed statement of the activities (mental and physical) involved in the job, and other relevant factors in the social and physical environment.

2.5 Information which should be elicited from a job appraisal is both task-orientated information, and also worker-orientated information, including the following.

(a) *Initial requirements* of the employee: aptitudes, qualifications, experience, training required, etc.

(b) *Duties and responsibilities:* physical aspects; mental effort; routine or requiring initiative; difficult and/or disagreeable features; consequences of failure; responsibilities for staff, materials, equipment or cash etc.

(c) *Environment and conditions:* physical surroundings, with particular features - eg. temperature or noise; hazards; remuneration; other conditions such as hours, shifts, benefits, holidays; career prospects; provision of employee services - canteens, protective clothing etc.

(d) *Social factors:* size of the department; teamwork or isolation; sort of people dealt with - senior management, the public etc; amount of supervision; job status.

Job description

2.6 A job description is a broad description of a job or position at a given time (since jobs are 'dynamic', subject to change and variation) formulated during job analysis. 'It is a written statement of those facts which are important regarding the duties, responsibilities, and their organisational and operational interrelationships.' (Livy - *Corporate Personnel Management*)

2.7 A job description should be clear and to the point, and so ought not to be lengthy. Typically, a job description would show the following.

(a) Title of job and department and job code number. The person to whom the job holder is responsible. Possibly, the grading of the job.

(b) *Job summary* - showing in a few paragraphs the major functions and tools, machinery and special equipment used. Possibly also a small organisation chart.

(c) *Job content* - list of the sequence of operations that constitute the job, noting main levels of difficulty. In the case of management work there should be a list of the *main* duties of the job, indicating frequency of performance - typically between 5 and 15 main duties should be listed. This includes degree of initiative involved, the nature of responsibility (for other people or machines etc).

(d) The extent (and limits) of the jobholder's authority and responsibility.

(e) Statement showing relation of job to other closely associated jobs, including superior and subordinate positions and liaison required with other departments.

(f) Working hours, basis of pay and benefits and conditions of employment, eg. location, pressure, social isolation, physical conditions, health hazards etc.

(g) Opportunities for training, transfer and promotion.

(h) Possibly, also, objectives and expected results, which will be compared against actual performance during employee appraisal.

Job description

MIDWEST BANK PLC
Job description: Clerk Grade 2

1. *Job title:*　　Clerk (Grade 2)

2. *Branch:*　　All branches and administrative offices

3. *Job summary:* To provide clerical support to activities within the bank

4. *Job content:*　　Typical duties will include:
   (a) cashier's duties;
   (b) processing of branch clearing;
   (c) processing of standing orders;
   (d) support to branch management.

5. *Reporting structure:*

Administrative officer/assistant manager

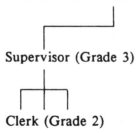

Supervisor (Grade 3)

Clerk (Grade 2)

6. *Experience/Education:* experience not required, minimum 3 GCSEs or equivalent.

7. *Training to be provided:* initial on-the-job training plus regular formal courses and training

8. *Hours:* 38 hours per week

9. *Personal characteristics required:* Age 16 years minimum, good communications skills and business-like attitude

10. *Objectives and appraisal:* Annual appraisal in line with objectives above.

11. *Salary:* refer to separate standard salary structure.

Job description prepared by: Head office personnel department

Date: March 19X9

2.8   A job description can then be used:

(a)   to decide what skills (technical, human, conceptual, design etc) and qualifications are required of the job holder (when formulating recruitment advertisements and interviewing an applicant for the job, the recruiter can use the job description to match the candidate against the job)

(b)   to ensure that the job:

(i)   will be a full-time job for the job holder and will not underutilise him by not giving him enough to do;

(ii)   provides a sufficient challenge to the job holder - job content is a factor in the motivation of individuals;

(c)   to determine a rate of pay which is fair for the job, if this has not already been decided by some other means.

Exercise 1

Draft a job description of what you currently do at present, on the lines suggested in paragraph 2.7. How does your description compare with that given to you by the bank?

Personnel specification

2.9   Once the job has been clearly defined, the organisation can decide what kind of person is needed to fill it effectively.

'If matching *[ie of demands of the job and the person who is to perform it]* is to be done satisfactorily, the requirements of an occupation (or job) must be described in the same terms as the aptitudes of the people who are being considered for it.'

Professor A. Rodger

2.10   A personnel specification identifies the type of person the organisation should be trying to recruit - their character, aptitudes, educational or other qualifications, aspirations in their career etc. Research has been carried out into what a personnel specification ought to assess. Two designs of specification are Rodger's Seven Point Plan (1951) and J Munro Fraser's Five Point Pattern of Personality (1966).

2.11   The Seven Point Plan draws the selector's attention to seven points about the candidate.

1	Physical attributes (neat appearance, ability to speak clearly and without impediment etc).
2	Attainment (educational qualifications etc).
3	General intelligence.
4	Special aptitudes (eg neat work, speed and accuracy etc).
5	Interests (practical and social).
6	Disposition (or manner, eg friendly, helpful).
7	Background circumstances.

2.12 The Five Point Pattern draws the selector's attention to these features.

1	impact on others, including physical attributes, speech and manner.
2	acquired knowledge or qualifications.
3	innate ability, including mental agility and aptitude for learning.
4	motivation, ie individual goals, demonstrated effort and success at achieving them.
5	adjustment, ie emotional stability, tolerance of stress, human relations skills.

2.13 Note that the personnel specification includes job requirements in terms of a candidate's:

(a) capacities (ie what he is capable of); and
(b) inclinations (ie what he will do).

In other words, behavioural versatility must be accounted for, by considering not only the individual's mental and physical attributes, but his current attitudes, values, beliefs, goals and circumstances - all of which will influence his response to work demands. It is not merely 'traits' that the recruitment officer should be interested in - they can only give a static and inflexible portrait of a dynamic process, the interaction of the individual and his (work and non-work) environment.

2.14 When matching a person against the specification, each feature should be judged according to what is:

(a) *essential*, for instance, honesty in a cashier is essential whilst a special aptitude for conceptual thought is not

(b) *desirable*, for instance, a reasonably pleasant manner should ensure satisfactory standards in a person dealing with the public

(c) *contra-indicated*, some features are actively disadvantageous, such as an inability to work in a team when acting as project leader.

Precision is necessary when completing a personnel specification - generalisation and vague impressions should be eradicated.

PERSONNEL SPECIFICATION: Assistant branch accountant

	ESSENTIAL	DESIRABLE	CONTRA-INDICATED
Physical attributes	Clear speech Well-groomed Good health	Age 25-30	Age 35+ Chronic ill-health and absence
Attainments	2 'A' levels GCSE Maths and English Thorough knowledge of branch banking	Degree (any discipline) Marketing training 2 years' experience in supervisory post	No experience of supervision or branch banking
Intelligence	High verbal intelligence		
Aptitudes	Facility with numbers Attention to detail and accuracy Social skills for customer relations	Analytical abilities (problem solving) Understanding of systems and IT	No mathematical ability Low tolerance of technology
Interests	Social: team activity		Time-consuming hobbies 'Solo' interests
Disposition	Team player Persuasive Tolerance of pressure and change	Initiative	Anti-social Low tolerance of responsibility
Circumstances	Able to work late, take work home	Located in area of bank	

Advertising job vacancies

2.15 After a job description and a personnel specification may have been prepared, the organisation should advertise the job vacancy (or vacancies). This is a matter of homing in on the target market of labour, and attracting interest in the organisation and the job. Even in a 'buyer's market', an employer must not think he will be doing someone a favour by giving him or her a job. Anyone answering an advertisement will want to know a bit about the job first, in particular:

(a) the salary or wage;
(b) what the job consists of;
(c) career prospects;
(d) qualifications required for the job;
(e) who is to apply for the job.

The recruiter will also have to present a true - but attractive - image and prospect of employment to potentially suitable applicants.

2: RECRUITMENT AND SELECTION

2.16 The way in which a job is advertised will depend on:

(a) the type of organisation; and
(b) the type of job.

A factory is likely to advertise a vacancy for an unskilled worker in a different way from a bank advertising vacancies for clerical staff. Managerial jobs may merit national advertisement or the use of 'executive search' agencies, whereas semi- or un-skilled jobs may only warrant local coverage, depending on supply in the local area. Specific attributes may be associated with particular sectors of the labour market that could be reached by special means eg advertising in *Banking World* for bank staff.

2.17 The choice of advertising medium will also depend on:

(a) the *cost* of advertising: it is more expensive to advertise in a national newspaper than on local radio, and more expensive to advertise on local radio than in a local newspaper etc;

(b) the *readership* and circulation (ie number and type of readers/listeners) of the advertising medium and its suitability for the number and type of people the organisation wants to reach;

(c) the *frequency* with which the organisation wants to advertise the job vacancy. A monthly magazine or weekly newspaper are probably only useful for advertising a vacancy once. This is probably only sufficient for a senior management position, since managers who are interested in changing their jobs will be on the look-out for vacancies advertised in certain magazines or newspapers.

2.18 The methods or media for advertising jobs are as follows.

(a) *In-house magazines and noticeboards.* An organisation might advertise vacancies for particular jobs through its own in-house magazine or journal, inviting applications from employees who would like a transfer or a promotion to the particular vacancy advertised.

(b) *Professional newspapers or magazines,* such as *Banking World* for bankers, *Computer Weekly* for data processing staff, *Accountancy Age* for accountants etc. Banks are increasingly having to recruit senior specialists eg, in taxation or international finance, to meet a widening range of competitors in various market segments, and professional bodies may be a good source of such applicants.

(c) *National newspapers,* especially for senior management jobs or vacancies for skilled workers, where potential applicants will not necessarily be found through local advertising.

(d) *Local newspapers,* for jobs where applicants are sought from the local area.

(e) *Local radio.*

(f) *Job centres.* On the whole, vacancies for unskilled work (rather than skilled work or management jobs) are advertised through local job centres, although in theory any type of job can be advertised here.

(g) *Recruitment agencies.* An organisation might leave the task of advertising a vacancy and selecting candidates for interview to a recruitment agency.

(h) *School and university careers offices.* When an organisation recruits school leavers or graduates, it would be convenient to advertise vacancies through their careers officers. Suitable advertising material (eg brochures) should be made available. Ideally, the manager responsible for recruitment in an area should try to maintain a close liaison with careers officers. Some large organisations organise special meetings or *careers fairs* in universities and colleges, as a kind of 'showcase' for the organisation and the careers it offers. This type of work may become more important as the number of young people falls during the 1990s and competition for high-calibre recruits becomes more intense, especially in industries like banking which has traditionally drawn the 'cream' of graduates into management trainee positions, and has drawn much of its more junior manpower from school-leavers.

A reminder of some of the manpower resourcing problems of banks

2.19 To date, the clearing banks have habitually recruited up to 4,000 school-leavers per year. School-leavers have represented a major resource for the banks, starting with basic processing and being developed into higher-grade employees if they stay.

(a) However, this pool of labour is shrinking, and although recent strategic reviews by banks have indicated that their manpower needs are falling with increased automation, there is still anticipated to be a shortfall. Recruitment among school-leavers is intensifying.

(b) In addition, banks are having:

(i) to meet manpower shortfalls by attracting new entrants to the job market eg. women returning after a career break

(ii) to meet specific skill shortfalls (created by a combination of the demographic downturn and increased specialisation in the deregulated banking environment) by recruiting specialists from outside the bank - at higher 'entry points' in the hierarchy, and often at a premium - rather than promoting 'all-rounders' from within.

2.20 In an article in *Banking World* (October 1989), David White noted that 'banking awareness is far from great among the young...Ask most people what they think of banks and the answer is "I don't think of banks". As noted above, banks in particular need a strong liaison with schools and universities, careers teachers and government careers officers. This liaison may be built up in the following ways.

(a) A bank should send managers and staff to talk to students, possibly with films.

(b) Careers literature should always be available for sending direct to people making enquiries and for making available to careers officers and teachers.

(c) Students should be invited with teachers to open evenings at branches to see practical demonstrations of banking work.

(d) A bank might provide a short course on banking at one of its training centres for groups of schoolchildren.

(e) A bank might send representatives to a careers convention, held by a school or government careers office, in which various employers are invited to take part.

(f)   A bank might offer a work experience scheme to students, to give them direct experience of working in a bank for about two weeks.

(g)   Students in further education (universities, polytechnics) might be given an industrial training project with the bank during a vacation or as part of a sandwich course.

The local branch manager can play a useful role in providing some of these contacts at a local level.

3.   SELECTION

3.1   Selection of employees (at all levels, but particularly for key posts) must be approached systematically if it is to be efficient and effective. The recruiting officer must know what the organisation's requirements are, and must measure each potentially suitable candidate against those requirements. He should not waste time and resources investigating candidates who are clearly disqualified from the post by some area of unsuitability ('if only...' is not a useful assessment). On the other hand, of those who are broadly suitable, summary rejection of someone who proves to be a considerable asset to another organisation is as much a danger as the incautious acceptance of a candidate who proves to be unsuitable.

A systematic approach can be illustrated by a flowchart like that on the following page.

Application forms

3.2   Applicants who reply to job advertisements are usually asked to fill in a *job application form*, or to send a letter giving details about themselves and their previous job experience (their CV or *curriculum vitae*) and explaining why they think they are qualified to do the job.

3.3   An application form should be used to find out relevant information about the applicant, in order to decide, at the initial 'sifting' stage:

(a)   whether the applicant is obviously unsuitable for the job; or
(b)   whether the applicant might be of the right calibre, and worth inviting to an interview.

3.4   The application form should therefore help the selection officer(s) to sift through the applicants, and to reject some at once so as to avoid the time and costs of unnecessary interviews. If the form is to be useful in the sifting process, it should be designed carefully.

(a)   It should ask questions which will elicit information about the applicant which can be compared with the key requirements of the job. For example, if the personnel specification requires a minimum of two 'A' level passes the application form should ask for details of the applicant's educational qualifications. Similarly, if practical and social interests are thought to be relevant, the application form should ask for details of the applicant's hobbies and pastimes, membership of societies and sporting clubs or teams etc.

(b)   It should give applicants the opportunity to write about themselves, their career ambitions or why they want the job. By allowing applicants to write in their own words at some length, it might be possible to obtain some information about their:

2: RECRUITMENT AND SELECTION

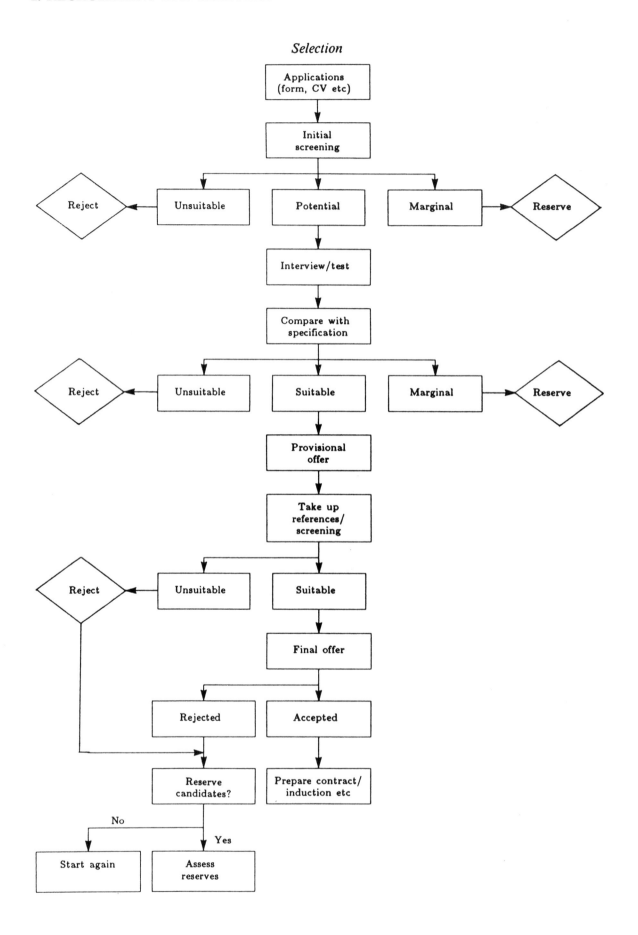

Selection

      (i)   neatness;
      (ii)   intelligence;
      (iii) ability to communicate in writing;
      (iv) motivation; and even
      (v)   character.

The selection interview

3.5   The interview is the second stage of the selection process. Interviewing is a crucial part of the selection process because:

    (a) it gives the organisation a chance to assess the applicant directly; and

    (b) it gives the applicant a chance to learn more about the organisation, and whether or not he or she wants the job.

3.6   The interview is a two-way process, but the interviewer must have a clear idea of what the interview is setting out to achieve, and he must be in sufficient control of the interview to make sure that every candidate is asked questions which cover the same ground and obtain all the information required.

3.7   The basis of the interview will be:

    (a) the job description, and what qualities are required of the job holder;

    (b) the personnel specification. The interviewer must be able to judge whether the applicant matches up to the personal qualities required from the job holder;

    (c) the application form.

3.8   The aim of the interview must be clear. It should have a three-fold purpose:

    (a) finding the best person for the job;

    (b) making sure that the applicant understands what the job is and what the career prospects are. He must be allowed a fair opportunity to decide whether he wants the job;

    (c) making the applicant feel that he has been given fair treatment in the interview, whether he gets the job or not.

3.9   *Interviewing* is a separate section of the Management in Banking syllabus. We discuss the techniques of interviewing in general, and for specific applications like selection, in Chapter 8. If you want to include the selection interview as part of your studies here, however, please turn to Chapter 8.

3.10 When the interviews have been conducted, the interviewers should have time straight away to evaluate the information and opinions they have obtained. They should discuss each candidate and compare their assessment of the individual with the job description, personnel specification and application form. The performance of the candidate in any aptitude test which might have been set should also be considered.

APPLICATION FORM

Post applied for: .... Date:

Surname: Mr/Mrs/Miss/Ms First names:

Address:

Post code: Telephone:

Age: Date of birth: / /
Nationality Marital status

EDUCATION AND TRAINING

Place of education (including schools after 11 years)	Dates	Examinations passed/qualifications

EXPERIENCE

Name of employer and main business	Position held	Main duties	From	To

---

OTHER INFORMATION
Please note your hobbies and interests, and any other information you would like to give about yourself or your experience.

State or health (include any disability)

May we contact any of your previous employers? Yes ☐ No ☐

If yes, please give the names of any managers to whom we may apply.

If selected, I would be available to start from / /

3.11 As a result of the evaluation process a decision will be taken whether or not:

  (a) to offer the candidate the job, subject to:

      (i)   taking up the references which the candidate was asked to supply in his job application;

      (ii) obtaining any evidence required of educational and professional qualifications;

      (iii) in some cases, a medical examination;

  (b) to invite the candidate to a second interview. Some organisations have a two-stage interview process, whereby first-stage interview candidates are reduced to a short-list for a second stage interview. The second stage of the interview might well be based on a group selection method.

Selection tests

3.12 In some job selection procedures, an interview is supplemented by some form of selection test. The interviewers must be certain that the results of such tests are reliable, and that a candidate who scores well in a test will be more likely to succeed in the job. The test will have no value unless there is a direct relationship between ability in the test and ability in the job. The test should be designed to be *discriminating* (ie to bring out the differences between candidates) and *standardised* (so that it measures the same thing in different candidates, providing a basis for comparison). There are four main types.

  (a) *Intelligence tests* aim to measure the applicant's general intellectual ability. They may test the applicant's memory, his ability to think quickly and logically and his skill at solving problems.

  (b) *Aptitude tests* are designed to predict an individual's potential for performing the job or acquiring new skills. There are various accepted areas of aptitude, eg. clerical, numerical and mechanical.

  (c) *Proficiency tests* are perhaps the most closely related to an assessor's objectives, because they measure ability to do the work involved. An applicant for an audio typist's job, for example, might be given a dictation tape and asked to type from it. This is a type of *attainment* test in that it is designed to measure abilities and skills already possessed by the applicant.

  (d) *Personality tests* may measure a variety of characteristics, such as an applicant's skill in dealing with other people, his ambition and motivation or his emotional stability.

3.13 This kind of testing must be used with care as it suffers from several limitations.

  (a) There is not always a direct (let alone 'predictive') relationship between ability in the test and ability in the job: the job situation is very different from artificial 'test' conditions.

  (b) The interpretation of test results is a skilled task, for which training and experience is essential.

(c) Particular difficulties are experienced with particular kinds of test. For example, an aptitude test measuring arithmetical ability would need to be constantly revised; otherwise, its content might become known to later applicants. Personality tests can often give misleading results because applicants seem able to guess which answers will be looked at most favourably. It is difficult to design intelligence tests which give a fair chance to people from different cultures and social groups, and which test the *kind* of intelligence that the organisation wants from its employees: the ability to score highly in IQ tests is not necessarily a desirable attribute.

(d) It is difficult to exclude bias from tests. Many are tackled less successfully by women than by men, or by immigrants than by native applicants: this is a particular problem in countries like the UK where there is legislation protecting applicants against discrimination.

Group selection methods

3.14 Group selection methods might be used by an organisation as the final stage of a selection process for management jobs. They consist of a series of tests, interviews and group situations over a period of two days, involving a small number of candidates for a job. Typically, six or eight candidates will be invited to the organisation's premises for two days. After an introductory chat to make the candidates feel at home, they will be given one or two tests, one or two individual interviews, and several group situations in which the candidates are invited to discuss problems together and arrive at solutions as a management team. Techniques in such programmes include:

(a) group role-play exercises, in which they can explore (and hopefully display) interpersonal skills and/or work through simulated supervisory tasks;

(b) case studies, where candidates' analytical and problem-solving abilities are tested in working through described situations/problems, as well as their interpersonal skills, in taking part in (or leading) group discussions of the case study.

> 'Among the qualities which neither the interview nor intelligence tests are able to assess accurately are the candidate's ability to get on with and influence his colleagues, to display qualities of spontaneous leadership and to produce ideas in a real-life situation.'
> Plumbley

3.15 These group sessions might be thought useful because:

(a) they give the organisation's selectors a longer opportunity to study the candidates;

(b) they reveal more than application forms, interviews and tests alone about the ability of candidates to persuade others, negotiate with others, and explain ideas to others and also to investigate problems efficiently. These are typically management skills;

(c) they reveal more about the candidates' personalities - eg stamina, interests, social interaction with others (ability to co-operate and compete etc) intelligence, energy, self confidence etc.

Since they are most suitable for selection of potential managers who have little or no previous experience and two days to spare for interviews etc, group selection methods are most commonly used for selecting university graduates for management trainee jobs.

Once selection has been made

3.16 Once an eligible candidate has found, a provisional offer can be made, by telephone or in writing, 'subject to satisfactory references'. The organisation should be prepared for its offer to be rejected at this stage. An applicant may have received and accepted another offer; he may not have been attracted by his first-hand view of the organisation, and may have changed his mind; he may only have been 'testing the water' in applying in the first place, ie gauging the market for his skills and experience for future reference, or seeking a position of strength from which to bargain with his present employer. A small number of eligible applicants should therefore be kept in reserve.

3.17 *References* provide further confidential information about the prospective employee. This may be of varying value, as the reliability of all but the most factual information must be in question. A reference should contain:

(a) straightforward factual information confirming the nature of the applicant's previous job(s), period of employment, pay, and circumstances of leaving;

(b) opinions about the applicant's personality etc. These should obviously be treated with some caution. Allowances should be made for prejudice (favourable or unfavourable), charity (ie withholding detrimental remarks), and possibly fear of being actionable for libel (although references are privileged, as long as they are factually correct and devoid of malice).

Exercise 2

The whole job selection process has been described from advertisement to interview. Think back to when you last applied for a job.

(a) Was the advert successful in describing the job?
(b) How did you learn about the vacancy?
(c) Did the application form enable you to describe yourself well?
(d) Do you think the interview was fair (with the benefit of hindsight)?

3.18 The process of induction, whereby the employee is made familiar with the new job, is described in Chapter 6.

4. DISCRIMINATION AND EQUAL OPPORTUNITIES

The law on discrimination

4.1 Various laws and directives have been passed to safeguard otherwise or hitherto disadvantaged groups, with regard to recruitment and selection (and subsequent training and career development opportunities).

(a) The Equal Pay Act 1970 entitles a woman to claim equal pay and terms of employment for work of 'equal value' (even if different) to that of a male employee.

(b) The Sex Discrimination Act 1975 forbids discrimination on grounds of sex or marital status.

(c)   The Race Relations Act 1976 forbids discrimination on grounds of race, colour, 'ethnic origin' or nationality.

(d)   In 1976 the EEC (now EU) issued a directive entitled 'Equal Treatment for Men and Women'.

4.2   In the British Acts, the obligation of 'non-discrimination' applies to all aspects of employment, including advertisements, recruitment and selection programmes, access to training, promotion, disciplinary procedures, redundancy and dismissal.

4.3   There are certain exceptions, in which 'discrimination' is permitted.

(a)   In relation to women, the most important of these are 'genuine occupational qualifications', which include:

(i)   reasons of physiology (not physical strength);

(ii)   reasons of decency or privacy, closely defined;

(iii)   special welfare consideration, or the provision of personal services promoting welfare or education (ie discrimination in *favour* of women); and

(iv)   jobs affected by legal restrictions, particularly jobs likely to involve work outside the UK, where 'laws or customs are such that the duties could not, or could not effectively, be performed by a woman'.

(b)   In the case of ethnic minorities, the exceptions are:

(i)   dramatic performances, where the *dramatis personae* requires a person of a particular racial group;

(ii)   artists or photographic models for advertising purposes, for reasons of authenticity;

(iii)   cafés and restaurants where the ethnicity of the food and drink require people of particular racial groups to maintain authenticity;

(iv)   where personal services are rendered for the welfare of a particular ethnic group.

4.4   The legislation does *not* (except with regard to training) permit 'positive discrimination' - ie actions which give preference to a protected person, regardless of genuine suitability and qualification for the job. In particular, there is no 'quota scheme' such as operates for registered disabled persons ie there is no fixed number or percentage of jobs that must be filled by women or members of ethnic minorities, regardless of other criteria. The organisation may, however, set itself *targets* for the number of such persons that they will *aim* to employ - *if* the required number of eligible and suitably qualified people can be recruited.

4.5   Both race relations and sex discrimination legislation allows *training* to be given to particular groups exclusively, if the group has in the preceding year been substantially under-represented. It is also permissible to *encourage* such groups:

(a)   to apply for jobs where such exclusive training is offered; and
(b)   to apply for jobs in which they are under-represented.

A training body (other than the employer) running such a scheme must be either permitted by the Act, or specially designated by application to the Secretary of State for Employment.

4.6 There are two types of discrimination, under the Acts.

(a) *Direct* discrimination occurs when one interested group is treated less favourably than another (except for exempted cases). It is unlikely that a prospective employer will practice direct discrimination unawares.

(b) *Indirect* discrimination occurs when requirements or conditions are imposed with which a substantial proportion of the interested group could not comply except to their detriment. The employer must, if challenged, justify the conditions on non-racial or non-sexual grounds. It is often the case that employers are not aware that they are discriminating in this way.

> The Commission for Racial Equality's Report of a Formal Investigation into Massey Ferguson Perkins Ltd concluded that: 'The main reason for the under-representation of blacks, we found, was not direct discrimination, but the company's method of recruitment for hourly paid jobs. They did not advertise or use Job Centres ... They simply relied on letters of application.'
>
> Similar decisions relate to discrimination against part-time workers (eg review of their contracts first, for redundancy) where the majority of part-time workers are women.

4.7 A further issue relates to equal opportunities although not directly to the current legislation. This is *sexual harassment*. The examiner has already set a question on this difficult and sensitive topic, in the October 1991 paper.

(a) There have also been a number of court cases about and the case law is still developing on the subject. However:

(i) if a person's promotion or job offer is made conditional on some sort of sexual relationship, then this might be classed as sexual discrimination under the Act;

(ii) a person whose life at work is made intolerable by persistent sexual harassment (or racial abuse for that matter) by a boss or by colleagues or even by the workplace culture, might be able to sue for compensation if it caused that person to resign.

(b) The management problem is a difficult one, especially as banks employ large numbers of women, and there is no definitive guide to every case. What must be considered is that people as a rule do not make complaints frivolously, that harassment by a boss is an abuse of authority, and that the principal judge as to whether someone's behaviour is 'only a bit of fun' is the person to whom that behaviour is directed.

4.8 The Equal Opportunities Commission and the Commission for Racial Equality have powers, subject to certain safeguards, to investigate alleged breach of the Acts, to serve a 'non-discrimination notice', and to follow-up the investigation until satisfied that undertakings given (with regard to compliance and information of persons concerned) are carried out.

Disability

4.9 Another area in which protection against discrimination is provided in law is that of *disability*. The Disabled Persons (Employment) Act 1944 defines a 'disabled person' as: 'A person who, on account of injury, disease, or congenital deformity is substantially handicapped in obtaining or keeping employment...of a kind which apart from the injury, disease or deformity would be suited to his age, qualifications and experience...'

There is a register of disabled persons who are capable of undertaking paid employment, kept by the Secretary of State for Employment.

4.10 The 1944 Act established a *quota scheme*, whereby any employer of more than 20 people must employ at least 3% (the 'standard percentage') of registered disabled persons, unless he has a permit to engage an able-bodied person instead. Appropriate records must be kept. If an employer fails to deep the quota, each new vacancy must be offered to a disable person: only if no-one is available can the vacancy be offered to non-disabled applicants. Certain jobs, eg lift attendant, have become traditionally designated for disabled persons.

4.11 In practice, however, public as well as private organisations frequently fail to meet quota requirements - many protected by bulk exemption permits. As Livy comments: 'Disabled persons, like ethnic minorities and other disadvantaged groups, are adversely affected in the increasingly competitive world of employment.' Livy also notes that the nature of disability is changing, with an increase in mental handicap, organic nervous diseases and psychiatric problems.

4.12 The quota scheme gives priority to disable applicants with equal qualifications, but gives no positive incentives to employers to re-examine job specifications and employ disabled people. It is also a fact that many disabled people are not protected by the quota scheme, because they fail to register themselves, for various reasons. Moreover, there is still no legal provision for access and other facilities for disabled people in work premises: places of employment are outside the scope of the Chronic Sick and Disabled Persons Act 1970!

Equal opportunities in practice

4.13 There is always a risk that a disappointed job applicant will attribute his lack of success to discrimination, especially if the recruiting organisation's workforce is conspicuously lacking in representatives of the same ethnic minority, sex or group. The implications for selection are obviously wide.

(a) *Advertising*. Any wording that suggests preference for a particular sector should be avoided (except for genuine occupational qualifications). Recruitment literature should state that the organisation is an Equal Opportunities employer. The placing of advertisements only where the readership is predominantly of one race or sex is construed as indirect discrimination.

(b) *Recruitment agencies*. Instructions to an agency should not suggest any preference.

(c) *Application forms*. These should include no questions which are not work-related (eg domestic details) and which only one group is asked to complete. Similarly at *interviews*, a non-work-related question must be asked of all subjects. It may be advisable to have a witness at interviews, or at least to take detailed notes, in the event that a claim of discrimination is made. Certainly, at least *one* representative of both sexes and all races of applicants should be invited for interview - even where *all* representatives of one group have unsuitable qualifications. (If none of the women applying, for example, has the required experience, *a* woman should still be interviewed - especially if the workforce is currently all male!)

(d) *Selection tests*. These must be wholly relevant, and should not favour those with limited cultural traditions.

(e) *Records*. Reasons for rejection etc should be carefully recorded, so that in the event of investigation the details will be available.

4.14 Banks are very aware of the need to recruit more women and members of minority groups.

(a) There is greater than ever social awareness of issues such as sexism, racism and opportunities for the disabled, and this forms part of the 'market environment' in which customers and potential customers of banks make their decisions. In other words, the *image* of the bank may suffer through society's perception of it as a white male preserve.

(b) Banks have traditionally relied on an ever-increasing supply of school leavers; now, with the effects of falling birth-rates in the 1970s, they are forced to re-consider their manpower resourcing. Women returning to work and older individuals are two major new sources of labour.

4.15 Most banks have appointed women as equal opportunities managers, and some have pushed the issue even higher up the agenda by appointing a Group Equal Opportunities Director or equivalent position reporting directly to the group Personnel Director. Some of the measures taken in the last ten years or so have included:

(a) flexible hours or part-time work - even 'term-time' contracts to allow for school holidays - to help women to combine careers with family responsibilities;

(b) career-break or return-to-work schemes for women;

(c) 'fast-tracking' school-leavers, as well as graduates, giving more opportunities for movement up the ladder;

(d) training for women-returners, 'women in management' etc to help women to manage their career potential;

(e) 'awareness training' for managers, to encourage them to think about equal opportunity policy;

(f) the provision of workplace nurseries for working mothers;

(g) positive efforts to short-list more minority representatives for job selection;

(h) alteration of premises to accommodate wheelchair users.

4.16 There is still a long way to go to change the culture, systems, and procedures of banks. Women have gained a lot of ground: the percentage of women in banking is much higher (and rising) in senior clerical - eg supervisory - positions than in management, but it is from these posts that future managers will emerge, so this higher proportion will soon be working its way into the system. There is more to do in the case of racial minorities and still more for the disabled.

5. CHAPTER ROUNDUP

5.1

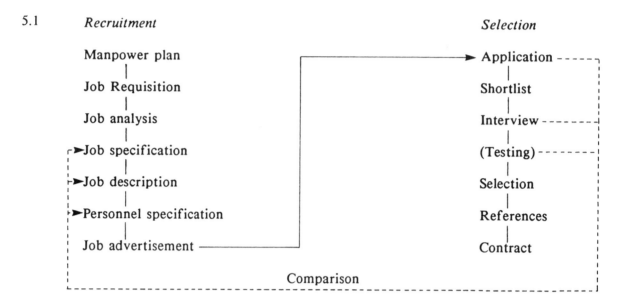

Recruitment	*Selection*
Manpower plan	Application
Job Requisition	Shortlist
Job analysis	Interview
►Job specification	(Testing)
►Job description	Selection
►Personnel specification	References
Job advertisement	Contract
Comparison	

5.2 Direct and indirect discrimination in recruitment and selection (and other personnel systems) can be very subtle. It is also illegal. The issue of Equal Opportunities can seem traumatic to traditional cultures such as banks, but must be addressed for reasons of:

(a) statutory obligation;
(b) public relations;
(c) manpower resourcing.

TEST YOUR KNOWLEDGE

The numbers in brackets refer to paragraphs of this chapter

1   Distinguish between recruitment and selection. (1.2)

2   Outline a comprehensive and systematic approach to recruitment and selection. (1.4)

3   What information would be included in a job description? (2.7)

4   What attributes are included in a personnel specification (any system of your choice)? What is its purpose? (2.9, 2.11, 2.12, 2.13)

5   What are some of the current pressures on bank recruitment policies and procedures? (2.10 - 2.20)

6   What are the four main types of selection and what are the problems associated with selection testing? (3.12, 3.14)

7   What can interviews and tests *not* tell the recruiter? Are there any methods of gathering this information? (3.14, 3.15)

8   Distinguish between direct and indirect discrimination, with examples. (4.6 and box)

9   Why should banks pay attention to equal opportunities? Why might they be reluctant to do so? What has *your* bank done to enhance the position of (a) women (b) disadvantaged groups employed by the bank? (4.13, 4.14, 5.2)

Now try question 2 at the end of the text

Chapter 3

MOTIVATION

This chapter covers the following topics.

1. What is motivation?
2. Need theories of motivation
3. Two-factor theory
4. Expectancy theory
5. The motivation calculus
6. Rewards
7. Motivation and performance

Introduction

A lot of effort can go into recruiting the right person, but in reality that is only part of the story. Once in work, the recruit needs to work efficiently and well, and a number of theories have been developed as to how people can be motivated into giving their best.

---

1. WHAT IS MOTIVATION?

1.1 The meaning of the words 'motives' and 'motivation' are commonly vary in different contexts.

    (a) *Goals, or outcomes* that have become desirable for a particular individual. These are more properly 'motivating factors' - since they give people a reason for behaving in a certain way (ie in pursuit of the chosen goal): thus we say that money, power or friendship are 'motives' for doing something.

    (b) The *mental process of choosing desired outcomes*, deciding how to go about them (whether the likelihood of success warrants the amount of effort that will be necessary etc.) and setting in motion the required behaviours. Our motivation to do something will depend on this 'calculation' of the relationship between needs/goals, behaviour and outcome;

    (c) The *social process* by which the behaviour of an individual is influenced by others. 'Motivation' in this sense usually applies to the attempts of organisations to get workers to put in more effort by offering them certain rewards (financial and non-financial) if they do so.

1.2 In short:

    (a) we 'are motivated' by our goals, the expected outcomes of certain behaviours;

    (b) we 'are motivated' when we decide to behave in a way that we believe will fulfil our goals;

(c) we 'are motivated' by other people to behave in a way that they desire.

1.3 One way of grouping the major theories of motivation is by distinguishing between *content theories* and *process theories*.

1.4 Content theories of motivation assume that human beings have a 'package' of motives which they pursue, ie they have a set of needs or desired outcomes. Maslow's need hierarchy theory and Herzberg's two-factor theory are two of the most important approaches of this type.

1.5 Process theories of motivation explore the process through which outcomes *become* desirable and are pursued by individuals. This approach assumes that man is able to select his goals and choose the paths towards them, by a conscious or unconscious process of calculation. Expectancy theory, and Handy's motivation calculus, are theories of this type. They take a 'contingency' approach by stressing the number of variables that influence the individual's decision in each case: there is no 'best way' to motivate people.

2. NEED THEORIES OF MOTIVATION

2.1 Need theories are content theories that suggest that the 'desired outcome' of behaviour in individuals is the *satisfaction of needs*.

2.2 The American psychologist Abraham Maslow argued that man has seven innate needs. Maslow's categories are:

(a) physiological needs — food, drink, sleep

(b) safety needs — freedom from threat, but also security, order, predictability

(c) social needs — for relationships, affection, sense of belonging

(d) esteem needs — for competence, achievement, independence, confidence and their reflection in the perception of others, ie recognition, appreciation, status, respect

(e) self-actualisation needs — for the fulfilment of personal potential: 'the desire to become more and more what one is, to become everything that one is capable of becoming'

(f) freedom of inquiry expression needs — for social conditions permitting free speech and encouraging justice, fairness and honesty

(g) knowledge and understanding need — to gain and order knowledge of the environment, to explore, learn, experiment etc.

According to Maslow, the last two needs are the channels through which we find ways of satisfying all the other needs, ie they are the basis of satisfaction. The first two needs are essential to human survival. Satisfaction of the next two is essential for a sense of adequacy and psychological health. Maslow regarded self-actualisation as the ultimate human goal, although few people ever reach it. We will discuss the 'hierarchy' into which Maslow put his needs below.

2.3 David McClelland, writing in the 1950s, identified three types of motivating need.

(a) *The need for power*. People with a high need for power usually seek positions of leadership in order to influence and control.

(b) *The need for affiliation*. People who need a sense of 'belonging' and membership of a social group tend to be concerned with maintaining good personal relationships.

(c) *The need for achievement*. People who need to achieve have a strong desire for success and a strong fear of failure.

Maslow's hierarchy of needs

2.4 In his motivation theory, Maslow put forward certain propositions about the motivating power of needs.

(a) People's needs can be arranged in a 'hierarchy of relative pre-potency'.

(b) Each 'level' of need is dominant until satisfied; only then does the next level of need become a motivating factor.

2.5 There is a certain intuitive appeal to Maslow's theory. After all, you are unlikely to be concerned with status or recognition while you are hungry or thirsty - primary survival needs will take precedence. Likewise, once your hunger is assuaged, the need for food is unlikely to be a motivating factor. Unfortunately, research does not bear out the proposition that needs become less powerful as they are satisfied, except at the very primitive level ie of 'primary' needs, hunger and thirst etc.

2.6 There are various problems associated with Maslow's theory.

(a) Empirical verification for the hierarchy is hard to come by.

(b) 'Maslow may simply have reflected American middle class values and the pursuit of the good life, and may not have hit on fundamental universal truths about human psychology.'
(Buchanan & Huczynski, *Organisational behaviour*)

(c) It is difficult to predict behaviour using the hierarchy: the theory is too vague. It is impossible to define how much satisfaction has to be achieved before the individual progresses to the next level in the hierarchy. Different people emphasise different needs. Also, the same need may cause different behaviour in different individuals.

(d) Application of the theory in work contexts presents various difficulties. The role of money or 'pay' is problematic, since it arguably acts as a representative or 'stand in' for other rewards - status, recognition, independence etc. Moreover, as Drucker notes, a want changes in the act of being satisfied: 'incentives' such as remuneration, once regularly provided, come to be perceived as 'entitlements', and their capacity to create dissatisfaction, to become a deterrent to performance, outstrips their motivatory power. Self actualisation, in particular, is difficult to offer employees in practice.

3. TWO-FACTOR THEORY

3.1 In the 1950s, the American psychologist Frederick Herzberg interviewed 203 Pittsburgh engineers and accountants and asked two 'critical incident' questions. The subjects were asked to recall events which had made them feel good about their work, others which made them feel bad about it. Analysis revealed that the factors which created satisfaction were different from those which created dissatisfaction.

3.2 In his book *Work and the nature of man* Herzberg identified the factors which cause job dissatisfaction and those which cause job satisfaction. He distinguished between 'hygiene factors' and 'motivator factors'. He saw two needs of individuals:

(a) the need to avoid unpleasantness, satisfied by 'hygiene factors'; and
(b) the need for personal growth, satisfied at work by 'motivator factors' only.

3.3 Hygiene factors include:

(a) company policy and administration;
(b) salary;
(c) the quality of supervision;
(d) interpersonal relations;
(e) working conditions;
(f) job security.

3.4 'When people are dissatisfied with their work it is usually because of discontent with the environmental factors'.

Herzberg calls such factors *hygiene factors* because they are essentially preventative. They prevent or minimise dissatisfaction but do not give satisfaction, in the same way that sanitation minimises threats to health, but does not give 'good' health. They are also called 'maintenance' factors because they have to be continually renewed. Satisfaction with environmental factors is not lasting. In time dissatisfaction will occur. For example an individual might want a pay rise which protects his income against inflation. If he is successful in obtaining the rise he wants, he will be satisfied for the time being, but only until next year's salary review.

3.5 *Motivator factors* create job satisfaction and are effective in motivating an individual to superior performance and effort. These factors give the individual a sense of self-fulfilment or personal growth, and consist of:

(a) status (although this may be a hygiene factor as well as a motivator factor);
(b) advancement;
(c) gaining recognition;
(d) being given responsibility;
(e) challenging work;
(f) achievement;
(g) growth in the job.

3.6 Herzberg suggested means by which motivator satisfactions could be supplied. Stemming from his fundamental division of motivator and hygiene factors, he encouraged managers to study the job itself (ie the type of work done, the nature of tasks, levels of responsibility) rather than conditions of work. 'Dissatisfaction arises from environment factors - satisfaction can only arise from the job.' If there is sufficient challenge, scope and interest in the job, there will be a lasting increase in satisfaction and the employee will work well; productivity will be above 'normal' levels. The extent to which a job must be challenging or creative to a motivator-seeker will depend on each individual ie. his ability and his tolerance for delayed success.

3.7 As will be discussed in Chapter 20, Herzberg specified three typical means whereby work can be revised to improve motivation.

(a) *Job enrichment,* or 'the planned process of up-grading the responsibility, challenge and content of the work'. Typically, this would involve increasing delegation to provide more interesting work and problem-solving at lower levels in the organisation.

(b) *Job enlargement,* the process of increasing the number of operations in which a worker is engaged and so moving away from narrow specialisation of work.

(c) *Job rotation,* or the planned operation of a system whereby staff members exchange positions with the intention of breaking monotony in the work and providing fresh job challenge.

Exercise 1

Are you affected more by hygiene than motivator factors? What about your colleagues?

---

4. EXPECTANCY THEORY

4.1 The expectancy theory of motivation is a process theory, based on the assumptions that human beings are purposive and rational, ie aware of their goals and behaviour. Essentially, the theory states that the strength of an individual's motivation to do something will depend on the extent to which he *expects* the results of his efforts, if successfully achieved, to contribute towards his personal needs or goals.

4.2 In 1964 Victor Vroom, an American psychologist, worked out a formula by which human motivation could actually be assessed and measured, based on an expectancy theory of work motivation. Vroom suggested that the strength of an individual's motivation is the product of two factors:

(a) the strength of his preference for a certain outcome. Vroom called this *valence*. It may be represented as a positive or negative number, or zero - since outcomes may be desired, avoided or considered with indifference; and

(b) his expectation that the outcome will result from a certain behaviour. Vroom called this *subjective probability*: it is only the individual's 'expectation', and depends on his perception of the probable relationship between behaviour and outcome. As a probability, it may be represented by any number between 0 (no chance) and 1 (certainty).

4.3 In its simplest form, the 'expectancy equation' therefore looks like this.

Valence ie strength of his preference for a certain outcome	×	**E**xpectation that behaviour will result in desired outcome	=	**F**orce or strength of motivation to do something

4.4 This is what you would expect: if either valence or expectation have a value of zero, there will be no motivation.

(a) If an employee has a high expectation that productivity will result in a certain outcome eg. promotion, but he is indifferent to that outcome (eg doesn't want the responsibility), $V = 0$, and he will not be motivated to productive behaviour.

(b) If the employee has a great desire for promotion - but doesn't believe that productive behaviour will secure it for him, $E = 0$, and he will still not be highly motivated.

(c) If $V = -1$, (eg because the employee fears responsibility and doesn't want to leave his work group), the value for motivation will be negative, and the employee may deliberately under-produce.

4.5 Expectancy theory attempts to measure the strength of an individual's motivation to act in a particular way. It is then possible to compare 'F' values for a range of different behaviours, to discover which behaviour the individual is most likely to adopt. It is also possible to compare 'F' values for different individuals, to see who is most highly motivated to behave in the desired (or undesirable) way.

5. THE MOTIVATION CALCULUS

5.1 Charles Handy (*Understanding organisations*) puts forward an 'admittedly theoretical' but attractive model not unlike the expectancy model. He suggests that it should be regarded 'as the way the individual deals with *individual* decisions, to do or not to do something... to apportion or not to apportion his time, energy and talents. This approach is based on the idea that man is a self-activating organism, and can, to some degree, control his own destiny and his own responses to pressures, that he can select his goals and choose the paths towards them'.

5.2 Handy suggests that for any individual decision, there is a conscious or unconscious 'motivation calculus' which is an assessment of three factors:

(a) the individual's own set of needs (these may be defined in any of the ways suggested by Maslow, Herzberg, McClelland and others);

(b) the desired results - ie what the individual is expected to do in his job;

(c) 'E' factors. Handy suggests that motivational theories have been too preoccupied with 'effort'. He notes that there seems to be a set of words, coincidentally beginning with 'e', that might be more helpful. As well as effort, there is energy, excitement in achieving desired results, enthusiasm, emotion, and expenditure (of time, money etc.).

5.3 The 'motivation decision' - ie how strong the motivation to achieve the desired results will be - will depend on the individual person's judgement about:

(a) the strength of his needs;
(b) the *expectancy* that expending 'E' will lead to a desired result; and
(c) how far achievement of the result will be 'instrumental' in satisfying his needs.

5.4 A man may have a need for power. To the degree that he believes (expectancy) that a particular result, eg a completed task, will gain him promotion *and* that promotion will in fact satisfy his need for power ('instrumentality') he will expend 'E' on the task. The higher his need for power the more 'E' he will put forth. If, however, experience has led him to believe that even if he completes the task, he will not be promoted (low expectancy) he will not think much 'E' expenditure worthwhile: the same will be true if he believes he *will* get promotion, but to a position that will not give him much power - (low instrumentality).

5.5 In terms of organisation practice, Handy suggests that several factors are necessary for the individual to complete the calculus, and to be motivated.

(a) *Intended results* should be made clear, so that the individual can complete his 'calculation', and know what is expected of him, what will be rewarded and how much 'E' it will take.

(b) Without knowledge of *actual results*, there is no check that the 'E' expenditure was justified (and will be justified in future). *Feedback* on performance - good or bad - is essential, not only for performance but for confidence, prevention of hostility etc.

6. REWARDS

6.1 You will notice that not all the 'rewards' or 'incentives' that an organisation can offer its employees are directly related to money. The satisfaction of any of the employee's wants or needs may be seen as a reward for past or future performance.

6.2 Different individuals have different goals, and get different things out of their working life: in other words they have different 'orientations' to work. Any one or combination of the 'needs' identified by Maslow and others may be the reason why a person works, or is motivated to work well.

(a) The human relations school, taking the 'Social Man' model, regarded work relationships as the main reward offered to the worker.

(b) Later writers adopted the 'Complex Man' model, and suggested a wide range of motivations, including:

(i) job satisfaction, ie interest and challenge in the job itself - 'rewarding' work;
(ii) participation in decision-making - responsibility and involvement;
(iii) the culture of the organisation, which itself can offer a range of psychological and physical rewards.

(c) Pay has always occupied a rather ambiguous position, but since people need money to live, it will certainly be *part* of the reward 'package' an individual gets from his work.

Job satisfaction

6.3 According to Herzberg, job satisfaction is offered by various factors at work which make employees 'feel good' about their work and jobs, and is a source of motivation and higher productivity.

6.4 Don't assume, however, that 'happiness' automatically means productivity!

(a) There is little evidence that a satisfied worker actually works harder - so increased productivity per se will not imply 'satisfaction' on the part of the work force. They may be motivated by fear, work methods may have been improved etc;

(b) There is, however, support for the idea that satisfied workers tend to be loyal, and stay in the organisation.

(i) *Labour turnover* (the rate at which people leave an organisation) may therefore be an indication of dissatisfaction in the workforce - although there is a certain amount of 'natural' loss (eg through retirement) in any case, as well as loss due to relocation, redundancy etc.

(ii) *Absenteeism* may also be an indication of dissatisfaction, or possibly of genuine physical or emotional distress;

(c) There is also evidence that satisfaction correlates with mental health - so that symptoms of stress, psychological failure etc. may be a signal to management that all is not well.

3: MOTIVATION

Participation as a means of motivation

6.5 There is a theory that if a superior invites his subordinates to participate in planning decisions which affect their work, if the subordinates voluntarily accept the invitation, and results about actual performance are fed back regularly to the subordinates so that they can make their own control decisions, then the subordinate will be motivated:

(a) to be more efficient;
(b) to be more conscious of the organisation's goals;
(c) to raise his or her planning targets to reasonably challenging levels;
(d) to be ready to take appropriate control actions when necessary.

6.6 What exactly does participation involve and why might it be a good thing? Handy commented that: 'Participation is sometimes regarded as a form of job enlargement. At other times it is a way of gaining commitment by workers to some proposal on the grounds that if you have been involved in discussing it, you will be more interested in its success. In part, it is the outcome of almost cultural belief in the norms of democratic leadership. It is one of those "good" words with which it is hard to disagree.'

6.7 The advantages of participation should perhaps be considered from the opposite end - ie what would be the disadvantages of *not* having participation? The answer to this is that employees would be told what to do, and would presumably comply with orders. However, their compliance would not be enthusiastic, and they would not be psychologically committed to their work.

6.8 Participation can involve employees and make them committed to their task, if certain conditions are satisfied.

(a) Participation should be genuine. It is very easy for a boss to pretend to invite participation from his subordinates but end up issuing orders. If subordinates feel the decision has already been taken, they might resent the falsehood of management efforts to discuss the decision with them.

(b) The efforts to establish participation should be continual and pushed over a long period of time and with a lot of energy. However, 'if the issue or the task is trivial, or foreclosed, and everyone realises it, participative methods will boomerang. Issues that do not affect the individuals concerned will not, on the whole, engage their interest'. (Handy).

(c) The purpose of the participation of employees in a decision should be made quite clear from the outset. If employees are consulted to make a decision, their views should carry the decision. If, however, they are consulted for advice, their views need not necessarily be accepted;.

(d) The individuals really have the abilities and the information to join in decision-making effectively.

(e) The manager wishes for participation from his subordinates, and does not suggest it because he thinks it is the 'done thing'.

6.9 'It is simply naive to think that participative approaches are always more effective than authoritarian styles of management or vice versa. The critics as well as the advocates of participative management would therefore be wise to direct their energies towards identifying the situations in which a variety of decision-making styles are effective, other than towards universalistic claims for the applicability or otherwise of any single approach.' (Hopwood)

Quality circles

6.10 Quality circles emerged first in the United States, but it was in Japan that they were adopted most enthusiastically. The modern success story of Japanese industry has prompted Western countries to imitate many of the Japanese working methods, with the result that quality circles are now re-appearing in American and West European companies, and some major banks.

6.11 A quality circle consists of a group of employees, perhaps about eight in number, which meets regularly to discuss problems of quality and quality control in their area of work, and perhaps to suggest ways of improving quality. The quality circle has a leader or supervisor who directs discussions and possibly also helps to train other members of the circle. Quality circles are not *random* groups of employees. To make the system work a number of factors must be considered.

   (a) A quality circle is a *voluntary* grouping. There is no point in coercing employees to join because the whole point is to develop a spontaneous concern for quality amongst workers.

   (b) Quality circles do not function automatically. Training may be needed in methods of quality control, problem solving techniques and methods of communication.

   (c) The right leader must be chosen. The person required is one who is capable of directing discussions and drawing out contributions from each member of the circle.

6.12 Ideally, quality circles should be given more responsibility than merely suggesting or even 'championing' improvements; commitment may be increased if the members of quality circles have responsibility for implementing their recommendations. In practice quality circles may become 'talk shops' for problem-solving, inter-disciplinary communication and suggestion/idea generation. Even so, their value should not be underestimated.

6.13 Benefits claimed to arise from the use of quality circles include:

   (a) greater motivation and involvement of employees;
   (b) improved productivity and quality of output;
   (c) greater awareness of problems by operational staff;
   (d) greater awareness of quality and service issues, market and individual customer needs etc.

Culture as a motivator

6.14 'Culture' is the shared value system of an organisation. Drucker speaks of the 'spirit of performance', which is the 'creation of energy' in the organisation. Peters and Waterman argue that employees can be 'switched on' to extraordinary loyalty and effort in some cases.

   (a) The cause should be perceived to be in some sense great – ie 'reaffirming the heroic dimension' of the work. Commitment comes from believing that a task is inherently worthwhile. Devotion to the *customer*, and his needs and wants, is an important motivator in this way. 'Owing to good luck, or maybe even good sense, those companies that emphasise quality, reliability, and service have chosen the *only* area where it is readily possible to generate excitement in the average down-the-line employee. They give people pride in what the do. They make it possible to love the product.' Shared values and 'good news swapping' - a kind of folklore of past success and 'heroic' endeavour - create a climate where intrinsic motivation is a real driving force.

(b) They should be treated as winners. 'Label a man a loser and he'll start acting like one.' Repressive control systems and negative reinforcement break down the employee's self-image. Positive reinforcement, 'good news swapping', attention from management etc. enhance the employee's self-image and create positive attitudes to work and to the organisation.

(c) They should satisfy their dual needs to:

(i) be a conforming, secure part of a successful team; and
(ii) be a 'star' in their own right.

This means giving control through firm central direction, and shared values and beliefs, but also maximum individual autonomy (at least, the *illusion* of control) - even competition between individuals or groups within the organisation. Peters and Waterman call this 'loose-tight' management. Culture, peer pressure, a focus on action, customer-orientation etc. are 'non-aversive' ways of exercising control over employees.

Pay as a motivator

6.15 Pay has a central - but ambiguous - role in motivation theory. It is not mentioned explicitly in any 'need' list, but it may be the means to an infinite number of specific ends, ie the satisfaction of many of the various needs. Individuals may also, however, have needs unrelated to money, which money cannot satisfy, or which the pay system of the organisation actively denies. So to what extent is pay an inducement to better performance, ie a motivator or incentive?

6.16 An employee needs income to live, and to attain and/or maintain a desired standard of living. However, people tend not to be concerned to *maximise* their earnings. They may like to earn more, but are probably more concerned:

(a) to earn *enough* pay; and
(b) to know that their pay is *fair* in comparison with the pay of others both inside and outside the organisation.

6.17 *Equity* (perceived fairness of pay in relation to the job and to the pay of others) is often more important than maximising income, once the individual has 'enough' pay to maintain a satisfactory lifestyle. Yet the 'Economic Man' model - which assumes that people will adjust their effort if offered monetary incentives - persists in payment-by-results schemes, bonuses, profit-sharing etc.

> Payment systems then have to tread the awkward path between equity (objective rate for the job, preserved differentials etc) and incentive (reward for extra effort and attainment by particular individuals and groups).

6.18 The 'Affluent Worker' research of Goldthorpe, Lockwood et al (1968) illustrated the 'instrumental' orientation to work (ie the attitude that work is not an end in itself, but a means to other ends). The highly paid Luton car assembly workers experienced their work as routine and dead-end. The researchers concluded that they had made a rational decision to enter employment offering high monetary reward rather than intrinsic interest: they were getting out of their jobs what they most wanted from them.

6.19 The Luton researchers, however, did not claim that *all* workers have an instrumental orientation to work, but suggested that a person will seek a suitable balance of:

(a) the rewards which are important to him; and
(b) the deprivations he feels able to put up with.

6.20 Even those with an instrumental orientation to work have limits to their purely financial aspirations, and will cease to be motivated by money if the 'deprivations' - in terms of working hours and conditions, social isolation etc - become too great, ie if the 'price' of pay is too high. High taxation rates may also weight the 'deprivation' side of the calculation; workers may perceive that a great deal of extra effort etc will in fact earn them little extra reward.

6.21 Pay is a 'hygiene' rather than a 'motivator' factor (Herzberg). It gets taken for granted, and so is more usually a source of dissatisfaction than satisfaction. Lawler suggested that in the absence of information about how much colleagues are earning, individuals guess their earnings and usually over-estimate. This then leaves them dissatisfied because they resent earning less than they *think* their colleagues are getting.

6.22 However pay is the most important of the hygiene factors, according to Herzberg. It is valuable not only in its power to be converted into a wide range of other satisfactions (perhaps the only way in which organisations can - at least indirectly - cater for individual employee needs and wants through a common reward system) but also as a consistent measure of worth or value, allowing employees to compare themselves and be compared with other individuals, occupational groups etc inside and outside the organisation.

Exercise 2

What types of motivational technique are used in your bank? How does your boss try to motivate you, and how do you try to motivate your subordinates?

---

7. MOTIVATION AND PERFORMANCE

7.1 You may be wondering whether motivation is really so important. It could be argued that if a person is employed to do a job, he will do that job and no question of motivation arises. If the person doesn't want to do the work, he can resign. The point at issue, however, is the *efficiency* with which the job is done. It is suggested that if individuals can be motivated, by one means or another, they will work more efficiently (ie productivity will rise) or they will produce a better quality of work. There is some debate as to what the actual effects of improved motivation are, efficiency or quality, but it has become widely accepted that motivation is beneficial to the organisation.

7.2 Barnard suggested that management needs to understand what motivates employees and act to encourage such motivation; otherwise, many employees will tend to act in a negative way, contrary to the aims of the organisation. 'If all those who may be considered potential contributors to an organisation are arranged in order of willingness to serve it, the scale descends from possibly intense willingness through neutral or zero willingness to intense opposition or hatred. The preponderance of persons in a modern society always lies on the negative side with reference to any existing or potential organisation.'

7.3 The case for 'job satisfaction' as a factor in efficiency is not proven. You should be clear in your own minds that although it seems obviously a 'Good Thing' to have employees who enjoy their work and are interested in it, there is no reason why the organisation should want a 'satisfied' work force unless it makes the organisation function better: it is good for 'human' reasons, but it is not necessarily relevant to organisational efficiency or effectiveness.

7.4 It is a point of debate whether 'intrinsic' satisfaction motivates employees to improved performance, or whether it works more the other way around - ie the perception of success and achievement from good performance is itself an important source of satisfaction.

8. CHAPTER ROUNDUP

8.1 'Motivation' is a term used in different contexts to refer to:

(a) goals or outcomes that have become desirable for a particular individual, as in 'he is motivated by money'

(b) the mental process of choosing a goal and deciding whether and how to achieve it, as in: 'he is motivated to work harder'

(c) the social process by which the behaviour of an individual is influenced by others, as in: 'the manager motivates his team'.

8.2 *Content* theories suggest that man has a 'package' of needs: the best way to motivate an employee is to find out what his needs are and offer him rewards that will satisfy those needs.

(a) Abraham Maslow identified seven innate needs of all individuals and arranged them in a hierarchy, suggesting that an individual will be motivated to satisfy each category, starting at the bottom before going on to seek 'higher order' satisfactions

(b) Frederick Herzberg identified two basic need systems: the need to avoid unpleasantness and the need for personal growth. He suggested factors which could be offered by organisations to satisfy both types of need: 'hygiene' and 'motivator' factors respectively.

8.3 *Process* theories do not tell managers what to offer employees in order to motivate them, but help managers to understand the dynamics of employees' decisions about what rewards are worth 'going for'. They are generally variations on the *expectancy* model which might work as follows.

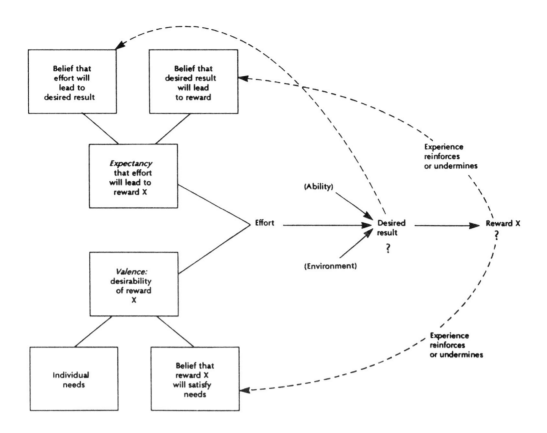

TEST YOUR KNOWLEDGE
The numbers in brackets refer to paragraphs of this chapter

1 What is the difference between process and content theories of motivation? (1.4, 1.5)

2 What are the seven needs identified by Maslow? Incorporate the relevant needs in a simple hierarchy. (2.2, 2.4)

3 List five motivator and five hygiene factors. (3.3, 3.5)

4 Explain the formula 'V × E = F'. (4.2, 4.3)

5 What are 'E' factors, and when are they put forth most strongly by an individual? (5.2, 5.3)

6 What are quality circles? Why might a bank want to use them? (6.9 - 6.13)

7 'People will work harder and harder to earn more and more pay.' Do you agree? Why (or why not)? (6.15 - 6.22)

Now try question 3 at the end of the text

Chapter 4

REWARD

This chapter covers the following topics.

1. Job evaluation
2. Remuneration
3. Salary structures
4. Salary planning and control
5. Incentives
6. Fringe benefits

Introduction

In the previous chapter, we introduced 'pay' (financial reward) and its role as a motivator. We noticed that there is a dilemma for management in the dual requirements in reward systems for:

(a) *equity* ie pay rates for a job that are fair in relation to others, that accurately reflect the relative worth of the job; and

(b) *incentive* ie the need to be able to offer extra reward for extraordinary effort and attainment: 'dangling the carrot'.

In this chapter we discuss how reward systems can be designed to fulfil both or either of these requirements.

---

1. JOB EVALUATION

1.1 Job evaluation is a systematic method of arriving at a wage or salary structure, so that the rate of pay for a job is felt to be *fair* in comparison with other jobs in the organisation.

The Institute of Administrative Management's *Office job evaluation* (1976) describes its purpose in the following way. 'Any job for which a wage or salary is offered has been evaluated in some way or other in order to arrive at the amount of payment to be made. To this extent it might be said that all organisations which pay employees have job evaluation. However, the term 'job evaluation' is mostly used nowadays with greater precision to describe a formal standardised method for ranking jobs and grouping them into grades. Invariably, such systems are used primarily as the basis for a payment structure....'

1.2 The British Institute of Management *(Job evaluation)* gives the following definition. 'Job evaluation is the process of analysing and assessing the content of jobs, in order to place them in an acceptable rank order which can then be used as a basis for a remuneration system.'

1.3 The advantages of a job-evaluated salary structure are as follows.

    (a) The salary structure is based on a formal study of work content, and the reasons for salary differentials between jobs has a rational basis that can be explained to anyone who objects to his salary level or grading in comparison with others.

    (b) The salary structure should be well balanced, even in an organisation that employs people with a wide range of different technical skills (eg engineers, accountants, salesmen).

    (c) The salary structure is based on job content, and not on the personal merit of the job-holder himself. The individual job-holder can be paid personal bonuses in reward for his efforts, and when he moves to another job in the organisation, his replacement on the job will be paid the rate for the job, and will not 'inherit' any personal bonuses of his predecessor.

    (d) Regular job evaluation should ensure that the salary structure reflects current changes in the work content of jobs, and is not outdated, so that pay differentials remain fair.

    (e) A job-evaluated salary structure might protect an employer from the accusation that rates of pay discriminate between different types of worker - eg between men and women, who by law (the Equal Pay Act 1970) should be paid the same rate for 'like work', 'work rated as equivalent' or 'work of equal value'.

    (f) Analysis of job content and worth are available for use in recruitment, selection, training etc.

1.4 Job-evaluated salary structures do have some flaws, however.

    (a) They pay a fair rate for a job only in the sense that differentials are set according to *relative* worth. Job evaluation does not make any recommendations about what the general level of pay ought to be, in money terms. Indeed it cannot do so without reference to outside factors such as rates fixed by collective bargaining, statutory obligation or local custom.

    (b) They pay a rate for the job irrespective of the personal merits of the job holder or fluctuations in his performance. If an organisation rewards individual merit with bonuses, evaluated differentials will again be distorted.

    (c) Many job evaluation methods suggest that job evaluation is a scientific and accurate technique, whereas in fact there is a large element of subjective judgement involved in awarding points or ratings, and evaluations can be unfair.

    (d) Job-evaluated salary structures can get out-of-date. There ought to be periodic reviews, but in practice, an organisation might fail to review jobs often enough.

4: REWARD

Methods of job evaluation

1.5 In large organisations, it is impossible to evaluate every individual job, because the process would be too long and costly. Instead, selected 'key' jobs are evaluated, and other similar jobs would be given the same evaluation without further analysis. In this way the 'key jobs' provide a benchmark for the evaluation of other jobs. Ideally, the key jobs chosen for analysis should be jobs comparable with jobs in other organisations, for which a 'market' rate of pay is known. (Some information may already be available in the form of *job descriptions*.)

1.6 It may be said that, even in its more 'quantitative' or 'analytical' forms, job evaluation is 'systematic' rather than 'scientific'. The number of different inputs and environmental variables make the element of subjectivity inevitable, despite refinements aimed at minimising it. 'Non-analytical' approaches to job evaluation make largely subjective judgements about the 'whole job', its difficulty, its importance to the organisation etc relative to other jobs. (Ranking and 'time span of discretion' are methods of this type.)

1.7 'Analytical' methods of job evaluation identify the component factors or characteristics involved in the performance of each job, eg skill, responsibility, experience, mental and physical efforts required. Each component is separately analysed, evaluated and weighted: degrees of each factor, and the importance of the factor within the job, are quantified. (Examples of such methods include 'points rating' and 'factor comparison'.) These methods involve detailed analysis and a numerical basis for comparing jobs as like to like. However, there is still an element of subjectivity, in that:

(a) the factors for analysis are themselves qualitative, not easy to define and measure. Mental ability and initiative are observable in job holders, but not easily quantifiable as an element of the job itself;

(b) assessment of the importance and difficulty of a job cannot objectively be divorced from the context of the organisation and job holder. The relative importance of a job is a function of the culture and politics of the organisation, the nature of the business and not least the personal power of the individual in the job. The difficulty of the job depends on the favourability or otherwise of the environment/technology/work methods/management etc;

(c) the selection of factors and the assignment of monetary values to factors remain subjective judgements.

1.8 It is undoubtedly desirable to achieve objectivity, to reduce the resentment commonly felt at the apparent arbitrariness of pay decisions. If job evaluation were truly objective, it would be possible to justify differentials on a rational basis, the organisation would have a balanced and economical pay structure based on contribution, and employers would be safe from accusations of unfair pay decisions.

1.9 Despite the element of subjectivity even in the 'analytical' methods of job evaluation, it may be true to say that *any* form of job evaluation is useful, minimising the (real or perceived) arbitrariness of pay decisions, removing personality issues from pay reviews etc. The four main methods of job evaluation are:

(a) ranking;
(b) classification;

(c) factor comparison;
(d) points rating.

Ranking method

1.10 In a ranking system of job evaluation, each job is considered as a whole (rather than in terms of job elements) and ranked in accordance with its relative importance or contribution to the organisation. Having established a list of jobs in descending order of importance, they can be divided into groups, and jobs in each group given the same grade and salary. The number of groups of jobs chosen will depend on how many grades in the management hierarchy the organisation's leaders want to have.

(a) The advantage of the ranking method is that it is simple and unscientific. In a small organisation, it might be applied with fairness.

(b) However, the job evaluators need to have a good personal knowledge of every job being evaluated and in a large organisation, they are unlikely to have it. Without this knowledge, the ranking method would not produce fair evaluations. This is why more complex methods of job evaluation have been devised.

Classification method

1.11 This is similar to the ranking method, except that instead of ranking jobs in order of mportance and then dividing them into grades, the classification method begins with deciding what grades there ought to be (eg grades A, B, C, D and E with each grade carefully defined) and then deciding into which grade each individual job should be classified - eg is the job a grade C or a grade D job?

1.12 Like the ranking method, the classification method evaluates each job as a whole, without analysing it into job elements. The disadvantage of the classification method is that the job evaluators require a good personal knowledge of each job being evaluated, otherwise the evaluation process is likely to be unfair and consequently unsatisfactory.

Factor comparison method

1.13 This is an analytical method of job evaluation, that begins with the selection of a number of qualitative factors on which each job will be evaluated. These qualitative factors might include, for example, technical knowledge, physical skill, mental skill, responsibility for other people, responsibility for assets, working conditions etc.

1.14 Key benchmark jobs are then taken, for which the rate of pay is considered to be fair (perhaps in comparison with similar jobs in other organisations). Each key job is analysed in turn, factor by factor, to decide how much of the total salary is being paid for each factor. So if technical skill is 50% of a benchmark job paying £10,000, the factor pay rate for technical skill (within that job) is £5,000.

When this has been done for every benchmark job, all the different rates of pay for each factor are correlated, to formulate a ranking and pay scale for that factor.

1.15 Other (non-benchmark) jobs are then evaluated by analysing them factor by factor. In this way a salary or grading for the *job* can be built up. For example, analysis of a bank clerk's job by factor by factor might be

Factor	Proportion of job		Pay rate for factor (as established by analysis of benchmark jobs)	Job value £
Technical skills	50%	×	£12,000 pa	6,000
Mental ability	25%	×	£16,000 pa	4,000
Responsibility for others	15%	×	£10,000 pa	1,500
Other responsibilities	10%	×	£5,000 pa	500
				12,000

1.16 The Institute of Administrative Management comments about the factor comparison method that: 'the system links rates closely to existing levels for key benchmark jobs and depends heavily on careful allocation of money values to each factor of the benchmark jobs. It is not easy to explain to employees, and is best suited to situations where the range of jobs is limited and of a fairly simple nature.' It is not well-suited to the evaluation of office jobs.

Points rating method

1.17 Points rating is probably the most popular method of formal job evaluation. It begins with listing a number of factors which are thought to represent the qualities being looked for in the jobs to be evaluated. (Note: remember that jobs are being evaluated, not job holders themselves, and the qualities listed should relate to the jobs themselves). In a typical evaluation scheme, there might be about 8-12 factors listed. The factors will vary according to the type of organisation, but they might include:

(a) skill - education, experience, dexterity, qualifications;
(b) initiative;
(c) physical or mental effort;
(d) dealing with others;
(e) responsibility for subordinates, or the safety and welfare of others;
(f) responsibility for equipment, for a process or product, for materials;
(g) job conditions - eg monotony of working, working in isolation, unavoidable work hazards.

1.18 A number of points is allocated to each factor, as a maximum score. In this way, each factor is given a different weighting according to how important it is thought to be . Each job is then examined, analysed factor by factor, and a points score awarded for each factor, up to the maximum allowed. The total points score for each job is found by adding up its points score for each factor. The total points scored for each job provides the basis for ranking the jobs in order of importance for grading jobs, if required, and for fixing a salary structure.

1.19 Points rating has the advantage of flexibility in that the factors selected are best suited for the particular types of job being evaluated.

4: REWARD

Introducing a job evaluation scheme

1.20 The following steps will be taken in introducing a job evaluation programme.

(a) Informing and involving staff - particularly where trade union attitudes need to be considered.

(b) Selecting benchmark jobs as a sample for internal and external comparison.

(c) Planning the programme itself, including:

(i) staffing - who is responsible? what training do they need?
(ii) information - to management, staff and unions;
(iii) procedures and methods, timetable etc;
(iv) techniques for pay comparison, job analysis etc as required.

(d) Communicating and negotiating the results and structure.

(e) Maintaining the scheme; regradings, appeals etc.

1.21 Job evaluation is a highly 'political' exercise, and will require openness and communication - not to mention diplomacy - throughout.

(a) Staff will have to be informed of the overall purpose, objectives and potential benefits of the system. It will, in particular, have to be made clear that the employees themselves are not being judged or evaluated. Increasingly, job evaluation *committees* are used, to involve staff in setting up, conducting and maintaining the scheme, to take advantage of the job holders' knowledge, and to minimise suspicion and demoralisation;

(b) The degree of consultation and participation will depend heavily on union attitudes (where unionisation exists). Unions may consider that job evaluation should be the true basis for *job* structuring only - otherwise it undermines the traditional role of collective bargaining. Others may simply insist on full communication between management and unions throughout the programme, the active participation of union members, and the institution of revision/appeals procedures.

(c) If an evaluation committee is used, there may be a delicate balance of power between management nominees, trade union representatives, and specialists (eg. from the personnel or, in larger organisations, salary administration department). This will have to be moulded into a 'team', by sorting out its collective responsibilities and its component interests.

(d) There are bound to be problems which will require appeal, and revision will in any case be necessary over time. Some of these situations may be 'sensitive', not only where unions are involved: managers may regard the grading of jobs in their jurisdiction to be part of their political 'power base', and may be sensitive to any perceived undervaluation.

2. REMUNERATION

2.1 Wages and salaries are to be considered as:

(a) a cost, which appears in the cost of the product or service to the market;

(b) an investment, ie. money spent on one factor of production (labour) in the hope of a return; and

(c) a potentially crucial environmental variable - ie in incentivating and motivational terms, a source of job satisfaction or dissatisfaction, political status or conflict etc.

2.2 The objectives of pay from the organisation's point of view are:

(a) to attract and retain labour of a suitable type and quality;
(b) to fulfil perceived social responsibilities;
(c) to motivate employees to achieve and maintain desired levels of performance.

2.3 From the point of view of the employee, the objective may be maximisation of earnings, but is more usually:

(a) equity - ie a fair rate for the job;

(b) relativity, or fair differentials, ie justified differences between the wages of individuals; and

(c) a 'steady' income.

2.4 We have discussed the role of job evaluation in determining the relative value of jobs, but there are other factors not related to job *content* which affect the rates an organisation will actually want to pay.

(a) *Equity*. Wilfred Brown defined equity as 'the level of earnings for people in different occupations which is felt by society to be reasonably consistent with the importance of the work which is done, and which seems relatively fair to the individual.' In other words, pay must be *perceived* and felt to match the level of work, and capacity of the individual to do it, ie 'felt-fair'. Pay structures should allow individuals to feel that they are being rewarded in keeping with their skill, effort and contribution, and with the rewards received by others for their relative contributions.

(b) *Negotiated pay scales*. Pay scales, differentials, minimum rates etc may have been negotiated at plant, local or national level, according to various environmental factors:

(i) legislation and government policy (eg on equal pay, or anti-inflation);

(ii) the economy (levels of inflation; unemployment, affecting labour supply and demand, and therefore market rates); and

(iii) the strength of the employers and unions staff associations in negotiation.

(c) *Market rates*. Market rates of pay will have most influence on pay structures where there is a standard pattern of supply and demand in the open labour market. If an organisation's rates fall below the 'benchmark' rates in the local or national labour market from which it recruits, it will have trouble attracting and holding employees. The concept of the market rate, however, is not exact. Different employers are bound to pay a range of rates for theoretically identical jobs, especially in managerial jobs, where the scope and nature of the duties will vary according to the situation of each organisation.

> As discussed in the chapter on recruitment and selection, banks are coming under new pressures in the fulfilment of their manpower needs. In particular, they are having to recruit specialists, who tend to enter the hierarchy higher up than staff used to under the banks' traditional policy of promotion from within, and tend to command higher rates of pay in the market. This alters the pay structure of the bank and may cause problems of perceived fairness where the imported specialist's salary is compared with that of a long-serving 'all-rounder' for whom the 'going rate' may not be so high.

2.5 Theoretically, an organisation could pay the absolute minimum rate consistent with meeting its manpower demands (by securing a willing supply): this is the 'market rate'. In practice, however, trade union pressure and/or social responsibility prevent employers from exploiting workers, where the market rate could be *very* low (eg in times of very high unemployment, or an influx of 'cheap' labour from abroad). In addition:

(a) the extent to which the organisation will have to adhere to the 'going rate' will vary according to the relative scarcity of supply of given skills: in a 'tight' labour market the need to recruit and retain qualified individuals will be greater, so the organisation may pay more;

(b) labour mobility in response to pay levels or differentials will also be important, from the point of view of the likelihood of attracting employees away from other organisations, and retaining existing employees.

2.6 One may list the general arguments for and against lower or higher rates as follows.

(a) The offer of a notably higher remuneration package than market rate may be assumed to generate greater interest in the labour market. The organisation will therefore have a wider field of selection for the given labour category, and will be more likely to have access to the most skilled/experienced individuals. If the organisation establishes a reputation as a 'wage leader' it may generate a consistent supply of high-calibre labour.

(b) There may be benefits of high pay offers for employee loyalty, and better performance resulting from the (theoretically) higher calibre and motivation of the workforce.

(c) If lower than market rates are offered, the employer may suffer from a lack of choice in selection, the recruitment of more marginal employees, the costs associated with labour turnover (as employees move in search of better-remunerated work elsewhere) and possibly lack of motivation: employees may be unwilling, in the terms of Handy's motivation calculus, to expand 'E' (energy, effort etc) on the job, if they know they will not be adequately rewarded in relation to their desire for monetary rewards.

(d) Social responsibility - or a concern for the organisation's public image - might prevent management from fixing low rates, even if they could 'get away with it'.

(e) On the other hand, there are substantial cost savings in paying lower rates. It cannot be assumed that high remuneration inevitably leads to higher motivation and better performance.

4: REWARD

Salary administration

2.7 'Salary administration' is not to be confused with 'payroll' administration, which is usually a financial function: it refers to the process by which levels of pay for staff employees are determined, monitored and controlled.

> 'Salary administration itself is not something that can be looked at in isolation. Salary administration is an attempt to achieve the objectives formulated in a salary *policy*, which itself ought ideally to be a plan - not simply to pay fair and equitable salaries, but to relate and reconcile career aspirations in terms of current and potential earnings, and personal commitment to total organisation objectives. A host of variables is involved.' Livy - *Corporate personnel management*

2.8 The aims of salary administration are therefore broadly concerned with:

(a) obtaining and retaining suitable staff, within the requirements of the manpower plan;

(b) developing and maintaining a *salary structure* which:

(i) is felt to be equitable, for jobs with similar responsibilities, and consistent in the differentials between differently valued jobs;

(ii) takes market rates into account;

(iii) is adjusted in line with cost-of-living increases;

(iv) is flexible enough to accommodate changes in market rates, organisational structure etc; and

(v) rewards performance and responsibility by providing for progression;

(c) *reviewing* salary levels and differentials;

(d) operating the system so that it is easily understood and seen to be fair by staff; and

(e) controlling salary and administrative costs to the organisation.

3. SALARY STRUCTURES

3.1 Armstrong identifies the main objectives in designing a coherent salary structure as being 'to provide for internal *equity* in grading and paying staff and to maintain *competitive rates* of pay' and notes that 'neither of those objectives can be achieved if a chaotic set of rates exists which has evolved over the years and is altered at whim or because of a panic reaction to difficulties in recruitment or retention.'

3.2 A salary structure may be designed using any, or a combination, of three main types:

(a) a graded structure, based on job evaluation;
(b) rate for age scales; and
(c) progression curves.

4: REWARD

We will discuss each of these briefly in turn.

Graded salary structure

3.3 A typical structure of this type consists of a series of salary grades, to which all jobs are allocated on the basis of job evaluation (ie an assessment of their value). For each grade, there is a salary *scale* or range, ie minimum and maximum salary levels for jobs in that grade.

3.4 The *range,* and *overlap* of the scales between grades, will require careful thought because of the consequences for promotions, and transfers between grades.

(a) The range must be wide enough to allow for progression: people in similarly-graded jobs may perform differently, and should be rewarded accordingly.

(b) There should be an overlap, in recognition that an experienced person performing well in a job may be of more value than a new or poor performer in the next grade up.

(c) There is a differential between the mid-points ('target salary') for each scale, providing scope for progression, on promotion to a higher grade, without creating too wide a gap between adjacent grades.

(d) The number of different scales in the structure will then depend on the number of distinct grades of jobs (according to job evaluation), the width and overlap of each scale, and the range of appropriate salaries in the organisation (ie. from the most junior to most senior job).

3.5 Flexibility must be built into the system.

(a) If a job changes in content and its assessed value alters, it must be re-graded within the structure. Similarly, if there is a change in market rates, a job may be re-graded, but it should be noted that this is an externally-imposed change and need not imply regrading of all similar jobs.

(b) Proportionate increases in the minima and maxima of scales should be provided for, to deal with cost of living increases, and increases in market rates.

(c) The main principle of the structure is that progression within a grade is *performance-related*, with the assumption that a normally competent individual eventually reaches the scale maximum, unless he is promoted out of the grade first. Again flexibility may be required eg in the case of an individual whose performance is outstanding, but for whom there are no immediate openings for promotion: discretionary payment of a salary *above* the grade maximum may be made, in order to maintain the individual's loyalty and motivation.

3.6 Progression through a grade is sometimes determined with reference to two (or three) stages of progression, which may be used to 'mark' entry points and salary levels *within each grade*.

(a) The *learning* stage or 'zone' is when an individual is still progressing towards full competence. Depending on past relevant experience, any point in this zone would be a likely entry point into a new grade.

(b) The *qualified* stage covers the mid-point of the scale and grade. The minimum salary in this zone should be the market rate; the mid-point represents the salary level for a competent employee, and should be *above* the market rate so that the organisation retains competent individuals (whose learning curve it may have financed so far); the maximum level is the normal maximum for the job, and it is expected that employees will be promoted out of the grade at or before this point.

(c) The *premium* zone provides the extra reward and encouragement to outstanding achievers for whom promotional opportunities do not presently exist.

Individuals may be allowed to progress through the zones at different speeds, according to managerial assessment of their ability and performance (although the Civil Service, for example, operates 'automatic progression' related to age and length of service.)

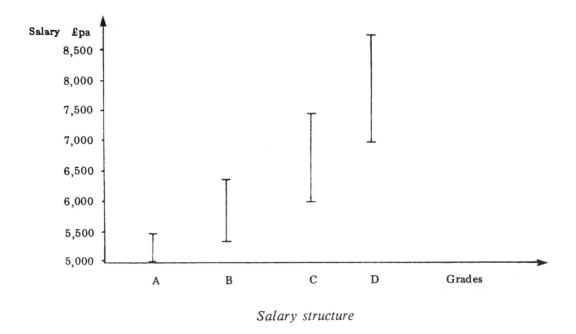

Salary structure

Rate for age systems

3.7 A rate for age system links the age of staff to defined scales or rates, for certain jobs, particularly where there are young employees who are being trained or carrying out junior, routine (eg clerical) work. Incremental scales for age are based on the assumption that the value of staff to the organisation is directly related to greater experience and maturity. They are, in their simplest form, easy to administer, because the evaluation of relative merit of trainees and junior employees etc do not have to be made: they are, therefore, perceived to be entirely equitable, but may not have a motivating effect unless a system is used which relates pay to performance as well as age, by applying scales for merit at each age.

4: REWARD

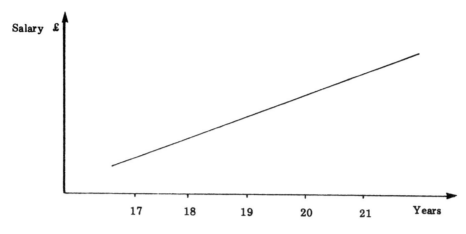

Simple incremental rate for age system

With added 'merit bands':

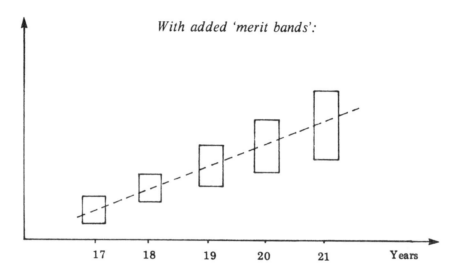

Salary progression curve

3.8   The 'salary progression' or 'maturity' curve also aims to relate salary increases to maturity and experience, but in the longer term. It is most relevant to staff whose value is measured in terms of their professional ability rather than pure job content, eg scientific and professional jobs. It is assumed that salary starts at the market rate for the employee's qualifications, and that staff will develop as a result of experience at a standard rate. In fact, some will develop faster than others, so the curve is only a guideline. It also differs from a rate for age curve by its relationship to market rates at various stages of the career progression.

3.9   Again, if a more incentivating approach is required thereby rewarding individuals for performance, parallel scales can be used, offering different starting rates (eg for different qualifications) and different rates of progression.

4: REWARD

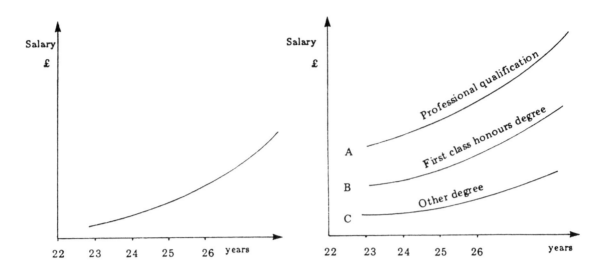

4. SALARY PLANNING AND CONTROL

4.1 A clearly designed salary structure, and defined rates of progress, will be important features of an effective salary control system. Other activities will include the following.

(a) *A salary budget,* ie a quantitative statement of the planned allocation of human resources, to meet the forecast requirements of the department and organisation. The budget will be based on:

   (i)   the planned level of activity and number of staff required (including number and categories of staff needed in the budget period);

   (ii) forecast salary levels, including general and incremental increases;

   (iii) forecast of staff mobility (ie. promotions, turnover) and its effect on salary costs (ie the balance of new, lower-paid recruits etc).

Comparison of actual and anticipated costs will disclose variance, which may be corrected by reduction in manning levels, reduction in the salary increase budget etc.

(b) Clear *lines of authority* for awarding and confirming salary changes, increments etc and for checking that any such changes are consistent with salary policies.

(c) *Salary review guidelines.* These must operate to define the limits for:

   (i)   increase in departmental payroll costs eg as a result of merit awards;
   (ii) maxima for increments;
   (iii) the distribution of awards between salary grades.

4.2 Salary reviews may be carried out as a general exercise, when all or most salaries have to be increased to keep pace with market rates, cost of living increases or negotiated settlements. *General reviews* are often carried out annually (government regulations permitting) during inflationary periods: this may or may not create problems in financing individual merit awards as well.

4.3 *Individual* salary reviews are carried out to decide on merit awards. Again, these are usually held annually - with interim reviews, possibly, for trainees and younger staff who are making fast progress. Some companies phase reviews throughout the year rather than hold them all at once; this is more difficult to administer but does diffuse the tension of a general review period.

4.4 Guidelines for salary review will be necessary to minimise the subjectivity of discretionary payments. The total cost of all merit increases, or minimum/maximum amounts for increases, might be specified. A *salary review budget* will determine the increase that can be allocated for awards, as a percentage of payroll costs for the department. The size of the budget will depend on:

(a) how average salaries in each grade differ from the target salary (the mid-point): ideally, they should correspond, but may be too high or low; and

(b) the amount the company estimates it will be able to pay, based on forecast revenue, profit, and labour cost savings elsewhere (eg. highly-paid employees leaving, and recruits entering at lower-paid levels).

> 'Salary structures, job evaluation schemes, progression policies and salary review procedures all aim to make salary administration a scientific process. But they cannot entirely succeed. Salary administration is as much art as science and, inevitably, there are problems which can only be solved by exercising judgement in the light of circumstances.'
>
> Armstrong, *Handbook of personnel management practice*

5. INCENTIVES

5.1 In our discussion of salary structures, we noted where 'incentives' could be built into fixed scales of pay - ie where payments could be linked directly to performance, so that employees could see a clear relationship between working well or better, and earning more. Various *incentive schemes* might be applied, including:

(a) payment by results;
(b) bonus schemes; and
(c) profit sharing.

Payment by results

5.2 Pay (or part of it) is related to output (in terms of the number of items produced, or time taken to produce a unit of work), or results achieved (ie performance to defined standards in key tasks, according to plan).

(a) For wage earners, the most common individual PBR scheme is 'straight piecework', ie payment of a fixed amount per unit produced, or operation completed.

(b) For managerial and other salaried jobs, a form of management by objectives will probably be applied so that:

(i) key results can be identified and specified, for which merit awards (on top of basic salary) will be paid;

(ii) there will be a clear model for evaluating performance and knowing when or if targets have been reached and payments earned;

(iii) the exact conditions and amounts of awards can be made clear to the employee, to avoid uncertainty and later resentment.

5.3 Sales results are more easily quantifiable than most key results of managerial jobs. They can be expressed as volume or value of sales, or new customer accounts opened etc. The sales 'culture' also tends to be more entrepreneurial and better suited to the challenge - and uncertainty - of performance-related pay. Typically, sales personnel receive a basic salary (which may be high or low) *plus* a percentage commission on the amount of sales *and/or* bonuses related to the achievement of sales targets or quotas. It may be that such a system will be adopted in banks for employees who are responsible for winning business in the marketplace.

5.4 For service and other departments, a PBR scheme may involve bonuses for achievement of key results, or 'points' schemes, where points are awarded for performance on various criteria (efficiency, cost savings, quality of service etc) and certain points totals (or the highest points total in the branch, if a competitive system is used) win prizes.

5.5 Another type of financial incentive directly linked with improved performance is the *suggestion scheme*, where payments or 'prizes' are offered to staff to come up with workable ideas on improving efficiency, new marketing initiatives etc. The theory is that there is in any case motivational value in getting staff involved in problem-solving and planning, and that staff are often in the best position to provide practical and creative solutions to their work problems or the customer's needs - but that an added incentive will help to overcome any reluctance on the part of staff to put forward ideas (because it is 'risky' etc).

5.6 Wherever possible, the size of the payment should be related to the savings or value added as a result of the suggestion - either as a lump sum or percentage. Payments are often also made for a 'good try' - an idea which is rejected but considered to show initiative, effort and judgement on the part of the employee. Suggestion schemes usually apply only to lower grades of staff, on the grounds that thinking up improvements is part of the supervisor's or manager's normal job.

5.7 Results-oriented payments should:

(a) offer 'real' incentives, ie sufficiently high after tax to make extraordinary effort worthwhile, perhaps 10-30% of basic salary;

(b) relate payments to criteria over which the individual has control (otherwise he will feel helpless to ensure his reward, and the 'expectancy' element in motivation will be lacking);

(c) make clear the basis on which payments are calculated, and all the conditions that apply, so that individuals can work out their 'motivation calculus', ie work out the reward for a given level of effort;

(d) be flexible ie sensitive enough to reward different levels of achievement in proportion, and with provision for regular review, and adaptation to the changing needs of the particular organisation.

4: REWARD

Bonus schemes

5.8 *Bonus schemes* are supplementary to basic salary, and have been found to be popular with entrepreneurial types eg. in marketing and sales, where the 'economic man' model can perhaps be applied with most accuracy. Bonuses are incentives and rewards.

5.9 *Group* incentive schemes typically offer a bonus for a group (equally, or proportionately to the earnings or status of individuals) which achieves or exceeds specified targets. Offering bonuses to a whole team may be appropriate for tasks where individual contributions cannot be isolated, workers have little control over their individual output because tasks depend on each other, or where team-building is particularly required. It may enhance team-spirit and co-operation as well as provide performance incentives, but it may also create pressures within the group if some individuals are seen to be 'not pulling their weight'.

Profit-sharing schemes

5.10 Profit-sharing schemes offer employees (or selected groups of them) bonuses, perhaps in the form of shares in the company, related directly to profits or 'value added'. The profit formula itself is not easily calculated - profit levels being subject to accounting conventions - so care will have to be taken to publish and explain the calculations to employees if the scheme is not to be regarded with suspicion or as simply another fringe benefit.

5.11 Profit sharing is in general based on the belief that all employees can contribute to profitability, and that that contribution should be recognised. If it is, the argument runs, the effects may include profit-consciousness and motivation in employees, commitment to the future prosperity of the organisation etc.

5.12 The actual incentive value and effect on productivity may be wasted, however, if the scheme is badly designed.

    (a) A perceivedly significant sum should be made available to employees - once shareholders have received appropriate return on their investment.

    (b) There should be a clear, and not overly delayed, link between effort/performance and reward. Profit shares should be distributed as frequently as possible - consistent with the need for reliable information on profit forecasts, targets etc and the need to amass significant amounts for distribution.

    (c) The scheme should only be introduced if profit forecasts indicate a reasonable chance of achieving the above: profit sharing is welcome when profits are high, but the potential for disappointment is great.

    (d) The greatest effect on productivity arising from the scheme may in fact arise from its use as a focal point for discussion with employees, about the relationship between their performance and results, areas and targets for improvement etc. Management must be seen to be committed to the principle.

4: REWARD

6. FRINGE BENEFITS

6.1 'Benefits' consist of items or awards which are supplementary to normal pay. Some benefits are essential, so the term 'fringe' is perhaps misleading, eg for pensions and sick pay. These provisions for the maintenance of adequate standards of living have been underwritten by the state, which has legislated for employees and employers alike to bear some of the cost. They are awarded to anyone who meets certain qualifying conditions and as such are independent of the employer's discretion. Other benefits, eg cars, medical insurance and a range of 'perks' for executives, are more in the nature of optional extras.

> 'The emphasis on benefits and the ingenuity shown in their provision vary with economic circumstances and with the impact of any incomes policy, but more recently they have appeared in conjunction with annual wage and salary demands. It must always be recognised, nevertheless, that, however generous they are, they can never be an adequate substitute for an inadequate base rate or an illogical salary structure or for tangible recognition of the effect of inflation.'
>
> Ream: *Personnel administration*

6.2 Some organisations operate on the belief that pay and benefits form a whole 'package', the composition of which is flexible and can be adapted to personal and organisational circumstances. This means that employees and employers alike get a more complete picture of the total value of the remuneration, and its cost to the company. Remuneration levels are set with consideration of bonuses and benefits as well: this may be important for senior staff, for whom there may be tax advantages in taking certain benefits instead of higher basic salary. The total remuneration concept has become so accepted that any decline in the value of 'perks' is seen as an erosion of remuneration.

6.3 An organisation might run what has been called a 'cafeteria' system, whereby a range of benefits are on offer, and employees can choose from among them up to their allowed budget. This offers the element of choice, and may increase the value of the benefit to the individual, since it answers his real needs or wants.

6.4 *Pensions* are generally regarded as the most important benefit after basic pay: they are a kind of 'deferred pay', building up rights to a guaranteed income on retirement (or to dependants, on death). They are financed by contributions from the company, with facilities for contribution by employees as well.

6.5 Most organisations see a need for more than token pension arrangements, because:

(a) social responsibility dictates the need to provide reasonable security especially for loyal and long-serving employees;

(b) a good pension scheme will be attractive to potential staff, and an inducement to loyalty for existing staff. (Note, however, that pensions are no longer the 'golden handcuff' they once were; pension rights must be preserved for early leavers, or transferred to another scheme. Pensions are more 'portable' than before recent legislative changes);

(c) a good pension scheme may have industrial relations benefits in demonstrating the organisation's long-term interest and care of its employees.

4: REWARD

Other benefits

6.6 *Sick pay* is generally provided on a sliding scale for length of service, eg:

Less than one year	Four weeks' full pay
1-5 years	13 weeks' full pay
More than five years	Add one week for each year of service
Managerial staff	Full pay for six months (or even more)

This can be costly, and may not always be appreciated, but ungenerous provision would certainly be a source of dissatisfaction.

6.7 *Holidays* are another benefit which is usually very much taken for granted. The UK average is three weeks' paid holiday, with four or five weeks for management.

6.8 There are few legal obligations governing entitlement in the UK. The 'right' to holidays is therefore whatever is set out and agreed in the terms and conditions of employment. The length of holidays has increased over the years in the UK: in a number of instances, additional holiday entitlement has been granted instead of reduction in working hours.

6.9 *Company cars* are another highly regarded benefit in the UK, and are increasingly necessary in order to attract and retain managerial staff. Cars for those whose work requires them to travel extensively (eg sales and service staff) are obviously a good investment for the company. A company car saves the user the cost of acquisition, and usually also running costs, although this advantage has been reduced by fiscal legislation in recent years. It is costly for the organisation to maintain a fleet, however, and there may be 'political' problems of preserving status differentials (not everybody can have a Porsche...).

6.10 Other benefits which might be on offer include the following.

(a) Transport assistance, eg season ticket loans; bulk buying of tickets by employers for distribution to staff.

(b) Housing assistance, eg:

   (i) allowances to staff who have been transferred or relocated - removal and travelling expenses, lodging, conveyancing fees etc;

   (ii) assistance with house purchase - bridging loan, preferential mortgage terms.

(c) Medical benefits - eg medical insurance with BUPA or Private Patients' Plan. Some medical services may also be provided at the workplace.

(d) Catering services - eg subsidised food and drink at the workplace or Luncheon Vouchers.

(e) Recreational facilities - eg subsidy and organisation of social and sports clubs, provision of facilities such as a gymnasium or bar.

(f) Home telephone subsidy, professional subscriptions, work-related reading matter and other allowances.

6.11 Bank employees may receive a number of additional benefits from their employers.

   (a) *Assistance with house purchase* in the form of a mortgage subsidy or reduced interest rate mortgage. The benefit will normally be available to employees after a qualifying period of service (eg two years), on attainment of a certain level in the bank (eg clerical Grade 3), and subject to borrowing limits.

   (b) *Discount* on a number of bank products, for example:

      (i)   unit trusts;
      (ii) insurance products, eg home or travelling insurance;
      (iii) leasing schemes for cars.

   (c) *Preferential terms* on a number of bank account products. For example:

      (i)   bonus interest on deposit and current accounts;
      (ii) bonus interest on term deposits and savings plans;
      (iii) no charges on current accounts (where charged to customers).

   (d) Some other *loan products* may also be given to staff under preferential terms, eg:

      (i)   reduced interest rate on overdraft or personal loans;
      (ii) reduced interest rate on credit or budget accounts.

Exercise

What 'fringe' benefits do you get as part of your remuneration package? Are any of these benefits that only a bank provides? How important are these benefits to you?

Do you feel your salary is fair for the job you do and in relation to others? Do you know how your job is evaluated? Do you know how your salary is worked out? What could your bank do to make the system:

(a) clearer?
(b) fairer?

---

7. **CHAPTER ROUNDUP**

7.1 'Job evaluation is the process of analysing and assessing the content of jobs, in order to place them in an acceptable rank order which can then be used as a basis for a remuneration system.'

Scheme	Characteristics	Advantages	Disadvantages
1. Ranking	Whole job comparisons are made to place them in order of importance.	Easy to apply and understand.	No defined standards of judgement - differences between jobs are not measured.
2. Job classification	Job grades are defined and jobs are slotted into the grades by comparing the whole job description with the grade definition.	Simple to operate and standards of judgement are provided in the shape of the grade definition.	Difficult to fit complex jobs into one grade without using excessively elaborate definitions.
3. Points rating	Separate factors are scored to product an overall points score for the job.	The analytical process of considering separate defined factors provides for objectivity and consistency in making judgements.	Complex to install and maintain - judgement is still required to rate jobs in respect of different factors.

Michael Armstrong *(A handbook of personnel management practice)*

7.2 'The constituents of a remuneration policy must therefore embrace such crucial factors as the objectives of the organisation, its finances, cash flow and profitability, the state of the labour market, expected demand and supply of various types of labour, any government regulations on pay, anticipated contraction or expansion of the organisation, as well as the personal aspirations and inclinations of the workforce.'

(Livy)

TEST YOUR KNOWLEDGE

The numbers in brackets refer to paragraphs of this chapter

1   Outline the advantages and disadvantages of job evaluation. (1.3, 1.4)

2   Distinguish between analytical/quantitative and non-analytical/qualitative approaches to job evaluation. (1.6, 1.7)

3   Outline the steps you would take if you were asked to introduce a job evaluation scheme in your branch. (1.20, 1.21)

4   Why might a bank not wish to offer very low rates of pay? (2.4 - 2.6)

5   What is salary administration? (2.7, 2.8)

6   Identify how performance-related awards can be built into:

   (a)   a graded salary structure; (3.4 - 3.6)
   (b)   a rate for age system; (3.7)
   (c)   a salary progression curve. (3.8 - 3.9)

7   What factors will be taken into account in fixing a salary budget? (4.1)

8   What are the requirements of an effective PBR scheme? (5.7)

Now try question 4 at the end of the text

Chapter 5

APPRAISAL

This chapter covers the following topics.

1. The purposes of appraisal
2. Appraisal procedures
3. Problems with appraisal
4. Identification of employee potential

Introduction

Appraisal is part of the management process of control. It involves a review of the employee's performance with a view to improving it, in the hope that the bank and the employee will both benefit from the process.

---

1. THE PURPOSES OF APPRAISAL

1.1 The general purpose of any staff appraisal system is to improve the efficiency of the organisation by ensuring that the individuals within it are performing to the best of their ability and developing their potential for improvement. Within this overall aim, staff appraisals are used in practice for:

(a) *reward review* - ie measuring the extent to which an employee is deserving of salary increase etc as compared with his peers;

(b) *performance review*, for planning and following-up training and development programmes, ie identifying training needs, validating training methods etc; and

(c) *potential review*, as an aid to planning career development, making promotions etc, ie predicting the level and type of work the individual will be capable of in the future.

1.2 In his book *Human Resource Management* George Thomason (1988) identifies the variety of objectives of appraisals.

(a) Establishing what actions are required of the individual in a job in order that the objectives for the section or department are realised.

(b) Establishing the key or main results which the individual will be expected to achieve in the course of his or her work over a period of time.

(c) Assessing the individual's level of performance against some standard, to provide a basis for remuneration above the basic pay rate. (Performance-related pay is a relatively new but increasing phenomenon in banks, especially for branch management.)

(d) Identifying the individual's levels of performance to provide a basis for informing, training and developing him.

(e) Identifying those persons whose performance suggests that they are promotable at some date in the future and those whose performance requires improvement to meet acceptable standards.

(f) Establishing an inventory of actual and potential performance within the undertaking to provide a basis for manpower planning.

(g) Monitoring the undertaking's initial selection procedures against the subsequent performance of recruits, relative to the organisation's expectations.

(h) Improving communication about work tasks between different levels in the hierarchy.

1.3 Whatever the purpose of appraising staff in a particular situation, the review should be a systematic exercise, taken seriously by assessor and subject alike. It may be argued that such deliberate 'stock-taking' is unnecessary, since managers are constantly making judgements about their subordinates and (should be) giving their subordinates feedback information from day to day. However, it must be recognised that:

(a) managers may obtain random impressions of subordinate performance (perhaps from more noticeable successes and failures), but rarely form a coherent, complete and objective picture;

(b) they may have a fair idea of their subordinates' shortcomings - but may not have devoted time and attention to the matter of improvement and development;

(c) judgements are easy to make, but less easy to justify in detail, in writing, or to the subject's face;

(d) different assessors may be applying a different set of criteria, and varying standards of objectivity and judgement, which undermines the value of appraisal for comparison, as well as its credibility in the eyes of the appraisees;

(e) unless stimulated to do so, managers rarely give their subordinates adequate feedback on their performance, especially if the appraisal is a critical one.

1.4 There is clearly a need for a system which tackles certain basic problems.

(a) The formulation and appreciation of desired traits and standards against which individuals can be consistently and objectively assessed. Assessors must be aware of factors which affect their judgements.

(b) Recording assessments. Managers should be encouraged to utilise a standard and understood framework, but still allowed to express what they consider important, and without too much 'form-filling'.

(c) Getting the appraiser and appraisee together, so that *both* contribute to the assessment and plans for improvement and/or development.

2.   APPRAISAL PROCEDURES

2.1 A typical appraisal system would therefore involve:

(a) identification of *criteria* for assessment, perhaps based on job analysis, performance standards, person specifications etc;

(b) the preparation by the subordinate's manager of an *appraisal report;*

(c) an *appraisal interview,* for an exchange of views about the results of the assessment, targets for improvement etc;

(d) review of the assessment by the assessor's own superior, so that the appraisee does not feel subject to one man's prejudices. Formal appeals may be allowed, if necessary to establish the fairness of the procedure;

(e) the preparation and implementation of *action plans* to achieve improvements and changes agreed; and

(f) *follow-up* ie monitoring the progress of the action plan.

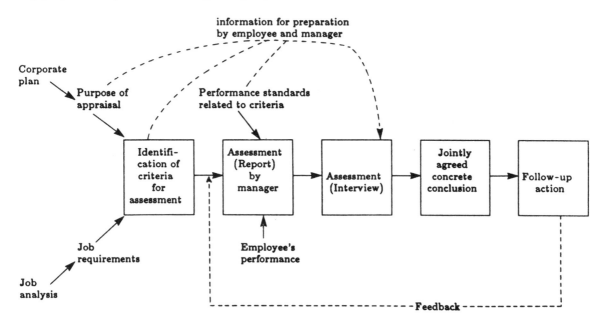

2.2 There may not need to be standard forms for appraisal - and elaborate form-filling procedures should be avoided - as long as managers understand the nature and extent of what is required, and are motivated to take it seriously. Most systems, however, provide for appraisals to be recorded, and report forms of various lengths and complexity may be designed for standard use.

5: APPRAISAL

The appraisal report

2.3 The basis of appraisal must first be determined. Assessments must be related to a *common* standard, in order for comparisons to be made between individuals: on the other hand, they should be related to meaningful performance criteria, which take account of the critical variables in each different job. A 'blanket' approach may provide a common standard, but may not offer a significant index for job performance.

2.4 In particular, there is the question of whether *personality* or *performance* is being assessed, ie what the individual 'is', or what he 'does'. According to Livy, 'Personal qualities have questionable validity as a measure of performance, and may introduce unreliability since they are prone to ambiguity and have moral connotations ... In practical terms, this ... has encouraged the use of results-based appraisals (such as management by objectives) and the development of job-related performance criteria.'

2.5 Various appraisal techniques have been formulated.

   (a) *Overall assessment.* This is the simplest method, simply requiring the manager to write in narrative form his judgements about the appraisee, possibly with a checklist of personality characteristics and performance targets to work from. There will be no guaranteed consistency of the criteria and areas of assessment, however, and managers may not be able to convey clear, effective judgements in writing. Kay Rowe studied several such schemes and concluded: 'A few suggested careful thought and a conscientious effort to say something meaningful, but the vast majority were remarkable for their neutrality. Glib, generalised, enigmatic statements abounded'.

   (b) *Guided assessment.* Assessors are required to comment on a number of specified characteristics and performance elements, with guidelines as to how the terms (eg 'application', 'integrity', 'adaptability') are to be interpreted in the work context. This is a more precise, but still rather vague method.

   (c) *Grading.* Grading adds a comparative frame of reference to the general guidelines, whereby managers are asked to select one of a number of levels or degrees to which the individual in question displays the given characteristic. These are also known as *rating scales*, and are much used in standard appraisal forms. Their effectiveness depends to a large extent on:

      (i) the relevance of the factors chosen for assessment, which may be nebulous personality traits, for example, or clearly defined job factors, eg job knowledge, performance against targets, decision-making etc;

      (ii) the definition of the agreed standards of assessment. Grades A-D might simply be labelled 'Outstanding - Satisfactory - Fair - Poor', in which case assessments are subject to much variation and subjectivity. They may, on the other hand, be more closely related to work priorities and standards, using definitions such as 'Performance is good overall, and superior to that expected in some important areas', or 'Performance is broadly acceptable, but employee needs training in several major areas and/or motivation is lacking.'

   Numerical values may be added to ratings to give rating 'scores'. Alternatively a less precise *graphic scale* may be used to indicate general position on a plus/minus scale, eg:

Factor: job knowledge

High:————————————————— Average ——————— ✓ ——————————Low

(d) *Behavioural incident methods.* These concentrate on employee behaviour, which is measured against 'typical' behaviour in each job, as defined by common *critical incidents* of successful and unsuccessful job behaviour reported by managers. Time and effort are required to collect and analyse reports and to develop the scheme, and it only really applies to large groups of people in broadly similar jobs. However, it is firmly rooted in observation of 'real-life' job behaviour, and the important aspects of the job, since the analysis is carried out for *key tasks*, (those which are identified as 'critical' to success in the job and for which specific standards of performance *must* be reached).

The behavioural equivalent of the graphic scale (illustrated above) for a branch manager's key task of 'marketing initiative' might appear as, for example:

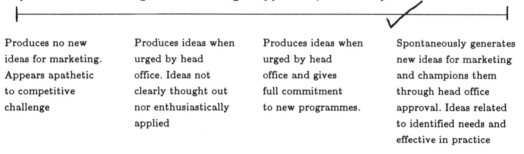

Produces no new ideas for marketing. Appears apathetic to competitive challenge	Produces ideas when urged by head office. Ideas not clearly thought out nor enthusiastically applied	Produces ideas when urged by head office and gives full commitment to new programmes.	Spontaneously generates new ideas for marketing and champions them through head office approval. Ideas related to identified needs and effective in practice

(e) *Results-orientated appraisal schemes.* All the above techniques may be used with more or less results-orientated criteria for assessment - but are commonly based on trait or behavioural appraisal. A wholly results-orientated approach (eg management by objectives) sets out to review performance against specific targets and standards of performance agreed in advance by manager and subordinate together. The advantages of this are that:

(i) the subordinate is more involved in appraisal of his own performance, because he is able to evaluate his success or progress in achieving specific, jointly-agreed targets;

(ii) the manager is therefore relieved, to an extent, of his role as critic, and becomes a 'counsellor';

(iii) learning and motivation theories suggest that clear and known targets are important in modifying and determining behaviour.

The effectiveness of the scheme will still, however, depend on the targets set (are they clearly defined? realistic?) and the commitment of both parties to make it work. The measurement of success or failure is only part of the picture: reasons for failure and opportunities arising from success must be evaluated.

> *Note*
> On an *individual* level, MBO or 'management by objectives' involves:
>
> - identification of job aims
> - identification of key results, and the key tasks involved in obtaining them
> - agreement on performance standards for key tasks
> - setting short-term goals and action plans (as part of an improvement plan, to achieve agreed standards)
> - progress monitoring and control.

2.6 Behavioural and results-oriented criteria for assessment in banks have focused increasingly on *marketing* skills and results, especially at managerial level, since this is the new orientation of much branch activity. Managers may be appraised on evidence of customer awareness, customer interview and selling skills, concern for staff training in selling and customer care, maintenance of branch environment etc. They may be appraised on results such as number of new customer accounts opened in a given period, or volume of business (or new business), number of new small-business or corporate clients or value of those accounts etc.

2.7 We will look at some of the pitfalls facing managers in making their assessments later. However, at this written stage of the assessment process, managers will need guidance, to help them make a relevant, objective and helpful report. Training sessions may be arranged. Most large organisations with standard review forms also issue detailed *guidance notes* to aid assessors with the written and discussion elements.

> Some notes which might refer to the written report element might include the following.
>
> 1 The immediate superior of each individual should write his report.
>
> 2 The report should be based on a job description prepared or agreed in consultation with the individual being reported on, as a fair reflection of his duties and responsibilities.
>
> 3 Spaces for 'comments' on this form should be used to explain grades awarded, and to describe special circumstances which have affected performance (eg. ill-health).
>
> 4 Grades should reflect actual performance during the past twelve months. There should be *no* reference to previous reports.
>
> 5 Reports are strictly confidential: their contents may only be disclosed to persons concerned with them in the course of official work.
>
> 6 Each report should be countersigned by a departmental manager or other appropriate executive, with additional comment where appropriate.
>
> 7 Report writers have a *continuous* responsibility to give performance information to their subordinates, positive and negative. No grading 'below average' should be recorded without the subordinate having received prior warning and opportunity to correct shortcomings.

Discussion of reports: interview and counselling

2.8 The extent to which any discussion or counselling interview is based on the written report varies in practice. For certain purposes - eg mutually agreed programmes for further training of the individual under review - the report may be distributed to the appraisee in advance of the interview, so that he has a chance to make an independent assessment, for discussion with his manager.

> The techniques and problems of interviewing, in general and as regards *appraisal* interviews, are covered in detail in Chapter 8.

2.9 Cuming suggests that encouraging a positive contribution from the subordinate is of prime importance.

'Why ... are so few managers able to use the full capacities of their staff to increase productivity by expanding their contributions to their jobs? Surely it is largely because they concentrate on what is wrong, on solving problems and overcoming obstacles, rather than on where they want to go and the prospects of getting there through the fuller use of the individual talents of their staff.'

2.10 Cuming suggests that, unlike the conventionally-used attitude surveys which concentrate on the 'compensatory' aspects of employment (on the basic assumption that work is intrinsically unpleasant, and that management's task is to render it more satisfactory by pay, fringe benefits, friendly treatment, pride in the company etc), the appraisal interview should ask positive and thought-provoking questions such as:

(a) Do you fully understand your job? Are there any aspects you wish to be made clearer?

(b) What parts of your job do you do best?

(c) Could any changes be made in your job which might result in improved performance?

(d) Have you any skills, knowledge, or aptitudes which could be made better use of in the organisation?

(e) What are your career plans? How do you propose achieving your ambitions in terms of further training and broader experience?

After counselling: follow-up

2.11 After the appraisal interview, the manager may complete his report, with eg overall assessment, assessment of potential, recommendations for follow-up action etc. The manager should then discuss the report with the counter-signing manager (usually his own superior), resolving any problems he has had in making the appraisal or report, and agreeing on action to be taken. The report form may then go to the management development adviser, training officer etc as appropriate for follow-up. The reviewing manager must implement any plans he has agreed with the appraisee and countersigning manager, and must provide feedback on progress to the appraisee.

APPRAISAL REPORT

Name:	Time in position:
Position:	Period of review:
Department:	Age:

	A	B	C	D	E	Comment
Overall assessment						
Job knowledge						
Effective output						
Co-operation						
Initiative						
Time-keeping						
Other relevant factors (specify)						

A = Outstanding, B = Above standard, C = To required standard
D = Short of standard in some respects   E = Not up to required standard

Potential	A	B	C	D	E	Comment

A = Overdue for promotion, B = Ready for promotion, C = Potential for promotion,
D = No evidence of promotion potential at present,
E = Has not worked long enough with me for judgement

Training, if any, required

Assessment discussed with employee?   Yes ☐   No ☐

Signed: Date:

Confirmed: Date:

2.12 *Follow-up* procedures will include:

(a) informing appraisees of the results of the appraisal, if this has not been central to the review interview. Some people argue that there is no point making appraisals if they are not openly discussed, but unless managers are competent and committed to reveal results in a constructive, frank and objective manner, the negative reactions on all sides may outweigh the advantages;

(b) carrying out agreed actions on training, promotion etc;

(c) monitoring the appraisee's progress and checking that *he* has carried out agreed actions, eg to improve time-keeping, attendance etc;

(d) taking necessary steps to help the appraisee to attain improvement objectives, eg by guidance, providing feedback, upgrading equipment, altering work methods etc.

3. PROBLEMS WITH APPRAISAL

3.1 In theory, such appraisal schemes may seem very 'fair' to the individual and very worthwhile for the organisation, but in practice the system often goes wrong.

(a) Appraisal interviews are often defensive on the part of the subordinate, who believes that any criticism will lessen the rewards for his/her performance (eg promotion will be missed). There may also be some mistrust of the validity of the scheme itself.

(b) Interviews are also often defensive on the part of the superior, who cannot reconcile the role of judge and critic with the 'human relations' aspect of the interview and may in any case feel uncomfortable about 'playing God' with the employee's future. The superior may therefore misrepresent the extent of the criticism of the subordinate which is contained in the report.

(c) The superior might show conscious or unconscious bias in his report (in the same way that an interviewer might show incorrect judgement in the interview process). Systems without clearly-defined standard criteria will be particularly prone to the subjectivity of the assessor's judgements, especially about personality traits, potential etc. It has also been noted that two managers required to rate the same person will vary not only in the standards used, but in the spread or 'scatter' of their ratings (showing different degrees of consistent judgement). Stereotyping, the 'halo effect' and other forms of perceptual selectivity or distortion (discussed in the chapter on Interviewing) may be operating.

(d) Reports from one department's managers might be more favourable or lenient than reports from another department - ie the general level of ratings may vary widely.

(e) There may be bias resulting from the interaction between appraiser and appraisee. This can be positive or negative, and may cast an influence back over the report as well: judgements are easy to make, but not easy to justify in writing, to be explained to the face of the appraisee.

(f) The manager may be reluctant to devote time and attention to appraisal. His experience in the organisation may indicate that the exercise is a waste of time, eg if there is a lot of form-filling and interviewing - but no reliable follow-up action. This may be an organisation-wide problem, or the bad example of the assessor's own superior.

(g) The organisational culture may simply not take appraisal seriously: interviewers are not trained or given time to prepare, appraisees are not encouraged to contribute, the exercise is perceived as a 'nod' to Human Relations with no practical results etc.

3.2 The affect of appraisal on motivation is a particularly tricky issue.

(a) Feedback on performance is regarded as vital in motivation, because it enables an employee to evaluate his achievement and make future calculations about the amount of effort required to achieve objectives and rewards. Even negative feedback can have this effect - and is more likely to spur the employee on to post-appraisal action.

(b) Agreement of challenging but attainable targets for performance or improvement also motivates employees by clarifying goals and the value (and 'cost' in terms of effort) of incentives offered.

(c) A positive approach to appraisal allows employees to solve their work problems and apply creative thinking to their jobs.

3.3 However, people rarely react well to criticism - especially at work, where they may feel that their reward or even job security is 'on the line'. In addition, much depends on the self-esteem of the appraisee.

(a) If the appraisee has a high self-image, he may be impervious to criticism: he will be able to deflect it - and the greater the criticism, the harder he will work to explain it away. If such a person is *not* criticised, he will be confirmed in his behaviour and sense of self-worth, which will motivate him to continue: this is fine if he is doing a good job, but *not* if he is doing a bad job, but being given a 'soft' appraisal.

(b) If the appraisee has a low self-image, he may be encouraged by low levels of criticism, and this may help to improve his performance. Heavy criticism of a person of low self-esteem can, however, be psychologically damaging.

3.4 The criteria for assessment of an appraisal scheme in the office may be broadly classified as follows.

(a) *Relevance*

(i) Does the system have a useful purpose? - eg to assess the skills and potential of employees, to reward them appropriately, to give feedback information for their development, to allow the appraisee to co-operate with his/her superior in planning the future.

(ii) Is the purpose clearly expressed and widely understood by all concerned, both appraisers and appraisees? (Otherwise, resentment and/or insecurity may result from the perceived 'threat' of appraisal.)

(iii) Are the appraisal criteria relevant to the purposes of the system? If the purpose is to assess performance, the appraiser should not focus on personality issues, his own feelings about the appraisee, the appraisee's life outside etc.

(b) *Fairness*

    (i)   Is there reasonable standardisation throughout the organisation - ie are employees of one branch being assessed by the same criteria and against the same standards of those of another?

    (ii)   Is there reasonable objectivity? There should be controls to ensure that personal bias does not colour the appraisal. The appraiser's style and attitude should be assessed from time to time. There should be some machinery for appeal to higher levels, in the event of alleged unfairness.

(c) *Genuineness* - is the system taken seriously by the organisation and by the individuals involved?

    (i)   Are the managers concerned committed to the system - or is it just something the personnel department thrusts upon them?

    (ii)   Who does the interviewing, and are they properly trained in interviewing and assessment techniques?

    (iii)   Is reasonable time and attention given to the interviews - or is it a question of 'getting them over with'?

    (iv)   Is there a genuine demonstrable link between performance and reward? If there isn't, the appraisals may be perceived as useless.

(d) *Co-operation*

    (i)   Is the appraisal a joint activity of appraiser and appraisee? - ie is it regarded as a co-operative problem-solving opportunity, or merely as a tool of management control?

    (ii)   Is the appraisee given time and encouragement to prepare for the appraisal, so that he/she can make a constructive contribution?

    (iii)   Does a jointly-agreed, concrete conclusion emerge from the interview? - ie in the form of a written summary or statement.

    (iv)   Are appraisals held at the appraisee's instigation or do management have to force them on employees? Are they held regularly - or once in a blue moon?

(e) *Efficiency*

    (i)   Does the system seem overly time-consuming compared to the value of its outcome?

    (ii)   Is it difficult and costly to administer? - ie are there efficient systems for the gathering, storage and retrieval of the performance information required, secretarial support for summaries etc arising from appraisals, Schedules for holding appraisal interviews etc?

A positive answer to the above questions will indicate a healthy, effective appraisal system.

Exercise

Do you have a formal or informal appraisal system at your place of work?

(a) Reviewing the techniques in paragraphs 2.5, which type of appraisal scheme do you think your employer operates?

(b) Do you think the appraisal system in your firm is relevant, fair, genuine, a co-operative exercise, and efficient?

---

4. IDENTIFICATION OF EMPLOYEE POTENTIAL

4.1 The review of potential is the use of appraisal to forecast the direction in which an individual is progressing, in terms of his career plans and skill development, and at what rate. It can be used as feedback to the individual, to indicate the opportunities open to him in the organisation in the future. It will also be vital to the organisation in determining its management succession plans.

4.2 Information for potential assessment will include:

(a) strengths and weaknesses in existing skills and qualities;

(b) possibilities and strategies for improvement, correction and development;

(c) the goals, aspirations and attitudes of the appraisee, with regard to career advancement, staying with the organisation, handling responsibility etc;

(d) the opportunities available in the organisation, including likely management vacancies, job rotation/enrichment plans and promotion policies for the future.

4.3 No single review exercise will mark an employee down for life as 'promotion potential' or otherwise. The process tends to be an on-going one, with performance at each stage or level in the employee's career indicating whether he might be able to progress to the next step. However, this approach based on performance in the current job is highly fallible: hence the 'Peter principle' of L J Peter, who pointed out that managers tend to be promoted from positions in which they are competent until one day they reach a level at which they are no longer competent - promoted 'to the level of their own incompetence'!

4.4 Moreover, the management succession plan of an organisation needs to be formulated in the long term: there is a long lead time involved in equipping a manager with the skills and experience needed at senior levels and the organisation must develop people if it is to fill the shoes of departing managers without crisis.

4.5 Some idea of 'potential' must therefore be built into appraisal. It is impossible to predict with any certainty how successful an individual will be in what will, after all, be different circumstances from anything he has experienced so far. However, some attempt can be made:

(a) to determine key indicators of potential, ie elements believed to be essential to management success; and/or

(b) to simulate the conditions of the position to which the individual would be promoted, to assess his performance.

Key indicators of potential

4.6 Various research studies (by employing organisations and by theorists) have been carried out into exactly what makes a successful senior manager (ie and could be identified in junior people to indicate that they might *become* successful senior managers). Some of the factors identified are:

(a) general effectiveness (track record in task performance and co-worker satisfaction);

(b) administrative skills (planning and organising, making good decisions);

(c) interpersonal skills or 'intelligence' (being aware of others, making a good impression, persuading and motivating);

(d) intellectual ability or analytical skills (problem-solving, mental agility);

(e) control of feelings (tolerance of stress, ambiguity etc);

(f) leadership (variously defined, but demonstrated in 'follower' loyalty and commitment);

(g) imagination and intuition (for creative decision-making and innovation);

(h) 'helicopter ability' (the ability to 'rise above' the particulars of a situation, to see the whole picture, sift out key elements and conceive strategies - the ability to 'see the wood for the trees');

(i) orientation to work (being motivated by *work* rather than non-work satisfactions; 'self-starting' rather than needing to be motivated by others);

(j) team work (ability and willingness to co-operate with others);

(k) taste for making money (empathy with the profit motive: ambition for self and business);

(l) 'fit' (having the mix of all the above skills, abilities and experience *that the business organisation needs* - ie being in the right place at the right time).

4.7 Various techniques can be used to measure these attributes, for example:

(a) written tests (for intellectual ability)

(b) simulated desk-top tasks or case studies (for administrative skills, analytical and problem-solving ability)

(c) role play (eg for negotiating or influencing skills, conflict resolution or team working)

(d) leadership exercises (testing the ability to control the dynamics of a team towards work-related objectives)

(e) personality tests (for work orientation, motivation etc)

(f) interviews (for interpersonal skills, motivation etc)

(g) presentations or speeches (for communication skills).

4.8 Note the use of *simulated* activity - case study, role play etc - to give potential managers 'experience' of managerial tasks. An alternative approach might be to offer them *real* experience (under controlled conditions) by appointing them to 'assistant to' or 'deputy' positions or to committees or project teams, and assessing their performance. This is still no real predictor of their ability to handle the *whole* job, on a continuous basis and over time, however, and it may be risky, if the appraisee fails to cope with the situation.

Assessment centres

4.9 *Assessment centres* are an increasingly used approach, growing out of the War Office Selection Board methods during the Second World War. The purpose of the method is to assess potential and identify development needs, through various *group* techniques. It is particularly useful in the identification of executive or supervisory potential, since it uses simulated but realistic management problems, to give participants opportunities to show potential in the kind of situations to which they would be promoted, but of which they currently have no experience.

4.10 Trained assessors - usually line managers two levels above the participants, and perhaps consultant psychologists - use a variety of games, simulations, tests and group discussions and exercises. Observed by the assessors, participants may be required to answer questionnaires about their attitudes, complete written tests, prepare speeches and presentations, participate in group role-play exercises, work through simulated supervisory tasks, and undertake self-appraisal and peer-rating. They are assessed on a range of factors, eg assertiveness, energy, initiative and creativity, stress-tolerance, sensitivity, abilities in persuasion, communication, decision-making etc.

An assessment report is then compiled from the assessors' observations, test scores and the participant's self-assessment. This is discussed in a feedback counselling interview.

4.11 Advantages of assessment centres include:

(a) a high degree of acceptability and user confidence; avoidance of single-assessor bias;

(b) reliability in predicting potential success (if the system is well-conducted);

(c) the development of skills in the assessors, which may be useful in their own managerial responsibilities;

(d) benefits to the assessed individual, eg experience of managerial/supervisory situations, opportunity for self-assessment and job-relevant feedback, opportunities to discuss career prospects openly with senior management.

4.12 The cost of a successful scheme must, however, be considered. A well-run centre with trained and practised assessors requires considerable expense of managerial time, and the time of participants, as well as the fixed costs of setting up the programme, whether it is designed internally or bought 'off the shelf'.

5. CHAPTER ROUNDUP

Performance appraisal

5.1

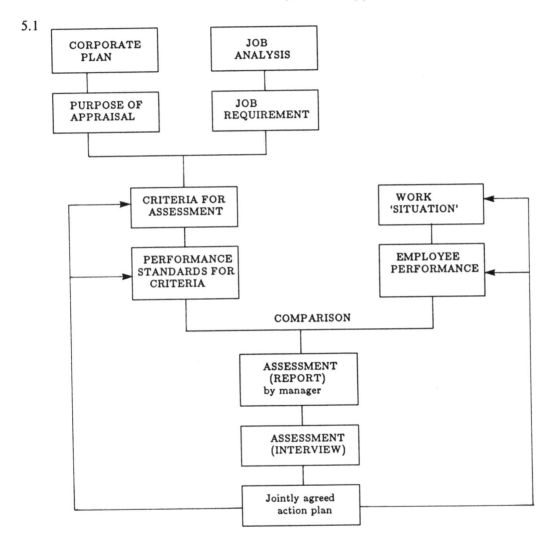

5.2 Potential appraisal indicates:

(a) the individual's promotability (present and likely future);
(b) the individual's training and development needs;
(c) the direction and rate of progress of the individual's development;
(d) the future (forecast) management resource of the organisation;
(e) the management recruitment, training and development needs of the organisation.

TEST YOUR KNOWLEDGE
The numbers in brackets refer to paragraphs of this chapter

1   What are the purposes of appraisal? (1.1, 1.2)

2   Why do organisations need a *formal* system of appraisal? (1.3, 1.4)

3   What bases or criteria of assessment might an appraisal system use? (2.3 - 2.5)

4   Outline a results-oriented approach to appraisal, and its advantages. (2.5)

5   What is the role of counselling in an appraisal system? (2.8 - 2.10)

6   What kinds of criticism might be levelled at appraisal schemes by a manager who thought they were a waste of time? (3.1, 3.3)

7   What techniques might be used to measure an employee's potential to become a successful senior manager? (4.7, 4.10)

Now try question 5 at the end of the text

Chapter 6

TRAINING AND DEVELOPMENT

This chapter covers the following topics.

1. Training
2. Training needs
3. The learning process
4. Approaches to training
5. Validation and evaluation of training
6. Management development

Introduction

As we will see in Chapter 24, providing the organisation with the most suitable human resources for the task and environment is an on-going process. It involves not only recruitment and selection, but the training and development of employees - prior to employment, or at any time during their employment, in order to help them meet the requirements of their current, and potential future job. Both selection and training are concerned with:

(a) fitting people to the requirements of the job;

(b) securing better occupational adjustment; and

(c) in methodological terms, setting and achieving targets, defining performance criteria against which the success of the process can be monitored.

---

1. TRAINING

1.1 The term 'industrial training', used in connection with training in a work context, includes a wide range of activities: commercial training, skills training, management development, apprenticeships etc. The main purpose of industrial training is to raise competence and therefore performance standards. From the perspective of personnel management, however, it is also concerned with personal development, helping individuals to expand and fulfil their potential, (also, theoretically, motivating them to higher performance through the opportunity for personal growth).

1.2 'Training is to some extent a management reaction to change, eg. changes in equipment and design, methods of work, new tools and machines, control systems, or in response to changes dictated by new products, services, or markets. On the other hand, training also induces change. A capable workforce will bring about new initiatives, developments and improvements - in an organic way, and of its own accord. Training is both a cause and an effect of change.'

Brian Livy, *Corporate personnel management*

1.3 This two-fold purpose of training may, however, encourage a certain conflict in the identification of training needs and priorities, where the perceived interests of organisation and individual differ. The organisation requires a fundamentally practical long-term training plan, explicitly geared to the requirements set out in the manpower plan.

1.4 Easy assumptions about training and, within each organisation, the training programme, should constantly be challenged, if the desired outcome from training is to be achieved.

(a) *Training is a personnel department matter.* Yes, it is - but not exclusively. Line managers are conversant with the requirements of the job, and the individuals concerned; they are also responsible for the performance of those individuals. They should be involved in:

(i) training need and priority identification;

(ii) training itself. A specialist 'trainer' may be used as a catalyst, but the experience of line personnel, supervisors and senior operatives will be invaluable in ensuring a practical and participative approach; and

(iii) follow-up of performance, for the validation of training methods.

(b) *The important thing is to* have *a training programme.* The view that training in itself is such a Good Thing that an organisation can't go wrong by 'providing some' is a source of inefficiency. The individual needs and expectations of trainees must be taken into account: the purpose of training must be clear, to the organisation (so that it can direct training effort and resources accordingly) and to the individual, so that he feels it to be worthwhile and meaningful - without which the motivatory factor will be lost. If the individual feels that he is training in order to grow and develop, find better ways of working, or become part of the organisation culture, he will commit himself to learning more thoroughly than if he feels he is only doing it to show willing, to fulfil the manpower plan, etc. It is too easy, also, to run old or standard programmes, without considering that:

(i) the learning needs of current trainees may be different from past ones;

(ii) the requirements of the job may not all be susceptible to classroom or study methods: are the most relevant needs being met?

(iii) the training 'group' may not be uniform in its needs: the training 'package' may be off-target for some members.

(c) *Training will improve performance.* It *might* - and *should,* all other things being equal - but a training course is not a simple remedy for poor performance. Contingency theory must be applied to situations where employee performance is below the desired standard: an employee who is adequately *trained* to perform may still not be *able* or *willing* to do so, because of badly designed working methods or environment, faulty equipment, inappropriate supervision, poor motivation, lack of incentive (poor pay scales or promotion prospects), or non-work factors, such as health, domestic circumstances etc. In particular, it must be remembered that performance is not just a product of 'the system', but a product, and manifestation, of human behaviour: training methods, and their expected results, must take into account human attitudes, values, emotions and relationships.

The systematic approach to training

1.5 According to the Department of Employment, training is 'the systematic development of the attitude/knowledge/skill/behaviour pattern required by an individual in order to perform adequately a given task or job.' The application of systems theory to the design of training has gained currency in the West in recent years. A 'training system' uses scientific methods to programme learning, from:

(a) the identification of training needs; this is a product of job analysis and specification (ie what is required to do the job) and an assessment of the present capacities and inclinations of the individuals (ie their 'pre-entry' behaviour); to

(b) the design of courses, selection of methods and media etc; to

(c) the measurement of trained performance against pre-determined proficiency goals - ie. the 'terminal behaviour' expected on the job.

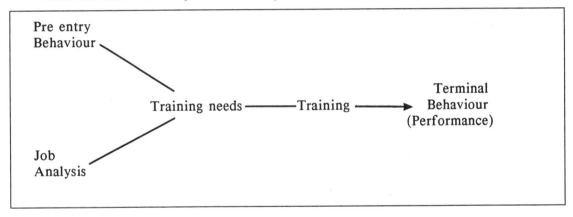

National vocational qualifications (NVQs)

1.6 The issue of training has been the subject of much political debate in recent years. Unfavourable comparisons have been drawn between the UK and Germany. The UK's poor economic performance has been linked, by some commentators, to its poor training record when contrasted with Germany.

1.7 A UK government review in the mid-1980s found there were too many vocational qualifications, offered by too many bodies, and based too much on 'knowledge' as opposed to actual competence.

1.8 The National Council for Vocational Qualifications was set up to *accredit* new qualifications, although it would not award them.

1.9 One of the important features of the scheme is that it should bring all vocational qualifications together on a 'competence basis'. This means that the qualification will describe what somebody is *capable of doing*, implying a certain level of *knowledge* and *understanding* behind it.

1.10 NCVQ will accredit qualifications to a number of levels (from level 1, the most junior, up to level 5 which reflects professional qualifications).

1.11 The following are the most important organisations in developing NVQs.

   (a) The National Council for Vocational Qualifications (NCVQ) which accredits new qualifications.

   (b) The Training, Enterprise and Education Directorate (TEED) of the Department of Employment is responsible for overseeing developing standards of occupational competence.

   (c) The *lead bodies*, which are funded by the TEED, develop standards. They are authoritative groups of practitioners in a particular area.

1.12 Some standards are industry specific ((eg the lead body for banking), whereas others cover broad occupational areas of the economy (eg lead bodies for administration).

1.13 What is the relevance for NVQs for the banking sector? There is a *lead body for banking*. Bank employees have already been on a pilot scheme at level 2 (as reported in *Banking World*). Draft standards for levels 3 and 4 are now under consideration.

1.14 To attain a standard, an employee must be competent in several *units of competence*. Each unit of competence is divided into *elements*. These are satisfied by *performance criteria*.

For example, the Banking Standards for level 2 include the following.

Unit CA3: set up, maintain and monitor customer accounts.
Element CA3.1: Open customer accounts/set up service by processing applications for products and services.

Performance criteria

   (a) Documentation obtained is in accordance with bank requirements.

   (b) Documentation and correspondence is legible, accurate and complete.

   (c) Identity of customer and all signatures/authorisations are confirmed in accordance with bank procedures.

   (d) Type of account/service is correctly identified and actioned without undue delay.

   (e) Progress of applications is monitored and undue delay is notified to the supervisor and the customer.

(f)   Irregularities, inaccurate/false information and problems are detected and reported to the supervisor promptly.

(g)   Contact with customer is tactful, courteous and such as to promote good relations and meet customer service standards.

(h)   Confidentiality procedures are observed at all times.

(i)   Security regulations with regard to initial transactions are observed.

1.15 The advantages of NVQs are given below.

(a)   The employee receives access to formal training opportunities, with qualifications that are understood and recognised throughout the industry.

(b)   A more skilled workforce might be more productive.

(c)   It is hoped the economic performance of the country at large will be improved.

1.16 There are worries, however:

(a)   that the system is costly and bureaucratic;
(b)   that training will be for today's, rather than tomorrow's, skills.

2.   TRAINING NEEDS

2.1   The training needs of individuals and groups will obviously vary enormously, according to the nature of the job and particular tasks, the abilities and experience of the employees etc. New recruits, in particular, may have:

(a)   no previous experience or training;
(b)   an 'academic' qualification in a related skill or discipline; and/or
(c)   experience in a similar job in another organisation.

The type and intensity of training will have to vary accordingly.

2.2   As suggested earlier, training should not be a 'shot in the dark'; the homogeneity of the training group cannot be assumed; clear and obtainable objectives are essential to the efficiency and effectiveness of the training programme.

(a)   Some training requirements will be obvious and 'automatic'. If a piece of legislation is enacted - say, the Financial Services Act 1986, which affected the way in which a bank could offer investment products - training in its provisions will automatically be indicated. The introduction of new technology similarly implies a training need.

(b)   Some qualitative indicators might be taken as symptoms of a need for training: absenteeism, high labour turnover, grievance and disciplinary actions, crises, conflict, poor motivation and performance. Such factors will need to be investigated to see what the root causes are, and whether training *will* solve the problem.

(c) Formal *training needs analysis* may be carried out. Training 'needs' should be identified as the gap between the requirements of the job and the actual current performance of the job-holders, ie

Required level of competence *minus* present level of competence.

This will obviously be different from individual to individual.

2.3 The present level of competence (which includes not only skill and knowledge, but inclination as well) of employees - ie their 'entry behaviour' - can be measured by an appropriate 'pre-test' of skills, knowledge, performance, attitude etc. Interviews and performance appraisals may also be used.

2.4 Job requirements can be determined in the following ways.

(a) Job analysis.

(b) Skills analysis, for more skilled jobs. Here, not only the task- and worker-oriented requirements of the job are identified, but the skill elements of the task, eg:

(i) what sensory information (cues and stimuli) need to be recognised?
(ii) what senses are involved? (ie vision, touch, hearing etc)
(iii) what left-hand/right-hand/foot operations are required?
(iv) what counter-balancing operations are required?
(v) what interactions with other operatives are required?

(c) Role analysis, for managerial and administrative jobs requiring a high degree of co-ordination and interaction with others.

(d) Existing records, eg job specifications and descriptions, person specifications, the organisation chart (depicting roles and relationships) etc.

2.5 The 'learning gap' between the two analyses can then be identified. Job requirements will indicate the 'terminal behaviour' desired from trainees at the end of the programme: ie the criteria for performance, probably divided into sub-goals (since some will take longer to develop than others).

2.6 The training department manager will have to make an initial investigation into the problem of the 'gap' between job requirements and current performance. As we noted earlier, it may be that shortcomings in the capacities and inclinations of employees would not be improved by training, but by a review of the work environment, systems and procedures, work methods, technology, industrial relations, leadership style, motivation and incentives etc.

2.7 If it is concluded that the provision of training would improve work performance, training *objectives* can then be defined. They should be clear, specific and related to observable, measurable targets, ideally detailing:

(a) behaviour - ie what the trainee should be able to do;
(b) standard - ie to what level of performance; and
(c) environment - ie under what conditions (so that the performance level is realistic).

This is usually best expressed in terms of active verbs: at the end of the course the trainee should be able to describe ...., or identify .... or distinguish x from y .... or calculate .... or assemble .... etc. It is insufficient to define the objectives of training as 'to give trainees a grounding in ....' or 'to encourage trainees in a better appreciation of ....': this offers no target achievement which can be quantifiably measured.

2.8 For example, the CIB's Scheme of Work for the *Management in Banking* syllabus lists the *objectives* of the learning programme. Objectives for this area of the syllabus include: '*describe* best practice in relation to training and career development'. They specify something you should be able to *do* at the end of a learning period, eg 'outline ... explain ... apply ... analyse ... identify ...'

3. THE LEARNING PROCESS

3.1 Having identified training needs and objectives, the manager will have to decide on the best way to approach training: there are a number of types and techniques of training, which we will discuss below. There are different schools of learning theory which explain and describe the learning process in very different ways.

(a) Behaviourist psychology concentrates on the relationship between 'stimuli' (input through the senses) and 'responses' to those stimuli. 'Learning' is the formation of *new* connections between stimulus and response, on the basis of experience or 'conditioning': we modify our responses in future according to whether the results of our behaviour in the past have been good or bad. We get *feedback* on the results of our actions, which may be rewarding ('positive reinforcement') or punishing ('negative reinforcement') and therefore an incentive or a deterrent to similar behaviour in future. Trial-and-error learning, and carrot-and-stick approaches to motivation work on this basis.

(b) The cognitive approach (or 'information processing') argues that the human mind takes sensory information and imposes organisation and meaning on it: we interpret and rationalise. We use feedback information on the results of past behaviour to make rational decisions about whether to maintain successful behaviours or modify unsuccessful behaviours in future, according to our goals and our plans for reaching them.

3.2 Whichever approach it is based on, learning theory offers certain useful propositions for the design of effective training programmes.

(a) The individual should be *motivated* to learn. The advantages of training should be made clear, according to the individual's motives - money, opportunity, valued skills etc.

(b) There should be clear *objectives and standards* set, so that each task has some 'meaning'. Each stage of learning should present a challenge, without overloading the trainee or making him lose confidence. Specific objectives and performance standards for each will help the trainee in the planning and control process that leads to learning, providing targets against which performance will constantly be measured.

(c) There should be timely, relevant *feedback* on performance and progress. This will usually be provided by the trainer (ie extrinsic feedback), and should be concurrent - or certainly not long delayed. If progress reports or performance appraisals are given only at the year end, for example, there will be no opportunity for behaviour adjustment or learning in the meantime.

(d) Positive and negative *reinforcement* should be judiciously used. Recognition and encouragement enhances the individual's confidence in his competence and progress: punishment for poor performance - especially without explanation and correction - discourages the learner and creates feelings of guilt, failure and hostility. Helpful or 'constructive' criticism, however, is more likely to be beneficial.

(e) Active *participation* is more telling than passive reception (because of its effect on the motivation to learn, concentration and recollection). If a high degree of participation is impossible, practice and repetition can be used to reinforce receptivity, but participation has the affect of encouraging 'ownership' of the process of learning and changing - committing the individual to it as his *own* goal, not just an imposed process.

Learning styles

3.3 It is believed that the way in which people learn best will be different according to the type of person, ie that there are *learning styles* which suit different individuals.

Peter Honey and Alan Mumford have drawn up a popular classification of four learning styles.

(a) *Theorist*

This person seeks to understand underlying concepts and to take an intellectual, 'hands-off' approach based on logical argument. Such a person prefers training:

(i)   to be programmed and structured;
(ii)   to allow time for analysis; and
(iii) to be provided by teachers who share his preference for concepts and analysis.

Theorists find learning difficult if they have a teacher with a different style (particularly an activist style), material which skims over basic principles and a programme which is hurried and unstructured.

(b) *Reflector*

People who observe phenomena, think about them and then choose how to act are called reflectors. Such a person needs to work at his own pace and would find learning difficult if forced into a hurried programme with little notice or information.

Reflectors are able to produce carefully thought-out conclusions after research and reflection but tend to be fairly slow, non-participative (unless to ask questions) and cautious.

(c) *Activist*

These are people who like to deal with practical, active problems and who do not have much patience with theory. They require training based on hands-on experience.

Activists are excited by participation and pressure, such as making presentations and new projects. Although they are flexible and optimistic, however, they tend to rush at something without due preparation, take risks and then get bored.

(d) *Pragmatist*

These people only like to study if they can see its direct link to practical problems - they are not interested in theory etc for its own sake. They are particularly good at learning new techniques in on-the-job training which they see as useful improvements. Their aim is to implement action plans and/or do the task better. Such a person is business-like and realistic, but may discard good ideas as being 'impractical' which only require some development.

3.4 The implications for management are that people react to problem situations in different ways and that, in particular, training methods should where possible be tailored to the preferred style of trainees.

The learning cycle

3.5 Another useful model is the 'experiential learning cycle' devised by David Kolb. Kolb suggested that classroom-type learning is 'a special activity cut off from the real world and unrelated to one's life': a teacher or trainer directs the learning process on behalf of a passive learner. 'Experiential learning', however, involves doing, and puts the learner in an active problem-solving role.

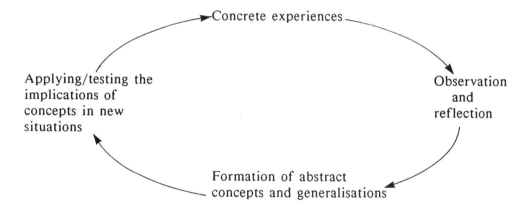

Say an employee interviews a customer for the first time (concrete experience). He observes his performance and the dynamics of the situation (observation) and afterwards, having failed to convince the customer to open an account, he analyses what he did right and wrong (reflection). He comes to the conclusion that he had failed to listen to what the customer really wanted and feared, underneath his general reluctance: he realises that the key to communication is listening (abstraction/generalisation). In his next interview he applies his strategy to the new set of circumstances (application/testing). This provides him with a new experience with which to start the cycle over again.

> Do actions
> Analyse actions
> Understand *principles*
> Apply principles

3.6 This is the model for many of the modern approaches to training, and particularly management development, which recommend experiential learning - 'learning by doing'. In effect, it involves elements of *all* the learning styles identified by Honey and Mumford.

4. APPROACHES TO TRAINING

4.1 Training methods and media must next be evaluated, and a programme designed. There are a variety of options, discussed below, including:

(a) formal learning; by internal or external residential courses, day courses or lectures, distance learning, programmed learning or computer-aided learning;

(b) on-the-job training; induction, coaching, job-rotation etc; and

(c) group learning.

4.2 The training course should only go ahead if the likely benefits are expected to exceed the costs of designing and then running the course. The problem here is not so much in estimating costs, but in estimating the potential benefits.

(a) Costs will be the costs of the training establishment, training materials, the salaries of the staff attending training courses, their travelling expenses, the salaries of training staff, etc.

(b) Benefits might be measured in terms of:

(i) quicker working and therefore reductions in overtime or staff numbers;
(ii) greater accuracy of work;
(iii) more extensive skills.

As you will appreciate, the benefits are more easily stated in general terms than quantified in money terms.

4.3 When the training course has been designed, it may be decided to have a pilot test of the course. The purpose of the test would be to find out whether the training scheme appears to achieve what it has set out to do, or whether some revisions are necessary. After the pilot test, the scheme can be implemented in full.

Formal training

4.4 Internal courses are often run by the training department of banks, which may have their own staff college. Skills may be taught at a technical level (eg foreign exchange, or lending decisions) or in aspects such as marketing, team building, interviewing or information technology management. Training is one of the aspects of banking management that is becoming more *decentralised* than it has traditionally been, being delegated to regional offices and even to branch level where there are particular training needs and resources.

4.5 One way of conveniently decentralising training (as well as quickly developing training courses to meet emerging needs) is the use of computer-based training (CBT) and interactive video (IV), through teaching equipment in each branch or strategically located branches. Training programmes are developed centrally by the bank's own trainers or by outside consultants - or bought 'off the shelf': the software (or 'courseware') can then be distributed to branches, so that large numbers of staff, dispersed around the country, can learn about new technology products or procedures quickly and simultaneously.

4.6 External courses vary, and may involve:

(a) day-release, which means that the employee works in the organisation and on one day per week attends a local college for theoretical teaching;

(b) evening classes, or 'distance learning', which make demand on the individual's time outside work;

(c) introductory or revision courses for examinations of professional bodies (like the CIB);

(d) a sponsored full-time course at a university or polytechnic for one or two years. This might be the case, for example, for a manager doing an MBA degree, such as the Lombard scheme.

Banks might use such facilities - perhaps with 'bespoke' programmes from business schools - to fill gaps in the training service offered in-house (ie specialist non-banking areas or qualifications) and/or to train bankers together with non-bankers, (eg in an open course on strategic planning for managers) in order to get wider perspectives and useful contacts.

4.7 The disadvantages of formal training might be as follows.

(a) An individual will not benefit from formal training unless he/she wants to learn. The individual's superior may need to provide encouragement in this respect.

(b) If the subject matter of the training course does not relate to an individual's job, the learning will not be applied, and will quickly be forgotten. Many training managers provide internal courses without relating their content to the needs of individuals attending them. Equally, professional examinations often include subjects in which individuals have no job experience, and these are usually difficult to learn and are quickly forgotten afterwards.

(c) Individuals may not be able to accept that what they learn on a course applies in the context of their own particular job. For example, a manager may attend an internal course on man-management which suggests a participatory style of leadership, but on returning to his job he may consider that what he has learned is not relevant in his case, because his subordinates are 'too young' or 'too inexperienced'.

(d) Immediate and relevant *feedback* on performance and progress may not be available from the learning process, which will lower the learner's incentive.

(e) It does not suit activists or pragmatists.

On-the-job training

4.8 On-the-job training is very common, especially when the work involved is not complex. Trainee managers require more coaching, and may be given assignments or projects as part of a planned programme to develop their experience. Unfortunately, this type of training will be unsuccessful if:

(a) the assignments do not have a specific purpose from which the trainee can learn and gain experience;

(b) the trainee is a 'theorist' or 'reflector' and needs to get away from the pressures of the workplace and think through issues and understand the underlying principles before he can apply new techniques;

(c) the organisation is intolerant of any mistakes which the trainee makes. Mistakes are an inevitable part of on-the-job learning, and if they are 'punished' the trainee will be reluctant to take further risks - will be de-motivated to learn.

In addition, there may be real risks involved in 'throwing people in at the deep-end': the cost of mistakes or inefficiencies may be high and the pressure on learners great.

4.9 An important advantage of on-the-job training is that it takes place in the environment of the job itself, and in the context of the work group in which the trainee will have to operate. The style of supervision, personal relations with colleagues, working conditions and pressures, the 'culture' of the office/shop floor etc will be absorbed as part of the training process.

(a) There will be no re-adjustment to make, as there will be when the trainee transfers his acquired knowledge, skills and 'academic' attitudes to the job, the work place and work group.

(b) The work group itself will be adapting to the dynamics of the trainee's situation: it will adjust to his new capacities and inclinations. All too often, a trainee returns from a course to find that he cannot apply his new-found ideas and skills: the supervisor is set in his ways, colleagues resent his perceived superiority, the tasks and methods stay the same.

(c) The perceived relevance of the training to the job and performance criteria is much greater, and therefore the training is felt to be of greater value.

(d) There is greater opportunity for relevant, performance-related *feedback*, which is an integral part of the learning process (both as the means by which the individual recognises the need for modified behaviour, and as a motivating factor, with the knowledge of progress, success etc). Feedback on performance in a non-work environment may still leave doubts in the trainee's mind as to the value of his progress when he returns to the job.

4.10 Different methods of on-the-job training include the following.

(a) *Induction:* introducing a new recruit or transferred employee to his job.

(b) *Coaching:* the trainee is put under the guidance of an experienced employee who shows the trainee how to do the job. The length of the coaching period will depend on the complexity of the job and the previous experience of the trainee.

(c) *Job rotation:* the trainee is given several jobs in succession, to gain experience of a wide range of activities. (Even experienced managers may rotate their jobs, to gain wider experience; this philosophy of job education is commonly applied in the Civil Service, where an employee may expect to move on to another job after a few years).

(d) *Temporary promotion:* an individual is promoted into his/her superior's position whilst the superior is absent due to illness. This gives the individual a chance to experience the demands of a more senior position.

(e) *'Assistant to' positions:* a junior manager with good potential may be appointed as assistant to the managing director or another executive director. In this way, the individual gains experience of how the organisation is managed 'at the top';

(f) *Project or committee work:* trainees might be included in the membership of a project team or committee, in order to obtain an understanding of inter-departmental relationships, problem-solving and particular areas of bank activity.

Induction training

4.11 From their first day in a job, new recruits must be helped to find their bearings. There are limits to what any person can pick up in a short time, so that the process of getting one's feet under the table will be a gradual one.

4.12 On the first day, a manager or other senior person should welcome the new recruit. The manager might discuss in broad terms what is required from people at work, working conditions, pay and benefits, training opportunities and career opportunities. The manager should then introduce the new recruit to the person who will be his or her immediate supervisor.

4.13 The immediate supervisor should then take over the process of induction.

(a) Pinpoint the areas that the recruit will have to learn about in order to start work. Some things (eg detailed technical knowledge) may be identified as areas for later study or training, while others (eg some of the office procedures and systems with which the recruit will have to deal) will have to be explained immediately. A list of learning priorities should be drawn up, so that the recruit, and the supervisor, are clear about the rate and direction of progress required.

(b) Explain first of all the nature of the job, and the goals of each task, of the recruit's job and of the department as a whole. This will help the recruit to work to specific targets and to understand how his tasks relate to the overall objectives of the department - or even the organisation as a whole.

(c) Explain about hours of work and stress the importance of time-keeping. If flexitime is operated, explain how it works.

(d) Explain the structure of the department - to whom the recruit will report, who deals with complaints or queries etc.

(e) Introduce the recruit to the people in the office, in particular to all the members of the immediate work team (and perhaps be given the opportunity to get to know them informally, over lunch in the canteen etc), and to the departmental manager (to identify who this person is). One particular colleague may be assigned to recruits as a *mentor* for their first few days - to keep an eye on them, answer routine queries, 'show them the ropes' etc. The layout of the office, procedures for lunch hours or holidays, rules about smoking or eating in the office etc will then be 'taught' informally.

(f) Plan and implement an appropriate training programme for whatever technical or practical knowledge is required. Again, the programme should have a clear schedule and set of goals so that the recruit has a sense of purpose, and so that the programme can be efficiently organised to fit in with the activities of the department.

(g) Coach and/or train the recruit. Check regularly on the recruit's progress, as demonstrated by performance, as reported by the recruit's mentor, and in the recruits own opinion. Feedback information will be essential to the learning process, correcting any faults at an early stage and building the confidence of the recruit.

(h) Integrate the recruit into the 'culture' of the office. Much of this may be done informally - the prevailing norms of dress, degree of formality in the office, attitude to customers are easily picked up this way etc. However, the supervisor should try to 'sell' the values and 'style' of the office - its 'mission statement' (if any) - and should reinforce commitment to those values by rewarding evidence of loyalty, hard work, desired behaviour etc.

4.14 There might be a supervisor or manager who is specifically responsible for the induction of new recruits. He should introduce himself to the new recruit, and may wish to deal with any paperwork on the first day, such as giving the recruit his contract of employment. He should repeat the information already given about training opportunities, hours of work, pay and conditions etc. He might arrange to introduce the new recruit to other recruits in other sections. He can provide information about the staff canteen, sports and social clubs, travel facilities to and from work, details about local shops etc. He should also encourage the recruit to come to him with any worries and problems he might have later which he cannot really discuss with his direct supervisor or his mentor.

4.15 Note that induction is a continuing process which might last for several months or even longer.

(a) The supervisor must arrange for the recruit's training programme to start.

(b) The recruit will only gradually learn his job through continued on-the-job training.

(c) The person responsible for induction should keep checking up on the new recruit, to make sure that he is settling in well and is learning the ropes.

(d) The senior manager should check on the recruit from time to time (in particular, to find out how his training is progressing).

4.16 After three months, six months or one year the performance of a new recruit should be formally appraised and discussed with him. Indeed, when the process of induction has been finished, a recruit should continue to receive periodic appraisals, just like every other employee in the organisation.

Coaching

4.17 Essential steps in the coaching process are as follows.

(a) Establish learning targets. The areas to be learnt should be identified, and specific, realistic goals stated. These will refer not only to the 'timetable' for acquiring necessary skills and knowledge, but to standards of performance to be attained, which should if possible be formulated by agreement with the trainee.

(b) Plan a systematic learning and development programme. This will ensure regular progress, appropriate stages for consolidation and practice. It will ensure that all stages of learning are relevant to the trainee and the task he will be asked to perform.

(c) Identify opportunities for broadening the trainee's knowledge and experience - eg by involving him in new projects, encouraging him to serve on interdepartmental committees, giving him new contacts, or simply extending his job, giving him more tasks, greater responsibility etc.

(d) Take into account the strengths and limitations of the trainee, and take advantage of learning opportunities that suit his ability, preferred style and goals. A trainee from an academic background may learn best through research-based learning - eg fact-finding for a committee, off-the-job study etc. Those who learn best by 'doing' may profit from project work, hands-on training etc.

(e) Exchange feedback. The supervisor will want to know how the trainee sees his progress and his future. He will also need performance information, to monitor the trainee's progress, adjust the learning programme if necessary, identify further needs which may emerge, and plan future development for the trainee.

All the above will require the commitment of the organisation, and the department manager in particular, to the learning programme. They must 'believe' in training and developing employees, so that they are prepared to devote money, opportunity and the time of all people concerned. The manager will largely dictate the department's attitude to these things. His own time and support will be required to give praise and constructive criticism, to show an interest etc.

Group learning: 'T' groups

4.18 Group learning is not common in industry but is more common in organisations such as social services departments of local government authorities. The purpose of group learning is to:

(a) give each individual in a training group (or 'T' group) a greater insight into his own behaviour;

(b) to teach an individual how he 'appears' to other people, as a result of responses from other members of the group;

(c) to teach an understanding of intra-group processes, ie how people inter-relate;

(d) to develop an individual's skills in taking action to control such intra-group processes.

'Encounter groups' for therapy are a development of the 'T' group principle.

4.19 Group learning may be of educational value to individuals whose job is dealing with other people. This process must have the full co-operation of all participants in the group if the training is to provide positive educational results.

5. VALIDATION AND EVALUATION OF TRAINING

5.1   Implementation of the training scheme is not the end of the story. The scheme should be validated and evaluated.

(a) *Validation* means observing the results of the course, and measuring whether the training objectives have been achieved.

(b) *Evaluation* means comparing the actual costs of the scheme against the assessed benefits which are being obtained. If the costs exceed the benefits, the scheme will need to be re-designed or withdrawn.

5.2   There are various ways of validating a training scheme. These are:

(a) *trainee reactions to the experience:* asking the trainees whether they thought the training programme was relevant to their work, and whether they found it useful. This form of monitoring is rather inexact, and it does not allow the training department to measure the results for comparison against the training objective;

(b) *trainee learning:* measuring what the trainees have learned on the course, perhaps by means of a test at the end of a course;

(c) *changes in job behaviour following training:* studying the subsequent behaviour of the trainees in their jobs to measure how the training scheme has altered the way they do their work. This is possible where the purpose of the course was to learn a particular skill;

(d) *organisational change as a result of training:* finding out whether the training has affected the work or behaviour of other employees not on the course - eg. seeing whether there has been a general change in attitudes arising from a new course in, say, computer terminal work. This form of monitoring would probably be reserved for senior managers in the training department;

(e) *impact of training on organisational goals:* seeing whether the training scheme (and overall programme) has contributed to the overall objectives of the organisation. This too is a form of monitoring reserved for senior management, and would perhaps be discussed at board level in the organisation. It is likely to be the main component of a cost-benefit analysis.

5.3   Validation is thus the measurement of 'terminal behaviour' (ie trained work performance) in relation to training objectives.

> 'The validation of training is really an assessment to see whether the training has achieved what it set out to achieve. To validate it scientifically, we would really need to compare various training methods to see which one produced the best result. Time and cost constraints may limit this luxury ...'
>
> Livy, *Corporate personnel management*

6: TRAINING AND DEVELOPMENT

6. MANAGEMENT DEVELOPMENT

6.1 You might subscribe to the trait theory of leadership, that some individuals are 'born' with the personal qualities to be a good manager, and others aren't. There might be some bits of truth in this view, but very few individuals, if any, can walk into a management job and do it well without some guidance, experience or training.

6.2 In every organisation, there should be some arrangement or system whereby:

(a) managers gain *experience*, which will enable them to do another more senior job in due course of time;

(b) subordinate managers are given *guidance* and *counselling* by their bosses;

(c) managers are given suitable *training* and *education* to develop their skills and knowledge; and

(d) managers are enabled to plan their future and the opportunities open to them in the organisation.

If there is a planned programme for developing managers, it is called a *management development programme*.

6.3 Drucker has suggested that management development should be provided for all managers, not just the ones who are considered promotable material. 'The promotable man concept focuses on one man out of ten - at best one man out of five. It assigns the other nine to limbo. But the men who need management development the most are not the balls of fire who are the ... promotable people. They are those managers who are not good enough to be promoted but not poor enough to be fired. Unless they have grown up to the demands of tomorrow's jobs, the whole management group will be inadequate, no matter how good ... the promotable people. The first principle of manager development must therefore be the development of the entire management group'.

6.4 On the other hand, Handy noted that '... it remains true that career planning in many organisations is not a development process so much as a weeding-out process'.

6.5 It is worth getting clear in your mind at the beginning why management training and development are needed.

(a) The prime objective of management development is improved performance capacity - from the managers *and* those they manage.

(b) Management development secures management succession, ie a pool of promotable individuals in the organisation.

(c) An organisation should show an interest in the career development of its staff, so as to motivate them and encourage them to stay with the firm, especially for banks, which have traditionally relied on internal promotion from lower ranks to fill senior management positions.

(d) Individual managers should be encouraged to 'own' their own careers and personal development plans.

6: TRAINING AND DEVELOPMENT

Management development, education and training

6.6 Approaches to management development fall into three main categories.

(a) *Management education* - study for an MBA (Masters in Business Administration) degree or DMS (Diploma in Management Studies), for example.

(b) *Management training* - largely off-the-job formal learning activities.

(c) *Experiential learning* - learning by doing.

6.7 The last of these categories has gained in popularity in recent years, with methods such as management by objectives being claimed to offer a higher degree of relevance to performance, and 'ownership' by the trainee.

> Constable and McCormick, however, in their influential report *The making of British managers*, suggest that there is still a place for a systematic education and training programme featuring study for professional qualifications and design of in-house training courses. Such a programme is the basis of efforts to ensure that managers are (and can demonstrate that they are) properly trained, through the Management Charter Initiative (MCI).

6.8 The report by Constable and McCormick found from a survey of UK employers that:

(a) most employers regard innate ability and experience as the two key ingredients of an effective manager. But education and training help, *especially in broadening the outlook of managers with only functional experience previously, and without experience of general management;*

(b) there was agreement that it would be both inappropriate and impossible to make management a controlled profession similar to accountancy and law. However, making a managerial career more similar to the professions and *having managers require specific competences appropriate to each stage of their career*, were seen as beneficial.

6.9 A useful distinction between management education, training and development was given by Constable and McCormick.

(a) '*Education* is that process which results in formal qualifications up to and including post-graduate degrees.'

(b) *Training* is 'the formal learning activities which may not lead to qualifications, and which may be received at any time in a working career', eg a course in customer interviewing or lending decision-making.

(c) '*Development* is broader again: job experience and learning from other managers, particularly one's immediate superior, are integral parts of the development process.' Development will include features such as:

    (i)   career planning for individual managers;
    (ii) job rotation;
    (iii) deputising for superiors;
    (iv) on-the-job training;

(v) counselling, perhaps by means of regular appraisal reports;

(vi) guidance from superiors or colleagues ie *'mentoring'*;

(vii) education and training;

(viii) job experience.

Recommendations for management development

6.10 A successful programme should involve both senior management and the individual managers. Constable and McCormick reported in 1987 that:

'the total scale of management training is currently at a very low level. The general situation will only improve when many more companies conscientiously embrace a positive plan for management development. This needs to be accompanied by strong demand on the part of individual managers for continuing training and development throughout their careers.'

Recommendations of the report 'The Making of British Managers'

Senior management

1. Create an atmosphere within the organisation where continuing management training and development is the norm.

2. Utilise appraisal procedures which encourage management training and development.

3. Encourage individual managers, especially by *making time available* for training.

4. Provide support to local educational institutes (eg colleges) to provide management education and training (E & T).

5. Integrate in-house training courses into a wider system of management E & T. *Make the subject matter of in-house courses relevant to managers' needs.* Work closely with academic institutions and professional institutions (eg. the CIB) to ensure that the 'right' programmes are provided.

Individual managers

1. Actively want and seek training and development. 'Own' their own career.

2. Recognise what new skills they require, and seek them out positively.

3. Where appropriate, join a professional institute and seek to qualify as a professional member.

6.11 Designing appropriate in-house courses and encouraging some managers to obtain a professional qualification should be two key features of an E & T programme for managers.

6.12 Although these recommendations focus on 'E and T', it is important to realise that this no longer implies bookwork, academic and theory-based studies. W A G Braddick *(Management for bankers)* suggests the kind of shift in focus that has occurred in management development methods in recent years. (The notes are ours.)

Notes

Principles	⟶ specifics	(Every organisation is unique)
Precepts	⟶ analysis/diagnosis	(Address the issues)
Theory-based	⟶ action-centred	(Understand it - but do it)
Academic	⟶ real time problems	(Tackle 'live' problems)
Functional focus	⟶ issue and problem focus	(Deal with 'whole' activities)
Excellent individual	⟶ team members and leaders	(Develop people-together)
Patient	⟶ agent	(Learn actively, take control)
One-off	⟶ continuous	(Keep learning)

Management education and training now tends to focus on the real needs of specific organisations, and to be grounded in practical skills. In-house programmes and on-the-job techniques have flourished, as have techniques of off-the-job learning which *simulate* real issues and problems: case study, role play, desk-top exercises, leadership exercises etc.

Career development

6.13 We will be discussing the individual's role in his own career management in Part E of this text, but note that management development includes *career development* and succession planning by the organisation. This will require attention to:

(a) the types of experience a potential senior manager will have to acquire. It may be desirable for a senior manager in a bank, for example, to have experience of:

(i) both line and staff/specialist management - in order to understand how authority is effectively exercised in both situations, and the potentially conflicting cultures/objectives of the two fields;

(ii) running a whole business unit (of whatever size) in order to develop a business, rather than a functional or sub-unit perspective. This is likely to be a vital transition in a manager's career, from functional to general management;

(iii) dealing with head office, from a subsidiary management position - in order to understand the dynamics of centralised/decentralised control;

(iv) international operations - if the bank is in (or moving into) the international arena, eg in post-1992 Europe. Understanding of cultural differences is crucial to effective strategic and 'man' management;

(v) other disciplines and organisations. Some banks offer secondment with business organisations, development agencies or the civil service. A diluted form of the same principle may be experience gained as a small business advisor or similar post in a branch;

(b) the individual's guides and role models in the organisation. It is important that an individual with potential should measure himself against peers - assessing weaknesses and strengths - and emulate role models, usually superiors who have already 'got what it takes' and proved it. Potential high fliers can be 'fast tracked' by putting them under the guidance of effective motivators, teachers and power sources in the organisation.

At any stage in a career, a *mentor* will be important. The mentor may occupy a role as the employee's teacher/coach/trainer, counsellor, role model, protector or sponsor/ champion, spur to action or improvement, critic and encourager;

(c) the level of opportunities and challenges offered to the developing employee. Too much responsibility too early can be damagingly stressful, but if there is not *some* degree of difficulty, the employee may never explore his full potential and capacity.

Exercise

Think about your employer's training schemes for a while.

(a) How relevant has your most recent training course been?

(b) What other benefits not related to your job do you think it has given you?

---

7. CHAPTER ROUNDUP

7.1 A systematic approach to training can be illustrated in a flowchart as on the opposite page.

7.2 Management development is a process whereby managers:

(a) gain experience;
(b) receive instruction and guidance from their superiors;
(c) enhance their ability and potential through training and education;
(d) plan their future and the opportunities open to them in the organisation.

This is obviously a collaborative activity of the organisation and the individual manager.

6: TRAINING AND DEVELOPMENT

Training

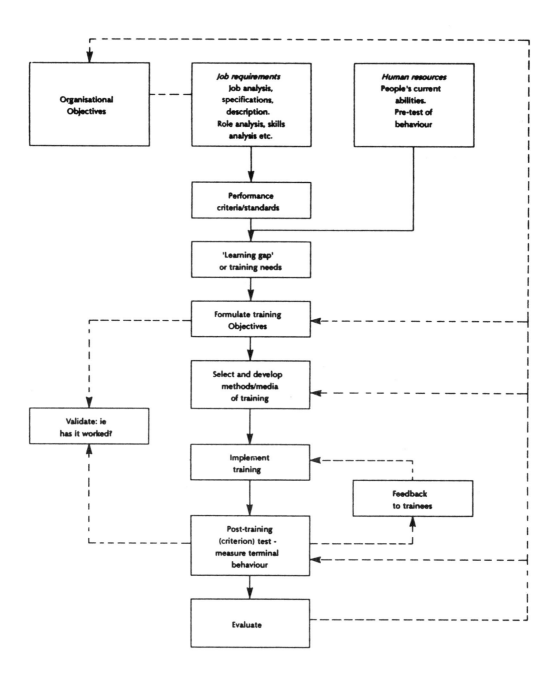

TEST YOUR KNOWLEDGE

The numbers in brackets refer to paragraphs of this chapter

1 Describe a systematic approach to training. (1.5)

2 How can a 'training need' be identified? (2.2 - 2.5)

3 Outline the role of:

    (a)   motivation;
    (b)   feedback; and
    (c)   'reinforcement'

    in the learning process. (3.1, 3.2)

4 List the four 'learning styles' identified by Honey and Mumford. Give examples of the type of training methods that would and would not appeal to a person who prefers each style. (3.3)

5 Draw the 'experiential learning curve' designed by Kolb. Choose any task you have done today, and show how the learning cycle would help you to do it better next time. (3.5)

6 Why might a bank send its employees to a training course at a local management centre or business school instead of to its own training facility? (4.6)

7 What are the advantages and disadvantages of 'on-the job' training methods? (4.8, 4.9)

8 Outline the process of:

    (a)   induction; (4.13)
    (b)   coaching. (4.17)

9 How can a training scheme be validated? (5.2)

10 What are the objectives of management development? (6.5)

11 Distinguish between management education, training and development, with examples of methods for each. (6.6)

12 What is a mentor? (6.13)

Now try question 6 at the end of the text

Chapter 7

DISCIPLINE, GRIEVANCE AND EXIT

This chapter covers the following topics.

1. Discipline
2. Grievance procedures
3. Exit from employment

Introduction

This chapter deals with what happens when things go wrong at work. An individual's conduct might breach work practices and call for censure, or someone might have a grievance. Large firms such as banks have procedures for dealing with these issues, to ensure fairness as far as possible.

1.   DISCIPLINE

1.1   Maintaining discipline among employees is an integral part of the directing function of management. It is used and understood in several different ways. The word discipline brings to mind the use of authority or force. To many, it primarily carries the disagreeable meaning of punishment. However, there is another way of thinking about discipline, a way which is far more in keeping with what has been said about good management. Discipline can be considered as a condition in an enterprise in which there is orderliness and in which the members of the enterprise behave sensibly and conduct themselves according to the standards of acceptable behaviour laid down by the organisation.

1.2   The best discipline is *self discipline*. Even before they start to work, most mature people accept the idea that following instructions and fair rules of conduct are normal responsibilities that are part of any job. Most employees can therefore be counted on to exercise self discipline. They believe in performing their work properly, in coming to work on time, in following the supervisor's instructions, and in refraining from fighting, drinking at work, or stealing etc. It is a normal human tendency to subordinate one's personal interests and personal idiosyncracies to the needs of the organisation.

1.3   Once employees know what is expected of them and feel that the rules are reasonable, self-disciplined behaviour becomes a part of 'group norms' (the way in which employees behave as a work group, and their collective attitudes). When new rules are introduced, the supervisor must try to convince employees of their purpose and reasonableness. If the work group as a whole accepts change, group pressure will act on possible dissenters, thus reducing the need for corrective action.

7: DISCIPLINE, GRIEVANCE AND EXIT

Types of disciplinary situations

1.4 However, there are always some employees in every organisation who, for various reasons, will fail to observe the established rules and standards even after having been informed of them. These employees simply do not accept the responsibility of self discipline. Since the job must be accomplished, the manager cannot afford to let the few 'get away' with violations. Firm action is required to correct those situations which interfere with the accepted norms of responsible employee behaviour. The test of a good line manager is how he deals with disciplinary situations, however caused.

1.5 There are many types of disciplinary situations which require attention by the supervisor or manager. For example:

(a) excessive absenteeism;

(b) excessive lateness in arriving at work;

(c) defective and/or inadequate work performance;

(d) poor attitudes which influence the work of others or which reflect on the public image of the firm;

(e) breaking rules regarding rest periods and other time schedules such as leaving work to go home early;

(f) improper personal appearance;

(g) breaking safety rules;

(h) other violations of rules, regulations and procedures;

(i) at times, open insubordination such as the refusal of an employee to carry out a legitimate work assignment.

1.6 In addition to these types of job situations supervisors might be confronted with disciplinary problems stemming from employee behaviour off the job. These may be an excessive drinking problem or involvement in some form of law-breaking activity. In such circumstances, whenever an employee's off-the-job conduct has an impact upon performance on the job, the supervisor must be prepared to deal with such a problem within the scope of the disciplinary process.

1.7 Managers must learn to deal with disciplinary situations rather than trying to avoid such issues by pretending to ignore them. If they do not take appropriate action when it is required, some employees who are on the borderline may be encouraged to follow the poor examples, and lack of discipline will become more extensive. In addition it is not fair on staff who do toe the line if others are seen to 'get away with anything'. When defects in employee self-discipline become apparent, it is the supervisor's responsibility to take action firmly and appropriately, however unpleasant it might be.

7: DISCIPLINE, GRIEVANCE AND EXIT

Disciplinary action

1.8 Any disciplinary action must be undertaken with sensitivity and sound judgement on the manager's part. The purpose of discipline is not punishment or retribution. Disciplinary action must have as its goal the improvement of the future behaviour of the employee and other members of the organisation. The purpose obviously is the avoidance of similar occurrences in the future.

1.9 Following ACAS guidelines for disciplinary action which emphasise no dismissal on first offence except for gross misconduct, many enterprises have accepted the idea of progressive discipline, which provides for an increase of the severity of the penalty with each offence. The following is a list of suggested steps of progressive disciplinary action and many companies have found these steps to be workable.

(a) *The informal talk*
If the infraction is of a relatively minor nature and if the employee's record has no previous marks of disciplinary action, an informal, friendly talk will clear up the situation in many cases. Here the supervisor discusses with the employee his or her behaviour in relation to standards which prevail within the enterprise.

(b) *Oral warning or reprimand*
In this type of interview between employee and supervisor, the supervisor emphasises the undesirability of the subordinate's repeated violation, and that ultimately it could lead to serious disciplinary action.

(c) *Written or official warning*
These are part of the ACAS Code of Practice. A written warning is of a formal nature insofar as it becomes a permanent part of the employee's record. Written warnings, not surprisingly, are particularly necessary in unionised situations, so that the document can serve as evidence in case of grievance procedures.

(d) *Disciplinary layoffs, or suspension*
This course of action would be next in order if the employee has committed repeated offences and previous steps were of no avail. Disciplinary lay-offs usually extend over several days or weeks. Some employees may not be very impressed with oral or written warnings, but they will find a disciplinary layoff without pay a rude awakening.

(e) *Demotion*
This course of action is likely to bring about dissatisfaction and discouragement, since losing pay and status over an extended period of time is a form of constant punishment. This dissatisfaction of the demoted employee may easily spread to co-workers, so most enterprises avoid downgrading as a disciplinary measure.

(f) *Discharge*
Discharge.is a drastic form of disciplinary action, and should be reserved for the most serious offences. For the organisation, it involves waste of a labour resource, the expense of training a new employee, and disruption caused by changing the make-up of the work team. There also may be damage to the morale of the group.

Relationship management in disciplinary situations

1.10 Each stage of this progressive discipline may involve a *disciplinary interview* - either to deliver warnings, to investigate complaints or to discuss with the employee the implications of written warnings and subsequent actions.

The *disciplinary interview* is discussed in more detail in Chapter 8.

1.11 Even if the manager uses sensitivity and judgement, imposing disciplinary action tends to generate resentment because it is an unpleasant experience. Following these basic rules will help the manager to reduce the resentment inherent in all disciplinary actions.

(a) *Immediacy*
Immediacy means that after noticing the offence, the supervisor proceeds to take disciplinary action as speedily as possible, while at the same time avoiding haste and on-the-spot emotions which might lead to unwarranted actions.

There are instances when an employee is clearly guilty of a violation, although full circumstances may not be known. Other cases will arise where the need for disciplinary action is unquestionable, but there is doubt as to the degree or amount of penalty which should be imposed. The nature of the incident may make it advisable to take some immediate action or to have the offender leave the premises quickly. However, the ACAS Code of Practice requires that *investigation* be made before action is taken. Consideration should be given to the employee's record and all pertinent details of the situation in preparation for the disciplinary interview.

(b) *Advance warning*
In order to maintain proper discipline and to have employees accept disciplinary action as fair, it is essential that all employees know in advance what is expected of them and what the rules and regulations are. Employees must be informed clearly that certain acts will lead to disciplinary action.

Many companies find it useful to have a disciplinary section in an employee handbook, which every new employee receives. However, each new employee should also be informed orally about what is expected. If a rule which was never enforced in the past (eg against wearing brown shoes) is now to be enforced, then the supervisor should not 'make an example' of the first employee he sees wearing brown shoes. Instead, he should tell his staff that brown shoes are forbidden from now on and explain why ('the new manager says so'). Ideally, a written memo should be used.

(c) *Consistency*
Consistency of discipline means that each time an infraction occurs appropriate disciplinary action is taken. Inconsistency in application of discipline lowers the morale of employees and diminishes their respect for the supervisor. Inconsistency also leads to employee insecurity and anxiety, and creates doubts in their minds as to what they can and cannot do.

(Consistency does not mean imposing the same standard penalty every time for a particular offence: there may be mitigating circumstances.)

(d) *Impersonality*

It is only natural for an employee to feel some resentment towards a supervisor who has taken disciplinary action against him. Yet the supervisor can reduce the amount of resentment by making disciplinary action as impersonal as possible. Penalties should be connected with the act and not based upon the personality involved.

Once a disciplinary action has been taken, the manager must let 'bygones be bygones'. He should treat the employee in the same way as before the infraction, and they should both try to forget about what has happened in the past. This is much easier said than done, since only a mature person can handle discipline without feeling hostility or guilt.

(e) *Privacy*

As a general rule (ie unless the manager's authority is challenged directly and in public) disciplinary action should be taken in private, to avoid the humiliation or 'martyrdom' of the employee concerned, and potential spread of the conflict.

Documentation

1.12 ACAS procedures require that in any form of disciplinary action, it is essential for the supervisor to keep records of what happened and the decision or response made to the situation. Documentation of the facts, including the reasoning involved in the decision, is necessary since the supervisor may be asked at some future time to justify the action he has since taken. Good documentation is vital because the burden of proof is usually on the supervisor, and it is not wise to try to depend on memory to defeat disciplinary actions at some time in the future. This is particularly true in unionised firms where grievance-arbitration procedures often result in a challenge of disciplinary actions meted out against employees.

The right to appeal

1.13 ACAS procedures require that the employee should have the opportunity to state his/her case, accompanied by a fellow employee or union representative, and have a right of appeal. The right to appeal against discipline is available through the various steps of the grievance procedure, if an employee belongs to a labour union. However, this right of appeal should also exist in non-unionised organisations, ie it should be possible for any employee to appeal to higher management against disciplinary action. Following the chain of command, the immediate superior's boss would be the one to whom an appeal should first be directed. Many non-union companies have provided for such a procedure which may include an appeal hierarchy through several levels of management.

1.14 This right of appeal must be recognised as being a real right and not merely a formality. There are managers who tell their employees that they can appeal to higher management, but who will actually hold it against the employee if he does. Such an attitude is indicative of the manager's own insecurity. It is management's obligation to provide an appeal procedure, and they should not feel that an appeal weakens their position as managers or leaders of their departments.

1.15 It may happen that as the result of an appeal, the disciplinary penalty imposed by a manager may be reduced or set aside by his boss. Under these circumstances, he may become discouraged, feeling that the boss has not 'backed him up'. However, managers who discipline properly will normally find their verdicts upheld by the boss.

7: DISCIPLINE, GRIEVANCE AND EXIT

ACAS Code of Practice

1.16 Disciplinary and grievance procedures should:

(a) be in written form*;

(b) specify to whom they apply (ie all, or some of the employees?);

(c) be capable of dealing speedily with disciplinary matters;

(d) indicate the forms of disciplinary action which may be taken (eg dismissal, suspension or warning);

(e) specify the appropriate levels of authority for the exercise of disciplinary actions;

(f) provide for individuals to be informed of the nature of their alleged misconduct;

(g) allow individuals to state their case, and to be accompanied by a fellow employee (or union representative);

(h) ensure that every case is properly investigated before any disciplinary action is taken;

(i) ensure that employees are informed of the reasons for any penalty they receive;

(j) state that no employee will be dismissed for a first offence, except in cases of gross misconduct;

(k) provide for a right of appeal against any disciplinary action, and specify the appeals procedure.

* The ACAS Code of Practice does not extend to informal 'first warnings'.

2. GRIEVANCE PROCEDURES

2.1 Grievance procedures are not at all the same as disciplinary procedures, although the two terms are often confused. A grievance occurs when an individual thinks that he is being wrongly treated by his colleagues or supervisor, eg he is being picked on, unfairly appraised in his annual report, unfairly blocked for promotion, discriminated against on grounds of race or sex, etc.

2.2 When an individual has a grievance he or she should be able to pursue the grievance and ask to have the problem resolved. Some grievances should be capable of solution informally by the individual's manager. However, if an informal solution is not possible, there should be a formal grievance procedure.

2.3 Formal grievance procedures, like disciplinary procedures, should be set out in writing and made available to all staff. These procedures should perform the following functions.

(a) State what *grades* of employee are entitled to pursue a particular type of grievance.

(b) State the *rights* of the employee for each type of grievance. For example, an employee who is not invited to attend a promotion/selection panel might claim that he has been unfairly passed over. The grievance procedure must state what the individual would be entitled to claim. In our example, the employee who is overlooked for promotion might be entitled to a review of his annual appraisal report, or to attend a special appeals promotion/selection board if he has been in his current grade for at least a certain number of years.

(c) State what the *procedures* for pursuing a grievance should be. A typical grievance procedure might be as follows.

   (i)   The individual should discuss the grievance with a staff/union representative (or a colleague). If his case seems a good one, he should take the grievance to his immediate boss.

   (ii) The first interview will be between the immediate boss (uncles he is the subject of the complaint, in which case it will be the next level up) and the employee, who has the right to be accompanied by his colleague or representative.

   (iii) If the immediate boss cannot resolve the matter, or the employee is otherwise dissatisfied with the first interview, the case should be referred to the next level of management (and if necessary, in some cases, to an even higher authority).

   (iv) Cases referred to a higher manager should also be reported to the personnel department. Line management might decide at some stage to ask for the assistance/advice of a personnel manager in resolving the problem;

(d) Distinguish between *individual* grievances and *collective* grievances. Collective grievances might occur when a work group as a whole considers that it is being badly treated.

(e) Allow for the involvement of an individual's or group's trade union or staff association *representative*. Indeed, many individuals and groups might prefer to initiate some grievance procedures through their union or association rather than through official grievance procedures. Involvement of a union representative from the beginning should mean that management and union will have a common view of what procedures should be taken to resolve the matter.

(f) State *time limits* for initiating grievance procedures and subsequent stages of them. For example, a person who is passed over for promotion should be required to make his first appeal within a certain time of his review, and his appeal to higher authority (if any) within a certain period after the first grievance interview. There should also be time scales for management to determine and communicate the outcome of the complaint to the employee.

(g) Require *written records* of all meetings concerned with the case to be made and distributed to all the participants.

2.4 All the major banks have a well-defined grievance procedure. The advantages of having formal grievance procedures are that:

(a) they are a means of referring problems for a solution without disrupting the flow of work. For example, if a work group, through its union, refers a grievance to a grievance procedure for solution, they will probably not go on strike until the matter is resolved and will continue to work normally;

(b) they are seen to give fair treatment to employees;

128

(c)   they allow for certain problems to be resolved objectively by a manager not directly involved in the dispute;

(d)   they allow a cooling-off period in which tempers can be forgotten, whilst the grievance is being studied and judged;

(e)   they protect the individual against the personal animosity of his boss;

(f)   they give the individual an opportunity to speak up for himself and to have his voice heard.

2.5   Grievance procedures should be seen as an employee's right. To this end, managers should be given formal training in the grievance procedures of their organisation, and the reasons for having them. Management should be persuaded that the grievance procedures are beneficial for the organisation and are not a threat to themselves (since many grievances arise out of disputes between subordinates and their boss).

2.6   Much will depend, however, not just on the manager's awareness of the formal procedures, but on his *attitudes* to the process, to the particular issue of complaint and to the employee. These attitudes may be shaped by past experience (perhaps even encounters with the same employee) and by the manager's own personality and leadership style. The grievance interview, in particular, will need to be carefully controlled to ensure that personal resentments and judgements do not interfere with the process: it *can* be made into a positive situation where the grievance is approached as a problem-solving, conflict-resolution opportunity in which 'everybody wins'.

> Grievance interviews will be discussed in the Chapter 8 on interviewing.

3.   EXIT FROM EMPLOYMENT

3.1   A 'contract of employment' is not necessarily a written document: all that is required to establish a contract is agreement of the essential terms by both parties. 'Fixed term' contracts may be made for a clearly defined period, but most contracts of employment are 'indefinite', ie they run until terminated by either party, subject to notice.

3.2   Circumstances in which the contract of employment comes to an end include the following.

(a)   *By mutual agreement,* eg. retirement, or possibly 'constructive dismissal', where the employee is forced to resign because of irreconcilable differences with the employer.

(b)   *By notice* eg:

(i)   resignation;
(ii)   dismissal, or
(iii) redundancy.

(c)   *By breach of contract*, entitling the employer to dismiss the employee without notice, eg

(i)   wilful disobedience to a reasonable order, representing total disregard for the terms of his contract;

(ii)   misconduct in employment, eg dishonesty;

      (iii)   misconduct *outside* employment which interferes with it, eg drunkenness;

      (iv)   serious negligence or incompetence;

   (d) *By frustration*, eg the death, illness or imprisonment of the employee or employer.

We will go on to discuss some of these circumstances.

Retirement

3.3   The average age of the working population has been steadily increasing, with higher standards of living and health care, and with emerging shortages in the number of young people entering employment. The problems of older workers and retirement are therefore commanding more attention. The time at which difficulties in obtaining or retaining jobs because of age occur will obviously vary according to the individual, his lifestyle and occupation, and the attitudes of his society and employers.

3.4   In later middle age, many workers try to move away from jobs which make demands on their agility, energy, muscular strength etc. However, they are capable of less strenuous work, and particularly in the office setting may be very valuable in jobs requiring mature judgement, conscientiousness, attention to detail, experience etc. They may make a great contribution to the training and coaching of more junior staff.

3.5   From the organisation's point of view, however, there are various arguments for enforcing retirement.

   (a) There is resistance to late retirement from younger workers, because it is felt that promotion opportunities are being blocked.

   (b) Younger employees with family responsibilities need to have their jobs secured, and in a redundancy situation, it is common for pensioners and those nearing retirement to be discharged first.

   (c) The age structure of an organisation may become unbalanced for future work requirements: there may have to be an injection of 'younger blood' through the compulsory retirement of older workers.

   (d) Engaging staff above middle age can be costly for the organisation: the cost of providing pensions rises according to the age at which the employee joins the superannuation scheme. Many pension funds exclude the entry of men and women above a specified age.

3.6   The personnel and/or line manager will have to consider how far any of the above factors apply in a given situation. It will depend to a large extent on the individual concerned, the type of work involved and the state of the local labour market. Retirement policies, and age limits on particular posts will have to be clearly communicated and decisions regarding particular cases discussed confidentially and tactfully with the individual concerned. Written confirmation of the decision to retire an employee should likewise be tactful, with expressions of regret and appreciation as appropriate. The final stage of employee training and development may take the form of courses to prepare employees for the transition to retirement and non-work.

7: DISCIPLINE, GRIEVANCE AND EXIT

Resignation

3.7 Employees may resign for any number of reasons, personal or occupational. Some or all of these reasons may well be a reflection on the structure, management style, culture or personnel policies of the organisation itself. When an employee announces his intention to leave, verbally and/or by letter, it is important for management to find the real reasons why he is leaving, in an *exit interview*. This may lead to a review of the existing policies on pay, training, promotion, the work environment, the quality and style of supervision etc.

3.8 The principal aspect of any policy formulated to deal with resignations must be the length to which the organisation will go to try and dissuade a person from leaving. In some cases, the organisation may decide to simply let the person go, but when an employee has been trained at considerable cost to the firm, or is particularly well qualified and experienced (no employee is irreplaceable - but some are more replaceable than others...), or has knowledge of information or methods that should not fall into the hands of competitors, the organisation may try to keep him.

3.9 Particular problems the employee has been experiencing may be solvable, though not always in the short term. It may be that the organisation will try to match or improve on a salary offer made to the individual by a new prospective employer. In that case, however, there may well be a problem of pay differentials and the individual's colleagues, doing the same work, may have to be given similar increases: can so large a cost be justified?

3.10 Various arrangements will have to be made when an employee decides to leave. There will have to be co-operation and full exchange of information between the personnel function and line managers so that procedures can be commenced upon notification of an intending departure.

(a) If attempts (if any) to make the employee stay have been unsuccessful, the exit interview will have to be arranged.

(b) The period of notice required for the employee to leave should be set out in his contract of employment, but some leeway may be negotiated on this. The time needed for recruitment and induction of a replacement may dictate that the leaving employee work out his full period of notice, and perhaps even longer if he is willing. On the other hand, if it is felt that he can be easily replaced, and that his continuing presence maybe destructive of morale (or possibly of advantage to competitors, as he continues to glean information), it may be possible to persuade him to accept pay in lieu of notice and leave immediately.

(c) Details of the departure will have to be notified to the wages clerk, pension fund officer, social secretary, security officer etc. so that the appropriate paperwork and other procedures can be completed by his date of leaving.

(d) The departmental head and/or supervisor should complete a leaving report form: an overall assessment of the employee's performance in the organisation. This can then be used to provide references to his future employer(s). NB - there is no obligation to give a reference to a former employee, but if one is given, care should be taken in the wording. If it can be proved that the employer acted maliciously, there may be a case for defamation of character.

7: DISCIPLINE, GRIEVANCE AND EXIT

Dismissal

3.11 If an employer terminates the contract of employment by giving notice, the minimum period of notice to be given is determined by the employee's length of continuous service with the employer.

Employee's length of service	*Minimum notice to be given by the employer*
1 month - 2 years	1 week
2 - 12 years	1 week for each year of service
12 years and over	12 weeks

This is the statutory minimum: longer periods may be written into the contract, at the employer's discretion, and by agreement. Either party may waive his right to notice, or accept payment in lieu of notice. If an employee asks, he is entitled to a written statement of the *reasons* for his dismissal within 14 days.

Unfair dismissal

3.12 An employee may bring a claim before the Industrial Tribunal if he considers that he has been 'unfairly' dismissed, under the Employment Protection (Consolidation) Act 1978. The employee first has to prove that he has been dismissed. The onus is then on the employer to prove that the dismissal was *fair*. Under the 1978 Act, dismissal is fair and justified if the reason for it was:

(a) redundancy (provided that the selection for redundancy was fair);

(b) legal impediment - ie the employee could not continue to work in his present position without breaking a legal duty or restriction (provided the employee was offered any suitable alternative employment);

(c) non-capability (provided adequate training and warnings had been given);

(d) misconduct (provided warnings suitable to the offence have been given - so the disciplinary procedures of the organisation are vitally important); or

(e) some other 'substantial' reason, eg that the employee is married to a competitor, or refused to accept a reorganisation made in the interests of the business and with the agreement of other employees.

3.13 Situations in which *unfair* dismissal can be claimed include:

(a) unfair selection for redundancy;

(b) dismissal because of membership (actual or proposed) and involvement in the activities of an independent trade union;

(c) dismissal because of pregnancy, *unless* by reason of it the employee becomes incapable of doing her work properly.

3.14 The Conciliation Officer or Industrial Tribunal to whom a complaint of unfair dismissal is made may order various remedies including:

(a) re-instatement - giving the employee his old job back;
(b) re-engagement - giving him a job comparable to his old one;
(c) compensation.

3.15 In deciding whether to order re-instatement or re-engagement the tribunal must take into account whether the complainant wishes to be reinstated, whether it is practicable for the employer to comply with such an order and whether if the complainant contributed to any extent to his dismissal it would be just to make such an order.

Redundancy

3.16 Redundancy is defined by the Act as dismissal where:

(a) the employer has ceased to carry on the business;
(b) the employer has ceased to carry on the business in the place where the employee was employed;
(c) the requirements of the business for employees to carry out work of a particular kind have ceased or diminished or are expected to. (This is the situation faced in many banks, with the automation of processes.)

3.17 Redundant employees are entitled to compensation:

(a) for loss of security; and
(b) to encourage employees to accept redundancy without damage to industrial relations. (Voluntary redundancy maybe offered to workers, with a financial incentive, thus avoiding the need for selection.)

3.18 The employee is *not* entitled to compensation if:

(a) the employer has made a 'suitable' offer of alternative employment and the employee has unreasonably rejected it. The 'suitability' of the offer will have to be examined in each case;

(b) the employee is of pensionable age or over, or has less than two years' continuous employment;

(c) the employee's conduct entitles the employer to dismiss him without notice.

3.19 Protective awards, ie an order of a tribunal that an employer shall continue to pay remuneration of employees, may be made against an employer who in a redundancy situation fails to consult trade unions 'at the earliest opportunity' or to give notice of impending redundancies.

3.20 In giving notice to the trade union the employer must give certain details in writing, including the reasons for the dismissals, the numbers employed and the number to be dismissed, the method of selecting employees for dismissal and the period over which the dismissals will take place. Information should be accurate, clear, realistic and positive as far as possible (ideas for retraining and redeployment, benefits and potential for voluntary redundancies or retirements should be far enough advanced that *some* 'good news' can be mixed with the bad). The employer should allow the trade union time in which to consider what he has disclosed and to make representations or counter proposals.

3.21 Measures which might be considered and discussed with employee representatives to avoid or reduce the numbers of forced redundancies that have to be made include:

(a) retirement of staff over the normal retirement age;

(b) offering early retirement to staff approaching normal retirement age;

(c) restrictions or even a complete ban on recruitment, so as to reduce the workforce over time by natural wastage;

(d) dismissal of part-time or short-term contract staff, once contracts come to sensible break-off points or conclusions;

(e) offering retraining and/or redeployment within the organisation;

(f) seeking voluntary redundancies.

3.22 Some banks claim that they have been able to achieve staff reductions by natural wastage alone, but there have been redundancies in recent years throughout the financial sector.

Exercise

How far does your employer's disciplinary procedures follow the ACAS code of practice in paragraph 1.16? Give one mark for each point it conforms with.

---

4. CHAPTER ROUNDUP

4.1 *Discipline* has the same end as motivation - ie to secure a range of desired behaviour from members of the organisation. Motivation may even be called a kind of 'self discipline' - because motivated individuals exercise choice to behave in the way that the organisation wishes. Discipline however, is more often related to 'negative' motivation, an appeal to the individual's need to avoid punishment, sanctions or unpleasantness.

4.2 *Grievance* procedures embody the employee's right to appeal against unfair or otherwise prejudicial conduct or conditions that affect him and his work.

4.3 *Exit* from employment takes several forms, voluntary and involuntary, but is likely to be traumatic in some degree to the leaving individual whatever the circumstances, because of the centrality of work and job security in most people's lives. The organisation should consider the sensitivity of the situation - not least because it may itself be traumatised by the exit of key individuals, the implications of and reasons for their leaving, the legal obligations with regard to employment protection etc.

TEST YOUR KNOWLEDGE

The numbers in brackets refer to paragraphs of this chapter

1   What is progressive discipline? (1.9)

2   What factors should a manager bear in mind in trying to control a disciplinary situation? (1.11)

3   Outline typical grievance procedures, or the grievance procedures of your own bank. (2.3)

4   What procedures will be called for when an employee resigns from a bank? (3.7 - 3.10)

5   For what reasons may a bank 'fairly' dismiss an employee? (3.12)

6   What is 'redundancy'? (3.16)

Now try question 7 at the end of the text

Chapter 8

INTERPERSONAL BEHAVIOUR: INTERVIEWING

This chapter covers the following topics.

1. Interpersonal behaviour
2. Interviewing
3. Selection and appraisal interviews
4. Disciplinary and grievance interviews
5. Customer interviews

Introduction

The syllabus for *Management* specifies as a topic area 'People as Individuals': we have not made that a separate unit of this study text, but have addressed the issues of individuality, personality conflicts, attitudes and motivations in the contexts in which the manager would have to consider and handle them: selection, discipline and grievance, motivation, control, communication etc. In this chapter, however, we'll draw together some of the points we've made about interpersonal processes, before applying them to the process of interviewing.

---

1. INTERPERSONAL BEHAVIOUR

1.1 The process of interpersonal behaviour may essentially be described as *communication*, ie the sending and receiving of messages in a continuous cycle. This is a deceptively simple description because, as we have already seen, there are many factors operating to interfere in the process: they frequently result in the 'wrong' message being sent, or the message being misinterpreted by the recipient, or even the failure by one or both parties to participate positively in the communication process.

1.2 Apart from difficulties inherent in the technical complexity of the communication process (language and image interpretation, transmission etc), there are problems arising from:

   (a) the differences between individuals and individual attitudes; and
   (b) the process of *perception*.

Individual differences

1.3 'Personality' is a term used to explain, describe and identify the differences between people. It has been defined as 'the total pattern of characteristic ways of thinking, feeling and behaving that constitutes the individual's distinctive method of relating to the environment [and other people.]'

1.4 There are different scientific approaches to the study of personality: one based on the idea that it is inherited and unalterable by experience (so people can be classed as a certain 'type' of person on the basis of certain 'personality traits') and one on the idea that it is determined by social and cultural processes and is therefore adaptive and changes with experience. An understanding of both approaches may be useful to the organisation.

   (a) Organisations will have to make certain generalised assumptions about the personalities of the individuals they employ and manage, about the 'type' of individuals they would wish to employ and to whom they would wish to allocate various tasks and responsibilities; but

   (b) It is important to recognise that an individual's behaviour is developed and adjusted through on-going evaluation of:

      (i) the effect of that behaviour on other people; and
      (ii) others' expectation of, attitudes and behaviour towards, him.

   (c) Relationship management at work *influences* worker personality, by 'socialising' the individual, whose behaviour is adapted to fit the environment. The manager must also be aware that individual personality has been and is being shaped by other factors: family, nationality, culture, religion, background etc.

1.5 The ability to assess the personality of others - with very little information - is an essential part of social behaviour, enabling individuals to interact with each other effectively in any number of contexts. A reasonably swift and accurate appraisal of personality consciously or unconsciously precedes any attempt at communication. We use our informal assessments of personality to explain and predict the behaviour of other individuals and to regulate the way in which we ourselves behave towards or around them.

1.6 We mainly do this by a process of simplification and generalisation, called *stereotyping*. Our perception of other people (as we will discuss below) is highly selective; on the basis of those characteristics that are most 'transparent', we form a generalised picture of their personalities which is simple enough to be of immediate use in social interaction. Stereotypes are at best over-simplified and at worst wildly inaccurate.

1.7 The reason why we are able to succeed in relating to other people despite our demonstrable lack of ability to assess personality accurately is that interaction generally works within a limited range of possible or permissible behaviours. In other words, individuals do behave in a 'simplified' way, according to the *role* they are in - ie the expectations, shared with the others concerned, of how a person in that social position or relationship should behave.

1.8 Individuals give hints as to the role they are playing at any given time by giving 'role signs' in their dress, manner, tone etc.

   In a recent advertising campaign, a major high street bank exploited stereotypical perceptions of roles and role signs. A young, fresh-faced, 'trendily' dressed man is seen entering a bank. The scene switches to the manager's office, where a forbidding, sombrely suited older man is seen shaking hands with the youngster. Which is the Bank Manager? *Not* as you'd expect....

1.9 When we interact, we are only faced with selected facets of the other individual's personality: we do not have to be accurate judges of the 'whole' person.

Perception

1.10 'Human beings do not behave in, and in response to, the world "as it really is"... Human beings behave in, and in response to, the world as they *perceive* it.'

Buchanan & Huczynski

The way an individual *perceives* people, events and the world around him will be highly subjective and selective, and will partly be influenced by his *expectations*. These in turn arise out of *past experience, personality* and the *social norms* to which the individual is accustomed. You may have noticed how the process of motivation in particular is based on the way in which the individuals concerned *perceive* themselves, other people and the world around them. The motivation calculus depends heavily on the perceived likelihood of achieving certain goals, and the perceived (highly subjective) desirability of those goals.

1.11 'Perception' is the psychological process by which stimuli or in-coming data are selected and organised into patterns which are meaningful to the individual. The 'selection' part of the process is what is happening when people seem to 'see only what they want to see', or stereotype others. The 'organisation' part of the process is where various forms of 'bias' and 'distortion' may affect a person's judgement: he interprets information wrongly.

1.12 *Attitudes* are linked to perception as the individual's 'standpoint' on things, part of the developing 'package' of assumptions and beliefs that each individual brings to his behaviour, decision-making and interactions with other individuals. Factors that might influence attitudes to work, or affecting work are outlined below.

(a) *Class and class-consciousness:* attitudes about the superiority or inferiority of others, owing to birth, political attitudes and so forth.

(b) *Age.* Attitudes about all sorts of issues may be formed by experience, and therefore by the era in which the they were formed: attitudes to sexual equality, morality, education etc. have varied widely from one generation to the next.

(c) *Race, culture or religion.* Attitudes *about* these areas will affect the way in which people regard each other - with tolerance, suspicion or hostility. Culture and religion are also strong influences on attitudes to work: the 'Protestant work ethic', Japanese concepts of the organisation family.

(d) *Lifestyle and interests.* Attitudes about these areas - where someone lives, what car he drives, what he does in his spare time - affect interpersonal relations, and the self concept of each individual. Is he 'fulfilled' and successful? Do other people *think* he is? Orientation to work itself is also affected by attitudes to money, leisure etc.

(e) *Sex.* Attitudes to the equality of the sexes, and their various 'roles' at work and in society, may be influential in:

(i) interpersonal relations (especially where women are in authority over men);

(ii) the self concept of the individual: women at work may be made to feel inferior, men may feel 'threatened' etc.

(iii) attitudes to work. Stereotyped roles ('a woman's place is in the home', 'the man has to support the family') may be held by both sexes and may create feelings of guilt or resentment.

1.13 Here to summarise, are some important things to remember about work relationships.

(a) *Goals*   What does the other person want from the process? What do you want from the process? What will both parties need and be trying to do to achieve their aims? Can both parties emerge satisfied (eg positive approach to appraisal interviews)?

(b) *Perceptions*   What, if any, are likely to be the factors causing 'selectivity' or 'distortion' of the way both parties see the issues and each other? (Attitudes, personal feelings, expectations?)

(c) *Roles*   What 'roles' are the parties playing? (Manager/subordinate, customer/server, complainer/soother?) What expectations does this create of the way they will behave?

(d) *Resistances*   What may the other person be 'afraid' of? What may he be trying to protect? (His ego/self-image, his attitudes?) Sensitivity will be needed in this area.

(e) *Attitudes*   What sources of difference, conflict or lack of understanding might there be, arising from attitudes and other factors which shape them (sex, race, specialism, hierarchy)?

(f) *Relationships* What are the relative positions of the parties and the nature of the relationship between them? (Superior/subordinate? Formal/ informal? Work/non-work)? What 'style' is appropriate to that relationship?p

(g) *Environment*   What factors in the immediate and situational environment might affect the issues and the people? (eg competitive environment → customer care; pressures of disciplinary situation → nervousness; physical surroundings → formality/ informality)

1.14 We'll now apply some of these factors by looking at interviews.

2. INTERVIEWING

2.1 You know, from your own experience, what an interview is, but if you had to define it, you might call it a *'planned interaction'* at work, characterised by *objectives'*. This indicates why an interview is not the same as a discussion or conversation.

(a) An interview is conducted in order to achieve a specific *purpose* for at least one - and ideally all - of the parties involved: information gathering, problem-solving, behaviour change, closure of sale etc. Classification (or anticipation) of the objectives will allow the content and conduct of the interview to be planned.

(b) An interview must be *planned* if it is to be effective. An agenda can be drawn up on the basis of objectives, and should be structured with an introductory phase, main body and concluding phase. Knowing what the opening will be (to start the interview off fluently), and knowing what you want from the close (to achieve objectives) are as important as drafting questions and topics for the main part of the interview.

(c) An interview is an *interaction,* not a monologue. Here are some of the characteristics of this in a business/work interview.

  (i)   Investigation/interrogation. The interviewer must ask questions that elicit *answers:* he must also *listen* to the answers.

  (ii) Roles. Interviews usually involve interaction between people not 'as themselves' but *in their roles* as appraiser/appraisee, selector/candidate, representative/ customer, superior/subordinate. Appropriate 'role signs' should be given. In addition, there is a role difference between interviewer and interviewee: the interviewer should take control of proceedings - although he may otherwise adopt a role as judge, counsellor, helper etc according to the nature of the interview, his personality, or organisation culture.

  (iii) *Formality.* The extent of formality of the interview will depend on the circumstances and personalities involved, but the interaction of 'roles' implies formality in the work/business context. The fine line between formality and tension/rigidity will need to be managed.

Conducting an interview

2.2   There are five basic stages to the interview process.

  (a) Preparation
  (b) Opening
  (c) Conducting
  (d) Closing
  (e) Follow-up

Preparation for an interview

2.3   First of all, the objectives of the interview must be determined. The interviewer should also be aware of any unstated objectives the interviewee may be bringing with him as a 'hidden agenda': scoring points off a supervisor, perhaps. The basic framework of the interview can then be planned, with ideas for any points that must be made or information that must be obtained or given: there should be enough flexibility, however, so that the interviewer can listen and respond to the interviewee's input and questions where relevant.

2.4   There may be some preparation to do for the content of the interview: information to be gathered on the interviewee or the topic under discussion. For a customer interview, for example, you will need to know what services the customer uses and requires, and you will need to know about the bank's products and services. Interviews for appraisal, grievance and discipline require considerable prior information and thought if they are to be handled constructively.

2.5 Physical preparations include obtaining suitable time and accommodation for the interview, usually somewhere private and free from distraction. The impression made by the setting on the interviewee may also be important: rooms, layout of chairs etc can be imposing and intimidating or informal and reassuring. So can the physical appearance of the interviewer.

Opening an interview

2.6 The *purpose* of the interview should be clearly laid out as a preliminary to engaging in any discussion. This puts everybody straight as to why they are there and what is expected of them. The 'tone' and *atmosphere* of the interview will also be established by the first impressions the parties have of each other, and the interviewer's opening remarks. The layout of the room, the number of interviewers and the formality of the proceedings should be carefully planned to manage the tension of the situation: it is usually desirable to put the interviewee at his ease, but the interviewer's strategy may be to maintain or even *increase* the experienced tension eg to test a candidate under pressure, to underline the seriousness of a disciplinary interview, or to assert control in other situations. A 'hot seat', across a desk (psychological barrier) from a large panel of hostile-looking interviewers will obviously set a certain tone for the interview.

2.7 In less extreme conditions, even the desk alone can be quite 'distancing', in reinforcing the superior role of the interviewer and separating him from the interviewee. If this is felt to be undesirable, eg in a customer interview, the physical setting may be changed (many branches now have interview rooms with less formal furniture and closer proximity) or the interviewer will have to take particular care to set a positive, supportive and welcoming tone in opening the interview.

Conducting an interview

2.8 Ask the right questions. Listen to the answers.

(a) Questions should be 'paced' and put carefully. The interviewer should not be trying to confuse the interviewee, plunging immediately into demanding questions or 'picking on' isolated points; nor should he allow the interviewee to digress or gloss over important points. The interviewer must retain control over the information-gathering process.

(b) 'Open' questions should be used, ie 'Who...? What...? Where...? When...? Why...?', so that interviewees have to put together their own responses in complete sentences. This is a lot more revealing than using 'closed' questions which invite 'yes' or 'no' answers. A closed question:

(i) elicits answers only to the question asked by the interviewer: there may be other questions and issues which have not been anticipated but will emerge if the interviewee is given the chance;

(ii) does not allow the interviewee to express his personality so that interaction can take place on a deeper level;

(iii) makes it easier for interviewees to conceal things ('you never *asked* me....');

(iv) makes the interviewer work very hard.

(c) The interviewer should not ask leading questions, giving the interviewee ideas about what the interviewer wants to hear: the response may be adjusted to please or impress. Leading questions include: 'Don't you think/agree that...?' and 'Surely...?'.

(d) The interviewer *must* listen to and evaluate the responses, to judge what the interviewee:

    (i)   wants to say;
    (ii)   is trying *not* to say;
    (iii) is saying - but doesn't mean, or is lying about;
    (iv) is having difficulty saying.

(e) In addition, the interview will have to be aware when he or she:

    (i)   is hearing something that will give useful information;

    (ii)   is hearing something he will not give useful information;

    (iii) is hearing only what he or she expects to hear;

    (iv) is not hearing clearly - ie when his own attitudes, perhaps prejudices, are getting in the way of a response to the interviewee and what are the interviewew is saying.

(f) Non-verbal signals or *body language* should also be taken as relevant feedback. Posture, position (intimate proximity or frosty distance), facial expression, gestures and 'sounds' (sighs, 'um's, murmurs) are signals of what the interviewee wants to say and of how he is feeling. The interviewer should look for signs of stress (nervous movements, pallor), dishonesty (failure to meet the eye), imitation (frown, tapping foot), positive response (smile, nod, leaning forward) etc as a kind of 'map' of the interaction situation. The interviewer himself can *use* non-verbal signs to:

    (i)   create a desired impression (smart appearance, smile, firm handshake); and
    (ii)   provide feedback (raised eyebrow, encouraging nod).

Closing an interview

2.9 A *summary* of proceedings or findings is usually a good way of confirming information, signalling the extent to which objectives have been achieved, and 'winding down' the interview towards closure. If a decision is required, it should be given: but only if the interviewee has the authority and has acquired the information to do so. The general 'position' of the parties should be clarified - ie if a compromise or agreement has been reached, or if one or both parties is not yet satisfied. Further action required should be agreed or communicated to the interviewee ('I'll get back to you...'; 'I'll have a decision for you in a few days...'; 'I'll put that in motion this afternoon...'; 'I need to know more about...'). A courteous closure (handshake, goodbye) should end the proceedings.

Following-up an interview

2.10 Once the interviewee has left, the interviewer should:

(a) assimilate the information gained;

(b) determine any action required or agreed as a result of the interview;

(c) make notes, or build notes up into a more complete record for the bank's files;

(d) initiate any actions agreed at or required by the interview, and monitor their effectiveness as necessary.

2.11 Let's see how these things work out in practice, in:

(a) selection
(b) appraisal
(c) disciplinary
(d) grievance, and
(e) customer interviews.

Remember that the general rules for conduct, and the dynamics of interviewing, are as discussed above.

3. SELECTION AND APPRAISAL INTERVIEWS

Selection interviews

3.1 Selection interviews are a crucial part of the selection process because they:

(a) give the organisation a chance to assess the applicant directly; and

(b) give the applicant a chance to learn more about the organisation, and whether or not he wants the job.

3.2 The aim of the interview must be clear. It should have a three-fold purpose:

(a) finding the best person for the job;

(b) making sure that the applicant understands what the job is and what career prospects are and so has the opportunity to make an informed decision;

(c) making the applicant feel that he has been given fair treatment in the interview, whether he gets the job or not.

3.3 The interview must be prepared carefully, to make sure that the right questions are asked, and relevant information obtained to give the interviewers what they need to make their selection.

(a) The job description should be studied to review the major demands of the job.

(b) The personnel specification should be studied and questions should be planned which might help the interviewer make relevant assessments of the applicant's character and qualifications.

(c) The application form of each applicant should be studied in order to decide on questions or question areas for each applicant.

3.4 The interview should be conducted in such a way that the information required is successfully obtained during the interview.

(a) The interview process should be efficiently run to make a favourable impression on the candidate: he should be clearly informed when and where to come, whom to ask for, what to bring with him etc and should be expected by the receptionist or other receiving staff. A waiting room should be available, with cloakroom facilities etc. Arrangements should have been made to welcome, escort and otherwise 'handle' candidates: they should not be placed under the extra stress of being left stranded, getting lost, or being ignored.

(b) The best way of finding out about a candidate is to encourage him to talk. It is necessary to ask relevant questions, but the time of the interview should be taken up mostly with the candidate talking, and not with the interviewers asking questions. Questions should therefore discourage short answers. The more a candidate talks, the easier it should be to assess his suitability for the job. A biographical approach is probably the easiest method, taking the candidate through his work history (concentrating most usefully on *recent* - rather than ancient - history).

(c) The candidate should be given the opportunity to ask questions. Indeed, a well-prepared candidate should go into an interview knowing what questions he may want to ask. His choice of questions might well have some influence on how the interviewers finally assess him. Moreover, there is information that the candidate will need to know about the organisation and the job, and about:

(i) terms and conditions of employment (although negotiations about detailed terms may not take place until a provisional offer has been made); and

(ii) the next step in the selection process - ie. whether there are further interviews, when a decision might be made, which references might be taken up etc.

The limitations of selection interviews

3.5 Interviews have often been criticised because they fail to select suitable people for the job vacancies. The main criticisms of selection interviews are as follows.

(a) Unreliable assessments. The opinion of one interviewer may differ from the opinion of another. They cannot both be right, but because of their different opinions, a suitable candidate might be rejected or an unsuitable candidate offered a job.

(b) They fail to provide accurate predictions of how a person will perform in the job.

(c) The interviewers are likely to make errors of judgement even when they agree about a candidate.

(i) The *halo effect* - a tendency for people (interviewers) to make an initial general judgement about a person based on a single obvious attribute, such as being neatly dressed, or well-spoken, or having a public school and Oxbridge education. This single attribute will colour later perceptions, and might make an interviewer mark the person up or down on every other factor in their assessment, according to the first impression received.

(ii) *Contagious bias* - a process whereby an interviewer changes the behaviour of the applicant by suggestion. The applicant might be led by the wording of questions or non-verbal clues from the interviewer and change what he is doing or saying in response.

(iii) A possible inclination by interviewers to *stereotype* candidates on the basis of insufficient evidence, eg on the basis of dress, hair style, accent of voice etc. Stereotyping is a form of perceptual organisation which groups together people who are assumed to share certain characteristics, then attributes certain traits to the group as a whole, and then (illogically) assumes that each individual member of the supposed group will possess that trait: ie all women are weak, all Scots are mean.

(iv) *Incorrect assessment* of qualitative factors such as motivation, honesty or integrity. Abstract qualities are very difficult to assess in an interview.

(v) *Logical error* - in other words, an interviewer might draw conclusions about a candidate from what he says or does when there is no logical justification for those conclusions. For example, an interviewer might decide that a young candidate who has held two or three jobs in the past for only a short time will be unlikely to last long in any job. Would this be a logical assumption, or not?

3.6 It might be apparent from the list of limitations above that a major problem with interviews generally is the skill and experience of the interviewers themselves. Any interviewer is prone to bias, but a person can learn to reduce this problem through training and experience. The problems with inexperienced interviewers are not only bias, but:

(a) inability to evaluate properly information about a candidate;

(b) inability to compare a candidate against the requirements for a job or a personnel specification;

(c) bad planning of the interview;

(d) inability to take control of the direction and length of the interview;

(e) a tendency to talk too much in interviews, and to ask questions which call for a short answer;

(f) a tendency to jump to conclusions on insufficient evidence, or to place too much emphasis on isolated strengths or weaknesses;

(g) a tendency to act as an inquisitor and make candidates feel uneasy;

(h) a reluctance to probe into facts and challenge statements where necessary.

Appraisal interviews

3.7 The interview is also a crucial part of the appraisal process. Its aims are:

(a) to review past performance as a basis for problem-solving and improvement planning;

(b) to set (or agree) goals for performance or improvement in the forthcoming period.

3.8 *Preparation* will be particularly important, since the interviewer (and ideally also the interviewee) should be aware of areas for praise and criticism, potential for improvement, problems to be solved etc. *Opening* phases will have to be carefully managed, because appraisal can (particularly in certain organisation cultures) be perceived as a threatening and judgemental exercise. Its purpose should be clearly explained, and the approach and roles of the participants established - since these can vary widely, as discussed below.

3.9 The conduct and culture of the appraisal interview will vary from organisation to organisation and individual to individual. Maier *(The appraisal interview)* identifies three types of approach to appraisal interviews.

(a) The *tell and sell* method. The managers tells the subordinate how he has been assessed, and then tries to 'sell' (ie gain acceptance of) the evaluation and the improvement plan. This requires unusual human relations skills in order to convey constructive criticism in an acceptable manner, and to motivate the appraisee to alter his behaviour.

(b) The *tell and listen* method. The manager tells the subordinate how he has been assessed, and then invites him to respond. The manager therefore no longer dominates the interview throughout, and there is greater opportunity for counselling as opposed to pure direction. The employee is encouraged to participate in the assessment and the working out of improvement targets and methods: it is an accepted tenet of behavioural theory that participation in problem definition and goal setting increases the individual's commitment to behaviour and attitude modification. Moreover, this method does not assume that a change in the employee will be the sole key to improvement: the manager may receive helpful feedback about how job design, methods, environment or supervision might be improved. Again, however, the interviewer needs to be a talented and trained listener and counsellor.

(c) The *problem-solving* approach. The manager abandons the role of critic altogether, and becomes a counsellor and helper. The discussion is centred not on the assessment, but on the employee's work problems. The employee is encouraged to think solutions through, and to commit himself to the recognised need for personal improvement. This approach encourages intrinsic motivation through the element of self-direction, and the perception of the job itself as a problem-solving activity. It may also stimulate creative thinking on the part of employee and manager alike, to the benefit of the organisation's adaptability and methods. Again, the interviewer will require highly-developed skills, and the *attitudes* of both parties to the process will need to be got right.

3.10 The Behavioural Sciences Research Division of the Civil Service Department carried out a survey of appraisal interviews given to 252 officers in a government department, in 1973. Findings included that:

(a) Interviewers have difficulty with criticising performance and tend to avoid it if possible.

(b) Criticism, however, is significant in the effective conduct and follow-up of interviews. It is more likely to bring forth positive post-appraisal action, and is favourably received by appraisees, who feel it is the most useful function of the whole process, if handled frankly and constructively,

(c) The most common fault of interviewers is talking too much. The survey recorded the preference of appraisees for a 'problem-solving' style of participative interview, over a one-sided 'tell and sell' style.

3.11 *Follow-up* is an integral part of the appraisal system. A jointly-agreed evaluation and future improvement plan should emerge from the interview, and will have to be implemented and monitored.

4. DISCIPLINARY AND GRIEVANCE INTERVIEWS

Disciplinary interviews

4.1 *Preparation* for the disciplinary interview will include:

(a) gathering of the facts about the alleged infringement;

(b) determination of the bank's position: how valuable is the employee, potentially? How serious are his offences/lack of progress? How far is the bank prepared to go to help him improve or discipline him further?

(c) identification of the aims of the interview: punishment? deterrent to others? improvement? Specific standards of future behaviour/performance required need to be determined.

4.2 In addition, preparation will involve the bank's disciplinary procedures, which should ensure that:

(a) informal oral warnings (at least) have been given;

(b) the employee has been given adequate notice of the interview for his *own* preparation;

(c) the employee has been informed of the complaint against him, his right to be accompanied by a colleague or representative etc.

4.3 The content of the interview will be as follows.

(a) The manager will explain the purpose of the interview.

(b) The 'charges' against the employee will be delivered, clearly, unambiguously and without personal emotion.

(c) The manager will explain the bank's position with regard to the issue involved: disappointment, concern, need for improvement, impact on others. This can be done frankly - but tactfully, with as positive an emphasis as possible on the employee's capacity and responsibility to improve.

(d) The bank's expectations with regard to future behaviour/performance should be made clear.

(e) The employee should be given the opportunity to comment, explain, justify or deny. If he is to approach the following stage of the interview in a positive way, he must not be made to feel 'hounded' or hard done by.

(f) The bank's expectations should be reiterated, or new standards of behaviour set for the employee. To be helpful when:

(i) they are specific and quantifiable, performance related and realistic. Increased output, improved timekeeping etc will be readily measurable;

(ii)   they are related to a practical but reasonably short time period. A date should be set to review his progress;

(iii) the manager agrees on measures to help the employee should that be necessary. It would demonstrate a positive approach if, for example, a mentor were appointed from his work group to help him check his work. If his poor performance is genuinely the result of some difficulty or distress outside work, other help (eg temporary leave, counselling or financial aid) may be appropriate.

(g) The manager should explain the reasons behind any *penalties* imposed on the employee, including the entry in his personnel record of the formal warning. He should also explain how the warning can be *removed* from the record, and what standards must be achieved within a specified timescale. There should be a clear warning of the consequences of *failure* to meet improvement targets.

(h) The manager should explain the bank's appeals procedures: if the employee feels he has been unfairly treated, there should be a right of appeal to a higher manager.

(i) Once it has been established that the employee understands all the above, the manager should summarise the proceedings briefly.

Records of the interview will be kept for the employee's personnel file, and for the formal follow-up review and any further action necessary.

4.4 Particular attention throughout should be given to interpersonal factors. The employee is likely to be defensive and resentful. The formality of proceedings may help to take the 'sting' out of it, but the manager's approach will need to be deliberately future-focused, positive and encouraging/supportive if possible.

Grievance interviews

4.5 The dynamics of a grievance interview are broadly similar to a disciplinary interview, except that it is the *subordinate* who primarily wants a positive result from it. Prior to the interview, the manager should have some idea of the complaint and its possible source. The meeting itself can then proceed.

(a) *Exploration*. What is the problem: the background, the facts, the causes (manifest and hidden)? At this stage, the manager should simply try to gather as much information as possible, without attempting to suggest solutions or interpretations: the situation must be seen to be 'open'.

(b) *Consideration*. The manager should:

(i)   check the facts;

(ii) analyse the causes - ie the problem of which the complaint may be only a symptom;

(iii) evaluate options for responding to the complaint, and the implication of any response made.

It may be that information can be given to clear up a misunderstanding, or the employee will - having 'got it off his chest' - withdraw his complaint. However, the meeting may have to be *adjourned* (eg for 48 hours) while the manager gets extra information and considers extra options.

(c) *Reply*. The manager, having reached and reviewed his conclusions, reconvenes the meeting to convey (and justify, if required) his decision, hear counter-arguments and appeals. The outcome (agreed or disagreed) should be recorded in writing.

4.6 The style of the interview will again depend very much on personality, situation and organisation culture: ideally it should be positive and constructive, with an emphasis on joint action to solve problems and avoid conflict. Otherwise, the scope for conflict and resentment is very wide.

Employee counselling

4.7 The major difference between 'advice' and 'counselling' is that counselling is directed at helping the subject to talk about himself and his problems and guiding him towards finding his own solution to them - rather than offering or urging solutions devised by the 'adviser'. The term 'non-directive' is often applied to modern counselling techniques.

4.8 The counselling approach involves:

(a) discerning need;

(b) ensuring privacy and time;

(c) encouraging openness (assurance of confidentiality);

(d) emphasis on interaction (personal rapport and trust);

(e) guidance in evolving the subject's own solutions - not advice (unless specifically requested, and even then, subject to exploration);

(f) supporting the solution devised (offering resources, help etc in implementation);

(g) monitoring the progress of the solution, and personal development/emotional improvement.

4.9 The 'culture' or ethos of counselling is now, as we have discussed, often applied to interviewing situations previously regarded as purely informative or judgemental - notably appraisal, but also discipline and grievance. An 'open door' management policy may require counselling of employees on a wide range of work and personal problems.

5. CUSTOMER INTERVIEWS

5.1 Customer interviews involve interaction with someone *outside the bank*, which alters the dynamics of the process somewhat.

(a) The roles of the parties will be defined more by the customer's expectations and the bank employee's sense of the bank/customer relationship than by the formally defined relationships of authority and purpose that characteristic intra-bank interview situations.

(b) The interview cannot assume that the customer is familiar with bank policy, practice, products or terminology and will have to adjust his style and vocabulary accordingly.

(c) The business relationship is generally characterised by a degree of formality. This may need to be reconciled with putting customers at their ease (since complaining, or requesting a loan, or visiting the bank in any circumstances can be stressful for some people) and with persuasive selling style.

(d) The marketing considerations of the bank/customer relationship will dictate a more pro-active approach, and a more positive, responsive (or conciliatory) style than would be required for interviews with subordinates in the organisation. The interviewer is projecting an image of the bank to an existing and/or potential customer/client: the human face of a bank may be a crucial factor in retaining customer loyalty in the highly competitive environment. Essentially, the interviewer needs to start with a 'the customer is always right' attitude - if only as an antidote to personal frustration and hostility when the customer is obviously wrong. *Courtesy* - as in intra-bank interviews - is the absolute minimum requirement.

5.2 Customer interviews may have a variety of purposes and may not be susceptible to planning in all circumstances. They therefore require more than usual *sensitivity* and *flexibility*.

5.3 You should be able to respond effectively to customer *queries*.

(a) Familiarise yourself thoroughly with: the range of services offered by the bank and branch; the procedures that you and the customer each have to complete for these services to be supplied; the services offered by other branches/banks/institutions, should comparisons be made or advice sought.

(b) Be aware of customers as *people*. Look out for signals that suggest stress, distress, perplexity, impatience. Be patient with non-bankers who don't understand what their statement means, why it takes time to arrange a personal loan, why they need a cheque guarantee card.

(c) Learn, from experience, ways of dealing with queries and situations that crop up over and over again. You can stay sensitive and responsive to individual cases *without* having to invent whole new ways of dealing with each one.

5.4 Handling *complaints* can be particularly awkward. Some customers may follow the rules of good communication when they complain (ie may have their facts straight, stay calm, not take their frustration out on the person answering the complaint - who is rarely the individual responsible). Most will not. As a banking professional, however, you are there to solve problems, either making it clear that there is no substance to the complaint, or putting things right if there is. You must not take a complaint personally - even if the customer seems to - but must handle it with dignity. A good strategy for doing that may be as follows.

(a) *Ask for the facts:* listen carefully; check that you have both got the facts *straight.* There may be some elementary misunderstanding that can be easily cleared up. If you look as if you're trying to get to grips with the substance of the complaint, you will reassure the customer that you intend to solve the problem and are taking it seriously. If you don't even appear willing to listen, you may invite further indignation and the situation may get out of control.

(b) *Sympathise.* You may not wish to open yourself or the bank to liability for an error by making placatory statements which sound like an admission of guilt. However, the customer may be quite overwrought (especially if he is not used to making complaints) and needs to hear that you appreciate how he feels, and that you recognise that he is justified in broaching the matter. Apologise for any inconvenience caused. If the customer is simply mistaken or confused about the complaint, explain firmly but politely, and give him time to adjust.

(c) *Be positive.* If a mistake *has* been made, apologise and tell the customer what you intend to do about it. You may be able to put it right immediately: if not, explain what steps will be taken and by whom. *Don't* make excuses, or blame others. *Don't* grovel. Be seen to be purposeful in dealing with the matter in hand.

(d) *Follow through.* Make sure your remedy has actually been carried out!

5.5 Of course, it isn't only in 'awkward' situations that fact-to-face encounters with the public can be hard work. Here are a few more hints that might be useful.

(a) *First contact.* It is important to 'engage' properly in a conversation. A smile and a 'Good morning, Sir [or madam]. Can I help you?' can make all the difference to the following exchange - and in *no* circumstances represents a waste of time or an excessive familiarity.

(b) *Attention.* Your time with the customer should be brief - so give him all your concentration. There is nothing more frustrating for a customer than encountering half an employee!

(c) *Information.* If you have to leave your position while dealing with a customer (eg to consult someone else), *don't* just walk away, leaving him to wonder whether he can go, whether there's 'a problem' etc. Explain briefly but patiently, if a customer wants to know what is going on and why. Give and request all the information required by the purpose of the interaction.

(d) *Language.* There may well be a 'language' problem on both sides. You must be aware that your technical vocabulary is simply not shared by most other people. The customer may not be using the 'right' vocabulary to voice a query or complaint: be patient, and listen carefully for what his problem or uncertainty is. When you reply to a customer, try and use laymen's terms.

(e) *Understanding.* Show willing. If a customer asks what a 'bank charge' is, don't act as if he's an imbecile and tell him it's-just-something-he's-got-to-pay-so-what's-the-point-of-asking?

(f) *Responsiveness.* Separate one customer from another in your mind. Each one is coming to you 'fresh'. He doesn't know - and doesn't care - that you've been answering queries all day, that you're busy, bored, tired, hungry, irritated from a string of awkward customers, plagued by the phone ringing etc etc etc. Don't 'take out' on one customer the emotions stirred up in you by another. Don't let the routine get to you so that you cease to see or hear the special case in front of you: to each customer, his transaction *matters*, and he is entitled to expect service from you as if he is your *first* and *only* customer.

(g) *Ending*. Agree any actions to be taken, information to be sent etc. 'Goodbye and thank you.'

Selling interviews

5.6 The aim of a selling interview is to win the customer over and to persuade him, for example, to buy unit trusts through the bank rather than direct from a unit trust company; or to take out holiday insurance through the bank rather than through the package tour operator selling the holiday. You might also be suggesting a product or service which the customer has not previously thought about (executorship, for example) and here your aim is not so much to persuade your customer not to go to a competitor as to persuade him of his need for your product. A final possibility is that you're trying to persuade a customer that he still needs a service (for example, that he shouldn't stop insuring his house contents on grounds of the expense of the premiums).

5.7 Many professional people find the idea of selling distasteful. It brings to mind images of pushy, insincere, aggressive salesmen who won't leave the house until they've closed on a sale. However, this is misleading. Everyone involved in dealing with customers is in some way involved in selling.

Selling doesn't (or shouldn't) mean persuading someone to buy something he doesn't need and/or can't afford and/or could buy more cheaply (or get a better version of) from someone else. As bankers you are hoping to build a *long-term* relationship with your customers. You can sell to your customers to increase your profits at the same time as providing them with a better service.

5.8 As the interviewer, you are in charge. If you were visiting the customer at his home or business you might lose some of your authority because you would be a guest and on unfamiliar ground, but in your own branch it is the customer who is ill at ease. You must take account of this and try to make the customer feel more relaxed; but the advantage of this position of control is that you can direct the interview and ask all the questions you need to.

5.9 An important reason for asking questions is to find out whether what the customer *perceives* as his needs are his *real* needs. He may, for example, have come in to discuss taking out a term assurance policy but what he really needs may turn out to be a personal pension with a lump sum payable on retirement: opportunities for *cross-selling*.

5.10 Once you know what the customer wants, you can select the product/service you think will be best tailored to his wants and needs. You must then must explain in as much detail as is required what the product you recommend is, how it works, how much it costs, and what its advantages are over other available options and, if the customer is considering a competitor's product, explain why, in your opinion, he would be better off with yours. This process of matching the customer's needs with the benefits of your product is called *benefit analysis*.

5.11 It is extremely important (especially in view of the constraints imposed by the Consumer Credit Act 1974, Financial Services Act 1986 etc) that you should not give false, misleading or incomplete information or advice.

5.12 Naturally your customers will not always agree to have your product without further discussion. However, you must be able to distinguish between simple queries and serious doubts. The former are easily dealt with: you provide further information. The latter are more difficult to deal with as the customer may not be coming out with his real objection to the product. Fundamental objections can either be overcome, or not - in which case you must give way with good grace. Some compromise may be required if, say, a business customer has the bargaining power of his custom, and wishes to negotiate the price of a loan. Reluctance to commit to an immediate decision may also be overcome - but may require the scheduling of a further meeting to give the customer time to 'think it over'.

5.13 When you have reached the point where the customer seems convinced, you must *close* (ie agree) the sale, or at least reach a point where further action is agreed. Devices to help close a sale may include the following.

(a) A *partnership approach* means summing up by going through the pros and cons of the product *with* the customer (instead of simply telling the customer what they are) and obtaining the customer's agreement at each point.

(b) An *incentive* can be offered, eg payment of legal fees for customers taking out mortgages within a certain period, which may or may not be generally advertised.

(c) A *step by step approach* involves gaining the customer's agreement at each stage that the product does have the benefits outlined for him personally. He thus begins to identify with the product at an early stage.

5.14 Regardless of the outcome, you should also ensure that you deal with the bank's internal procedures (eg to record the details of the interview) and that you review how successfully you handled the interview. If you didn't succeed in convincing the customer, was that because of lack of experience, product knowledge or stiff competition? You may be able to pass useful information on to the marketing department about the competition and you will always be able to improve your own performance by trying to spot your mistakes and thinking about how to correct them.

Customer care

5.15 Of course, customer relationship management is not just about effective interviewing and complaints handling. The relationship should be managed through:

(a) the range and quality of products offered - their suitability to customer needs, consistent delivery, fair pricing etc;

(b) the quality of service offered, in terms of personal assistance from bank staff, availability of services in locations and at times to suit customers etc;

(c) the culture of the bank, and its implied attitude to customers as people - including the atmosphere of branches, the comfort/convenience of facilities (wheelchair access, seating etc), the use of 'personal bankers', 'personal business managers' etc;

(d)   training of bank staff in communication and customer service methods and awareness: customers should receive courteous, consistent and considerate treatment;

(e)   provision of clear, non-technical information to customers about products and services and about the bank's policies and procedures - taking the 'mystique' to an extent (and potential for suspicion) out of banking. Information about bank charges, for example;

(f)   provision of information to customers about their rights as customers; complaints procedures, role of the Ombudsman etc.

5.16   Many banks now manage their relationships with customers by offering customers *guidance* leaflets on how to approach interview/contact situations with the bank eg 'how to complain about bank services', 'how to apply for a loan' - including the psychological as well as procedural implications of such situations). This type of information helps to set the positive tone of bank-customer dealings, and helps customers to do their part in effective preparation and conduct of subsequent interviews.

5.17   Note that customer care involves both:

(a)   provision of the 'right' products and services; and
(b)   delivery of products/services in a considerate, customer-oriented way.

The bank's legal obligations of care and trust (as well as specific provisions related to procedures and the provision of services) have a similar orientation.

Exercise

Here is a playlet, set in the local head office of a bank.

MRS PITT: *[Timidly, glancing at her watch]* Um... excuse me... that young man knows that I've arrived, doesn't he?

RECEPTIONIST: *[Not looking up]* Oh yes. He said he'll be along in a minute.

[Several minutes pass by]

DAVID: *[Ambling out of the reception area and winking at the receptionist.]* Ah. Mrs...um. I see you've found some magazines! Would you like to finish reading that?

MRS PITT: *[Putting down Banking World and looking rather frightened.]* Hello. I had an appointment to see a Mr Laxe. I hope I'm...

DAVID: That's me - you can call me David. Mrs... *[flicks through file]* Pitt, ah yes, that's right - problems with loan repayments. Would you like to come this way?

[DAVID walks quickly down the corridor, pausing half way down to check that MRS PITT is following.]

DAVID: *[In doorway, to three junior staff in suits, smoking and laughing]* Could you clear out for ten minutes, please chaps: I've got an F104.

[MRS PITT arrives in the room. The three 'chaps' pick up their papers, put out their cigarettes and leave. DAVID leans his head out of the door before closing it and makes an inaudible remark which is greeted with loud laughter.]

DAVID: Well Mrs Pitt, Pitt the Younger is it? *[leans forward and leers]*. How can we help you?

MRS PITT: Well actually you wrote to me and asked me to come in and see you. I'm sorry.

[The phone rings.]

DAVID: Oh, put him through. John! How are you? How's business?... Yes I did ring you, its about that ten grand you were after. I just wanted to say, no problem mate. Yes, I thought you'd be pleased. How's Caroline? *[Lengthy silence while DAVID listens to the person on the other end of the line.]* I'm sorry... I had no idea, mate. So its completely... um... there's no chance of you getting back together?... Well, give it time, you know what they say. Look, I've got to go - I'll see you on Friday, OK? Bye. *[Looks down at the file on the table.]* Now then, Mrs Pitt. You borrowed £2,000, when was it... nearly four years ago. Monthly repayments... £60-ish. Three months arrears. Now we're a caring bank, Mrs Pitt, but we do like people to keep up with their repayments. Is there a problem?

MRS PITT: Well, I suppose it was because my husband lost his job and there was no money in our joint account. It was you who wouldn't do the transfers, actually.

DAVID: Um... it depends on your... er... overdraft facility. But... um... I take it your husband's trying to find another job?

MRS PITT: Well he will do, but we're going on holiday actually - his redundancy money was held up but it's just come through *[scrabbles in her handbag.]* I've got some cash here. I was going to pay off the arrears and settle the loan, if I'm allowed to do that. I don't want to break the rules.

DAVID: *[Completely thrown.]* Um... yes, of course. I'll take you down to the front office and we'll work out what the outstanding amount is. *[Trying to recover.]* Well that is good news - I wish all our customers were like you! Was it... er... how... if it's a large sum we....

MRS PITT: Oh I'm not sure. My husband's dealing with all that - he just gives me pocket money *[She waves a large bundle of notes and smiles very sweetly]*.

David clearly does not deal with Mrs Pitt very well. What criticisms would you make of his handling of this case?

Solution

David (and the organisation generally) handle Mrs Pitt badly from start to finish.

(a) Mrs Pitt is kept waiting for some while after the appointed time before she receives any attention. Even the receptionist is offhand with her.

(b) When he does arrive David does so in a very unbusinesslike manner. He does not greet Mrs Pitt by name. He does not apologise for being late. His comment about the magazine appears to be at the expense of Mrs Pitt and the magazine (his trade's journal) itself.

(c) His tone of friendliness ('you can call me David') is belied by his complete lack of interest in Mrs Pitt's case.

(d) He is quite oblivious to any desire that Mrs Pitt may have for her business to be handled confidentially. He blurts out her financial problems in front of the receptionist.

(e) He acts discourteously in not showing Mrs Pitt the way to the interview room. He should have let her go first and made some attempt to put her at her ease.

(f) He is more polite to the three juniors who appear to be wasting time then he has so far been to his customer. He becomes conspiritorial in referring to her, mysteriously, as 'an F104'. This tells Mrs Pitt that the organisation regards her as a number and that her case, however harrowing its circumstances may be, are about to be swallowed up by bureaucracy.

(g) David's private joke with his colleagues may have nothing to do with Mrs Pitt, but by now she is likely to be feeling that, when the organisation is not being seriously inconvenienced by her, it regards her as a laughing matter.

(h) David's joke at the expense of Mrs Pitt's name appears to be a corny attempt at a compliment. She has given no indication so far that either jokes or compliments are appropriate. The joke is not funny and the accompanying language is quite out of place.

(i) Once more David's lack of interest in the case is shown by his 'How can I help you?' He is pulled up by Mrs Pitt's reply but then 'saved by the bell'.

(j) He should not have accepted the telephone call – it could have been diverted to a colleague or he could have called back later.

(k) As it is, it is quickly apparent to Mrs Pitt that she is far less valued as a customer than David's caller, who also appears to be a personal friend. The organisation's time and Mrs Pitt's is wasted by the discussion of the caller's domestic circumstances. Mrs Pitt will hardly be able to feel that her own affairs are being handled confidentially if David is prepared to have conversations about his friend's circumstances in front of her.

(l) When David does at last get down to business he is very unsympathetic to Mrs Pitt's problem.

(m) David's change of tone when he realises that Mrs Pitt is far from penniless rings totally false. He is quite unable to cope with unexpected information.

6. CHAPTER ROUNDUP

6.1 *Interview*

Objectives
Preparation
Conduct: personal factors - information needs - open questions - objectivity
Closing: summary - conclusion
Follow up

6.2 *Contact with customers*

First impression
Attention
Information
Language   it won't be!
Understanding
Responsiveness
Ending

TEST YOUR KNOWLEDGE
The numbers in brackets refer to paragraphs of this chapter

1   What might influence a person's attitudes? (1.12)

2   What are the characteristics of an interview that distinguish it from a 'conversation'? (2.1)

3   Outline the *types* of questions that ought to be asked in an interview in order to elicit information? (2.8)

4   Why do selection interviews sometimes fail to result in selection of the right person? (3.5, 3.6)

5   What possible approaches may an interviewer adopt in an appraisal interview? (3.9)

6   Outline the content of a disciplinary interview. (4.3)

7   How would you approach an interview with a personal customer of the bank who has a current and deposit account with your branch and, being just about to buy a house for the first time, has come to ask you about a loan to buy furniture? (5.9)

8   What is 'customer care'? Why do banks have 'customer care' programmes? What procedures are there in your own bank for customer care? What training is involved for staff? (5.15 and your own experience)

Now try question 8 at the end of the text

Chapter 9

PEOPLE IN GROUPS

This chapter covers the following topics.

1. What is a group?
2. Group cohesion and conflict
3. Creating an effective group
4. Participating in meetings

Introduction

In the work situation, people are less likely than before to operate independently as isolated indivdiuals. Skills in teamworking are becoming increasingly important.

---

1. WHAT IS A GROUP?

1.1 Handy in *Understanding Organisations* defines a group as 'any collection of people who perceive themselves to be a group'. The point of this definition is the distinction it implies between a random collection of individuals and a 'group' of individuals who share a common sense of identity and belonging.

1.2 A group has certain attributes that a random 'crowd' does not possess.

(a) *A sense of identity.* Whether the group is formal or informal, its existence is recognised by its members: there are acknowledged boundaries to the group which define who is 'in' and who is 'out', who is 'us' and who is 'them'. People generally need to feel that they 'belong', that they share something with others and are of value to others.

(b) Loyalty to the group, and acceptance within the group. This generally expresses itself as *conformity* or the acceptance of the 'group norms' of behaviour and attitude that bind the group together and exclude others from it.

(c) *Purpose and leadership.* Most groups have an expressed purpose, aim or set of objectives, whatever field they are in: most will, spontaneously or formally, choose individuals or sub-groups to lead them towards the fulfilment of those goals.

Why people form groups

1.3 People in organisations will be drawn together into groups by:

(a) a preference for small groups, where closer relationships can develop;
(b) the need to belong and to make a contribution that will be noticed and appreciated;
(c) familiarity: a shared office, canteen etc;
(d) common rank, specialisms, objectives and interests;
(e) the attractiveness of a particular group activity (eg joining an interesting club);
(f) resources offered to groups (eg sports facilities);
(g) 'power' greater than the individuals alone could muster (eg trade union, pressure group).

Formal and informal groups

1.4 Some such groupings will be the result of *formal* directives from the organisation: for example, specialists may be 'thrown together' in a committee set up to investigate a particular issue or problem; a department may be split up into small work teams in order to facilitate supervision.

(a) *Informal* groups may spring up as a result of these formal arrangements, (eg if the members of the committee become friends), and will invariably be present in any organisation. Informal groups include workplace 'cliques', and networks of people who regularly get together to exchange information, groups of 'mates' who socialise outside work etc. They have a constantly fluctuating membership and structure, and leaders emerge usually through personal (rather than 'positional') power. The purposes of informal groups are usually related to group and individual member satisfaction, rather than to a task.

(b) *Formal* groups will have a formal structure; they will be consciously organised for a function allotted to them by the organisation, and for which they are held responsible - they are task oriented, and become *teams*. Leaders may be chosen within the group, but are typically given 'legal' authority by the organisation. Permanent formal groups include standing committees, management teams (eg the board of directors) or specialist services (eg information technology support). *Temporary* formal groups include task forces, designed to work on a particular project, ad hoc committees etc.

The functions of groups

1.5 From the organisation's standpoint the functions of groups or teams include:

(a) performing tasks which require the collective skills of more than one person;

(b) testing and ratifying decisions made outside the group;

(c) consulting or negotiating, especially to resolve disputes within the organisation;

(d) creating ideas (acting as a 'think tank');

(e) exchanging ideas, collecting and transmitting information;

(f) co-ordinating the work of different individuals or other groups;

(g) motivating individuals to devote more energy and effort into achieving the organisation's goals.

1.6 There may be no strict division between these different functions. They will inevitably overlap in practice. But the effectiveness with which a group acts is likely to be greater if they are not attempting to cope with different functions simultaneously.

1.7 From the individual's standpoint groups also perform some important functions.

(a) They satisfy social needs for friendship and belonging.

(b) They help individuals in developing images of themselves (eg a person may need to see himself as a member of the corporate planning department or of the works snooker team).

(c) They enable individuals to help each other in matters which are not necessarily connected with the organisation's purpose (eg people at work may organise a baby-sitting circle).

(d) They enable individuals to share the burdens of any responsibility they may have in their work.

The formation of groups

1.8 Groups are not static. They mature and develop. Four stages in this development are commonly identified:

(a) forming
(b) storming
(c) norming and
(d) performing.

1.9 During the first stage (*forming*) the team is just coming together, and may still be seen as a collection of individuals. Each individual wishes to impress his personality on the group, while its purpose, composition, and organisation are being established. The individuals will be trying to find out about each other, and about the aims and norms of the team. There will at this stage probably be a wariness about introducing new ideas. The objectives being pursued may as yet be unclear and a leader may not yet have emerged.

This settling down period is essential, but may be time wasting: the team as a unit will not be used to being autonomous, and will probably not be an efficient agent in the planning of its activities or the activities of others. It may resort to complex bureaucratic procedures to ensure that what it is doing is at least something which will not get its members into trouble.

1.10 The second stage is called *storming* because it frequently involves more or less open conflict between team members. There may be changes agreed in the original objectives, procedures and norms established for the group. If the team is developing successfully this may be a fruitful phase as more realistic targets are set and trust between the group members increases.

1.11 The third stage (*norming*) is a period of settling down. There will be agreements about work sharing, individual requirements and expectations of output. The enthusiasm and brain-storming of the second stage may be less apparent, but norms and procedures may evolve which enable methodical working to be introduced and maintained. Group norms are discussed further below.

1.12 Once the fourth stage (*performing*) has been reached the team sets to work to execute its task. Even at earlier stages some performance will have been achieved but the fourth stage marks the point where the difficulties of growth and development no longer hinder the group's objectives.

1.13 It would be misleading to suggest that these four stages always follow in a clearly-defined progression, or that the development of a group must be a slow and complicated process. Particularly where the task to be performed is urgent, or where team members are highly motivated, the fourth stage will be reached very quickly while the earlier stages will be hard to distinguish.

Group norms

1.14 A work group establishes 'norms' or acceptable levels and methods of behaviour, to which all members of the group are expected to conform. This team attitude will have a negative effect on an organisation if it sets unreasonably low production norms (anyone producing more is made the social outcast of the group).

1.15 The general nature of group pressure is to require the individual to share in the team's identity, and individuals may react to group norms, customs etc with:

(a) compliance - 'toeing the line' without real commitment;
(b) internalisation - full acceptance and identification; or
(c) counter-conformity - rejecting the group and/or its norms.

1.16 Pressure is strongest on the individual when:

(a) the issue is not clear-cut;
(b) he lacks support for his own attitude or behaviour; and
(c) he is exposed to other members of the group for a length of time.

1.17 From the findings that an individual's opinions can be changed or swayed by group consensus, it may be argued that it would be more effective, and probably also easier in practice, to change group norms than to change individual norms. Motivation should therefore involve the work group as a whole, because changes agreed by a group are likely to be more effective and longer-lasting.

2. GROUP COHESION AND CONFLICT

2.1 In an experiment reported by Deutsch (1949), psychology students were given puzzles and human relation problems to work at in discussion groups. Some 'co-operative' groups were told that the grade each individual got at the end of the course would depend on the performance of his group. Other 'competitive' groups were told that each student would receive a grade according to his own contributions.

2.2 No significant differences were found between the two kinds of group in the amount of interest and involvement in the tasks, or in the amount of learning. But the co-operative groups, compared with the competitive ones, had greater productivity per unit time, better quality of product and discussion, greater co-ordination of effort and sub-division of activity, more diversity in amount of contribution per member, more attentiveness to fellow members and more friendliness during discussion.

2.3 However another experiment, conducted in 1949 by Sherif and Sherif, set out to investigate how groups are formed, and how relationships between groups are created. The experimenters used teams of schoolboys to investigate the effects of conflict and competition between rival groups. The results suggested that *inter-group competition may have a positive effect on group cohesion and performance.*

Inter-group conflict

2.4 Within each competing group:

(a) members close ranks, and submerge their differences; loyalty and conformity are demanded;

(b) the 'climate' changes from informal and social to work and task-oriented; individual needs are subordinated to achievement;

(c) leadership moves from democratic to autocratic, with the group's acceptance;

(d) the group tends to become more structured and organised.

2.5 Between competing groups:

(a) the other group begins to be perceived as 'the enemy'; and
(b) inter-group communication decreases.

2.6 In a 'win-lose' situation (ie where one group can only benefit at the expense of another), the 'winning' group will:

(a) retain its cohesion;
(b) relax into a complacent, playful state ('fat and happy');
(c) return to group maintenance, concern for members' needs etc; and
(d) be confirmed in its group 'self-concept' with little re-evaluation.

2.7 The losing group will:

(a) deny defeat if possible, or place the blame on the management, the system etc;

(b) lose its cohesion and splinter into conflict, as 'blame' is apportioned;

(c) be keyed-up, fighting mad ('lean and hungry');

(d) turn towards work-orientation to regroup - rather than members' needs, group maintenance etc;

(e) tend to learn by revaluating its perceptions of itself and the other group. It is more likely to become a cohesive and effective unit once the 'loss' has been accepted.

2.8 All members of a group will act in unison if the group's existence or patterns of behaviour are threatened from outside. Cohesion is naturally assumed to be the result of communication, agreement and mutual trust - but in the face of a 'common enemy' (competition, crisis or emergency) cohesion and productivity benefit.

Problems of establishing cohesion in groups

2.9   In an ideal functioning group:

(a)   each individual gets the support of the team, a sense of identity and belonging which encourages loyalty and hard work on the group's behalf;

(b)   skills, information and ideas are 'pooled' or shared, so that the team's capabilities are greater than those of the individuals;

(c)   new ideas can be tested, reactions taken into account and persuasive skills brought into play in group discussion for decision-making and problem-solving;

(d)   each individual is encouraged to participate and contribute and thus becomes personally involved in and committed to the team's activities;

(e)   goodwill, trust and respect can be built up between individuals, so that communication is encouraged and potential problems more easily overcome.

2.10   Unfortunately, team working is rarely such an undiluted success. There are certain constraints involved in working with others:

(a)   awareness of group norms and the desire to be acceptable to the group may restrict individual personality and flair. This may perhaps create pressure or a sense of 'schizophrenia' for the individual concerned who can't 'be himself' in a team situation;

(b)   conflicting roles and relationships (where an individual is a member of more than one group) can cause difficulties in communicating effectively, especially if sub-groups or cliques are formed in conflict with others;

(c)   the effective functioning of the group is dependent upon each of its members, and will suffer if one member:

(i)   dislikes or distrusts another;
(ii)   is so dominant that others cannot participate; or
(iii)   is so timid that the value of his ideas is lost; or
(iv)   is so negative in attitude that constructive communication is rendered impossible;

(d)   rigid leadership and procedures may strangle initiative and creativity in individuals;

(e)   differences of opinion and political conflicts of interest are always likely and if all policies and decisions are to be determined by consultation and agreement within the group, decisions may never be reached and action never taken.

Group cohesion and 'group think'

2.11   It is possible for groups to be *too* cohesive, too all-absorbing. Handy notes that 'ultra-cohesive groups can be dangerous because in the organisational context the group must serve the organisation, not itself'. If a group is completely absorbed with its own maintenance, members and priorities, it can become dangerously blinkered to what is going on around it, and may confidently forge ahead in a completely wrong direction. I L Janis describes this as 'group think'.

2.12 The cosy consensus of the group prevents consideration of alternatives, constructive criticism or conflict. Symptoms of 'group think' include:

(a) sense of invulnerability - blindness to the risk involved in 'pet' strategies;
(b) rationalisations for inconsistent facts;
(c) moral blindness - 'might is right';
(d) tendency to stereotype 'outsiders' and 'enemies';
(e) strong group pressure to quell dissent;
(f) self-censorship by members - not 'rocking the boat';
(g) perception of unanimity - filtering out divergent views;
(h) mutual support and solidarity to 'guard' the decision.

2.13 Victims of 'group think' - which is rife at the top and centre of organisations - take great risks in their decisions, fail to recognise failure, and are highly resistant to unpalatable information. Such groups must:

(a) actively encourage self-criticism;
(b) welcome outside ideas and evaluation; and
(c) respond positively to conflicting evidence.

3. CREATING AN EFFECTIVE GROUP

3.1 The criteria of group effectiveness are:

(a) fulfilment of task and organisation goals; and
(b) satisfaction of group members.

3.2 The management problem is how to create an effective, efficient work team. If managers can motivate groups (and individuals) to work harder and better to achieve organisational goals, the sense of pride in their own competence might create job satisfaction through belonging to the team and performing its tasks.

3.3 Handy takes a contingency approach to the problem of team effectiveness, which, he argues, depends on:

(a) the group	}	
(b) the group's task	}	The 'givens'
(c) the group's environment	}	
(d) motivation of the group	}	
(e) leadership style	}	The 'intervening factors'
(f) processes and procedures	}	
(g) productivity of the group	}	The 'outcomes'
(h) satisfaction of the group members	}	

These factors are important, and are worth learning carefully. They are considered in more detail below.

The givens

3.4   The personalities and characteristics of the individual members of the team, and the personal goals of these members, will help to determine the group's personality and goals. An individual is likely to be influenced more strongly by a small group than by a large group in which he may feel like a small fish in a large pond, and therefore unable to participate effectively in team decisions.

3.5   It has been suggested that the effectiveness of a group depends on the blend of the individual skills and abilities of its members. A project team might be most effective if it contains:

    (a) a person of originality and ideas;
    (b) a 'get-up-and-go' person with considerable energy, enthusiasm and drive;
    (c) a quiet, logical thinker, who ponders carefully and criticises the ideas of others;
    (d) a plodder, who is happy to do the humdrum routine work;
    (e) a conciliator, who is adept at negotiating compromises or a consensus of thought between other members of the group.

Group roles

3.6   Belbin, in a study of business-game teams at Carnegie Institute of Technology in 1981, discovered that a differentiation of influence among team members (agreement that some members were more influential than others) resulted in higher morale and better performance. Belbin's picture (which many managers have found a useful guide to team working) of the most effective character-mix in a team involves eight necessary roles which should ideally be balanced and evenly 'spread' in the team:

    (a) the *co-ordinator* (formerly *chairman*) - presides and co-ordinates; balanced, disciplined, good at working through others;

    (b) the *shaper* - highly strung, dominant, extrovert, passionate about the task itself, a spur to action;

    (c) the *plant* - introverted, but intellectually dominant and imaginative; source of ideas and proposals but with disadvantages of introversion;

    (d) the *monitor-evaluator* - analytically (rather than creatively) intelligent; dissects ideas, spots flaws; possibly aloof, tactless - but necessary;

    (e) the *resource-investigator* - popular, sociable, extrovert, relaxed; source of new contacts etc. but not an originator; needs to be made use of;

    (f) the *implementer* (formerly *company worker*) - practical organiser, turning ideas into tasks - scheduling, planning etc. Trustworthy and efficient - but not excited (or exciting, often); not a leader, but an administrator;

    (g) the *team worker* - most concerned with team maintenance - supportive, understanding, diplomatic; popular but uncompetitive - noticed only in absence;

    (h) the *finisher* - chivvies the team to meet deadlines, attend to details etc; urgency and follow-through important, though not always popular.

9: PEOPLE IN GROUPS

The group's task

3.7 The nature of the task must have some bearing on how a group should be managed. If a job must be done urgently, it is often necessary to dictate how things should be done, rather than to encourage a participatory style of working. Jobs which are routine, unimportant and undemanding will be insufficient to motivate either individuals or the group as a whole. If individuals in the team want authoritarian leadership, they are also likely to want clearly defined targets.

The group's environment

3.8 The group's environment relates to factors such as the physical surroundings at work and to inter-group relations. An open-plan office, in which the members of the group are closely situated, is more conducive to cohesion than a situation in which individuals are partitioned into separate offices, or geographically distant from each other. Team attitudes will also be affected, as described previously, by the relationship with other teams, which may be friendly, neutral or hostile.

Intervening factors

3.9 Of the 'intervening factors', motivation and leadership (especially of groups - see Handy and Fiedler in Chapter 14) have already been discussed. With regard to processes and procedures, research indicates that a team which tackles its work systematically will be more effective than one which lives from hand to mouth, and muddles through.

Outcomes

3.10 High productivity may be achieved if work is so arranged that *satisfaction* of individual and group needs coincides with *high output*. Where teams are, for example, allowed to set their own improvement goals and methods and to measure their own progress towards those goals, it has been observed that they regularly *exceed* their targets.

3.11 Individuals may, however, bring their own 'hidden agendas' to groups for satisfaction - goals which may have nothing to do with the declared aims of the team - such as protection of a sub-group, impressing the boss, inter-personal rivalry etc. The danger is that the more cohesive the group, the more its own maintenance and satisfactions may take precedence over its task objectives, and the more collective *power* it may have - even to sabotage organisational goals (eg by 'freezing out' disliked supervisors or restricting output to whatever level the group feels is 'fair').

3.12 Like organisations, therefore, groups have 'cultures' which will contribute importantly to the effectiveness or otherwise of their operation and member satisfaction.

Peters and Waterman *(In search of excellence)* outline the cultural attributes of successful *task force* teams. They should:

(a) be small - requiring the trust of those who are not involved

(b) be of limited duration and working under the 'busy member theorem' - 'get off the damned task force and back to work'

(c) be voluntary - which ensures that the business is 'real'

(d) have an informal structure and documentation - no bulky paperwork, and open communication

(e) have swift follow-up - be *action*-oriented.

The characteristics of effective and ineffective work groups

3.13 If a manager is to try to improve the effectiveness of his work group he must be able to identify the different characteristics of an effective and an ineffective group. No one factor on its own will be significant, but taken collectively the factors may indicate how well or badly the group is doing.

The value of groups as work units

3.14 It is worth noting that for all its opportunities for exchanged ideas and knowledge, immediate feedback, 'brainstorming' etc, the 'group' as a work unit is not necessarily superior to the individual in terms of performance in all situations.

(a) Decision-making may be a cumbersome process where consensus has to be reached - and it has been shown (rather surprisingly) that teams take *riskier* decisions than the individuals comprising them, perhaps because of the sense of shared responsibility. Still, decisions reached by consensus have the advantage of acceptance - not merely compliance - and can show the benefit of share creativity and output.

(b) Group norms may work to lower the standard rate of unit production - though, again, individuals need groups psychologically; isolation can produce stress and hostile behaviour, and can impair performance just as surely as 'rate fixing'.

(c) Group cohesion may provide a position of strength - solidarity - from which to behave in hostile or deviant (from the organisation's point of view) ways. On the other hand, teams can be committed to organisational objectives, and many provide a much stronger impetus for change than individuals.

(d) Groups have been shown to produce less ideas - though better evaluated - than the individuals of the group working separately. However, a group *will* often produce a better solution to a problem than even its best individual, since 'missing pieces' can be added to his performance.

Effective groups	Ineffective groups
Quantifiable factors	
• Low rate of labour turnover	• High rate of labour turnover
• Low accident rate	• High accident rate
• Low absenteeism	• High absenteeism
• High output and productivity	• Low output and productivity
• Good quality of output	• Poor quality of output
• Individual targets are achieved	• Individual targets are not achieved
• There are few stoppages and interruptions to work	• Much time is wasted owing to disruption of work flow
	• Time is lost owing to disagreements between superior and subordinates
Qualitative factors	
• There is a high commitment to the achievement of targets and organisational goals	• There is no understanding of organisational goals or the role of the group
• There is a clear understanding of the group's work	• There is a low commitment to targets
• There is a clear understanding of the role of each person within the group	• There is confusion and uncertainty about the role of each person within the group
• There is free and open communication between members of the group and trust between members	• There is mistrust between group members and suspicion of group's leader
• There is idea sharing	• There is little idea sharing
• The group is good at generating new ideas	• The group does not generate any good new ideas
• Group members try to help each other out by offering constructive criticisms and suggestions	• Group members make negative and hostile criticisms about each other's work
• There is group problem-solving which gets to the root causes of the work problem	• Work problems are dealt with superficially, with attention paid to the symptoms but not the cause
• There is an active interest in work decisions	• Decisions about work are accepted passively
• Group members seek a united consensus of opinion	• Group members hold strongly opposed views
• The members of the group want to develop their abilities in their work	• Group members find work boring and do it reluctantly
• The group is sufficiently motivated to be able to carry on working in the absence of its leader	• The group needs its leader there to get work done

---

Exercise

How far are groups used in your work place, or in your training college, to analyse problems or give effect to management decisions?

(a) What roles (as in paragraph 3.6) did you play?
(b) Do you think the groups you have participated in have been effective?

---

4. PARTICIPATING IN MEETINGS

4.1 Meetings play an important part in the life of any organisation, whether they are required by government legislation or the Articles of a company, or held informally for information exchange, problem-solving and decision-making.

4.2 Company directors meet for strategic planning and performance review; the members of trade unions, and other associations and societies of all kinds meet regularly to discuss general policy or particular up-coming events; representatives of various levels or departments in an organisation meet to exchange information, think creatively and hammer out solutions to problems.

4.3 Face-to-face communication in general and group discussion in particular offer several advantages for:

(a) generating new ideas;
(b) 'on the spot' feedback, constructive criticism and exchange of views;
(c) encouraging co-operation and sensitivity to personal factors;
(d) spreading information quickly through a group of people.

4.4 However, meetings can be non- or counter-productive if:

(a) the terms of reference (defining the purpose and power of the meeting) are not clear;
(b) the people attending are unskilled or unwilling communicators;
(c) there is insufficient guidance or leadership to control proceedings; or
(d) the participants lack the information necessary for discussion and decision.

4.5 To achieve their purpose, those who attend a meeting must generally conform or respond to a measure of *organisation* and *procedure*.

(a) There is usually a *chairman*, assisted by a *secretary*, who guides the proceedings of the meeting and aims to maintain order. A meeting can hardly function efficiently if it is or is allowed to become a sort of Tower of Babel in which everybody talks at once and nobody listens.

(b) There is often a *sequence of business*, or at least of speeches, to express points of view or reach decisions on the common purpose of the meeting. It is not essential to formalise this point with an *agenda*, but private meetings usually do have one.

(c) The *purpose* of the meeting (which should be clearly defined) is usually achieved by reaching some *decision or expression of opinion* at the end of the discussion. In some circumstances this may lead to taking a vote to determine what is the majority view.

4.6 An informal meeting, such as might be called from time to time by a department head or working party, may take the form of a group discussion 'chaired' by a leader, and informally documented: notes handed round or taken during the meeting, a summary of arguments and decisions reached provided afterwards. Formal meetings, however, are governed by strict rules and conventions, and generate formal documentation, for the announcement, planning, conduct and recording of the proceedings. Principle among such documents are:

(a) *notice:* the announcement of and 'invitation' to the meeting;
(b) *agenda:* the list of items of business to be discussed at the meeting;
(c) *minutes:* the written record of a meeting, approved by those present.

Notice of a meeting

4.7 There are two main ways of calling together or 'convening' a meeting:

(a) 'automatically', without initiating action by the organiser on each occasion, if a meeting is one of a regular series or cycle of meetings;

(b) by issuing a *notice* of the meeting.

Unless a meeting is convened in accordance with requirements laid down, *it is not a proper meeting and its proceedings may be invalid on that account.*

Agenda of a meeting

4.8 A meeting should (and can effectively) only discuss one subject at a time. If its business includes more than one item, the items will have to be taken in sequence. Hence it is standard practice to draw up a list (called an *agenda* - Latin for 'things to be done') of the various items of business of a meeting.

4.9 The agenda is usually distributed to those participating in the meeting, so that:

(a) everyone knows the *subject* of the business to be covered at the meeting, and can prepare speeches, questions etc. accordingly;

(b) everyone knows the *order* of business, and can if necessary arrange to attend only the relevant session of the meeting;

(c) the chairman can keep the meeting to a schedule, and within a framework for debate, of which everyone is already aware.

4.10 The drawing up of the agenda is usually the task of the person calling the meeting, its elected 'chair' or secretary: items for inclusion may be invited from the participants in advance. Agendas will vary according to the type and formality of the meeting and the business to be discussed. General considerations in drafting them, however, will include:

(a) *length:* too many items on an agenda will mean either superficial coverage of each, or a very long, ponderous and expensive meeting; keep it short and relevant;

(b) *formality:* all the 'apparatus' of formal meetings (election of the Chair, vote of thanks to Chair and secretary, replies of same etc.) may not be necessary in informal ones;

(c) *approach:* there may be one or two important items of business on an agenda among other more routine ones. It will be up to the Chair to decide whether the latter are best 'got out of the way first', or whether the important items will require the participants to be fresh.

4.11 For a formal meeting, the agenda will usually contain the following elements.

(a) *Membership.* This is an optional item which allows the Chair to introduce new members or allude to retirements or resignations.

(b) *Apologies for absence.* Once the meeting has been declared open, apologies sent to the secretary by members unable to attend are read out.

(c) *Minutes of the last meeting.* The previous minutes are read out, or have more probably been sent in advance to the members. It is then considered whether or not the wording of those minutes is accurate in fact and implication, and a true record of the meeting. If so, the Chair signs the minutes as approved; if not, amendments may be made.

(d) *Matters arising.* If a situation has developed, or action been taken in response to the previous meeting, the fact should be reported. This item should *not* be an excuse for disputes to be re-opened.

(e) *The new business of the present meeting.* It may include plans to be made, information reports to be delivered and discussed or particular proposals to be debated and decided on. It is always helpful if each item of business is put before the meeting in the form of a *proposal* which defines:

(i) the matter for discussion; and
(ii) the point to be decided, in straightforward 'yea or nay' terms.

The proposal put to a meeting is a 'motion' and if it is 'carried' (approved) it becomes a 'resolution' (decision).

(f) *Any other business (AOB).* If a topic has been overlooked, or has arisen between the drafting of the agenda and the meeting, it may be dealt with at this point. 'AOB' should not be considered an excuse to 'spring' items on an unprepared (and probably tired) meeting: if the matter is sufficiently important, it may be carried over to the next meeting.

(g) *Date of the next meeting.* The meeting is then formally declared closed. The secretary should have recorded start and finish times for the proceedings.

4.12 *The chairman's agenda* is slightly different from that circulated to everyone else, in that:

(a) each item on the agenda is followed by brief notes: information updates, background detail, explanations, reminders of when an item was previously discussed, any problems that might arise between members and need sensitive handling etc.

    (b) a wide right hand margin is left for the chairman to make his/her own notes as the meeting progresses.

This means that the Chair is fully prepared to provide all necessary information to the meeting, and can also conduct the proceedings with tact and authority.

Constitution of the meeting

4.13 A meeting which has been properly *convened* may only proceed to business if it has been properly *constituted*, ie if it is 'made up' in a certain way.

    (a) A meeting must have a *chairman*, whose duties are described in detail later. A 'chairman' may of course be of either sex, and is sometimes called 'a chairperson' (and addressed merely as 'Chair'). We shall be using the less cumbersome term 'chairman' in this study text, referring equally to both sexes.

    (b) A minimum number of persons (called a *quorum*), as prescribed by the regulations, must be present.

Conducting the meeting

4.14 The conduct of the general discussion is the most demanding test of a chairman's skill and judgement. He is concerned:

    (a) to preserve order in the meeting, so that its business can proceed without hindrance. To this end, he must prevent people from growing frustrated or angry, interrupting or heckling etc;

    (b) to appear fair and impartial.

4.15 His task will be much more difficult if the meeting becomes antagonistic towards him or even loses confidence in his ability to keep the situation under control. He should be conciliatory but firm, perhaps letting some minor point of procedure pass unchallenged rather than provoke indignation.

4.16 In terms of procedure, the chairman should:

    (a) *keep the meeting to the agenda.* Business should be taken in the set order, kept to the point, and kept as brief as possible;

    (b) *insist that only one person at a time may address the meeting.* If more than one person at a time indicates that he wishes to speak eg. by rising in his place or raising a hand, the chairman decides who is to speak next and usually calls on him by name;

    (c) *insist that speakers address the chair.* If individuals start arguing among themselves, the meeting will degenerate into a brawl.

4.17 *Voting* is the means by which participants in a meeting may inform the chairman of their decision with regard to a motion, by a 'show of hands' or a 'poll', a secret 'ballot' (like government elections) or a 'voice vote' (shouting 'Aye' or 'No'). In some small informal meetings it is not considered necessary to have a vote on the motion. The chairman may look round the table, saying something like: 'Well, I think we are all agreed ...' and, unless there is dissent, the discussion will close at that point; the minutes will record that 'It was resolved'.

Minutes of a meeting

4.18 The minutes or written record of the meeting are extremely important if the meeting is to be an effective means of communication in any organisation. The production of minutes tests the secretary's skill in:

(a) forming an accurate, complete but concise record of business;

(b) filtering out personality clashes and 'heat of the moment' expressions that are later regretted, and do not enhance the reputation of the meeting;

(c) giving a correct account of participants' views and words, especially since the minutes will be jealously inspected for error or misrepresentation by the people concerned.

4.19 Minutes, as a written record of the proceedings at a meeting, act as:

(a) *a source of reference.* This will be important as an aid to remembering the decisions reached orally at the meeting: they cannot be 'conveniently' forgotten or distorted afterwards. The record also provides precedent and authority for future proposals: procedures and attitudes may be progressively accepted and developed according to each change documented in the minutes;

(b) *a check on ill-considered contributions.* Participants will know that their views and remarks are going into the minutes: this may cause them to think carefully before they speak, and will also enable them to 'go on record' with views they hold particularly strongly, or wish to be recalled later.

4.20 Minutes may take three forms.

(a) *Resolution minutes.* Here only the resolutions (or decisions) are recorded, without describing the debate preceding the vote.

(b) *Narrative minutes.* Here a concise summary of the discussion leading up to the resolution is added. This enables individuals to go on record with their views, and also enables the organisation to thereafter assess their soundness of judgement: the individual gains the satisfaction of 'making his mark' but also makes himself accountable for his words.

(c) *Action minutes.* Where the meeting has clear authority to direct members' actions, 'action minutes' may be used to indicate explicitly what is expected as a result of resolutions, and who is responsible. A right hand column may be used to note the name of the person who has undertaken or been asked to perform the necessary action.

The chairman of a meeting

4.21 There are a number of recognised qualities of a good chairman (though common sense may dictate many others, varying with the circumstances of the meeting).

(a) He will have to give immediate rulings on points of dispute or doubt, so he should have:

    (i)   a sound knowledge of the relevant regulations;

    (ii)   an ability to make up his mind without dithering; and

    (iii) skill in communicating his rulings clearly, but tactfully and in a courteous manner.

(b) He should be, and be seen to be, impartial. There will be times when criticism is expressed which he personally may find unfair, or when there is a strong clash of opinion between other members present. In either situation, whatever his personal views, the chairman should treat opponents with equal fairness - and his *own* opponents with as much consideration as his supporters. In particular, he should give them a reasonable opportunity to express their views, along with any minority interests at the meeting.

(c) He should have the discretion to know when to insist on strict observance of correct procedure, and when a certain amount of relaxation will ease the tension. (If in doubt, proper adherence to procedure may on the whole be safer.)

(d) He should be punctual and regular in his attendance at meetings. If he cannot give his duties the appropriate amount of time and attention, he should consider resigning.

4.22 The chairman's tasks are as follows.

(a) Before starting the meeting the chairman should be satisfied that it has been *properly convened* by notice and is *properly constituted* by the attendance of a quorum.

(b) He should do his best to *maintain order and harmony* (or at least courtesy). He should take appropriate action in face of disorder.

(c) He should *guide the meeting through its business*:

    (i)   taking one subject at a time, in the order set out in the agenda (or any modification of it which may be agreed by the meeting); and

    (ii)   making sure that only those who are eligible to speak are invited to do so.

(d) He should *permit an adequate amount of discussion* on each motion, giving sufficient (but not excessive) opportunity for the expression of different points of view. He should deal firmly with irrelevance, long-windedness, interruption, and signs of temper.

(e) If *'points of order'* are raised, ie complaints or queries regarding procedure, he should give immediate rulings on them.

(f) At the end of a debate he must *ascertain 'the sense of the meeting'* in an appropriate way, by summing up or taking a vote.

(g) When the minutes of the meeting have been prepared, the chairman should satisfy himself that they are an accurate and complete record. If he is satisfied, he should *sign the minutes*.

The secretary of a meeting

4.23 Much of the day-to-day work of a salaried secretary of an organisation is *not* concerned with meetings, but work incidental to meetings is one of the most important recognised duties of a secretary. This work may include:

(a) duties before the meeting:

(i) fixing the date and time of the meeting;
(ii) choosing and preparing the location of the meeting;
(iii) preparing and issuing various documents;

(b) duties at the meeting: eg. assisting the chairman, making notes;

(c) duties after the meeting: eg. preparing minutes, acting on and communicating decisions.

5. CHAPTER ROUNDUP

5.1 A group is 'any collection of people who perceive themselves to be a group'.

An 'effective' group is one which:

(a) achieves its allotted task *and*
(b) satisfies its members.

5.2 *Givens* ⟶ *Outcomes*

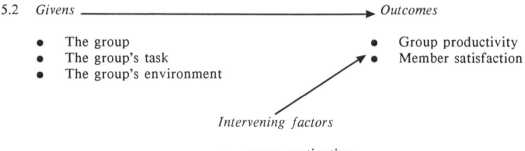

- The group
- The group's task
- The group's environment

- Group productivity
- Member satisfaction

Intervening factors

- group motivation
- leadership style
- processes and procedures

5.3 *Meetings* are often not highly regarded in banks as an effective method of communication. They can be improved by attention to:

(a) the purpose and agenda of the meeting
(b) the members and their potential contribution
(c) the members and their potential contribution
(d) the secretary and his preparation for the meeting
(e) the organisation - its support and facilities

TEST YOUR KNOWLEDGE
The numbers in brackets refer to paragraphs of this chapter

1   Why do individuals tend to form groups? (1.3)

2   What are the four stages of group formation? (1.8 - 1.13)

3   What effects does competition have on group performance? (2.4 - 2.8)

4   Describe some of the constraints which affect teamwork. (2.10)

5   What types of people should a leader try to recruit into his team? (3.6)

6   What are the twin objectives of a team, ie what makes a team 'effective'? (3.13)

7   What are:
(a)   the notice; (4.7)
(b)   the agenda; (4.8)
(c)   the minutes, (4.18 - 4.20)
of a meeting?

8   What does the chairman of a meeting do? How can he make the debate smooth-running and effective? (4.14 - 4.16, 4.22)

Now try question 9 at the end of the text

Chapter 10

MANAGING CHANGE

This chapter covers the following topics.

1. Change
2. Managing change
3. Resistance to change

Introduction

Management today is faced with rapid change on all sides. Traditionally it has earned profit for the owners through efficient control of essentially repetitive activities. Increasingly, this is no longer true. Technology, markets, people's attitudes etc are all changing at an accelerating pace and management which is geared solely to effective operating control of an existing business is less likely to be successful in the future.

---

1. CHANGE

1.1 The ability to control existing operations will continue to be one of the principal criteria for a successful business, management must also acquire the skills to identify the long-term opportunities that can emerge from this process of change, and devise a management structure for their organisations which will enable those opportunities to be seized and exploited. This is true for any organisation and its management.

1.2 For a bank, which has long operated within a highly regulated market and developed the bureaucratic culture system best suited to those relatively stable conditions, change may be even more traumatic. Yet banks *must* change to survive.

   (a) New markets and market segments are proliferating in the deregulated competitive climate: new products must be developed and innovation is therefore vital.

   (b) Information technology is still accelerating the pace of change for banking services and procedures.

   (c) Customers are changing - becoming more sophisticated in their financial awareness and more demanding of quality of service.

   (d) New competitors, within and outside the financial services sector, are entering the market.

   (e) Financial services is becoming an increasingly international arena.

1.3 Change, in the context of organisation and management, could involve any of the following.

(a) *Changes in the 'environment'.* These could be changes in what competitors are doing, what customers are buying, how they spend their money, changes in the law, changes in social behaviour and attitudes, economic changes, and so on.

(b) *Changes in the products the organisation makes, or the services it provides.* These are made in response to changes in customer demands, competitors" actions, new technology, and so on.

(c) *Changes in how products are made (or service provided) or by whom. Changes in working methods.* These changes are also in response to environmental change - eg new technology, new laws on safety at work etc.

(d) *Changes in management and working relationships, cultural change.* For example, changes in leadership style, and in the way that employees are encouraged to work together. Also changes in training and development.

(e) *Changes in organisation structure or size.* These might involve creating new departments and divisions, greater delegation of authority or more centralisation, changes in the way that plans are made, management information is provided and control is exercised, and so on. Organisation re-structuring will be made in response to changes in (a), (b), (c) or (d) above.

1.4 Change in the environment creates opportunities and threats: the organisation must respond with internal change in order to maximise its strengths and minimise its weaknesses.

1.5 Further implications of change for the organisation are discussed in Chapter 16.

2. MANAGING CHANGE

2.1 A step-by-step model for change and development is shown below.

1 Determine need or desire for change in a particular area, and so the *objectives* of the change

2 Prepare a tentative plan.
- Brainstorming sessions a good idea, since alternatives for change should be considered (Lippitt 1981)

3 Analyse probable reactions to the change

4 Make a final decision from the choice of alternative options
- Decision taken either by group problem-solving (participative) or by manager on his own (coercive)

5 Establish a timetable for change
- 'Coerced' changes can probably be implemented faster, without time for discussions
- Speed of implementation that is achievable will depend on the likely reactions of the people affected (all in favour, half in favour, all against etc)
- Identify those in favour of the change, and perhaps set up a pilot programme involving them. Talk with the others who resist the change

6 Communicate the plan for change
- This is really a continuous process, beginning at Step 1 and going through to Step 7

7 Implement the change. Review the change
- Continuous evaluation and modifications

2.2 Management must make sure that:

(a) they have the resources to make the change:

  (i) they have the money to buy the new equipment or premises or other assets they will need;

  (ii) they have the staff, properly *trained in advance* to deal with the new systems;

(b) the change is worth doing. The major test of whether a change is worthwhile is a cost-benefit analysis. The benefits from the change - which might be non-money benefits as well as money-benefits - must justify the costs of making the change. The costs of change include the time and effort it takes, as well as the money cost.

2.3 External consultants are sometimes brought in by organisations to investigate and formulate strategies for organisational development and change.

(a) *Benefits of using external consultants*

  (i) They will use analytical techniques and specialist knowledge, in which internal staff do not have the training.

(ii)   They bring experience from dealing with similar problems in other organisations.

(iii)   They can help with the resolution of internal conflicts within the organisation, by acting as an 'independent referee'.

(iv)   They are 'neutrals', outside departmental politics.

(v)   They are not tied by status or rank, and can discuss problems freely with the people involved, at all levels within the organisation.

(vi)   They can look at problems objectively, and unlike internal managers don't have to worry about the consequences of their recommendations for their jobs or career prospects.

(b) *Disadvantages of using consultants*

(i)   They might be seen as top management's 'poodles', or 'outside meddlers'.

(ii)   They might show an inclination to bring a standard solution to a unique problems, and fail to resolve the problem properly.

(iii)   They might be too academic, and lack experience in 'actual' management.

(iv)   They will need time to learn about an organisation, and 'acclimatise' themselves. The client organisation will have to pay consultancy fees for this learning process!

Evaluating change management

2.4   Change management will be judged to have been effective in much the same way that training effectiveness is validated (since organisational change is also a 'learning' process), ie by assessing:

(a) the impact of the change on organisational goals: has the change contributed to the overall objectives of the organisation as defined by the corporate plan?

(b) the success of the change in meeting its specified objective (and short-term targets set for progress measurement): has the change solved the problem?

(c) the behaviour of people in the organisation: has the change programme resulted in the behavioural changes planned (eg higher output, better teamwork, more attention to customer care)?

(d) the reaction of the people in the organisation: has the change programme been implemented without arousing hostility, fear, conflict, and its symptoms (absenteeism, labour turnover etc)?

2.5   Note that, like any management process, change management should be judged on two criteria:

(a) task effectiveness
(b) people satisfaction

2.6   There are many reasons why an organisation might fail to manage change successfully, including:

(a)   failure to identify the *need* to change (typically a failure to pay attention to change in the environment);

(b)   failure to identify the *objectives* of change, so that the wrong areas are addressed;

(c)   failure to identify correctly the strategy required, out of all the options, to achieve the objectives - so that change takes place, but not in the relevant direction. New technology, for example, is sometimes regarded as a universal solution to organisational problems - but won't necessarily improve productivity or profitability if the product/market strategy or workforce is the real problem;

(d)   failure to commit sufficient resource to the strategy;

(e)   failure to identify the appropriate method of implementing change, for the situation and the people involved (typically, failing to anticipate resistance to change);

(f)   failure to implement the change in a way that secures acceptance, because of the leadership style of the change agent (typically, failure to consult and involve employees).

2.7   The first four of the above reasons for failure are to do with strategic planning generally: they are potential shortcoming in any planning exercise. The peculiar difficulties of introducing *change*, however, are the human factors. We will now look more closely at human reactions to change, and how they affect change management.

3.   RESISTANCE TO CHANGE

3.1   Changes may affect individuals and groups in several areas.

(a)   There may be *physiological* changes, from changing work routines and patterns, location etc, and *circumstantial* changes - living in a new area, travelling a new route, establishing new relationships etc.

(b)   There may be *social* effects: the group membership dispersed, relationships disrupted, relative positions altered etc.

(c)   Above all, change affects individuals and groups *psychologically*.

   (i)   There is a sense of disorientation before new circumstances have been assimilated.

   (ii)   Uncertainty is increased, and this can lead to insecurity - especially in changes involving work, where pressures for continuity, progression and short learning curves can be acute.

   (iii) New relationships, challenges and pressures can radically affect people's self image and sense of competence: many people feel guilty and inadequate as 'beginners' or 'newcomers'.

   (iv)   Change imposed from without can seem particularly threatening if it is perceived to be outside the individual's or group's control and power to choose.

3.2 *Resisting* change means attempting to preserve the existing state of affairs – the status quo – against pressure to alter it. Despite the possibly traumatic effects of change *per se*, as discussed above, most people do *not* in fact resist it on these grounds alone. Many people – think of your own work situation – long for change, and have a wealth of ideas about how it should be achieved.

3.3 Sources of resistance to change itself may include age and inflexibility, strong needs for security, emotional instability etc. Sources of resistance to particular proposed changes – eg in location, methods of working, pay structure – may include the following.

(a) *Attitudes or beliefs*, perhaps arising from cultural, religious or class influences (eg resistance to change in the law on Sunday trading).

(b) *Loyalty to a group and its norms*, perhaps with an accompanying rejection of other groups, or 'outsiders' (eg in the case of a relocation so that two departments share office space). Groups tend to close ranks if their independent identity is threatened.

(c) *Habit, or past norms*. This can be a strong source of clinging to old ways, whether out of security needs, respect for tradition, or the belief that 'you can't teach an old dog new tricks' (eg resistance to the introduction of new technology).

(d) *Politics* – in the sense of resisting changes that might weaken the power base of the individual or group, strengthen a rival's position etc. Changes involving increased delegation may be strongly resisted by senior management, for example.

(e) The *way* in which any change is put forward and implemented – as we will discuss later.

Overcoming resistance to change

3.4 Three factors which might be helpful to managers in introducing change include:

(a) the pace of change;
(b) the manner of change; and
(c) the scope of change.

The pace of change

3.5 Changes ought generally to be introduced slowly. Apart from 'people problems', there may be a long planning and administrative process and/or financial risks to be considered, eg in a relocation of offices or a factory: a range of alternatives will have to be considered, information gathered etc. Change is, however, above all a 'political' process: relationships are changed, and must be reformed, old ways have to be unlearned and new ways learned.

3.6 The more gradual the change, the more time is available for questions to be asked, reassurances to be given and retraining (where necessary) embarked upon. People can get used to the idea of new methods – can get acclimatised at each stage, with a consequent confidence in the likely success of the change programme, and in the individual's own ability to cope.

Reasons for resisting change	Reasons for welcoming change
(a) Fear of personal loss	(a) Expectations of personal gain

(i)   security
    (ii)   money (eg. travelling costs to work, when a change of office location is proposed)
    (iii) pride and job satisfaction
    (iv) friends and contacts
    (v)   freedom
    (vi) responsibility
    (vii) authority/discretion
    (viii) good working conditions
    (ix) status	

(b) Can't see the need for change	(b) Change provides a new and welcome challenge
(c) Believes change will do more harm than good	(c) Change will reduce the boredom of work
(d) Lack of respect for the person initiating the change	(d) Likes/respects the source of the change
(e) Objection to the manner in which the planned change was communicated	(e) Likes the manner in which the change was suggested
(f) No participation 'We weren't asked'	(f) Participation in the decision
(g) Negative attitude to the job	(g) Wants the change
(h) Belief that the change is a personal criticism of what the individual has been doing	(h) The change improves the employee's future prospects
(i) Change requires effort	(i) The change comes at a good time
(j) The change comes at a bad time 'We have enough on our plate already'	
(k) Challenge to authority in the act of resisting change	

10: MANAGING CHANGE

The manner of change

3.7 The *manner* in which a change is put across is very important: the climate must be prepared, the need made clear, fears soothed, and if possible the individuals concerned positively motivated to embrace the changes as their own.

(a) Resistance should be confronted - not swept under the carpet to emerge later.

(b) There should be free circulation of information about the reasons for the change, its expected results and likely consequences. The information should appear sensible, clear, consistent and realistic.

(c) The change must be 'sold' to the people. Objections must be overcome - but it is also possible to get people *behind* the change in a positive way, if:

   (i) the reason for it can be put across. If those involved understand that there is a problem, which is real and poses a threat to the organisation and themselves, *and* that the solution is a sensible one and will solve the problem, there is a firm rational basis for change. Changes in *crisis* face far less resistance than *routine* changes;

   (ii) the organisation makes the change seem 'heroic' and exciting, emphasising the challenge and the opportunity, perhaps adding incentives or competitions for groups adapting best and quickest, coming up with ideas etc.

(d) Individuals must be helped to learn. Training must be given to prepare employees and to give them confidence. The 'big picture' of change should be communicated.

(e) The effects of insecurity, helplessness and resentment can be lessened if the people can be involved in planning and implementing the change. Change must be initiated from the top (otherwise the politics are too complicated) but consultation and participation should be used as much as the organisation culture and circumstances allow: employees will in any case have some valuable input.

3.8 A brief guide is outlined below

(a) *Tell* the people: clearly, realistically, openly.

(b) *Sell* the pressures which make change necessary and desirable, *and* the vision of successful, realistically attainable change.

(c) *Evolve* the people's attitudes, ideas, capacity to learn new ways.

(d) *Involve* the people where possible in planning and implementation.

Lewin's model of planned change

3.9 In the words of John Hunt (*Managing people at work*): 'Learning also involves re-learning - not merely learning something new but trying to unlearn what is already known.' This is, in a nutshell, the thinking behind Lewin/Schein's three stage approach to changing human behaviour, which may be depicted as follows.

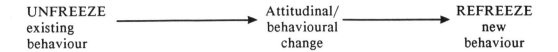

UNFREEZE   Attitudinal/   REFREEZE
existing   behavioural   new
behaviour   change   behaviour

3.10 *Unfreeze* is the most difficult (and in many cases neglected) stage of the process, concerned mainly with 'selling' the change, ie with giving individuals or groups a *motive* for changing their attitudes, values, behaviour, systems or structures. The method of 'unfreezing' existing behaviour will vary from situation to situation. If the need for change is immediate, clear and perceived to be associated with the survival of the individual or group (eg change in reaction to an organisational crisis), the unfreeze stage will be greatly accelerated. Routine changes may be harder to 'sell' than transformational ones, if they are perceived to be unimportant and not survival-based.

3.11 Various techniques may be used, depending on the nature of the change, the power of the change agent and the method likely to appeal to the individuals and groups involved: some will respond to conceptualisations, others respond to 'hands-on' trials, other emotive and cultural appeals etc. Group norms and peer pressure may be used.

3.12 Kurt Lewin's 'forcefield' theory can be used to indicate how 'unfreeze' works. The theory suggests that there is an equilibrium between opposing forces in the perception of those involved in change situations: driving forces for change, and restraining forces resisting change. People generally attempt to use driving forces for change - persuasion, threat etc - yet this often causes the restraining forces to become stronger, ie encourages resentment. Lewin suggested that a more effective way is to remove the restraining forces by identifying, discussing and mitigating the sources of resistance to change.

3.13 *Change* is the second stage, mainly concerned with identifying what the new, desirable behaviour or norm should be, communicating it and encouraging individuals and groups to 'own' the new attitude or behaviour.

3.14 *Refreeze* is the final stage, implying consolidation or reinforcement of the new behaviour. Positive reinforcement - praise, reward etc - or negative reinforcement - sanctions applied to those who deviate from the new behaviour - may be used.

3.15 The important point about Lewin's model is that it is designed to show how *attitudes* - not just behaviour - can be changed.

(a) People *will* change their *behaviour* if change is forced on them, presented as a 'fait accompli' without consultation, or 'sold' to them. But this only secures *compliance* - not acceptance - and resistance will still be there.

(b) People will change their *attitudes* only if the sources of resistance are confronted. This secures *acceptance*, which is harder to win, but provides more lasting and genuine commitment.

Exercise

Identify three changes (large or small) that have been introduced in your bank in the last year. How were they introduced? Did you know about them beforehand, or even help to plan them? Were they resisted?

---

4. CHAPTER ROUNDUP

'Dos' and 'don'ts' for the would-be 'change master'.

4.1 Tune into the company's external environment much more effectively. Only then will you be able to identify new needs.

4.2 Use 'kaleidoscope thinking' to create new approaches, by combining known facts and fragments to form different patterns. (This is one of the various definitions of creativity). This way of thinking can be stimulated throughout an organisation by encouraging playfulness and irreverence.

4.3 Develop the ability to create and communicate a clear vision. The importance of this is underlined by the fact that venture capitalists place more weight on the person behind a project than on the project itself.

4.4 Build coalitions, and don't spring new things on people.

4.5 Work through highly-motivated teams. 'Successful change efforts are associated with heightened teamwork.'

4.6 Persevere and persist. 'Everything looks like a failure halfway through, which is when the political problems arise.'

4.7 Share credit and recognition - 'make everyone a hero.'

The Change Masters, Rosabeth Moss Kanter
(as reviewed by Christopher Lorenz)

TEST YOUR KNOWLEDGE

The numbers in brackets refer to paragraph numbers of this chapter

1   In what areas is change most likely to be found? (1.3)

2   Outline the process of planning change. (2.1)

3   Why use external consultants? (2.3)

4   Why do individuals resist change? (3.3)

5   How can the *manner* of change help to overcome resistance? (3.7)

6   Outline the unfreeze/refreeze model of change. How would you apply it if you had to introduce new technology into your department, and you know your staff were feeling insecure and worried about it? (3.9 - 3.14)

Now try question 10 at the end of the text

PART C
MANAGEMENT PROCESSES, THEORIES, MODELS, SKILLS AND TECHNIQUES

Chapter 11

THE MANAGER

This chapter covers the following topics.

1. The functions of management
2. Managerial 'roles'
3. The managerial job

Introduction

In this chapter we re-introduce some of the concepts outlined in Chapter 1. However, we also identify some of the problems that arise with the descriptions of managerial functions. The manager's day to day activities are not characterised by uniformity but variety.

---

1. THE FUNCTIONS OF MANAGEMENT

1.1 The process of managing and the functions of management have been analysed many times, in various ways and by various writers, who have taken the view that:

(a) management is an operational process, which can be understood by a close study of management functions; and

(b) the study of management should lead to the development of certain principles of good management, which will be of value in practice.

1.2 The *Management in Banking* syllabus divides the processes of management into two sets:

(a) *managing the system*, ie forecasting, planning, organising, monitoring and controlling; and

(b) *managing the people*, ie relationship management with individuals and groups inside and outside the organisation.

The classical view

1.3 The ideas of Henri Fayol, the French industrialist and management theorist working in the early decades of this century, were one of the first systematic approaches to defining the manager's 'job'. According to Fayol, the process of management consists of five functions.

(a) *Planning*. This involves selecting objectives and the strategies, policies, programmes and procedures for achieving the objectives, either for the organisation as a whole or for a part of it. Planning might be done exclusively by line managers who will later be responsible for performance; however, *advice* on planning decisions might also be provided by 'staff' management who do not have 'line' authority for putting the plans into practice. Expert advice is nevertheless a part of the management planning function.

(b) *Organising*. This involves the establishment of a structure of tasks, which need to be performed to achieve the goals of the organisation, grouping these tasks into jobs for an individual, creating groups of jobs within sections and departments, delegating authority to carry out the jobs, providing systems of information and communication and co-ordinating activities within the organisation.

(c) *Commanding*. This involves giving instructions to subordinates to carry out tasks over which the manager has authority for decisions and responsibility for performance.

(d) *Co-ordinating*. This is the task of harmonising the activities of individuals and groups within the organisation, which will inevitably have different ideas about what their own goals should be. Management must reconcile differences in approach, effort, interest and timing of these separate individuals and groups. This is best achieved by making the individuals and groups aware of how their work is contributing to the goals of the overall organisation.

(e) *Controlling*. This is the task of measuring and correcting the activities of individuals and groups, to ensure that their performance is in accordance with plans. Plans must be made, but they will not be achieved unless activities are monitored, and deviations from plan identified and corrected as soon as they become apparent.

1.4 Several writers followed Fayol with broadly similar analyses of management functions. Other functions which might be identified, for example, are *staffing* (filling positions in the organisation with people), *leading* (unlike commanding, 'leading' is concerned with the interpersonal nature of management) and acting as the *organisation's representative* in dealing with other organisations (an ambassadorial or public relations role). Note the changing emphasis from classical to human relations ideas: many theorists now reject Fayol's concept of 'commanders', arguing instead that managers should approach the same function by being *communicators, persuaders* and *motivators*.

1.5 Another important role which we have mentioned elsewhere, but is not included in Fayol's model, is the *sustaining of corporate values*, ie the creation and maintenance of the *culture* of the organisation. Recent influential management books (eg *In Search of Excellence* by Peters and Waterman) have suggested that this is the vital role of management in today's business environment, since it determines how planning, organising, control and the other functions are carried out.

> 'A company is more than a legal entity engaged in the production and sale of goods and services for profit. It is also the embodiment of the principles and beliefs of the men and women who give it substance, it is characterised by guiding principles which define its view of itself and describe the values it embraces. Such values have, for our company, existed implicitly for very many years - [the company] is what it is and as good as it is because a great many individuals over a long period of time have contributed their own best efforts to preserving and enhancing the values that cause it to endure.'
>
> *Ethics and Operating Principles Handbook*, United Biscuits plc

11: THE MANAGER

The approach of Peter Drucker

1.6 Peter Drucker worked in the 1940s and 1950s as a business advisor to a number of US corporations, and was also a prolific writer on management. Drucker (in *The practice of management*) adds explicitly to Fayol's analysis the function of *communication*. It is a manager's task to communicate ideas, orders and results to different people, both within and outside the organisation. Communication is essential for planning, organising, motivating and controlling.

1.7 Drucker grouped the *operations* of management into five categories.

   (a) *Setting objectives* for the organisation. Managers decide what the objectives of the organisation should be, and quantify the targets of achievement for each objective. They must then communicate these targets to other people in the organisation.

   (b) *Organising the work.* The work to be done in the organisation must be divided into manageable activities and manageable jobs. The jobs must be integrated into a formal organisation structure, and people must be selected to do the jobs.

   (c) *Motivating employees* and communicating information to them to enable them to do their work.

   (d) *The job of measurement.* Management must:

   (i)   establish objectives or yardsticks of performance for every person in the organisation;

   (ii) analyse actual performance, appraise it against the objectives or yardsticks which have been set, and analyse the comparison;

   (iii) communicate the findings and explain their significance both to subordinate employees and to superiors.

   (e) *Developing people.* The manager 'brings out what is in them or he stifles them. He strengthens their integrity or he corrupts them'.

   Every manager performs all five operations listed above, no matter how good or bad a manager he is. A bad manager performs these functions badly, whereas a good manager performs them well.

1.8 Drucker has also argued that the management of a *business* has one overriding function - *economic performance*. In this respect, the business manager is different from the manager of any other type of organisation. Management of a business can only justify its existence and the legitimacy of its authority by the economic results it produces, however significant the non-economic results which occur as well.

1.9 Drucker described the jobs of management within this basic function of economic performance as follows.

   (a) *Managing a business.* The purposes of a business are:

   (i)   to create a customer; and

(ii)   innovation. (This is a very important concept for the modern business environment in conditions of change and competitive pressure. It emphasises the *entrepreneurial* aspect of management).

(b)   *Managing managers.* The requirements here are:

(i)   management by objectives;
(ii)   proper structure of managers' jobs;
(iii)   creating the right spirit in the organisation;
(iv)   making a provision for the managers of tomorrow;
(v)   arriving at sound principles of organisation structure.

(c)   *Managing the worker and work.*

1.10   Drucker called attention to the fact that these three jobs of management are carried out within a *time dimension.*

(a)   Management must always consider both the short-term and longer-term consequences of their actions. A business must be kept profitable into the long-term future, but at the same time, short term profitability must be maintained to avoid the danger that the long term will never be reached, (and in banks, immediate liquidity is also a conflicting priority).

(b)   Decisions taken by management are for the future, and some have a very long 'planning horizon': the time between making the decision and seeing the consequences of that decision can be very long. For example, if a decision is made to enlarge the ATM network of a bank, it might be years before the network is designed, equipped and in operation, and years more before it generates sufficient business to pay back the investment.

2.   MANAGERIAL 'ROLES'

2.1   Another way of looking at the manager's job is to observe what managers actually do, and from this to draw conclusions about what 'roles' they play or act out. This is known as the *managerial roles* approach.

2.2   Henry Mintzberg identified ten managerial roles, which may be taken on as appropriate to the personality of the manager and his subordinates and the nature of the task in hand.

(a)   *Interpersonal roles*

(i)	Figurehead	(performing ceremonial and social duties as the organisation's representative eg. at conferences)
(ii)	Leader	(of people, uniting and inspiring the team to achieve objectives)
(iii)	Liaison	(communication with people outside the manager's work group or the organisation)

(b)   *Informational roles*

| (i) | Monitor | (receiving information about the organisation's performance and comparing it with objectives) |
| (ii) | Disseminator | (passing on information, mainly to subordinates) |

(iii)	Spokesman	(transmitting information outside the unit or organisation, on behalf of the unit or organisation)

(c) *Decisional roles*

(i)	Entrepreneur	(being a 'fixer' - mobilising resources to get things done and to seize opportunities)
(ii)	Disturbance - handler	(rectifying mistakes and getting operations - and relationships - back on course)
(iii)	Resource allocator	(distributing resources in the way that will most efficiently achieve defined objectives)
(iv)	Negotiator	(bargaining - eg for required resources and influence)

2.3 The mix of roles varies from job to job and situation to situation: a manager will, as it were, put on the required 'hat' for his task. A manager will, however, wear some hats more than others: senior officials (say, the branch manager at local level, and the directors and general managers at corporate level) are more likely to be called upon to act as figureheads than sectional managers and supervisors, who will be more concerned with resource allocation and disturbance-handling.

2.4 In modern management theories, particular emphasis has been placed on leadership and entrepreneurship, at *all* levels of management. The cultural effects of both work at team as well as organisational level: involving and committing employees to achieving goals, and focusing on creative action and resource mobilisation to get things done.

3. THE MANAGERIAL JOB

3.1 What makes a manager's job different from a worker's? The difference can be expressed in terms of the functions and roles (discussed above) which are the prerogative of management. However, there are also particular *characteristics* of the managerial job.

3.2 The characteristics of the managerial job include the following.

(a) A *high level of activity*. Managers are very 'busy' in the sense that they tend to perform a high number of separate activities, and have a high number of interpersonal contacts, in the course of a day.

(b) *Discontinuity*. As the number of activities suggests, managers tend not to be able to spend long on single, continuous tasks. They are constantly interrupted by personal contacts and matters arising for their attention: telephone calls, meetings, people bringing information or problems, and 'deskwork' resulting from all of them. Managerial activity tends to be a rather unpatterned mixture of routine/planned and unplanned tasks.

(c) *Variety*. The nature and diversity of the managerial roles mean that managers have more job variety than most of their subordinates, covering differing types of activity including:

(i) paperwork (dealing with it *and* generating it);
(ii) telephone calls (taking and making);

(iii) meetings (formal - especially in more senior posts - and informal)

(iv) interpersonal contacts - (internal and - especially in senior and 'liaison' posts - external)

For each of these types of activity, the potential range of matters to be dealt with - ie job *content* - is extremely wide, since it is management's responsibility to handle the unforeseen and discretionary areas of business as well as the routine.

(d) *Separation* from the location and detail of operational work. The more senior the manager, the less he will be involved 'at the coal face' (relying on feedback through subordinates) and the more time he will spend outside his office, his department and even the organisation.

(e) *Talking and thinking*. Managers are expected (and paid) to perform much more 'brain' activity (such as thinking, planning, decision-making and problem-solving) than subordinates. They are not, in other words, expected to be as immediately and visibly productive as workers. In addition, up to 90% of total work time may be taken up in primarily *oral* activity: telephone calls, discussions, meetings etc.

(f) *Time span of discretion*. This was a term devised by Elliot Jaques to describe the amount of time between a decision or action taken by an individual, and the checking up on it and evaluation of it by the individual's superior. Low level employees are frequently monitored - in so far as they are allowed to exercise their own discretion at all - but managers perform actions and take decisions whose consequences may not emerge for a long time.

(g) *Networks*. The more senior a person is - and the more 'broad' his concerns in the organisation - the wider is the network of information in which he participates. Lower employees 'network' with peers in their immediate sphere of work, and with immediate superiors and subordinates. At higher levels, information for decisions, planning and control will be drawn from a wider set of contacts, including many sources outside the organisation.

Being a manager: the views of Handy

3.3 Charles Handy suggested that a definition of a 'manager' or a 'manager's role' is likely to be so broad as to be fairly meaningless. His own analysis of being a manager was divided into three aspects, based on the practice and experience of being a manager:

(a) the manager as a general practitioner;

(b) managerial dilemmas;

(c) the manager as a person.

The manager as a general practitioner

3.4 A manager is the first recipient of an organisation's health problem and he must:

(a) identify the symptoms in the situation (eg. low productivity, high labour turnover, severe industrial relations problems etc);

(b) diagnose the disease or cause of the trouble;

(c) decide how it might be dealt with - developing a strategy for better health; and

(d) start the treatment.

3.5 Typical strategies for improving the organisation's health might be as follows.

(a) *People*: changing people, either literally or figuratively, by:

    (i)   hiring and firing;
    (ii)   reassignment;
    (iii) training and education;
    (iv) selective pay increases;
    (v)   counselling or admonition.

(b) *The work and the structure*:

    (i)   re-organisation of reporting relationships;
    (ii)   re-definition of the work task;
    (iii) job enrichment;
    (iv) re-definition of roles.

(c) *The systems and procedures*, to amend or introduce:

    (i)   communication systems;
    (ii)   reward systems (payment methods, salary guides);
    (iii) information and reporting systems;
    (iv) budgets or other decision-making systems (eg stock control, debtor control).

Managerial dilemmas

3.6 The job of a manager is different from that of a worker, and managers are paid more than workers, because they face constant dilemmas which it is their responsibility to resolve. These dilemmas are as follows.

(a) *The dilemma of the cultures.* It is the manager's task to decide which 'culture' of organisation and management is required for his particular task and the people involved. As a manager rises in seniority, he will find it necessary to behave in a culturally diverse manner to satisfy the broader requirements of his job and the more diverse abilities, personalities and expectations of his employees. The manager 'must be flexible but consistent, culturally diverse but recognisably an individual with his own identity. Therein lies the dilemma. Those ...... who relapse into a culturally predominant style will find themselves rightly restricted to that part of the organisation where their culture prevails. Middle layers of organisations are often overcrowded with culturally rigid managers who have failed to deal with this cultural dilemma'.

(b) *The dilemma of time horizons.* This is the problem of responsibility for both the present and the future at the same time. Concentration on short-term success may be at the expense of the evolution and innovation required for survival and growth in the long term.

(c) *The trust-control dilemma.* This is the problem of the balance between management's wish to control the work for which they are responsible, and the necessity to delegate work to subordinates, implying trust in them to do the work properly. The greater the trust a manager places in subordinates, the less control he retains himself, which can be risky and stressful. Retaining control implies a lack of trust in subordinates which may create human relations problems. 'The managerial dilemma is always how to balance trust and control'.

(d) *The commando leader's dilemma.* In many organisations, junior managers show a strong preference for working in project teams, with a clear task or objective, working outside the normal bureaucratic structure of a large formal organisation and then disbanding. Unfortunately, there can be too many such 'commando groups' for the stability of the total organisation. A manager's dilemma is to decide how many entrepreneurial groups he should create to satisfy the needs of his subordinates and the demands of the task, and how much bureaucratic organisation structure should be retained for efficiency, consistency and 'safety'.

The manager as a person

3.7 Management is developing into a 'semi-profession' and managers expect to be rewarded for their professional skills. The implications for individual managers are that 'increasingly it will come to be seen as the individual's responsibility to maintain, alter or boost his skills, to find the right market for his skills and to sell them to the appropriate buyer'. The manager must be regarded as an individual in his own right, with his own objectives: he does not exist solely within and for the benefit of the organisation.

3.8 Another consequence of this is that the 'traditional' view that an organisation should employ 'raw recruits' and nurture them into its management structure might in future no longer be accepted. 'There will be no obligation to continue to employ the individual when the benefits of his skills begin to be less than their costs'.

3.9 As employees of banks, which still tend to retain the traditional view of management development, promotion, seniority and job security, you might well disagree with Handy's analysis in this matter: you may also not feel very confident about your 'mobility' or 'ownership' of your own career. However, increased specialisation, competition, technology and skill shortages are gradually eroding traditional structures and cultures of employment. Individual managers are starting to regard themselves (and be regarded) as human *resources*. They must be effective and efficient - like any other resource employed by the organisation - but they themselves are free to move elsewhere if the organisation does not satisfy their needs.

Exercise

Do you do 'managerial work'? In your own experience, is Mintzberg right? How much of your time is taken up with Fayol's five managerial functions, and with Mintzberg's managerial 'roles'.

---

4. CHAPTER ROUNDUP

4.1

Managerial

Functions	Roles	Characteristics
	Interpersonal	
Planning	Figurehead	Volume of work
Organising	Leader	Discontinuity
Controlling	Liaison	Variety
Co-ordinating	*Informational*	Talking/thinking
Commanding	Monitor	Discretion
[Leading/motivating]	Disseminator	Networks
Communication	Spokesman	Dilemmas
Economic performance	*Decisional*	
Culture creation	Entrepreneur	
	Disturbance-handler	
	Resource allocator	
	Negotiator	

TEST YOUR KNOWLEDGE
The numbers in brackets refer to paragraphs of this chapter

1   List Fayol's five functions of management. Indirect where you disagree or would add to with his analysis. (1.3 - 1.5)

2   What three 'jobs' of management, according to Drucker, are necessary in the management of a business, in the interests of economic performance? (1.9)

3   List the ten managerial roles identified by Mintzberg (2.2) and for each of them, identify the area of *your own job* in which you perform such a role.

4   Choose three characteristics of managerial jobs. (3.2) How do they apply to *your own job?*

5   What are the dilemmas facing a manager? (3.6)

6   What are the implications of regarding a manager as a person, rather than as the 'role' in the organisation, for:

    (a)   the manager himself; and
    (b)   the organisation? (3.7 - 3.9)

Now try question 11 at the end of the text

Chapter 12

DECISION-MAKING AND PROBLEM-SOLVING

This chapter covers the following topics.

1. What is a decision?
2. The decision sequence
3. Decision-making in practice
4. Delegation

Introduction

The earliest management authors highlighted decision-making as one of the key differences between management and workers. (Remember our early definition of management as deciding what should be done and getting people to do it.) However, as we shall see in Chapter 16, there are pressures to make front-line employees take more decisions and this means change to the manager's role.

1. WHAT IS A DECISION?

1.1 A decision may be defined as 'a formal judgement' or 'resolving to carry out a particular course of action'. In a business sense, a decision is usually the result of choosing between available or anticipated 'options' and is often taken on the grounds of future projections, subject to uncertainty and risk. The decision-making process is thus one involving value judgements and risk-taking.

1.2 Managers have varying levels of responsibility according to their positions in the organisation structure. They are expected to act within their responsibilities and to take required decisions within their scope of authority. Matters which cannot be adequately dealt with by a manager should be referred to more senior management.

1.3 The extension of this idea is that managers should *only* refer to more senior management decisions which are outside the scope of their own authority and/or ability. This is the principle of *exception*. A senior manager is only informed by his subordinates when there is a need, ie when there is some unplanned event, or some deviation from plan: he need not get unnecessarily involved or duplicate the decision-making delegated to his subordinates. This is the concept of delegation and referral, which we will be discussing later.

12: DECISION-MAKING AND PROBLEM-SOLVING

Types of decision

1.4 *Scientific decision-making* depends on the quantitative techniques of management. In this way, attempts are made to measure and express all viable alternatives. This approach depends upon the view that full and complete information will lead to the 'ideal solution'. It is generally agreed that this is an over-simplification and ignores individual flair or 'hunch'. It should also be recognised that many management decisions have to be taken in haste without the luxury of time in which to evaluate alternatives; otherwise events will continue to evolve and will enforce a decision which may not be the right one. If the manager were to postpone taking a decision until he obtained further information, he would be abdicating his responsibility.

['Analysis paralysis' is a catchy term for the inertia that sets in when managers attempt to get 'all' the information they think they need for a decision.]

1.5 *Reaction decisions* theory assumes that once policies and corporate plans are established, decisions that are required follow as a natural result of those plans. In this way, decision-making is regarded as an extension of the process of implementing corporate plans. Decisions therefore are partly predetermined by the detail of the plans.

1.6 Another way of looking at the decision structure of an organisation is to identify *levels* of decision-making:

(a) strategic decisions;
(b) administrative decisions; and
(c) operating decisions.

1.7 *Strategic decisions* are concerned with the problems raised by the environment in which the organisation operates and the courses of action open to it, specifically relating to product range and market potential, which will best achieve its objectives.

1.8 *Administrative decisions* are concerned with the development and structuring of the firm's resources to give effect to the strategic decisions. This involves recognising the operating needs created by the product-market strategy and providing the necessary framework within which these needs can be fulfilled. The administrative problem is concerned, therefore, with:

(a) organisation - the structuring of functional relationships, with attendant lines of authority and divisions of responsibility, workflows, information flows, distribution channels and location facilities; and

(b) resource acquisition and development - personnel training and development, financing and the acquisition of facilities and equipment.

1.9 *Operating decisions* occupy the greatest part of the managerial effort. These decisions tend to be repetitive and are capable of being programmed. Operating decisions are delegated to a large extent to lower management and are concerned with achieving the greatest revenue at the lowest cost within the constraints of the strategic decisions. The application of operating decisions relates to:

(a) allocation of resources among functional areas and product or service lines;
(b) scheduling of operations; and

(c) supervision of performance.

1.10 Another useful framework puts decisions into five categories.

(a) *Routine planning decisions;* typically, budgeting and scheduling.

(b) *Short-run problem decisions;* typically, decisions of a non-recurring nature. For example, a manager might have to deal with a staff problem, or give instructions to a subordinate about what to do next.

(c) *Investment or disinvestment decisions.* For example, should an item of equipment be purchased? Should a department be shut down? Decisions of this nature often have long-term consequences. For a banker, we might add a sub-category: *lending* decisions.

(d) *Longer-range decisions:* decisions made once and reviewed infrequently, but which are intended to provide a continuing solution to a continuing or recurring problem. These include decisions about selling and distribution policies (What type of customer should the branch attempt to attract? Should a new product or service be launched? Should staff be trained in customer service and selling skills?)

(e) *Control decisions;* decisions about what to do when performance is disappointing and below expectation.

Decisions as the solutions to problems

1.11 Decisions are not taken for the sake of it. If there was no uncertainty, dilemma or need, a decision would not have to be reached: activity would simply carry on as planned. Decisions can thus be seen as the *solutions to problems.*

1.12 Decisions are needed to resolve problems, when there is a choice about what to do. Problems vary, not just according to what they are about, but also according to:

(a) how easy or complex they are to resolve;

(b) how frequently they arise;

(c) whether the problem can be quantified, or whether there are qualitative matters of judgement involved;

(d) how much information is available to help the manager to make the decision;

(e) how serious the consequences would be if a bad decision were made;

(f) whose job it is to make the decision about how to deal with them.

1.13 Some problems are recurring, and have to be resolved fairly regularly. Other problems are occasional, perhaps unique, and difficult to foresee.

(a) *Recurring problems.* Problems which recur regularly can be dealt with in a routine or standardised way, with the help of *rules and procedures.* For example:

(i)   if a member of staff is continually late for work, a disciplinary code of practice should be available to give guidance to the employee's supervisor about what steps to take;

(ii)   if a supplier is late with a delivery, there should be procedures in the purchasing department for chasing it up.

(b) *One-off problems*. Problems of a non-recurring and non-foreseeable nature cannot be provided for in a book of rules and procedures. A higher decision-making ability is usually needed from managers to deal with such problems.

1.14 *Quantifiable* problems are problems where the likely outcome of each decision option can be measured and quantified, and the option which offers the 'best numbers' will be selected.

The outcome of a decision might be measured in:

(a) money terms - eg revenue, costs, profits;

(b) units of output or work - eg value or number of transactions processed, number of accounts opened, hours worked, number of employees or items of equipment utilised;

(c) productivity or efficiency - volume of work produced per unit of resource employed.

1.15 However, not all problems can be dealt with mathematically. Even with quantifiable problems, there will often be matters of doubt and uncertainty, where 'qualitative' factors will affect the outcome too.

Qualitative factors include risk, human behaviour and attitudes.

1.16 For example, a branch manager has to decide whether to introduce changes the procedures for handling routine transactions. These ideas for change would involve some re-grouping of staff, and some need for training with new computer software. They would improve the productivity of the back office and enable it to handle more work each week. However, the manager suspects that the work force will resist the change, and will insist on alterations to the proposals, and create a hostile atmosphere in the branch. Quantifiably, the decision should be in favour of change, but a qualitative factor that could change the decision is what the reaction of staff might be.

The need for judgement in decision-making

1.17 The more qualitative issues are involved in a decision, the more 'judgement' (or even intuition) will be needed. One final way of classifying decisions is according to how much judgement they require.

(a) *Programmed* decisions are decisions that conform to a standard pattern because they relate to a standard situation or problem. Programmed decisions might be incorporated into rule books or procedure manuals. For example, deciding what to do when a customer's cheque is not covered by sufficient funds can be made into a standardised procedure.

(b) *Non-programmed* decisions are decisions which call for managerial judgement, and which usually deal with non-standard situations. There is no rule or procedure that can be used to make a good decision. Decisions on how to launch a new service or product with maximum publicity impact would be non-programmed.

1.18 Programmed decisions lend themselves to automation, so that a computer can make the decision instead of humans. For example, if a bank wishes to send a reminder letter to every customer whose overdraft exceeds their agreed limit, a computer can 'decide' when to issue it.

2. THE DECISION SEQUENCE

2.1 There is a generally accepted rational model of decision-making and problem-solving.

	Action
We have a problem	Identify and specify the problem
	Analyse the problem
What solution can we find?	Appraise available resources
	List and compare alternative solutions
	Select the optimum solution
Now implement the solution	Draw up action plan to implement solution
	Carry out decisions required
	Check that solution has worked

Defining a problem

2.2 You can't find an answer unless you are *asking the right question*. If you regard the 'symptoms' of a disease as your problem and treat them, you will still not necessarily have cured the disease. Careful definition of the problem and examination of its causes frequently produce a definition of the solution. 'Indeed, the most common source of mistakes in management decisions is the emphasis on finding the right answer rather than the right question'.   (Drucker)

2.3 *Find the real problem and define it*. This involves finding the 'critical factor' in the situation. For example, a bank which is concerned about low profitability might apply all its efforts to cost-cutting, whereas the real problem might be a poor product mix, and insufficient attention to the needs of key segments in the market.

Two ways of helping managers to identify the critical problem are:

(a) assume that nothing will be done to deal with the problem, and ask the question: 'what will happen in due time?';

(b) look back in time and ask the question 'what would the situation be now if we had taken such-and-such action in the past?'

2.4 *Determine the conditions for the solution of the problem*. There may be certain constraints on the solution to the problem.

(a) Financial constraints. Expenditure limits are an obvious example. Another would be banks' need to maintain liquidity (ie sufficient cash and near-liquid funds to be able to repay depositors if necessary): this is a constraint on profitability, since the quicker an asset can be turned into cash, the lower interest it earns.

(b) Employee constraints. The abilities and willingness of employees (or lack thereof) may act as a constraint on proposed action. Management might be unable to recruit outside help (eg by hiring the services of a specialist organisation) without considering the consequent effects on internal morale and employee relations.

(c) Social or ethical constraints. There may be some restrictions on the decision imposed by the law, or by the requirement to uphold certain social or ethical standards.

Analysing a problem

2.5 The next stage in the decision process is to classify the type of problem faced and examine it. Classification of the problem is necessary in order to determine who will be responsible for dealing with it. It might be appropriate to classify problems according to the following.

(a) The *futurity of the decision*. Decisions which will have a long-term effect on the organisation should be taken by senior management, whereas decisions which have a short-term effect, or which can be reversed quickly if they are found to be wrong, can be taken by more junior managers. Decisions which have a longer-term effect usually *cost* the organisation more if they are wrong, and a related classification of decisions is according to the *cost of error*.

(b) The *impact of the decision on other areas or functions of the business*. Where other areas will be affected, decisions should be taken at a level of management which has authority over all the areas affected (or, if necessary, by joint agreement of two or more managers who pool their authority).

(c) The *number of qualitative factors involved in the decision*. Decisions calling for the exercise of careful management judgement should be taken by more senior managers.

(d) Whether the decision is 'one-off' or *unique*, or whether it is a decision involving a problem of a *routine nature*.

2.6 It is also necessary to find out as many facts about the situation as it is possible to obtain with reasonable effort and at reasonable cost. Most decisions are based on incomplete information, because:

(a) 'all' the information is not available; or

(b) beyond a certain point, the gathering of *more* information would not be worth the extra time and cost involved.

A good decision can be made without all the facts, but a manager must know what information is missing in order to evaluate the amount of *risk* he is taking with his decision.

Appraising available resources

2.7 The resources available to a manager to provide a solution to a problem may be not only financial.

(a) *Human:* numbers of personnel available and also their skills, training and experience. This information should be readily available to an organisation which has a manpower planning system.

(b) *Technical and physical resources:* including premises and computer capacity, information systems (the 'distribution' systems of many bank services), suppliers etc.

2.8 In evaluating resources, it is sensible to relate the *time-scale* of the problem to the time scale of the resources. For example, there is little relevance in attempting to solve an immediate short-term problem by deciding to use resources which will only become available over a longer-term period.

Listing and evaluating alternative solutions

2.9 There is rarely only one solution to a problem and much of a manager's skill will be exercised in framing, comparing and finally selecting between alternative solutions. Ways of generating alternative solutions are these.

(a) Sometimes the solution will be suggested by the way the problem is defined. If a fraud results from poor internal controls, then the solution will be to improve them. Where creative or innovative approohces to problem solving are required, it is advisable to generate as many options as possible.

(b) 'Brainstorming' is a technique usually involving a group, where ideas as 'thrown out' at random, without any critical evaluation or comment at this stage: people simply 'bounce' ideas off each other, hook into each other's train of thought to produce new ideas - so creativity is not stifled. It is a mistake to regard such techniques as a potential waste of time: they are a potential source of effective solutions.

(c) Lateral thinking exercises help the manager to see the problem in a new light.

2.10 In comparing the alternatives available, the manager must weigh the advantages and disadvantages of each course of action with the extent to which it satisfies the *objectives* of the decision. Any decision is based on risks and 'probabilities', especially where information is limited. Decision-makers can only speculate about the consequences of alternative courses of action, to compare their 'risk-gain' properties - but it is important to do so. It is the *consequences* of decisions that make a solution effective or ineffective, and desirable or undesirable for the organisation. (Even if a certain decision solves 'its' problem, it may *create* problems elsewhere).

Selecting the optimum solution

2.11 The criteria for selecting the best of the alternatives available are as follows.

(a) *Risk*. The size of the risk should be compared to the expected benefits. High-benefit, low-risk decisions are obviously preferable to low-benefit, high-risk decisions. However, it might be necessary to compare alternative A with a higher potential benefit, but higher risk of failure, against alternative B, which has a lower potential benefit but a greater chance of success.

(b) *Timing*. If the problem demands an urgent solution, a decision that 'dramatises' the decision might be best. On the other hand, if the problem requires a long-term approach to a solution, a decision which involves a slow start and a gradual gathering of momentum might be better. For example, if an organisation is faced with liquidation, the solution might be a dramatic cost-cutting exercise, or 'wielding the surgeon's knife' to get rid of unprofitable activities. On the other hand, if it is faced with a gradual decline in business, the decision might be of a gradual development of new products and new markets, or a gradual overhaul of the company's 'out-of-date' image etc.

(c) *Economy of effort*. A decision option which achieves the required results with the minimum of effort should be preferred to a decision which makes a 'song and dance' about arriving at a solution.

(d) *Limitations of resources*. As indicated earlier, a decision option must be feasible, and must not demand the consumption of resources (people, money, machines, materials) which the organisation does not have. Furthermore, a decision option which uses up smaller quantities of a scarce resource might be preferred to one which uses up more of it.

2.12 Quasi-mathematical and related quantifying techniques may be used to recommend a solution. Techniques which are widely used include:

(a) cost benefit analysis:
(b) discounted cash flow (DCF);
(c) simulation techniques; and
(d) probability theory and risk analysis.

The aim in using any such techniques is to quantify the risk, costs and benefits of a course of action.

2.13 If the information available is substantial and the risk-gain (or cost-benefit) equation is clear-cut, the decision maker is unlikely to overrule the objective evaluation with a subjective one of his own. However, it should be remembered that - particularly in highly qualitative problems, mainly 'people' problems - the manager *should* draw on his own:

(a) experience - for models and precedents and understanding;
(b) imagination - for envisaging decision options and potential consequences; and
(c) intuition - ie 'gut feeling'.

Implementation and follow-up

2.14 An action plan to implement the chosen decision should be drawn up by the manager responsible in consultation with the subordinate managers or workers who must put it into action. If a manager has to 'sell' his decision to his subordinates, it probably means that he has not consulted them properly in the evaluation of alternatives, and that he has made a decision which they are unwilling or unable to accept as a 'naturally' good choice out of the options available. We will discuss 'concensus' decision-making, and how managers can gain acceptance of decisions, a bit later.

2.15 Once a decision has been put into action, the decision process has not yet ended. It is necessary to make a subsequent check that;

(a) the decision was implemented fully, as intended; and

(b) the problem has been solved in the manner and to the extent anticipated.

This is a normal element of the management *control process*.

3. DECISION-MAKING IN PRACTICE

3.1 In practice, decision-making never seems as simple as the decision model makes it look - even taking into account the uncertainties and risks inherent in choosing options. The fact is that personality and organisational influences affect the decision-making process. Decision support systems may fail to provide the manager with timely and relevant information. The culture of the organisation, and the manager's own personality, may be resistant to the use of imagination and the taking of risks. Politics and employee relations may put human constraints on the manager's freedom to make decisions. Decision-making can be a stressful and emotional process - but few organisation cultures allow it to be seen as such.

Common faults in decision-making

3.2 Poor quality decisions most often arise from the following shortcomings of decision-makers.

(a) Failure to identify goals or objectives clearly. Poor quality decisions will result from failure to identify and state expected outcomes, or to recognise the short- or long-term nature of a decision. Proper evaluation of alternative options will not be possible in a vacuum.

(b) 'Analysis paralysis'. Decision-makers may not recognise the bounded rationality of decision-making, ie the fact that decision must be made with imperfect information. They may therefore keep delaying the point of decision (and action), pleading the need for more information and analysis. Opportunities may be lost in the meantime, and the waste of time and information search resources will be costly.

(c) Hurried decisions made with insufficient information. The decision-maker may feel unable to wait until full and relevant information is available, or he may be pressured into making a decision without giving sufficient attention to the information that has been given to him.

(d) Risk-aversion. Safe decisions have a certain 'negative' value in that they do not invite errors, but an element of adventure in decision-making is necessary for higher returns, and also to keep the organisation innovative and creative.

(e) Communication failure. This may apply both to the communication of decisions to those who have to implement them (in which case the decisions will be ineffective) and to the seeking of feedback information by which the outcomes of the decision can be monitored and controlled if necessary.

3.3 Following from the above, various factors may help to improve a manager's decision-making ability.

    (a) Managers should be trained and/or coached by more experienced colleagues to understand the structure of decision-making, ie the decision process discussed earlier.

    (b) The formal systems of the organisation - for planning, control, communication etc - should support the decision. The corporate plan, rules and policies etc may give guidelines; the control system should provide information; communication for and of decisions should be efficient.

    (c) Managers should receive the best possible information for decision-making, ie timely, relevant, accurate, sufficient but not excessive. This applies to the information needed for the decision, and also to feedback information which will help the manager and organisation to evaluate the quality of the decision. Operational research, organisation and methods, personnel and other management service departments might help to provide decision-support information.

    (d) Managers should receive the support of colleagues and superiors for innovative and risky decisions. Small failures should be permitted, if innovation and an action focus are not to be inhibited by fear of failure. Successful decisions should be recognised and rewarded: this is another reason why feedback information will be important in the learning process.

4. DELEGATION

4.1 *Delegation* is the process whereby a manager gives his subordinate(s) the authority to make decisions within a given sphere of influence. In other words, it is the way in which responsibility for decision-making is shared in the organisation.

4.2 It is generally recognised that in any large complex organisation, management must delegate some authority because:

    (a) there are physical and mental limitations to the work load of any individual or group in authority;

    (b) routine or less important decisions can be passed 'down the line' to subordinates, freeing the superior to concentrate on the more important aspects of the work (eg planning);

    (c) the increasing size and complexity of organisations calls for specialisation, both managerial and technical;

    (d) employees in today's organisations have high expectations with regard to job satisfaction - including discretion and participation in decision-making;

    (e) the managerial succession plan depends on junior managers gaining same experience of management processes in order to be 'groomed' for promotion.

4.3 Effective delegation consists of four stages.

    (a) The expected *performance levels* of the subordinate should be clearly specified. These should be fully understood and accepted by the subordinate.

(b) *Tasks should be assigned* to the subordinate who should agree to do them.

(c) *Resources should be allocated* and authority delegated to the subordinate to enable him to carry out his tasks at the expected level of performance

(d) *Responsibility should be exacted* from the subordinate by the superior for results obtained (because ultimate responsibility remains with the superior) – but within the scope of his delegated authority, the subordinate should have discretion to make decisions without requiring ratification by the superior.

Problems of delegation

4.4 In practice many managers are reluctant to delegate and attempt to handle many routine matters themselves in addition to their more important duties. Amongst the reasons for this reluctance one can commonly identify the following.

(a) Low confidence and trust in the abilities of the subordinates, ie the suspicion that 'if you want it done well, you have to do it yourself'.

(b) The burden of responsibility and accountability for the mistakes of subordinates, aggravated by (a) above.

(c) A desire to 'stay in touch' with the department or team – both in terms of workload and staff – particularly if the manager does not 'feel at home' in a management role, and/or misses aspects of the subordinate job, camaraderie etc.

(d) An unwillingness to admit that subordinates have developed to the extent that they could perform some of the manager's duties. The manager may feel threatened by this sense of 'redundancy'.

(e) Poor control and communication systems in the organisation, so that the manager feels he has to do everything himself, if he is to retain real control and responsibility for a task, and if he wants to know what is going on.

(f) An organisational culture that has failed to reward or recognise effective delegation by superiors, so that the manager may not realise that delegation is positively regarded (rather than a 'shirking' of responsibility).

(g) Lack of understanding of what delegation involves – ie *not* giving subordinates total control, making the manager himself redundant etc.

4.5 Handy writes of a 'trust-control dilemma' in a superior-subordinate relationship, in which the sum of trust + control is a constant amount:

$$T + C = Y$$

where T = the trust the superior has in the subordinate, and the trust which the subordinate feels the superior has in him;
C = the degree of control exercised by the superior over the subordinate;
Y = a constant, unchanging value.

Any increase in C leads to an equal decrease in T, ie if the superior retains more 'control' or authority, the subordinate will immediately recognise that he is being trusted less. If the superior wishes to show more trust in the subordinate, he can only do so by reducing C, by delegating more authority.

4.6 To overcome the reluctance of managers to delegate, the following is necessary.

(a) Provide a system of selecting subordinates who will be capable of handling delegated authority in a responsible way. If subordinates are of the right 'quality', superiors will be prepared to trust them more.

(b) Have a system of open communications, in which the superior and subordinates freely interchange ideas and information. If the subordinate is given all the information he needs to do his job, and if the superior is aware of what the subordinate is doing:

(i) the subordinate will make better-informed decisions;
(ii) the superior will not 'panic' because he does not know what is going on.

Although open lines of communication are important, they should not be used by the superior to command the subordinate in a matter where authority has been delegated to the subordinate; in other words, communication links must not be used by superiors as a means of reclaiming authority.

(c) Ensure that a system of control is established. Superiors are reluctant to delegate authority because they retain absolute responsibility for the performance of their subordinates. If an efficient control system is in operation, responsibility and accountability will be monitored at all levels of the management hierarchy, and the 'dangers' of relinquishing authority and control to subordinates are significantly lessened.

(d) Reward effective delegation by superiors and the efficient assumption of authority by subordinates. Rewards may be given in terms of pay, promotion, status, official approval etc.

When to delegate

4.7 A manager should be coached, if necessary, about the particular instances in which he should or should not delegate. He will have to consider the following issues.

(a) Whether he requires the *acceptance* of subordinates - for morale, relationships, ease of implementation of the decision etc. If so, he would be advised at least to consult his subordinates; if acceptance is the primary need and the decision itself is largely routine, eg in the case of canteen arrangements, office decor etc he should delegate.

(b) Whether the *'quality'* of the decision is most important, and acceptance less so. Many financial decisions may be of this type, and should be retained by the superior, who alone may be capable of making them. If acceptance and quality are equally important, eg for changes in work methods or the introduction of new technology, consultation may be advisable.

(c) Whether the *expertise or experience* of subordinates is relevant or necessary to the task, or will enhance the quality of the decision. If a manager is required to perform a task which is not within his own specialised knowledge, he should delegate to the appropriate person: the office manager may delegate repair and maintenance of machinery to an operations supervisor, perhaps.

(d) Whether, being as objective as possible, he feels he can trust in the competence and reliability of his subordinates. As Handy notes, there is bound to be a dilemma here, but the manager is accountable for his own area of authority, and should not delegate if he *genuinely* lacks confidence in his team (in which case, he has other problems to solve).

(e) Whether the task or decision requires tact and confidentiality, or, on the other hand, maximum exposure and assimilation by employees. Disciplinary action, for example, should not be delegated (ie to a peer of the individual concerned), whereas tasks involving new procedures to which employees will have to get accustomed may be delegated as soon as possible.

(f) His own personality and leadership style.

4.8 In instances where *reference upwards* in the scalar chain to the manager's own superior may be necessary, the manager should consider:

(a) whether the decision is *relevant* to the superior, ie will it have any impact on his area of responsibility, eg strategy, staffing, or the departmental budget?

(b) whether the superior has *authority* or *information* relevant to the decision that the manager does not possess: eg authority over issues which affect other departments or inter-departmental relations, or information only available at senior levels;

(c) the *political climate* of the organisation, ie will the superior expect to be consulted, and resent any attempt to make the decision without his authority? Are there, on the other hand, useful 'points' to be scored for showing initiative and independence (especially if the decision is a success)?

4.9 The general structure and accepted practices of the organisation will partly decide the extent to which a manager will delegate decisions to subordinates, or refer them to his superior: eg if the corporate culture favours participation, group decision-making, a consultative style of management etc.

Exercise

Have you ever had to delegate? Did you feel reluctant to delegate (see paragraph 4.4)? How about your boss? Does your boss find it easier in your opinion to delegate than you?

Groups and decision-making

4.10 *Group* decision-making is another possibility for a manager who wishes to delegate decisions. It may be of benefit in some instances.

(a) Pooling skills, information and ideas - perhaps representing different functions, specialisms and levels in the organisation - could increase the quality of the decision. Groups have been shown to produce better evaluated (although fewer) decisions than individuals working separately: even the performance of the group's best individual can be improved by having 'missing pieces' added by the group.

(b) Participation in the decision-making process makes the decision acceptable to the group, whether because it represents a compromise or consensus of all their views, or because they have simply been consulted and given a sense of control and input.

4.11 However, group decision-making might be dangerous.

(a) Groups can suffer from 'group think' - 'the psychological drive for concensus at any cost, that suppresses dissent and appraisal of alternatives in cohesive decision-making groups'. In other words, a close-knit group may become blinkered to what is going on around it and maintain its sense of unity by ignoring divergent views and facts which shake its sense of invulnerability, creating a support for 'pet' decisions regardless of risk.

(b) Groups may have their own 'agenda' and make decisions to further their own - rather than the organisation's - objectives.

(c) Individuals in groups tend to take greater risks than they would on their own. The explanations of this 'risky-shift' phenomenon are:

(i) the sharing - and therefore diffusion - of any sense of responsibility for the outcome of the decision;

(ii) the reinforcing during discussion of cultural values associated with risk: courage, boldness, strength etc. In some cultures - including those fostered by contemporary ideas on 'excellence', innovation, entrepreneurship etc - such values may be put forward as desirable and 'risk aversion' derided.

4.12 With critical decisions, where quality is the prime objective, it may be more helpful for a manager to involve work groups in areas such as problem definition and formulation of alternative solutions to take advantage of the collective skills and experience of group members and the creativity of group idea-generation.

4.13 The choice of decision might be best left to the manager responsible. Some 'acceptance' advantages might still have been gained by the consultative process.

4.14 The concept of empowerment is relevant here; it is discussed in Chapter 20.

5. CHAPTER ROUNDUP

5.1

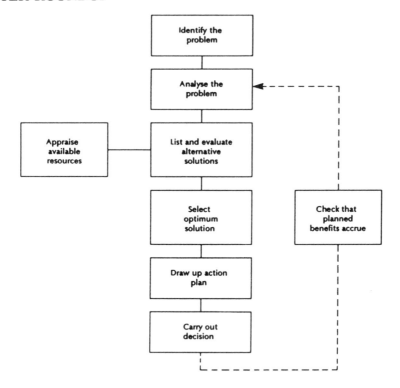

5.2 The extent to which decision-making is shared will depend on:

(a) the need for quality (whether or not the manager will be able to make the best decision on his own);

(b) the need for acceptance (whether or not the manager can and must secure the co-operation of the people affected by the decision);

(c) the culture and structure of the organisation.

'Two heads are better than one' *vs* 'Too many cooks spoil the broth'

5.3 Common faults in decision-making are:

Communication failure
Insufficient information
Goal-lessness
Analysis paralysis
Risk-aversion

TEST YOUR KNOWLEDGE
The numbers in brackets refer to paragraphs of this chapter

1   What are the classifications of types of decision based on:

    (a)   level in the decision structure? (1.6, 1.7)
    (b)   amount of human judgement required? (1.17)

    Give examples.

2   List the stages in the sequence of problem-solving. (2.1)

3   How can managers go about 'defining the problem' effectively? (2.2, 2.3)

4   What is 'brainstorming'? (2.9)

5   What criteria should a manager use when selecting his best decision option? (2.11)

6   What organisational conditions give a manager the best possible support for decision-making? (3.3)

7   Why is delegation necessary? (4.2)

8   Why are managers often reluctant to delegate? (4.4, 4.5)

9   When should a manager delegate a decision to his subordinates? (4.7, 4.9, 4.13)

10   What tendencies of work groups might discourage a manager from delegating authority for decision-making to a group? (4.12)

Now try question 12 at the end of the text

Chapter 13

PLANNING AND CONTROLLING

> **This chapter covers the following topics.**
>
> 1. The management functions of planning and control
> 2. Planning
> 3. An approach to planning and control
> 4. Project management
> 5. Management by objectives
> 6. Control systems
> 7. Cost management and budgetary control
>
> **Introduction**
>
> In this chapter, we look more closely at planning as a management activity, and at some of the processes of monitoring and 'controlling' subordinates that arise naturally out of the planning process. In this context, we also cover 'management by objectives' as an approach to planning and control.

1. THE MANAGEMENT FUNCTIONS OF PLANNING AND CONTROL

1.1 There is a convenient, theoretical break-down of management decisions into planning decisions and control decisions.

1.2 Robert N Anthony argued, however, in his book *Planning and Control Systems: a Framework for Analysis* (1965) that 'although planning and control are definable abstractions and are easily understood as calling for different types of mental activity, they do not relate to separate major categories of activities actually carried on in an organisation either at different times, or by different people, or for different situations'.

1.3 In fact, managers carry out planning and control activities at the same time; control action responds to deviations from plan, and plans must be made or altered in order to effect control measures. Anthony developed his framework of 'strategic planning/management control/ operational control' (discussed in Chapter 22) as a way of categorising areas of decision-making *without* using what he thought of as a false distinction between 'planning' and 'control' decisions.

1.4 How does this relate however to Mintzberg's 'roles'? Planning involves resource allocation, a manager's responsibility. The manager might delegate some of the mechanics of planning to subordinates, so this will be an aspect of the manager's *decisional* role.

2. PLANNING

2.1 If individuals and groups within an organisation are to be effective in working for the achievement of the organisation's objectives, they need to know what it is that they are expected to do. This is the purpose of planning:

    (a) to decide objectives for the organisation;
    (b) to identify alternative ways of achieving them; and
    (c) to select from amongst these alternatives for both the organisation as a whole, and also for individual departments, sections and groups within it.

2.2 Planning involves decisions about:

    (a) what to do in the future;
    (b) how to do it;
    (c) when to do it;
    (d) who is to do it.

2.3 The future cannot be foreseen with certainty, and even the best-laid plans will go wrong to a greater or lesser degree; nevertheless, plans give direction to an organisation. Without plans, events will be left to chance.

Barriers to good planning

2.4 Planning is obviously essential and an all-round 'good thing' for the organisation. In practice, however, many managers are reluctant to make formal plans, and prefer to operate without them, dealing with problems only when and if they arise. The reason for their reluctance to plan might be as follows.

    (a) *A lack of knowledge (or interest) about the purpose and goals of the organisation.* However, unless a manager knows what the organisation's goals are, and how other departments and sections are trying to work towards those goals, his own efforts might well either:

        (i) duplicate the efforts of someone else, thereby causing a waste of time and resources;
        (ii) conflict with the efforts of someone else; or
        (iii) simply be useless to the organisation.

    Good planning encourages the co-ordination of efforts within an organisation.

    (b) *A reluctance to be committed to one set of targets.* Planning involves making a choice about what to do, from amongst many different alternative courses of action. A manager might want to keep his options open, especially where the business environment is changing rapidly and the future is (even more than usually) uncertain: he will not want to have specific goals. Whereas this is understandable, and might be feasible in a very small organisation, it is unsatisfactory in any organisation where managers must co-ordinate their efforts and work together for the achievement of organisational goals. Freedom of choice could well be a recipe for *lack* of preparation for environmental changes, and a lack of co-ordinated response to economic, technological, social and political developments etc with which the organisation will be faced.

    (c) *A fear of blame or criticism for failing to achieve planned targets.* By setting targets or plans, and later comparing actual performance against plans, it is possible to identify success or failure. When failure is 'punished' in any way (eg in the form of lower salaries or bonuses, thwarted promotion prospects and career ambitions, or even the displeasure of superior managers) managers might resent planning, because planning is the start of a process by which they might later be labelled as failures. (The motivation to plan for inefficient performance will also be strong, since the likelihood of 'failure' will then be relatively low).

(d) *A manager's lack of confidence in himself to perform his job efficiently and effectively,* or a lack of confidence in the organisation's senior management to provide him with the resources he needs to achieve his planned targets.

For example, suppose that the manager of a bank branch is asked to plan the target volume of turnover and profits in the next two or three years. The manager might lack confidence in head office to provide him with enough resources (staff, equipment, product ranges, money for sales promotion etc) to achieve a reasonable targeted performance; or if he did have sufficient resources, he might doubt his own ability to ensure that the targets are achieved. The manager would then prefer instead not to have any plans or targets at all.

(e) *A manager's lack of information about what is going on in the 'environment'.* Managers need to know about the needs of customers, the nature of their markets and their competition, the strength of public opinion or government pressures, the state of the economy etc. Without such information, they will be unable to make plans for the future which are achievable in view of environmental conditions. For example, when the Monopolies and Mergers Commission announced its intention to investigate credit cards, banks needed to know about the timing, nature and enforcement of its report before they could plan properly for its consequences.

(f) *A manager's resentment of plans made on his behalf.* Some managers have plans imposed upon them without any prior consultation at all. If a manager is told what he must do and what his targets are, he is likely to resist the plan, and find reasons why it is not achievable - especially if the politics of the situation, and his relationship with his superiors, are already 'sensitive'.

2.5 The barriers to good planning must be overcome.

(a) All levels of staff should be involved (to a greater or less degree) in the planning process. Imposing plans on staff without their participation, or without their opinions being sought, is a barrier to successful planning. A thorough-going approach to participation in planning, and integration of all plans in the organisation, is management by objectives (MBO).

(b) Planners must be provided with the information they need (and access to sources of future information, when it arises) to plan properly. The source of information might be:

(i) outside the organisation, concerning environmental factors;

(ii) inside the organisation, concerning facts about the organisation itself. This information is called 'feedback'.

(c) A system of rewards for successful achievement of plans might be beneficial. However, a system of rewards is also a system of punishment for those managers who fail to earn rewards. The motivational problems of rewards and punishments are not easily overcome, and are likely to be a continual barrier to good planning: again, MBO attempts to address this issue.

(d) Managers should be taught the virtues of planning, and the techniques of good planning. For example, managers should learn the value of co-ordinating efforts for the achievement of common goals; and the managers should also learn that a subordinate can only be expected to achieve certain targets if he is given sufficient resources to do his job properly.

Types of plan

2.6 The most important types of plan for our purposes are as follows.

(a) *Objectives* for the organisation as a whole. An objective is an end goal towards which all activities should be aimed. This might be to earn a profit, or provide a certain service. It might also be possible to distinguish between a mission for the organisation (eg to provide a certain type of product in order to satisfy a certain type of customer need or need of society) and an objective (eg to make a profit whilst accomplishing the organisation's mission). Individual departments or divisions may also have objectives.

(b) *Strategies* follow on from the determination of long-term goals and objectives. Strategies are plans of activity (mainly long-term) and plans for the allocation of resources which will achieve the organisation's objectives. There are different types of strategy. For example:

    (i) a product/market strategy is a plan about the types of product or service an organisation should provide and about the types of market in which it should be trying to sell those products or services;

    (ii) a manpower strategy is a plan about the number and types of staff which will be required in the long term to achieve the organisation's goals.

(c) *Tactics*. These are the means by which strategies are implemented, at a detailed level.

(d) *Policies* are general statements or 'understandings' which provide guidelines for management decision-making. Policy guidelines should allow managers to exercise their own discretion and freedom of choice, but within certain acceptable limits. Company policies might be, for example:

    (i) to promote managers from within the organisation wherever possible instead of recruiting managers to senior positions from 'outside';

    (ii) to encourage all recruits to certain jobs within the organisation to work towards obtaining an appropriate professional qualification;

    (iii) to grant loans to individuals fulfilling certain criteria of credit-worthiness.

(e) A *budget* is a plan for carrying out certain activities within a given period of time, in order to achieve certain targets. The budget indicates how many resources will be allocated to each department or activity in order to carry out the planned activities. Budgets are formal statements of expected results, set out in numerical terms and summarised in money values.

The steps in planning

2.7 The steps in a planning decision are given below.

(a) Recognising an opportunity to be exploited or a problem to be dealt with.

(b) Establishing goals or objectives as the end result of exploiting the opportunity or solving the problem.

(c) Forecasting relevant information (eg about products, markets, competition, prices, wage rates, technology etc). Planning premises should be established which are agreed and used by managers throughout the organisation. An accepted set of premises about the environment in which the organisation will operate, and the resources it will have at its disposal, will provide guidelines for planning decisions.

(d) Considering alternative 'realistic' courses of action for the achievement of the objectives.

(e) Comparing the alternative courses of action, and selecting the best course.

(f) Formulating detailed plans for carrying out the chosen course of action.

2.8 In fact, however, 'planning' does not really stop at this stage.

(a) In order to complete the planning process (as with any type of decision) it is necessary to verify whether or not the plan has worked or is working, and whether the objectives of the plan have been/are being achieved. This is where 'control' becomes part of the planning process.

(b) Actual results and performance are therefore compared to the plan. If there are deviations, weaknesses or errors, control measures will be taken - which involves adjusting or setting further plans for ongoing action. This is where 'planning' becomes part of the control process.

3. AN APPROACH TO PLANNING AND CONTROL

3.1 An integrated approach to planning and control in practice provides the basis for:

(a) the scheduling and allocation of *routine* tasks in your section, so that they are completed on time and without 'bottlenecks' or idle periods for people or equipment;

(b) the handling of *high-priority* tasks and deadlines - working into the routine urgent tasks which interrupt the usual level of working (eg preparation of a report, completion of a project);

(c) adapting to changes and unexpected demands - ie having the 'machinery' to deal with emergencies, as far as possible;

(d) establishing standards for working, against which actual performance can be measured;

(e) the co-ordination of individual and combined efforts;

(f) efficient use of premises, equipment, information and human effort in the achievement of goals.

Components of the integrated approach

3.2 The *aims* of the section and each job within it, and therefore the results that are to be achieved will be defined.

3.3 *Key tasks* will be identified (ie those which are 'critical' to successful completion of the work: if they are not done on time and to the required standard, other tasks will be affected and results not achieved). Another term for this process may be '*prioritising*', ie considering tasks in the order of their importance for the objective concerned. A job will be critical or 'high-priority' compared to other tasks, if:

(a) it has to be completed by a 'deadline' in order to fulfil its objective;
(b) other tasks depend on its completion;
(c) the potential consequences of failure are long-term, difficult to reverse, far-reaching and costly.

3.4 *Performance standards*, will be set ie indicators that the job is being done 'well' and contributing to the fulfilment of objectives.

(a) Standards should be quantified as far as possible so as to be measurable and specific. They should also be:

(i) relevant to the attainment of objectives; and
(ii) attainable - yet challenging (so as not to encourage sub-optimal performance).

(b) Effective standards usually relate to specific targets for cost, time taken, quantity and quality of output, or all of them together, eg X staff should process Y items per hour, under normal conditions, with an error rate of no more than 1%.

(c) *Work measurement* is the application of techniques to establish the standard time it takes an average worker under normal conditions to perform a specified task at a specified level of performance. (Allowances are built in for rest and relaxation periods and fluctuations in performance due to fatigue, emotional state etc.)

(d) Note that not all types of work will be measurable in terms of 'output' (jobs completed). Routine, repetitive and mechanised jobs will be fairly easy to set quantified standards for, but jobs involving meetings, telephone calls, customer contact, planning, research, 'thinking' and other non-routine, non-repetitive tasks will be harder: what is their value to the organisation relative to the time they take? Even overall 'time spent' on such tasks may be hard to measure, because they tend to be more interrupted and various.

3.5 Setting *short-term goals* for key tasks, so that progress towards longer-term goals can be monitored at suitable intervals for control action to be taken.

3.6 *Action-planning.* On an operational work planning level, this may means *scheduling* or timetabling tasks, and *allocating* them to people within appropriate timescales so that the flow of work within and through the section is smooth and continuous as far as possible. Some 'slack' or flexibility should be allowed for unscheduled events (aided by the prioritising exercise: some other tasks may be temporarily pushed aside by higher-priority intervening tasks). 'Contingency plans' may be used to cope with some 'rogue' events that can be envisaged (eg a 'virus' attacking the branch's computer system).

Other tactical action plans will specify and initiate the tasks required to achieve goals in the short and longer term: staff may require training in order to maintain or improve performance standards; new equipment or systems may need to be implemented etc;

3.7 *Monitoring and control.* Control information should be fed back to the planner to indicate:

(a) whether short-term goals are being met, and performance is therefore 'on target' to meet its objectives;

(b) whether performance standards are being maintained;

(c) the extent of any shortfall or deviation, eg if a 'critical' activity has started running late, if there is a backlog of work, if any of the assumptions in the plan, (eg about work volume or staff availability) are not borne out in practice;

3.8 *Control action.* The range of possible responses may be:

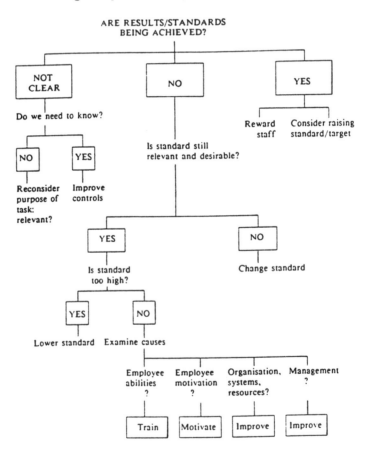

4. PROJECT MANAGEMENT

4.1 Project management is a particularly complex exercise in planning and control, because it involves:

(a) staff possibly from different disciplines and levels of the organisations used to different objectives, timescales and cultures of work;

(b) a complex sequence of inter-related tasks, over a potentially long time-span;

(c) elements of 'matrix' organisation: the project manager will not necessarily be seen as the 'rightful leader' of the group, at first.

A project team is said to be a co-ordinating mechanism in the organisation: first, however, it needs to be co-ordinated itself!

> We will discuss some of the uses of project teams in banking in Chapter 17.

4.2 A project by definition has a purpose or aim, and the project team will be disbanded once its purpose has been fulfilled. The first requirement, therefore, is for *terms of reference*. The project manager needs a concise and specific statement of:

(a) objectives;
(b) timetable; and
(c) estimated/acceptable costs.

4.3 The *management structure* of the project team mirrors the roles requires in the organisation as a whole.

(a) The project needs a 'sponsor' or 'champion' in the organisation, someone in a position of influence who wants to achieve the project's aims, and will push for resources etc on its behalf.

(b) A project manager will have overall control. For a small project, this may be sufficient but more complex operations may have a *director* - in an overseeing, co-ordinating role - who delegates areas of activity to *project leaders*.

4.4 *Group members* should be selected on the basis of expertise (although special training or briefings may be given) and potential for contribution to the aims of the project: this includes their ability to work together as a team. A project group will not necessarily be 'continuous', ie it may meet infrequently, and will not necessarily naturally unite under its chosen leader. Careful attention will therefore need to be given to the followning.

(a) *Co-ordination*. Team members working independently will need to be allocated clearly defined tasks and timetables.

(b) *Motivation*. Focus should be on the challenge of the task. Team identity may be a source of motivation if it can be exploited. Reward according to results is likely to be the system used.

(c) *Control*. Progress and development should be regularly checked, particularly for key or 'critical' tasks and stages of the project.

(d) *Communication*. This will be essential between team members, but the project manager will also have to be aware of people outside the project who need to be kept informed of changes to the timetable, or implications of the project work which will effect their work. A project team created, say, to prepare guidance notes on a new piece of legislation affecting banking might offer advance warning to relevant departments, or might refer to them for information about the current procedures that would be affected.

4.5   *Planning* will follow the general sequence discussed earlier, with performance standards, reporting procedures, review dates and targets etc. There are various ways of planning for sequences of actions. Simple methods include:

(a)   *Activity scheduling* (lists of necessary activities in the order in which they must be completed, like a checklist).

(b)   *Time scheduling* adds timescales for each activity and is useful for setting deadlines and review dates.

   The time for each step is estimated; the total time for the task can then be calculated, allowing for some steps which may be undertaken simultaneously by different people or departments.

(c)   *Job cards* or *action sheets:* detailed work programs for each person or task, based on time schedules and final deadlines.

	Activity	Days before	Date	Begun	Completed
1	Request file	6	3.9		
2	Draft report	5	4.9		
3	Type report	3	6.9		
4	Approve report	1	8.9		
5	Signature	1	8.9		
6	Internal messenger	same day	9.9		

Network analysis

4.6   A more sophisticated approach to the planning and control of complex projects is *network analysis*. The basis of network planning is the representation of the *sequential* relationship between tasks using linking lines. The optimum pattern of links, whereby the total time spent on the project is as short as possible, is called the 'critical path'. Here are the two most common techniques of network planning.

(a)   Critical Path Analysis (CPA), used in large, complex projects eg in construction and manufacturing;

(b)   Programme Evaluation and Review Technique (PERT), which tends to be applied to one-off projects of a complex nature or where time or cost are of overriding importance.

4.7   The basic network is a combination of the following.

(a)   *Events:* the start or end points of an activity (finished reading a chapter, done the 'test your knowledge' quiz). Events are shown as a circle or *node*, usually identified by a short description of the event, or a code number.

(b)   *Activities:* actions which proceed through time (eg reading chapter, doing quiz). Activities are shown as arrows and are usually designated by letters.

(c) *Dummy activities:* actions which do not take time, but link other activities (eg applying your reading of the chapter to the questions in the quiz), and so must be shown to maintain the logic of the network. Dummy activities are shown by dotted arrows.

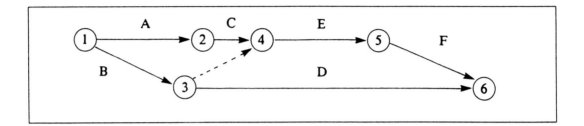

4.8 The 'critical path' is the longest sequence of activities through the network from beginning to end: there is only *one* start event and *one* finish event. Events on the critical path must be carefully monitored: if they are behind schedule or below standard, the whole network is affected. Another convention is that an event is not complete until all activities leading to it are themselves complete, ie the network always moves forward in time: you cannot go back along the critical path to 'polish off' unfinished business, but must redraw the network.

4.9 Times and costs and other relevant information can be added to the model as it is built up. Events may be marked, for example, with the earliest date on which each can start and the last date by which it must be finished if the critical path is not to be broken.

4.10 Networks can be useful in:

(a) providing a logical picture of the sequence of a complex project, its 'layout' over time and the relationships between its components;

(b) identifying activities and events which are critical to the success of the whole project;

(c) estimating the times, costs and resources involved in the project;

(d) providing the project manager with a tool for co-ordination and motivation;

(e) planning and controlling complex sequences of interdependent activities in projects.

Exercise 1

Take a task or project you have been allocated in your work. Draw up a plan, following the steps identified in paragraph 4.7.

---

5. MANAGEMENT BY OBJECTIVES

5.1 We have already talked about the 'hierarchy' of objectives in the organisation, from company objectives and strategic plans down through sub-unit plans for management control, to short-term operational control targets.

Management by objectives (MBO) is a comprehensive approach to planning and control which attempts:

(a) to co-ordinate short-term plans with longer-term plans and goals;
(b) to co-ordinate the plans (and commitment) of junior with senior management;
(c) to co-ordinate the efforts of different departments;
(d) to focus on *results* (system outputs) rather than on *activity* (system processes); and
(e) to improve management performance.

5.2 There are two possible approaches to establishing a hierarchy of objectives that will achieve the above aims.

(a) Senior managers (perhaps the managing director himself) can tell managers what to do and set up control procedures. John Humble, a leading advocate of MBO, comments that 'this apparently sensible and logical approach often misses the spark of vitality, challenge and involvement on which the real use of human beings depends'. It is 'top-down' management.

(b) Develop the contribution and motivation of each manager in the business by involving him in the planning process. This approach introduces an element of 'bottom-up' management, organised within the framework of corporate objectives and strategic plans, and offers the opportunity to integrate organisational goals (such as profit and growth) with the needs of individual managers to contribute to the organisation and to their own self development.

5.3 Advocates of MBO (Drucker, Humble etc) argue that managers will only be committed to their objectives if they are allowed to assume responsibility for setting them. Higher management should:

(a) reserve the right to approve or disapprove the manager's objectives, set by himself;

(b) help the manager to set his objectives by communicating to him the goals and broad strategies of the organisation over the corporate planning period;

(c) give the manager the information he needs to control his own performance, as soon as the information can be made available (economically) for him to use. The control information should go directly to him, and not to his boss. Control should not be seen to come down from above.

Management development is a key feature of MBO and it will only be successful if managers are given the responsibility for setting their own objectives (in consultation perhaps with their superiors).

Management by objectives : the approach in more detail

5.4 Humble described the typical sequence of events for the introduction of a scheme of management by objectives as follows.

(a) The objectives of the 'sub-units' of the organisation (subsidiaries, departments, sections etc) are identified, in accordance with the overall corporate plan.

(b) An analysis must be prepared, in consultation with each manager, of the *key results* that are critical to the successful performance of his job and the *key tasks* by which these results are achieved. (Unlike an ordinary job description, this analysis does not simply list *all* the tasks of the manager's job, but identifies the critical and potentially most productive elements of it, for which specific objectives must be reached.)

(c) *Performance standards* and *short-term targets* are agreed for the key tasks of each manager.

(d) Top management assesses the 'unit' objectives and the key results for each manager:

   (i)   to ensure that unit objectives are consistent with each other and with overall corporate objectives;

   (ii) to identify common areas for improvement and ensure that the best joint approach is being taken to deal with them;

   (iii) to assign priorities for improvement schemes and objectives;

   (iv) to check that every key area of business performance is the responsibility of one manager, and that there are no gaps in the control system.

(e) Top management formulates the *unit improvement plan*. From this, *job improvement plans* for individual managers are agreed. These set out the actions which need to be taken in the short term to ensure that key tasks are accomplished to the required standard, by target dates.

(f) Each manager must be given sufficient authority and opportunity to achieve his job improvement plan. A timescale for achievement must be decided. 'Once it is agreed and issued, the job improvement plan is vitally important. The manager is committed to achieving the results and his boss is committed to providing any agreed resources and information.'   (Humble)

(g) There must be a systematic performance review of each manager's results, together with a performance review for the 'unit' as a whole. MBO sets standards and specifies results for managers, and allows them to see how well they are performing in key areas of their jobs. Reviews should be:

   (i)   participative;
   (ii) focused on *performance* and
   (iii) forward-looking, concentrating on goals for improvement.

(h) There must be a continuing management development programme (potential reviews, training, career development, selection etc.) MBO provides a realistic system for discussing managers' aspirations and progress.

5.5 As a management process, the approach works as follows.

(a) Clarify with each manager the *key results* and *performance standards* he should achieve.

(b) Agree with each manager a *job improvement plan* for himself.

(c) Provide conditions which will help managers to achieve their key results and job improvement plans: feedback, authority, resources etc.

(d) Carry out systematic *performance and potential review* of each manager's results.

(e) Formulate *management training plans* to develop potential.

(f) Secure commitment by effective salary and career development plans.

Advantages and disadvantages of MBO

5.6 The advantages of MBO may be summarised briefly as:

(a) clarification of organisational goals within the framework of a long-term plan;

(b) converting strategic plans into management action plans and budgets;

(c) the co-ordination of individual management targets into the overall scheme, so that each individual manager knows what is expected of him;

(d) identifying 'key' areas of managerial jobs, for improvement plans, analysis of training needs etc;

(e) committing individual managers to their targets by encouraging participation and 'ownership';

(f) providing a framework for results-based appraisal of managers, and management development;

(g) encouraging co-ordination and unity of purpose within the organisation;

(h) helping to identify the need for change in organisational goals or individual managers' performance.

5.7 The disadvantages of MBO are, briefly, that:

(a) it will not be as effective as it should be if corporate plans have not been properly established;

(b) there is a danger of inflexibility, if individual objectives, once set, are not changed because the overall plan is rigidly adhered to. There must be flexibility and a willingness to accept amended objectives in the light of changing circumstances;

(c) it can be a time-consuming exercise which might not justify the benefit achieved;

(d) it might call for a significant change in the attitudes of senior managers, the style of leadership and the organisation structure if it is to function effectively as a system;

(e) it requires considerable inter-personal skills by managers throughout the organisation (in setting objectives and in reviewing performance with subordinates);

(f) it might overstress the need for individual achievements, at the expense of teamwork.

6.   CONTROL SYSTEMS

6.1 Control is an integral part of the planning process. Here we will cover the basics of control systems theory, as a preparation for looking at budgetary control in the following section of this chapter.

6.2 Control is one of the 'maintenance' systems of the organisation, helping it to keep a steady state, and to absorb change without trauma. It is also, like many management processes, about *risk management*. Control is required because unpredictable events occur and actual performance deviates from what was expected and planned: consider the effect, for example, of the entry of a powerful new competitor into the market, an unexpected rise in labour costs etc. Control aims to ensure that the business is capable of surviving such disturbances, by allowing managers to identify deviations from plan in time to do something about them, before they have adverse consequences.

6.3 The basic control process or control cycle in management has six stages.

(a) Making a plan; deciding what to do and identifying the desired results. Without plans there can be no control.

(b) Recording the plan formally or informally, in writing or by other means, statistically or descriptively. The plan should incorporate standards of efficiency or targets of performance.

(c) Carrying out the plan, or having it carried out by subordinates, and measuring actual results achieved.

(d) Comparing actual results against the plans. This is sometimes referred to as the provision of 'feedback'.

(e) Evaluating the comparison, and deciding whether further action is necessary to ensure the plan is achieved.

(f) Where corrective action is necessary, this should be implemented. Alternatively, the plan itself may need adjusting (eg if targets were unrealistic or have been overtaken by events - or if actual results are *better* than planned).

6.4 At its simplest the cycle would look like this:

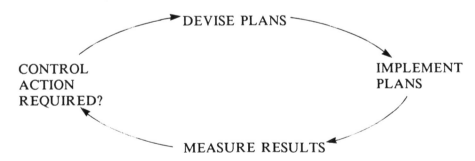

6.5 We will be discussing information systems in the Chapter 18, but you can see that at each stage of the control cycle information is required to support the decisions.

6.6 A particular feature of control information is *feedback*, information gathered from the operations of the business and reported to the managers responsible for them, for the purposes of control. *Negative feedback* is information which indicates that results are deviating from their planned or prescribed course, and that some re-adjustment is necessary to bring the plan back on to course. This feedback is called 'negative' because control action would seek to reverse the direction or movement of the system back towards its planned course.

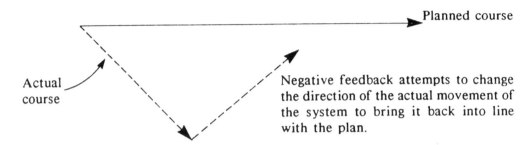

6.7 In designing the control system, the following decisions will have to be made.

(a) What key targets are identified in the plan, how clearly they are defined and how realistic they are. A control system is not designed to compensate for bad planning: it requires clear and realistic goals - or managers will not be able to compare actual results against plan in any meaningful way.

(b) What elements need to be checked or monitored regularly to show up significant variations from plan.

(c) What size of variation in any given area will be considered significant. Variations which are greater than a specified margin of 'tolerance' (within which they need not be reported) and smaller variations which may indicate a trend, should be reported. If a branch processes fewer transactions on Tuesday than on Monday, the manager will probably not be perturbed - but if the number of transactions has decreased every Tuesday for three weeks, he will want to know about it.

(d) Who should get the control information, ie someone who has the authority to act on it. Control is carried out at all levels of management.

(e) How frequently monitoring and reporting are required. The *timeliness* of control information is critical; it is not necessarily better late than never! Frequency will depend on factors such as the likelihood of the operation going out of control (ie the risks it is subject to), and the availability and cost of gathering control information.

(f) What types of controls are available/suitable. For example, computerised processes may be able to apply *automatic* controls, which are triggered by a specified degree of variation from plan. Banking examples would be an automatic change in the rate of interest on funds in a deposit account when a certain balance is reached, or a letter created and sent to a customer when a set level of overdraft is reached.

(g) How complex a control system will be *economical*. Controls should be worth their costs in terms of benefits obtained, risks averted etc. They should if possible be directed only at critical control points, ie elements of performance that require special attention because they are points of greatest risk, and generally indicate better than other factors whether results are working according to plan.

6.8 The *human* factor in the control system will also have to be considered.

(a) The control system should be acceptable to the organisation's members.

(i)   Employees who are used to a rigid, disciplinarian management will perhaps accept strict measures of control and procedures or rules for investigating exceptional variations between actual results and plans.

(ii)   Employees who are accustomed to participating in planning decisions, and are encouraged to use their initiative, will react unfavourably to rigid controls 'imposed' on them by senior management.

The purpose of control information is to stimulate control action, and it must therefore be tailored to the 'culture' of the organisation or the department within the organisation.

(b)   Controls should be tailored to the capabilities and personalities of individual managers. If a manager cannot or will not understand control information given to him, he will not trust it, and if he does not trust it, he will not use it. Some managers, (eg bankers, accountants) might prefer numerical reports of some complexity, whereas other managers might prefer simpler reports, perhaps with charts or diagrams.

(c)   A control system will serve no useful function at all unless it leads management into taking corrective action. Information should be related to relevant indicators of performance. Managers should be assessed on their ability and willingness to make effective use of the system.

6.9   John Child developed the basic control cycle to show some of the human activities and influences at work in the management control system of an organisation.

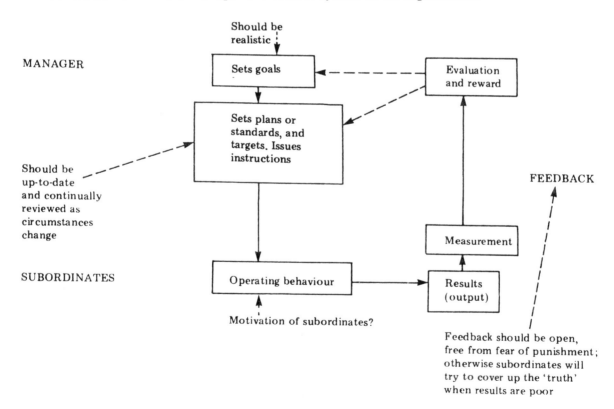

6.10 We cover *budgetary control* (a typical form of control system) in the following section, as a control application of 'management information systems'. You should be aware however, that the cycle/system epitomised by budgetary control is not the only form of control employed in organisations. The term 'control' is used in two ways in the discussion of organisation and management: one to refer to operations and the other to refer to people.

(a) Control (or management control) is the process through which plans are implemented and objectives achieved, by setting targets and standards, measuring performance, comparing actual performance with standards and taking corrective action where necessary. (This sense of the word is the basis of the 'control system').

(b) Control is a psychological and political process in which powerful individuals and groups dominate others and establish an 'order' of behaviour. It can be perceived as *positive* and psychologically necessary, creating stable and predictable conditions in which people can function effectively, or as *negative*, in the form of coercion and manipulation. Control in this sense can be applied through:

(i)   rules, procedures, 'norms' of behaviour and automated processes

(ii) personal centralised decision-making, leadership and direct supervision

(iii) culture, by fostering in individuals a strong personal identification with the goals of the organisation: there may be few formal controls but strong 'central guiding values'.

7. COST MANAGEMENT AND BUDGETARY CONTROL

7.1 A budgetary control system is part of the management information system of the organisation, and its application in planning and control.

(a) A *budget* is 'a plan quantified in monetary terms, prepared and approved prior to a defined period of time, usually showing planned income to be generated and/or expenditure to be incurred during that period, and the capital to be employed to attain a given objective.'

(b) *Budgetary control* is '(a) the establishment of budgets, relating the responsibilities of executives to the requirements of a policy, and (b) the continuous comparison of actual with budgeted results, either to secure the objective of that policy or to provide a basis for its revision.

The purpose of budgets

7.2 'Budgets are designed to carry out a variety of functions: planning, evaluating performance, co-ordinating activities, implementing plans, communicating, motivating, and authorising actions. The last-named role seems to predominate in government budgeting and not-for-profit budgeting, where budget appropriations serve as authorisations and ceilings for management actions.'

(Horngren, *Cost accounting: a managerial emphasis*)

7.3 The purpose of budgets is as follows.

(a) To *compel planning*. Horngren regards this as the most important feature of budgeting because management is forced to look ahead, setting targets, anticipating problems and giving the organisation purpose and direction.

(b) To *communicate ideas and plans to everyone affected by them.* A formal system is necessary to ensure that each person is aware of what he or she is supposed to be doing.

(c) To *co-ordinate* the activities of different departments or sub-units of the organisation. This concept of co-ordination implies, for example, that the purchasing department should base its budget on production requirements and that the production budget should in turn be based on sales expectations.

(d) To *establish a system of control* by having a plan against which actual results can be progressively compared.

(e) To *motivate employees to improve their performance.* Two levels of attainment could be set:

(i) a minimum expectations budget; and
(ii) a 'desired standards' budget, which provides some sort of challenge to employees.

7.4 Because of the 'human' problems associated with budgets, many organisations have implemented 'participative' budgeting, where the responsible individual is invited or encouraged to participate in the budgeting process: this is considered to enhance the motivatory effect, since people 'own' their objectives and targets more than if they were imposed from above.

7.5 A budget, since it has different purposes, might mean different things to different people.

(a) As a *forecast* of the expected performance of the organisation, it helps managers to look into the future. Given conditions of rapid change and uncertainty, however, this function will only be helpful over short periods of time. Budgets will be updated or superseded.

(b) As a *means of allocating resources* it can be used to decide how much resource is needed - cash, labour etc - and how much should be given to each area of the organisation's activities. Resource allocation is particularly important when some resources, usually finance and qualified staff, are in short supply. Budgets often set ceilings or limits on how much administrative and service departments - or project teams - are allowed to spend in the budget period.

(c) As a *yardstick* against which to compare actual performance, the budget provides a means of indicating where and when control action may be necessary (and possibly where some managers or employees are open to censure for achieving poor results).

(d) As a *target* for achievement, a budget might be a means of motivating the workforce to greater personal accomplishment.

The purpose of budgetary control

7.6 The main uses of budgetary control (not only budgeting, but comparing actual results with the budget plan, and - if there are discrepancies - initiating either corrective action or revision of the budget) are:

(a) to define the objectives of the organisation as a whole, and within this overall framework, to define the results which each department (and its personnel) should achieve;

(b) to communicate overall objectives and sub-objectives to responsibility centres within the organisation, aiding co-ordination and unit awareness of organisational goals;

(c) to reveal the extent by which actual results have exceeded or fallen short of the budget;

(d) to indicate, with variances or other measures of performance, the reasons why actual results differ from those budgeted, and to establish the magnitude of the differences;

(e) to provide a basis for executive action to correct adverse trends and to take full advantage of any beneficial trends which are revealed by the results;

(f) to provide a basis for the revision of the current budget, or for the preparation of future budgets;

(g) to provide a system whereby the resources of the organisation are used in the most efficient way possible;

(h) to indicate the efficiency with which the various activities of the organisation have been co-ordinated (and therefore to prevent or reduce the problems of 'sub-optimality' where the objectives of some units are attained at the expense of others and of the organisation as a whole);

(i) to provide some centralising control, (especially control over expenditure and costs) where activities and responsibilities are decentralised.

Information required for budgetary control

7.7 The management information system will provide information for the budgeting process.

(a) Planning information will be required before the budget is formulated.

(i) 'Budget centres' need to be selected - ie sections of the organisation for which 'sub-budgets' will be prepared. For each, the type of budgets required will be determined: key objectives should be chosen that can be used as meaningful measures of performance (quantity or quality of output, expenditure limit, project completion to deadline etc).

(ii) Required *improvements* in quality, productivity and/or cost effectiveness will be determined (with reference to internal standards or external requirements eg competition based on quality or price).

(iii) A time-scale in which targets are meaningful and control required (ie a budgetary period) should be fixed.

(b) The budget itself should state:

(i) responsibility for attainment;

(ii) time period of the budget (and intervening reporting requirements, if any);

(iii) quantified, clearly expressed targets related to (a) (vi) above, including identification of targeted improvements where required;

(iv) assumptions made (eg in relation to rates of inflation, volume of work);

(v) comparison with the previous (or *a* comparable previous) budget;

      (vi) the date of formulation of the budget;

      (vii) at a later stage, if necessary, revised forecasts/targets.

(c) Feedback information on productivity, costs, income, quality and all other relevant performance indicators will be required in order to compare 'actual' with 'plan', and to assess progress towards plan during the budgetary period so that operations - or the budget itself - can be adjusted accordingly.

All this information should have the qualities of good information listed in paragraph 2.8(h).

Problems in budgeting

7.8 Planning for the future of an organisation, even in the relatively short term, is bound to create numerous difficulties. For example:

(a) external factors such as the rate of inflation or supplier changes might be hard to predict, so that budgeting for price levels will be largely guesswork;

(b) the volume of activity cannot be foreseen with certainty: a budget might quickly be outdated as demand for services either exceeds or falls short of expectations;

(c) there will be problems of organisation in the attempt to co-ordinate the plans of different departments into an optimal master budget.

7.9   The information aspects of budgetary control may also cause problems.

(a) Budgets may be expressed in terms which managers find difficult to understand or relate to.

(b) Information may reach unmanageable volumes in order to 'feed' the budgetary control system: not every item of control data will be relevant and 'exception' or 'variance' reporting should be used.

7.10 In addition, there are 'human' problems in budgeting.

(a) Managers are often hostile to budgeting because:

      (i)   it is time-consuming (and not always perceived to be worthwhile, especially in unpredictable circumstances);

      (ii)   it is restrictive, stifling creativity and flexibility, and allowing no room for manoeuvre in operational decisions;

      (iii)   it is a form of control imposed from above - and can be seen as threatening and judgemental rather than motivating and the basis for reward;

      (iv)   it puts them under pressure to achieve.

(b) Managers uncommitted to budgeting tend to 'do it badly'.

      (i)   Future plans may be based on past results, without appraisal of new opportunities, threats, alternatives etc.

      (ii)   Short-term planning may distract attention from long-term goals and the long-term consequences of short-term decisions.

      (iii) Slapdash or deliberately 'fiddled' analysis and recording of actual results/costs etc may be tolerated to make a department 'look better'.

      (iv) Managers may fail to co-ordinate their budgets with those of related functions in the organisation.

      (v)   If the budget-setter is not highly respected by subordinates, there will be no motivating effect on performance. (Accountants often suffer from this feeling in operational units.)

      (vi) Managers might put in - and secure from their staff - just enough effort to achieve budget targets, without trying to do better. This is called 'satisficing' performance.

      (vii) Managers under pressure to achieve may deliberately lower their targets to ensure success.

  (c) Politics is rife in budgeting: competition for resources is endemic in organisations.

      (i)   Managers may build 'slack' into expenditure estimates to boost their department's expenditure allowance (as a kind of status symbol, as well as for the greater share of resources).

      (ii)   There may be jealousy and hostility between departments - especially over expenditure, or when one seems to be 'pushed' harder than other for results.

      (iii) Managers often 'spend up' to their full expenditure allowance, even if it is not necessary, to ensure that it will not be reduced next year.

7.11 Although budgeting might seem to be a technical process, it depends heavily on the expectations, guesses, opinions and aspirations of managers because the future is always uncertain. The more uncertain the future, the more valuable a budget will be for an organisation, but there will also be more scope for political bargaining over resource allocations.

Budgets and motivation

7.12 The behavioural consequences of budgeting can, however, also be advantageous.

  (a) People can be better motivated if they have clearly-stated realistic targets for performance or improvement. They can more easily make the calculation of what effort will be involved, and so how worthwhile that effort will be, in terms of the rewards on offer.

  (b) People may be particularly well motivated if they have participated in setting targets, since there is less resentment and sense of threat. Also the individual is more likely to 'own' and stick by targets which he has determined himself: the psychological discomfort (or 'dissonance') involved in failing to meet targets which he has set and agreed as achievable would be too great.

(c) Feedback on actual results achieved also helps in the motivation and learning processes, because individuals adjust their future behaviour in accordance with the degree of success attained by present performance.

7.13 Budgets as motivators, however, occupy a rather precarious position, because of the number of purposes to which budgeting information is put.

(a) If individuals are paid according to results, or have a high need to achieve, they will tend to set their targets lower if they can (thus increasing the likelihood of success).

(b) One sophisticated approach is to offer two sets of reward - one for the difficulty of the target, and one for meeting the target - so that the risk of *failure* with a higher target is offset by the reward for setting it so high, and the rewards of *meeting* a high target are very great.

(c) Other organisations have a set of targets for their sales staff that are greater than the figures actually used for operational planning: the assumption is that not all targets will be met - while still offering a challenge to sales staff.

Exercise 2

How do you know how well you are performing in your job? Who (if anyone) tells you what you are expected to achieve? What (if any) are the key factors on which your performance is judged? Choose one or two of your tasks: if things 'started going wrong', or you discovered an error, how big would the problem or error have to be before you had to report it to your superior? Are you aware of a 'budget' that your department or section is trying to keep to: if so, what kind of budget is it and do you know how your department/section is doing?

Cost control

7.14 In addition to planning resources, budgets are also used to control costs. Banks have been slashing costs, to reduce their cost/income ratio. This means that if revenues suddenly fall, there is at least a 'cushion' on which to land.

7.15 Banks are using more sophisticated approaches to managing risk. Any loan a bank makes has a risk that it will not be repaid - and this risk increases dramatically in an economic recession. There is an argument that in good times, banks lend over-enthusiastically and the debts go bad. Bank profits tend to see-saw. Better assessment of the risks, including the overall exposure to particular sectors, would cut the losses.

7.16 Some bank branches are being closed. This is particularly the case after mergers, and there have been a number of mergers in the financial services sector. It is likely that if the merger between Lloyds Bank and the TSB goes through the branch network of each bank will be 'rationalised'. This is mainly supposed to save on staff costs.

7.17 Technological innovations are being developed to reduce the need for expensive branch networks or to make better use of the resources available. Information technology enables staff to take a front office role.

7.18 To reduce the costs of handling money and cheques the banks have introduced the following.

(a) Debit cards, such as Switch and Connect, are cheaper than cheques, which is why banks are encouraging their use.

(b) The banks are advertising *direct debits* as a means of payment - again this is cheaper than cheques.

(c) The banks are also investigating *electronic cash*. Trials of *Mondex* have been taking place in Swindon. This should increase security and reduce cash handling expenses.

(d) Banks are encouraging consumers to use telephone banking. First Direct, a subsidiary of the Midland, was set up with this in mind.

(e) Many banks are redesigning their business processes.

7.19 The problem, from the banks' point of view, is consumers' attitudes to cost saving innovations. The *Financial Times* (6 October 1995) reported an interview with Lloyds Bank chairman Sir Brian Pitman.

'He said that Lloyds intended to keep reducing the number of staff working in branches. At present there was an average of 18 people in each branch, but it was planned to cut the number to 15 by removing processing work.'

Sir Brian said that Lloyds would like to cut costs by introducing electronic banking, but there was considerable resistance among customers to such delivery methods. Most people still wanted to talk to another human.

"Customers are not interested in cutting-edge technology," he said. "I would love to change customer behaviour, so people would use gizmos instead of wanting to deal with a member of staff, but customers do not want it."

7.20 The article also mentions another way of controlling costs. Following public sector practice, which is to abandon *national* pay bargaining systems in favour of local arrangements, the article suggests that Lloyds is finding it difficult to recruit in urban areas, but easy in more rural ares.

'"When you get out of the urban areas, nearly the only staff turnover we get is when someone dies," he said. Staff were now being recruited on less attractive contracts than those held by its existing employees.'

8. CHAPTER ROUNDUP

8.1

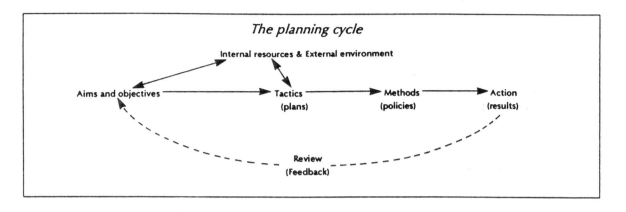

8.2 A practical approach to operational planning involves:

(a) *aims*, which dictate

(b) *priorities*, or 'key tasks', for which there should be

(c) *standards* and

(d) *goals*, so that

(e) *action plans* can be formulated and implemented, subject to

(f) *monitoring* and

(g) *control* action where required.

8.3   *MBO as a system of management*

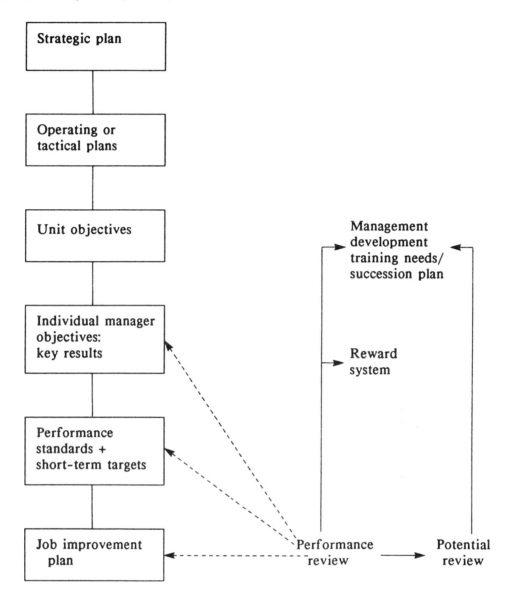

8.4   *A basic control system*

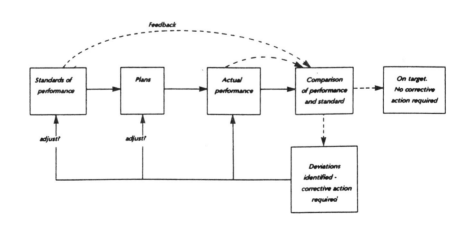

8.5   *Budgetary control* is '(a) the establishment of budgets relating the responsibilities of executives to the requirements of a policy, and (b) the continuous comparison of actual with budgeted results, either to secure the objective of that policy or to provide a basis for its revision.'

8.6   A *budget* is 'a plan quantified in monetary terms, usually showing planned income to be generated and/or expenditure to be incurred during that period and the capital to be employed to attain a given objective.'

8.7   Note, however, that budgets carry out a variety of functions: planning, control, co-ordination, motivating, authorising. They can be perceived in different ways by different people.

TEST YOUR KNOWLEDGE
The numbers in brackets refer to paragraphs of this chapter

1   Why might managers be reluctant to make formal plans? (2.4)

2   Define three different types of 'plan'. (2.6)

3   Why is a systematic approach to planning and control useful? (3.1)

4   What makes a task 'critical' or 'high priority'? (3.3)

5   What are the desirable attributes of performance standards? (3.4)

6   What are the requirements for successful management of a project team? (4.2 - 4.5)

7   What are the benefits of network analysis for project managers? (4.10)

8   Outline the advantages and disadvantages of MBO. (5.6, 5.7)

9   List the stages of the control cycle. (6.4)

10   Outline five of the considerations that would be taken into account when designing a control system. (6.7, 6.8)

11   What are the uses to which budgets can be put? (7.2)

12   What are the positive and negative 'behavioural' consequences of budgetary control? (7.10 - 7.12)

Now try question 13 at the end of the text

Chapter 14

MANAGEMENT AND LEADERSHIP

> **This chapter covers the following topics.**
>
> 1. The manager as leader
> 2. Individual differences: implications for leaders
> 3. Theories of leadership.
> 4. The usefulness of leadership theories
>
> **Introduction**
>
> Leading and managing are not the same, although the most successful managers are good leaders. After all, a leader can be opposed to the management. A leader is somebody in a group who is frequently or persistently seen to exercise acts of influence. Some people are appointed in order to lead; other leaders are elected.

1. THE MANAGER AS LEADER

1.1 Leadership is the process of influencing others to follow willingly. 'The essence of leadership is *followership*. In other words it is the willingness of people to follow that makes a person a leader' (Koontz, O'Donnell, Weihrich).

In an organisation, a manager should exercise leadership to ensure his followers work to the organisation's goals and to the best of their abilities.

1.2 Leadership comes about in a number of different ways.

   (a) A manager is appointed to a position of authority within the organisation. He relies mainly on the (legitimate) authority of that position. Leadership of his subordinates is a function of the position he holds (although a manager will not necessarily be a 'leader', if he lacks leadership qualities).

   (b) Some leaders (eg in politics or in trade unions) might be elected.

   (c) Other leaders might emerge by popular choice or through their personal drive and qualities. Unofficial spokesmen for groups of people are leaders of this style.

1.3 Leaders are *given* their roles by their putative followers; their 'authority' may technically be removed if their followers cease to acknowledge them. The *personal, physical* or *expert* power of leaders is therefore more important than position power alone.

1.4 Leaders are the creators and 'sellers' of culture in the organisation. 'The [leader] not only creates the rational and tangible aspects of organisations, such as structure and technology, but is also the creator of symbols, ideologies, language, beliefs, rituals and myths.'

(Pettigrew)

1.5 If a manager had indifferent or poor leadership qualities his subordinates would still do their job, but they would do it ineffectually or perhaps in a confused manner. By providing leadership, a manager should be able to use the capabilities of subordinates to better effect: leadership is the 'influential increment over and above mechanical compliance with the routine directives of the organisation' (Katz and Kahn, *The social psychology of organisations*).

> 'Leadership over human beings is exercised when persons with certain motives and purposes mobilise, in competition or conflict with others, institutional, political and other resources so as to arouse, engage and satisfy the motives of followers.'
>
> Gregor Burns

1.6 Since leadership is concerned with influencing others, it is necessary to have some understanding of what motivates people to work. Motivation is the subject of a later chapter of this text, but it may be summarised briefly as the effort, energy and excitement which a person is prepared to expend in his work. Koontz, O'Donnell and Weihrich formulate the principle that 'since people tend to follow those whom they see as a means of satisfying their own personal goals, the more managers understand what motivates their subordinates and how these motivations operate, and the more they reflect this understanding in carrying out their managerial actions, the more effective leaders they are likely to be.'

2. INDIVIDUAL DIFFERENCES: IMPLICATIONS FOR LEADERS

2.1 If we agree that the effectiveness of leadership depends on 'followership', it is clear that managers must pay attention to their subordinates in order to formulate a leadership strategy. The trouble with this is that all people are different.

2.2 Each individual may be involved in the organisation which employs him in many different roles:

(a) as an employee, but also as a manager of others - ie in a subordinate and superior role;

(b) as a friend of other individuals, and as part of a specifically work-centred team;

(c) as a provider of man hours, skill and experience - and as a seeker of money, satisfaction and/or other needed or desired benefits;

(d) as a committed member of the organisation, sharing its aims, and as a person with other allegiances - to family, leisure interests etc - who may be working simply to support his non-work life; some allegiances, eg to class or trade union may lead to outright conflict with the interests of the organisation as a whole;

(e) as a unique individual with particular attitudes, beliefs, perceptions, aspirations and lifestyle - as well as a component, 'conforming' part of the organisation.

2.3 Charles de Gaulle once said of France: 'How can anyone govern a country that has 246 different kinds of cheese?' Much the same problem faces the manager in an organisation: the organisation itself may seem 'as one' - but it is made up of individuals, each of whom has his own perceptions of reality and other people, and each of whom desires and expects different things from his work life. How then is the organisation - and more specifically its managers - to 'govern' its human resources, to get the best possible performance from them? How can it know what they need and want from the organisation in return?

2.4

> 'Managers, if one listens to the psychologists, will have to have insights into all kinds of people. They will have to be in command of all kinds of psychological techniques. They will have to understand an infinity of individual personality structures, individual psychological needs, and individual psychological problems ... But most managers find it hard enough to know all they need to know about their own immediate areas of expertise, be it heat-treating or cost accounting or scheduling.'
>
> Drucker, *Management*

2.5 In organisations, particularly large organisations, it is often essential to concentrate on the characteristics which most individuals have in *common*. This is necessary because large organisations must develop rules, procedures and standards with which employees in general must conform. But individuals are unique. Unless this point is recognised there is a danger that general principles of management will be misapplied because they are inappropriate in particular cases.

2.6 Managers themselves have this dilemma of how far they can deal with their subordinates on an individual basis, and how far they will need to make generalisations and assumptions about 'the workers' or 'the team'.

In practice, a manager's approach to the motivation, direction and control of workers depends on the *assumptions* he makes about them, since he will not have time to interact at a significant level with all the individuals around him. We have already seen how the 'picture' of the worker and what he wants and expects from work changed from the scientific management to human relations models.

2.7 Two interesting analyses of the different 'models' of and assumptions about 'the workers' that management might have are:

(a) the four managerial models of Edgar Schein;
(b) Douglas McGregor's Theory X and Theory Y.

Schein's managerial models

2.8 Edgar Schein identified four models of individuals commonly believed by management. The models have implications for the role employees are given in the organisation, and the type of leadership and motivation they are given.

2.9 The *rational-economic man* is primarily motivated by economic incentives. He is mainly passive and can be manipulated by the organisation; he is emotional and unpredictable, and organisations will have to control him. In the context of an employing organisation, such a man would be influenced in his behaviour mainly by salary and fringe benefits. Fortunately, not all men are like this, and the self-motivated, self-controlling individuals must assume responsibility for those that are.

2.10 The *social man* looks for self-fulfilment in social relationships. In the context of an employing organisation, this would imply that an individual's major motivation would be not so much the job itself as the opportunity to mix with other people.

2.11 The *self-actualising man* is influenced by a wider range of motivations. At the simplest level, these may include the need for food and security; but they range beyond this to the need felt by self-actualising man to realise his own full potential. He is capable of maturity and autonomy and will (given the chance) voluntarily integrate his goals with the organisation.

2.12 The *complex man* represents Schein's own view of people. According to his model, individuals are variable and driven by many different motives. The motives influencing a particular individual may change from time to time, and their relative importance may also vary, depending on the situation. The complex man will respond to no single managerial strategy, but will consider its appropriateness to circumstances and his own needs.

Theory X and Theory Y

2.13 Douglas McGregor, in his book *The human side of enterprise,* discussed the way in which managers handle people according to the assumptions they have about them, and about what kind of management 'style' will obtain their efforts. He identifies two extreme sets of assumptions (Theory X and Theory Y) and explores how management style differs according to which set of assumptions is adopted.

2.14 Theory X is the theory that the average human being has an inherent dislike of work and will avoid it if he can. The human being prefers to be directed, wishing to avoid responsibility. He has relatively little ambition and wants security above all. He is self-centred, with little interest in the organisation's needs. He is resistant to change, gullible and easily led. He must be coerced, controlled, directed, offered reward or threatened with punishment to get him to put forth adequate effort towards the achievement of organisation objectives.

2.15 According to Theory Y, however, the expenditure of physical and mental effort in work is as natural as play or rest. The ordinary person does not inherently dislike work: according to the conditions it may be a source of satisfaction or punishment. Extensive control is not the only means of obtaining effort. Man will exercise self-direction and self-control in the service of objectives to which he is committed: he is not naturally passive, or resistant, to organisational objectives, but has been made so by experience.

2.16 Under Theory Y, the most significant reward that can be offered in order to obtain commitment is the satisfaction of the individual's for personal growth and development needs. The average human being learns, under proper conditions, not only to accept but to seek responsibility. At present the potentialities of the average person are not being fully used: management's responsibility is to create conditions and methods that will enable individuals to integrate their own and the organisation's goals, by personal development.

2.17 You will have your own viewpoints on the validity of Theory X with Theory Y. In fact McGregor intentionally polarised his theories, and recognises that people are in reality too complex to be categorised in this way and that managers' assumptions may be somewhere along the line between the two extremes.

2.18 McGregor also recognised that the assumptions were self-perpetuating, even where the 'types' of employee did not exist. If people are treated *as though* they are 'Theory X' people, because of management assumptions, 'Theory X' behaviour will in fact be induced - thus confirming management in its beliefs and practices (eg. 'clocking on', timekeeping systems, close supervision and management controls etc), ie: 'Theory X explains the *consequences* of a particular managerial strategy'.

2.19 We will continue to address the issue of employees as different individuals as we proceed to topics such as motivation and employee goals, management of change, interviewing and teamwork. It will underpin most of the personnel systems discussed in Part D of this text.

Exercise 1

(a) Do you think you have a Theory X or Theory Y view of people under your supervision? What theory do you think your boss holds?

(b) A firm uses a video monitor to check that its employees are working hard, when the video is switched off the employees relax. That managing directors says that this proves the truth of Theory X. Does it?

Solution

No. This is a self-fulfilling prophecy, perpetuating close supervision. It is an extension of the managing director's prejudice, and the employees quite possibly are responding to a situation where they are denied responsibility.

Transactional analysis

2.20 One model of some of the forces underlying boss:subordinate relationships is transactional analysis. In brief, this theory suggests that each person has three ego states, or states of mind, which correspond with three ways of feeling and behaving.

(a) *Parent ego state.* The 'parent' in us corrects and criticises, but also develops and nurtures. It is based on how our teachers and parents behaved towards us. It is controlling.

(b) The *child ego state* is fixated in early childhood but is still active. It is based on feelings in early life. It is exemplified by feelings of dependence, fear and insecurity, perhaps even defensiveness. It is spontaneous and emotional.

(c) The *adult ego state* is based upon an objective appraisal of reality. It contains experience of problem solving, and includes the ability to 'read' other ego states.

2.21 In the work environment, it is sometimes helpful to know which ego state a person is in. The theory holds that communication will only be smooth if the transaction between the individuals is complementary, ie:

(a) adult to adult;
(b) parent to child;
(c) child to parent.

2.22 In other words an appropriate behavioural response must be made to the other person's ego-state. For example, a 'child' might work most effectively when 'parented'.

2.23 Crossed communications occur when the inappropriate response is made. For example if Mr Smith talks to Mr Jones in an 'adult' mode, but Mr Jones responds as a 'child' or a 'parent' the substance of the communication would be lost in the anticipated role play.

2.24 Each person can play each of these roles, although their strengths might vary. Furthermore, a 'child' or 'parent' might use the organisational environment as a means of satisfying those psychological needs rather than acting for the wellbeing of the organisation.

2.25 An effective leader needs to know when to adopt each role. Authoritarian leaders might be behaving as a 'parent', when the subordinates respond best when treated as 'adults'.

3. THEORIES OF LEADERSHIP

Trait theories of leadership

3.1 Early writers like Taylor believed that the capacity to 'make others do what you want them to do' was an inherent characteristic: you either had it, or you didn't: leaders were 'born, not made'. Studies on leadership concentrated on the personal *traits* of existing and past leadership figures.

3.2 One study by Ghiselli did show a significant correlation between leadership effectiveness and the personal traits of intelligence, initiative, self assurance and individuality. This is logical enough, and what you would expect. However:

(a) the approach does not take account of the individuality of the subordinates and other factors in the leadership situation: 'A person does not become a leader by virtue of the possession of some combination of traits, but the pattern of personal characteristics of the leader must bear some relevant relationship to the characteristics, activities and goals of the followers' (Stodgill);

(b) Jennings (1961) wrote that 'Research has produced such a variegated list of traits presumed to describe leadership, that for all practical purposes it describes nothing. Fifty years of study have failed to produce one personality trait or set of qualities that can be used to distinguish between leaders and non-leaders';

(c) the 'great man' approach does not help organisations to make better managers or leaders - it merely attempts to help them recognise a leader when they see one;

(d) the full list of traits is so long that it appears to call for a man or woman of extraordinary, even superhuman, gifts to be a leader.

Though superficially attractive, trait approaches are now largely discredited.

3.3 *Charisma* is frequently identified as a leadership trait. It is certainly accepted as an ingredient of leadership (as opposed to management), since it enables a person to get work done through others without the exercise of pure positional authority: ie it relates to *'personal power'*. It has traditionally been surrounded by a certain 'mystique', but House *(A Theory of charismatic leadership*, 1976) suggests that this power can be acquired and developed, through training in:

(a) role modelling (setting an example to followers);

(b) image creation (engaging in behaviour designed to create an impression of competence and success);

(c) confidence building (communicating confidence in and high expectations of followers);

(d) goal articulation (voicing goals laden with moral overtones);

(e) motive arousal (behaving in an inspiring manner).

Style theories of leadership

3.4 The conclusion was that if leadership is not an innate gift, a *style* of leadership appropriate to a given work situation could be learned and adopted.

3.5 Four different types or styles of leadership were identified by Huneryager and Heckman (1967).

(a) *Dictatorial style:* the manager forces subordinates to work by threatening punishment and penalties. The psychological contract between the subordinates and their organisation would be coercive.

Dictatorial leadership might be rare in commerce and industry, but it is not uncommon in the style of government in some countries of the world, nor in the style of parenthood in many families.

(b) *Autocratic style:* decision-making is centralised in the hands of the leader himself, who does not encourage participation by subordinates; indeed, subordinates' ideas might be actively discouraged and obedience to orders would be expected from them.

The autocratic style is common in many organisations, and you will perhaps be able to identify examples from your own experience. Doctors, matrons and sisters in hospitals tend to practise an autocratic style; managers/directors who own their company also tend to expect things to be done their way.

(c) *Democratic style:* decision-making is decentralised, and shared by subordinates in participative group action. To be truly democratic, the subordinate must be willing to participate.

(d) *Laissez-faire style:* subordinates are given little or no direction at all, and are allowed to establish their own objectives and make all their own decisions.

The leader of a research establishment might adopt a laissez-faire style, giving individual research workers freedom of choice to organise and conduct their research as they themselves want (within certain limits, such as budget spending limits).

The Ashridge studies

3.6 The research unit at Ashridge Management College carried out studies in UK industry in the 1960s and identified four styles.

(a) The autocratic or *tells* style. There is only a one-way communication between the manager and the subordinate: the manager tells the subordinate what to do, and expects his or her decisions and instructions to be obeyed without question.

(b) The persuasive or *sells* style. The manager still makes all the decisions, but tries to explain and justify them in order to motivate subordinates.

(c) The *consultative* style. This involves discussion between the manager and the subordinates involved in carrying out a decision, but the manager retains the right to make the decision himself. By conferring with his subordinates before making any decision, the manager will take account of their advice and feelings. Consultation is a form of limited participation in decision-making for subordinates, but there might be a tendency for a manager to appear to consult his subordinates when really he has made up his mind beforehand. Consultation will then be false and a facade for a 'sells' style of leadership whereby the manager hopes to win acceptance of his decisions by subordinates by pretending to listen to their advice.

(d) The democratic or *joins* style. This is an approach whereby the leader joins his group of subordinates to make a decision on the basis of consensus or agreement. It is the most democratic style of leadership identified by the research study. Subordinates with the greatest knowledge of a problem will have greater influence over the decision. The joins style is therefore most effective where all subordinates in the group have equal knowledge and can therefore contribute in equal measure to decisions.

3.7 The Ashridge studies made some interesting findings with regard to leadership style and employee motivation. (Compare these with the other views described in this chapter.)

(a) Subordinates clearly preferred the *consultative* style of leadership but managers were most commonly thought to be exercising the 'tells' or 'sells' style.

(b) Subordinate's attitudes towards their work varied according to the style of leadership they thought their boss exercised. The most favourable attitudes were found amongst subordinates who thought their boss was exercising the *consultative style*.

(c) The least favourable attitudes were found amongst subordinates who were unable to perceive a consistent style of leadership in their boss. In other words, subordinates are unsettled by a boss who chops and changes between autocracy, persuasion, consultation and democracy. The conclusion from this finding is that *consistency* in leadership style is important.

3.8

			Strengths		Weaknesses

(a) *Tells style*

(1) Quick decisions can be made when speed is required

(1) It doesn't encourage the subordinate to give his opinions when these might be useful.

(2) It is the most efficient type of leadership for highly-programmed routine work.

(2) Communications between the manager and subordinate will be one-way and the manager will not know until afterwards whether his orders have been properly understood.

(3) It doesn't encourage initiative and commitment from subordinates.

(b) *Sells style*

(1) Employees are made aware of the reasons for decisions

(1) Communications are still largely one-way. Subordinates might not buy his decisions.

(2) Selling decisions to staff might make them more willing to co-operate.

(2) It does not encourage initiative and commitment from subordinates.

(3) Staff will have a better idea of what to do when unforeseen events arise in their work because the manager will have explained his intentions.

(c) *Consultative style*

(1) Employees are involved in decisions before they are made. This encourages motivation through greater interest and involvement.

(1) It might take much longer to reach decisions.

(2) An agreed consensus of opinion can be reached and for some decisions consensus can be an advantage rather than a weak compromise.

(2) Subordinates might be too inexperienced to formulate mature opinions and give practical advice.

(3) Employees can contribute their knowledge and experience to help in solving more complex problems.

(d) *Joins style*

(1) It can provide high motivation and commitment from employees

(1) The authority of the manager might be undermined.

(2) It shares the other advantages of the consultative style.

(2) Decision-making might become a very long process, and clear decisions might be difficult to reach.

(3) Subordinates might lack enough experience.

3.9 It is important to get the consultative and 'joins' styles in perspective. A leader cannot try to forget that he is the 'boss' by being friendly and informal with subordinates, or by consulting them before making any decision. Douglas McGregor (*Leadership and motivation*) wrote about his own experiences as a college president that : 'It took a couple of years, but I finally began to realise that a leader cannot avoid the exercise of authority any more than he can avoid responsibility for what happens in the organisation.' A leader can try to avoid acting dictatorially, and he can try to act like 'one of the boys', but he must accept all the consequences of being a leader. McGregor wrote that 'since no important decision ever pleases everyone in the organisation, he must also absorb the displeasures, and sometimes severe hostility, of those who would have taken a different course'.

Task and people: Blake's grid

3.10 By emphasising style of leadership and the importance of human relations, it is all too easy to forget that a manager is primarily responsible for ensuring that tasks are done efficiently and effectively. Robert R Blake and Jane S Mouton attempted to address the balance of management thinking, with their *'management grid'* (1964) based on two aspects of managerial behaviour, namely:

(a) concern for production, ie the 'task'; and
(b) concern for people.

3.11 The results of their work were published under the heading of 'Ohio State Leadership Studies', but are now commonly referred to as *Blake's grid*.

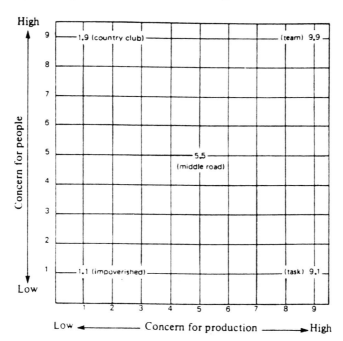

The extreme cases shown on the grid are defined by Blake and Mouton as follows.

(a) 1.1 *impoverished:* the manager is lazy, showing little effort or concern for staff or work targets.

(b) 1.9 *country club:* the manager is attentive to staff needs and has developed satisfying relationships. However, there is little attention paid to achieving results.

(c) 9.1 *task management:* almost total concentration on achieving results. People's needs are virtually ignored and conditions of work are so arranged that people cannot interfere to any significant extent.

(d) 5.5 *middle of the road or the dampened pendulum:* adequate performance through balancing the necessity to get out work while maintaining morale of people at a satisfactory level.

(e) 9.9 *team:* high performance manager who achieves high work accomplishment through 'leading' committed people who identify themselves with the organisational aims.

3.12 The conclusion is that the most efficient managers combine concern for the task with concern for people.

3.13 It is worth being clear in your own mind about the possible usefulness of Blake's grid. Its primary value is obtained from the appraisal of a manager's performance, either by the manager himself or by his superiors. For example, a manager rated 3.8 has further to go in showing concern for the task itself than for developing the work of his subordinates. However the grid is rather 'two-dimensional' compared to:

(a) contingency approaches which bring in other variables; and

(b) W J Reddin's 3-dimensional version of the grid, which recognises that whether a manager's concern for task and concern for people is high or low, he may still be effective *or* ineffective, depending on the circumstances. Blake assumes that a 1.1 manager is ineffective - but he may be effective if he is a rule-follower or bureaucrat in a bureaucratic environment.

3.14 Reddin's point is most important in limiting the effectiveness of the grid as a tool for management development. There is a tendency for Blake's framework to look as if concern for people and concern for task are ends in themselves, whereas the crucial consideration in leadership behaviour is the propensity to produce results (whether in terms of group satisfaction or task achievement), ie 'effectiveness'. A 9.9 manager on Blake's scale is, according to Blake, by definition effective, but Reddin points out that a 9.9 can still be ineffective, if he is a 'compromiser': his *concern* for human relations and the task will not necessarily translate into positive action.

Tannenbaum and Schmidt's continuum

3.15 Tannenbaum and Schmidt built on several contemporary theories to the effect that managers adopt either a task-centred or an employee-centred approach, an authoritarian or democratic approach. On these polarised dimensions Tannenbaum and Schmidt constructed a continuum, somewhere along which will be shown a manager's style in given circumstances. They include elements of contingency thinking in recognising that managers make *choices* in selecting and exercising a leadership style, affected by 'forces' including the manager himself, the subordinates and the situation.

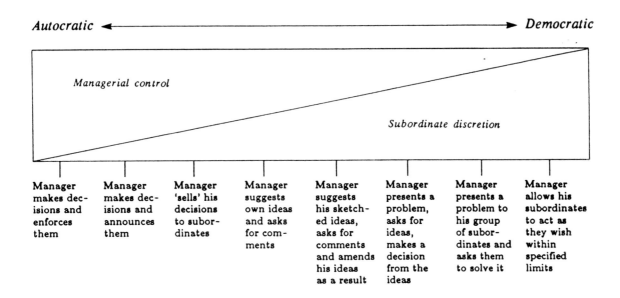

3.16 The continuum is a flexible model which addresses a range of situations, although only on one dimension - ie the extent to which the manager retains and exercises control. The theory has the advantage of getting managers to recognise that management style is a flexible thing, and has been used to this end in management development programmes.

Rensis Likert's systems of management

3.17 Rensis Likert's model is another style theory, a further variation on the authoritarian/ democratic polarisation and the combined concern for task and people. He distinguished four systems of management:

(a) *System 1: Exploitative-authoritative:* use of hierarchical position power, no teamwork, poor communication, use of sanctions for discipline. Mediocre productivity.

(b) *System 2: Benevolent-authoritative:* similar to 1, but with some leeway for consultation and decentralisation. Productivity fair to good - but not 'happy'.

(c) *System 3: Consultative authoritative:* good communication, some teamwork, consultation in goal-setting and decision making, positive reinforcement used. Good productivity.

(d) *System 4: Participative group management:* Likert's 'ideal' system. Participation, good communication, growth needs catered for, commitment secured. Excellent productivity.

3.18 Effective management, for Likert, was a combination of:

(a) expecting high levels of performance;
(b) being employee-centred, taking time to get to know workers and develop trust;
(c) not practising close supervision;
(d) operating a participative style of management as a natural style.

3.19 He emphasised that all four features must be present for a manager to be truly effective. For example, if a manager is employee-centred, if he delegates and is participative, then he will have a happy working environment but he will not produce a high performance unless he also establishes high standards. A manager's concern for people must be matched by his concern for achieving results.

3.20 This linking of the human relations approach with scientific management targets provides the recipe for effective performance. It is important to remember that management techniques such as time and motion study, financial controls etc are used by high producing managers 'at least as completely as by the low producing managers, but in quite different ways.' The different application is caused by a better understanding of the motivations of human behaviour.

Contingency or 'situational' theories

John Adair: action-centred leadership

3.21 J Adair's action-centred, or 'functional' leadership model (1973) is part of the *contingency* school of thought. Like other contingency thinkers, Adair saw the leadership process in a context made up of three main variables, all of which are interrelated and must be examined in the light of the whole situation.

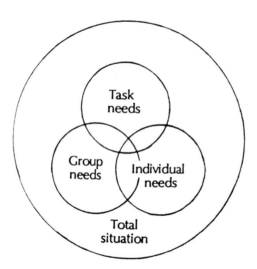

3.22 The total situation dictates the relative priority that must be given to each of the three sets of needs. Effective leadership is identifying and acting on that priority to create a balance between the needs. Meeting of the various needs can be expressed as specific management roles:

Task roles	*Group maintenance roles*	*Individual maintenance roles*
Initiating	Encouraging	Goal-setting
Information-seeking	Peace-keeping	Feedback
Diagnosing	Clarifying	Recognition
Opinion-seeking	Standard-seeking	Counselling
Evaluating		Training
Decision-making		

3.23 Around this framework, Adair developed a scheme of leadership training based on precept and practice in each of eight leadership activities as applied to task, team and individual.

    (a) defining the task
    (b) planning
    (c) briefing
    (d) controlling
    (e) evaluating
    (f) motivating
    (g) organising
    (h) setting an example.

3.24 Adair argued that the common perception of leadership as 'decision-making' was inadequate to describe the range of action required by the complex situation in which the manager finds himself. This model is therefore more practical.

F E Fiedler's contingency theory of leadership

3.25 Perhaps the leading advocate of contingency theory is F E Fiedler. He studied the relationship between style of leadership and the effectiveness of the work group. Two styles of leader were identified in terms of their psychological distance.

    (a) *Psychologically distant managers* (PDMs) who maintain distance from their subordinates by:

        (i)   formalising the roles and relationships between themselves and their superiors and subordinates;

        (ii)   being withdrawn and reserved in their inter-personal relationships within the organisation (despite having good inter-personal skills);

        (iii) preferring formal consultation methods rather than seeking opinions of their staff informally.

    PDMs judge subordinates on the basis of performance, and are primarily task-oriented: Fiedler found that leaders of the most effective work groups tend to be PDMs.

    (b) *Psychologically close managers* (PCMs) who:

        (i)   do not seek to formalise roles and relationships with superiors and subordinates;

        (ii)   are more concerned to maintain good human relationships at work than to ensure that tasks are carried out efficiently;

        (iii) prefer informal contacts to regular formal staff meetings.

3.26 Fiedler went on to develop his contingency theory in *A theory of leadership effectiveness*. He suggested that the effectiveness of a work group depended on the *situation*, made up of three particular variables:

    (a) the relationship between the leader and his group - the amount of trust and respect they have for him;

(b) the extent to which the task is defined and structured; and

(c) the power of the leader in relation to the group (his authority, and power to reward and punish).

3.27 A situation is 'favourable' to the leader when:

(a) the leader is liked and trusted by the group;
(b) the tasks of the group are clearly defined;
(c) the power of the leader to reward and punish with organisation backing is high.

3.28 Fiedler concluded that:

(a) a structured (or psychologically distant) style works best when the situation is either very favourable, or very unfavourable to the leader;

(b) a supportive (or psychologically close) style works best when the situation is moderately favourable to the leader.

> 'Group performance will be contingent upon the appropriate matching of leadership styles and the degree of favourableness of the group situation for the leader, that is, the degree to which the situation provides the leader with influence over his group members.'
> (Fiedler)

Charles Handy: the leadership 'environment'

3.29 Handy has also suggested a contingency approach to leadership. The factors in any situation which contribute to a leader's choice of style (on a scale from 'tight' to 'loose' control) and effectiveness are:

(a) the leader himself - ie his personality, character and preferred style of operating;

(b) the subordinates - ie their individual and collective personalities, and their preference for a style of leadership;

(c) the task - the objectives of the job, the technology of the job, methods of working;

(d) the environment.

3.30 The *environment* of leadership is important, and it features are outlined below.

(a) *The position of 'power' held by the leader in the organisation and the relationship of the leader and his group.* A person with great power has a bigger capacity to set his own style of leadership, select his own subordinates and re-define the task of his work group.

(b) *Organisational 'norms' and the structure and technology of the organisation.* No manager can flout convention and act in a manner which is contrary to the customs and standards of the organisation. If the organisation has a history of autocratic leadership, it will be difficult to introduce a new style. If the formal organisation is highly centralised, there will be limits to how far a task can be re-structured by an individual manager.

(c) *The variety of tasks and the variety of subordinates.* In many groups, tasks vary from routine and simple to complex 'one-off' problem-solving. Managing such work is complicated by this variety. Similarly, the individuals in a work group might be widely different. One member of the group might seek participation and greater responsibility, whereas another might want to be told what to do. Furthermore, where labour turnover is frequent, the individuals who act as leaders or subordinates are constantly changing; such change is unsettling because the leadership style will have to be altered to suit the new situation.

3.31 The 'environment' can be improved for leaders within an organisation if top management act to ensure that:

(a) leaders are given a clear role and 'power';
(b) organisational 'norms' can be broken - ie the culture is responsive and adaptive;
(c) the organisational structure is not rigid and inflexible;
(d) subordinates in a work group are all of the same quality or type;
(e) labour turnover is reduced, especially by keeping managers in their job for a reasonably lengthy period of time.

4. THE USEFULNESS OF LEADERSHIP THEORIES

4.1 Few of the concepts discussed above attempt to distinguish 'leadership' behaviour from 'management' behaviour, other than peripherally in the form of 'motivation' or 'setting an example'. It is arguable, therefore, that although they may encourage better management - through their application in management assessment and development - they are incapable of making better *leaders,* other than by adding insight to management functions for those who are leaders already.

4.2 It is also doubtful to what extent study of a concept, even where it is built into a training scheme, can in fact change a given individual's behaviour. Individual managers/leaders will not change their values in response to a theory, especially where it is one of many - often conflicting - frameworks. Even if *willingness* to change management values and style exists, conditions in the organisation may not allow it.

4.3 The trouble with theories is that many of them do *not* take relevant organisational conditions into account, and for a manager to model his own behaviour on a formula which is successful in theory or in a completely different situation will not necessarily be helpful. In addition, it may be that:

(a) the manager's personality (or 'acting' ability) is simply not flexible enough to utilise leadership theories by attempting to change styles to suit a situation. A manager may not be able to be participative in some circumstances and authoritative in others where his personality and personal goals are incompatible with that style;

(b) the demands of the task, technology, organisation culture and other managers constrains the manager in the range of 'styles' and leadership behaviours open to him. If the manager's own boss believes in and practises an authoritarian style, and the group members are incompetent and require close supervision, no amount of theorising on the desirability of participative management will be effective;

(c)   consistency is important to subordinates. If a manager practises a contingency approach to leadership, subordinates may simply perceive him to be 'fickle', or may suffer insecurity and distrust the 'changeful' manager.

> 'There is therefore no simple recipe which the individual manager can use to decide which style to adopt to be most effective. Management style probably can be changed, but only if management values can be changed ... It is not enough to present managers with research findings and try to convince them with logical argument that change is necessary.'
>
> Buchanan and Huczynski: *Organisational behaviour*

4.4   Moreover, it must be reiterated that 'the essence of leadership is *followership*' (Koontz et al). It is follower response that will ultimately decide the competence of leadership - and follower response is not necessarily subject to leadership theory, however well supported with research findings from other situations.

Exercise 2

Some firms have introduced 'upwards appraisal' of managers. This means that a manager's subordinates comment on his or her performance. Which theory of leadership do you think this practice subscribes to? What benefits could the manager gain from such a service? What benefits would accrue to the organisation as a whole?

Solution

The contingency theory holds that *followers* are important in ensuring that a leader is effective. The benefit for a manager is that he or she gets some sort of feedback, especially on management style and problems caused by communication failure. For senior management it is important to know how staff actually feel, as it might be an indication of their attitudes to customers: unhappy or badly led employees, especially in service industries, with face to face contact with customers and clients, are perhaps unlikely to give excellent service.

14: MANAGEMENT AND LEADERSHIP

5. CONCLUSION

5.1 *Style theories*

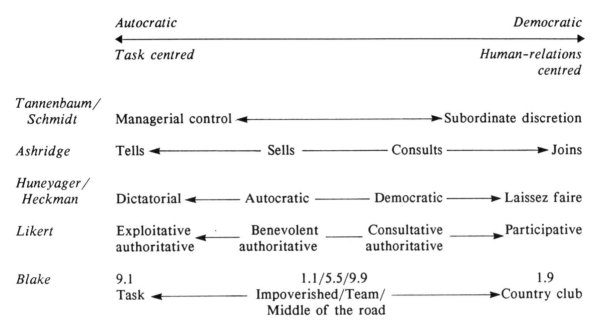

5.2 *Contingency approaches*

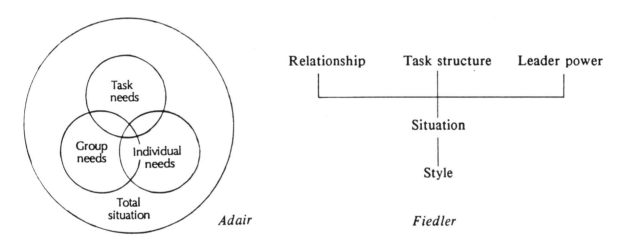

TEST YOUR KNOWLEDGE
The numbers in brackets refer to paragraphs of this chapter

1　'Leader' is just another word for 'manager'. Do you agree? (1.1 - 1.6)

2　Describe Schein's managerial models. (2.9 - 2.12)

3　Outline Theory X and Theory Y. What kind of management style and techniques would be appropriate if a manager thought his subordinates were as Theory X describes? What elements in your own job might lead you to suspect that the bank retains Theory X views of people? (2.14 - 2.17)

4　Choose a figure you consider to be a great leader. What traits does/did he or she possess? Why might such an approach to the study of leadership not be very helpful in practice? (3.2)

5　Outline the tells-sells-consults-joins style of leadership. (3.6)

6　What is Blake's grid useful for, and what does it *not* tell us? (3.13)

7　What factors, according to various contingency theories, influence leadership effectiveness? (3.22, 3.26, 3.29, 3.30)

8　If you really liked the idea of a particular leadership style, and wanted to 'adopt' it, what problems might you have in practice? (4.1 - 4.4)

Now try question 14 at the end of the text

PART D
ORGANISATIONS AND THEIR SYSTEMS

Chapter 15

THE NATURE OF ORGANISATIONS

This chapter covers the following topics.

1. Work organisations
2. Formal and informal organisations
3. Authority, responsibility and power in organisations
4. Organisation and management theory
5. Aspects of the organisation

Introduction

Having dealt with individuals and groups, we can now take a wider view over the organisation as a whole. Rather than go directly into how organisations are designed, we discuss in more general terms what organisations are for, some common features and then some approaches to designing them.

---

1. WORK ORGANISATIONS

1.1 Buchanan and Huczynski (*Introduction to Organisational Behaviour*) put forward the following definition of organisation: 'Social arrangements for the controlled performance of collective goals.' They point out that the difference between organisations (and particularly work organisations) and other social groupings with collective goals (eg the family or the bus stop queue) is:

(a) the preoccupation with performance; and
(b) the need for controls.

1.2 In general terms, organisations exist because they can achieve results which individuals cannot achieve alone. By grouping together, individuals overcome limitations imposed by both the physical environment and also their own biological limitations. Chester Barnard (1956) described the situation of a man trying to move a stone which was too large for him:

(a) the stone was too big for the man (environmental limitation) and
(b) the man was too small for the stone (biological limitation).

By forming an organisation with another man, it was possible to move the stone with the combined efforts of the two men together.

1.3 Barnard further suggested that the limitations on man's accomplishments are determined by the *effectiveness* of his organisation.

1.4   In greater detail, the reasons for organisations may be described as follows:

(a) *social reasons:* to meet an individual's need for companionship;

(b) to *enlarge abilities:* organisations increase productive ability because they make possible both:

(i)   specialisation; and
(ii)   exchange or sharing

of knowledge, skills, experience etc. Unlike most individuals, in other words, organisations have the capacity to achieve the depth of specialisation across a breadth of activity;

(c) to *accumulate knowledge* (for subsequent re-use and further learning);

(d) to *save time* in achieving objectives.

1.5   The need for *controls* arises because organisation is very complex in practice.

(a) Organisations are collections of interacting individuals, occupying different roles but experiencing common membership. However, this embraces a wide variety of behaviours: the relationship between them may be co-operative or coercive; their roles may be ill-defined or clearly-defined, overlapping, conflicting etc.

(b) Organisations are created because individuals need each other in order to fulfil goals which they consider worthwhile. However, one individual's goals may be very different from another's and from those of the organisation as a whole.

(c) Performance must be controlled in order to make best use of human, financial and material resources, for which individuals, groups and organisations compete. In work organisations, management is usually accountable for the use of these resources, eg to the owners of the business. The need for controlled performance leads to a deliberate, ordered environment, allocation of tasks (ie division of labour), specialisation, the setting of standards and measurement of results against them etc. This implies a whole structure of 'power' or 'responsibility' relationships, whereby some individuals control others.

1.6   Barnard described an organisation as a 'system of co-operative human activities' and it is important to be aware that:

(a) an organisation consists of members, ie people who inter-react with each other;

(b) the way in which people inter-react is designed and ordered by the organisation structure so as to achieve joint (organisational) objectives. Each individual has his own view of what these organisational objectives are;

(c) each person in the organisation has his own personal objectives;

(d) the organisational objectives as gauged by an individual need to be compatible with personal objectives of the individual if he is to be a well-integrated member of the organisation.

The task of recognising and reconciling organisational and individual objectives, and making optimal use of resources to achieve both, is the basic task of management.

1.7 It may be added that another characteristic peculiar to *work* organisations is the system of rewards, compensations and incentives that centres mainly on 'pay' and other benefits. Pay is seen in different ways:

(a) as a reward for services rendered to the organisation;

(b) as an incentive to act in the interests of the organisation (with the implied threat of deprivation) - and therefore as a means of *control* within the organisation;

(c) as compensation for deprivations endured in the interests of the organisation;

(d) as a necessary and desirable commodity for life outside the organisation, irrespective of the quality of life inside (whether bad - 'at least it's a living' - or good - 'I'm doing it for love, not money').

1.8 The way in which rewards are determined - on seniority or contribution, as incentive or compensation, as a rate for the job or for individual performance in the job, on effort or achievement, time spent or value added - has been discussed in detail in an earlier chapter. Be aware, however, of the extent to which reward may be the *only* factor integrating individual and organisational objectives. As we discuss the 'hierarchical' structure of organisations and the nature of managerial jobs, too, it is worth thinking about what makes a particular job 'worth' more than another to the organisation and how this translates itself into reward for the individual in the job: we'll deal with that when we cover 'job evaluation'.

2. FORMAL AND INFORMAL ORGANISATIONS

2.1 Louis A Allen, in his books *Management and Organisation* and *The Management Profession*, tells us that 'organisation' is a mechanism or structure that enables living things to work effectively together. The basic elements of organisation are:

(a) division of labour, ie specialisation ('who does what?');
(b) a source of authority ('who is responsible for seeing that they do it?'); and
(c) relationships ('how does it fit in with what everyone else is doing?').

2.2 Formal organisations have an explicit hierarchy of authority in a well-defined structure. Division of labour is more or less fixed in the form of job design, expressed in job specifications. Communication channels for reporting 'upward' as well as passing information and instructions 'downward' are also well-defined.

The 'bureaucracy' is the purest form of the formal, rational organisation designed on classical principles: we will examine its nature and effectiveness in the following chapter.

Informal organisation

2.3 It is important to recognise, however, that the structure of an organisation is affected by the people working within it, and an *informal* organisation exists side by side with the formal one.

The informal organisation of a company is so important that a newcomer has to 'learn the ropes' before he can settle effectively into his job, and he must also become 'accepted' by his fellow workers.

2.4 When people work together, they establish social relationships and customary ways of doing things. They:

(a) form social groups, or cliques (sometimes acting against one another);

(b) develop informal ways of getting things done - norms and rules which are different from those imposed by the formal organisation.

Social groups, or cliques, may act collectively for or against the interests of their company; the like-mindedness which arises in all members of the group strengthens their collective attitudes or actions. Whether these groups work for or against the interests of the company depends to some extent on the type of supervision they get. If superiors involve them in decision-making, they are more likely to be management-minded.

2.5 The informal organisation of a company, given an acceptable social atmosphere:

(a) improves communications by means of a 'grapevine' or 'bush telegraph' system;

(b) facilitates the co-ordination of various individuals or departments and establishes 'unwritten' methods for getting a job done. These may 'by-pass' communication problems, eg between a manager and subordinate, or lengthy procedures; they may be more flexible and adaptable to required change than the formal ways of doing things.

2.6 Disadvantages of the informal structure, however, are that:

(a) individuals may put more energy and loyalty into the group than the organisation;

(b) the 'grapevine' tends to operate by distortion and rumour, more than fact;

(c) the group may have objectives (eg having fun) which run counter to organisational requirements;

(d) close-knit groups tend to feel very 'cosy' and invincible, and can make bad decisions;

(e) some individuals may be left out of the informal structure, or not have as much influence there as they ought to have according to their position in the formal structure. A manager who is not respected or liked may have his authority undermined by the informal group or leader.

2.7 A conclusion might therefore be that management should seek to harness the informal organisation to operate to the benefit of the formal organisation. In practice, however, this will be difficult because unlike formal organisation, which does not change even when individual employees move into and out of jobs (by promotion, transfer, appointment, resignation or retirement etc) most informal organisations depend on individual personalities. If one member leaves, the informal organisation is no longer the same, and new informal organisations will emerge to take its place.

2.8   D Vander Weyer (in *Management and people in banking*, ed Livy) suggests that in Britain, large banks tend to shy away from publishing formal organisation structures (eg as organisation charts) because they stifle management flexibility in the face of environmental change and interpersonal relations. In practice, however, managers function more effectively if they are clear as to the exact extent of their authority, responsibility and objectives.

2.9   In the same article, Vander Weyer argued the importance of the informal organisation in banking. The formal authority which a manager has on paper might be powerless in practice to overcome resistance from subordinate individuals within the organisation. For example, even chief general managers have little real power to extend bank opening hours, no matter that they have the apparent authority to do so. To some extent, there is a 'doctrine of acceptability'. Managers must 'sell' their authority to subordinates and peers and must win acceptance of their ideas before they can be successfully implemented. The doctrine of acceptability makes for managerial weakness, but depending on the negative power of the informal organisation, it may be inevitable, especially in large organisations such as banks. The informal organisation therefore acts to place limits on formal authority, and it is a test of the personal skills of a senior manager to achieve his business aims against this sort of resistance.

2.10   As we are beginning to see, even in formal work organisations, 'authority' takes many forms and is not exclusively bestowed by position in the organisation. Let's look at this more closely.

3.   AUTHORITY, RESPONSIBILITY AND POWER IN ORGANISATIONS

3.1   *Authority* is the right to do something. In an organisation, it refers to the scope and amount of discretion given to a person to make decisions, by virtue of the position he or she holds in the organisation: it is conferred 'from the top down' because each manager can pass on some of his or her authority to subordinates in assigning tasks to them.

However, authority is not *only* bestowed by the organisation (ie by more senior people in it). Authority can be bestowed 'from the bottom up', when it is conferred on a leader figure by people at *lower* levels in the hierarchy eg by election: trade union officials have this kind of authority.

3.2   *Responsibility* is the liability of a person to be called to account for his or her exercising of authority, actions and results. It is therefore a formal obligation to do something.

Accountability is the duty of an individual to report to his or her superior how he has fulfilled his or her responsibilities.

3.3   It is important to realise that responsibility cannot be 'delegated' or passed on to a subordinate. A manager may delegate *authority* to a subordinate (if that authority is within his *own* power to delegate) – but he remains *responsible* to his own boss for seeing that the work gets done, albeit by the subordinate rather than by himself personally. The subordinate will be responsible to him for the result, but he will also still be responsible to his own boss.

3.4   *Delegation* thus refers to the process whereby a superior gives a subordinate the authority to carry out a given aspect of the superior's own task. It is delegation that shapes the hierarchical structure of the formal organisation, where authority is passed down the 'chain of command' and accountability passes back up.

3.5 There should be a careful balance between delegated authority and responsibility in the organisation.

   (a) A manager who is not held accountable for any area of his authority is free to exercise it in a capricious way: he is not bound to do otherwise.

   (b) A manager who is held responsible for aspects of performance, but has not been given authority to control them, is in an impossible position. Sufficient authority must be given to enable the individual to do what is expected of him.

3.6 It should be evident that the boundaries of each manager's authority should be clear, to avoid ambiguity and overlap. This is an argument for 'unity of command' ie that each individual should report to only one superior, so as to avoid conflicts and doubts created by dual command. Dual command systems have, however, proved workable in practice, eg where there is project/product management: either clarified boundaries of authority or consensus management is required.

Power and influence

3.7 Influence is the process by which one person in an organisation, A, directs or modifies the behaviour or attitudes of another person, B. Influence can only be exerted by A on B if A has some kind of power from which the influence emanates. Power is therefore the ability to influence, whereas influence is an active process. Note that *power* is not the same as *authority*. A manager may have the right to expect his subordinates to carry out his instructions, but may lack the ability to make them do it. On the other hand, an individual may have the ability to make others act in a certain way, without having the organisational authority to do so: informal 'leaders' are frequently in this position.

3.8 Power and influence are clearly important factors in the structure and operations of an organisation. They help to explain how work gets done. In addition, it has also been suggested that:

   (a) an individual who believes he exerts some influence is likely to show greater interest in his work. The research of writers, such as Likert, who support the principle of management by participation suggests that employees may be more productive when they consider that they have some influence over planning decisions which affect their work;

   (b) some individuals are motivated by the need for power, and show great concern for exercising influence and control, and for being leaders.

3.9 Charles Handy (*Understanding organisations*) identified six types of power from different sources.

   (a) *Physical power* - ie the power of superior force. Physical power is absent from most organisations (except the prison service and the armed forces), but it is sometimes evident as bullying or harrassment.

   (b) *Resource power* - ie the control over resources which are valued by the individual or group to be influenced. Senior managers may have the resource power to grant promotion or pay increases to subordinates; trade unions possess the resource power to take their members out on strike. The *amount* of power a person has then depends on how far he controls the resource, how much the resource is valued by others, and how scarce it is.

(c) *Position power* - ie the power which is associated with a particular job in an organisation. Handy noted that position power has certain 'hidden' benefits:

(i) access to information;

(ii) the right of access: eg entitlement to membership of committees and contact with other 'powerful' individuals in the organisation;

(iii) the right to organise conditions of working and methods of decision-making.

(d) *Expert power* - ie the power which belongs to an individual because of his expertise, although it only works if others *acknowledge* him to be an expert. Many staff jobs in an organisation (eg computer systems analysts, organisation and methods analysts, accountants, lawyers or personnel department managers) rely on expert power to influence line management. If the expert is seen to be incompetent (eg if an accountant does not seem to provide sensible information) or if his area of expertise is not widely acknowledged (which is often the case with personnel department staff) he will have little or no expert power.

(e) *Personal power*, or *charisma* - ie the popularity of the individual. Personal power is capable of influencing the behaviour of others, and helps to explain the strength of informal organisations.

(f) *Negative power* is the use of disruptive attitudes and behaviour to stop things from happening. It is associated with low morale, latent conflict or frustration at work. A subordinate might refuse to communicate openly with his superior, and might provide false information; a colleague might refuse to co-operate; a typist might refuse to type an urgent letter because she is too busy; a worker might deliberately cause his machine to break down. Negative power is destructive and potentially very damaging to organisational efficiency.

3.10 Influence, the act of directing or modifying the behaviour of others, may then be achieved through:

(a) the application of force, eg physical or economic power;

(b) the establishment of rules and procedures - enforced through position and/or resource power;

(c) bargaining and negotiation - depending on the relative strengths of each party's position, (expert, resource or personal power etc);

(d) persuasion, again associated with various sources of power.

3.11 Handy identified two further, 'unseen' methods of influence.

(a) *Ecology*, or the environment in which behaviour takes place. The physical environment can be altered by a manager, who may be able to regulate noise levels at work, comfort and security of working conditions, seating arrangements, the use of open-plan offices or segregation into many small offices, the physical proximity of departments as well as individuals.

> 'The design of work, the work, the structure of reward and control systems, the structure of the organisation, the management of groups and the control of conflict are all ways of managing the environment in order to influence behaviour. Let us never forget that although the environment is all around us, it is not unalterable, that to change it is to influence people, that ecology is potent, the more so because it is often unnoticed.'
>
> (Handy)

(b) *Magnetism,* ie the unseen application of personal power. 'Trust, respect, charm, infectious enthusiasm, these attributes all allow us to influence people without apparently imposing on them.'

3.12 According to Amitai Etzioni, authority and power are exercised differently according to the environment, relationships and type of subordinates involved. He suggests that there are three forms of power that might be used, depending on the situation:

(a) *coercive* (eg that used in prisons): power based on fear of physical punishment;

(b) *remunerative* (eg that used in most work organisations); power based on control and administration of the reward system; and

(c) *normative* (eg in professional or religious organisations): power based on the application of norms and standards.

3.13 Max Weber, the organisational theorist most closely associated with the analysis of bureaucracy, was also interested in why individuals obeyed commands, and identified three grounds on which legitimate authority could exist.

(a) *Charismatic leadership,* based on non-rational allegiance to a leader figure who is regarded as having some special power or attribute.

(b) *Traditional or patriarchal leadership,* where authority is bestowed by virtue of hereditary entitlement and 'precedent' for decisions.

(c) *Bureaucracy:* authority is bestowed by dividing the organisation into jurisdictional areas, each with specified duties, and delegating authority to individuals to fulfil those defined roles, controlled by rules and regulations. Power is therefore of a purely 'rational-legal' nature.

Organisational politics

3.14 Organisational 'politics' is all about power and influence in an organisation. Banks, like other systems, are comprised of individuals and groups with their own interests and goals. There is competition and rivalry for finite resources, power and influence; there are cliques, alliances, pressure groups and blocking groups.

3.15 There are inevitable disparities of power and influence in organisations - and despite the rational hierarchical structure, events are often decided by certain dominant individuals or coalitions within and/or outside the organisation. Other individuals tend to want to influence, join or overthrow the dominant coalition, in order to gain power to further their own objectives, or to protect their own 'territory' (authority, specialism etc) against encroachment: interdepartmental rivalry is often of this kind.

3.16 Mintzberg (*Power In And Around Organisations*) identifies various political games, which can be stimulating for the organisation, but can also degenerate into harmful, all-absorbing conflict:

(a) games to resist authority - ie to sabotage the aims of superiors

(b) games to counter this resistance - ie the imposition of rules and controls by superiors

(c) games to build power bases - ie associating with useful superiors, forming alliances among colleagues, gaining the support of subordinates, getting control of information or resources

(d) games to defeat rivals - ie inter-group or inter-departmental conflict; and

(e) games to change the organisation - ie higher power struggles or rebellion.

4. ORGANISATION AND MANAGEMENT THEORY

4.1 It is worth noting that ideas of what organisations are, and how they should be analysed, designed and managed, have changed over the years. Organisations have been likened to 'tribes', 'organisms', 'systems', 'kingdoms' etc.

4.2 Theories about organisations tend not to be 'theories' at all, strictly speaking, but 'approaches' offering ways of looking at issues such as organisational structure, management functions or motivation. None of them can be used to predict with certainty what the 'behaviour' of an organisation, manager or employee will be in any given situation. Nor can they guarantee that application of the principles they put forward will result in effectiveness and efficiency for the organisation.

They can however provide helpful and/or thought-provoking ways of analysing organisational phenomena, and 'frameworks' within which practical problems and situations can be tackled.

The 'scientific management' and 'classical' approaches

4.3 The main early theorists who put forward ways of understanding organisations were practising managers, who analysed their own experience in management to produce a set of what they saw as 'principles' of organisation, applicable in a wide range of situations. Their approach was essentially prescriptive, ie it attempted to suggest what is good - or even best - for organisations, and contributed techniques for studying the nature of work more systematically than ever before, and solving problems of how it could be organised more efficiently.

4.4 Frederick W Taylor (1856 - 1915) pioneered the *scientific management* movement. He argued that management should be based on 'well-recognised, clearly defined and fixed principles, instead of depending on more or less hazy ideas'. This involved the development of a 'true science of work', where all the knowledge gathered and applied in the work should be investigated and reduced to 'law' and techniques.

4.5 The practical application of the approach was the use of work study techniques to break each job down into its smallest and simplest component parts: these single elements became the newly-designed 'job'. Workers were selected and trained to perform their single task in the most efficient way possible, as determined by techniques such as time and motion study to eliminate 'wasted motions' or unnecessary physical movement. Workers were paid incentives on the basis of acceptance of the new methods and output norms.

4.6. Hicks writes: 'by the end of the scientific management period, the worker had been reduced to the role of an impersonal cog in the machine of production. His work became more and more narrowly specialised until he had little appreciation for his contribution to the total product... Although very significant technological advances were made....the serious weakness of the scientific approach to management was that it de-humanised the organisational member who became a person without emotion and capable of being scientifically manipulated, just like machines'.

4.7 The *classical* approach was pioneered by Henri Fayol, who we have encountered already. It was primarily concerned with the structure and activities of the formal organisation. Effective organisation was seen to be mainly dependent on factors such as the division of work (ie specialisation); the establishment of a rational hierarchy of authority (and responsibility) and communication; span of control (the number of subordinates one manager can reasonably control); and unity of command.

Fayol popularised the concept of the 'universality of management principles', although he recognised that 'allowance must be made for different changing circumstances'.

The human relations approach

4.8 In the 1930s, a critical perception of scientific management, in particular, emerged.

'We have failed to train students in the study of social situations: we have thought that first-class technical training was sufficient in a modern and mechanical age. As a consequence, we are technically competent as no other age in history has been; and we combine this with utter social incompetence.'
Elton Mayo

4.9 Mayo (1880-1949) was pioneer of a new approach, which emphasised the importance of human attitudes, values and relationships for the efficient and effective functioning of work organisations. This was called the 'human relations' approach. It was developed mainly by social scientists - rather than practising managers - and based on research into human behaviour, with the intention of describing and thereafter predicting behaviour in organisations. Like classical theory, it was essentially prescriptive in nature.

4.10 The human relations approach concentrated mainly on the concept of "Social Man" (*Schein*): man is motivated by 'social' or 'belonging' needs, which are satisfied by the social relationships he forms at work.

Hawthorne studies

4.11 This emphasis resulted from a famous set of experiments (the 'Hawthorne Studies') carried out by Mayo and colleagues for the Western Electric Company in the USA. The company was using a group of girls as 'guinea pigs' to assess the affect of lighting on productivity: they were astonished to find that productivity shot up *whatever* they did with the lighting. The conclusion was that the girls' sense of being a group singled out for attention raised their morale. The next stage involved interviews, and revealed that work relationships were considered very important. A later stage of the research studied group behaviour specifically, and noted how a powerful and self-protecting informal organisation, with its own goals, rules and norms, was operating - even to the detriment of the company (eg by restricting output, falsifying reports and 'freezing out' disliked supervisors).

4.12 Mayo's ideas were followed up by various social psychologists - eg Maslow, Herzberg, Likert and McGregor, whose theories on motivation and leadership we discuss later - but with a change of emphasis. People were still considered to be the crucial factor in determining organisational effectiveness, but were recognised as having more than merely physical and social needs. Attention shifted towards man's 'higher' psychological needs for growth, challenge, responsibility and self-fulfilment. Herzberg suggested that only these things could positively motivate employees to improved performance: work relationships and supervisory style, along with pay and conditions, merely ward off *dis*satisfaction (and then only temporarily).

This phase was known as the 'neo-Human Relations' school.

4.13 The human relations approaches contributed an important awareness of the influence of the human factor at work (and particularly in the work group) on organisational performance. Most of its theorists attempted to offer guidelines to enable practising managers to satisfy and motivate employees and so (theoretically) to obtain the benefits of improved productivity.

4.14 However, the approach tends to emphasise the importance of work to the workers without really addressing the economic issues: there is still no proven link between job satisfaction and motivation, or either of these and productivity or the achievement of organisational goals. Employee counselling (prescribed by Mayo) and, for example, job enrichment (prescribed by Herzberg) have both proved at best of unpredictable benefit to organisations applying them in practice.

The systems and contingency approaches

4.15 The *systems approach* to organisations was developed at the Tavistock Institute of Human Relations in the 1950s, although general system theory, in which it has its scientific roots, was pioneered in the 1930s. The approach was based on the idea that a work organisation can be treated as an open system, which takes in 'inputs' (capital, labour, information, materials) from its environment and converts them into 'outputs' to the environment (information, products, satisfied customers) in a continuing cycle.

4.16 The 'system' analogy can be helpful in that it:

(a) draws attention to the *dynamic* aspects of organisation;

(b) creates an awareness of *sub-systems*, each with potentially conflicting goals to be integrated; and

(c) focuses on interrelationships between aspects of the organisation, and between the organisation and its *environment*.

4.17 A diagram of the organisation as a open system with sub-systems might appear as follows.

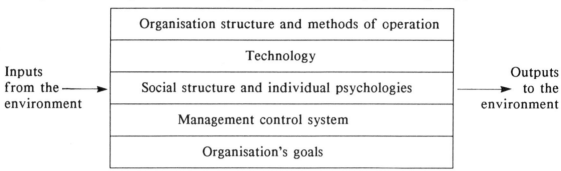

| Organisation structure and methods of operation |
| Technology |
| Social structure and individual psychologies |
| Management control system |
| Organisation's goals |

Inputs from the environment → [diagram] → Outputs to the environment

4.18 There are many sub-systems of the organisation: social systems, technology, reward systems, control systems etc. Following traditional systems theorists, Charles Handy (*Understanding organisations*) groups them into four sets of systems.

  (a) *Adaptive systems* - concerned with fitting the organisation into its environment, deciding policies, dealing with external influences, analysing and managing risk at the corporate level (see Chapter 10)

  (b) *Operating systems* - concerned with the daily existence and functions of the organisation, the basic logistics of the process of work (sales systems, production systems, transaction processing systems)

  (c) *Maintenance systems* - concerned with keeping the organisation together and healthy: integration, control and communication systems (covered in this chapter) and various personnel systems: compensation or reward systems (Chapter 4); training and career development systems (see Chapters 1 and 6); appraisal systems (Chapter 5) etc

  (d) *Information systems* - (Chapter 18) concerned with serving all of the above, providing the lifeblood of the whole organisation system: information.

4.19 Trist and Bamforth developed a more complex approach which suggested that an organisation can be treated as an open 'socio-technical' system. Any production system requires material technology (tasks, layout, equipment and tools etc) and social organisation (relationships between people): these two sub-systems are linked, and the system design must find a 'best fit' between the needs of both components.

4.20 This is called *socio-technical systems* theory. It made the very important point that technology cannot be viewed in isolation: it is not effective or ineffective (or good or bad in its affect on employees) in itself, but according to the organisation of work and social relationships *around* it, which are the subject of managerial choices. Technology does not determine organisation: decisions can and must still be made about job and task design, work place layout etc. You might consider this in relation to the effects of new technology on your own work in the bank.

4.21 Arising out of the open systems approach and its recognition of environmental influences, an essentially pragmatic view was developed which argued that *no* single theory can guarantee the organisation's effectiveness. Essentially, 'it all depends'.

4.22 This *contingency approach* aims to suggest the most appropriate organisational design and management style *in a given set of circumstances*. It rejects the universal 'one-best-way' approach, in favour of analysis of the internal factors and external environment of each organisation, and the design of organisational structure as a 'best fit' between the tasks, people and environment in the particular situation. As Buchanan and Huczynski put it: 'With the coming of contingency theory, organisational design ceased to be "off-the-shelf", but became tailored to the particular and specific needs of an organisation.'

4.23 Awareness of the contingency approach will be of value in:

(a) encouraging managers to identify and define the particular circumstances of the situation they need to manage, and to devise and evaluate appropriate ways of handling them;

(b) encouraging responsiveness and flexibility to changes in environmental factors through organisational structure and culture. Task performance and individual/group satisfaction are more important design criteria than having a single, unchanging type of organisational design. Within an organisation, there may be bureaucratic units, side by side with task-centred matrix units which can respond to particular pressures and environmental volatility.

Exercise

Paragraph 3.9 identifies six types of power. On a scale of 1 to 10 identify the extent to which each form of power is exercised in the working environment of your branch.

---

5. ASPECTS OF THE ORGANISATION

5.1 One way in which we can discuss the organisation is by using the McKinsey 7'S' approach. This describes all the various aspects of organisational life that have to be managed for the organisation to be successful. They are outlined in the diagram below.

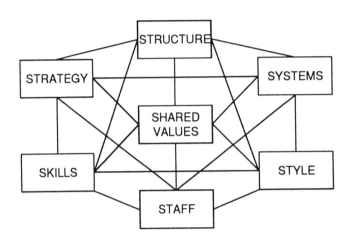

In brief, the elements in the diagram can be described as follows.

(a) *Structure*. This refers to the formal organisation structure (eg the division of tasks).

(b) *Systems*. An important example of a system is an accounting system which processes financial data and produces information. The whole gamut of information and data processing systems is referred to here, including the marketing information system.

(c) *Style* refers to how the organisation presents itself.

(d) *Staff*. This is self-explanatory.

(e) *Skills*. This is what the organisation does well. They are more than just the aggregate of individual skills, but are the ways in which these are deployed in pursuit of organisational objectives.

(f) *Strategy* in this context refers to the organisation's business and competitive strategies.

(g) *Shared values*. These are the guiding beliefs as to why the organisation exists. They refer to mission and culture.

5.2 You can use this as a checklist to review organisational life and practices. Here are some examples as to how the banks are dealing with the various 'Ss' outlined.

(a) *Structure*. Developments in how banks are organising themselves are covered in the next chapter. Examples include:

    (i)   branch closures;
    (ii) siting of cashpoint machines away from branches (eg supermarkets and airports);
    (iii) concentrating business accounts in key branches.

(b) *Systems*. Banks have been very heavy investors in information technology:

    (i)   to reduce costs;
    (ii)   to enable front line staff to take decisions;
    (iii) to provide customer databases.

(c) *Style*. Most of the banks and building societies have a distinct approach to their appearance - Barclays has a distinctive turquoise for example. But it can also refer to how managers go about their job, and how staff are treated.

(d) *Staff*. Many banks have been cutting overall staff numbers to save money, and redeploying those remaining into front line 'selling' roles. Although it is possible to exaggerate the widespread claims that there is no longer a 'job for life' many more jobs are characterised by insecurity than before. Furthermore, the promotion paths have been shortened. Staff are expected to be more flexible in the jobs they do. At the same time, banks have become less rigid in the categories of people they employ. This means allowing for women returners.

(e) *Skills*. In a way this follows on from 'staff'. Banks as a whole have needed new skills. For example, many banks have had to re-think their approaches to marketing and dealing with their customers, from an environment of little competition to one of high competition.

(f) *Strategy*. A recent example of a strategic development is the proposed merger between Lloyds and the TSB. Lloyd's customer base is deeper in the South of England, whereas the TSB is stronger in the North. The building society sector is going through a spate of mergers. Another strategy seems to be to attract more business from the existing customer base. Some banks are reducing their investment banking and money-market operations. There is some caution about overseas organisation.

(g) *Shared values*. In a time of disruption and change, talking about shared values can often result in cynicism, especially where the old value system requires change. Whilst trying to enhance commitment to quality and customers, banks are scaling down their commitment to the staff, leading to short term working. Squaring the circle of requiring more customer-orientated staff but offering them less is likely to prove difficult.

6. CHAPTER ROUNDUP

6.1

'School'	Interest in	Names to note
Scientific	Organisation, analysis of work, methodical approach	F W Taylor
Classical	Organisation	Henri Fayol
Human relations	Social relationships between workers as the prime factor in motivation	Elton Mayo (Hawthorne studies)
Neo-human relations	'Complex man' - capable of a range of motivations at work; intrinsic satisfactions	Abraham Maslow Frederick Herzberg Peter Drucker
Systems/socio-technical systems	Organisations as open systems, interacting with the environment: social (relationships) and technical (technology and work methods) sub-systems	Katz and Kahn Eric Trist (Tavistock Institute)
Contingency	No 'one best way': 'it all depends'	Laurence and Lorsch Burns and Stalker Joan Woodward

6.2 Here are some rules of thumb.

(a) *Authority* is the right to act.
(b) *Responsibility* is the duty to act.
(c) *Power* is the ability to influence others to act.
(d) *Influence* is the process by which you get others to act.

6.3 The sources of power may be:

(a) physical or coercive;
(b) resource or remunerative;
(c) positional, legal, rational or bureaucratic;
(d) expert;
(e) personal or charismatic;
(f) negative;
(g) traditional or patriarchal;
(h) ecological.

TEST YOUR KNOWLEDGE

The numbers in brackets refer to paragraphs of this chapter

1   Why do individuals form or join organisations? (1.4)

2   What does a manager pass on when he 'delegates'? What does he *not* pass on, and why? (3.3)

3   List the types of power available to an individual. Give an example of the source of each type of power. (3.9, 3.11)

4   Give five examples of 'political' activity in an organisation - perhaps in your own bank. (3.16)

5   What aspects of:

(a)   scientific management; and
(b)   the human-relations approaches

can you recognise in your own bank and job?
(4.6, 4.10, 4.12 - but think about your own experience)

6   What are the contributions to management of:

(a)   systems theory; and
(b)   the contingency approach?   (4.16, 4.19, 4.22)

Now try question 15 at the end of the text

Chapter 16

ORGANISATION DESIGN AND CULTURE

This chapter covers the following topics.

1. What do we mean by organisational structure?
2. Bases of organisational design
3. Bureaucracy
4. The structure of banks
5. Organisational culture
6. The adaptive organisation

Introduction

As we saw in the previous chapter, there have been several theories about what the best approach to discussing organisation might be, but all theorists agree that organisation design is important - whether as the prime factor of controlled performance, or as part of the organisational system, or as one of the contingent facts in organisational behaviour.

---

1. WHAT DO WE MEAN BY ORGANISATION STRUCTURE?

1.1 Organisational design or structure implies a framework or mechanism intended:

(a) to link individuals in an established network of relationships so that authority, responsibility and communications can be controlled;

(b) to group together (in any appropriate way) the tasks required to fulfil the objectives of the organisation, and allocate them to suitable individuals or groups;

(c) to give each individual or group the authority required to perform the allocated functions, while controlling behaviour and resources in the interests of the organisation as a whole;

(d) to co-ordinate the objectives and activities of separate units, so that overall aims are achieved without 'gaps' or 'overlaps' in the flow of work required;

(e) to facilitate the flow of work, information and other resources required, through planning, control and other systems.

1.2 The advantages of having a formal organisation structure therefore include:

(a) unity or 'congruence' of objectives and effort;

(b)   clarity in expressing objectives;

(c)   control over interpersonal relationships, exercise of authority, use of resources, communication and other systems (eg promotion, planning, reward, discipline), offering predictability and stability for planning and decision-making;

(d)   controlled information flow throughout the structure to aid co-ordination and (arguably) employee satisfaction;

(e)   the establishment of precedents, procedures, rules and norms to facilitate decision-making and interpersonal relations in recurring situations.

1.3   Many factors influence the structural design of the organisation.

(a)   *Size.* As an organisation gets larger, its structure gets more complex: specialisation and subdivision are required. The process of controlling and co-ordinating performance, and communication between individuals, also grows more difficult as the 'top' of the organisation gets further from the 'bottom' ie with more intervening levels. The more members there are, the more potential there is for interpersonal relationships and the development of the *informal* organisation.

(b)   *Task,* ie the nature of its work. Structure is shaped by the division of work into functions and individual tasks, and how these tasks relate to each other. Depending on the nature of the work, this can be done in a number of ways. The complexity and importance of tasks will affect the amount of supervision required, and so the ratio of supervisors to workers. The nature of the market will dictate the way in which tasks are grouped together: into functions, or sales territories, or types of customer etc.

(c)   *Staff.* The skills and abilities of staff will determine how the work is structured and the degree of autonomy or supervision required. Staff aspirations and expectations may also influence job design, and the amount of delegation in the organisation, in order to provide job satisfaction.

(d)   Legal, commercial, technical and social *environment.* Examples include: economic recession necessitating staff 'streamlining' especially at middle management level; market pressures in the financial services sector encouraging a greater concentration of staff in specialised areas and at the bank/customer interface; new technology reducing staff requirements but increasing specialisation.

(e)   *Age* - ie the time it has had to develop and grow, or decline, whether it is very set in its ways and traditional or experimenting with new ways of doing things and making decisions.

(f)   *Culture and management style* - how willing management is to delegate authority at all levels, how skilled they are in organisation and communication (eg in handling a wider span of control), whether teamwork is favoured, or large, impersonal structures accepted by the staff etc.

(g)   *Customers.* Marketing considerations can influence organisation structure. This partly explains the move by some of the banks to set up regional business centres for business clients offering a wider range of relevant expertise and services than would have been available at a small local branch.

1.4 We'll discuss specific recent influences on the structure of banks a bit later in this chapter. First, we look at some of the concepts associated with organisational design.

2. BASES OF ORGANISATIONAL DESIGN

Scalar chain

2.1 The *scalar chain* or *chain of command* is the term used to describe the organisation's formal management hierarchy, that is the chain of superiors from lowest to highest rank. Formal communication runs up and down the lines of authority, eg E to D to C to B to A in the diagram below. Note that if communication between different branches of the chain is necessary (eg D to H) the use of a 'gang plank' of horizontal communication saves time and is likely to be more accurate, so long as superiors know that such communication is taking place.

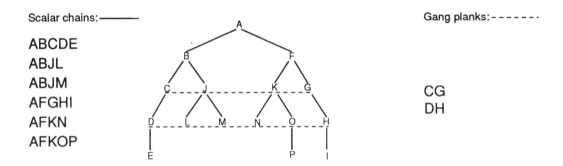

2.2 There might be a tendency for chains of command within a single organisation to get longer as the organisation grows older, larger, and its activities more complicated. The length of the chains of command is a function of:

(a) the size of the organisation;
(b) the type and complexity of the products it makes or services it provides;
(c) the diversity of its products and services;
(d) its geographical spread;
(e) the number and complexity of controls required; and
(f) the type of people it employs.

2.3 No rules have been (or can be) laid down for how chains of command should be structured, but a few general principles are as follows. Chains of command should:

(a) reflect the business organisation, its environment, products, employees, diversity, spread and controls (so that managers can concentrate on the business rather than on purely internal organisational issues);

(b) be as short as possible consistent with efficiency and effectiveness, so that news can be communicated quickly and be met with a swift response;

(c) be short enough to provide a training ground for developing managers, which encourages a tendency towards guiding some operations into divisions or subsidiaries.

Span of control

2.4 The span of control is the number of people under the direct control of a given 'delegator' or superior official. In other words, if a manager has five subordinates responsible directly to him, the span of control is five.

2.5 Various classical theorists suggest that:

(a) there are physical and mental limitations to any given manager's ability to control people, relationships and activities, but that

(b) there needs to be tight managerial control from the top of an organisation downward.

The span of control should therefore, they argued, be restricted, to allow maximum control consistent with the manager's capabilities: usually between three and six. If the span of control is too wide, too much of the manager's time will be taken up with routine problems and supervision, leaving less time for planning: even so, subordinates may not get the supervision, control, communication etc that they require.

2.6 On the other hand, if the span is too narrow, the manager may fail to delegate, keeping too much routine work to himself and depriving subordinates of decision-making authority and responsibility. There may be a tendency to interfere in or over-supervise the work that is delegated to subordinates - and the relative costs of supervision will thus be unnecessarily high. Subordinates tend to be dissatisfied in such situations, having too little challenge and responsibility and perhaps feeling that the superior does not trust them.

2.7 The appropriate span of control will depend on various factors.

(a) *Ability of the manager.* A good organiser and communicator will be able to control a larger number. The manager's work-load will also be relevant, as will be his ability to handle interruptions to his own work.

(b) *Ability of the subordinates.* The more able, intelligent, trustworthy and well-trained subordinates are, the easier it is to control large numbers, as they need less support and advice to work on their own.

(c) *Nature of the task.* It is easier for a supervisor to control a large number of people if they are all doing routine, repetitive or similar tasks. Where closer control is necessary, the span would have to be smaller. The *technology* of the task may also make control easier (eg if the task is highly automated) or more necessary (eg if it is complex and specialised).

(d) The *geographical dispersal* or grouping of the subordinates, and the communication system of the organisation. These may or may not facilitate control.

2.8 The span of control has implications for the 'shape' of the organisation. An organisation with a narrow span of control will have more levels in its management hierarchy than an organisation of the same size with a wide span of control: the first organisation will be narrow and 'tall', while the second will be wide and 'flat'. In fact, it is the 'flat' organisation that reflects a greater degree of delegation in the structure: the more a manager delegates, the wider his span of control can be, and authority is shared among more people, further down the organisation. A 'tall' organisation reflects tighter supervision and control, and lengthy chains of command and communication.

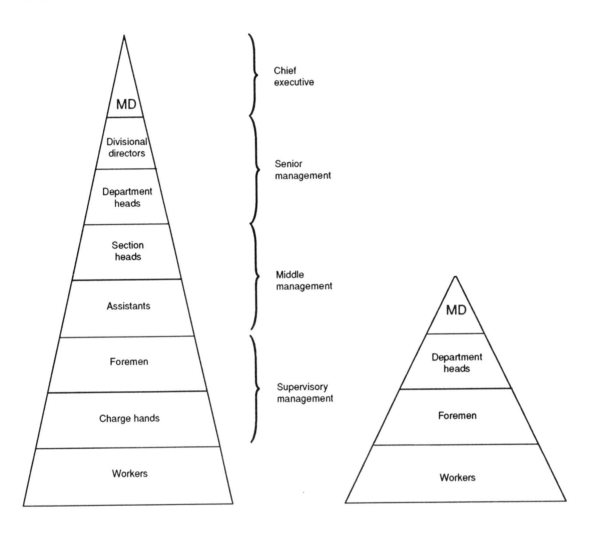

Exercise 1

Draw an organisation chart for your branch indicating the chain of command and the spans of control.

Centralisation and decentralisation

2.9   Centralisation and decentralisation refer to the degree to which authority is delegated in an organisation. The terms are thereby used to describe the level at which decisions are taken in the management hierarchy.

2.10 A number of factors which influence the appropriate degree of centralisation can be listed as follows.

(a) *Cost.* By delegating authority there is the potential cost of mistakes which the subordinate might make. On the other hand, the failure to delegate sufficient authority has a hidden cost of low morale among subordinates and poor management succession.

(b) *The status of the organisation's planning, control and information systems:* when an organisation has a well established system of planning (eg management by objectives), and when control information is reported regularly and efficiently, it will be safer to decentralise.

(c) *The environment of the organisation:* if the organisation is faced with rapid change, competition etc, there will be a greater reliance on the flexibility, local knowledge and 'on-the-spot' decisions which characterise decentralisation.

(d) *The culture and personnel of the organisation:* the skill, knowledge and attitudes of subordinates will help to decide how much delegation will be wanted by the subordinates, and how far superiors trust them.

(e) *Technology of the organisation.* It is possible to exercise better and cheaper central control by means of a computerised information system for management. However, developments in technology (eg remote micro-computers linked to a central computer) have also facilitated decentralisation.

(f) *Uniformity:* where a high level of uniformity and co-ordination is required throughout the organisation, there is likely to be more centralisation of authority.

(g) *The decision itself.* Broadly, the scope importance of the decision should be matched to the authority and skill of the manager taking it.

(h) *Management philosophy:* the philosophy of senior managers might favour either centralisation or delegation, and they will give authority to subordinates in accordance with these views.

Arguments in favour of centralisation and decentralisation

Pro centralisation

1 Decisions are made at one point and so easier to co-ordinate.

2 Senior managers in an organisation can take a wider view of problems and consequences

3 Senior management can keep a proper balance between different departments or functions - eg by deciding on the resources to allocate to each

4 Quality of decisions is (theoretically) higher due to senior managers' skills and experience

Pro decentralisation/delegation

1 Avoids overburdening top managers, in terms of workload and stress

2 Improves motivation of more junior managers who are given responsibility - since job challenge and entrepreneurial skills are highly valued in today's work environment.

3 Greater awareness of local problems by decision makers. Geographically dispersed organisations should often be decentralised on a regional/area basis.

---

5 Possibly cheaper, by reducing number of managers needed and so lower cost of overheads	4 Greater speed of decision making, and response to changing events, since no need to refer decisions upwards. This is particularly important in rapidly changing markets.
6 Crisis decisions are taken more quickly at the centre, without need to refer back, get authority etc	5 Helps junior managers to develop and helps the process of transition from functional to general management.
7 Policies, procedures and documentation can be standardised organisation-wide	6 Separate spheres of responsibility can be identified: controls, performance measurement and accountability are better.
	7 Communication technology allows decisions to be made locally, with information and input from head office if required.

2.11 Banks have attempted both centralisation and decentralisation. There was a trend for some processing to be centralised, and also for some branches to be converted into 'hubs' dealing with business clients. However some banks have reversed this trend.

Line and staff management

2.12 'Line' and 'staff' can be used to denote functions in the organisation.

(a) *Line* management consists of those managers directly involved in achieving the objectives of an organisation (eg all production and sales managers).

(b) Every other manager represents staff management (eg accounting, personnel, research and development). Staff activities are those which primarily exist to provide advice and service.

2.13 The terms are also used to denote authority relationships. A manager (even a personnel - staff - manager) has 'line' authority over his own subordinates: authority passed down the chain of command. 'Staff' authority depends on persuasion and 'expert' power, and crosses departmental boundaries.

2.14 Accountants, personnel administrators, economists, data processing experts and statisticians are all experts in a specialised field of work. Where this expertise is 'syphoned off' into a separate department, the problem naturally arises as to whether:

(a) the experts *advise* line managers, who may accept or reject the advice given; or
(b) the experts can step in to *direct* the line managers in what to do.

2.15 'Staff authority' is now usually considered to be purely advisory: the organisation and methods department, for example, or the 'personal assistant' are such roles.

2.16 The term *functional authority* is a step further in the recognition that some 'staff' management has become highly specialised in areas of work which form a fundamental part of line management. This 'expert' power becomes formally recognised in the organisation/management structure, merging line and staff authority: the expert has formally delegated to him the authority to influence specific areas (those in which he is a specialist) of the work of other departments and their managers.

2.17 This is a move towards dual authority, since the line manager retains ultimate authority for the functioning of his department. For this reason, and to avoid complex political problems, functional authority is usually exercised through the establishing of systems, procedures and standards, rather than by on-going direct intervention on the part of functional specialists.

2.18 There are drawbacks to using staff departments.

(a) There is a danger that staff experts may, intentionally or not, undermine the authority of line managers.

(b) Friction may also occur when staff managers report on the line departments' performance, over the heads of line managers, eg to the managing director.

(c) Staff managers have no line authority and are therefore not accountable for the effect of their advice.

2.19 The solutions to these problems are easily stated, but not easy to implement in practice.

(a) Authority must be clearly defined, and distinctions between line, staff and functional authority clearly set out (eg in job descriptions).

(b) The use of experts should become part of the organisational culture - with emphasis on the building of multi-disciplinary teams if possible.

(c) Staff managers must be fully informed about the operational aspects of the business, so they will be less likely to offer impractical advice.

Different types of structure

2.20 The grouping of organisational activities (usually in the form of 'departments') can be done in different ways. The most common forms of departmentation are based on:

(a) *Function*: this is a widely-used method of organisation. Primary functions in a manufacturing company might be production, sales, finance, and general administration. In a bank, they might be domestic banking, international banking, executor and trustee, staff, marketing. Functional organisation is logical and traditional and accommodates the division of work into specialist areas. Apart from the problems which may arise when 'line' management resents interference by 'staff' advisers in their functional area, the drawback to functional organisation is simply that more efficient structures might exist which would be more appropriate in a particular situation.

Departmentation by function

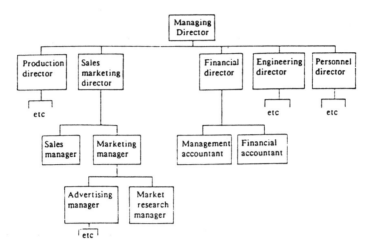

(b) *Territory*. This method of organisation is suitable when similar activities are carried out in widely different locations. Many sales departments are organised territorially. The branch structure of a bank works in the same way, to offer local provision of services.

(i)   The *advantage* of territorial departmentation is better local decision-making at the point of contact between the organisation (eg a salesman) and its customers. Localised knowledge is put to better use. In a personal service industry like banking, the close relationship between the local branch and the community will be important - although 'remote' centralised banking by telephone and post (eg First Direct) are also being explored.

(ii)   The *disadvantage* of territorial departmentation might be the duplication of management effort, increasing overhead costs and the risk of dis-integration. For example, a national organisation divided into ten regions might have a customer liaison department at each regional head office.

Departmentation by territory

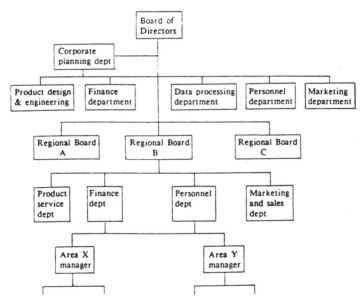

Functional divisions within areas

(c) *Product.* Some organisations group activities on the basis of products or product lines. Functional division of responsibility remains, but under the overall control of a manager with responsibility for the product, product line or brand (eg in a bank, pensions, portfolio management, mortgages etc.)

    (i)   The *advantages* of product departmentation are that:

        (1)   individual managers can be held accountable for the *profitability* of individual products;

        (2)   specialisation can be developed. For example, salesmen can be trained to sell a specific product in which they may develop technical expertise;

        (3)   the different functional activities and efforts required to make and sell each product can be co-ordinated and integrated by the product manager.

    (ii)   The *disadvantage* of product departmentation is that it increases the overhead costs and managerial complexity of the organisation;

Departmentation by product

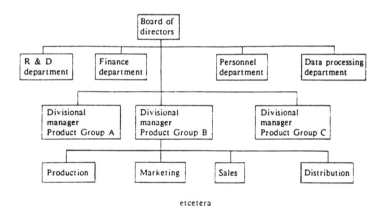

etcetera

(d) *Customer or market segment.* Departmentation by customer is commonly associated with sales departments and selling effort, but it is increasingly used at the product development stage. The internal structure of a bank branch, for example, might reflect the division of business between domestic and foreign, or personal, small businesses and corporate customers.

(e) *Common processes or technology.* The most obvious example is the data processing department of large organisations. Batch processing operations are conducted for other departments at a computer centre (where it is controlled by DP staff) because it would be uneconomical to provide each functional department with its own large mainframe computer.

Matrix organisation

2.21 In recent years, the awareness of internal and external influences on organisational structure and operation has contributed to a new emphasis on flexibility and adaptability in organisational design, particularly since the pace of the change in the technological and competitive environment has put pressure on businesses to innovate, to adopt a market orientation.

2.22 Part of this shift in emphasis has been a trend towards task-centred structures, eg multi-disciplinary project teams, which draw experience, knowledge and expertise together from different functions to facilitate flexibility and innovation. In particular, the concept of 'matrix' organisation has emerged, dividing authority between functional managers and product or project managers or co-ordinators - thus challenging classical assumptions about 'one man one boss' and the line/staff dilemma.

2.23 Matrix management first developed in the 1950s in the USA in the aerospace industry. Lockheed-California, the aircraft manufacturers, were organised in a functional hierarchy. Customers were unable to find a manager in Lockheed to whom they could take their problems and queries about their particular orders, and Lockheed found it necessary to employ 'project expediters' as customer liaison officials. From this developed 'project co-ordinators', responsible for co-ordinating line managers into solving a customer's problems. Up to this point, these new officials had no functional responsibilities. With increasingly heavy customer demand, Lockheed eventually created 'programme managers', with full authority for project budgets and programme design and scheduling. This dual authority structure may be shown diagrammatically as a management *grid*; for example:

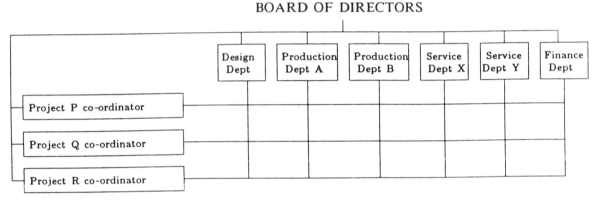

Functional department heads are responsible for the internal organisation of their departments, but project co-ordinators are responsible for the aspects of all departmental activity that affects their particular project.

2.24 The authority of product or project managers may vary from organisation to organisation. J K Galbraith drew up a range of alternative situations, as shown.

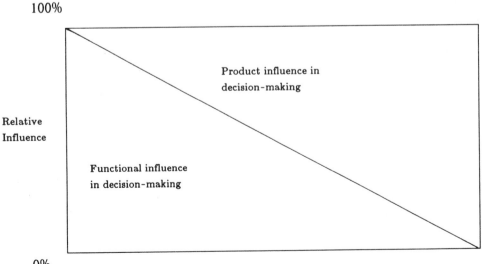

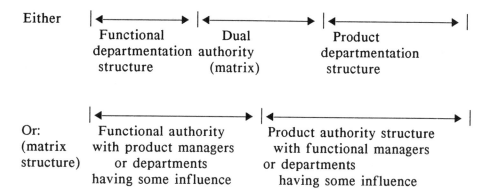

2.25 The *advantages* of a matrix structure are said to be:

(a) greater flexibility:

    (i) of people. Employees develop an attitude geared to accepting change, and departmental monopolies are broken down;

    (ii) of tasks and structure. The matrix structure may be short-term (as with project teams) or readily amended;

(b) re-orientation. A functional department will often be production-oriented: product management will create a market orientation;

(c) a structure for allocating responsibility to managers for end-results;

(d) inter-disciplinary co-operation and a mixing of skills and expertise;

(e) arguably, motivation of employees by providing them with greater participation in planning and control decisions.

2.26 The *disadvantages* of matrix organisation are said to be as follows.

(a) Dual authority threatens a conflict between functional managers and product/project managers. Where matrix structure exists it is important that the authority of superiors should not overlap and areas of authority must be clearly defined. A subordinate must know to which superior he is responsible for a particular aspect of his duties.

(b) One individual with two or more bosses is more likely to suffer stress at work.

(c) Matrix management can be more costly - eg product management posts are added, meetings held etc.

(d) It may be difficult for the management of an organisation to accept a matrix structure and the culture of participation, share authority and ambiguity that it fosters.

3. BUREAUCRACY

3.1 Max Weber (1864-1920) is the organisational theorist most closely associated with the analysis of bureaucracy.

3.2 Bureaucracy is a formal organisation structure built on a high degree of specialisation and delegation, legal authority, rules and procedures. To a layman, the term has unpleasant associations, but Weber was inclined to regard it as the ideal form of organisation, which is 'from a purely technical point of view, capable of attaining the highest degree of efficiency and is in this sense formally the most rational means of carrying out imperative control over human beings'.

3.3 Weber specified several general characteristics of bureaucracy, which he described as 'a continuous organisation of official functions bound by rules'.

   (a) *Hierarchy*: each lower office is under the control and supervision of a higher one.

   (b) *Specialisation and training*: there is a high degree of specialisation of labour, and an emphasis on ability.

   (c) *Impersonal nature*: employees work within impersonal rules, regulations and procedures.

   (d) *Rationality*: the 'jurisdictional areas' of the organisation are determined rationally. The hierarchy of authority and office structure is clearly defined. Duties are established and measures of performance set.

   (e) *Uniformity* in the performance of tasks is expected, regardless of who is engaged in carrying them out.

   (f) *Technical competence* in officials, which is rarely questioned within the area of their expertise.

   (g) *Stability*.

3.4 The potential advantages of bureaucracy may be apparent. Weber was impressed with the development and accomplishments of bureaucracy, and especially with the role of technical knowledge in bureaucratic administration, which he regarded as the primary source of the superiority of bureaucracy as an organisation. He did however, fear that its success would have a 'deadening' effect on people, creating an organisation of 'little cogs, little men, clinging to little jobs and striving towards bigger ones.'

3.5 Weber argued that bureaucracy was the most efficient form of organisation because:

   (a) it is supposedly free from the personal bias of individual managers (although some bureaucracies are intensely *political*);

   (b) its authority system is based on merit;

   (c) it is based on the rational achievement of its objectives;

   (d) it is free from human friction and relationships in pursuing the organisation's objectives - that is, the personal element (which can be destructive) is taken out;

   (e) it makes full use of technical knowledge;

   (f) it encourages close control and co-ordination of activities;

    (g)   employees find the working environment stable and secure;

    (h)   it is very useful for businesses where operations are routine, because situations are categorised in order to reach decisions, and decision-making is therefore simplified;

    (i)   it provides a hierarchy for structured career development.

3.6   Criticisms of bureaucracy, however, have included the following.

    (a)   Rules have a tendency to take on a life of their own, so they are applied without reference to the specific objectives they are supposed to achieve.

    (b)   Decision-making is 'routinised' by rules and categorisations, but the routine may be unable to cope with non-routine situations. This in turn means that decisions tend to be referred upwards - 'passing the buck'.

    (c)   The above disadvantages contribute towards a rigidity of behaviour which may create reliability, but increases difficulties with regard to response to the needs of customers/clients.

    (d)   Bureaucracies are unable to adapt to conditions of change. They tend to discourage innovation and initiative on the part of individuals. According to Michael Crozier, the control mechanism (whereby feedback on errors is used to initiate corrective action) is hampered: bureaucracies cannot learn from their mistakes! Because of delays in taking action, and the cultural resistance to change caused by the type of people attracted and recruited to bureaucracies, Crozier suggests that bureaucracies cannot adjust to inevitable environmental changes without 'deeply-felt crisis'.

3.7   This is undoubtedly the most serious disadvantage of bureaucracy, especially in a fast-changing environment.

4.   THE STRUCTURE OF BANKS

4.1   The major UK clearing banks have broadly similar organisational structures, with a central or head office in London, regional offices around the UK and branch networks controlled by the regional offices. From this wide viewpoint, then, they are structured territorially. However, the *management* structure of a clearing bank is a mixture of functional and product/market organisation. For example:

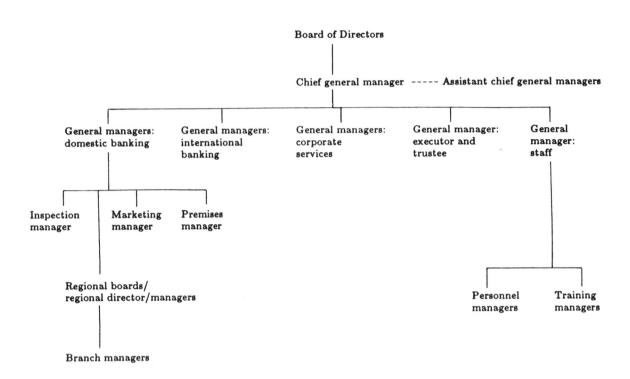

4.2 At the regional level, management structure tends to vary from bank to bank. Most banks however, do delegate authority to regional units. This helps to establish a local identity for the bank and provides a framework for controlling branch activity: there are 'ceilings' on the authority of branch managers (eg to approve or renew overdraft or loan facilities) and any decision too 'big' for them to take on their own must be sanctioned by regional office. Only very large transactions would require regional office to refer back to head office.

4.3 *Support* departments of the bank - personnel, training, inspection, marketing, premises management, computing, organisation and methods etc - provide specialist services of benefit to the bank as a whole. These may operate at national level, reporting to the general managers, or at regional level. Marketing, for example, is a function which has permeated deep into the branch structure.

4.4 At branch level, organisation again varies from bank to bank, and with the size of the branch. Job titles also differ, but an example of a traditional medium-sized branch structure might be:

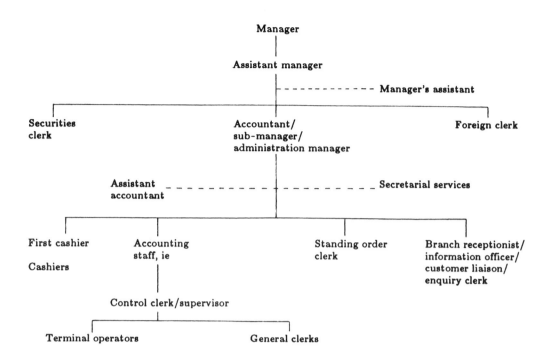

Trends in banking structures

4.5 Fierce competition, interest-bearing current accounts, the slowdown in personal lending and other pressures have prompted cost reduction exercises in many banks. The automation of many processes has contributed to radical restructuring which has effected staff from back-office to upper management level, with retraining and transfers, early retirements, bar on recruitment, and redundancies.

It is not just a question of reducing 'head-count' but of restructuring - in most cases to take processing operations out of the branches and to centralise them, and to reorientate the staff and management structure towards selling activities.

4.6 Sub-branches (branches provided with a skeleton staff from other branches) have been closed, and other branches down-graded from 'full manager' to 'sub-manager' status: a sub-manager has limited lending powers and may need authorisation from the manager of the nearby 'full' branch.

4.7 Thus at local level there has developed a structure of support (*satellite*) branches run by a 'clerk in charge', under the control of a main/key branch and its manager, or the local area office. The support branches offer basic banking services - paying in, drawing out and very limited lending: lending managers, and specialists such as foreign business and securities clerks, work at or from the key branch. The customer must go the *main branch* to make use of specialist services or arrange loans, although the specialists are increasingly willing to attend a support branch by appointment.

4.8 The costs of the branch network are thus reduced, and there are advantages in specialisation, in faster and more knowledgeable service to the customer. However, there is a loss of convenience for the customer of a support branch, and a weakening of the traditional relationship between the customer and his branch manager, who used to be an 'all rounder' and stable point of contact with the bank. This was one of the criticisms of banks mentioned in an earlier chapter.

4.9 Some banks have tried to market the advantages of the 'cluster' concept: rather than free-standing branches, each a self-contained unit providing a range of products and services, there will be a cluster of units, with a team of managers specialising in particular disciplines, eg personal sector services, business services, corporate services etc. This is intended to free managers from administrative burdens (since there will be an operations manager as well) and allow them to provide more focused management attention, and to respond flexibly to the needs of their customers (and potential customers).

4.10 The role of the branch has changed in other ways.

(a) Technological advances have eroded the person-to-person contact and administrative processing roles of branches. Automated Teller Machines (ATMs) are often installed in the public areas of branches or in a separate 'card access lobby' to which customers gain access using their ATM or credit card. Some branches have been entirely replaced by ATMs. The concept of 'automated delivery channels' has developed as far as 'remote only' services such as First Direct, with no branch network at all.

(b) The automation of clerical procedures has 'liberated' bank staff for a role which competitive pressures have necessitated: selling. Staff are to be redeployed from clerical to sales/customer service positions, just as managers are developing their roles in seeking new business.

4.11 The traditional view of the bank as a bureaucratic structure and culture is thus beginning to be eroded.

(a) The tall, highly 'tiered' vertical structure characteristic of bureaucracy is less in evidence now - there are more flexible, 'slimmed-down' staffs. Whole layers of head office management have been abolished, shortening lines of communication between senior management and the regions, which have a great deal more input and autonomy. In other words, the scalar chain has shortened, and spans of control are wider, leading to flatter organisations.

(b) Increased competition in the financial services market has re-emphasised the importance of the customer in banking, and the need for greater responsiveness, at least at the interface between the bank and its customers/clients. The emergence of 'the action bank', 'the bank that likes to say yes', 'the listening bank' etc as banking cultures illustrates this recognition, as do the various attempts by banks to encourage greater face-to-face contact between customers and 'personal bankers' in open plan reception areas of branches.

(c) Increased competition has also encouraged a wider range of products and aggressive marketing policies. Quick reaction to competitors' actions and innovations has been a feature of recent years, with banks following each other swiftly into areas such as extended banking hours, Saturday (and even Sunday) opening, debit cards, ATM expansion, interest on current accounts etc. Branding of products and tailoring of product ranges to suit market segments (eg small business, corporate personal, 'high-net-worth') and locality areas are further evidence of increasing flexibility. Branches are being restructured on this basis.

(d) The management structures required to create and maintain the above flexibility and speed of reaction - and also product innovation - tend to be non-bureaucratic. Product development task forces, for example, need to be used. Communication upwards from the 'front line' needs to be speeded up, as does the decision-making process. Elements of matrix structure are now used at Citibank, for example, and quality circles eg at Nat West. Smaller units are being utilised, with more autonomy in certain areas of new business development, ie more decentralisation to branch levels where managers are being made responsible for performance. Segmentation (eg separating the management of corporate and retail services) is being applied throughout bank structures.

4.12 Two examples are given by the National and Provincial Building Society and the Leeds Permanent which called off a proposed merger. The Financial Times reported (29 October 1993):

'Leeds is seen in the industry as having a more traditional and hierarchical management structure, while N&P has adopted an approach which is based more on teamwork, and emphasises a focus on the customer rather than on the product.

Mr O'Brien's redesign of the management structure at N&P since he became chief executive in 1990 has produced a sharp reduction in the number of management grades.'

Exercise 2

Would you say that your bank is centralised or decentralised? What type of organisation structure does it have? Identify the changes in structure that have taken place over the past few years.

---

5. ORGANISATIONAL CULTURE

5.1 Every organisation is different, as you will readily appreciate if you have worked in more than one. Why is this so? After all, two organisations such as banks may be similarly structured and involved in similar activities - and *still* be quite unlike to work for or deal with. The concept of organisational 'style' or 'climate' has been developed to explore such differences: the most current term for it is 'culture'. Culture is important. The Financial Times (29 October 1993) reported that the Leeds Permanent and the National Provincial Building Society called off a proposed merger because 'it would be too difficult to combine the different cultures, on top of the need to bring together two complex businesses'.

5.2 Culture may be defined as *the complex body of shared values and beliefs of an organisation.* Handy sums up 'culture' as 'that's the way we do things round here'. For Schein, it is 'the pattern of basic assumptions that a given group has invented, discovered, or developed, in learning to cope with its problems of external adaption and internal integration, and that have worked well enough to be considered valid and, therefore, to be taught to new members as the correct way to perceive, think and feel in relation to these problems.'

> 'I believe that the real difference between success and failure in a corporation can very often be traced to the question of how well the organisation brings out the great energies and talents of its people. What does it do to help these people find common cause with each other? And how can it sustain this common cause and sense of direction through the many changes which take place from one generation to another?...I think you will find that it owes its resiliency not to its form of organisation or administrative skills, but to the power of what we call *beliefs* and the appeal these beliefs have for its people.'
>
> Watson (IBM) quoted by
> Peters and Waterman

5.3 All organisations will generate their own cultures, whether spontaneously or under the guidance of positive managerial strategy. The culture will consist of the following.

(a) The *basic, underlying assumptions* which guide the behaviour of the individuals and groups in the organisation, eg customer orientation, or belief in quality, trust in the organisation to provide rewards, freedom to make decisions, freedom to make mistakes, and the value of innovation and initiative at all levels. Assumptions will be reflected in the kind of people employed (their age, education or personality), the degree of delegation and communication, whether decisions are made by committees or individuals etc.

(b) *Overt beliefs* expressed by the organisation and its members, which can be used to condition (a) above. These beliefs and values may emerge as sayings, slogans, mottos etc. such as 'we're getting there', 'the customer is always right', or 'the winning team'. They may emerge in a richer mythology - in jokes and stories about past successes , heroic failures or breakthroughs, legends about the 'early days', or about 'the time the boss...'. Organisations with strong cultures often centre themselves around almost legendary figures in their history. Management can encourage this by 'selling' a sense of the corporate 'mission', or by promoting the company's 'image'; it can reward the 'right' attitudes and punish (or simply not employ) those who aren't prepared to commit themselves to the culture.

(c) *Visible artefacts* - the style of the offices or other premises, dress 'rules', display of 'trophies', the degree of informality between superiors and subordinates etc.

5.4 'Positive' organisational culture may therefore be important in its influence on:

(a) the motivation and satisfaction of employees (and possibly therefore their performance) by encouraging commitment to the organisation's values and objectives, making employees feel valued and trusted, fostering satisfying team relationships, and using 'guiding values' instead of rules and controls;

(b) the adaptability of the organisation, by encouraging innovation, risk-taking, sensitivity to the environment, customer care, willingness to embrace new methods and technologies etc; and

(c) the image of the organisation held by its customers. The cultural attributes of an organisation (attractive or unattractive) will affect its appeal to potential employees, customers etc. For example, the moves of banks to modernise and beautify branch design are meant to convey a 'style' that is up-to-date, welcoming, friendly but business-like, with open-plan welcome areas, helpful signposting, lots of light and plants etc.

Cultural problems and how to change culture

5.5 Not all organisation cultures are so 'positive' in their nature and effect, however. The symptoms of a negative, unhealthy or failing culture (and possibly organisation as a whole) might be as follows.

(a) No 'visionary' element: no articulated beliefs or values widely shared, nor any sense of the future.

(b) No sense of unity - because no central driving force. Hostility and lack of co-ordination may be evident.

(c) No shared norms of dress, habits, ways of addressing others etc. Sub-cultures may compete with each other.

(d) Political conflict and rivalry, as individuals and group vie for power and resources and their own interests.

(e) Focus on the internal workings of the organisation rather than opportunities and changes in the environment. In particular, disinterest in the customer.

(f) Preoccupation with the short term.

(g) Low employee morale, expressed in low productivity, high absenteeism and labour turnover, 'grumbling' etc.

(h) Abdication by management of the responsibility for doing anything about the above - perhaps because of apathy or hopelessness.

(i) No innovation or welcoming of change: change is a threat and a problem.

(j) Rigorous control and disciplinary systems have to be applied, because nothing else brings employees into line with the aims of the business.

(k) Lacklustre marketing, company literature etc.

5.6 There are many factors which influence the organisational culture, including the following.

(a) *Economic conditions*
In prosperous times organisations will either be complacent or adventurous, full of new ideas and initiatives. In recession they may be depressed, or challenged. The struggle against a main competitor may take on 'heroic' dimensions.

(b) *Nature of the business and its tasks*
The types of technology used in different forms of business create the pace and priorities associated with different forms of work, eg the hustle and frantic conditions for people dealing in the international money market compared with the studious life of a research officer. Task also to an extent influences work environment, which is an important visual cultural indicator.

(c) *Leadership style*
The approach used in exercising authority will determine the extent to which subordinates feel alienated and uninterested or involved and important. Leaders are also the creators and 'sellers' of organisational culture: it is up to them to put across the vision.

(d) *Policies and practices*
The level of trust and understanding which exists between members of an organisation can often be seen in the way policies and objectives are achieved, eg the extent to which they are imposed by tight written rules and procedures or implied through custom and understanding.

(e) *Structure*
The way in which work is organised, authority exercised and people rewarded will reflect an emphasis on freedom or control, flexibility or rigidity.

(f) *Characteristics of the work force*
Organisation culture will be affected by the demographic nature of the workforce eg manual/clerical division, age, sex, personality.

5.7 It is possible to 'turn round' a negative culture, or to change the culture into a new direction.

(a) The overt beliefs expressed by managers and staff can be used to 'condition' people, to sell a new culture to the organisation eg by promoting a new sense of corporate mission, or a new image. Slogans, mottos ('we're getting there'), myths etc can be used to energise people and to promote particular values which the organisation wishes to instil in its members.

(b) Leadership provides an impetus for cultural change: attitudes to trust, control, formality or informality, participation, innovation etc will have to come from the top – especially where changes in structure, authority relationships or work methods are also involved. The first step in deliberate cultural change will need to be a 'vision' and a sense of 'mission' on the part of a powerful individual or group in the organisation.

(c) The reward system can be used to encourage and reinforce new attitudes and behaviour, while those who do not commit themselves to the change miss out or are punished, or pressured to 'buy in or get out'.

(d) The recruitment and selection policies should reflect the qualities desired of employees in the new culture. To an extent these qualities may also be encouraged through induction and training.

(e) Visible emblems of the culture – eg design of the work place and public areas, dress code, status symbols etc – can be used to reflect the new 'style'.

5.8 The difficulties, though, of changing a culture should not be underestimated.

(a) It is all very well insisting that supervisors take a nurturing caring interest in staff, if the supervisors themselves are managed in an authoritarian and high handed way. Cultural change depends on the active and visible commitment of senior management. The cultural change must extend right up to the Board of Directors.

(b) Changes in culture must overcome employee uncertainty and cynicism. You cannot simply command a change of morale. BT's change of culture went hand in hand with redundancies. A much larger number of people asked for voluntary redundancy than BT needed to shed.

(c) Above all, it must be seen as a quick fix or as overlay. Attention to detail is important.

Types of culture

5.9 Different writers have identified different types of culture, based on particular aspects of organisation and management. Charles Handy discusses four cultures and their related structures. He recognises that while an organisation might reflect a single culture, it may also have elements of different cultures appropriate to the structure and circumstances of different units in the organisation. (The customer service or marketing units may, for example, have a more flexible, and dynamic 'style' than administrative units, which tend to be more bureaucratic.)

(a) The *power culture*. Mainly in smaller organisations, where power and influence stem from a central source, through whom all communication, decisions and control are channelled. The organisation, since it is not rigidly structured, is capable of adapting quickly to meet change; however, the success in adapting will depend on the luck or judgement of the key individuals who make the decisions. Political competition for a share of power is rife, and emotional behaviour is encouraged by the 'personality' cult surrounding the leader.

(b) The *role culture* or bureaucracy, discussed earlier.

(c) The *task culture*, reflected in a matrix organisation, in project teams and task forces. The principal concern in a task culture is to get the job done; therefore the individuals who are important are the experts with the ability to accomplish a particular aspect of the task. Such organisations are flexible and constantly changing as tasks are accomplished and new needs arise. Innovation and creativity are highly prized. Job satisfaction tends to be high owing to the degree of individual participation, communication and group identity.

(d) The *person culture*, in an organisation whose purpose is to serve the interests of individuals within it. Organisations designed on these lines are rare, but some individuals may use any organisation to suit their own purposes; to gain experience, further their careers, express themselves etc.

5.10 Dale and Kennedy (*Corporate cultures*) consider cultures to be a function of the willingness of employees to take risks, and how quickly they get feedback on whether they got it right or wrong.

High risk

BET YOUR COMPANY CULTURE ('slow and steady wins the race') Long decision-cycles: stamina and nerve required eg oil companies, aircraft companies, architects	**HARD 'MACHO' CULTURE** ('find a mountain and climb it') eg entertainment, management and consultancy, advertising
PROCESS CULTURE ('it's not what you do, it's the way that you do it') Values centred on attention to excellence of technical detail, risk management, procedures, status symbols eg Banks, financial services, government	**WORK HARD/PLAY HARD CULTURE** ('find a need and fill it') All action - and fun: team spirit eg sales and retail, computer companies, life assurance companies

Slow feedback — *Fast feedback*

Low risk

5.11   In 1987 the Halifax building society began a review of its pay and grading structure. Outside consultants were brought in to carry out a programme of *job evaluation* to which pay scales were to be linked. The society also planned to recruit outside specialists for the new business areas (insurance, housing development etc) into which it intended to expand. The Halifax also published a list of the aspects of management which were likely to change as a result of the cultural upheaval.

CHANGING CULTURE AT THE HALIFAX

	Aspects of management	*'Old' culture (appropriate for stable controlled environment)*	*'New' culture (appropriate for dynamic competitive environment)*
1	Objectives	Social	Commercial
2	Key tasks	Administration	Business development
3	Promotion and power	Seniority, general skills and experience	Expertise, specialisation and training - more external recruitment
4	Structure	Centralised and bureaucratic	Decentralised and flexible
5	Planning	Short-term based on tradition	Long-term based on research
6	Decision making	Rules and regulations	Greater personal initiative
7	Relationships	Status and individual roles	Job content and teamwork
8	Appraisal systems	Based on effort, loyalty and criticism of mistakes	Based on performance, results and praise
9	Staff attitudes	Loyal and pround of the society	Hopefully the same
10	Employment	Secure, well paid, successful and caring	Striving for achievement to ensure success, while still caring.

6.   THE ADAPTIVE ORGANISATION

Flexible structure

6.1   Most organisations exist in a changing environment and must adapt in order to survive. Although formalisation and bureaucratic organisation helps a small company to develop into a large one, it may be insufficient to enable the organisation to survive continuing environmental changes.

Burns and Stalker identified the need for a different organisation structure when the technology of the market is changing, and innovation is crucial to the continuing success of any organisation operating in the market.

6.2   For rapid-change conditions, they recommended an *organic structure* (also called an 'organismic structure') which has the following characteristics.

(a)   There is a 'contributive nature' of specialised knowledge and experience to the common task of the organisation, rather than a less integrated functional approach.

(b)   Each individual has a realistic task which can be understood in terms of the common task of the organisation.

(c)   There is a continual re-definition of an individual's task, through interaction between the individual and others, rather than rigid job descriptions.

(d)   There is a spread of commitment to the concern and its tasks - ie it is not only management who are 'switched on' to overall objectives.

(e)   There is a *network* structure of authority and communication, directed at getting things done rather than formal channels.

(f)   Communication tends to be *lateral* rather than vertical, and takes the form of information and advice rather than instructions and decisions.

6.3   Burns and Stalker contrasted the organic structure of management, which is more suitable to conditions of change, with a *mechanistic* system of management, which is more suited to stable conditions. A mechanistic structure is essentially a 'bureaucracy', with all its formal and inflexible characteristics (see Chapter 6).

Flexible culture

6.4   You can see how the flexible and adaptive 'organic' structure carries with it cultural elements, such as the sharing of knowledge, skills and ideas, the common task focus rather than activity focus, the free informal communication etc. Culture is considered crucial in the organisation's ability to adapt and innovate to meet environmental pressures, because it is the 'people system' of the organisation - and it is people's attitudes that support or stifle flexibility, creativity and change.

6.5   Charles Garfield (*Peak performers: the new heroes in business*) writes of the change in ethos which now celebrates innovation and adaptability, opportunism and flair - the attributes of the entrepreneur.

> 'Entrepreneurs and intrapreneurs (the internal entrepreneurs who pull together diverse strengths within their organisations to promote innovation) are the new stars.'

6.6 Peters and Waterman, in their influential anecdotal study of successful American companies – *'In search of excellence'* – define 'excellent' as 'continually innovative'. They, too, note that the promotion of exploration, experimentation, willingness to change, opportunism and internal competition create an entrepreneurial 'culture' or 'climate' in organisations that keeps them adaptive to their environment and enables consistent success.

6.7 Management can give *encouragement* to innovation.

(a) Give it financial backing, by spending on market research and risking capital on following through viable new ideas.

(b) Give employees the opportunity to work in an environment where the exchange of ideas for innovation can take place. Management style and organisation structure can help here.

    (i) Management can actively encourage employees and customers to put forward new ideas. Participation in development decisions might encourage employees to become more involved with development projects and committed to their success.

    (ii) Development teams can be set up and an organisation built up on project team-work.

    (iii) Quality circles and brainstorming groups can be used to encourage creative thinking about work issues.

(c) Recruitment policy should be directed towards appointing employees with the necessary skills for doing innovative work. Employees should be trained and kept up to date.

(d) Certain managers should be made responsible for obtaining information from outside the organisation about innovative ideas, and for communicating this information within it.

(e) Strategic planning should result in targets being set for innovation, and successful achievements by employees should if possible be rewarded.

7. CHAPTER ROUNDUP

Some organisation structures

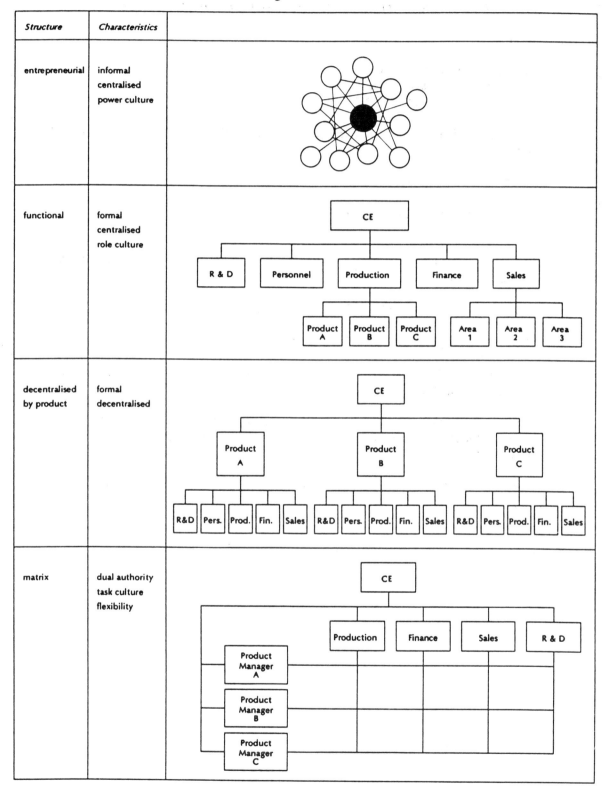

Structure	Characteristics	
entrepreneurial	informal centralised power culture	
functional	formal centralised role culture	
decentralised by product	formal decentralised	
matrix	dual authority task culture flexibility	

TEST YOUR KNOWLEDGE

The numbers in brackets refer to paragraphs of this chapter

1 Define:

    (a)   span of control (2.4)
    (b)   functional authority (2.16)
    (c)   matrix organisation (2.21)

2 Why might a bank want a greater degree of decentralisation in its structure? (2.10 box)

3 What are the advantages of:

    (a)   a matrix structure; (2.25)
    (b)   a bureaucratic system (3.5)

4 What are the disadvantages of bureaucracy, and to what extent have they affected banks? (3.6, 4.11)

5 Why is organisational culture important? (5.4, 5.5)

6 How can an organisation change its culture? (5.7)

7 What terms might you use to describe the culture of your bank, or different units within it? (5.8, 5.9)

8 What kind of organisation structure was thought by Burns and Stalker to be best suited to conditions of rapid change? (6.2) Does the structure of your bank have any of these elements?

9 How can management of an organisation encourage innovation? (6.7)

Now try question 16 at the end of the text

Chapter 17

COMMUNICATION AND CO-ORDINATION

This chapter covers the following topics.

1. Communication
2. Formal and informal communication systems
3. Co-ordination
4. Conflict

Introduction

Communication is important to the individual manager, in order to carry out his functions (in Fayol's terms), or indeed his roles (according to Mintzberg). For the organisation as a whole, communication is necessary so that people know what to do.

---

1. COMMUNICATION

1.1 The most basic definition of communication is the transmission or exchange of information. It is a universal human activity, which may be directed at:

(a) initiating action - eg by request, instruction or persuasion;
(b) making known needs and requirements;
(c) exchanging information, ideas, attitudes and beliefs;
(d) establishing understanding - and perhaps also exerting influence or persuasion;
(e) establishing and maintaining relationships.

1.2 Communication therefore embraces a wide spectrum of activities in organisations, both in the way the organisation as an entity communicates or 'projects itself' to people who come into contact with it, and in the way that individuals within and around the organisation communicate with each other.

The importance of communication in organisations

1.3 Among the more important roles of communication in an organisation are as follows.

(a) Providing information for *planning, co-ordination and control* activities of management. Managers need to be aware of what their departments *should* be achieving, and what they are and are not achieving. Information in organisations should initiate or support a decision or action.

(b) Providing information about the organisation and its services (or as an integral part of its services) to people in the outside would.

(c) Encouraging the formulation, swapping and testing of *ideas*. Communication - in forms such as quality circles or brainstorming sessions - can contribute to innovation and the flexibility of the organisation in the face of change.

(d) *Co-ordination* of the activities of all the interdependent sub-systems of the organisation, so that the overall objectives of the organisation are met. This will also be important in the control of conflict. Co-ordinatory mechanisms such as committees and project teams depend on communication (see section 3 below).

(e) Fulfilling the needs of *employees* for information about their task, the standards expected of them, how their performance measures up to standard etc. Information is important for learning and development, because 'feedback' is necessary for the change or correction of behaviour. It has also been claimed to have benefits for employee job satisfaction and motivation: without performance information, the employee may be working without understanding or sense of purpose, without commitment and without the satisfaction of feeling that he is contributing to the achievements of the organisation.

(f) Creating, developing and maintaining interpersonal relations between subordinates, supervisors, peers and also customers, suppliers etc.

1.4 Systematic efforts can and should be made:

(a) to educate employees in the processes and techniques of communication

(b) to help employees identify and overcome barriers to communication

(c) to encourage communication through organisational structure, procedures, systems and culture, and

(d) to evaluate the effectiveness of communication (including its *perceived* value to employees).

The communication cycle

1.5 Effective communication is a two-way process, perhaps best expressed as a cycle. Signals or 'messages' are 'sent' by the communicator and 'received' by the other party, who 'sends' back some form of confirmation that the 'message' has been received and understood. This is enormously complicated in practice, especially in face-to-face communication: you may send a letter and receive an acknowledgement back, which would correspond to a single cycle of communication, but face-to-face, the workings of two or more minds and bodies (eg nodding, understanding, gesturing etc) complicate the picture.

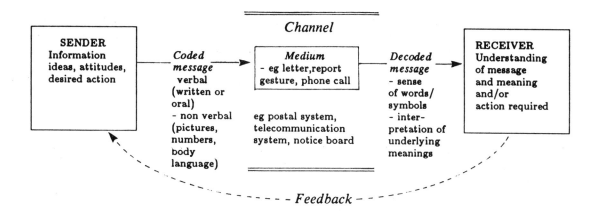

1.6   As illustrated in the above diagram, it is *feedback* that makes communication a two-way process rather than a series of send-receive events. Feedback is a vital and often neglected aspect of the process, which indicates to the sender whether or not his message has been successfully received, understood and interpreted. Failure to seek or offer feedback, or ignoring feedback offered, is one of the major problems in communication.

1.7   The management of interpersonal relations - inside and outside the organisation - depends on effective communication, and on the correct understanding and interpretation. It is easy to misinterpret not only the surface meaning of words and numbers (eg for a customer who is not familiar with the terminology used in a bank brochure, or his statement) but the underlying meaning: tone of voice, metaphorical language, sarcasm, associations not shared by the receiver etc can all make someone 'get the wrong idea', which defeats the purpose of communication.

1.8   Feedback can alert the sender, if this is happening. It may consist of:

Positive feedback

- Action being taken as requested
- A letter/note/memo confirming receipt of message and replying in an appropriate way
- Accurate reading-back of message
- Smile, nod, murmur of agreement, 'I've got that' etc

Negative feedback

- No action or wrong action being taken
- No written response where expected
- Request for more information, clarification or repetition
- Failure to read back message correctly
- Silence, blank look, sound or gesture of protest or perplexity

Communication problems

1.9   Two technical terms related to communication problems are distortion and noise.

1.10   *Distortion* refers to the way in which the meaning of a communication is lost in handling. It occurs mainly at the 'encoding' and 'decoding' stages of the process, where:

(a) the precise intention of the sender, ie what he wants to communicate, fails to translate itself accurately into language that is suitable for its purpose and its intended recipient, so that the 'wrong' message is being sent; or

(b) the language used is not translated into proper understanding by the receiver, ie the wrong message is received.

1.11 *Noise* refers to distractions and interference in the environment in which communication takes place, obstructing the process by affecting the accuracy, clarity or even the 'arrival' of the message. Examples include physical noise (of talk or machinery etc) preventing a message from being heard clearly; a breakdown in a computer printer or phone line; bad handwriting; barriers to understanding created by differences in personality, culture and outlook; excessive emotion, nerves or prejudice etc interfering with sending or receiving.

1.12 Other potential problems in the process include the following.

(a) *Not* communicating. (Bear in mind that even 'tactful' or 'thoughtful' silences are open to misinterpretation).

(b) Sending the 'wrong' message - ie one that is meaningless, irrelevant or unsuitable to the purpose, recipient and context of the communication.

(c) Distortion or omission of information by the sender.

(d) Misunderstanding due to lack of clarity, use of technical jargon etc.

(e) Non-verbal signals (gestures, facial expression, appearance, posture etc) contradicting the verbal message, confusing the recipient.

(f) 'Overload' - giving the recipient more information than he can digest in the time available.

(g) Differences in social, racial or educational background, compounded by general age and personality differences, which may create barriers to understanding and even to the *desire* to communicate.

(h) Perceptual bias or selectivity - ie people hearing only what they want to hear.

1.13 Additional problems may be caused in communication between managers and subordinates in organisations because of the following.

(a) A subordinate mistrusting his superior and looking for 'hidden meanings' in a message.

(b) Hostility or resentment of subordinates towards management, resulting in deliberate attempts to 'sabotage' communication.

(c) Subordinates otherwise giving superiors incorrect or incomplete information (eg to protect a colleague, or to avoid 'bothering' the superior).

(d) People from different job or specialist backgrounds (eg bankers, marketing managers, engineers) having difficulty in talking on the same wavelength. Managers may, unintentionally or to assert their superiority, talk 'over the heads' of their subordinates. On the other hand, operating staff may be frustrated by general management's lack of understanding of their functions and needs.

(e)   Managers who are prepared to make decisions on a 'hunch' without proper regard to the communications they may or may not have received. This may cause frustration for those subordinates who offer management information.

(f)   Lack of opportunity, formal or informal, for subordinates to say what they think or feel.

(g)   Employees may not take an interest in organisational matters which do not affect them personally.

Improving communication in the organisation

1.14   It may be apparent from the preceding paragraphs that communication problems fall into three broad categories.

(a)   There may be a bad formal communication system.

(b)   There may be misunderstanding about the actual content of a message.

(c)   There may be inter-personal difficulties causing a break-down even though the formal communications of the organisation may be adequate under normal circumstances.

1.15   Bad organisation must be improved. The ways in which this may be achieved will depend on the individual circumstances of each problem, but the aim should be to set up more or better communication links in all 'directions'. Standing instructions should be recorded in easily accessible manuals which are kept fully up-to-date; management decisions should be sent to all people affected by them, preferably in writing.

1.16   To improve upward communication, regular staff meetings or formal consultation with staff associations/trade union representatives should be held. A house journal might be issued regularly. For the same reason, there should be formal 'appraisal' interviews between a manager and his subordinates, to discuss not only the job performance and career prospects of the subordinates but also how they feel about their work, and how it could be improved - ie feedback upwards to management. The *informal* organisation should supplement this increased freedom of communication: if status consciousness can be reduced in management (as in Japanese companies) there will be more opportunity for exchange of views, motivatory 'good news swapping', and general 'keeping in touch', in the open plan office, the canteen, the corridor etc.

1.17   Some techniques of communication, and general awareness (eg of the need to avoid 'jargon' and overload) can be *taught*, but inter-personal communication difficulties cannot really be improved by teaching skills on formal courses. The best solution might be for top management to set an *example* by expressing their intentions openly to subordinate managers, to make 'personableness' an important criterion in selection for jobs, and to set up facilities within the organisation (eg a comfortable canteen and coffee lounge, or a sports and social club) to improve the likelihood of a good atmosphere at work and better informal communications.

1.18 Communication between superiors and subordinates will be improved when an interpersonal trust exists. Exactly how this is achieved will depend on the management style of the manager, the attitudes and personality of the individuals involved, and other environmental variables. Peters and Waterman have suggested that a strong central 'culture' is the key to uniting employees to their manager's objectives, and removing the resentment inherent in some methods of managerial control. They advocate 'management by walking around' (MBWA) and informality in superior/subordinate relationships as a means of establishing closer links.

2. FORMAL AND INFORMAL COMMUNICATION SYSTEMS

2.1 Various media and channels of communication may be used in the formal communication system. Here are some examples.

(a) Face-to-face communications:

(i) formal meetings;   } (discussed in earlier chapters);
(ii) interviews.

(b) Oral communications:

(i) the telephone - the most commonly used method of everyday business communication;
(ii) public address systems.

(c) Written communication:

(i) letters: via the external mail system (or internal, as a more personal equivalent of a memorandum);

(ii) memoranda; via the internal mail system;

(iii) reports; routine and non-routine, for management to give subordinates (and others) information - eg in the Annual Report of a company - or for subordinates to report to superiors;

(iv) forms;

(v) notice boards;

(vi) house journals, bulletins, newsletter;

(vii) organisation manual;

(viii) fax (facsimile transfer);

(ix) printout or on-screen messages computer-to-computer.

(d) Visual communications:

(i) charts;
(ii) films and slides;
(iii) graphs etc 'sent' from terminal to terminal of the computer system.

2.2 The most appropriate method in any given circumstances will depend on the following.

(a) The time necessary to prepare and transmit the message, considering its urgency. A phone call, for example, is quicker than a letter: a memo is quicker than a full-scale report.

(b) The complexity of the message: what channel will enable it to be most readily understood. A written message, for example, allows the use of diagrams, figure workings etc - but if something needs to be explained and questions answered on the spot, a discussion may be preferred.

(c) The distance the message is required to travel and in what condition it must arrive.

(d) The need for a written record, eg for confirmation of transactions, legal documents. Bank transactions usually need a written element, because of the need for secure identification and authorisation.

(e) The need for 'interaction' or immediate exchange, eg question and answer, instant 'feedback' etc. It is often preferable to meet customers, for example, in order to discuss complex problems or attempt to 'sell' the benefits of a service.

(f) The need for confidentiality or, conversely, the dissemination of information widely and quickly. A notice board is obviously different in application from a private interview or confidential letter.

(g) Sensitivity to the effect of the message on the recipient: the need for tact, personal involvement, or impersonality. The effect of a letter and a face-to-face discussion in announcing redundancies, for example, will be quite different.

(h) Cost, considered in relation to all the above, for the best possible result at the least possible expense. The cost of using the system (materials, maintenance, charges etc) is not the only consideration: staff time is also an expense - which is why face-to-face discussion with a customer at the 'window' is not always an effective option for bank staff when the branch is busy.

2.3 In early 1986, a survey was carried out by Vista Communications, an employee consultancy company. The most popular methods of communication proved to be:

(a) internal memos, circulars and notice boards (used by 92% of companies who completed the questionnaire)

(b) team or line briefings (86%)

(c) the company newspaper (81%)

(d) management conferences (65%)

(e) employee reports (63%) and

(f) communication via trade union representatives (62%).

2.4 It is noticeable that these formal elements of the communication systems are designed almost exclusively for *downward* communication (from superiors to subordinates) and *lateral* communication (ie between managers or departments).

2.5 Formal *upward* communication (from subordinates to superiors) is an important – and perhaps the most neglected – part of the communication system. Formal mechanisms for meetings of employee representatives and management are useful, but tend to be applied in a limited number of situations: negotiation, grievance etc. The organisation needs a system which offers a channel for employee complaints, comments and – crucially – suggestions from lower levels as to how work practices, systems or technology might be improved or problems solved. This may be achieved through:

(a) more regular non-negotiatory meetings with employee representatives;

(b) team meetings for 'brainstorming' solutions to problems or discussing work issues;

(c) 'suggestion schemes', perhaps with incentives for positive contributions;

(d) 'open door': a manager might be always available, or establish 'surgery' hours when employees are welcome to bring problems, suggestions or feedback to him.

2.6 Whichever methods are used, the important feature of formal communication systems is the existence of 'channels', in the sense of defined routes by which communications pass.

These channels are usually formed by the structure of the organisation. The 'chain' up and down which authority and responsibility passes is also the chain of communication.

2.7 Say your branch was structured as follows.

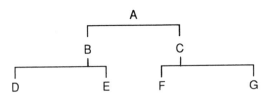

(a) If A wanted to issue instructions to D, the communication would have to go through B, who would pass it to D.

(b) If F has a problem that can only be solved by A, or requires authorisation, he would have to refer it to C : C would then approach A.

(c) If D has a task or problem that affect G, he would have to refer it to B: B might be able to discuss it with C – but might have to approach him through A, if it is outside the bounds of his own authority. C would then tell G.

2.8 The third of these situations is clearly inefficient. In practice, there should be a horizontal 'gangplank' between B and C, and between D-E-F-G, so that interdepartmental issues can be tackled direct by the people involved without constant reference back.

2.9   The first two situations, however, describe the policy of most formal - and especially bureaucratic - organisations, and reflect immense structural and political pressures. Efficient delegation means that A *shouldn't* have to get involved in work at D's level and, after all, B is D's immediate boss and knows him and his work best.

2.10 However, speeding up the process and cutting out 'red tape' are attractive ideas: why 'go through channels' if you can, as a senior manager, go direct to a subordinate down the line, or if you can, as an employee, go over your immediate superior's head (especially if you are appealing against his decision, or want to impress a more senior manager, or simply do not respect your superior)?

2.11 Middle management, in particular, tend to get 'passed over' where formal channels are eroded, which is a source of conflict and stress in many organisations. That being said, there are many situations where middle managers need to communicate with their equivalents in different functions to ensure the coordinated implementation of corporate strategy. Middle managers might end up developing informal communication networks of their own.

How to communicate effectively

1   Clarify ideas before attempting to communicate.

2   Examine the purpose of communication. The purpose of the communication may affect the way in which the message should be conveyed.

3   Understand the physical and human environment when communicating. Choices can then be made about where and how the message is conveyed.

4   In planning communication, consult with others to obtain their support as well as the facts. The consultation may produce helpful additional information or a new insight on how to approach the communication.

5   Consider the content and the overtones of the message. The content may be distorted by non-verbal factors, or the choice of language.

6   Whenever possible, communicate something that helps, or is valued by, the receiver. Effective communication depends partly on action performed by the person receiving the message: the reaction of the receiver is therefore important.

7   Communication, to be identified as effective, requires feedback and follow-up.

8   Communicate messages that are of short-run and long-run importance. One of the difficulties that may arise in communication is conflict between long-term and short-term objectives.

9   Actions must be congruent with communications. Subordinates will not act in accordance with communications unless their superior is seen to be doing so.

10 Be a good listener. Understanding other people's viewpoints is an important element in communicating effectively.

'Ten commandments of good communication'
by American Management Associations Inc

Informal communication systems

2.12 The *formal* system of communication in an organisation is always supplemented by an *informal* one: talks in the canteen, at the pub, on the way home, on the telephone etc. The danger with informal communication is that it might be malicious, full of inaccurate rumours or wild speculation. This type of gossip in the organisation can be unsettling, and make colleagues mistrust one another.

2.13 Formal communication systems do, however, need the support of a good - accurate - informal system, which might be encouraged by:

(a) setting up 'official' communications to feed information into the informal system, eg house journals or briefings, (though these will have to earn the attention and trust of employees); and

(b) encouraging and offering opportunities for 'networking'. A network is a collection of people, usually with a shared interest, who tend to keep in touch to exchange informal information. Ordinary social exchanges should not be stifled at work (unless they start interfering with performance, eg by distracting or delaying a cashier in a bank, in the middle of seeing a customer!)

2.14 The *grapevine* or 'bush telegraph' is one aspect of informal communication. The grapevine works very fast - 'word gets around' often before the formal structure has conveyed news - and is selective: information is not divulged randomly but in a network of interested parties. The problem with the grapevine is that it tends to communicate rumour and gossip, which become further distorted in the retelling. Much of this inaccurate information will be negative in its effect, although the satisfaction involved in participating in the system may actually have a positive effect on morale.

2.15 Perhaps surprisingly, the grapevine is only active when the formal communication network is also active: the grapevine does not fill a gap created by an ineffective formal communication system, but co-exists with it.

2.16 Since the grapevine exists, and cannot be got rid of, management should learn both to accept it and to use it, ie harness it towards achieving the objectives of the organisation. It is important for managers themselves to 'hook into' the grapevine, to be aware of what is going on - and what their subordinates *think* is going on.

Exercise 1

Identify the various means of communication used by your organisation and in your branch.

(a) Are you genuinely better informed by them?
(b) Can they be improved?

---

3. CO-ORDINATION

3.1 Co-ordination is the process of integrating the work of different individuals, sections and departments of the organisation towards effective achievement of its goals. As we've already suggested, co-ordination is closely connected with communication in the organisational system.

3.2 Co-ordination is vital for the following reasons.

(a) The *timing* of activities is synchronised for efficient use of labour, machine hours and effort (so that no-one is 'hanging around' waiting for another job to be finished before they can complete their own tasks). In banking, for example, transactions consist of complex sequences of tasks which may cross departmental boundaries, but need to be brought to completion on time.

(b) The *direction* of activities contributes to overall objectives. If the efforts of individuals and groups are not united, or are actually 'pulling' in different directions, those efforts will be wasted or even counter-productive; eg if the marketing function is trying to project an 'upmarket' modern image of the bank, while the premises section's objectives are to cut costs by buying cheap furniture and materials and refurbishing branches less frequently.

(c) *Control* procedures can be implemented to evaluate the efficiency and effectiveness of inter-disciplinary activity.

3.3 There are various reasons why co-ordination might be difficult to achieve.

(a) There might be poor communication in the organisation both horizontally and vertically, which is both a *source* and a *symptom* of conflict and lack of co-ordination. The left hand may not know what the right hand is doing.

(b) There may be an inadequate system of planning and objective setting for the organisation as a whole, so that sub-unit objectives conflict or overlap, and are unrelated to each other and to the overall objectives of the organisation.

(c) It is difficult co-ordinating the tasks and workflows of departments and groups working under different time pressures. Operational departments produce output quickly and regularly and need quick decisions - but project planning exercises (eg for the restructuring of the branch or introduction of new systems) are concerned with the long term: if a project team has designed a new system - without tight time pressures - and then tries to implement it in an 'up and running' operational department, there will be a clash of culture and priorities.

(d) Differences in leadership style can aggravate problems, by creating different cultures, ways of working and priorities in departments. Staff of an authoritarian disciplinarian manager will be frustrated by co-operating with staff who have absorbed a 'laid back' or *laissez-faire* attitude from their own leader.

(e) The organisation structure may be badly designed so that:

(i) communication channels are complex and lengthy;

(ii) there is an imbalance of power for 'line' and 'staff' functions, with political rivalries ensuing';

(iii) there is insufficient use of structural opportunities for co-ordination such as liaison positions, product management (ie an element of matrix organisation), interdisciplinary committees and project teams etc.

(f) There may be personal and/or political hostility and rivalry between managers, or between groups and departments, in the competition for scarce resources, power and influence.

(g) The culture of different units may make integration difficult. Innovation specialists often have problems being accepted into the mainstream of a traditional bureaucratic organisation. 'Selling' and customer service units are often very different in their outlook and priorities from administrative units, personnel management units etc. (This has in fact created significant cultural 'trauma' in banks, in the attempt to re-integrate the overall culture of the institution in its new market orientation.)

Improving co-ordination

3.4 So how can management go about improving co-ordination? Jane Thompson (*Organisation in action*) suggests that there are three types and methods of integration.

(a) *Standardisation.* Policies, procedures, systems and documentation can to an extent be standardised, at least for similar activities in different divisions or branches of the organisation. (Bank staff, for example, should find documents, forms and procedures the same from branch to branch. As well as inter-branch co-ordination, this ensures consistency of service.)

(b) *Plans and schedules* should be used to contribute to co-ordination from the highest level (strategic planning) downwards, so that the objectives of each unit are clearly defined and related collectively to the overall objectives of the organisation.

(c) *Mutual adjustment* is more difficult to apply in practice, involving the exchange of information and mutual response to it. (Thompson argued that this method of integration is best for dealing with complex procedures.) Two essential strategies for achieving mutual agreement will be:

(i) improving organisational communication; and
(ii) controlling conflict.

3.5 The organisation *structure* can be designed or adjusted to aid co-ordination.

(a) The 'cross-over' point (at all levels) at which one manager is responsible for two or more individuals in different departments should represent a co-ordinating role.

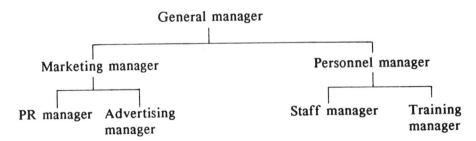

(b) Special 'liaison' or co-ordinatory posts may be created. These may be incorporated in a matrix structure, eg having a project or product manager.

3.6 *Mechanisms* can be set up to improve communication and to erode inter-departmental barriers, including committees (discussed in more detail below) and project groups - temporary interdisciplinary teams with a matrix structure, brought together to achieve specified objectives.

3.7 *Cultural* change will be required to aid co-ordination by reducing inter-group conflict and political rivalry. This may centre on the following.

(a) Incorporating a belief in *co-operation* in the central value system of the organisation. Co-operation, 'working together', 'teamhood' etc is in fact a common cultural belief, and one that is thought to be satisfying to man's need for fellowship and belonging. Co-operation has an emotional appeal, because it incorporates values about unity, teamwork, comradeship and the organisational 'family': it also has a rational appeal, since it is demonstrable that a suitable number of people co-operating on a task will achieve a better result than an individual doing the same task. What needs to be 'sold' by the culture-creators is the concept that co-operation extends to the whole organisation - not just to the work group or department.

(b) Focusing the attention of groups and departments beyond their own maintenance activities and other objectives. The *end-product* of overall organisational goals - ideally expressed in terms of customer satisfaction - should be the focus of activity, offering greater unity of direction, and a motivation to co-operate.

(c) Using the career development and reward systems of the organisation to reward task-centred, co-operative behaviour and awareness of co-ordination. This will also gradually help to ensure that departmental leaders will be committed to the belief that sub-unit interests and goals are less important than organisational performance.

The internal customer

3.8 An alternative method is to use *market forces* to compel departmental reappraisal of the nature of the relationship between one department and other.

Some units may focus on their activity for its own sake - as if it had no objective, no purpose outside the unit. Some may take for granted the relationship of their task to others, having a 'take it or leave it' attitude to the 'service' they provide other units, being complacent about its quality because they have an effective monopoly on that service or task ('if we don't do it - it doesn't get done'). The concept of the *internal customer* aims to change all that.

3.9 As the term implies, the concept of the 'internal customer' is that:

(a) any unit of the organisation whose task contributes to the task of other units (whether as part of a process, or in a 'staff' or 'service' relationship) can be regarded as a supplier of services like any other supplier used by the organisation. The receiving units are thus *customers* of that unit;

(b) the concept of *customer choice* operates within the organisation as well as in the external market environment. If an internal service unit fails to provide the right service at the right time and cost, it cannot expect customer loyalty: it is in *competition* with other internal and external providers of the service. Although there are logistical and control advantages to retaining the provision of services within the organisation, there is no room for complacency;

(c) the service unit's objective thus becomes the efficient and effective *satisfaction of customer needs* - as much within the organisation as outside it. This has the effect of integrating the objectives of service and customer units throughout the organisation. (It also makes units look at the *costs* of providing their services and what *added value* they are able to offer.)

3.10 For example:

(a) the training department of a bank must offer cost-effective training programmes to meet the demand from managers: it is in competition with external training providers and consultants;

(b) the premises management section of the bank must likewise fulfil the objectives derived by senior management for the acquisition, maintenance and sale of bank premises; it is in competition with premises consultants, chartered surveyors etc;

(c) the systems design and maintenance/information technology support/computer department must evaluate the services it offers in comparison with external systems consultancies, computer bureaux and specialist processing operations (eg for credit card processing).

Committees

3.11 Committees are groups to whom authority is delegated, to be exercised collectively. The extent of that authority will vary according to the committee's terms of reference, but may embrace discussion only, decision-making for recommendation to management, decision- making binding on management, and even implementation of decisions.

3.12 Committees are flexible. They may be made up of individuals from a single unit or many different disciplines, and from all levels of the organisation. They may exist for the duration of particular tasks, reporting and then disbanding ('ad hoc' committees) or they may be a permanent feature of the organisation structure, reporting regularly ('standing' committees).

3.13 Some reasons why committees are an important organisational mechanism are as follows.

(a) They can undertake larger and more complex projects and workloads than single managers. The individual may not be able to cope with the volume of work or the diversity of demands made on his skills, or may lack authority to make an individual decision.

(b) They embrace a variety of specialisms, knowledge and attitudes. This may be important for the following reasons.

(i) Co-ordination. An awareness of the inter-relationship of tasks and objectives is fostered.

(ii) Competence. Multi-disciplinary tasks can be dealt with, without 'gaps' in the knowledge and experience of the decision-makers.

(iii) Perspective. A wider range of attitudes and experience can avoid a 'blinkered' outlook, especially where an issue would otherwise be politically complicated and open to polarised viewpoints. Where creative thinking is required to define and solve problems, a range of thought is valuable.

      (iv)   Representation. The participation of different interest groups will ensure all-round consideration of issues. At the same time, consensus decisions or representative deliberations are perceived to carry greater weight than individual equivalents. Where the *acceptability* of decisions is important (eg on issues affecting staff morale, working conditions etc) this may be particularly valuable.

      (v)   Communication. Committees can be a formal - and informal - focal point for communication of views, performance feedback, policy decisions etc.

3.14 The *potential advantages* of committees follow on from this.

(a) Achievement of acceptable decisions or compromises. Where compromise or consensus decisions might be beneficial, or where they are the only way out of a problem (eg industrial relations), a committee might provide a useful forum in which to negotiate the problem's solution.

(b) Consolidation of power and authority: whereas an individual may not have sufficient authority to make a decision himself, the pooled authority of a committee (eg a board of directors) may be sufficient to enable the decision to be made.

(c) They are a means of upward, downward and lateral communication. This frequently leads to the generation of creative ideas (eg by 'brainstorming'). It may also be useful ground for staff development in team-working and interpersonal skills.

(d) Combining abilities: committees enable the differing skills and outlooks of its various members to be brought together to deal with a problem. In theory the quality of committee decisions should be of a high standard.

(e) Co-ordination: they should help management achieve the maximum co-ordination of all parties involved in a committee decision, eg compiling master budgets.

(f) Through a greater degree of participation, they may improve the morale and motivation of committee members.

3.15 The *disadvantages* of committees may be summarised as follows.

(a) The time taken by a committee to resolve a problem tends to be in direct proportion to its size.

(b) Committees are time consuming and expensive. In addition to the cost of highly-paid executives' time, secretarial costs will be incurred.

(c) Incorrect or ineffective decisions may be made, owing to the fact that members of a committee are unfamiliar with the deeper aspects of issues under discussion. Compromise decisions and solutions to problems may not (where *quality* is more important than *acceptability*) be the best.

(d) There is no individual responsibility for decisions. This may invite compromise instead of clear-cut decisions, besides weakening individual responsibility throughout the organisation. Moreover, members may be able to avoid direct responsibility for poor results arising from decisions taken in committee.

(e) Committees lack conscience. Each individual can pass the blame for unethical or harsh actions to the others.

Exercise 2

Identify one example of good co-ordination and one of bad co-ordination in your branch in the past month.

Project groups

3.16 A *project group or team* is similar to an ad hoc committee. It is temporary and focused on achievement of a particular task, usually related to the planning and implementation of change.

3.17 In banking, for example, a project group might be set up to handle the following.

(a) major strategic developments, such as the reorganisation of the branch network, the implementation of centralised processing systems etc. There are likely to be sub-groups looking at aspects of such a large project, and each will be multi-disciplinary, to gain the benefits of shared expertise and representation.

(b) individual 'cases' or customer projects eg offering liaison and financial advice for a multi-organisational venture such as the Channel Tunnel.

(c) industry specialisation: gathering experts in particular customers' fields to manage tasks and customer relationships in a small, specialised sector (eg aircraft manufacture or farming).

(d) 'seasonal' tasks at branch levels, eg the review of half yearly charges to customer accounts, which requires fairly wide expertise and intensive work - but only for short and infrequent periods of time.

3.18 Successful project management is covered in Chapter 13.

Networking

3.19 *Network* is a rather vague term, probably as vague as the social group it is supposed to denote.

(a) In some circumstances, the word describes a set of external relationships (eg alliances, joint ventures).

(b) More often, the term describes informal or semi-formal alliances among managers.

3.20 A network, then, is a group of managers and will sometimes be recognised as such by the formal organisation structure. The members may be drawn from a number of corporate functions and geographical areas.

3.21 A network might be a group of middle managers whose day-to-day jobs are important in influencing and coordinating the implementation of corporate plans and strategies.

3.22 A network might be institutionalised in regular meetings to discuss matters of mutual importance, to obviate the need for operating decisions to pass up and down the management hierarchy, and to ensure the relevant coordination of activities. However, you should note that:

(a) networks are not 'task forces' or teams brought together to solve a particular problem;

(b) networks do not simple deal with issues presented to them by senior management, but instead identify issues for examination.

3.23 The network is not a structure but instead, in the words of Chandra, a 'social architecture'. Senior management identifies key tactical and operational decision makers. Network membership may not correspond with functional position.

3.24 Finally, a network is not simply an exercise in teamwork or the raising of group morale. it deals with the fundamentals of the business, and is a means by which information and experiences can be *shared*, across functional and geographical lines, so that the organisation can learn from them.

3.25 Networks, then, are semi-formal, permanent arrangements of managers and decision-makers are tactical and operational levels, which cross over functional boundaries.

4. CONFLICT

4.1 We have included conflict in this part of the text, because part of the role of the manager as integrator, co-ordinator and controller is to *reconcile differences*.

People are different. They have different attitudes, values and opinions. Yet to an extent they must put aside or reconcile those differences in order to function in teams and in the organisation as a whole, and in order to sustain workable interpersonal relationships.

4.2 Handy identified three ways in which differences are expressed.

(a) By *argument*: this is the constructive exchange of ideas with the positive intention of reaching an agreement.

(b) By *competition*:

(i) constructive competition between individuals or groups has the beneficial effect of:

(1) setting or improving standards of achievement;
(2) stimulating activities;
(3) sorting out the good, successful employees from the bad, unsuccessful ones;

(ii) harmful competition occurs when one person or group can only do well at the expense of another; this is known as 'zero-sum' competition, because if one person gains, another loses an equal amount. Competition for resources, recognition and better results, if zero-sum, will degenerate into conflict;

(c) By *conflict*.

4.3 Argument and competition are forms of what is usually considered to be 'conflict' which are potentially beneficial and fruitful for the organisation. They can energise relationships and clarify issues, clear the air, encourage the challenging of ideas and assumptions. In Handy's definition, however, 'conflict' itself is a destructive and negative concept which can distract attention from the task, split teams, encourage 'spoiling' behaviour and interpersonal hostility, prevent communication etc.

4.4 Conflict in this sense may be caused by:

(a) clashes or divergence in the objectives of individuals or groups;
(b) disputes over power and the boundaries of authority;
(c) poor management of situations involving argument and competition (eg for resources) so that they get emotional and 'win-lose'.

4.5 According to Handy, the observable *symptoms* of conflict in an organisation will be:

(a) poor communications, in all 'directions';
(b) interpersonal friction;
(c) inter-group rivalry and jealousy;
(d) low morale and frustration;
(e) proliferation of rules, norms and myths; especially widespread use of arbitration, appeals to higher authority, and inflexible attitudes towards change.

Managerial response to conflict

4.6 Hunt identifies five different management responses to the handling of conflict - not all of which are effective.

(a) *Denial/withdrawal*, or 'sweeping it under the carpet'. If the conflict is very trivial, it may indeed 'blow over' without an issue being made of it, but if the causes are not identified, the conflict may grow to unmanageable proportions.

(b) *Suppression* - 'smoothing over', to preserve working relationships despite minor conflicts. As Hunt remarks, however: 'Some cracks cannot be papered over'.

(c) *Dominance* - the application of power or influence to settle the conflict. The disadvantage of this is that it creates all the lingering resentment and hostility of 'win-lose' situations.

(d) *Compromise* - bargaining, negotiating, conciliating. To some extent, this will be inevitable in any organisation made up of different individuals. However, individuals tend to exaggerate their positions to allow for compromise, and compromise itself is seen to weaken the value of the decision, perhaps reducing commitment.

(e) *Integration/collaboration.* Emphasis must be put on the task, individuals must accept the need to modify their views for its sake, and group effort must be seen to be superior to individual effort. Not easy.

4.7 Handy suggests two types of strategy which may be used to turn conflict into competition or argument, or to manage it in some other acceptable way.

(a) *Environmental (ecological) strategies.* These involve creating conditions in which individuals may be better able to interact co-operatively with each other: they are wide-ranging, time-consuming, and unpredictable, because of the sheer range of human differences. Such strategies involve:

    (i)   agreement of common objectives;
    (ii)   reinforcing the group or 'team' nature of organisational life, via culture;
    (iii) providing feedback information on progress;
    (iv) providing adequate co-ordination and communication mechanisms;
    (v)   sorting out territorial/role conflicts in the organisational structure.

(b) *Regulation strategies.* These are directed to control conflict - though in fact they make it so much a part of the formal structure of the organisation that they tend to legitimise and even perpetuate it. Possible methods include:

    (i)   the provision of arbitration to settle disputes;

    (ii)   the establishment of detailed rules and procedures for conduct by employees;

    (iii) appointing a person to 'manage' the area of conflict - a liaison/co-ordination officer;

    (iv) using confrontation, or inter-group meetings, to hammer out differences, especially where territorial conflicts occur;

    (v)   separating the conflicting individuals; and

    (vi) ignoring the problem, if it is genuinely likely to 'go away', and there is no point in opening fresh wounds.

Exercise 3

Do you know of any instances of conflict:

(a) within your branch?
(b) between your branch and another?

What were the causes of the conflict? Do you feel it was constructive or destructive? Why?

---

5. CHAPTER ROUNDUP

5.1

The communication process

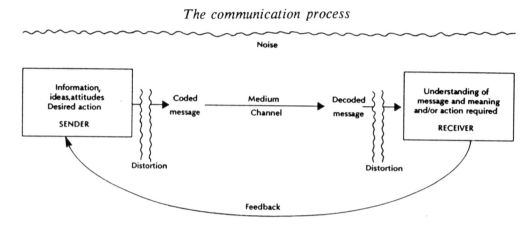

5.2

'Technical' problems in the process itself	Problems in the context of communication at work
• Failure to communicate • Communicating too much (ie 'over load') • Sending the 'wrong' message (eg one that is irrelevant or meaningless) • Encoding or decoding the message wrongly (so that misunderstanding occurs) • Choosing an unsuitable medium or channel of communication • Failure to feed back	• Differences or conflict between objectives and/or individuals • Different 'vocabulary' of different disciplines • Subordinate's fear of transmitting 'bad news' to a superior • Giving more importance to communication from 'above' than from 'below' • Incorrect or incomplete information available within time constraints • Lack of opportunity and encouragement for subordinates to communicate 'upwards'

5.3 Co-ordination can be improved in organisations by:

(a) standardisation
(b) integrated planning at all levels
(c) improved communication
(d) controlling conflict
(e) co-ordinating positions in the structure
(f) co-ordinating mechanisms
   (i) meetings
   (ii) project groups
(g) cultural emphasis on co-operation
(h) applying the 'internal customer' concept

TEST YOUR KNOWLEDGE

The numbers in brackets refer to paragraphs of this chapter

1 Why is communication important in a bank? (1.3)

2 Select five communication problems. (1.10 - 1.13) How can they be overcome? (1.15 - 1.18)

3 What criteria would you use to select a medium and channel of communication appropriate to your purpose? (2.2)

4 What factors cause poor co-ordination? (3.3)

5 Give three examples of functions in a bank, and identify their internal customers? (3.10 or your own examples)

6 What are the potential advantages of committees? (3.14)

7 In what sense is conflict a good thing in an organisation? (4.2, 4.3)

8 How can conflict be managed? (4.6, 4.7)

Now try questions 17 and 18 at the end of the text

Chapter 18

INFORMATION SYSTEMS

This chapter covers the following topics.

1. Information systems
2. Management information systems
3. Databases

Introduction

In this chapter we will look at information systems, concentrating on management information systems in general, and databases in particular. We will not deal with the technological implications of such systems in this chapter. Information technology is treated separately in Chapter 19.

---

1. INFORMATION SYSTEMS

1.1 Information systems can be divided into two broad categories:

    (a) transaction processing systems; and
    (b) management information systems.

1.2 As the terms imply, transaction processing involves the routine handling of data transactions, often 'clerical' work, whereas management information involves the formulation of information for managers to use.

Transaction processing systems

1.3 Transaction processing could be said to represent the lowest level in an organisation's use of information systems. They are used for routine tasks in which data items or transactions must be processed so that operations can continue. Examples include daily account transactions, standing orders, safe custody ledgers, and payroll.

1.4 Transaction processing systems generally contain at least two categories of files:

    (a) a file (or files) of master records; and
    (b) a file of transactions to be used in updating the master records.

1.5 Consider a bank: the master records would consist of some identification data, historical transactions, the current balance for all the accounts and - in recent years - customer information to be used in the selection of relevant services for 'cross-selling' purposes. The transactions file would consist of a day's transactions and would include deposits, withdrawals, cheques, direct debits, bank charges etc. The transactions file would then be used to update the master file records of customer accounts. (Note that a 'file' of transactions could start off as a pile of forms, cheques and letters on a clerk's desk.)

1.6 Transaction processing systems are primarily *operational* systems but also provide 'raw material' which is often used more extensively by management information systems, databases or decision support systems. In other words, they might be used to produce *management information*, ranging from customer data (for strategic marketing) to the total salary bill of the branch (for manpower planning).

1.7 An example of the multi-purpose nature of transaction or operational information is customer records.

   (a) Customer details are essential operationally, not only to maintain account balances, standing orders and direct debits etc, but also for the verification of identity (signature authentication etc), the provision of addresses for statements etc.

   (b) Customer details are now a major *marketing* tool of banks, enabling banks:

       (i) to identify customers who may be in a particular market 'segment' (ie homeowners for mortgages, 'homeowner loans' and contents insurance; students for student accounts; 'high net worths' for investment accounts, taxation advice, pensions etc);

       (ii) to produce 'personalised' mail, offering relevant products/services to selected customers, and co-ordinate mailshots of brochures etc;

       (iii) to analyse their customer base in terms of its location, age, sex, occupational and socio-economic group, for the purpose of marketing and image-creation, branch location and specialisation (ie so that only branches in strategic areas have a small business manager) etc.

       It should be noted, however, that the bank's duty of confidentiality requires caution in the use and disclosure of customer details; the Code of Banking Practice restricts its use, and advocates that customers should have the option to refuse its use for marketing purposes.

   (c) Customer details support managerial decisions, eg about lending, offering historic and current information about income (and growth or decline trends therein), repayment record etc.

1.8 Another important example is personnel records, which offer:

   (a) statutory records, for provision of data to government and other agencies on health and safety, equal pay, earnings and benefits etc; and

   (b) operational information for payroll administration, administration of benefits, record of holidays etc; but also

(c) management information in the shape of a personnel audit, for manpower planning in its widest sense, including demand and supply forecasting, identification of training needs, performance appraisal, evaluation of selection/training/health and safety policies etc.

> The Data Protection Act 1984 seeks to protect the subjects of data held on computer; this is relevant both for customers and employees and is covered fully in the *Law Relating to Banking Services* syllabus.

Redesigning transaction systems: business process re-engineering

1.9 Many firms are seeking to improve the efficiency with which they process transactions or go about their business. However, there is no use simply automating existing procedures rather than redesigning them from scratch.

1.10 *Business process re-engineering* (BPR), also known as *process innovation* and *core process re-design*, is the introduction of radical changes in business processes to achieve breakthrough results in terms of major gains in levels of performance plus reductions in costs.

1.11 The concept of BPR was originally formulated in 1990 by Michael Hammer in a seminal article for the *Harvard Business Review*. He contended that 'In a time of rapidly changing technologies and ever-shorter product life cycles, product development often proceeds at a glacial pace. In an age of the customer, order fulfilment has high error rates and customer enquiries go unanswered for weeks. In a period when asset utilisation is critical, inventory levels exceed many months of demand. The usual methods of boosting performance - process rationalisation and automation - haven't yielded the dramatic improvements companies need. In particular, heavy investments in information technology have delivered disappointing results - largely because companies tend to use technology to mechanise old ways of doing business. They leave the existing processes intact and use computers simply to speed them up.'

1.12 The chief BPR tool is a clean sheet of paper. Re-engineers start from the future and work backwards. They are unconstrained by existing methods, people or departments. In effect, they ask, 'If we were a new company, how would we run the place?' Hammer points out that 'At the heart of re-engineering is the notion of discontinuous thinking - of recognising and breaking away from the outdated rules and fundamental assumptions that underlie operations.'

1.13 Re-engineers ask two fundamental questions about everything that happens in organisations: 'Why?' and 'What if?'. Only when they receive satisfactory answers to these questions do they then begin to explore better ways of doing things. The critical questions they then ask are:

What is done?	Why do it?
How is it done?	Why do it that way?
Where is it done?	Why do it there?
When is it done?	Why do it then?
Who does it?	Why that person?

1.14 The difference between traditional approaches to efficiency improvement and BPR is that BPR more typically breaks away from conventional wisdom and the constraints of organisational or departmental/functional boundaries. BPR is more concerned, too, with exploiting the power of information technology – not to automate existing processes, but to facilitate new ones.

2. MANAGEMENT INFORMATION SYSTEMS

2.1 A management information system (MIS) is 'an information system making use of available resources to provide managers at all levels in all functions with the information from all relevant sources to enable them to make timely and effective decisions for planning, directing and controlling the activities for which they are responsible.' A distinction can be made between:

(a) *data* (perhaps the result of processing) which is raw input material; and

(b) *information.* In a management information system, data can be the output of a transactions processing system, which is then converted into management information relevant to the planning and control of a business.

2.2 A management information system is therefore a system for gathering and communicating information which will enable managers to do their job. Since managers must have information, there will always be a management information system in any organisation: each manager will (depending on his drive and initiative) make sure he gets the data he thinks he needs from the other people with whom he interacts.

2.3 In large organisations, however, formal design and construction of an MIS may be required, not only to reduce risk by *ensuring* that good quality information is obtained at the right time, but also because computerisation has forced management to consider its information needs systematically and in detail.

The role of an MIS

2.4 The various functions performed by a management information system include the following.

(a) *Channelling* internal and external (environmental) data, and converting it into information which is appropriate for application in the planning and control systems and decision-making of the organisation. The MIS provides a formal structure for the processing and transmission of feedback arising from the organisation's transactions and operations, and for external information gathering.

(b) *Database* management, providing a 'stock' of information for all the organisation's communication, co-ordination, planning and control requirements (and for application in various decision support programmes, in a computerised system).

(c) *Control.* The MIS provides operation/results monitoring and feedback information which should act as a 'trigger' of control action, planning and decision-making. Variance and exception reports (ie where results are significantly different from the plan or budget) should stimulate corrective action; periodic performance reports and *ad hoc* reports of non-routine jobs or occurrences will provide a check on progress and a basis for performance assessment.

(d)   *Co-ordination* (ie linking parts and activities of the organisation) by contributing to the overall communication system of the organisation, and providing consistent (and consistently available) information to different departments and divisions.

(e)   *Planning and decision support.* Quantitative and qualitative information can be provided to support planning at all levels in the hierarchy - strategic, tactical and operational. Routine, recurring decisions may be automated. An MIS may also provide means by which alternative plans or strategies may be 'tried out' (without risk) in order to arrive at a decision, eg simulation models or spreadsheets.

(f)   *Culture and motivation.* Information, eg on targets and objectives and the organisation generally, can be used to create and sell the culture of the organisation, and to give individuals/groups more involvement.

2.5   In other words the role of the MIS is both:

(a)   organisational (controlling information exchange with the environment, the structure of communication and the extent of co-ordination) and

(b)   managerial (enabling managers to fulfil their functions).

2.6   The managerial role of information systems covers the three basic levels of managerial activity that we will discuss in Chapter 22.

(a)   *Strategic information* is that used by senior managers to plan the objectives of the organisation, and to assess whether they are being met in practice (ie for *strategic planning*). Such information includes overall profitability, the profitability of different segments of the business, future market prospects, opportunities and threats arising from new technologies and new markets and other environmental trends/events, the availability and cost of raising funds, manning levels. Much of this information will be broad in scope rather than deeply detailed: it will come primarily from environmental sources, although internally generated information will also be used. It will be long-term in focus.

(b)   *Tactical information* is that used in *management control*, at the senior or middle management level, concerned with the acquisition and use of resources in order to accomplish strategic plans. Such information includes departmental productivity measurements (profit per branch), budgetary control reports, cash flow forecasts, manning levels and profit results, labour turnover statistics, short-term purchasing requirements etc. A large proportion of this information will be generated from within the organisation (ie as feedback) and is likely to have an accounting emphasis. Tactical information is usually more detailed, and is prepared more regularly - perhaps weekly or monthly - than strategic information.

(c)   *Operational information* is used for *operational planning* and control by junior management, ensuring that specific functions and tasks are carried out efficiently and effectively. Information is required frequently - daily, hourly, 'on the spot' for some decisions - and at a much greater level of detail than tactical or strategic information: this is the 'nitty gritty' of the information system.

Features of an MIS

2.7 As you can see from the above, different types of information are required by different people for different purposes. Considerations in the design of an effective MIS include:

(a) what levels of manager or status of persons need information?
(b) what functions can they be divided into?
(c) what should be the frequency of the information provided?
(d) what information does each level or status of person need?
(e) from what sources should the information be obtained?
(f) what sort of computer system is needed?

2.8 The basic features of an MIS may be summarised as follows.

(a) Information flows *horizontally and vertically*, but it is with the *vertical flow* (between superiors and subordinates and vice versa) that management information systems are most concerned.

(b) Reports generated by an information system will range between:

(i) information for low-level management about the small area of the company under their control ie *operational* information; and

(ii) reports of a broader nature for top-level management concerned with overall control, ie *strategic* information.

The central core of an MIS is likely to be *tactical* information for management control.

(c) The *control* application of the MIS (the comparison of actual results against a plan and the production of exception reports to show where control action may be needed) cannot be effective unless the initial *plan* is carefully prepared. The integration of aspects of the MIS must therefore be considered.

(d) A precise and carefully drawn up specification of the areas of management responsibility is essential to ensure that information will flow to the managers who need it.

(e) There are many sources of information, internal and external, and the MIS will not only channel internally generated transaction and administrative data, but will be used to access data such as government statistics, market reports, technological reports, demographic data etc.

(f) Information can be gathered formally (eg by a system of budgetary control) or informally. Managers and employees *informally* gather information from external sources relevant to the business and its markets (eg by reading newspapers and personal experience), from internal sources (talking to colleagues in other departments etc) and from each other (especially if there is a policy of 'Open Door' management or 'management by walking around' which stimulates 'upward' communication).

(g) Information may be:

(i) quantitative (measurable in numerical terms) - eg statistics, amount of money, numbers of people or transactions; or

(ii)   qualitative (difficult or impossible to measure in quantitative terms) – eg employee morale and motivation, customer loyalty, social trends and attitudes.

Management information systems will use both types, but attempts should be made to *quantify* information as far as possible (eg to evaluate the monetary cost of poor morale, in terms of low productivity, costs of replacing and training employees who leave etc).

(h)   Information may be good or bad quality. Good quality information should:

(i)   have a clearly defined purpose
(ii)   be relevant to its purpose
(iii)   be complete for its purpose - without being excessive
(iv)   be sufficiently accurate for its purpose (correct, but not too detailed)
(v)   be quantitative where possible (vi) be clear to its intended user
(vii) be confidence-inspiring to its user (ie trustworthy)
(viii) be communicated to its user - not to someone else
(ix)   be timely - ie while relevant to the user
(x)   in the right format for its purpose (figures or words, written or oral)
(xi)   be provided at a cost which is justified by its value.

Exercise

Examine two of the reports produced on a regular basis by your branch. To what extent:

(a)   are they mere records of data?
(b)   do they offer good information?
(c)   can they be used to inform the decision making process?

2.9   With reference to point (h) above, the purpose of the MIS is to provide *good* quality information. What if it fails?

2.10 Finally, an effective management information system is necessary to enable banks to manage their risks more effectively, which as we saw in Chapter 13, is where the banks are trying to improve their effectiveness. A MIS can assist in risk management in the following ways.

(a)   It enables the bank to take a view of the organisation as a whole, so enabling the bank to see if it is becoming over-exposed to particular industry sectors or in particular financial instruments.

(b)   It can identify key indicators for the business.

The importance of MIS: effect of poor information on management

Quality of information	Consequences	
	Planning	*Control*
1. Inaccurate	Planning decisions might be misguided	Managers won't be told about what is really going on, and so won't take control action when it is needed.
2. Too late	Decisions will be taken without all the necessary facts being available - decisions could be misguided.	Managers won't be told what is going on until too late, or until after unnecessary damage has been done.
3. Unclear	Managers might misunderstand what they have been told, and so make misguided decisions.	Managers might overlook or misunderstand what they have been told, and so be unaware that control action is needed.
4. Incomplete	Decisions will be taken without all the facts being available.	Decisions will be taken without all the facts being available.
5. Irrelevant	Managers might be confused by data which is irrelevant to decisions they have to take, and waste time with it unnecessarily.	Managers might be confused by data which is irrelevant to their needs, and waste time unnecessarily.
6. Subjective	Managers might refuse to accept subjective opinions, or worse still, might make decisions based on subjective opinions that other people might resent and resist.	Managers might refuse to accept the subjective opinions given to them.
7. Control information is not directed at critical points	–	Managers will not have their attention directed towards key issues, and might overlook them. Control action that should be taken might therefore be missed.

3. DATABASES

3.1 The concept of the database, in an extreme form, says that *all* data is potentially useful and should be stored away for possible use in the future. In practice, only the data likely to be of use is captured, because the additional expense and effort involved in having a completely comprehensive database would be greater than the value of the extra data. However, the database concept is that there should be a single set of integrated data files which can be used for a wide range of applications.

3.2 Because information needs are constantly changing, it is of great importance that a database system should be flexible, allowing additional types of data to be stored when the need arises. Information which turns out never to be used should also be removable from the database.

3.3 A database is a collection of data files which is integrated and organised so as to provide a single comprehensive file system. The data is governed by rules which define its structure and determine how it can be accessed. The purpose of a database is to provide convenient access to the common data for a wide variety of users and user needs.

3.4 A database should have four major objectives.

(a) It should be *shared*. Different users should be able to access the same data in the database for their own processing applications, and at the same time if required. This removes the need for duplicating data on different files.

(b) The *integrity* of the database must be preserved. This means that one user should not be allowed to alter the data on file so as to spoil the database records for other users. However, users must be able to update the data on file, and so make valid alterations to the data.

(c) The database system should provide for the *needs of different users*, who each have their own processing requirements and data access methods. In other words, the database should provide for the operational requirements of all its users.

(d) The database should be capable of *evolving*, both in the short term (it must be kept updated) and in the longer term (it must be able to meet the future data processing needs of users, not just their current needs).

What data should a database contain?

3.5 A database for strategic planners will include information about the *environment*, ie about all the factors - competitive, economic, legal, social, technological and 'stakeholder' - that may have implications for the demand or supply of the organisation's products/services.

3.6 A database can also be built up of *internal* data about the business itself. The data can be used:

(a) to carry out a *resource audit* ie a survey of what resources the business has in each of its functions or divisions;

(b) to assess and plan *resource utilisation* ie the efficiency with which resources are used, and the effectiveness of their use in achieving the planning objectives of the business;

(c) to *control* the use of resources.

Using databases

3.7 The advantages of database systems are that:

(a) data only has to be input and stored once - no matter how many different uses and users it will have;

(b) data is flexible and can be applied, selected, sorted etc for many different uses;

(c) management are encouraged to regard data as an organisational resource to be managed - and shared;

(d) data is more widely available and 'integrated' than in systems of independent departmental files;

(e) data can be updated centrally, so that all units of the organisation are using consistent data.

3.8 There are disadvantages, however, the effects of which need to be carefully controlled.

(a) There are problems of data security and privacy: there is potential for unauthorised access to personal data (protected under the Data Protection Act) such as the personal and financial details of customers. Software controls (eg restricted access to certain programs, user identification codes etc) should be supplemented with administrative safeguards.

(b) Since there is one central store of information, it is essential that data be accurate, up-to-date and free from corruption (eg notorious computer 'viruses' which wipe out files).

(c) A system with users spread over a wide geographical area must rely on the communications network, which can be expensive and unreliable.

3.9 Account details have for some time been held in bank databases, so that balances of account and other details can be obtained via the system of any branch of the account-holding bank in 'real time' (rather than in overnight batches), ie quickly enough to respond to a customer request, assess availability of funds for withdrawal, or credit available on a credit card etc. A wide range of transactions can now be processed through ATMs and staff terminals in the modern branch, calling up and altering account data as required.

Banks have also utilised external data in database systems, eg for foreign exchange and taxation rates.

3.10 It is comparatively recently, however, that banks have realised the full potential of the system for *marketing* - particularly 'cross-selling' purposes. In *Banking World* (September 1990) there is an article about how "the 'relational database' systems now being introduced in banks and financial institutions can provide marketing staff with powerful new selling tools". The new systems are *customer-based* rather than *account-based*, with a much wider range of information available at local level on the existing customer base (now regarded as potential customers for other and/or new services).

(a) This data is used to select and sort customers into market segments: particular parameters (job, income, balance in current account, financial services used etc) can be selected to identify, say, all people aged 25-30 with earnings over £15,000 pa who do not yet have any pension arrangements. The bank can then - as if by 'intuition' - offer those individuals pensions advice or products.

> 'Traditional marketing practice involved sending mail shots to all customers. There might be a five percent response, but the cost of obtaining that resource was enormous. The new systems allow the rifle rather than the shot-gun to be used to pick off likely targets'.
>
> *Banking World*, September 1990

(b) Such 'parameter-driven' systems also enable new *products* to be created and defined quickly, in response to competitor action and other factors - eg the current proliferation of mortgage products according to size of mortgage, first-time buyer etc.

> 'Another factor that makes customer-based systems so important is that, with increased competition in the financial services sector, customers are becoming a scarce resource. Many institutions believe it is more effective to sell additional products to existing customers than to spend resources on drumming up new ones. To do this, institutions need to know a good deal about their customers and the type of products that they might be likely to buy.'
>
> *Banking World*, September 1990

4. CHAPTER ROUNDUP

4.1 A management information system is 'an information system making use of available resources to provide managers at all levels in all functions with the information from all relevant sources to enable them to make timely and effective decisions for planning, directing and controlling the activities for which they are responsible.'

4.2 One of the most important recent developments in the management information systems of banks is the use of databases for marketing and product design applications, reflecting the move from account-based to information-based systems, and the exploitation of extensive and accessible customer information.

TEST YOUR KNOWLEDGE

The numbers in brackets refer to paragraphs of this chapter

1   Give an example of the use of transaction/operational information as management information. (1.5 - 1.7)

2   What is the role of an MIS? (2.4)

3   What 'levels' of information are required by management and for what sorts of management activity? Give examples. (2.6)

4   What is 'good' information? (2.8)

5   What are the advantages of a database for a bank? (3.7, 3.9, 3.10)

Now try question 19 at the end of the text

Chapter 19

INFORMATION TECHNOLOGY

This chapter covers the following topics.

1. What is information technology?
2. General applications of information technology
3. IT: some banking applications
4. Issues and trends in banking technology

Introduction

The management of information technology is one of the option subjects of the syllabus. For this paper, you are not expected to have a detailed knowledge but you should understand the significance of IT developments.

---

1. WHAT IS INFORMATION TECHNOLOGY?

1.1 'Information technology' is:

> 'the acquisition, processing, storage and dissemination of vocal, pictorial, textual and numeric information by a micro-electronics based combination of computing and telecommunications.'

1.2 Technology has impacted on other areas of the business environment than information processing. Micro-electronics has revolutionised product design, with new products such as compact disks and electronic games, redesigned products such as digital watches and improvements in products such as TVs, videos and microwave ovens. In manufacturing processes robotics, computer aided design (CAD) and manufacture (CAM) and computerised stock and production control processes are being used to save labour and labour costs, improve control and increase innovation.

1.3 Meanwhile the administration systems of much less automated organisations are being changed by the advent of facsimile transfer ('fax'), electronic mail, networking etc: 'the electronic office'. For a bank, however, the prime operational activity *is* information processing: it is not just the administrative support systems but the whole function of the organisation that has been revolutionised by IT.

> 'Information technology, or IT, is at the heart of modern banking. It is difficult to envisage a bank operating without IT, indeed, I would go so far as to say it would be impossible in today's environment. Outside banking, IT is affecting, some might say intruding into our lives in so many ways. We haven't yet got to the situation where

'if it isn't in a computer it doesn't exist', but like it or loathe it... IT is here to stay. In the banking industry, the *challenge* is how to manage IT cost effectively and use it for the benefit of the customer, and, through that, the company.'
Sir John Quinton's Presidential Address: Banking World January 1990

2. GENERAL APPLICATIONS OF INFORMATION TECHNOLOGY

2.1 The essence of information technology has been summed up by G A Cole (*Management: theory and practice*):

'Whereas, in the past, information-handling involved massive dependence on paper, the emphasis has now shifted to the creation, storage and transmission of tiny electrical impulses.'

The 'paperless office' may not be as imminent as some pundits predict (since computers actually turn out to generate quite a lot of 'hard copy' on paper), but the dependence on paper formats for data *transmission* and *storage* is a thing of the past.

2.2 Let's look very briefly at some of the concepts and terms associated with information technology. There are three main areas of information technology:

(a) computers;

(b) microelectronics - the design and application of very small-scale electronic devices and components, eg 'microchips' used in microcomputers and many modern telecommunication devices such as fax, telephone exchange etc; and

(c) telecommunications.

2.3 A computer system is made up of two basic elements: hardware and software.

(a) *Hardware* means the physical devices and components that make up a computer system, such as the Central Processing Unit (CPU), storage units (disc drives etc), Visual Display Unit (VDU) with screen for output, keyboard for input etc.

(b) *Software* is needed to make the hardware process data in the ways the user wants. It is created by a *programmer*, who can use a computer language (eg BASIC, COBOL etc) to give it instructions: how to work as a computer, and how to perform specific tasks for the user. Ready-written programs for standard applications can be bought 'off the shelf': these are called software 'packages'.

2.4 The hardware provides for four broad activities.

(a) *Input:* some means of entering data eg a keyboard, and instructions to the computer (programs). This can be done at a desk-top terminal which is separate from the main processing unit of the computer. Input can be largely automated (eg in cheque processing).

(b) *Processing:* a central processing unit where all calculations are done and the main 'memory' is housed.

(c) *Backing storage:* a means of holding the data which is not being worked on eg on magnetic tape or disk.

(d) *Output:* display of the processed information eg on a VDU screen, or in 'hard copy' format via a printer.

The separate (optional) components of the computer - like a printer - are called 'peripherals'.

2.5 Software are the instructions which get the work done. Application software includes word processing spreadsheets, account processing, credit scoring systems, risk assessment and management.

2.6 'Telecommunications' means transmitting information by means of electric cables (telephone and telegraph) or by means of radio waves. Telephone links are based on electronics and so have become naturally integrated with more complex forms of IT, for example electronic mail and electronic data interchange (EDI), which allow computers to exchange data - to 'talk to each other' - via the phone line. Networks of computers (and fax and telex machines) in remote locations can transmit, receive and share information, being connected by cable (eg within an office) or telephone lines (if dispersed). ISDN allows more complicated data to be sent down the line.

2.7 The *nature* of data processing is essentially the same, no matter whether it is done manually or electronically. The main differences between manual and computerised data processing, however, can be outlined as follows.

(a) *Speed:* computers can process data much more quickly than a human. This means that a computer has a much higher productivity and so ought to be cheaper for large volumes of data processing than doing the work manually. As computer costs have fallen, this cost advantage of the computer has become more accentuated. The ability to process data more quickly means that a computer can produce more timely information, when information is needed as soon as possible. Telecommunications have also meant that the *transmission* of information is much faster (or almost instantaneous).

(b) *Accuracy:* computers are generally accurate, whereas humans are prone to error.

(c) *Volume and complexity:* as businesses grow and become more complex, the data processing requirements increase in volume and complexity too. More managers need greater amounts of information. More transactions have to be processed. The volume of information processing work is often beyond the capability of even the largest clerical workforce to do manually. Clearing banks would be unable to function nowadays without electronic data processing to ease the demands on their workforce.

(d) *Flexibility:* computers are highly versatile in the number of processing operations and presentational formats that can be used. They can be used for automatic reporting by exception, the production of operational control reports, planning and decision support (using complex modelling where required) etc. Database systems are particularly well-suited to management applications for marketing, product/service design etc.

(e) *Accessibility:* information is stored electronically, saving enormous amounts of physical space, and making data quickly accessible through terminals. 'Interrogation systems' allow instant access to stored data from a remote terminal, and are the basis of many bank services.

2.8 The power and speed of information technology have increased dramatically over years. Computers are now portable - enabling pensions advisers to draw up a quote on client's premises, or to communicate with head office.

The Internet

2.9 An important development linking computers and communications system is the *Internet*. The Internet is a network governed by certain rules which anybody with a personal computer, a modem and a telephone line can access. There are a large number of Internet terminals in the US and Europe. Every member has a unique 'address'.

2.10 The Internet has two implications for bank management.

(a) In the long term, it is possible that payment for services might be made over the Internet. However, there are major problems with security. Ever more advanced encryption technology is defeated by ever more sophisticated hackers.

(b) In the medium term it might be used as a means of marketing communications.

(i) Banks can open a 'site' on the Internet, so that Internet users can obtain information, or even order services.

(ii) Advertising (ie sending 'mail-shots' to other people's Internet addresses) is more problematic. Reports have come in about advertisers being 'mail-bombed'; in other words, their own Internet addresses have been swamped with messages from Internet users outraged at having received 'junk email'.

3. IT: SOME BANKING APPLICATIONS

The changing role of IT in banks

3.1 The first phase of automation in banks, in the 1960s and 1970s, concerned the *back office*. Technology was introduced primarily to replace processes carried out manually, as the explosion in the volume of business threatened to send staffing levels out of control. It had a limited role, since:

(a) little thought was given to restructuring the underlying processes themselves;

(b) the change was internally motivated and had little effect on the front office, or loan, securities and management teams in branches, or on customers, although it did start to open the way for new products such as credit cards and cash dispensers;

(c) it was confined to 'data processing'. Little thought had yet been given to 'information' - and the translation of data into information for management remained a manual process.

Nevertheless, this basic role of IT in transaction processing is still crucial: account-holding and money transmission business is still the bread and butter of clearing banks.

3.2 During the 1980s there were radical changes, with the development of more powerful computer processing at lower costs. Spreadsheets and database management software re-oriented the system towards the production of *information*, rather than the processing of transaction *data*, with more flexible and valuable applications. These changes also focused attention on the possibilities of integrating systems. 'Data processing' was largely part of internal bank operations, but database management and communications facilities started to connect the bank more closely with its environment and the demands made by that environment.

3.3 In broad terms, IT has now been applied in banks to:

(a) the administrative infrastructure of banking;

(b) the provision of management information;

(c) development of customer databases for marketing, market segmentation etc;

(d) the provision of services to customers: offering greater speed and convenience of service, greater diversity and 'tailoring' of products;

(e) communications (including payments systems etc);

(f) risk evaluation and management both at customer level (eg lending) and at corporate level (strategic planning and the management of change).

We will look at some of the specific current applications of technology in the services offered to customers, and then at larger trends and influences within banks and bank management.

Money transmission systems

3.4 Money transmission is one of the key activities of banks. Although the means of money transmission most familiar to customers is probably the cheque, automated systems have significantly reduced the need for vast volumes of paper to be transferred throughout the banking system - reducing the time and cost of the service to banks and their customers. Money transmission services include BACS, CHAPS, EFTPOS and SWIFT.

3.5 BACS (Bankers Automated Clearing Services) was set up by the banks in the 1960s to reduce paper flows for payments. BACS services payment methods such as standing orders, direct debits and bank giro credits. Banks or companies sponsored by banks make payments through BACS by means of data held on computer media which might be a disk or tape. The data may be physically taken to the BACS processing centre or transmitted to banks through the telephone network using a service called BACSTEL. (There is also a trial scheme for sending BACS payments via EDI - electronic data interchange-systems - called 'BACSNET'.)

Perhaps the biggest application of BACS has been to corporate customers paying salaries, wages and trade debts.

3.6 The Clearing House Automated Payment System or CHAPS was established in 1984 by the banks to automate the transfer of funds for amounts of £5,000 and over between banks. CHAPS settlement takes place on the same day, a great advantage where large amounts are being settled for which interest, even if only over night, can be a significant amount. The system operates between CHAPS settlement banks, which are all the major English and Scottish banks. The banks' CHAPS computers are 'networked' using sophisticated software and telecommunications links, so there is no centre point for CHAPS processing - it is a decentralised system. The banks' links into the system are called 'gateways'. Institutions which are not CHAPS settlement banks may use the system, but only through a settlement bank's gateway. Security of the system is of paramount importance, as no signatures or paper records are actually transferred, only electronic instructions.

3.7 The promotion of Electronic Funds Transfer at the Point of Sale, or EFTPOS, is set to revolutionise money transmission in the retail environment. The idea behind the system is that a customer wishing to make a payment in a shop, for example, uses a plastic card (debit card) containing his bank account details in a magnetic strip. The card is 'wiped' through a terminal in the shop and the data for the transaction transmitted to the bank's computer centre, which generates the appropriate payment instruction to the retailer's bank, without the need for vouchers, cheques etc. The customer's account is debited directly, and the retailer's is credited: this and the administrative convenience are considered the main advantages for retailers.

3.8 SWIFT (the Society for Worldwide Interbank Financial Telecommunications) is a Belgian-registered co-operative society used by all major banks in the developed world, linked with domestic inter-bank networks. SWIFT facilitates the transmission between members of international payments, statements and other messages (previously 'documents') concerned with international banking. The SWIFT system has enabled faster, safer and more efficient international money transmission services by banks. It is still growing and developing. The promotion of globally based personal banking has encouraged the introduction of inter-branch file transfer (IFT) so that banks can send automated instructions across national frontiers to pay dividends, salaries and pensions to expatriates.

Electronic data interchange (EDI)

3.9 Corporate customers will soon be able to settle transactions between themselves by means of EDI. This technology will allow SWIFT to become a much more widely-used medium for settlement. Instead of having to use paper messages to link the flow of funds between corporate accounts (payment) with communication between companies (remittance advices), EDI allows the two - money and information - to flow simultaneously. Very prompt payments will also be facilitated.

Cash management systems

3.10 Corporate customers are usually more sophisticated in their approach to financial management than personal customers, and as a large potential market, they have seen a lot of effort made on their behalf in the development of electronic banking services, known as *office banking*.

3.11 The essence of a cash management service is that a company with any number of UK and/or international accounts can obtain up-to-date information by means of data transmission from its bank's computer to a PC in the company treasury department. The service includes the following.

    (a) *Account reporting:*

        (i) information about the balances on the accounts, including details of the cleared balance for the previous day;

        (ii) forecast balance reports, which take into account uncleared items and automated entries (eg BACS credits and debits, standing orders and direct debits);

        (iii)   reports giving individual transaction details;

        (iv)   summary reports of transactions, balances and forecast balances;

        (v)   cheque reconciliation programmes.

   (b) *Funds transfer service:* The customer can initiate payments through his terminal, and movements from one account to another.

   (c) *Decision support services:*

        (i)   information on foreign exchange rates and interest rates; and
        (ii)   balance history reports.

3.12 It is obviously important for a corporate customer to be assured that an office banking system is secure, and that unauthorised persons are unable to access the systems and, in particular, move funds. Most office banking systems use 'smart cards' for this purpose.

3.13 The equivalent facility for personal customers is *home banking*, where bank customers have access to information about their account from the bank computer, through a home terminal (or even via the telephone, using voice recognition technology). The services provided are similar to those provided by the most advanced ATMs (except of course, cash dispensing): customers can make balance enquiries, statement and chequebook requests, inter-account transfers and bill payments.

3.14 More user-friendly, but less technology-based, forms of home and office banking are available via the 'branchless' banks, where 'callers speak to staff at special banking centres where they can draw on a complete range of banking products.' *(Banking World,* January 1991).

ATMs

3.15 Transaction automation has changed the way in which branch staff work, but has also revolutionised the role of the branch network itself by making possible extra-mural and unstaffed delivery of services. Of all the technological advances in banking in recent years, the most well-known to the general public must be the development of automated teller machines (ATMs).

3.16 To use an ATM, a customer inserts his or her card into the machine, keys in a Personal Identification Number (PIN) and then keys in instructions to the machine under guidance from a visual display in the machine itself. The latest ATMs can be used:

   (a) to withdraw cash;

   (b) to find out the current balance on the customer's account;

   (c) in some cases, to ask for a statement of account or new cheque book to be sent;

   (d) in some cases, to deposit cash or cheques in the customer's account;

   (e) to carry out simple bill payment facilities;

(f) in some cases, to obtain a mini-statement showing the last few transactions on the account;

(g) to request financial services information (not so much transaction as *sales* automation).

3.17 ATMs have evolved fairly rapidly from 'cash dispensers' into sophisticated information devices for the retail customer. Most newer ATMs are usable 24 hours per day, seven days per week, although some earlier machines have more limited hours of service, and a bank might restrict usage as a matter of general policy.

3.18 Most ATMs are through-the-wall machines which can be used in the street, but there are some in the public areas of branches or in self-contained 'lobbies' to which the card gives access. The installation of through-the-wall ATMs at bank branches is now slowing down, and the emphasis is switching to providing:

(a) ATMs at 'stand-alone' locations away from branches; and
(b) rapid cash dispensers and staff-operated computer terminals in the branches themselves.

3.19 Important developments have taken place to link up the ATM networks of different banks. The term 'ATM reciprocity' refers to arrangements between banks and financial institutions to allow customers to use the ATMs of all the participating organisations using a card issued by any one of them. Credit cards can also be used to obtain cash from ATMs.

3.20 The advantages of ATMs to banks are:

(a) improved competitiveness, by improving the quality of services to customers;
(b) labour-cost savings, provided that customer usage of ATMs is high enough;
(c) prevention of unauthorised overdrafts, since the funds are not dispensed if the balance is (or would be after the transaction) overdrawn beyond the agreed limit.

3.21 The advantages of ATMs to customers are:

(a) unrestricted hours of service;

(b) accessibility of banking services, when the link-ups between the ATMs of banks develop, and ATMs are extended to more non-bank sites.

Smart cards

3.22 Smart cards are similar to magnetic stripe cards used in ATMs, which the major difference that they contain a microchip, instead of a magnetic stripe, and are thus able to store a great deal more information. Smart cards might contain the entire amount of transactions on a particular account in certain circumstances, or other personal details. They will thus be an entire personal file, which the bank can review automatically.

Electronic cash

3.23 Banks have been trying for some years to reduce the risk and expense of dealing with cash, and to increase security. This is one reason why the banks have been experimenting with electronic cash.

3.24 At the time of writing, *Mondex* has been introduced on an experimental basis to the town of Swindon. Mondex is a type of electronic cash. In brief, the principles are these.

(a) The customer has a plastic card, which is effectively used as a purse. The customer puts the card in the Mondex terminal (either at a high street site or an attachment to the customer's telephone), and transfers electronic cash from his or her bank account to the card.

(b) Security devices ensure that the card stays locked; a PIN is needed to activate it.

(c) When the customer wishes to 'spend' the money, he or she swipes the card through the retailer's terminal, and the electronic cash is collected by the retailer.

3.25 Just as Switch and Connect operate as electronic cheques, Mondex works as electronic cash. The bank is not offering credit by offering the card, and the customer is not incurring any additional debt (other than overdraft facilities arranged in the normal way).

3.26 Given that consumers have taken well to all types of plastic cards, and the fact that they are worried about carrying around large amounts of cash, it is probable that Mondex is the 'way forward'.

Planning and control applications

3.27 Risk assessment and management in *transactions* (ie not at the strategic planning level) has also been aided by the application of technology.

(a) *Credit scoring.* This is a method of assessing a potential borrower's creditworthiness (or indeed a potential employee's suitability in a post). The system used to be manually performed by unskilled labour. The loan applicant, say, gives details on a form, relating to age, marital status, property ownership, length of time at present address and employment, income, bank accounts held, loan details etc. In the manual system a 'master scoring table' was matched to the form to derive marks scored on each criterion: according to score, the loan could be accepted, declined or referred to a senior official. The computer system can make the same 'programmed decisions'. It is even anticipated that knowledge-based systems technology could in the future provide a credit-scoring system that can 'learn' from previous loan applications and their performance.

(b) *Signature authentication* in the attempt to control credit card and cheque fraud. Signatures can be scanned and stored electronically: terminal users in the bank can access the signature for visual comparison. This might be used increasingly in EFTPOS systems.

(c) *Fraud detection.* Given the extent of credit card fraud, banks have used software to monitor accounts for unusual patterns of transactions which might indicate fraudulent use of a card.

3.28 Underpinning most of the UK banks' investment in branch automation is the development of *database management*. As discussed in the previous chapter, databases offer quick on-screen access to stored data; a reduction in paper-work; the provision of 'real time' customer and product information; and the ability to design tailored services to defined market segments. In *Banking World* in September 1991 it was stressed that relational databases represented a big step forward, being huge customer information systems which allow staff:

(a) to handle an unlimited number of products and services; and
(b) to access all a customer's relationships with the bank on-screen.

3.29 Databases have also opened up much greater possibilities for strategic planning, which is the only way banks can prepare themselves to cope with uncertainty and change in their business environment. Internal and external information is available for strategic planning: information about the customer base, the bank's employees, social and political trends and economic forecasts.

3.30 Hand in hand with sheer data availability has come the development of sophisticated management information systems for strategic, tactical and operational planning.

3.31 At the strategic level forecasting, modelling, sensitivity analysis and other techniques have been significantly enhanced by computerisation. The range of variables that can be introduced into models, for example, is very much wider than would ever have been possible on paper, allowing managers to assess the effect on bank operations and results of different scenarios incorporating both external circumstances and managerial decisions. Managers can 'try out' strategies and tactics using models and simulations, and assess their consequences without having to risk damage or cost to the 'real' business. The risks of complex lending and investment decisions can be assessed by modelling 'worst case scenarios', and safety margins can be determined.

3.32 Calculations are faster more accurate and less prone to human subjectivity. Graphs and charts and other planning aids can be created from input figures at the touch of a button.

4. ISSUES AND TRENDS IN BANKING TECHNOLOGY

4.1 'For the chief executive, IT presents strategic issues for competitive positioning, organisation and staffing; for the account executive it can be a help or a hindrance in successful relationship management; for our staff it can be the difference between slavish routine or liberation... The impact of IT upon banking is...radical.'

Presidential address, *Banking World* January 1990

The effect of technology on competition and market strategies

4.2 New technology has changed, and continues to change, the structure of competition faced by banks, the markets they serve and the products they offer.

(a) Technology involves high set-up costs, but once it is in place, the marginal cost of processing are much reduced by lowering staff levels and costs for a given volume of output. Such a cost structure offers opportunities to reap 'economies of scale'; a reduction in the unit cost of high-volume business. This has created even stiffer competition in the market place for services, particular *price* competition, as providers battle for market share. Technology has contributed to the over-supply of services in the market, but also offers solutions in terms of opportunity for increased market segmentation and price competition.

(b) IT also reduces the 'barriers of entry' which might otherwise deter new competitors from entering the market. In particular, smaller institutions have been offered several new opportunities.

   (i) Electronic funds transfer systems are now open to smaller and non-bank institutions, which are banding together in joint schemes or joining existing bodies to gain access to networks. Widespread services can thus be offered by small institutions without the massive investment in administrative structures that would once have been necessary.

   (ii) When ATMs were introduced, they favoured the large operators who could afford, and had the concentration of customers to justify, the investment required. Now, however, networks are being linked, and smaller institutions can have access to a major ATM network without substantial capital investment. Capital can be redirected to more sophisticated applications supporting market-segmentation, direct marketing and cross-selling etc - thus compensating for a smaller branch presence. A customer base can be served through ATM networks that would otherwise be inaccessible due to lack of branches.

(c) The definition of the marketplace is changing. Segments have been made more distinct through the use of IT, and with basic cash transactions automated, banks can direct financial and human resources to the sale of more profitable financial services. There is thus fierce competition at market segment level, with opportunities to gain higher market share in smaller, but highly profitable, markets.

(d) Globalisation of the financial markets has been made possible by IT, and has produced a new potential customer base. A bank which positions itself in this market requires sophisticated telecommunications networks, integrated databases and global delivery systems.

(e) With its possibilities for market segmentation and diversification, IT reveals the extent to which 'banking' is not a single service, but a 'bundle' of services offered to disparate groups of customers. IT has affected the answer to the question 'What business are we in?'. The different answers also produce different competitors - especially among non-banking institutions. For example, an expanding role for banks is anticipated to be the processing and provision of information itself (previously seen only as part of other mechanisms for payment and transfer): in this business, the competitive peer group includes management consultancies, telecommunications companies and IT vendors.

(f) In the past, it was possible for banks to equate customer 'inertia' with customer loyalty. Now, however, the combination of competition and technology has reduced the cost of switching between institutions, and customer turnover rates are becoming a critical performance indicator.

The effect of technology on the bank branch

4.3 We have suggest how remote transaction systems such as ATMs and home banking have down-graded the importance of the branch network as the 'place' element of the marketing mix. Many branches have been shut down or downgraded in status and staffing. However, this is to underestimate the change in the *role* of branches.

(a) Developments in IT have taken the majority of data processing and basic transactions out of the branch: with further growth in home banking, 'smart cards' and high-tech ATMs, this trend is likely to continue. Institutions - or units within them - concentrating exclusively on core banking functions are moving towards branchless banking (eg First Direct). Meanwhile prime space and staff in branches are liberated to become a sales outlet marketing more complex financial instruments.

(b) There has been a cycle in the relationship between bankers and customers. IT applications have removed the need for customers to visit the branch to transact business, as well as scaling down branch presence, and creating a 'mass market' for banking: they have thus 'de-personalised' the relationship since the (pre-technology) days of personal contact banking. IT has also, however, *re*personalised the relationship, since database technology supports the tailoring and marketing of specialist products to specific segments of the customer base: it refocuses attention on the customer, rather than the account.

(c) Technology supports high and consist service levels for the customer.

   (i) Transaction times are speeded up.

   (ii) The branch environment is growing more customer-friendly. The barriers created by 'bandit screens' are being dismantled and replaced by teller-assisted units. More space is liberated for open-plan public and 'personal banking' areas.

   (iii) The range of services offered by the branch is widening: integrated systems can offer related relevant products to the customer and handle applications together, moving towards 'one-stop shopping' in financial products.

The effect of technology on bank staff

4.4 Information technology affects many areas of organisational life.

(a) It changes the work environment. There are now problems for premises managers in adapting the environment to technology in terms of space, heat, noise, ventilation, control of static electricity, wire and cable management etc. For employees, however, the change is generally seen to be beneficial: a 'high tech' environment is often cleaner, safer and more 'designed' than pre-technology offices.

(b) It changes the nature of work and structure of the workforce by:

   (i) requiring new skills in technology management and operation;

   (ii) making human intervention unnecessary for some processes (but possibly liberating staff for different roles eg sales or consultancy); and

   (iii) reinforcing these new roles through competitive pressures and opportunities.

(c) Use of portable 'laptop' computers allow bank staff greater mobility, so personal financial advisers can provide 'on-the-spot' point of sale demonstrations wherever consultations with the customers take place (eg in their homes).

4.5 One of the main concerns about the application of IT is 'replacement' - ie the substitution of 'intelligent' machines for people at work. Redundancies *have* resulted from the labour- saving automation of processes and the contraction of the branch network in favour of automated transaction units. However, new job opportunities have also arisen in marketing and consultancy roles, supported by database technology. Technological advance must also be seen as a way of *preserving* jobs in the face of intense competitive pressures in the financial services industry: any institution which falls behind is going to face problems.

4.6 Another fear associated with technology is *deskilling*, ie the fear that skills will be wasted and die out. However, Buchanan and Huczynski suggest that: 'as machines do more, people do not necessarily do less. Computer technology may be tools that *complement* human skills and create more interesting and meaningful work ... The outcome depends to a large extent on *management decisions* on how to organise the work around the new devices.'

In addition, there are frequently *new* skills to be learned - eg in systems operation and maintenance, 'house-keeping' routines etc, skills in a constantly developing and high-status field.

4.7 Even where employees' traditional roles have disappeared, there is the new challenge to improve the level of skills in the areas in which IT frees them to participate, eg sales or consultancy. Since IT has simultaneously freed the customer from the need to enter branch premises, selling bank services has become a much more pro-active process - with new skills in information provision, interpersonal relationship management and sale closure to be acquired or upgraded. Previously, sales training consisted of preparing staff to handle queries and spot opportunities of cross-selling - essentially reactive processes. Now there is emphasis on identifying and seeking out new markets and businesses.

4.8 So what has the effect of IT actually been on job satisfaction in banking? Has it freed employees from the drudgery of data processing - or re-enslaved them to impersonal machines which rob them of discretion and meaning in their jobs? Two sides have been argued as to whether technology is 'good' or 'bad' for the worker.

(a) Process operators are victims of management's use of technology to create work that is unskilled - and unlikely to offer any learning opportunities - boring, repetitive, tightly controlled, lacking meaning, and socially isolating. Microelectronic extension of automation may alter the demand for operators' human skills, and may damage the quality of working life: it may replace the exercise of human mental capacity altogether.

(b) Process operators are skilled, knowledgeable decision makers, with responsibility, discretion and prosperous working conditions. Process automation eliminates dirt and hazard, and can offer a motivating work environment with task variety, meaning, learning opportunities and discretion. Electronic controls lack human flexibility and creativity: systems can enhance job skills and interest.

4.9 You may have your own opinions about this. The essential point is that the introduction of technology *per se* cannot be seen in isolation from *managerial choices* about organisation work, job design, workplace layout, control systems, the culture of the organisation etc. It is these considerations that make technology acceptable or unacceptable to workers, good or bad for job satisfaction and effective or ineffective.

The challenge of the future

4.10 In an article in *Banking World* (December 1990) Joseph de Feo stressed the fact that IT managers in banks will have to be seen as mainstream business managers so that IT is integral to the services offered by the bank, such as EDI and home banking. IT will be central to the quality of the bank's products and services, since it allows segmentation of the market.

'IT management must accept a new role in the organisation as business managers who just happen to have specific expertise in, and knowledge of, IT, and should no longer view themselves as somehow 'outside' the mainstream of the bank.'

Exercise

Choose an example, from your own experience, of technological change in a bank. How was it introduced? How did it affect your work? What are its disadvantages and advantages for you, the bank and the customer?

---

5. CHAPTER ROUNDUP

5.1 IT is the use of computer, micro-electronics and telecommunications to produce, store, obtain and send information in the form of pictures, words or numbers, more reliably, quickly and economically.

5.2 The qualities of electronic data and information processing are:

S peed
A ccuracy
V olume
V ersatility
I nterrogation

5.3 Banking applications include:

(a) money transmission and other services
(b) transaction automation
(c) marketing
(d) planning and control
(e) database management.

5.4 'Mere possession of sophisticated IT will not guarantee success in the future. The ability to apply IT effectively, ie to increase profits by reducing costs or adding value, will be the key. The early implementation of IT has produced a generation of managers for whom computers were for the back-office and thus were something you were promoted away from. There is a need to overcome the resulting resistance and IT used for the powerful tool that it can be.'

(Sir John Quinton, CIB President)

TEST YOUR KNOWLEDGE

The numbers in brackets refer to paragraphs of this chapter

1   What are the general advantages of computerised as opposed to manual data processing? (2.7)

2   Outline the historical change in the role of IT in banking. (3.1,3.2)

3   What are:

(a)   BACS
(b)   EFTPOS, and
(c)   SWIFT? (3.5, 3.7, 3.8)

4   What are the advantages of ATMs to customers and banks? (3.20, 3.21)

5   How has IT contributed to risk assessment and control? (3.27)

6   How has IT brought smaller institutions and non-banks into greater competition with the large banks? (4.2)

7   How have ATMs changed the role of the bank branch? Has technology therefore eroded the bank-customer relationship? (4.3)

8   How does IT affect:

(a)   the structure of the workforce in banks; (4.4, 4.5, 4.9)
(b)   job satisfaction of bank staff. (4.8, 4.9)

Now try question 20 at the end of the text

Chapter 20

THE DESIGN OF WORK

This chapter covers the following topics.

1. Job design
2. Job enrichment
3. Job enlargement
4. Job rotation

Introduction

Our consideration of the bank as an organisation and as a complex system would not be complete without some discussion of the 'people' element of the socio-technical system. The way in which work is organised around the technology, methods or processes of an organisation is *job design*. It is part of the organisation structure, because it embodies decisions about specialisation, decentralisation of authority etc.

---

1. JOB DESIGN

1.1 There is no particular mystique about 'job design': it is merely the way in which tasks are fragmented or grouped to form a given job, and what decisions are made about specialisation, discretion, autonomy, variety and other job elements.

Early job design

1.2 Frederick Taylor ('scientific management') was an early exponent of systematic job design. His technique was:

(a) to decide on the optimum degree of task fragmentation, ie breaking down a complex job into its simplest component parts;

(b) to decide the most efficient way of performing each component; and

(c) to train employees to carry out a single task in the 'best' way.

1.3 This micro-division of labour is based on a production line organisation of work, and offers some efficiencies.

(a) Each task is so simple and straightforward that it can be learned with very little training.

355

(b) Since skills required are low, the effects of absenteeism are minimised: workers can be shifted from one task to another very easily.

(c) Similarly, high labour turnover is not critical, because replacements can be found and trained without difficulty.

(d) Tasks are closely defined, standardised and timed, so output and quality are more easily predicted and controlled.

Problems of task fragmentation

1.4 The question of 'job design' acquired its prominence when human relations theorists became interested in the motivational aspects of the job itself, and the role of 'job satisfaction' in employee performance. It was recognised that jobs made up of low-skilled, repetitive tasks (of which there will inevitably be some, in any organisation's operations) could offer little satisfaction to the workers performing them, being socially isolating, meaningless and monotonous.

1.5 Studies of human behaviour at work also suggested that the existence of such tasks poses problems for management.

(a) Monotony, and the experience of boredom, is part of what may be called 'industrial *fatigue*', an element which interferes with the 'steady state' in which workers work best. Tasks which provide little mental stimulation for the worker may result in inattention, daydreaming or preoccupation with social interactions and diversions. Errors and even accidents may result from this. If the worker has *no* social outlet, however, the strain of monotony is even worse.

(b) Stress is related to high workload, low discretion jobs. Its symptoms - including nervous tension, withdrawal and low moral - will invariably affect performance.

(c) Motivation will suffer, unless particular efforts are made to compensate the workers for lack of satisfaction in the work itself.

(d) If such tasks are perceived to be the lot of the worker ('us'), under the control of management ('them'), interpersonal relations between manager and workers will be hampered.

1.6 The general conclusions of studies of monotony have been that it is less likely to arise if:

(a) the activity is changed from time to time, and rest pauses allowed. The Health and Safety Executive suggest that short, frequent breaks seem to prevent fatigue and that natural pauses are preferable to fixed rest break schedules, giving workers some control;

(b) tasks are grouped into whole, self-contained 'jobs' with a sense of 'meaning' and completeness, and involving co-operation with others - rather than the repetition of a single part of a job by each individual in isolation;

(c) workers are permitted the outlet of social interaction, ie are allowed to form groups, rather than being isolated by the way the work place is designed; 'chatting' is usually permitted within reason and a decision-making role may even be given to the work group.

1.7 Such areas of interest focused attention on job design as a factor in employee motivation, satisfaction and performance. A systematic approach to job satisfaction and its relationship to job design was first put forward by Frederick Herzberg, in the 1950s.

Job satisfaction and its implications for job design

1.8 Frederick Herzberg formulated a 'two factor' theory of motivation, drawing a distinction between:

(a) 'maintenance', 'hygiene' or 'environmental' factors which are taken for granted as the basis of continuing to work at an acceptable level, offering freedom from dissatisfaction (temporarily) but not positive satisfaction; and

(b) 'motivator factors' which satisfy employees and offer them an incentive to achieve higher levels of performance.

In the first group, Herzberg put supervision, work relationships and even pay. In the second, he put 'intrinsic' satisfactions including recognition, responsibility, challenge, achievement and personal growth. He suggested that these positive motivator factors, which alone give lasting satisfaction, can only be supplied by the job itself.

1.9 The job itself can be interesting and exciting. It can satisfy the desire for a feeling of 'accomplishing something', for responsibility, for professional recognition, for advancement and the need for self-esteem. The extent to which a job *must* be challenging or creative to a motivator seeker will depend on each individual, ie

(a) his ability and intelligence; and
(b) his tolerance for delayed success, or delayed gratification of his needs.

1.10 Herzberg specified three means whereby job design can be revised to improve motivation. These are:

(a) job enrichment;
(b) job enlargement;
(c) job rotation.

Relevance of job design theories

1.11 Job enrichment and enlargement became popular techniques throughout the 1970s. The former, in particular, contributed to the 'quality of working life' movement. However, the world economic recession of the 1980s diverted management theorists' attention away from such issues. As Buchanan and Huczynski note: 'The quality of working life is less important when there is little work to be had.'

1.12 Nevertheless, the theories have offered managers ideas about what their subordinates look for and get out of their work, and what variables can be manipulated to give them greater challenge and satisfaction in their work. Relatively simple managerial changes, eg giving more direct feedback on performance, or reducing the number of formal controls on employee behaviour, can affect the employee's experience of the core job dimensions. Introducing new tasks and increased involvement in client relationships are two techniques positively *forced* on management by changes in the banking environment. Task significance is being enhanced for many bank employees by the automation of basic repetitive processes, and the relatively new market- and customer-orientation of banking work.

1.13 Increased delegation and the offering of autonomy may be more difficult for managers to introduce into existing structures and cultures, especially in banks where accuracy and security of work is still paramount - but elements of it may be available, eg where there are places available on project teams and committees, so that selected employees can learn to participate in decision-making processes.

2. JOB ENRICHMENT

2.1 Job enrichment is planned, deliberate action to build greater responsibility, breadth and challenge of work into a job. It is thus a 'vertical' extension of the job design, and Herzberg suggested the application of various 'vertical job loading factors' which would enrich a job:

(a) remove controls;
(b) increase accountability;
(c) create natural work units;
(d) provide direct feedback;
(e) introduce new tasks;
(f) allocate special assignments.

2.2 A similar prescription was drawn up by later motivation theorists. Concepts such as combining of tasks, formation of natural work units, establishing of client relationships, vertical loading (ie increased delegation, reduced controls) and feedback were said to result in enhancement of work experience in five *core job dimensions:*

(a) skill variety;
(b) task identity;
(c) task significance;
(d) autonomy;
(e) feedback.

The experience of these dimensions was said to meet employee growth needs and lead to high motivation and satisfaction, high quality performance and low absenteeism/turnover rates.

2.3 Current trends in banking to give staff a selling, consultancy and customer service role in branches - explaining a wider range of financial products, giving information etc - instead of or in addition to traditional transaction processing roles (which are now heavily automated) represent job enrichment.

2.4 It would be wrong, however, to suppose that job enrichment alone will automatically make employees more productive.

> 'Even those who want their jobs enriched will expect to be rewarded with more than job satisfaction. Job enrichment is not a cheaper way to greater productivity. Its pay-off will come in the less visible costs of morale, climate and working relationships'.
> (Handy)

Empowerment

2.5 In order to curtail costs and improve responsiveness, many organisations, including banks are seeking to reduce the number of management layers and to devolve decision-making down to the customer.

2.6 Empowerment is the devolution of decision-making power in certain areas to the workplace. It is stronger than mere delegation.

2.7 The information processing Max Hand (*Management Accounting*, January 1991) refers to the place of *empowerment* in the quality control process: 'the people lower down the organisation possess the knowledge of what is going wrong within a process but lack the authority to make changes. Those further up the structure have the authority to make changes but lack the profound knowledge required to identify the right solutions. The only solution is to change the culture of the organisation so that everyone can become involved in the process of improvement and work together to make the changes'. This approach risks conflicts and requires discipline.

2.8 Empowerment has two key aspects.

(a) Allowing workers to have the freedom to decide how to do the necessary work, using the skills they possess and acquiring new skills as necessary to be an effective team member.

(b) Making those workers personally responsible for achieving production targets and for quality control.

2.9 In a banking context it might mean that an employee, using IT, can authorise a loan if it has been credit scored automatically, without referral to a manager.

3. JOB ENLARGEMENT

3.1 Job enlargement is frequently confused with job enrichment though it should be clearly defined as a separate technique. Job enlargement, as the name suggests, is the attempt to widen jobs by increasing the number of operations in which a job holder is involved. This has the effect of lengthening the 'time cycle' of repeated operations: by reducing the number of repetitions of the same work, the dullness of the job should also be reduced. Job enlargement is therefore a 'horizontal' extension of an individual's work, whereas job enrichment is a 'vertical' extension.

3.2 Arguably, job enlargement is limited in its ability to improve motivation since, as Herzberg points out, to ask a worker to complete three separate tedious, unchallenging tasks is unlikely to motivate him more than asking him to fulfil one single tedious, unchallenging task.

4. JOB ROTATION

4.1 Job rotation might take two forms.

(a) An employee might be transferred to another job after a period in an existing job, in order to give him new interest and challenge.

(b) Job rotation might be regarded as a form of training. Trainees might be expected to learn a bit about a number of different jobs by spending 6 months or 1 year in each job before being moved on. The employee is regarded as a 'trainee' rather than as an experienced person holding down a demanding job.

4.2 No doubt you will have your own views about the value of job rotation as a method of training or career development. It is interesting to note Drucker's view: 'The whole idea of training jobs is contrary to all rules and experience. A man should never be given a job that is not a real job, that does not require performance from him.'

It is generally accepted that the value of job rotation as a motivator is limited.

> We have looked at other aspects of personnel systems - namely job evaluation, discipline and grievance procedures and appraisal systems - in Part B of this text.

Exercise

To what extent do you think your job has been consciously *designed*? How far are job enlargement, job enrichment and job motivation used in the organisation of work in your current branch, or in the career planning advocated by your bank?

5. CHAPTER ROUNDUP

5.1 *Job design* had been the focus of attention under the 'scientific management' school of thought, with the emphasis on task fragmentation and specialisation. Each job was broken down into its smallest and simplest components, each of which was then allocated to one individual trained to perform it in the most efficient manner.

5.2 Under 'human relations' influences, however, the issue of job design focused on the 'rebuilding' of jobs to reconcile the efficiencies of specialisation with worker satisfaction. Herzberg recommended three possible approaches:

(a) *job rotation* - task variety through changing jobs regularly

(b) *job enlargement* - a 'horizontal' extension of the job to embrace more tasks of the same kind

(c) *job enrichment* - a 'vertical' extension of the job to embrace more tasks with added responsibility, discretion or difficulty.

TEST YOUR KNOWLEDGE
The numbers in brackets refer to paragraphs of this chapter

1   What are the advantages of job design on scientific management principles? (1.3)

2   What problems are posed for management by the existence of low-skilled, repetitive tasks in their organisation? (1.5)

3   How useful are job design theories? (1.10 - 1.12)

4   What sort of 'vertical job loading factors' can be used to enrich a job? (2.1)

5   Distinguish between job enlargement and job enrichment. (3.1)

6   Describe two methods of job rotation. (4.1)

Now try question 21 at the end of the text

PART E
THE BUSINESS ENVIRONMENT

Chapter 21

THE ORGANISATION AND THE ENVIRONMENT

This chapter covers the following topics.

1. Introduction to organisation and the environment
2. The commercial and economic environment
3. The political and legal environment
4. The technological environment
5. The social and ethical environment
6. The stakeholder view

Introduction

As an open system, a bank is involved in constant exchange with the environment. The environment provides *inputs* - of finance, labour, materials etc - to the system which are converted by the system's activities into *outputs* back to the environment - finance, services, products etc.

---

1. INTRODUCTION TO ORGANISATION AND THE ENVIRONMENT

1.1 There are many ways of looking at and talking about 'organisations'. One influential modern approach is to use the analogy of a 'system'.

1.2 A system may be defined as a collection of parts into a complex unity, or as 'organised complexity', but in systems theory a distinction is made between:

(a)   *closed systems*, whose processes are contained within the boundaries of the system, without any interaction with the 'outside'; and

(b)   *open systems*, whose processes influence and are influenced by the world outside the system's own boundaries - the *environment* of the system.

1.3 In other words, an organisation such as a bank may have boundaries, giving it a 'shape' and identity, but they are neither rigid nor impenetrable. Employees of the bank, for example, are also part of its environment - as customers (if they use the services of the bank), as part of the socio-political system (as voters, members of a trade union) etc.

1.4 Another way of looking at the relationship between an organisation and its environment identifies three linking mechanisms.

(a) The organisation imports *resources* from the environment (eg employees, equipment, finance).

(b) There are different *groups* in the environment, or connected with the environment, who may have some rights or claims with regard to the activities of the organisation, ie who may be 'stakeholders' in the organisation. These groups include customers, employees, the government, the general public, suppliers, competitors and shareholders.

(c) The environment provides *opportunities* which an organisation can exploit (eg for a bank, new markets opening in Europe or other areas of financial services) and *threats* which endanger the organisation's survival (eg competitors' actions, restrictive legislation, political unrest in debtor countries, demographic changes shrinking the labour 'pool').

1.5 You can see from the above just how many and varied are the elements of the environment that impact on the organisation - and need to be *managed*. The organisation 'meets' its environment at different points: some units deal with customers and 'the market', others deal with the pool of labour in the employment market, while others again are at the forefront when it comes to technological change etc. The term *boundary management* is used for how the relationship is handled at these points, at the 'interface' between the organisation and the outside world.

1.6 In following chapters, we look at some aspects of boundary management in more detail, but first we will get an overview of what the environment of a bank is, and how it affects the banking organisation.

General pressures on the banking system

1.7 In *Banking World* (January 1995), David Llewellyn identified some trends in banking which he thinks will influence its long-term future.

(a) There will be increased competition in the markets for deposits and loans.

(b) Entry barriers will decline further - in other words, it will be easier for new competitors to enter financial services markets. For example, Marks and Spencer now sells personal pensions.

(c) Services will be *deconstructed*. In other words processes will be decomposed into their component parts which might be provided separately. A loan involves three processes:

(i) originating the loan;
(ii) administrating the loan;
(iii) holding the asset.

For example, banks have securitised some of their mortgage loans, by selling them to investors, even though they still administer them.

(d) Direct banking (eg over the phone) will grow in importance as the branch network deteriorates.

1.8 Banking's future evolution might be as follows.

(a) Profitability rather than size of the balance sheet will be the banks' main concern.

(b) Banks will see themselves as in the business not so much as borrowing and lending, but as managing risk.

(c) Banks will become less able to use profits from some services to subsidise others.

(d) Banks will lose market share to capital markets.

(e) Fee income will become more important than interest margin.

2. THE COMMERCIAL AND ECONOMIC ENVIRONMENT

2.1 The commercial environment consists of:

(a) the wider economy and society in which the banks operates;

(b) other individuals or groups with whom the bank has a specific relationship or whose activities affect the bank (ie investors, suppliers, competitors, customers, the government and labour).

The wider economy and society

2.2 The UK banks are profit-orientated organisations. The clearing banks are quoted on the Stock and must report their results every year. Some building societies aim to make a surplus for their members.

2.3 It is hardly surprising, therefore, that banks and building societies will look for profit opportunities like other commercial organisations. However, in some respects banks are peculiarly sensitive to conditions in the wider economy, whereas in others they are relatively immune to them.

2.4 As far as the domestic economy goes, some of a bank's services are steady and secure. For example, despite a severe recession, those in work, who still form the majority of the working-age population, need to be paid by their employers, and need to pay their bills. The funds provided by basic account-holding are still available. Moreover, it is arguable that a bank's interest income might increase from interest on distress lending. However, the wider economic recession can reduce profitability in the following ways.

(a) Reducing the amount of new business a bank can win. Consumers are currently nervous about borrowing, thus reducing the amount of interest a bank can earn on loans and credit card balances.

(b) Increasing the level of non-performing loans (bad debts) which means that banks have to 'provide' against profits. An example is given by loans to property companies. When property values are rising, and the general activity of the economy is reflected in high levels of occupancy company and rent, such loans will earn interest like any other. However, if property values fall, and the owners are unable to service the interest on the debt, then the entire debt must be written off, with a hefty blow to a bank's profits. If the original loan advanced was large, then the damage can be quite significant.

2.5 Furthermore, the extent to which banks are affected by domestic economic conditions will depend on how much they are exposed to a particular sector.

(a) Financial institutions, such as the Abbey National, which have concentrated on the domestic retail business have been hit less hard by the collapse of the property sector than some other banks.

(b) Some clearing banks have invested considerable sums, with mixed success, in activities which would once have been the preserve of merchant banks or investment houses. Barclays has been fairly successful with BZW, but NatWest has had problems with County Bank. The TSB's forays into uncharted waters have been quite costly.

(c) Banks with severe exposure to the property sector have chalked up losses. Also, the increase in business failures in a recession means that banks might be exposed to losses on other business loans. Some of the clearing banks felt that they ought to offer the widest variety of services.

2.6 Banks are affected by the *international* economic environment in a number of ways.

(a) The economic conditions of foreign economies can turn profits into severe losses. An example is 'sovereign debt'. In the 1970s, banks lent a great deal to governments and public sector institutions in Latin America and Eastern Europe. Since 1982 there countries have had difficulty servicing these debts: banks have had to cope with a number of low performing loans. Although the situation is now better than it was, the banks have been exposed to worrying losses. Banks have also been exposed to losses resulting from property-lending in the US.

(b) World trade indirectly affects the demand for some of the banks' financial services products, such as the arrangement of hedging instruments.

(c) Some banks, which have securities businesses however, can profit from trading in foreign exchange and other financial instruments. Should a single European currency eventually arrive, the banks would lose out on the business of trading in intra-European currencies, which would disappear in the interests of greater stability.

2.7 So a bank's exposure to wider economic conditions can be:

(a) *direct*, in that it affects what a bank actually does (eg the interest rates on the loans it supplies to its customers are determined by the rate at which they borrow funds);

(b) *indirect* as:

(i) it affects the bank's customers and hence the demand for the bank's services;

(ii) it affects the bank's competitors. An example would be the growth in the presence of Japanese banks, perhaps as a reflection of that country's economic success.

Investors

2.8 Every organisation needs money, to invest or to spend. Companies raise funds from shareholders and other investors (in the form of loans), or by retaining profits for re-investment instead of paying them as dividends. Nationalised industries raise much of their capital from the government. Charitable organisations raise most of their funds from donations or through grants. Banks require deposits from customers in order to lend to borrowers.

2.9   The environment with regard to sources of capital is continually changing. High interest rates will make borrowing more expensive, and companies may then prefer to raise short-term loans, in the hope that interest rates will eventually fall before long-term loans have to be negotiated. A reduction in the liquidity of companies or the disposable income of the general public is likely to have a severe effect on the income of charitable organisations.

Suppliers

2.10 Suppliers are an important part of the commercial environment. Manufacturing companies, for example, need to ensure that they can obtain sufficient raw materials and components for their needs, which are satisfactory with regard to both price and quality. Similarly, a bank requires materials, equipment and services: computer systems, design and printing of publicity material, stationery supplies etc. Managers need to be aware of changes which affect suppliers.

Competitors

2.11 Competitors are a threat in the commercial environment, as you should be readily able to appreciate. Banks and building societies face competition not only from each other, but also from other financial organisations. In the UK, competition in the banking markets has been influenced in recent years by the following.

(a)   The influx of competition from foreign banks setting up new business in the UK. American and Japanese banks have been particularly active in this respect.

(b)   The way in which building societies have been seeking to extend their activities to providing customers with a form of banking service. Banks, too, have encroached on territory traditionally occupied by building societies.

Customers

2.12 Every organisation has its customers. A bank's customers pay for banking services, whereas the customers of a school are students, customers of a hospital are patients, customers of a government department are members of the general public and customers of a charitable organisation are the people in need of aid. You might also be aware that there is a trend in organisations towards thinking of other departments and functions as the *internal customer* - so that, for example, the accounts department or information technology support department regard other departments as their customers, and offer services on that basis - in competition with outside agencies offering the same services.

2.13 An organisation must be very aware of what its customers want, otherwise it will produce the wrong goods and services. A bank which fails to recognise changes in customer needs (eg for longer banking hours), wants (eg interest on deposits *plus* accessibility of the funds) and perceptions (eg of how open and 'welcoming' a bank branch is) might lose business to competitors (other banks, building societies, accountancy firms etc). The current mood in banking is that the customer's needs, wants and perceptions must be at the centre of any bank's strategy. The clearing banks, like other financial institutions, have been attempting to extend the range of their *markets and services* in recent years, and we should expect the trend to continue in the future. Recent developments have been:

(a) some expansion into new overseas markets, eg North America;

(b) extending the insurance services offered by banks - eg underwriting more policies setting up pension schemes;

(c) the provision of services (eg Mergers and Acquisitions) which would previously have been provided by merchant banks;

(d) the development of mortgage lending business, accountancy services and estate agency networks;

(e) the development of special services for 'wholesale' banking customers, separate from traditional 'retail' banking;

(f) a greater awareness of marketing, and providing services to suit the needs of particular customer segments: special saving schemes for pensioners, special offers for school leavers and university students, high-interest savings accounts, interest on current accounts etc.

Government

2.14 The government influences the commercial environment by means of taxation. Value added tax, for example, raises the price of goods in shops, and therefore to some extent affects consumer demand. The Government also influences interest rates, which can greatly affect a bank's operation.

Labour

2.15 An aspect of the commercial environment which currently attracts considerable attention is the availability of a (skilled) pool of labour from which to recruit employees at the 'right' price. Again, this will be discussed in detail later, but briefly, the organisation will have to respond to changes for the following reasons.

(a) To be able to attract skilled workers. This will be harder when there is a shortage of such workers 'on the market': the organisation will have to enter into competition with other employers to offer incentives to potential recruits, and/or will have to give attention to training and developing individuals who may not yet be of the desired calibre.

(b) To retain skilled workers within the organisation. In times of skill shortage, the potential for worker 'mobility' is higher, as organisations compete for employees.

(c) To train and develop from within the organisation a calibre of employee that may be scarce in the environment.

(d) To manage employee relations. In times of high unemployment, for example, employee representatives may be concerned to protect jobs, with resistance to labour-saving technological innovations, abolition of overtime, pressure for shorter working hours etc.

2.16 Two issues for banks' employment practices stand out.

(a) A major challenge for banks in the 1990s (and indeed for all commercial concerns) is the fall in birth rate over the last twenty years, and therefore the fall in the number of young people eligible for employment (set to reduce by a third by 1995). This means that greater emphasis is placed on attracting and keeping employees. These demographic changes are also likely to cause general and specific *skill* shortages, so that increased emphasis will need to be placed on *training and development* and on employing women who have had time of work to have children.

(b) Although there is still a need for banking staff to provide 'traditional' banking services, and opportunities for a lifetime career in banking for many employees, there is now also a number of employees who do not work at traditional banking tasks, but who are *specialists* in the new areas into which banks have moved - eg accountants, stockbrokers, computer specialists etc. These individuals cannot necessarily see a lifetime career in working for a bank and have specialist skills that they can offer to other organisations. Career and manpower planning will have to take into account the need to attract and retain such individuals *or* to recognise and allow for 'short-stay' employment and high labour turnover in certain positions *or* to use these people to extend the range of services the bank offers.

The housing market in the UK

2.17 Of particular concerns to building societies is the state of the UK housing market.

(a) Mortgages are still the building societies' main product. If there is low demand for mortgages, then building societies will be affected.

(b) The state of the housing market directly affects customers' ability to pay their debts. A poor housing market means that customers cannot sell their way out of high indebtedness, and so loan loss provisions have to rise.

2.18 Furthermore, the rate of interest affects building societies in two ways, as well as their general effect on consumer confidence and the housing market.

(a) Building societies depend more on customer deposits than do banks, which have more freedom to borrow from the wholesale money markets. If interest rates are low, customers might prefer to invest in shares.

(b) High interest rates hurt borrowers and reduce demand, but they enable higher rates to be paid to depositors.

3. THE POLITICAL AND LEGAL ENVIRONMENT

3.1 The political environment changes in response to social pressures, and, in the UK, with the views of the political party in power. It both reflects and influences public (and therefore potential customer) opinion.

3.2 The *legal* controls affecting the management of an organisation come from the Companies Acts and a wide range of other legislation and case law, and can be categorised under five broad headings.

(a)   *Personnel*: minimum wages, sexual and racial discrimination, employment protection, formal worker participation etc.

(b)   *Operations*: health and safety at work, product safety standards etc.

(c)   *Marketing*: there are restrictions on the description of goods and services, sending unsolicited goods to customers, misleading advertising, etc.

(d)   *Ecology*: certain products or production operations might be banned because they are damaging to mind and health, or pollute the environment.

(e)   *Finance*: eg foreign exchange controls and taxation, where the organisation has a dual role:

   (i)   acting as tax collectors for the government (PAYE income tax, VAT etc);
   (ii) paying tax to the government (corporation tax etc) and avoiding tax.

   There are also legal requirements to produce financial information (eg annual returns, annual report and accounts). The financial affairs of banks are, of course, heavily regulated, for the protection of depositors.

(f)   *Production:* the law can affect the type of services a bank offers.

3.3   Organisations also influence the legal environment. Their activities may (regrettably) make legislation necessary, or they may actively promote legislation which benefits their interests or enhances their public image. They may also act to prevent changes in the law from taking place: cigarette manufacturers, for example, have successfully postponed anti-smoking legislation in the UK.

The political and legal environment of banks

3.4   The political and legal environment of banks is the same in general as for other organisations although there are specific items of legislation and specific political opinions or events that are unique to the banking industry, for example the Banking Act, the Consumer Credit Act, the Financial Services Act and the attitude of people generally that bankers should act philanthropically, not commercially. The threat of further legislation in the area of the banker-customer relationship hangs over banks following the Jack Committee report (February 1989). The Code of Banking Practice (reproduced at the back) addresses some of these problems.

3.5   Through the Bank of England the government influences and directs the activities of banks and other financial institutions. Control over interest rates, taxation, public spending and membership of the European Community are just a few aspects of government influence over the economic environment in the UK which affect banks.

3.6   Banks and financial institutions are perhaps subject to greater official scrutiny than other commercial organisations. The Bank of England's role is an informal but powerful one in reviewing banks' policies, and the Bank of England has even laid down criteria for judging the amount banks should provide against bad debts. There are several reasons for this.

(a) Banks are places where depositors store money. A bank failure can lead to loss and hardship for perhaps millions of people. The collapse of BCCI is an example.

(b) The collapse of a large bank, because of the size and nature of its cash flows, can have a serious, damaging and *sudden* affect on the wider economy, and lead to the collapse of other financial institutions. Companies will be unable to pay their debts and wages. It will affect people quite unrelated to the bank. It was the collapse of a small bank that *triggered* the great depression of 1929 (although this was not the fundamental cause).

(c) The City of London is still one of the world's major financial centres. The Bank of England acts, with varying success, as a sort of referee to ensure minimum standards are adhered to.

Example: the legal environment and building societies

3.7 Until 1986, building societies in the UK were restricted in the types of financial service they could offer to customers: in effect, they were restricted to offering secured loans to personal customers for house purchases and home improvements. They were also limited to deposits from savers as their source of funds.

3.8 In 1986, the Building Societies Act (with further amendments in 1988) allowed the building societies to do more things than they had been able to do before. They can now:

(a) raise *some* funds from the 'wholesale' money markets;

(b) offer 'retail banking'-type services, such as:

    (i) cheque accounts, cheque cards;
    (ii) credit cards (Visa, Access etc);
    (iii) unsecured personal loans;
    (iv) personal loans for purposes other than house purchase;
    (v) cash cards and cash dispenser machines;
    (vi) travellers' cheques and foreign money;
    (vii) standing orders and direct debits;

(c) become limited companies, and so turn themselves into banks.

3.9 The implications of these changes for the strategic plans of the building societies should be apparent.

(a) The building societies have had to decide what financial services to offer. They do not have to provide 'banking services' if they do not want to, and many of the largest societies do not offer all the services listed above.

(b) By challenging the retail banks the competition between the building societies and the banks has taken on a sharper edge.

    (i) Banks have the powerful competitive advantages of being the traditional providers of banking services, and still having the exclusive right to serve corporate customers.

    How can a building society take market share from the retail banks?

   (ii)   Anything that the building societies do to stir up competition will provide a response from the banks. For example:

   (1)   the banks now provide large amounts of mortgage finance;
   (2)   in response to the success of the interest-bearing current accounts provided by two of the largest societies, the clearing banks announced their intention (1988) of doing the same from 1989.

(c)   Each building society must decide whether it wishes to become a bank, or whether to retain building society status.

3.10   Building societies have responded in a number of ways.

(a)   Some offer cheque accounts. Building societies pioneered the concept of 'free banking'.

(b)   They also provide loans and other services traditionally provided by banks, as the differences between the two types of institution fade.

(c)   Some building societies, such as the Abbey National, have become banks. Many more are following this trend.

(d)   There have been many mergers in the building society sector.

4.   THE TECHNOLOGICAL ENVIRONMENT

4.1   Technology refers to the ways of 'getting things done' - not only to scientific inventions and developments, but also to methods of working. Examples of technological developments are mechanisation, automation, and the use of the micro-chip to control the operations of modern equipment, computerisation of data processing and information systems, nuclear and solar energy, new synthetic materials and greater speed of travel.

We will be discussing technology in banking in more detail in Part B, but the following will give you an idea of its importance in the initiating and controlling of change in banking.

Banks and technology

4.2   Developments in information technology have had a major impact on banking services.

(a)   Existing services can be improved and developed. Automated Teller Machines (ATMs) have changed the way in which many existing bank services are delivered to customers, and one implication of ATMs for the future is that banking services can be provided at 'stand alone' service points away from traditional bank branch premises. As another example, automated links to credit centres allow better facilities for checking credit card fraud. The BACS and BACSTEL services have introduced more automation and a quicker service into credit clearing services.

(b)   New services can now be provided. Electronic Funds Transfer at the Point of Sale (EFTPOS) is developing as the new system of money transfer for the future. Home and office banking is another service of the moment with some schemes already in operation in the UK.

(c)   Automation has eased pressures for ever-increasing staff numbers to cope with the volume of administrative work. BACS, for example, has significantly released bank staff for a more customer service-orientated role. However, the danger of overstaffing is now very real and most banks are making some employees redundant.

(d) The management of banking organisations has also been transformed by awareness of the value of computers, computer software and information technology in general to assist with many routine operations and with planning, controlling and decision-making responsibilities. Foreign exchange dealings are a particular area of banking operations which rely heavily on a sophisticated information service.

(e) The use of customer databases has made the 'cross-selling' of bank services increasingly possible, eg mailing brochures on insurance and pensions to existing current account customers or savers. It has also enabled banks to tailor eg mortgage products more closely to the needs of specific customer segments.

4.3 New technology provides opportunities for banks, but threats too. If banks do not take advantage of the available technology to provide new and better services, competitors (eg building societies or other banks) will. Adjusting to technological change means that a bank's management must:

(a) be flexible and willing to adapt;

(b) be prepared to change a bank's organisation structure in order to take on new wings to their business (eg to assimilate Stock Exchange dealings or estate agency services into their network);

(c) be on the lookout for new services, new markets and new competitors (eg the establishment of telephone banking by *Firstdirect*);

(d) use computer technology to improve management planning and control systems;

(e) be aware of the need to adapt staff recruitment, training and retraining to meet the current needs of their markets. Banks will not succeed against competition unless they have suitable skilled and qualified staff to provide the changing services.

5. THE SOCIAL AND ETHICAL ENVIRONMENT

5.1 Whereas the political environment consists of laws, regulations and government agencies:

(a) the social environment consists of the customs, attitudes, beliefs and education of society as a whole, or of different groups in society;

(b) the ethical environment consists of a set (or sets) of well-established rules of personal and organisational behaviour: justice, respect for the law and a 'moral code' (which may differ from culture to culture).

5.2 Social attitudes, such as a belief in the merits of education, progress through science and technology, and fair competition, are significant for the management of a business organisation. Other beliefs which have either gained strength or been eroded in recent years include the following.

(a) There is a growing belief in preserving and improving the quality of life by reducing working hours, reversing the spread of pollution, developing leisure activities etc.

Pressures on organisations to consider the environment are particularly strong because most environmental damage is irreversible and some is fatal to humans and wildlife.

(b) Many pressure groups have been organised in recent years to protect social minorities and under-privileged groups. Legislation has been passed in an attempt to prevent racial discrimination and discrimination against women and disabled people. In the wider arena, pressure is put on organisations to withdraw or withhold support for regimes which have a poor human rights or environmental record.

(c) Differences in social class between management and workers, has bedevilled British industry for many years and shows signs of abating only in restricted areas. To some extent, this view is the product of social conditions which also exist outside *a particular* work situation.

(d) There have been significant changes to social attitudes to debt. At one time this was something to be avoided. Now, consumer credit is an important aspect of the economy as a whole. Credit cards are profitable business for banks.

(e) Other trends relate to *demography* or changes in the population. Fewer younger people are entering the labour market. The consequences of this are discussed in chapter 24.

(f) The marketing strategies of banks and building societies will be influenced by changes in the population structure (eg there will be more services directed to the elderly) and changes in culture.

5.3 It is worth noting the extent to which the ethical environment is a matter of public perception. Many companies are suspected or greed and corruption, or of a willingness to pollute the environment or endanger lives in the pursuit of profit. However, while the bribery of government officials would be regarded as unethical in the UK, such a course of action might be socially acceptable - indeed, essential for success - in the pursuit of business in various other countries of the world.

5.4 The British Institute of Management has published a *Code of Conduct* giving guidance on the ethical standards required of managers on the basis that managers should:

(a) comply with the law;
(b) respect the customs and practices of any country in which they work as managers; and
(c) not misuse their authority or office for personal or other gains.

'The law is a floor - ethical business conduct should normally exist at a level well above the minimum required by law.'

5.5 Some organisations issue their own code of conduct, whether as part of the general 'mission statement' or guiding principles of the organisation and its culture, or as a set of detailed prescriptions for managers in situations where they may have to choose between an 'ethical' and an 'expedient' option (eg whether or not to take a bribe, in a country where it is accepted practice to do so).

5.6 The issue of ethics has become increasingly important for the financial services sector, following the financial deregulation of the mid-1980s. There have been a number of highly publicised trials.

(a) The Maxwell affair is only the most significant scandal affecting the pensions industry. More generally, financial services organisations are having to examine the selling of personal pensions: did customers receive best advice? The Goode report recommended tightening up on pensions.

(b) Despite the failure of many 'insider dealing' prosecutions, the climate in the City has become more concerned with regulation. The aim is to strike a balance between protecting the individual consumer, and excessive red tape unnecessary for professional investors.

5.7 For banks which have purchased their own securities houses, the main conflicts are between:

(a) employees who act in an advisory capacity to the bank's clients;
(b) employees who try and sell a company's shares;
(c) employees who manage investment funds on behalf of customers or clients.

Exercise 1

The Bank of Albion (a fictitious bank) has two departments.

(a) A pension fund investment department. This invests money on behalf of clients and customers eg in bonds, shares and so on.

(b) A merchant bank department. Amongst other things, this underwrites share issues. One of its clients is the prestigious and dynamic Blakes Severn plc, which is to offer a new tranche of shares to the investment community.

Required

Identify the potential conflict of interest.

Solution

The management of the pension fund will seek to get the best possible return on the funds invested. They must put the interests of their customers first. However, the 'merchant bank' department will wish to ensure that as many as possible of Blakes Severn plc's new shares are purchased by investors. The conflict of interest lies in the fact that, *without proper regulation*, the fund managers in the pension fund investment department might feel under pressure to buy the shares in Blakes Severn plc *against their better judgement*.

5.8 Other areas of concern and ethics have been brought to light with complaints about the banks' handling of small business clients (eg promising an increased overdraft if security is given, obtaining the securities, then going back on the promise). These and other ethical questions merge into issues about the banks' duty of social responsibility, which is discussed below.

The social responsibility of organisations and managers

5.9 Since organisations have an effect on their environment, it is arguable that, morally, they should act in a way which shows social awareness and responsibility. From a less idealistic point of view, it can be noted that in recent years there has been an upsurge in *public* awareness of concern with social and environmental issues, placing market pressure on organisations to respond if they are to retain the approval of their existing and potential customers, suppliers etc.

> 'A society, awakened and vocal with respect to the urgency of social problems, is asking the managers of all kinds of organisations, particularly those at the top, what they are doing to discharge their social responsibilities and why they are not doing more.'
> *Koontz, O'Donnell and Weihrich*

5.10 The twentieth century has seen a shift in the relationship between society and business.

   (a) Businesses have become *bigger* and more anonymous: there is a fear that this makes them less accountable.

   (b) Businesses are less rooted in the *local* community - especially with the emergence of multinationals: there is a fear that local interests are being ignored.

   (c) People are generally better *educated* and better *informed* about business and social issues, and more *articulate* in expressing their concern.

   (d) Public awareness has joined with spreading democratic values to encourage *pressure groups* which attempt to counterbalance the economic power of business.

   (e) Organisation have themselves recognised the need to take account of *interest groups* other than those (the shareholders) with a direct stake in the financial success of the business.

   (f) At the same time, there has been an enhanced role for the state in *monitoring businesses*.

5.11 There are different views on the extent to which social and ethical constraints modify business objectives.

   (a) One view advocates that society allow market forces and the economic objectives of business unrestricted freedom: business will then be effective and generate profit: profit benefits society via taxation, sponsorship, employment, new services, technological advancement etc.

   (b) An opposing view suggests that the means of production, distribution and control are too important to society to be left to the forces in the free market, and should be controlled by the State on behalf of the people.

5.12 Whichever of these attitudes is held, it is important to relate social responsibility to business objectives, because managers are judged by a set of results - profits, sales growth, market share, earnings per share etc - which may or may not include achievements for society. After all, why should Company A incur high costs on improving the safety standards of its product when a competitor, Company B, does not spend any money on such improvements, and would therefore be able to undercut Company A's prices on the market?

6. THE STAKEHOLDER VIEW

6.1 One important way of looking at this issue is the 'stakeholder view' of organisations. This suggests that several groups of people have an interest or 'stake' in what the organisation does, being affected by its activities. Shareholders may *own* the business, but other people are involved with it as well, and each of these groups has its own objectives. Management's task is to balance the profit objective of the shareholders with pressures from non-shareholder groups, in order to determine the strategic targets of the business.

6.2 The organisation may be said to be responsible to:

(a) its shareholders;
(b) employees;
(c) customers;
(d) suppliers;
(e) competitors;
(f) the local community;
(g) the general public;
(h) the state.

6.3 The four major stakeholders of a bank are: shareholders, employees, customers and the State. Its responsibility to these may be as follows.

(a) *Shareholders*

(i) Generate profits sufficient to give shareholders a return on their investment (ie dividends).

(ii) Provide honest and efficient management and control of the resources (monetary and non-monetary) of the bank.

(iii) Be accountable for the bank's performance; to provide true and sufficient information to shareholders to enable them to assess its performance.

(b) *Employees*. The Social Chapter of the Maastricht Treaty allows for the creation of Works Councils, which are elected by employees. Although the UK has opted out of the Social Chapter, large UK firms, especially those with operations elsewhere in the EU, have set up works councils. NatWest is an example.

(i) Ensure at least a minimum wage, perhaps with appropriate differentials to reward skilled labour.

(ii) Offer job security (perhaps over and above the protection afforded by legislation).

(iii) Provide safe, healthy and, ideally, pleasant conditions of work (ie above the legal minimum).

(iv) Avoid discrimination in recruitment, selection, training and career development policies.

(v) Offer job satisfaction, training, career development, participation.

     (vi) Operate procedures for communication, consultation, collective bargaining, discipline and grievance handling etc involving employees as members of trade unions, staff associations, professional bodies etc.

     (vii) Preserve the confidentiality of information held for personnel purposes, and to use such information responsibly (in accordance with Data Protection legislation).

     (viii) Offer fair provisions for retirement, redundancy etc.

(c) *Customers*

     (i)   Provide products/services of a nature that customers want and a quality they expect.

     (ii) Deal honestly and fairly with customers. (This is especially relevant in cases of hardship. The various schemes by which building societies and banks deal with mortgage arrears are examples of social responsibility in that eviction is a last resort, rather than a kneejerk reaction to a person's financial difficulties.)

     (iii) Secure and manage resources entrusted to the bank by customers with utmost integrity.

     (iv) Provide information to customers and potential customers that is true, and adequate to enable them to assess the merits of the products/services on offer, and the integrity of transactions (under the Consumer Credit Act).

(d) *The State*

     (i)   Conform with legislation on employment, health and safety, marketing, organisation (eg duties of directors), provision of financial information etc.

     (ii) Conform with taxation requirements (ie paying taxes, administering employee taxation, PAYE, National Insurance etc - being accountable to the IR for tax deducted at source etc).

     (iii) Comply with regulation by the Bank of England, to promote and maintain the nation's financial stability.

     (iv) Inform authorities of suspicions relating to the source or use of funds (as under the Drug Trafficking Offences Act) and otherwise to cooperate with the authorities.

The State's concern in more than an interest which must be appeased. The state's dictates must be followed.

6.4   In some areas, the interests of stakeholders will coincide. Taking account of customer needs is believed to be essential in success - fulfilling shareholder objectives. Obeying state legislation on employment safeguards the interests of employees.

Conflict between stakeholders

6.5   However, it should be clear that, in some cases, there will be conflict. The allocation of profit between *shareholders* (in the form of dividends), *customers* (in the form of reinvestment or price reductions) and *employees* (in the form of pay and benefits) is the most obvious. There may be conflict between customer and employee interests eg in the case of longer banking hours and Saturday opening. Refusal to allow Sunday trading may be an example of conflict between state, and customers and shareholders.

6.6 The conflicting interests of a bank's customers and shareholders represent a problem for banks. Whereas shareholders expect a good return on investment and the proper stewardship of their funds in order for profits to be generated, customers expect banks to operate in a way which can be said to be non-commercial; not charging for services, providing impartial advice, acting always in the interests of the community even where this conflicts with the bank's - and its shareholders' - interests.

6.7 Management will have to be aware of stakeholders' interests, and changes in them - monitoring public opinion and employee attitudes etc. Corporate planning - discussed in the following chapter - should take stakeholder groups seriously as a source of opportunities and threats to the business.

6.8 Less obvious, perhaps, are the organisation's responsibilities towards suppliers and competitors.

(a) *Suppliers* should be able to expect fair and consistent trading relationships. A large organisation, for example, may have considerable power as a buyer, and should not use it unscrupulously. Information obtained from a supplier should be kept confidential. Payment should not be unreasonably delayed. Long-standing relationships should be maintained where possible, but any competition for business from new suppliers should be treated fairly.

(b) *Competitors* should expect ethical and honest competition. No organisation should undermine another's position with false disparagement, or attempt improperly to acquire its trade secrets or other confidential information.

6.9 Responsibility to the *community* covers a variety of local needs and expectations. An organisation should:

(a) uphold the social and ethical values of the community;

(b) contribute towards its well-being, eg by sponsorship of events and/or causes;

(c) respond constructively to any complaints or concerns with regard to eg pollution, traffic control, premises design etc;

(d) provide information, where decisions and activities affect the community, (such as a bank's plan to shut down or relocate a local branch).

It is true to say that historically banks have been particularly good and conscientious corporate citizens.

Exercise 2

In times of recession, it is the banks ultimately who decide whether a particular business survives or fails. There is a widespread view that banks should support small businesses come what may, as not to do so would be socially irresponsible.

Give reasons both for an against this view.

Solution

Here are some possible arguments either way. You might have thought of some more.

For

1   A small business might be viable in the future, and to liquidate it because of a temporary problem may in the long term be deleterious to the national economy and the local community.

2   A great deal of personal hardship will be caused.

3   In the long term it may not be good for the banks' image to be seen to be calling in debts.

Against

1   Money is a scarce resource, and by supporting non-viable small businesses, help might be diverted from businesses which have a better chance of growth.

2   The bank has responsibility to other stakeholders as well as customers. Its shares may be owned by investment institutions or pension funds, whose return on the investments they make on behalf of their clients will be less.

---

7.   CONCLUSION

7.1   INFLUENCES (OPPORTUNITIES AND THREATS)

IN THE ENVIRONMENT

INPUTS FROM THE ENVIRONMENT (Resources) → THE ORGANISATION → OUTPUTS TO THE ENVIRONMENT

The organisation as an open system

7.2 *Key elements of the environment of an organisation*

Political/legal factors
Economic/commercial factors
Social/cultural factors
Technological factors

7.3 *Stakeholders in the organisation*

'Success' is spelt with three 'C's!

Shareholders
Unions/staff associations
Customers
Community
Competitors
Employees
Suppliers
State.

TEST YOUR KNOWLEDGE
The numbers in brackets refer to paragraphs of this chapter

1   What, in general, are the ways in which the organisation and the environment inter-relate? (1.1 - 1.6)

2   What aspects of the commercial environment are commonly identified? (2.1)

3   Identify some of the challenges posed to banks by changes in economic conditions. (2.6 - 2.7)

4   Give two examples each of how new technology:

   (a)   enables improvement of existing services;
   (b)   enables development of new services;
   (c)   releases bank staff from paperwork;
   (d)   contributes to management functions. (4.2 - and your own experience)

5   Identify three changes in social attitudes that might affect banks. (5.2)

6   What has changed society's attitude to business in general? (5.10)

7   Who are the stakeholders of a bank, and what are some of the bank's responsibilities to them? (6.2, 6.3)

Now try question 22 at the end of the text

Chapter 22

ACHIEVING CORPORATE GOALS

This chapter covers the following topics.

1. Mission
2. Corporate objectives
3. Corporate appraisal
4. Planning for the achievement of corporate goals
5. Change and strategic management in banks

Introduction

If management is deciding what to do and getting others to do it, managers need to decide on the most general level what the organisation should be achieving.

---

1. MISSION

1.1 The activities of 'corporate appraisal' and 'strategic management' are part of a complex process whereby organisations set *objectives* for themselves and *plan* how to meet them in a systematic fashion.

1.2 This process is called 'corporate planning' or 'strategic planning'. The purpose of corporate planning is:

(a) to reduce uncertainty in decision-making (as far as possible) by anticipating and planning for future events;

(b) to make management think in a systematic fashion, and from a long-term perspective, about business concerns and short-term decisions;

(c) to ensure that the external environment, and trends in it, are being monitored for potential opportunities and threats;

(d) to provide a mechanism for systematic appraisal of the internal strengths and weaknesses of the organisation;

(e) to provide a framework against which new ideas for business development can be checked.

1.3 Despite recent theories about 'ad hocracy', 'thriving on chaos' and the dangers of 'analysis paralysis' in an environment of rapid change, a coherent framework for strategic development needs to be formulated. It should not stifle creativity or remove managerial discretion, but keep managers' eyes on the overall goals of the organisation, preserving unity of direction. Rapid change and response to unexpected events in the environment (eg the sudden collapse of the Iron Curtain, or the Gulf Crisis from August 1990 causing the freezing of Iraqi and Kuwaiti funds in foreign banks) may call for modifications to plan, or entirely new initiatives and projects: even so, reactions to such events must be measured against organisational objectives, and some form of planning will be essential.

The main stages in corporate planning are as follows.

1. Define the 'business' or 'purpose' of the organisation and its overall objectives. Sometimes this is termed the 'mission' of a business.

2. Corporate appraisal, including:
   - external analysis of opportunities and threats
   - internal analysis of strengths and weaknesses

3. Define strategic objectives.

4. Develop, evaluate and select alternative strategies.

5. Formulate budget plans and operating plans.

6. Establish policies, procedures and rules for the organisation.

7. Monitor progress and effectiveness.

1.4 Identifying and defining 'what business we are in' might seem a simple exercise. Banks are in 'the banking business', just as car manufacturers are in the business of making cars. Unfortunately, this begs several questions. In particular, it is legitimate to ask the question 'what is the banking business?' anyway, as banks' perception of their roles and purpose have changed.

(a) Is banking a profession, like the law, with long-term clients ('relationship banking')?

(b) Is banking, especially to the consumer sector, more like a *retailing* business: 'an under-exploited distribution system, through which more product could be sold'? (*Bankers' World* June 1992)

(c) Is *banking* a single and identifiable 'business' at all, given that it contains so many disparate elements?

1.5 The mission statement is simply a statement of what an organisation is aiming to achieve through the conduct of its business. It can even be thought of as a statement of the organisation's reason for existence. The purpose of the mission statement is to provide the organisation with focus and direction.

1.6 The commonest approach to determining the corporate mission is to rely on the product/market scope. The mission statement is then essentially based on customer groups, needs served and technology employed.

1.7 It is not sufficient for a firm to identify its mission as being 'banking' – it would be more appropriate to identify that mission as being, for example, 'meeting consumer needs for financial transactions'. A mission statement of this nature can offer guidelines to management when considering how the business should develop and in which directions.

1.8 Once a clear statement of the corporate mission has been achieved and corporate objectives have been determined, this information, in conjunction with further detailed analysis of the environment, provides the input for the next stage in the planning process.

Exercise 1

Look at the statement below, which the National Westminster Bank publishes (untitled) every year on the first page of its annual report and accounts. It is a mission statement or a statement of objectives? What do you think is NatWest's aim in publishing it?

The NatWest Way is to bring:

QUALITY TO OUR CUSTOMERS

We value our customers as the foundation of our business. Our relationships with customers and suppliers are based on principles of respect and mutual benefit.

We aim to develop profitable and lasting relationships. We want to build on what we do well and to innovate to meet changing customer needs.

QUALITY TO OUR INVESTORS

We have a long term responsibility to everybody who has a stake in the Group to operate with care, efficiency and at a profit.

Our objective is to earn the profits needed to provide a consistent increase in the value of our shareholders' investment, obtain the highest credit ratings and finance the development of our business.

QUALITY TO OUR PEOPLE

We respect each other's experience and skills and value the contribution each of us makes to the NatWest team. We recognise that pride and enjoyment in the job come from commitment, leadership by example and accomplishment.

Our goal is to work together to reward, train and develop people in ways that acknowledge performance and individual abilities.

QUALITY TO THE COMMUNITY

We recognise that our actions must acknowledge our responsibilities for the well-being and stability of the community.

We aim to support the community through the involvement of our people and the contribution of 1% of our group profits.

---

2. CORPORATE OBJECTIVES

2.1 'Corporate objectives' are those which are concerned with the goals of the organisation as a whole: they outline the expectations of the firm, which strategic planning is concerned to fulfil. The determination of corporate objectives is a reiterative process: the objectives are constantly, or as the need arises, being refined, as new information becomes relevant and available.

2.2 So why is it important for an organisation to *have* objectives?

(a) The business needs a sense of direction in order for strategies and policies, operational plans and budgets to be formulated and implemented and in order to assess whether these are sufficient to achieve the stated objectives. This should be provided by mission.

(b) Where desired ends conflict - eg profit maximisation and employee motivation through pay - a defined hierarchy of objectives will clarify the relative importance of each, as a guide to decision-making.

(c) Objectives help management to predict organisational behaviour, to an extent.

(d) Clearly stated objectives aid co-ordination of the different functions of the business in pursuit of a common aim.

(e) Objectives are required in order to control performance: the organisation needs a yardstick against which success, or lack of it, can be measured. (If it doesn't know where it's going, it won't know when it's arrived).

(f) Objective-setting encourages managers to adopt a long-term prospective (which is essential in matters such as capital investment, staff training, automation etc) and a realistic approach (since objectives should be achievable).

(g) Clearly stated, realistically achievable objectives are an important element in learning and motivation, enabling individuals to appreciate their role, gauge their progress and calculate the extent to which their effort and energy is being constructively spent.

(h) Objectives may help managers to 'justify' or explain the purpose and direction of the business to the community, potential investors, potential employees etc: they are an important part of the organisation's image.

Types of objective

2.3 Types of objective could be listed under the following broad headings.

(a) *Financial*: eg profitability, return on capital employed, return on shareholders' equity, return on trading assets employed, earnings per share.

(b) *Market position*: eg total market share of each market segment, growth of sales, customers or potential customers, the need to avoid relying on a single customer for a large proportion of total sales, what markets should the company be in.

(c) *Product development*: eg to bring in new products, develop a product range, spend money on research and development, to provide products of a certain quality at a certain price level.

(d) *Technology*: eg to acquire the latest technology in equipment for production, to improve productivity and reduce the cost per unit of output.

(e) *Employees and management*: eg to pay employees a wage above the industry's average, to provide job satisfaction and career development, to look after staff welfare, to train employees in certain skills, to reduce labour turnover.

(f) *Organisation*: eg to create an organisation where much authority is delegated and employees, lower and middle management have a greater degree of participation in planning and decision-making.

(g) *Public responsibility*: eg to acknowledge the social responsibilities of the company to protect the environment and support their local communities.

2.4

> 'Objectives are needed in every area where performance and results directly and vitally affect the survival and prosperity of the business'   *Drucker*.

2.5 There has been considerable disagreement about the choice of the *overall* corporate objective, although it is often agreed that for a company it must be a financial objective. Various financial objectives would include:

(a) profitability;
(b) return on capital employed (ROCE);
(c) survival, (the avoidance of loss);
(d) (growth in) earnings per share (EPS);
(e) (growth in) dividends to shareholders.

So, for example, a bank may translate its general aspirations into a specific objective such as: 'We will become the largest bank in Europe, judged on return on investment, by the year 1995.'

2.6 It is generally accepted now that in many organisations, especially large ones, managers do not operate on the principle of maximising profits. They are content to achieve a level of profits or return on capital which will appear acceptable and realistic to all managers in the organisation, shareholders, employees, government and public opinion! In other words, they will seek a satisfactory or satisficing level of profits, given the restrictions imposed by other considerations. As we discussed in the previous chapter, purely financial objectives may be modified by (usually subsidiary) objectives related to the perceived social and ethical responsibilities of the organisation. A bank might be able to maximise its profits by allowing a very high level of borrowing, but in addition to prudential reasons, may not wish to do that on grounds of social responsibility.

3.   CORPORATE APPRAISAL

3.1   In order to formulate realistic objectives, and - even more crucially - to turn these into strategic plans (which pave the way for shorter-term budgets and operating plans), management will require a thorough understanding of exactly:

(a)   what is required;
(b)   what is possible; and
(c)   what needs to be done if there is a 'gap' between the two.

3.2   This is where 'corporate appraisal' comes in. It is a study of:

(a)   the organisation's internal strengths and weaknesses; and

(b)   threats and opportunities in its business environment (eg. the changing nature of markets, competition, technology, legislation, age structure of the population, leisure time etc).

Together, these studies are known as SWOT analysis.

S - strengths W - weaknesses O - opportunities T - threats

Internal appraisal: strengths and weaknesses analysis

3.3   In essence the internal appraisal seeks to identify:

(a)   shortcomings in the company's present skills and resources; and
(b)   strengths on which the company can build its expansion.

3.4   A company undertaking a strengths and weaknesses analysis will endeavour to consider all main areas of the company so that there is no weak link left unidentified. A judgement should be made about:

(a)   management ability;
(b)   personnel skills;
(c)   systems and organisational capabilities;
(d)   resources and equipment;

in each of the main functions of the organisation.

3.5   The corporate appraisal project team, usually made up of people from different functions in the organisation, might consider information in the following areas.

(a)   Marketing:

(i)   the fate of new product launches;
(ii)   success or failure of advertising campaigns.

(b) Current products and services:

    (i)   profit margin and overall profit contribution;
    (ii)   price elasticity of demand of products;
    (iii) growth or decline of product, indicating its stage in the 'product life cycle'.

(c) Distribution (eg branch network, telephone banking):

    (i)   delivery services standards;
    (ii)   geographical availability of products.

(d) Research and development:

    (i)   the costs of R & D;
    (ii)   benefits of R & D in new products/new variations on existing products.

(e) Finance:

    (i)   how investment is deployed, and at what level of risk
    (ii)   availability of short-term and long-term funds, cash flow;
    (iii) contribution of each product.

(f) Plant and equipment and other facilities:

    (i)   valuation of all assets;

    (ii)   location of land and buildings, their value, area, use, length of lease, current book value;

    (iii) potential for cost savings from investment in technology.

(g) Management and staff:

    (i)   age spread, succession plans;
    (ii)   training and recruitment facilities.

(h) Business management - organisation:

    (i)   organisation structure;
    (ii)   communication links.

3.6   The purpose of the analysis is to express, qualitatively or quantitatively, which areas of the business have strengths to exploit and which areas have weaknesses which must be improved or protected against. Although every area of the business should be investigated, only the areas of significant strength or weakness should warrant further attention. Strengths and weaknesses show up the organisation's current *potential* for exploiting opportunities and resisting threats which the environment offers.

External appraisal: opportunities and threats

3.7   An external appraisal is required to:

(a) identify opportunities which can be exploited; and

(b) anticipate environmental threats against which the organisation must protect itself.

3.8 The external areas which should be investigated at a local, national and international level include the following. (You should be familiar with the 'PEST' framework from the previous chapter).

(a) *Political/governmental*. Opportunities may include taxation incentives, investment grants or the opening of new markets eg within the EC and Eastern Europe. Threats may include the widening of competition (eg allowing building societies to enter traditional banking preserves) or restriction/regulation of practices.

(b) *Economic/commercial*. At local or national level, threats and opportunities would include unemployment, the level of wages and salaries, increases in local government rates and fuel costs, the expected total market behaviour for products, total customer demand, the growth and decline of industries and suppliers, general investment levels etc. At an international level, world production, demand recessions and exchange controls must be considered. Particular aspects include the following.

   (i) *Competitors*. Possible competitors' actions in the future must be considered, and their comparative strengths and weaknesses evaluated. (In Britain, it has been especially important to identify where competitors are weak in export markets, and where foreign competitors might threaten domestic industry with cheaper or better imports.) Banks need to identify their direct and indirect competitors: competitors for deposits are not necessarily other banks, nor even financial services institutions, since people may be investing in art, cars - or not at all. The bank also needs to assess what areas of its activity might attract *new* competitors into the market: eg retailers such as Marks and Spencer offering credit cards.

   (ii) *Customers*. Who are they, what do they want from the organisation and do they feel they are getting it? What existing needs is the organisation not yet satisfying? What future needs could it satisfy? Who are the non- and (therefore potential) customers? What can the organisation offer them?

   (iii) *Suppliers*. The services provided by banks are dependent on outside assistance, eg with ancillary services (printing, mail, power, security etc) as well as funding for advances, much of which is nowadays acquired 'in the market'. The organisation will need to assess present and likely future standard and reliability of service, the risk and cost of relying on other organisations etc.

(c) *Social*. Opportunities include greater affluence, more women in the labour force, and the perceived value of financial careers. Threats include the declining and ageing population, skill shortages, inflation reducing the value of savings, pressure for employment protection and equality and high unemployment figures which influence the total available spending power of consumers.

(d) *Technology*. Technological changes must be forecast so as to identify the possibility of new products appearing, or cheaper means of production or distribution being introduced. The micro-chip has far-reaching effects on both producers (eg the use of robots), service industries (eg communication and information services) and markets (eg the use of databases to identify new market segments).

4. PLANNING FOR THE ACHIEVEMENT OF CORPORATE GOALS

4.1 Once internal strengths and weaknesses are assessed in relation to external opportunities and threats, it should be possible to identify a number of discrepancies. The organisation may be weak in areas required to capitalise on opportunities or avoid threats: in other words, its *current* capabilities may not be equal to what it wants or needs to achieve. A bank's competitors may have started to offer a popular 'lobby' service, with a wide range of 'through the wall' facilities through ATMs: the bank will need to respond - but may find that it lacks the technological expertise, or management flexibility, to implement such a scheme itself. Bridging that gap will dictate the formulation of interim strategic objectives with regard to investment in ATMs and associated information systems, managerial developments etc

4.2 Gap analysis is a technique to establish:

(a) the organisation's targets over the planning period;
(b) what the organisaton would be expected to achieve if it carried on, without any change;
(c) the differences between (a) and (b).

4.3 The difference is the 'gap'. New strategies, (eg developing new products) must be developed to fill the gap. Examples are:

(a) the redeployment of resources (eg banks increasingly shifting their staff into customer service and selling roles);

(b) product development (eg special accounts, telephone banking);

(c) merger or acquisition, to enter other markets (eg banks entering stockbroking or estate agency);

(d) structural re-organisation (eg the erosion of the traditional branch structures in favour of 'slimline' service units).

The evaluation of alternative strategies

4.4 Proposed strategies should be tested against a list of criteria for acceptance.

(a) To what extent will the strategy contribute towards financial objectives in both the short and long term?

(b) Is the strategy consistent with the organisation's social/ethical objectives?

(c) Does the strategy conform to other strategies pursued, or is it a completely new direction?

(d) Is the element of risk high compared with the potential rewards? If the strategy can only be successful under the most favourable conditions, then the risk is probably too great - but some organisations are less 'risk averse' than others.

(e) Is the strategy capable of succeeding in spite of the likely reaction by competitors?

(f) Will there be adequate control techniques? A new strategy needs a careful check on performance to put any necessary corrective steps into effect.

(g) Is the strategy preferable to other, mutually exclusive strategies? Is there an option to combine two separate strategies into one action?

(h) Are the technology and resources available to carry out the strategy? Among the resources, *time* must be allowed for new organisational and communication patterns to develop and operate freely, and for personal abilities and relationships to mature.

(i) Is the new strategy flexible and capable of adjusting to change in the business environment?

Monitoring strategic plans

4.5 Once the strategic decision has been made and the plans approved (say, by the bank's chief executive, on the recommendation of a planning group which has carried out the corporate appraisal and strategy evaluation stages), the broad strategies are 'filtered' down through the organisation, through a hierarchy of managerial control budgets, and operational action plans. Each unit of the organisation has a detailed budget and plan for its part of the whole.

4.6 Unit plans should be reviewed at this stage, to ensure that the whole is in fact the sum of its parts. Once finally approved, unit objectives can be translated into key tasks and *performance*.

However, senior management will need to monitor the progress of strategic plans, in order to evaluate:

(a) the success of the *corporate planning exercise* itself. Has the strategy been communicated to the right people in the right way, so that it is relevant, clearly understood, acceptable to (and even capable of motivating) those who have to implement it?

(b) the success of the *strategy*. Does it in practice live up to the evaluation made earlier of its consistency, feasibility etc? Has the element of risk associated with it become more or less acute? Has it, in fact, exploited the opportunity, or minimised the threat, it was intended for?

4.7 The problems in corporate planning can be overcome if management organises its planning processes correctly.

(a) Corporate objectives must be defined clearly.

(b) Quantified corporate plans should be prepared for a period within which changes in the business environment can be foreseen with some realism. A planning period of five years might be appropriate, in which plans are quantified in some detail.

(c) Plans should be reviewed regularly, typically once each year (so that there will be, say, a rolling five year plan).

(d) Within the corporate plan, very detailed short-term plans (budgets) should be prepared. The link between long-term plans and budgets is critically important for the successful implementation of the corporate plan.

(e) The information system of the organisation should be developed so that it is capable of providing sufficient information from the environment for the preparation of realistic plans.

(f)　Ideally, management throughout the organisation should participate in the corporate planning process, at their own level. This will:

    (i)　encourage the commitment of management to corporate plans; and

    (ii)　make easier the conversion of strategic plans into detailed action plans for every section and manager in the organisation.

Levels of planning

4.8　You may have noted above the way in which corporate planning 'filters' down through the organisation, with planning decisions being taken at different levels. We will briefly discuss here Robert Anthony's influential model of this process as consisting of:

(a)　strategic planning;
(b)　management control; and
(c)　operational control.

4.9　*Strategic planning* (as we have seen) is the process of deciding on objectives of the organisation, on changes in these objectives, on the resources used to attain these objectives and on the policies that are to govern the acquisition, use and disposition of these resources. It is essentially an imprecise and long-term process.

4.10　*Management control* is the 'process by which managers ensure that resources are obtained and used effectively and efficiently in the accomplishment of the organisation's objectives'.

In other words, it sets up the framework within which the broad product-market strategy can work. This involves organisation (ie the structuring of communication and authority relationships) as well as resource acquisition and development. Management control is a managerial activity (ie at a fairly high level) but operates within the framework of strategic plans and objectives already formulated. Drafting and co-ordinating functional budgets are largely a management control planning process. Another term for the same type of planning might be 'tactical' or 'administrative'.

4.11　*Operational control* is the lower-level process of ensuring that specific tasks are carried out effectively and efficiently. It focuses on detail and the short-term and is carried out within the parameters established by management control decisions. Many operational control decisions are repetitive and can be 'programmed' or even automated: mathematical models can be designed to provide optimal solutions to recurring problems (eg the assessment of customer credit-worthiness) and many physical procedures can be controlled by automatic devices.

5.　CHANGE AND STRATEGIC MANAGEMENT IN BANKS

5.1　We have already discussed various aspects of change in the banking environment and how they affect banks. In the following chapters, we discuss marketing strategy as a response to customer and competitor influence, and human resource strategies as a response to changes in the employment market.

5.2 You should try to be aware of change in the banking environment, which is on-going and constant. Consider the strategic implications of events such as: the Gulf Crisis from August 1990; the UK's entry into and departure from the Exchange Rate Mechanism of the European Monetary System within the space of 18 months; the completion of the European Market in 1992; the ever-nearer deadline for a single European currency; the recent crisis in Mexico which gave the world financial system the 'jitters'; the 'opening up' of Eastern Europe with its hunger for investment; the fluctuation of industrial power with the rise of the Pacific Basin countries (Japan, Korea etc) and the decline of the West's traditional manufacturing base; the ever-present volatility of the world financial system, with high foreign debt; the 'demographic downturn' predicted to starve the British workforce of skilled young people by the mid-90s; the introduction of new technology; the advertising 'war' between banks in response to increased competition; and the increasing sophistication of potential customers for financial services.

5.3 Supplement your study of such examples in this study text with *regular* reading of *Banking World* and the management section of quality newspapers.

Exercise 2

Review recent changes in your bank either by observing what has happened at your branch or by reading your in-house company magazine.

(a) How many of them resulted from a change of strategy (eg to fill a gap) as opposed to just routine management?

(b) What environmental impact (ie on the bank's environment, not the natural environment) will these changes have?

---

6. CHAPTER ROUNDUP

6.1 A corporate mission statement states the business a company is in, and sometimes it contains management's view of the corporate ethos.

6.2 Objectives are set to flesh out and quantify the mission. They usually refer to a specific time period.

6.3 Plans are made to allocate resources and direct activities towards the achievement of objectives.

6.4 Corporate appraisal is a process of determining an organisation's current situation.

TEST YOUR KNOWLEDGE

The numbers in brackets refer to paragraphs of this chapter

1   What is a mission statement? (1.5)

2   Why does an organisation need to define its objectives? (2.2)

3   Suggest some areas in which internal analysis of a bank may reveal strengths and/or weaknesses. (3.5)

4   Identify two opportunities and two threats from each of the 'PEST' aspects of the external environment of a bank. (3.8)

5   What can senior management do to try and make the planning process effective? (4.7)

6   Briefly outline the three levels of planning decision identified by R N Anthony. (4.9 - 4.11)

Now try question 23 at the end of the text

Chapter 23

CUSTOMERS, COMPETITION AND QUALITY

This chapter covers the following topics.

1. Marketing
2. Marketing planning
3. Identifying customers: market segmentation
4. Reaching customers: the marketing mix
5. The branch marketing plan
6. The competitive environment of banks and building societies
7. Problems in bank marketing: the role of quality

Introduction

The importance of the customer and increased competition has led to an increase in marketing activities by banks. Again, this is the subject of a CIB associateship option paper.

1. MARKETING

1.1 Banks and building societies compete for customers. They are beginning to use the marketing techniques of other consumer organisations to attract customers.

What is marketing?

1.2 First of all, it is necessary to recognise that 'marketing' is not the same as simply 'selling' goods and services - nor is it exclusively the preserve of the marketing function of the organisation. 'Marketing is not only much broader than selling, it is not a specialised activity at all. It encompasses the entire business. It is the whole business seen from the point of view of the final result, that is, from the customer's point of view. Concern and responsibility for marketing must therefore permeate all areas of the enterprise.'

(Peter Drucker)

The marketing concept

1.3 The *marketing concept* has been defined as a management outlook that accepts that the key task of the organisation is to determine the needs, wants and values of a target market of customers and to adapt the organisation as necessary to deliver the desired satisfaction more effectively and efficiently than its competitors. There are, however, alternative outlooks or 'orientations', eg towards:

(a) *production:* concentrating on manufacture, cost and volume, which works well when demand outstrips supply;

(b) *product:* concentrating on product design and quality, so that the product 'sells itself'. (in conditions of competition and/or over-supply of the product in the market, however, demand will have to be stimulated with a 'product push' to convince customers of the product's desirability);

(c) *sales:* concentrating on selling product in the face of assumed customer inertia, with heavy investment in sales promotion.

Orientation	Assumption
Product	Customers know (and buy) a 'good thing' when they see it.
Sales	Customers will not know (or buy) a 'good thing' without being told by the sales function.
Market	A 'good thing' is by definition one that customers will want to buy.

Emergence of the marketing concept in banks

1.4   Banks seem to have done little in the way of advertising or promoting their services until the late 1960s, when joint advertising campaigns emerged, designed rather to promote banking itself than one particular bank. The 1970s saw separate advertising campaigns for banks, and the beginnings of a newly active approach to the marketplace.

1.5   In the 1980s, however, there was considerable change in the range of products and services offered by banks and building societies, and by their competitors, who were growing in number, with the convergence of interest between different financial service providers (accountants, insurance companies etc). This created new pressures for banks and building societies to consider more carefully who their customers were (and whether groups of customers might form particular markets for particular services); what were their customers' needs, wants and values; who their competitors were; and how they could satisfy their customers more efficiently and effectively than their competitors.

1.6   Kevin Gavaghan, in an article in March 1990 *Banking World*, outlines some of the changes in bank marketing in the 1980s.

(a) 'In the beginning there was *market planning* and there was *public relations and advertising.* In most British banks these two functions (or similar entities by different names) reported to different general managers and argued about the only word they had in common - budget. The winner was clearly seen in the advertising.' In the 1980s, however, the marketing function was reconstructed, so that research analysis, product management and communications worked together to build new products and profitable services based on researched needs.

(b) Meanwhile, greater socio-economic emphasis on wealth accumulation and small business enterprise shifted the banks' attention away from gaining *new* customers among the 'unbanked' population, to 'cross-selling' services to *existing* customers who had and wanted more: a shift from 'product orientation' to 'customer orientation'. This process was aided by the development of detailed customer databases.

(c) Competition from foreign banks and other institutions increased dramatically under deregulation, making winning new customers a difficult and costly business, and increasing the attractions of the cross-selling option. 'New strategies for both personal and corporate markets now clearly distinguish between recruitment (finding new customers) and retention/cross-sale (keeping and offering further services to existing customers).'

(d) 'In banks everywhere, the heterodox and often unco-ordinated ranks of sales staff, relationship managers, providers of expert services, product managers, researchers and internal suppliers of processing, operations and administration services should heed the concept of "service, relationships and database management", and build it into their vision, their mission and their strategy.'

(e) The drive to meet customers' needs in a systematic way - and at a profit - requires four integrated components.

    (i) The *service proposition:* is the service 'mass-market', 'off the peg', or brought to customers personally, ie a 'bespoke' service?

    (ii) *Products:* designed to meet needs, to make a profit and to differentiate themselves from others eg by branding and distinctive product 'features'.

    (iii) *Delivery:* traditional bank branch, special small business or corporate outlets, or direct (mail or phone) services and sales. In addition, bankers are starting to 'go out' into the market place - rather than waiting for customers to come to them.

    (iv) *Credit authorisation and control procedures:* so the bank can provide fast and efficient services at a controlled level of risk.

In each case, developments in technology and staff training will need to keep pace.

(f) 'Prioritisation of effort, resource and management focus requires a clear understanding of the size, nature and attainable share of all appropriate markets.'

(g) 'Marketing departments can no longer operate tactically or in isolation and have therefore to involve themselves in the development of business strategies to meet current and future needs.'

(h) Environmental changes forecast for the 1990s will make the need for such a marketing out-look more acute. Bank customers, like the workforce as a whole, will be wealthier and more mobile, including more older people and working women. The climate for enterprise startups will be less favourable. Community concerns will emerge as a priority for all targeted customer groups. 'Marketing departments that cannot adapt to, and profit by, the pressures to innovate, for each market they serve, will fail, and their business with them.'

1.7 Banking activity in branches has, in the past, been commonly associated with lending rather than marketing other services, such as savings and investment schemes. However, banks are beginning to take major lending away from the branches and giving the responsibility for it to specialised centres. Where this has happened, branches should have more time to devote to marketing, especially since many of the data processing tasks of the branch are now automated.

1.8 To help with the process of using retail bank branches more as places for selling ranges of financial services, the banks have:

(a) developed specialist corporate branches, to deal with large company customers, and so allow the retail branches to concentrate more on the 'mass-market' of individual customers;

(b) trained branch staff to be salespeople;

(c) redesigned the layout of branches, to put more staff on the 'customer's side of the counter' - ie not separating customer from bank employee with screens;

(d) spent heavily on computer systems, which allow the banks to analyse customer data for marketing purposes.

1.9 As David Pirie, director of UK retail banking at Lloyds Bank, said in an article entitled *Service and costs* in *Banking World* December 1990:

'The key factors differentiating banks in the future will be quality of service and management of costs. Today's customer expects much more from his or her bank, spurred on by the growing competition between financial institutions. This same competition has eroded margins, highlighting excessive cost structures. Banks have responded by putting greater emphasis on sales activity and increased used of technology.'

1.10 Before we go on to look at specific aspects of marketing planning, it is worth noting that marketing by banks differs in certain respects from marketing by other organisations.

(a) The banker is a person on whom a customer usually relies for advice that he can trust. In other words, there is a *fiduciary relationship* between the banker and his customer. The banker must be careful to maintain the trust of his customer, and so he should consider the customer's wider interests and not just try to 'hard sell' banking services to the customer, whether or not they are needed. Indeed, the effects of hard selling and of stepping outside the fiduciary relationship have been seen in the increasing number of complaints received by and about banks.

(b) The banker should consider the long-term relationship with the customer, not just an 'immediate sale'. For example, what is the value of persuading a new customer to open an account if the customer soon becomes disillusioned with the service because it does not meet his needs? Banks should try to create 'clients' (who will come to the bank for a wide range of their financial needs) rather than just 'customers' for a particular product.

2. MARKETING PLANNING

2.1 The objective of marketing must be seen within the framework of the corporate plan as a whole, in that marketing plans can only be made with the organisation's overall goals in mind.

2.2   The marketing planning activity at its most basic consists of:

(a)   identifying present and future markets for services;

(b)   selecting which markets to serve (on the basis of market potential, taking into account competitor activity, and the capability of the organisation to capitalise on that potential);

(c)   identifying the needs, wants and 'market environment' of the selected markets;

(d)   defining marketing objectives for new and existing services;

(e)   selecting strategies for manipulating factors in the 'marketing mix' (price, product, promotion and place) so as to achieve objectives;

(f)   monitoring progress and success of strategies.

Marketing strategy

2.3   The organisation will have to make a number of strategic choices about:

(a)   which markets (or segments of markets) to be in;

(b)   what the marketing objective is to be: market share, sales volume?

(c)   which products/services to offer, and how they should be 'positioned' in the market (eg as value-for-money, or bespoke/quality service);

(d)   the relationship between the quality and price of the product;

(e)   how the product is to be delivered to the customer;

(f)   how the product is to be promoted.

2.4   These decisions will be complicated by the fact that the organisation will, as it grows, develop a portfolio of different products in different markets. Ansoff developed a matrix to show possible product/market strategies as follows.

	Existing products		*New products*
Existing markets	Consolidation or 'segment protection' *(capitalising on existing strengths)*	Market penetration *(increased competition for market share)*	Product development
New markets	Market development or extension *(eg by more detailed market segmentation and targeting, generating new demand through promotion or finding new customers on the strength of product improvements)*		Diversification

2.5 The process is still further complicated if the organisation has objectives related to *market share*, which may be declining or growing, in a market which itself may be declining or growing: how do you decide whether you are actively 'gaining ground' or not? A market growth rate/market share matrix such as that designed by the Boston Consulting Group can be used to indicate how a product is 'doing' in these terms. If it has a low market share of a fast-growth market, for example, it's clearly falling behind. A high share of a slow-growth market will offer a ready source of revenue, which can be used to finance products with more work to do.

Boston Consulting Group matrix

Market growth rate \ Market share	HIGH	LOW
HIGH	STAR	QUESTION MARK
LOW	CASH COW	DOG

'Cash cows' primarily supply finance for activities such as 'question marks'. A 'question mark' may be developed into a 'star' by increasing its market share, but if it fails to fulfil its potential, it will be a 'dog'.

2.6 The kinds of strategies employed in the market of financial services are substantially similar to those of organisations in other areas, including the following.

(a) *Consolidation*, or 'segment protection'. This may involve capitalising and building on existing strengths, eg experience, specialist expertise, a database of customers for direct mailing, high street retail outlets etc.

(b) *Market penetration*. This may involve increased competition for market share within existing markets/segments, as indicated by the advertising campaigns of the major banks. It may also involve the expansion of the market itself eg by encouraging home ownership, full insurance etc.

(c) *Breaking into new markets* by further market segmentation, and targeting of specific segments: 'niche' marketing. Insurance companies, for example, may specialise in high-risk forms of insurance which would be less viable for banks who also sell insurance services. Building societies diversified, with mixed results, into estate agency.

(d) *Introducing new products*, complementary to existing products or completely new.

(e) *Diversification*. Building societies diversifying into estate agency services; the merger of the Nationwide and Anglia Building Societies (Nationwide Anglia) to widen their scope. The Building Societies Act 1986 enabled building societies to diversify away from their original function of secured loans, and to offer a wide range of facilities similar to those offered by other institutions.

23: CUSTOMERS, COMPETITION AND QUALITY

Marketing information

2.7 The strategic decisions outlined above clearly require information and analysis about:

(a) the size and potential size of target markets ie their value and rate of growth;

(b) environmental factors that might affect the market;

(c) the needs, wants and values of target customers and likely influences on them;

(d) the current and potential share of the market obtainable by the given product/service, based on:

  (i) competitor activity;
  (ii) the organisation's ability to develop competitive products;

(e) the current and likely future performance of the product, and its stage in its life cycle;

(f) the organisation's strength and weaknesses with regard to developing new products for existing markets and/or new markets for existing products and/or diversification into new territory altogether (perhaps by merger or acquisition);

(g) opportunities and threats in the market.

2.8 *Marketing research* is the term for 'the objective gathering, recording and analysing of all facts about problems relating to the marketing of goods and services' including eg situational analysis (like SWOT analysis), competitive analysis, market share analysis etc.

2.9 It should be distinguished from *market research*, which is the aspect of marketing research concerned with assessing potential sales, ie the size of the overall market and the size and nature of 'segments' within the market (based on distinguishing characteristics of a group of consumers, and how they perceive and differentiate between different products/brands).

2.10 Note that 'marketing research' not only looks *outwards* to existing and potential markets, the customer (or market place), the competitive environment etc but also *inwards*, at the way in which the organisation *responds* to the demands of the market place. An analysis of the organisation's marketing system and capabilities would look at:

(a) the market environment (particularly customers, competitors, suppliers, technology etc);

(b) marketing strategy (corporate and marketing objectives, strategies, resources, strengths and weaknesses);

(c) marketing plans and controls (sales forecasting, market plans, product development, control procedures, marketing research);

(d) the marketing mix (evaluation of products, pricing policy, promotion, channels of distribution and the sales force);

(e) profitability and cost-effectiveness (of products and of the marketing function itself);

(f)   marketing organisation (management structure, staff training and motivation, efficiency, co-ordination etc).z

3.   IDENTIFYING CUSTOMERS: MARKET SEGMENTATION

3.1   'Market segmentation is the subdividing of a market into distinct subsets of customers, where any subset may conceivably be selected as a target market to be reached with a marketing mix' (P Kotler, *Marketing Management*).

The concept of market segments is that different groups of potential customers have their own characteristic needs, and so a special variation of a basic product or service, or a new product or service, might be the best way of winning their custom. A product or service might need to be sold to each different market segment in a different way (eg perhaps by emphasising the low cost of the service, or the high interest rate for savers, or perhaps by advertising through different media, such as direct mailshots, poster advertising, newspaper advertising etc).

3.2   For example, the market for banking services as opposed to traditional building society services is clearly divided between *personal customers* and *corporate customers*.

Individuals' needs	*Corporate needs*
● Ready access to money. ● Small personal loans to buy consumer products or household improvements. ● Savings for future income, or a 'rainy day' - protection of the value of savings against inflation. ● Interest on credit balances in their current account(?) ● To buy a home with a mortgage. ● Security and personal wealth (insurance, pensions). ● Convenience in paying for goods in shops etc (credit cards) or in obtaining cash (cash dispensers). ● Planning personal finances sensibly (eg budget accounts). ● Help with wills: making financial provisions for death and sorting out finances after a death. ● Instalment credit (eg personal loans, hire purchase). ● Revolving credit (eg credit cards, overdrafts).	● Deposit facilities for large quantities of short term funds. ● Large loans or other methods of finance for working capital or fixed assets. ● To find an organisation that will relieve it of burdensome administrative tasks, such as invoicing and debt collection (factors), share registration, payroll (BACS) etc. ● Assistance on specialist matters such as foreign trade (foreign exchange, bills of exchange, documentary credits, collections etc). ● Business advice. ● Instalment credit and revolving credit on a larger scale than for personal customers.

3.3   Corporate customers can in turn be segmented, perhaps into small businesses, medium-sized businesses and large businesses; or into exporters, importers and domestic traders. The same business can belong to several different potential market segments at the same time, and so sub-segmentation can take place (eg small businesses in importing, medium-sized export businesses etc).

3.4 Personal customers and potential customers can be segmented too, by age group, income level, social class, marital status. All of these are potential savers and borrowers, but each has characteristic needs in the market for depositing funds, saving and borrowing. Remember, through, that a bank is trying to establish a *lifelong relationship* with a personal customer, and so the same individual will, throughout his or her life, move through several market segments. A bank will therefore emphasise that its products are appropriate for both the customer's *current needs* and the customer's *future needs*.

(a) Students are offered free overdrafts and gifts. Apply this to the working population, and the bank would be ruined.

(b) However, the bank hopes that a student who benefits now will buy the bank's other products at a later date.

3.5 The bases for segmenting 'personal' or 'consumer' markets might be listed briefly as follows.

(a) *Geographic* (region/country, town or rural area, town size, population density, etc). Many building societies have a strong regional identity.

(b) *Demographic* (age, sex, family life cycle - ie young and single, young and married with no children, young and married with children, retired etc).

(c) *Social class, occupation or income.* Retail banks have generally divided their personal customers into two broad groups: 'mass market' customers, to whom a bank will sell services through the branch network and/or customer mailshots, and 'wealthy individual' customers, who are thought likely to be in the market for financial advice, tax management, 'personal banking' etc.

(d) *Life style and personality* - useful mainly for determining the style of advertising used.

(e) *Behavioural characteristics* of the potential customers such as:

(i) usage rate: how often they would use the product or service;

(ii) user status - non-user, ex-user, potential user, first-time user, regular user;

(iii) benefits sought from the product/service (economy, convenience, prestige etc);

(iv) readiness stage - unaware of the product or service, aware, well-informed, interested, very interested etc.

For example, there are certain defined stages in the house buying process - most customers go to an estate agent. This is a place where financial services can be sold. Surveys and conveyancing must be arranged. Building societies have been interested in carrying out this type of service.

3.6 The requirements for an effective segmentation of the market are as follows.

(a) The size and potential value of each market segment be *measurable*. Share registration services, for example, might appeal to large public companies with a large number of shareholders, and banks can readily assess the existing and potential size of the market.

    (b)   Customers and potential customers in the market segment must be *accessible.*

    (c)   The market segment must be sufficiently *substantial* in size to make it worth the while of a supplier to develop a product or service, or launch an advertising campaign etc for that segment. In banking, market segments can be very large, eg the unbanked - and the clearing banks continue to look for ways of attracting new customers into banking (eg offering interest-bearing current accounts or persuading companies not to offer payment of wages in cash).

4.   REACHING CUSTOMERS: THE MARKETING MIX

4.1   The 'marketing mix' has been defined as 'the balanced blend of marketing ingredients best calculated to achieve a defined marketing objective as economically as possible.' (McIver & Naylor, *Marketing Financial Services*).

4.2   The marketing mix has been *traditionally* identified with 'the Four Ps': product, place, promotion and price.

4.3   *Product* (or service) is concerned with the features of bank products and services, and any options available to the customer. Product features in bank lending for example, would include the term of loans, variable or fixed interest rates and the option to switch from variable to fixed rates or vice versa. Product is determined according to the needs, wants and values of the targeted market segment, as interpreted by market research, and in accordance with feedback from the market (eg if a product becomes 'stale' or subject to competitive pressure, or is rendered obsolete by events).

4.4   *Place* is concerned with where the product or service is made available to the customer, or how the customer can obtain the service. In banking, the existence of a branch network and an ATM network are aspects of place, and so too are:

    (a)   the widespread acceptance of credit cards by shops, hotels, restaurants etc;

    (b)   the ability of customers to obtain personal loans by written application to their bank, without the need for a personal interview;

    (c)   telephone 'branchless' banking;

    (d)   visiting of business customers by bank representatives.

4.5   *Promotion* is concerned with advertising, direct selling and other forms of sales promotion. Bank advertising has had a particularly high profile in recent years, and is generally aimed at image creation for the bank as a whole, as well as creating and improving customer awareness of new and existing services, stimulating demand etc. Forms of sales promotion other than advertising include direct selling by bank staff, 'direct mail' (ie sending promotional material to potential customers using databases), exhibitions and conferences, public relations, sponsorship of sporting and cultural events etc.

4.6   *Price*, in banking, refers to interest rates offered to depositers and borrowers and bank charges and commissions for individual services. Prices have to be fixed at levels which take into account cost of provision, competitor charges, perceived 'added value' for the customer, the strategic importance of the service regardless of profitability (eg for PR) etc.

4.7 In addition to the Four Ps, factors in the overall marketing mix, especially for service businesses, are now recognised to include three other Ps.

4.8 *Physical evidence.* This is particularly important in retailing and branding. Physical evidence comprises logos, colour schemes and so forth which help give and institution its particular image. These include:

(a) branch layout (eg intimidating security grills or friendly desks);
(b) lighting (and 'atmosphere');
(c) convenience of use.

4.9 *Process.* These are the efficiency with which a bank's services are delivered. For example, while a bank loan is a product, the design of the application form and the speed with which the request is dealt with, are procedural matters. The process involves:

(a) technology (eg ATMs make it quicker to withdraw money);

(b) bureaucracy (the bank's procedures affect the speed with which a customer's request is dealt with).

4.10 *People.* If banks see themselves as service businesses, then 'people' issues are important. The people element of the marketing mix includes:

(a) the bank's personnel, who might have to be trained to sell the bank's products rather than simply process transactions;

(b) the bank's customers, in that customers' needs must be understood.

5. THE BRANCH MARKETING PLAN

5.1 Branches of each bank will develop a marketing plan or programme with the framework of a head office plan and in consultation with district control. The ultimate responsibility for a branch marketing plan, however rests with the branch manager.

5.2 The development of a branch marketing plan must begin with an assessment of the branch's operating area, its customers and potential customers, the services the bank can provide and the strengths and weaknesses of the individual branch.

(a) There might be some value in giving branch staff supplementary marketing education and training at branch level. There is likely to be inexperience in selling, and perhaps even inadequate knowledge of the increasing range of services on offer.

(b) A customer 'database' should be created by the branch, which contains whatever information about customers can be gathered together (eg from interview notes, newspaper cuttings, account history as described in bank statements, credit enquiries received about the customer etc). Many banks have already done this on a bank-wide basis.

(c)   The database information can be used to match services to customer groups. For example, high-earning customers might be suitable for the marketing of investment advice, life assurance, an executorship service or taxation advice. Young professionals might be suitable 'targets' for marketing mortgage loans etc.

(d)   Information should be gathered (from local chambers of commerce or the local authority rates office) about local businesses, especially new businesses moving into the area, that do not bank with the branch. A direct marketing approach to these businesses might be planned, to win their custom.

(e)   Managers should analyse the strengths and weaknesses of their branch - eg the convenience of the branch site to customers. They should consider ways of exploiting the strengths and minimising the weaknesses.

(f)   Realistic targets for achievement should be drawn up for the branch marketing plan, taking these items into consideration. The branch plan should be formulated in consultation with district control.

(g)   The rewards of marketing success should be real, built into the reward system of the branch and communicated to staff.

(h)   The plan should not be rigid, and the branch staff should retain a flexible approach to exploit any marketing opportunities that may unexpectedly arise.

(i)   Marketing should be timed carefully. There is little point, for example, in marketing travellers' cheques after the holiday season has ended. The timing of national promotional campaigns should also be taken into account.

(j)   Attention should be given to the method of reaching target customers. Leaflets detailing bank services should be made available to customers on the branch premises, but the branch should also use mail-shots, eg sending out leaflets with bank statements. Mail-shots could be supplemented by local advertising.

(k)   A branch should keep a constant eye on the local competition, namely other banks, building societies and retailers who develop their own credit facilities for customers (eg Marks and Spencer). The marketing plan may have to include defensive, 'follow the leader' initiatives to match competitor action.

(l)   Performance should be monitored and compared with the marketing plan: if there is deviation from plan, either the practice or the plan itself may need to be adjusted.

5.3   In a *Banking World* article in December 1990 entitled *Marketing ... and the branches*, Frank Abramson stressed how important premises design was to marketing:

'If the team in charge of premises is deciding what branches should look like, two of the most pressing points for consideration will be what customers want and what products and services have to be sold in the new branch ... After spending valuable time and money researching customers' needs and designing product and promotional literature, the marketing department needs to be sure that its work does not fall at the final fence by appearing in a branch that is inconvenient, unwelcoming or outdated.'

5.4   However, branches must be careful not to overstep the mark when it comes to their marketing plans.

(a) Some customers feel alienated by the 'one stop shopping', 'financial supermarket' attitude in which the traditional banking activities of cashing cheques, depositing money and taking out loans have become depersonalised. Customers appreciate being known and recognised, and find the 'selling' atmosphere uncomfortable if it is not also a 'service' atmosphere.

(b) The nature of the banker/customer relationship requires that the bank should maintain a duty of confidentiality, which may restrict the amount of cross-selling by group companies. In addition, the Consumer Credit Act 1974 places legal restrictions on marketing to minors and requires adherence to special procedures for certain other types of transaction.

5.5 The Code of Banking Practice, whose second edition is reproduced as an Appendix to this Study Text, requires the following.

(a) Banks must tell customers if information on them may be used for direct marketing purposes by banking, financial and investment members of the group.

(b) Where requested, banks will *not* send direct marketing material to customers.

(c) Direct mail will not be used indiscriminately. Restraint will particularly be used where customers are minors and where loans and overdrafts are being marketed.

(d) In all advertising and promotional material it must be made plain that lending is subject to appraisal of each customer's financial standing, taking into account prior knowledge from past dealings, information obtained from credit reference agencies, the information provided by applicants and credit scoring. All material must comply with relevant codes of practice and must be fair and reasonable.

5.6 Consumer groups have also asked for:

(a) transparency of charges (ie people should be able to work out why they have paid charges);

(b) more willingness to rectify errors.

Exercise

Identify three different products/services offered by the bank for which you work. As a comparative exercise, visit the branch of a bank or financial institution which also provides these services to find out how your three choices of products/services are offered there. Compare:

(a) the physical layout of the competitor's branch to your own;
(b) what you perceive to be the marketing approach of each.

---

6. THE COMPETITIVE ENVIRONMENT OF BANKS AND BUILDING SOCIETIES

6.1 The key word in any consideration of the bank environment today - and looking into the future - is 'competition'. There are five factors in the competitive environment of organisations. These are sometimes referred to as the five competitive forces.

(a) *Barriers to entry*. Organisations entering the banking industry in the UK must comply with strict requirements, if they want to act as deposit-takers. This is a barrier to entering the market for these services.

(b) *Substitute products*. Banks and building societies offer different types of money, to put it simply. It is unlikely that any 'substitute' can be found for this basic commodity. It could be argued, moreover, that banks' enhancements of their traditional services involve substitutes which are hardly threats (eg the debit card is a substitute for the cheque). There are some substitutes in the corporate sector: some companies can borrow direct from the money markets (eg by issuing certificates of deposit) rather than borrowing money (on a loan basis) from a bank.

(c) The *bargaining power of customers*. Customers can pick and choose. Yet a bank is in a strong position in relation to the individual customer. Banks and customers are in a relationship. The bank will suffer if its behaviour destroys the relationship.

(d) The *bargaining power of suppliers*. Suppliers provide the organisation with goods and services. Customers are suppliers for the banking sector, as they deposit money. A bank which loses customers' confidence will collapse. The bargaining power of suppliers would seem high: but customers who are the same people and/or firms depend on the bank's stability.

(e) The *state of competition within the industry*. This is very intense in the UK financial services sector as we shall see.

6.2 In the financial services sector, banks and building societies are in competition with:

(a) each other;
(b) insurance companies;
(c) merchant banks;
(d) foreign and international banks;
(e) private banks;
(f) finance companies and store cards;
(g) unit and investment trusts.

In addition there is competition from:

(h) National Savings;
(i) investment in stock (as opposed to interest-bearing deposit accounts);
(j) other professionals: solicitors, accountants, estate agents, insurance brokers and computer bureaux (for advice).

6.3 In response, banks (excluding building societies) have had to widen *their* service range to include other financial services: mortgages, portfolio management, insurance services etc. Building societies have widened their activities to include cheque accounts, personal loans, pensions and insurance.

6.4 A restricted service range may dilute customer loyalty, in the face of increased competition from organisations offering, in effect, 'one-stop shopping' for financial services. Customer loyalty may already be eroded by the increasing financial sophistication of the personal sector and increasing price-sensitivity: attention to the cost of delivering services to the customer (eg through the increased use of technology) may be a bank's principal approach to competition from other banks, whose services overlap to a great extent.

6.5 New entrants to the market also now include retailers offering in-store credit cards, charge cards etc, as well as financial service outlets.

6.6 One complex aspect of the competitive environment has arisen from the 'polarisation' between independent and tied agents under the Financial Services Act 1986, affecting the way in which banks and other institutions sell personal investments (eg unit trusts), pensions and life assurance. These products can only be sold:

(a) through a *tied agency*, in which the supplier sells his own services/products direct to customers or through intermediaries who *only* sell that one supplier's services/ products (the limited nature of the selection for the customer is made clear); or

(b) through an *independent agent*, a licensed intermediary who must offer an unrestricted range of products/services and is bound by the Act to offer 'best advice' according to the needs of the customer. A tied agent cannot be an independent agent as well.

6.7 Independent agents are able (and bound) to offer wide choice to customers. Suppliers who continue to sell their own brands/service lines, therefore, are under increasing pressure to secure their market position, reputation, visible performance and competitiveness. Their promotional and selling initiatives will also be crucial, which is why corporate sponsorship and aggressive media advertising have been used to raise their profile.

6.8 Companies selling through independent agents will also have to increase their marketing efforts, so that they gain or maintain a 'high profile' and their brand or service will be asked for by name when customers go to their brokers. They may also have to lend promotional support to the independent brokers themselves, on whom they now rely, in order to compete with the suppliers who are going direct to the market.

Changes in bank marketing and services

6.9 The 1988 Ernest Sykes Memorial Lecture, delivered by Barry Reed, was reported in *Banking World* June 1988. The article stressed the changing role of the high street bank, and the ways in which bankers and retailers can learn from each other, in the context of consumerism, competition, deregulation and technology. Some of the developments discussed include:

(a) the new importance of product knowledge and selling skills, with increased financial services range and competition;

(b) consumerism: the move of banks towards retailers in their willingness to seek out, and make themselves readily available to, customers (Saturday banking, flexible opening hours, banker visits etc);

(c) the changing role of the branch, with:

      (i)   a wider range of delivery points for bank services;

      (ii)   remote cash dispensers, home banking etc;

      (iii)   the moving of the branch's traditional work load (with its emphasis on successful lending) to specialist branches, liberating staff time and premises for customer service and selling roles;

(d)   the awareness of the potential of prime high-street premises as genuine sales outlets: branch decor and design as a new issue with a more welcoming and personal air;

(e)   the adoption of direct mail marketing by banks using their existing customer database;

(f)   cross-selling and diversification of the product range; relationship banking as a basis for developing customer loyalty and cross-selling potential, (eg regarding 'customers' as 'clients');

(g)   customer segmentation; 'high-net-worths', personal, corporate, small business etc;

(h)   the move of retailers into banking preserves, eg charge cards, credit cards, personal loans, share shops, fund transfer: an example being Marks & Spencer. Retailers, however, suffer from several weaknesses, eg:

      (i)   lack of experience and expertise;
      (ii)   a limited product range hindering their image as a provider;
      (iii)   lack of banks' sophisticated information base;

(i)   the reduction of banks' dependence on paper handling (if only as a percentage of total business volume), increasing service quality, volume and cost-effectiveness.

6.10   Barry Reed envisaged a future in which banks go even further in improving sales and distribution, eg by:

(a)   taking segmentation right up through the organisation structure to director level;
(b)   extending sales-related reward schemes to include commission;
(c)   speeding up the transition to open-plan flexible branch layouts;
(d)   freeing managers to sell, rather than to administer/process;
(e)   emphasising presentation and merchandising of bank products;
(f)   exploring profitable use of branch floor space (eg leasing to outside franchises).

This presupposes a profound cultural change in banks, staff and managerial attitudes, and market perception. It is starting to happen, and you will probably recognise many of the above ideas are coming into being in your own bank or branch.

The international market

6.11   Banks are increasingly operating in a *global market*. Internationalisation means increased competition from foreign banks, particularly Japanese and American banks which have moved into the UK in the 1980s. UK banks are in a favourable position, however, for the following reasons.

(a)   London is still a leading financial centre, so UK banks are well placed to provide international financial services.

(b) UK banks are able to channel profits into new markets and ventures, both at home and overseas. The UK home market is quite profitable.

(c) Britain has a long history of international trading and diplomacy which may form a basis for banking activity. Many UK banks are already involved in international markets.

(d) British banks have a reputation for stability; allegations of fraud and financial malpractice amongst London's financial institutions have been countered by legislation on investor protection and insider dealing. How that reputation will survive the Barings affair is a matter for speculation.

(e) In particular, British banks have responded swiftly to the challenge of new technology (eg EFTPOS, electronic data interchange (EDI) etc) and so are known for the speed and efficiency of their transaction processing.

(f) International trade and finance of international trade should be expected to develop, with new markets and demand for new products opening up (eg with the completion of the European Market in 1992, the opening up for business of Eastern Europe). The Cecchini Report estimated that up to one-third of the growth anticipated from the creation of a single European Market in the first six years will be directly attributable to the expansion of financial services.

(g) Global strategies are increasingly important for success. The management and staff of banks are more aware of the international arena than ever before, especially with the publicity given to 1992, and professional training is more geared to the international marketplace. Above all, the 'culture' of UK banks no longer favours the parochial and insular. Hence many banks are linking up with banks in other countries to form a pan-European network, such as Bank of Scotland with the Greek Dorian Bank.

6.12 But there is still a chance that UK banks will be left behind.

(a) The developments in bank awareness and experience of international markets and operations are still relatively recent and not yet universal.

(b) London as a financial centre is under threat from other centres such as New York and Tokyo, (and perhaps Paris or Frankfurt, post-1992).

(c) The competitive instinct that has developed in UK banks with regard to international markets is not exclusive to UK banks. Other nations are also preparing for fierce competition in domestic and overseas markets.

(d) Many banks are large bureaucracies, and British banks in particular have a long institutional history: this makes them relatively slow to respond to change and inflexible in their attitudes. Their relative security might also encourage a complacent and conservative attitude. They may find that their 'culture' simply doesn't export: the style of staffing and management that is successful in the UK may not work among foreign nationals etc.

(e) Banks tend to be risk-averse, and the potential for expensive mistakes is far greater outside the domestic market.

(f) There may be constraints placed on foreign banks by some countries which want to maintain a protected domestic market, or which are simply suspicious of foreign banks.

6.13 Many of the disadvantages for UK banks in the international arena are such that they can be overcome by management; there must be preparedness to innovate, to adapt, to develop a more international culture etc. Fierce competition is not in itself a constraint: it may stimulate the necessary changes in the outlook of British banks. You should look carefully in *Banking World* and the quality press for on-going plans for the *single European market* and its implications for banking.

6.14 It is anticipated that the implications of deregulated European banking will include:

(a) opportunities in the wider market for services;

(b) cheaper and administratively simpler ways of setting up branches in Europe;

(c) potential cost benefits to customers, ie falling prices - and squeezed margins for the banks;

(d) increased complexity of retail banking, since the implications of the single market are equally great for the banks' corporate and individual customers and their financial affairs: credit and risk assessment systems (especially for corporate lending) will need revision;

(e) opportunities arising from free movement of trade and travel facilities (eg eurocheque cards or travellers cheques), but also threats and changes eg new competitors, the ECU (European Currency Unit) etc.

6.15 Moreover, should there emerge a common European currency, this will facilitate cross-border operations.

Building societies and competition

6.16 The UK retailing banking sector is dominated by the 'Big Four'. The same is not so true of the building society industry. While Abbey National, Halifax and so forth have a UK-wide presence, there are a large number of regionally-based societies.

6.17 An article by Patrick Frazer (*Banking World* November 1993) identifies a number of forces which will lead to a shakeout in this sector.

(a) There are 'too many' societies: 'business has collapsed by 50% since 1988 .. yet .. the number of staff has defied gravity'.

(b) 'Societies are caught in a battle for market share on both sides of the balance sheet.'

(c) 'Customers are now looking elsewhere for the best rates on their savings'. In particular, unit trusts (in which banks, as opposed to building societies, have the dominant share) are becoming more popular. Between 1980 and 1990, the value of unit trusts rose nine-fold.

(d) Societies are less able than banks to survive an outflow of deposits. Competitors are better able to rely on the wholesale moneymarket, perhaps to fund mortgages at rates which undercut those offered by the building societies.

(e) Fixed rate mortgages are hard to fund.

Consequently 'squeezed between unit trusts and banks, societies face a serious loss of market share and must juggle their interest rates so that the pain is evenly divided between deposits and loans'.

6.18 Building societies have made up for a shortfall by selling endowment mortgages: 'a product which is arguably no longer suitable for most borrowers in a world where long-term investment returns may be much lower than in the past'. Some societies (eg the Cheltenham and Gloucester) have abandoned endowment policies.

6.19 Building societies can also become banks, thereby ensuring greater access to money market funds.

6.20 Frazer predicts that a possible way forward to the problem of overcapacity is a series of mergers. This, however, may not be too effective. The Leeds and N&P were going to merge, but this fell through owing to differences in management style.

6.21 Two sorts of 'mergers' can be suggested.

 (a) *Acquire and eliminate.* In this case a smaller rivals' capacity is closed down, once it has been acquired.

 (b) *Combine and cut.* In this case, two building societies merge and cut costs and capacity.

6.22 Historically, the trends is for a smaller number of institutions. There were 3,642 building societies in 1895, but only 89 were active at the end of 1992.

6.23 It seems likely, therefore that the excess of capacity and low cost competition will lead to significant changes in the building society sector in future.

7. PROBLEMS IN BANK MARKETING: THE ROLE OF QUALITY

7.1 Millions of people have some sort of connection with banks and financial institutions. Even if half the population of the UK has a bank account, this amounts to up to 30 million accounts. Huge numbers of financial transactions are processed each day.

7.2 However hard a bank tries to market itself there is always a danger in that particular cases will cloud the reputation of the whole bank. Tom Lloyd wrote in *Banking World*, June 1992 that 'the same people who would previously have described banks as "courteous", "secure", "efficient" and "reliable", are more likely to see them nowadays as "irresponsible", ignorant", "importunate", "uncaring" and "selfish"'.

7.3 This might seem unfortunate given the amount and effort banks spend on market research, direct mail and so forth. Also, banks give considerable amounts as sponsorship to the arts and to charities.

7.4 Why might this state of affairs have come about?

(a) Lloyd believes that 'the problem with the contemporary banking culture is that it is confused. The rapid commercialisation has been laid over the old professional ethos, rather than integrated with it'.

(b) Ian Lindsay, also writing in *Banking World* (June 1992), has some other ideas as to why banks frequently seem to be criticised.

(i) 'What customers really want may be ignored because it is too inconvenient for the bank or building society to provide.'

(ii) 'All to often banks are not prepared to accept they have made mistakes and are slow to correct them. Very often, they deny liability, not because they are in the right but because their lawyers advise them to do so'.

Taking a forgiving attitude may cost money occasionally, but can generate enormous goodwill.

(iii) Banks fail to manage their relations with the press very well.

(c) Other reasons, quoted by Lloyd, include:

(i) 'staff are moved round too fast for good banking relationships to develop';

(ii) 'banks are no longer seen as sources of objective advice and have acquired a hard sell profiteering image';

(iii) 'they charge too much, they change charges without warning'.

(d) Other well publicised stories include:

(i) the Maxwell affair, in which banks had acquired legal assets which had otherwise belonged to the pension funds;

(ii) other scandals such as BCCI taint the image and reputation of banks generally.

7.5 Clearly, the service delivered depends very much on the way in which small individual matters are handled. The problem of bank marketing, then, is that the quality of service at individual level must support the bank's desired image.

Quality management programmes

7.6 In an article in *Banking World* (December 1992) Gorden Henderson (head of corporate quality at Girobank) stated that: 'quality is the key to the success of banks of the future but it was not always seen this way'.

7.7 Quality management techniques, such as TQM (total quality management) have been first introduced in manufacturing companies. Quality has two aspects.

(a) *Design quality.* The product or service must be designed in such a way as to satisfy customer needs.

(b) *Conformance quality*. The product or service must be 'built' or provided according to specification. In other words, for example, a customer's direct debits must be processed correctly on the required date.

7.8 Most *customer complaints* probably derive from failings in conformance quality, in that the service provided has fallen down in some way. In addition, for more complex financial products, the 'design quality' may be poor if the customer does not understand it. Customer complaints however can be seen as an opportunity for learning.

7.9 For banks, quality issues are particularly appropriate to the process element of the marketing mix. Customer care programmes are fine, but are not enough. As Henderson says: 'charm wears rather think when a customer's electricity is cut off because a processing error leaves his bill unpaid'.

7.10 Total quality management is defined by Holmes as 'a culture aimed at continually improving performance in meeting the requirements in all functions of a company'. In other words, it is an approach to management, not just a set of techniques. TQM can involve the following.

(a) Quality monitoring. A survey should be done to assess the bank's actual quality of service (eg customer complaints).

(b) Implementation of quality targets (eg the percentage of calls answered within 20 seconds).

(c) Training of staff.

(d) Continual review, improvement and redesign of processes to ensure quality targets are met.

(e) The establishment of systems of quality control. BS EN ISO 9000 (formerly BS5750) is a recognised standard of quality management. To achieve BS EN ISO 9000, an organisation has to 'establish, document and maintain an effective quality system which will demonstrate to [the] customers that [it] is committed to quality and are able to satisfy their quality needs.

7.11 Holmes proposes an eight stage model for improving quality.

(a) *Step 1*. Find out the problems (eg from customer and employees).

(b) *Step 2*. Select action targets from the number of improvement projects identified in *Step 1*, on the basis of cost, safety, importance, feasibility (with current resources).

(c) *Step 3*. Collect data about the problem.

(d) *Step 4*. Analyse data by a variety of techniques to assess common factors behind the data, to tease out any hidden messages the data might contain.

(e) *Step 5*. Identify possible causes (eg using brainstorming sessions). No ideas are ruled out of order.

(f) *Step 6*. Plan improvement action.

(g) *Step 7*. Monitor the effects of the improvement.

(h) *Step 8.* Communicate the result.

7.12 Henderson reports some of the features of quality improvement programmes at Girobank. 'In each area, the emphasis was on identifying and eliminating errors and waste, improving processes, defining and meeting customer needs and establishing a clear procedure for handling complaints and appropriate corrective actions. Hundreds of groups of project workers broke down processes into small manageable pieces, corrected them and then put them together again.'

7.13 The results of Girobank's quality improvement programme have been as follows.

(a) 'A 63 per cent improvement in the number of calls answered within 20 seconds between 1989 and 1991. Now the target is even higher.'

(b) 'A 13% improvement in operator productivity.'

(c) 'A fall in customer complaints of more than 50 per cent.'

(d) 'Operational cost savings from implementing quality improvement projects have saved some £12m.'

(e) 'Savings from implementing staff suggestions account for another £2m.'

8. CHAPTER ROUNDUP

8.1 Marketing is broader than selling, and embraces the whole business. This is particularly true where an organisation has a 'marketing orientation' based on *determining* and *meeting* the needs and wants of the target market. Banks are rapidly having to acquire such an orientation.

8.2 Key activities for bank marketing include:

(a) the identification of subsets of customers as distinct target markets, ie market segmentation;

(b) application of the 'marketing mix', ie

Product
Place   + People
Promotion   + Process
Price   + Physical evidence

8.3 The competitive environment of banks has grown more complex in recent years, with:

(a) convergence of the activities of various institutions in the financial services sector;

(b) polarisation of independent and tied agents under the Financial Services Act;

(c) the increasing internationalisation of the market for financial services;

(d) opportunities and threats posed by new technology;

(e) the increasing sophistication of the market place, and the range of personal expectations and values brought to bear on the bank–customer relationship.

TEST YOUR KNOWLEDGE
The numbers in brackets refer to paragraphs of this chapter

1 Outline the changes in banks' orientation to the marketing activity in recent decades. (1.4 - 1.6)

2 Outline the process of marketing planning. (2.2)

3 What alternative product/market strategies does a bank have, in relation to new and existing products and new and existing markets? (2.4)

4 What information is required in order to formulate marketing strategies? (2.7 - 2.10)

5 Choose three traditional bank product/services and identify the market segment at which they might be targeted. (3.2)

6 Give two examples from the banking world of each of the 4Ps of the 'marketing mix', plus 'the marketing environment'. (4.2 - 4.10)

7 What restrictions are there on banks' marketing of financial services? (5.5)

8 List six potential providers of services which compete with those provided by a bank. (6.2)

9 Outline five recent changes in branch banking that you know of or have experienced in your own bank - in any aspect of its activity. Identify influences or events to which each change might have been designed to respond. (6.9)

Now try question 24 at the end of the text

Chapter 24

HUMAN RESOURCE MANAGEMENT

This chapter covers the following topics.

1. What is human resource management?
2. Personnel planning
3. Management succession and promotion
4. Labour turnover
5. Employee relations in banking

Introduction

'Staff' are a major input to the organisation: perhaps *the* major resource which an organisation imports from its environment, since the organisation is made up of people and depends on them for all its functions. This is especially true of service companies. We have already discussed individual recruitment: now for the context.

---

1. WHAT IS HUMAN RESOURCE MANAGEMENT?

1.1 The organisation's interface with the *labour* market is therefore crucial. Within the organisation, all levels of management, the employees themselves, and the specialist personnel function (if there is one) are involved in the process of managing interpersonal relations and individual and group activity: we will discuss these aspects in the section on 'Managing other people'. However, at the *boundary* between the organisation and the environment, there must be a specialised form of management, concerned with importing, retaining or releasing human resources, according to the strategic requirements of the organisation.

1.2 This has come to be called 'human resource management', and embraces the personnel functions of manpower planning and resourcing, recruitment, retention, development and the control of labour turnover.

1.3 Since the bank's interface with the employment environment also includes employee relations, we will include that topic here. Statutory intervention in the employee–employer relationship (eg employment protection, discrimination laws etc) is also relevant, but will be covered in other chapters, in the particular contexts to which pieces of legislation apply.

Human resource management

1.4 The term 'human resource management' is fairly new, and some people have suggested that it is just a way of saying 'personnel management' (or even 'manpower planning'), which reflects the desire of personnel managers to upgrade their status and sense of self-esteem. In many organisations, this may be so.

1.5 However, a precise and positive interpretation of HRM would include the following two admissions.

(a) Personnel management has been changing in various ways in recent years. Many of its activities have become more complex and sophisticated and, particularly with the accelerating pace of change in the business environment, less narrowly concerned with areas previously thought of as personnel's sole preserve (hiring and firing, training, industrial relations, manpower planning etc); the personnel function has become centrally concerned with issues of broader relevance to the business and its objectives, such as change management, the introduction of technology, the implications of falling birthrates and skill shortages for the resourcing of the business etc.

(b) Personnel management can and should be integrated with the strategic planning of the business, ie with management at the broadest and highest level. The objectives of the personnel function can and should be directly related to achieving the organisation's goals for growth, competitive gain and improvement of 'bottom line' performance.

1.6 In a survey of 20 top personnel directors (reported in *Personnel Management*, October 1989) Michael Armstrong identifies the key issues for the personnel function of the future.

(a) HRM implies a shift of emphasis in personnel management from the peripheral 'staff' role of the past to mainstream business management. Armstrong suggests that 'twenty years ago people in equivalent positions would have been more likely to talk about [personnel activities] as if these were techniques or areas of knowledge which had intrinsic value and did not need to be considered in terms of fit with business strategies or impact on business results.'

(b) The definition of entrepreneurship is the 'shifting of economic resources out of the area of lower and into an area of higher productivity and greater yield' (J B Say), and this is essentially what HRM embodies, in terms of finding, obtaining and developing - getting the best out of - the human resources of the business.

(c) This implies a close match between corporate objectives and the objectives of the human resource function. *All* business planning should recognise that the ultimate source of 'value' is people, and should appreciate the human resource implications and potential constraints associated with any long-term strategies evolved.

(d) The integration of personnel and overall corporate objectives firmly establishes personnel as an *enabling* function, creating a framework and culture within which effective contributions can be made.

(e) This 'enabling' role brings us back to the term 'HRM'. A major part of personnel's relatively new-found concern for performance management is the re-orientation towards '*resourcing*' in its broadest sense. Personnel's strategic contribution to a business is the definition of relationships between business requirements and organisational and human requirements: the human *resourcing* of the business is how this works in practice, and includes not only the obtaining of an increasingly scarce resource (people) but the maximisation of their contribution through development, reward, organisational culture etc.

1.7 Personnel management is the key to many service industries as the services are delivered by staff in a personal encounter.

2. PERSONNEL PLANNING

What is personnel planning?

2.1 Labour is one of the resources of an organisation which management must plan and control. Compared to machines and money, labour is a relatively unpredictable and uncontrollable resource.

    (a) People have their own goals. Individuals might pursue their own interests at the expense of the organisation's efficiency, if their goals are in conflict with those of the organisation.

    (b) Environmental factors, such as government decisions or fluctuating markets, create uncertainties in the *demand* for labour, whereas other factors (such as education, unemployment levels or demographic changes) create uncertainties in the *supply* of labour.

    (c) Constant changes in job content - with new technology and market changes - require managerial and employee flexibility. The career and retraining *potential* of the individual will be at least as important as his basic qualifications and skills', but not so readily assessible.

2.2 Manpower planning can be seen in simple terms as the closing of the gap between an organisation's need for labour, and the supply which exists within and outside the organisation. The object of manpower planning is to have the right people in the right jobs at the right time.

2.3 The supply/demand equation is complicated in practice, and cannot be left to chance.

    (a) Jobs often require skills and experience which are scarce in the market place: *training* and *development* may be required within or outside the organisation to make these skills available.

    (b) Employment legislation, employee aspirations and expectations and trade unionism make it difficult for organisations to pursue haphazard and simplistic measures to control over-supply (eg redundancies), or under-supply (eg external recruitment without attention to internal promotion policies).

    (c) The rate of change in the environment creates uncertainties about the future in many areas. Risk assessment and control, in order to reduce uncertainty to an acceptable level, requires systematic forecasting and planning: management needs to be able to recognise likely opportunities and threats, anticipate consequences and act accordingly - without day-to-day reactive 'fire-fighting'.

2.4   A systematic approach is therefore required.

    (a)   Forecast of manpower *requirements*, by grades and skills, to meet the long- and short-term needs of the organisation (the manpower strategy). The forecast will be based on the objectives of the organisation (and any likely changes), present (and anticipated future) manpower utilisation - productivity etc - and any external factors which will influence demand for labour (technology, market expansion or recession, employee demands for longer holidays etc).

    (b)   Forecast of the available *supply* of labour to meet these needs, taking into account labour turnover, the potential capacity of the existing labour force, and the 'pool' of labour in the environment.

    (c)   Acquire manpower (where necessary) and controls its 'flow' through the organisation (through conditions of employment, pay, job enrichment, career development, employee relations, termination of employment etc).

    (d)   Develop required skills and abilities within the organisation, to enhance the workforce's capacity.

2.5   The general aim of corporate personnel planning is to reduce the risk of either surplus or shortage of particular kinds of manpower, because any imbalance between personnel and other resources or corporate needs is likely to involve waste.

2.6   The *demand* for labour must be forecast by considering the following.

    (a)   The *objectives* of the organisation, and the long and short-term plans in operation to achieve those objectives. Where plans are changed, the effect of the changes must be estimated: proposed expansion or contraction of the organisation's activities, diversification etc will obviously affect the demand for labour or particular skills and may be estimated by market research, competitive analysis, trends in technological advances etc.

    (b)   *Personnel utilisation* - how much labour will be required, given the expected productivity or work rate of different types of employee and the expected volume of business activity. Note that productivity will depend on capital expenditure, technology, work organisation, employee motivation and skills, negotiated productivity deals and a number of other factors.

    (c)   *Services provided*. Some categories of people may be better suited to banking jobs than others. Service industries depend on the right people being employed. A bias in favour of young employees, might be a simple prejudice on behalf of recruiters, rather than a realistic match of possible employees with the jobs available.

    (d)   The *cost* of labour - including overtime, training costs etc - and therefore what financial constraints there are on the organisation's manpower levels.

    (e)   *Environmental* factors and trends in technology and markets that will require organisational change.

2.7   The *supply* of labour will be forecast by considering the following

(a) Wastage (turnover through resignations, retirement etc), promotion, absentee and productivity levels etc. This will require information on:

    (i) age structure of staff (forthcoming retirement or family start-up);
    (ii) labour turnover for a comparable period;
    (iii) promotion potential and ambitions of staff.

(b) The production potential of the existing work force, and its structure (age distribution, grades, location, sex, skills, hours of work and rates of pay).

(c) The potential supply of new labour with the relevant skills from the 'environment' - ie the labour market.

2.8   Demand and supply must be compared in a review we could call a *manpower position survey*. Forecast discrepancies in the numbers required/available, their grade, skills or location can be removed through the application of an integrated manpower strategy.

Closing the manpower gap between demand and supply

2.9   Shortages or surpluses of labour which emerge in the process of formulating the position survey may be dealt with in various ways.

(a) A *deficiency* may be met through:

    (i) internal transfers and promotions, training and development etc;

    (ii) external recruitment;

    (iii) reducing labour turnover, by reviewing possible causes, including pay and conditions;

    (iv) productivity bargaining.

(b) A *surplus* may be met by:

    (i) running down manning levels by natural wastage (or 'accelerated wastage' - encouraging labour turnover by reducing job satisfaction, pay or other incentives to stay);

    (ii) restricting recruitment;

    (iii) redundancies - as a last resort, and with careful planning.

2.10   Manpower strategy thus requires the integration of *policies* for:

    (a) pay and conditions of employment;
    (b) promotion;
    (c) recruitment;
    (d) training;
    (e) industrial relations.

Tactical plans can then be made, within this integrated framework, for pay and productivity bargaining; management and career development; organisation and job specifications, recruitment and redundancies etc.

2.11 Once a personnel plan has been established, regular control reports should be produced.

(a) Actual numbers recruited, leaving and being promoted should be compared with planned numbers. If actual levels seem too high, action can be taken by stopping recruitment temporarily. If levels seem too low, recruitment, promotions or retaining activity should be stepped up.

(b) Actual pay, conditions of employment and training should be compared with assumptions in the manpower plan. Do divergences explain any excessive staff turnover?

(c) Periodically the manpower plan itself should be reviewed and brought up to date.

The personnel plan

The personnel plan is prepared on the basis of the analysis of manpower requirements, and the implications for productivity and costs. The plan may consist of various elements, according to the circumstances.

(a) *The recruitment plan:* numbers and types of people, and when required; the recruitment programme.

(b) *The training plan:* numbers of trainees required and/or existing staff needing training; training programme.

(c) The redevelopment plan: programmes for transferring, retraining employees.

(d) The productivity plan: programmes for improving productivity, or reducing manpower costs; setting productivity targets.

(e) The redundancy plan: where and when redundancies are to occur; policies for selection and declaration of redundancies; redevelopment, retraining or relocation of redundant employees; policy on redundancy payments, union consultation etc.

(f) *The retention plan:* actions to reduce avoidable labour wastage.

The plan should include budgets, targets and standards. It should allocate responsibilities for implementation and control (reporting, monitoring achievement against plan).

How 'scientific' is personnel planning?

2.12 Personnel planning is regarded as a scientific, statistical exercise, but it is important to remember that:

(a) statistics are not the only element of the planning process, and are subject to interpretation and managerial judgements (about future growth, potential innovation etc) that are largely qualitative and even highly speculative;

(b) *trends in statistics are the product of social processes*, which are *not* readily quantifiable or predictable: staff leave for various social reasons in (unpredictable) individual cases, to get married, relocate etc. The growth of the temporary and freelance workforce is a social trend, as are the buying patterns which dictate demand for goods and services.

2.13 Forecasting is not an exact science. Few exponents of even the most sophisticated techniques would claim that they are wholly accurate, although:

(a) the element of guesswork has been substantially reduced by the use of computer and other models to test various assumptions, and to indicate trends;

(b) the general principles can still be applied to indicate problems, and stimulate control action.

The uncertainty of the future is the main problem for personnel planning of any long-range nature. This is not to say that the exercise is in itself futile (indeed it will be even *more* necessary, in order to assess and control the *risk* of manpower resourcing problems in the future) but a measure of flexibility should be built into the plan, so that it can be adapted to suit likely or even unforeseen contingencies. Above all, it should not be seen and communicated as an inflexible plan, as if it were based on certainty.

2.14 *Statistical methods* are varied in their approach and degree of sophistication. Computerisation has greatly enhanced the speed, ease and accuracy with which they can be applied. Simple extrapolation, regression analysis, sensitivity analysis etc can be used to create a more accurate model of the future than simple subjective estimates. Even so, there are a number of assumptions involved. Moreover, the results are limited in value: they are quantitative - eg numbers of staff required - where *qualitative* information may be required as well: the effects of change, re-staffing, or management style on the culture of the organisation and individual/group behaviour etc.

2.15 *Work study methods* aim to set standards of man-hours per unit of output in order to achieve maximum productivity. Where end-products are measurable, work-study techniques can offer a reasonably accurate forecast of manpower requirements, for direct workers at least. In banking work, however, end products and 'output' may not be easily subject to standard-setting: the number of telephone calls, customer interviews, customers served etc is likely to fluctuate widely with the flow of business and the nature of particular transactions.

2.16 *Managerial estimates* form the simplest and cheapest method of assessment: as such, they may be the most appropriate - and are the most common - method for small organisations. At the best of times, however, this method has the disadvantage of a high degree of subjectivity, and although this can, to an extent, be controlled (eg by requiring managers to support their estimates with reasons and to reconcile their estimates with those of senior management), it is a source of potential risk.

Manpower planning in today's banking environment

2.17 There are, as we indicate above, problems in manpower planning - especially where there are long planning horizons for manpower requirements (eg with long training periods required for specialist employees) or where the market for the organisation's products/services is volatile.

2.18 Particular features of today's banking environment, however, that affect the process include the following.

Technology

2.19 The availability of microchip technology has in some ways made manpower planning easier, through the provision of more and better information. The speed and accuracy of data gathering and processing and the availability of a range of formats and facilities (eg spreadsheets and 'models') have taken much sheer labour out of forecasting and risk assessment, and facilitated more penetrating analysis of current situations and future trends.

2.20 On the other hand, the impact of technological innovation on markets (and demand for products/services and therefore demand for labour) is not easily identified in advance, and can render long-term manpower plans swiftly obsolete. The sudden expansion of technology in banking has reduced demand not only for much administrative, paper-handling labour, but more advanced decision-making roles as well: risk assessment for lending, and analysis of investment prospects, are carried out using computerised models; many of the over-the-counter services in the bank are offered by Automated Teller Machines without human intervention etc. Some banks have had to approach this problem with staff lay-offs, while others carry out a policy of 'natural wastage', relying to an extent on the reduced discretion and interest in the newly-automated jobs to accelerate the rate of employee wastage. Many organisations try to reduce 'management layers' to enhance flexibility.

The demographic downturn

2.21 The labour market is getting increasingly difficult, particularly for the recruitment and retention of young workers, and those in skilled occupations. Falling birthrates mean that although the labour force will still be growing in the coming decade, it will not be growing fast enough to meet demand for labour. Growth in demand is expected to be concentrated among the higher skilled occupations - but the main source of supply to such occupations (ie graduates) is constrained by the demographic factors and by educational policy. In addition, the average age of the workforce will rise and employers such as banks who rely particularly on young people, eg school leavers, in certain jobs or entry grades will have to rethink their manpower plans.

2.22 Because population growth is not 'feeding' the workforce to the same extent, *readiness* of individuals to work will be the key to holding off labour and specific skill shortages: employers will need to attract more women and more mature people into the workforce - overcoming prejudice and tradition along the way. This demands a radical cultural change in 'traditional' banking sectors, and also has implications for the overall age structure of the bank, and for the rewards and benefits required if the banks are to compete for the skilled individuals they require.

2.23 Shortage of supply not only forces employers to rethink their recruitment and retention strategies from the outset, but creates a tendency to greater career mobility, which complicates the manpower planners' assumptions about wastage rates. This is likely to be a particularly acute problem for banks, which are already having to adjust to greater mobility in their workforce arising from the increasing employment of specialists (eg in information technology or taxation) rather than career bankers.

Economic conditions

2.24 These tend to be unpredictable at the best of times, but the personnel planners' task will be complicated in coming years by factors such as the increased amount and variety of markets - and competition - following the unification of the European market (which will also effect the size, composition and mobility of the labour force); the economic unification of Germany; the opening of markets in Eastern Europe etc. Fluctuating interest rates, a slump in the housing market, and the economic recession and increased competitive pressures in the early 1990s have all led to cost-reduction programmes in many banks, including branch closure and staff reduction.

Competition

2.25 The re-orientation of banks in the face of *competition* has created demand for a new set of skills, primarily in marketing, selling and customer service, as well as technology operation and management, and specialist areas of financial service provision. For instance, in *Banking World* December 1990 John Berry of Abbey National revealed that 'all job structures and descriptions within our branches (have been reorganised) so that each function justified itself in relation to the customer - not the paperwork.' Planning for an organisation's increased need for 'personal financial advisors' is obviously a different matter to planning for the recruitment and retention of old-style banking generalists.

Cost cutting

2.26 Banks and building societies still employ almost 500,000 people. The 1980s saw a major increase. Numbers have fallen as a result of:

(a) mergers;
(b) productivity pressures leading cuts in branches.

2.27 The fall in numbers has largely been met by 'natural wastage' (ie not replacing employees who leave or retire).

2.28 Another important trend has been an increase in part-timers, now 20% of building society staff (*Banking World*, June 1994). This makes the increased marketing emphasis within banks, including longer operating hours, easier to sustain.

2.29 In common with many areas of the economy, banks will rely more often on part time staff.

3. MANAGEMENT SUCCESSION AND PROMOTION

3.1 Promotion and succession policies are a vital part of the manpower plan, because they are a form of risk management associated with the internal supply of labour. The planned development of staff (not just skills training, but experience and growth in responsibility) is essential to ensure the *continuity* of performance in the organisation. This is particularly so for *management* planning. The departure of a senior manager with no planned or 'groomed' successor could leave a gap in the organisation structure: the lead time for training and developing a suitable replacement may be very long.

3.2 Promotion is not only useful from the firm's point of view - ie in establishing a management succession, filling more senior positions with proven, experienced and loyal employees. It is also one of the main forms of reward the organisation can offer to its employees, especially where, in the pursuit of 'equity', employees are paid a rate for the job rather than for performance: pay ceases to be a prime incentive. In order to be a motivator, promotion must be seen to be available, and fair. It can also cause political and structural problems in the organisation if it is not carefully planned.

3.3 A coherent policy for promotion is needed. This may vary to include provisions such as the following.

(a) All promotions, as far as possible, and all things being equal, are to be made from within the firm; this is particularly important with reference to senior positions if junior ranks are not to be discouraged and de-motivated. Although the organisation will from time to time require 'new blood' if it is not to stagnate, it will be an encouragement to staff to see that promotion is open to them, and that the best jobs do not always go to outsiders.

(b) Merit and ability (systematically appraised) should be the principal basis of promotion, rather than seniority (ie years of service). Loyalty and experience will obviously be considered but should not be the sole criterion. Younger staff may grow impatient if they feel that are simply waiting to grow old before their prospects improve. Promotion on ability is more likely to have a motivating effect. Management will have to demonstrate to staff and unions, however, that their system of appraisal and merit rating is fair and fairly applied if the bases for promotion are to be trusted and accepted.

(c) Vacancies should be advertised and open to all employees.

(d) There should be full opportunities for all employees to be promoted to highest grades.

(e) Personnel and appraisal records should be kept and up-dated regularly.

(f) Training should be offered to encourage and develop employees of ability and ambition in advance of promotion.

(g) Scales of pay, areas of responsibility, duties and privileges of each post etc should be clearly communicated so that employees know what promotion means - ie. what they are being promoted *to*.

3.4 The decision of whether to promote from within or fill a position from outside will hinge on many factors. If there is simply no-one available on the current staff with the expertise or ability required (eg if the bank is venturing into new areas of activity, or changing its methods by computerisation etc), the recruitment manager will obviously have to seek qualified people outside. If there is time, a person of particular potential in the organisation could be trained in the necessary skills, but that will require an analysis of the costs as compared to the possible (and probably less quantifiable) benefits of promoting an insider.

3.5 Where the organisation has the choice, it should consider the following points.

(a) Management will 'know' the promotee: there will be detailed appraisal information available from employee records. The outside recruit will to a greater extent be an 'unknown quantity' - and the organisation will be taking a greater risk of unacceptable personality or performance emerging later.

(b) A promotee has already worked within the organisation and will be familiar with its:

    (i)   culture, or philosophy; informal rules and norms as well as stated policy etc;

    (ii)   politics; power-structures and relationships;

    (iii) systems and procedures;

    (iv) objectives;

    (v)   other personnel (who will likewise be familiar with him).

(c) Promotion of insiders is visible proof of the organisation's willingness to develop people's careers. This may well have an encouraging and motivating effect. Outsiders may well invite resentment. Banks have traditionally 'home grown' their branch managers through a well-established career structure, perhaps starting at school-leaver level, and rising to accountant, assistant manager, small branch manager, large branch manager etc.

(d) On the other hand, an organisation must retain its ability to adapt, grow and change, and this may well require 'new blood' - ie wider views, fresh ideas etc. Insiders may be too socialised into the prevailing culture to see faults or be willing to 'upset the applecart' where necessary. In the banking environment, the traditional career ladder has been somewhat disrupted by the need to employ specialists to cope with the diversification of bank activities: there are more 'entry points' at which people are recruited into the bank, higher up the structure than previously.

3.6   A comprehensive *promotion programme,* as part of the overall manpower plan (ie for getting the right people into jobs at the right time) will include:

(a) establishment of the relative significance of jobs, by analysis, description and classification, so that the line and consequence of promotion are made clear;

(b) establishment of methods of assessment of staff and their potential for fulfilling the requirements of more senior positions;

(c) planning in advance for training where necessary to enhance potential and develop specific skills;

(d) policy with regard to internal promotion or external recruitment and training.

4.   LABOUR TURNOVER

4.1   There are different ways of measuring labour turnover. Most simply, 'actual gross numbers' of people leaving may provide a basis for identifying recruitment numbers - but does not say anything about whether or not these people *need* replacing. To measure labour turnover in a more systematic and useful way, an index may be used, allowing managers to make comparisons between, for example, different organisations in the same industry, or different department in the same organisation: the *significance* of the wastage figures then emerges. Here are some examples.

(a) Crude labour turnover rate

Here we express turnover as a percentage of the number of people employed.

$$\frac{\text{Number of leavers}}{\text{Average number of people employed}} \times 100 = \% \text{ turnover}$$

This is normally quoted as an annual rate and may be used to measure turnover per organisation, department or group of employees. The disadvantage of this index is that it does not indicate the length of service of leavers, which makes it impossible to identify long term employees and therefore the size of the *stable* workforce.

(b) Labour stability

Here we try to eliminate short-term employees from our analysis, thus obtaining a better picture of the significant movements in the workforce.

$$\frac{\text{Number of employees with one or more years service}}{\text{Number of employees employed at the beginning of the year}} \times 100\% = \% \text{ stability}$$

Advantages and disadvantages of labour turnover

4.2   It would be wrong to think of labour turnover as purely disadvantageous to every organisation. Here are some potential advantages.

(a) Opportunities to inject 'new blood' into the organisation, ie new people bringing new ideas and outlooks, experience in different situations etc (absence of labour turnover would simply create an increasingly aged workforce).

(b) The creation of opportunities for promotion and succession. If there were no labour turnover, junior staff and management would face a long career without development, waiting for someone higher up the ladder to retire, with no incentives or encouragement to ambition.

(c) The ability to cope with labour surpluses, in some grades of job, without having to make redundancies. Natural wastage can save industrial relations problems in this way.

4.3   However, disadvantages of labour turnover include the following.

(a) It breaks the continuity of operations, culture and career development. It is generally recognised by employers that continuity offers stability and predictability, which is beneficial to efficiency. When people leave, there is bound to be a hiatus while a replacement is found and - through induction, training, experience etc - brought 'on line' to the same level of accustomed expertise of the previous job-holder.

(b) It may be perceived by other employees as a symptom of job-dissatisfaction, causing the problem to escalate. High labour turnover can foster a culture low in morale and loyalty.

(c) The costs of turnover can be high: the cost of recruiting, selecting and training replacements; loss of output or efficiency during this process; possible wastage, spoilage, etc because of inexperience in new staff.

(d) High turnover can result in poor service, if staff are uncommitted to staying.

4.4 It is common to hear that turnover is bad when it is 'high' – but this cannot be assessed in isolation. What is an acceptable rate of turnover and what is excessive? There is no fixed percentage rate of turnover which is the borderline between acceptable and unacceptable. Labour turnover rates will be a signal that something is possibly wrong when:

(a) they are higher than the turnover rates in another similar department of the organisation. (eg if the labour turnover rate is higher at branch A than at branches B, C and D in the same area, something might be wrong at branch A);

(b) they are higher than they were in previous years or months (ie the situation might be deteriorating);

(c) the costs of labour turnover are estimated and are considered too high – although they will be relative to the costs of *preventing* high turnover by offering employees rewards, facilities and services that will keep them in the organisation.

Otherwise, the organisation may 'live with' high rates because they are the norm for a particular industry or job, because the organisation culture accepts constant turnover, or because the cost of keeping employees is greater than the cost of replacing them.

Causes and control of labour turnover

4.5 A systematic investigation into the causes of undesirable turnover will have to be made, using a variety of techniques.

(a) Information is given in *exit interviews* with leaving staff, which should be the first step after an employee announces his intention to leave. It must be recognised, however, that the reasons given for leaving may not be complete, true, or those that would be most useful to the organisation. The interviewer should be trained in interview techniques, and should be perceived to be 'safe' to talk to and objective in his appraisal of the situation (ie. rather than being the supervisor against whom the resigning employee has a complaint, the manager who is going to write a reference etc).

(b) Information can be gleaned from interviews with leavers, in their homes, shortly after they have gone. This is an occasionally-used practice, intended to encourage greater objectivity and frankness, but one which requires tact and diplomacy if it is not to be resented by the subject.

(c) Attitude surveys, to gauge the general climate of the organisation, and the response of the workforce as a whole to working conditions, management style etc. Such surveys are notoriously unreliable, however.

(d) Information gathered on the number of (interrelated) variables which can be *assumed* to correlate with labour turnover. Some of these are listed below.

4.6 Labour turnover might be influenced by any of the following factors.

(a) The economic climate and the state of the jobs market. When unemployment is high and jobs are hard to find, labour turnover will be much lower.

(b) The age structure of the work force. An ageing workforce will have many people approaching retirement. However, it has been found in most companies that labour turnover is highest amongst:

(i)   young people, especially unmarried people with no family responsibilities;

(ii) people who have been in the employment of the company for only a short time.

(c) The organisation 'climate' or 'culture', and the style of leadership. An organisation might be formal and bureaucratic, where employees are expected to work according to prescribed rules and procedures. Other organisations are more 'organic' and flexible, and allow more scope for individual expression and 'creativity'. Individuals will prefer - and stay with - one system or the other.

(d) Pay and conditions of employment. If these are not good enough, people will leave to find better terms elsewhere.

(e) Physical working conditions. If working conditions are uncomfortable, unclean, unsafe, or noisy etc, people will be more inclined to leave.

(f) Career prospects and training. If the chances of reaching a senior position before a certain age are low, an ambitious employee is likely to consider leaving to find a job where promotion is likely to come more quickly. The same may be true where an employee wants training for a qualification or skill development, and opportunities are limited in his current job.

4.7 Some reasons for leaving will be genuine and largely unavoidable, or unforeseeable, eg:

(a) illness or accident, although transfer to lighter duties, excusing the employee from shiftwork etc might be possible;

(b) a move from the locality for domestic reasons, transport or housing difficulties;

(c) marriage or pregnancy. Many women still give up working when their family situation changes;

(d) retirement;

(e) career change.

4.8 However, where factors such as those discussed in paragraph 4.6 above are identified as sources of employee dissatisfaction and departure, those problems can be addressed, eg by offering competitive pay and conditions, training and development opportunities etc. In addition, recruitment and selection systems will be revised to ensure that individuals are compatible with the culture and leadership of the organisation, and with the demands of their jobs (since some people will be able to handle monotony, pressure, responsibility or lack of it etc better than others).

5. EMPLOYEE RELATIONS IN BANKING

5.1 'Employee relations' represents the interface between the business organisation and another organisation: in this case, the employees as an organised group - a trade union or staff association - whose objectives may not be in harmony with those of the employing organisation.

5.2 Employers and employees, through their representatives, come to agreements on pay and conditions of employment. The process of negotiation is often referred to as *collective bargaining*, which may take place at national (industry-wide) level, company level, or local (branch or plant) level, which is called 'domestic bargaining'.

5.3 Negotiations tend to cover not only pay and conditions of employment such as holidays, hours of work, etc but also promotion, training, discipline, manning agreements, job demarcation etc. The subject matter of collective bargaining might be clearly defined in some companies or industries; but in others unions might press to have some say in an increasing number of areas that used to be managerial preserves (eg work procedures).

5.4 Collective bargaining has also been extended to more groups of employees, particularly 'white collar' workers, as:

(a) white-collar workers saw the pay differentials between their salaries and the wages of blue-collar (manual) workers being eroded. They attributed much of this erosion to the union organisation of manual workers;

(b) membership of a trade union has become more socially acceptable to white-collar staff, especially since there has been a shift from manual work to desk or 'knowledge' work;

(c) new technology and economic recession are seen as a threat to jobs, and collective power is required to defend job security;

(d) organisational change has accelerated, and requires discussion and negotiation with staff: this would be impossible on an individual basis.

However, collective bargaining has perhaps retreated in recent years.

5.5 The 'paternalistic' view of organisations is that the interests of the organisation as a whole and the interests of its employees are really one and the same. What is good for the organisation will be good for its employees, so there should be a common aim for management and unions, and everyone in the organisation should pull together as a team.

5.6 There are many people who still hold this view. However, an alternative view is that employers and employees have completely different interests and objectives: the organisation is seen as a pluralistic society consisting of many related but separate interest groups, and the task of management is to find an equilibrium in which both the organisation and its employees get the best they can from each other under the circumstances.

Employee involvement

5.7 Section I of the Employment Act 1982 provides for a (still largely voluntary) increase in worker involvement. Any company employing more than 250 persons must include in its directors' report a statement describing 'the action that has been taken during the financial year to introduce, maintain or develop arrangements aimed at:

(a) providing employees systematically with information on matters of concern to them as employees;

(b)   consulting employees or their representatives on a regular basis, so that the views of employees can be taken into account in making decisions which are likely to affect their interests;

(c)   encouraging the involvement of employees in the company's performance through an employees' share scheme or by some other means;

(d)   achieving a common awareness on the part of all employees of the financial and economic factors affecting the performance of the company'.

5.8   This is not a requirement to *perform* any of the above - only to *report* whether or not the company has done so! Nevertheless, auditors, general management and personnel management will have to confer over this, and the awareness of the extent of involvement may at least increase.

5.9   There are different degrees and methods of involvement, reflecting the extent to which organisations wish to involve employees in decision-making, for the following reasons.

(a)   The perceived need to obtain a higher level of identification with organisational goals - ie '*commitment*'. Communication to employees, a consultative management style, the use of teams etc may be used at all levels.

(b)   *Legislation.* Most of the legislative proposals on participation have been put forward by the EC, including the draft Fifth Directive, which (in its revised form) requires limited companies to adopt:

(i)   collective bargaining on decisions; or

(ii)   a two-tier board structure, with elected worker representatives on the senior or 'supervisory' board to which the management or executive board is responsible; or

(iii) a unitary board structure with worker representatives as non-executive directors (worker-directors); or

(iv)   a sub-board level company council, with worker representation (on the model of a German 'works council', which is an employee-only body with legal rights to information, consultation and co-determination on personnel issues).

Some of these will be introduced in continental Europe. The UK's opt out of the Social Chapter of the Maastricht Treaty makes these developments unlikely in the UK in the short term.

(c)   *Trade union pressure.* According to the TUC (*Industrial Democracy* 1977), 'industrial democracy' means 'the achievement by workpeople collectively of a greater control over their work situation'. The main progress has been towards extending collective bargaining into areas traditionally considered as management concerns - eg manning levels, training etc.

Industrial relations in banking

5.10 There are major unions in UK banking.

(a) The Banking, Insurance and Finance Union (which used to be NUBE, the National Union of Bank Employees). The original union was formed after the First World War, and (as the change of name suggests) was exclusively involved in banking, until it recognised the potential membership in the finance sector more generally (in 1979). It has both widened and increased its membership to include building society and insurance company employees. This may have contributed to the sense of convergence between financial services providers, with claims for comparability (eg over hours of work, Saturday opening).

(b) The Clearing Bank Union, formed in 1980 from the staff associations of three major clearing banks - but since dissolved and replaced by staff unions, eg at Barclays, Natwest.

(c) Other more 'marginal' unions, such as the Management Scientific and Finance Union (MSF), which has limited bargaining rights, and the Association of Scientific Technical and Managerial Staffs (ASTMS).

The social and legal responsibilities of organisations

5.11 Quite apart from the formal machinery of industrial relations, there are social and legal aspects to the preservation of constructive relationships between the state, the employee and the employer. The law, and 'best practice' (not necessarily the same thing) with regard to employment and dismissal, equal opportunities and discrimination in the work place, employment conditions etc, are undoubtedly relevant to the process and 'climate' of human resource management. However, we will be discussing them later, in the particular contexts in which they are most relevant.

Exercise

Review your own branch over the period you have been working there and identify the following changes in personnel requirements.

(a) The number of people the branch needs in order to function. Has it grown or fallen?

(b) The change in the type of jobs people do in the branch. Is there a higher proportion of people in selling jobs than there was before? Is there a lower proportion of people in 'back office' processing than before?

(c) Has your bank communicated its personnel strategy to you recently?

---

6. CHAPTER ROUNDUP

6.1 'We've moved through periods when money has been in short supply and when technology has been in short supply. Now it's the people who are in short supply. So personnel directors are better placed than ever before to make a real difference - a bottom-line difference. The scarce resource, which is the people resource, is the one that makes the impact at the margin, that makes one firm competitive over another.'

Barry Curnow, IPM President

6.2

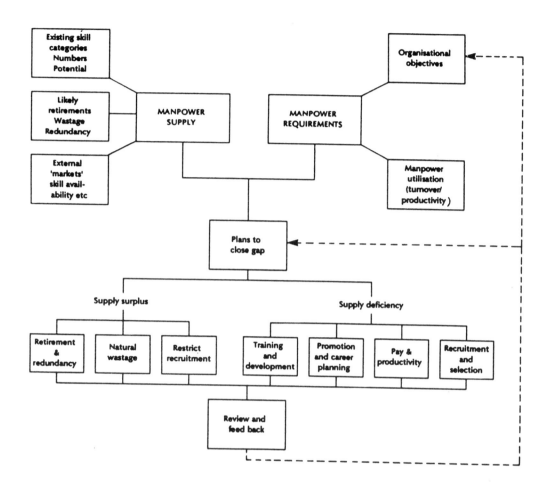

6.3 Employee relations is not only an element in the bank's strategy for recruiting and retaining manpower. It also represents the interface between the bank and other organisations in its environment: including those, such as trade unions and staff associations, of which its own employees are members. Control of the potential conflict of interests arising from this situation, and if possible harnessing the positive contributions available in employee involvement, are key tasks of human resource management.

TEST YOUR KNOWLEDGE

The numbers in brackets refer to paragraphs of this chapter

1   Why might 'human resource management' be different from the traditional role of the personnel function? (1.5, 1.6)

2   Why is it not as easy for organisations to close the gap between labour demand and supply as it might appear in theory? Giving banking examples of complicating factors. (2.3, 2.18)

3   Outline a systematic approach to manpower planning. (2.4)

4   List three types of method used in manpower forecasting. Indicate to what degree each is a 'scientific' method. (2.13 to 2.16)

5   Outline the effects of the 'demographic downturn' on bank manpower supply and demand. (2.18)

6   List four reasons why an organisation might wish to promote an existing employee rather than recruit someone from outside to fill the post. What might make this a less desirable option, from a bank's point of view? (3.5)

7   When is labour turnover to be regarded as a bad thing? (4.4)

8   List the factors that might contribute to your leaving the bank where you work. What (if anything) could or should the bank do to keep you? (4.6 for ideas, but think about *your* situation)

9   Why might an organisation involve its employees in decision-making? What forms of involvement might it use? List six of them in order of the amount of power given to employees. (5.9)

Now try question 25 at the end of the text

APPENDIX: THE CODE OF BANKING PRACTICE (SECOND EDITION)

Preface

This Code sets out the standards of good banking practice to be observed by banks, building societies and card issuers in their relations with personal customers in the United Kingdom. Individual customers will find the Code helpful in understanding how every bank, building society or card issuer subscribing to the Code is expected to behave towards them.

It is a voluntary Code which allows competition and market forces to operate to encourage higher standards for the benefit of customers.

The Code first came into effect on 16 March 1992 and it was stated then that it would be reviewed from time to time. This second edition is issued in the light of the first review. It will be effective from 28 March 1994, except for paragraph 5.3.

All institutions subscribing to the second edition of the Code will ensure that their staff are aware of it. They have also agreed to make copies of the Code available or to inform customers about how to obtain them.

This Code will be reviewed from time to time and another revision will be completed by March 1997.

Code of banking practice

Introduction

1.1 This second edition of the Code has been prepared by the British Bankers' Association (BBA), The Building Societies Association (BSA), and the Association for Payment Clearing Services (APACS) in the light of a review carried out by an independent committee following the receipt of submissions from Government Departments, consumer and other organisations, the Banking and Building Societies Ombudsmen and members of the public.

1.2 The Code is written to promote good banking practice. Specific services may have their own terms and conditions which will comply with the principles contained in the Code.

1.3 The Code is in three parts.

Part A - Governing principles.

Part B - Customers, their banks and building societies - is addressed to banks and building societies who adopt the Code and offer personal customers ('customers' for short throughout the Code) banking services such as current accounts, deposit and other savings accounts, overdrafts and loans, and various services delivered by the use of plastic cards.

Part C - Customers and their cards - is addressed to banks, building societies and others who adopt the Code and provide financial services by means of plastic cards. All such providers are called card users in the Code.

APPENDIX: THE CODE OF BANKING PRACTICE (SECOND EDITION)

Part A - Governing principles

2.1 The governing principles of the Code are:

  (a) to set out the standards of good banking practice which banks, building societies and card issuers will follow in their dealings with their customers;

  (b) that banks, building societies and card issuers will act fairly and reasonably in all their dealings with their customers;

  (c) that banks, building societies and card issuers will help customers to understand how their accounts operate and will seek to give them a good understanding of banking services;

  (d) to maintain confidence in the security and integrity of banking and card payment systems. Banks, building societies and card issuers must recognise that their systems and technology need to be reliable to protect their customers and themselves.

2.2 Banks, building societies and card issuers will comply with all relevant legislation, judicial decisions and codes of conduct or similar documents which are observed by members of the BBA, BSA and APACS.

2.3 The Code requires banks, building societies and card issuers to provide certain information to customers. This will usually be at the time when an account is opened. Information will also be available to customers from branches, if any, of the bank, building society or card issuer. Banks, building societies and card issuers will provide additional information and guidance about specific services at any time on request.

Part B - Customers, their banks and building societies

Opening an account

3.1 Banks and building societies are required by law to satisfy themselves about the identity of a person seeking to open an account to assist in protecting their customers, members of the public and themselves against fraud and other misuse of the banking system.

3.2 Banks and building societies will provide to prospective customers details of the identification needed.

Terms and conditions

4.1 Written terms and conditions of a banking service will be expressed in plain language and will provide a fair and balanced description of the relationship between the customer and bank or building society.

4.2 Banks and building societies will tell customers how any variation of the terms and conditions will be notified. Banks and building societies will give customers reasonable notice before any variation takes effect.

4.3 Banks and building societies should issue to their customers, if there are sufficient changes in a 12 month period to warrant it, a single document to provide a consolidation of the variations made to their terms and conditions over that period.

4.4 Banks and building societies will provide new customers with a written summary or explanation of the key features of the more common services that they provide. This will include an explanation, when accounts are held in the names of more than one customer, of the rights and responsibilities of each customer.

4.5 Banks and building societies will not close customers' accounts without first giving reasonable notice.

4.6 To help customers manage their accounts and check entries, banks and building societies will provide them with regular statements of account. Except where this would be inappropriate to the nature of the account (eg where passbooks are issued) this should be at no less than 12 monthly intervals but customers will be encouraged to request statements at shorter intervals.

Charges and debit interest (payable by customers)

5.1 Banks and building societies will provide customers with details of the basis of charges, if any, payable in connection with the operation of their accounts. These will be in the form of published tariffs covering basic account services which will

- be given or sent to customers:
  (a) when accounts are opened;
  (b) at any time on request;
- and be available in branches.

Details of any changes will also be given or sent to customers and be available in branches before the changes are implemented.

5.2 Charges for services outside the tariff will be advised on request or at the time the service is offered.

5.3 Banks and building societies will introduce systems to come into effect by 31 December 1996 to ensure that they will give no less than 14 days' notice of the amount to be deducted from their customers' current and savings accounts in respect of interest and charges for account activity that have accumulated during the charging period.

Banks and building societies which have not introduced such systems will disregard the charges to be applied to customers' accounts for any charging period if those were incurred solely as a result of the application of charges for the previous charging period.

5.4 Banks and building societies will tell customers the interest rates applicable to their accounts, the basis on which interest is calculated and when it will be charged to their accounts. These will include the rates applicable when accounts are overdrawn without prior agreement or exceed the agreed borrowing limit. Banks and building societies will explain also the basis on which they may vary interest rates.

5.5 When banks and building societies change interest rates with immediate effect they will effectively publicise those changes, for example by notices in their branches, if any, or in the press, or on statements.

Credit interest (payable to customers)

6.1 Banks and building societies will make information about the rates on interest bearing accounts which they offer (whether or not these are open to new customers) freely available and accessible to customers by one or more effective means, for example:

(a) notices and/or leaflets in branches;
(b) press advertisements;
(c) personal notice;
(d) a branch/central telephone service.

6.2 Banks and building societies will tell customers the interest rates applicable to their accounts, the basis on which interest is calculated and when it will be paid to their accounts. Banks and building societies will explain also the basis on which they may vary interest rates.

6.3 When banks and building societies change interest rates with immediate effect they will effectively publicise those changes, for example by notices in their branches, if any, or in the press, or on statements.

Handling customers' complaints

7.1 Each bank and building society will have its own internal procedures for handling customers' complaints fairly and expeditiously.

7.2 Banks and building societies will inform their customers that they have a complaints procedure. Customers who wish to make a complaint will be told how to do so and what further steps are available if they believe that the complaint has not been dealt with satisfactorily either at branch or more senior level within the bank or building society.

7.3 Banks and building societies will ensure that all their staff who deal directly with customers are made aware of their institution's internal complaints procedure and are able to help customers by giving correct information about it.

7.4 Banks subscribing to the Code will be expected to belong to one or other of the following:

(a) the Banking Ombudsman Scheme;
(b) the Finance and Leasing Association Conciliation and Arbitration Schemes; or
(c) the Consumer Credit Trade Association Arbitration Scheme.

Building societies have to belong to the Building Societies Ombudsman Scheme or another authorised scheme.

Banks and building societies will provide details of the applicable scheme to customers using such methods as leaflets, notices in branches or in appropriate literature, showing their current addresses and telephone numbers.

APPENDIX: THE CODE OF BANKING PRACTICE (SECOND EDITION)

Confidentiality of customer information

8.1 Banks and building societies will observe a strict duty of confidentiality about their customers' (and former customers') affairs and will not disclose details of customers' accounts or their names and addresses to any third party, including other companies in the same group, other than in the four exceptional cases permitted by the law, namely:

(a) where a bank or building society is legally compelled to do so;
(b) where there is a duty to the public to disclose;
(c) where the interests of a bank or building society require disclosure;
(d) where disclosure is made at the request, or with the consent, of the customer.

8.2 Banks and building societies will not use exception (c) above to justify the disclosure for marketing purposes of details of customers' accounts or their names and addresses to any third party, including other companies within the same group.

8.3 Banks and building societies will give customers at least 28 days' notice if they intend to disclose to Credit Reference Agencies information on undisputed personal debts which are in default and where no satisfactory proposals for payment have been received following formal demand.

Banks and building societies will inform customers that, where they have acquired the legal right to sell mortgaged or charged property, this information may be disclosed to Credit Reference Agencies.

Any other disclosure to Credit Reference Agencies shall be with the customer's consent.

8.4 Banks and building societies will at all times comply with the Data Protection Act when obtaining and processing customers' data.

Banks and building societies will explain to their customers that customers have the right of access, under the Data Protection Act 1984, to their personal records held on computer files.

Status enquiries (bankers' references)

9.1 Banks and building societies will on request:

(a) advise customers whether they provide bankers' references or bankers' opinions in reply to status enquiries made about their customers;

(b) explain how the system of status enquiries (bankers' references) works.

Marketing of services

10.1 Except in response to a customer's specific request, banks and building societies will not pass customers' names and addresses to other companies in the same group for marketing purposes, in the absence of express written consent. Banks and building societies will not make the provision of basic banking services conditional on customers giving such written consent. For this purpose 'basic banking services' include the opening and the maintenance of accounts for money transmission by means of cheques and other debit instruments.

10.2 Banks and building societies will give new customers at the time they open their accounts the opportunity to give instructions that they do not wish to receive marketing material.

10.3 Banks and building societies will remind customers from time to time, and at least once every three years, of their right to give instructions at any time that they do not wish to receive marketing material.

10.4 Banks and building societies will not use direct mail indiscriminately and in particular will exercise restraint and be selective.

(a) where customers are minors; and
(b) when marketing loans and overdrafts.

Marketing and provision of credit

11.1 Banks and building societies in their advertising and promotional material will tell customers and potential customers that all lending will be subject to appraisal of their financial standing by the banks and building societies concerned.

11.2 Banks and building societies will act responsibly and prudently in marketing. All advertising will comply with the British Code of Advertising Practice, the British Code of Sales Promotion Practice, and other relevant Codes of Practice of similar standing.

In particular banks and building societies will ensure that all advertising and promotional literature is fair and reasonable, does not contain misleading information and complies with all relevant legislation.

11.3 In considering whether or not to lend, banks and building societies will take account of information which may include:

(a) prior knowledge of their customers' financial affairs gained from past dealings;
(b) information obtained from Credit Reference Agencies;
(c) information supplied by applicant;
(d) credit-scoring;
(e) age of applicants; and
(f) applicants' ability to repay, with the aim of avoiding over-commitment by an applicant.

11.4 Banks and building societies will give due consideration to cases of hardship. They will encourage customers who are in financial difficulty to let them know as soon as possible and will use their best endeavours to give practical information and, subject to normal commercial judgement, will try to help.

Availability of funds

12.1 Banks and building societies will provide customers with details of how their accounts operate, including information about:

(a) how and when they may stop a cheque or countermand other types of payments;

(b) when funds can be withdrawn after a cheque or other payment has been credited to the account;

(c) out of date cheques.

Foreign exchange services and cross-border payments

13.1 Banks and building societies will provide customers with details of the exchange rate and the commission charges which will apply to foreign exchange transactions or, when this is not possible, the basis on which they will be calculated.

13.2 Banks and building societies will provide customers wishing to effect cross-border payments with details of the services they offer. In doing so, they will provide, as a minimum:

(a) a basic description of the appropriate services available and the manner in which they can be used;

(b) information as to when money sent abroad on customers' instructions will usually reach its destination or, when an exact date cannot be given, the latest date by which the money might be expected to arrive;

(c) the details of any commission or charges payable by customers to their bank or building society including a warning where agents' charges may also be incurred.

Guarantees and other types of third party security

14.1 Banks and building societies will advise private individuals proposing to give them a guarantee or other security for another person's liabilities:

(a) that by giving the guarantee or third party security he or she might become liable instead of or as well as that other person;

(b) whether the guarantee or third party security will be unlimited as to amount or, if this is not the case, what the limit of the liability will be;

(c) that he or she should seek independent legal advice before entering into the guarantee or third party security.

14.2 Guarantees and other third party security documentation will contain a clear and prominent notice to the above effect.

APPENDIX: THE CODE OF BANKING PRACTICE (SECOND EDITION)

Part C – Customers and their cards

Opening an account

15.1 Card issuers are required by law to satisfy themselves about the identity of a person seeking to open an account or to obtain a card to assist in protecting their customers, members of the public and themselves against fraud and other misuse of the banking and card processing systems.

15.2 Card issuers will provide to prospective customers details of the identification needed.

Terms and conditions

16.1 The written terms and conditions of a card service will be expressed in plain language and will provide a fair and balanced description of the relationship between the customer and the card issuer.

16.2 Card issuers will tell customers how any variation of the terms and conditions will be notified. Card issuers will give customers reasonable notice before any variation takes effect.

16.3 Card issuers should issue to their customers, if there are sufficient changes in a 12 month period to warrant it, a single document providing a consolidation of the variations made to their terms and conditions over that period.

16.4 Card issuers will publish changes to their credit card interest rates in their branches or in the press or in the statement of account sent to credit card holders, or by all those methods when such changes are made with immediate effect.

16.5 Card issuers will tell credit card holders how frequently they will receive a demand for payment and the period within which payment should be made.

Issue of cards

17.1 Card issuers will issue cards to customers only when they have been requested in writing or to replace or renew cards that have already been issued.

17.2 Card issuers will tell customers if a card issued by them has more than one function. Card issuers will comply with requests from customers not to issue Personal Identification Numbers (PINs) where customers do not wish to use the functions operated by a PIN.

Security of cards

18.1 Card issuers will issue PINs separately from cards and will advise the PIN only to the customer.

18.2 Card issuers will tell customers of their responsibility to take care of their cards and PINs in order to prevent fraud. Card issuers will emphasise to customers that:

(a) they should not allow anyone else to use their card and PIN;

(b) they should take all reasonable steps to keep the card safe and the PIN secret at all times;

(c) they should never write the PIN on the card or on anything usually kept with it;

(d) they should never write the PIN down without making a reasonable attempt to disguise it;

(e) they should destroy any PIN advice promptly on receipt.

18.3 When customers are provided with an opportunity to select their own PIN, card issuers should encourage them to do so to help them remember the PIN.

Lost cards

19.1 Card issuers will inform customers that they must tell their card issuers as soon as reasonably practicable after they find that:

(a) their card has been lost or stolen;
(b) someone else knows their PIN.

19.2 Card issuers will tell customers, and will remind them at regular intervals on their statement or by other means, of the place and the telephone number where they can give the details of a lost or stolen card at any time of the day or night. Card issuers will arrange for that telephone number to be included in British Telecom Phone Books.

19.3 Card issuers will act on telephone notification but may ask customers also to confirm in writing any details given by telephone.

19.4 Card issuers, on request, will inform customers whether they accept notification of loss or theft of a card from card notification organisations.

19.5 Card issuers on being advised of a loss, theft or possible misuse of a card or that the PIN has become known to someone else will take action to prevent further use of the card.

Liability for loss

20.1 Card issuers will bear the full losses incurred:

(a) in the event of misuse when the card has not been received by the customer;

(b) for all transactions not authorised by the customer after the card issuer has been told that the card has been lost or stolen or that someone else knows or may know the PIN (subject to 20.4 below);

(c) if faults have occurred in the machines, or other systems used, which cause customers to suffer direct loss unless the fault was obvious or advised by a message or notice on display.

20.2 Card issuers' liability will be limited to those amounts wrongly charged to customers' accounts and any interest on those amounts.

20.3 Customers' liability for transactions not authorised by them will be limited to a maximum of £50 in the event of misuse before the card issuer has been notified that a card has been lost or stolen or that someone else knows the PIN (subject to 20.4 below).

20.4 Customers will be held liable for all losses if they have acted fraudulently. They may be held liable for all losses if they have acted with gross negligence. Gross negligence may be construed as including failures to comply with any of the requirements of paragraph 18.2 if such failures have caused those losses.

20.5 In cases of disputed transactions the burden of proving fraud or gross negligence or that a card has been received by a customer will lie with the card issuer. In such cases card issuers will expect customers to co-operate with them in their investigations.

Records

21.1 To help customers manage their accounts and check entries, card issuers will provide customers with a written record on their statement of account of all payments and withdrawals made.

21.2 Card issuers will inform customers that they should tell them as soon as reasonably practicable if they receive a statement of account that includes an item which seems to be wrong.

Handling customers' complaints

22.1 Each card issuer will have its own internal procedures for handling customers' complaints fairly and expeditiously.

22.2 Card issuers will inform their customers that they have a complaints procedure. Customers who wish to make a complaint will be told how to do so and what further steps are available to them if they believe that the complaint has not been dealt with satisfactorily by the card issuer.

22.3 Card issuers will ensure that all their staff who deal directly with customers are made aware of their internal complaints procedures and are able to help customers by giving correct information about them.

22.4 Card issuers subscribing to the Code will be expected to belong to one or other of the following:

(a) the Banking Ombudsman Scheme;
(b) the Building Societies Ombudsman Scheme or another authorised scheme;
(c) the Finance and Leasing Association Conciliation and Arbitration Schemes;
(d) the Consumer Credit Trade Association Arbitration Scheme; or
(e) the Retail Credit Group Mediation and Arbitration Schemes.

Card issuers will provide details of the applicable scheme to customers using such methods as leaflets, notices or in appropriate literature, showing their current addresses and telephone numbers.

ILLUSTRATIVE QUESTIONS

AND

SUGGESTED SOLUTIONS

1 KEEPING TIME

Reg Reynolds was promoted to supervisor of his section in the bank when Makebridge was a small country town. In recent years it has become an overspill town. It has developed around the nucleus of the original town which still forms the centre of the new development. The building in which the branch is housed was large enough to accommodate more staff and it has become the central branch for Makebridge. Staff increased as business boomed and Reg found himself running a very large section.

At first he coped but recently he has been showing increasing signs of strain. Once punctual, he now sometimes arrives late. He often stays late in the evening, takes work home, worries his boss for decisions he should take himself and delays making decisions on matters referred to him by his staff. As a result, work piles up and this makes him more anxious. Staff are demoralised; one or two key people have left and this has increased performance problems.

Required

As the manager of the branch:

(a) identify the main problems;
(b) what action would you take?

2 SCHOOL LEAVERS

John Hoskins is the manager of a branch of a business in which your bank has acquired an interest. As the local bank personnel officer you discover John Hoskins's branch has a very large turnover of staff - significantly higher than colleagues who recruit in the same vicinity.

Closer examination reveals that the bulk of the turnover is among young trainees recruited locally by Mr Hoskins himself. 60% tend to leave in the first month of employment.

Mr Hoskins recruits on the basis of a ten minute interview because he believes you can sum anyone up in that time. He blames the turnover on local schools who fill kids' heads with ideas above their station.

Required

What selection methods would you introduce to John Hoskins to help him to improve his selection? What would you suggest in terms of his attitude to local schools?

3 KNOWLEDGE OF MOTIVATION

How can a knowledge of motivation help managers? Illustrate and explain your answer with examples.

4 MERIT RATING

As part of its policy of improving efficiency, your branch has decided to introduce merit rating for its salaried staff. The standard salary for each grade is evaluated by using a points system specially designed for the organisation by specialist consultants in this field. In order to provide a genuine incentive, the merit awards range from minus 10% to plus 15% of the standard salary. This means that the potential range of salaries for adjoining grades may overlap. The assessment of the merit rating is to be made by an employee's immediate superior, on the basis of how well previously-set targets have been met.

C is a young supervisor who has just been informed of his job 'value' in terms of points, including the number of points allocated for individual factors such as know-how. C is worried because he does not know the maximum points available for each factor, and thus cannot assess whether the evaluation of his job is reasonable.

He has just been to see his superior to discuss the targets on which his merit rating will be decided at the next review. He gets on well with his manager, who simply told him 'I am not concerned with setting you targets. I am very pleased with the way you are doing your job. Just carry on as you are.'

You are required:

(a) to appraise the introduction of this job evaluation and merit rating scheme;
(b) to discuss what effect is it might have on performance.

5 WASTED APPRAISAL

'Despite the many apparent advantages of what should be an intrinsic and critical part of management control, there is much evidence both in the UK and abroad to suggest that many appraisals are largely a waste of time.' (Williams) What are these 'apparent advantages'? Why is appraisal often a 'waste of time', and what could be done to make it a worthwhile exercise?

6 TRAINING NEEDS

How do 'training needs' arise in an organisation? How would you carry out a 'training needs analysis' if required to do so?

7 POP GROUP BANKER

James Dixon has worked in the city centre branch of your bank for just over a year and he has been given study leave for one week to follow a course of business studies at the local technical college. The attendance record submitted by the college to the manager reveals that he has attended only three times out of a possible fourteen. His record is poor in other respects: his time keeping has been poor; his work record has been barely adequate, but not bad enough for him to have been warned; his appearance has left much to be desired; and he has seemed more interested in the pop group for which he plays three times a week than in his banking duties.

Required

What course of action would you recommend? Give reasons for your recommendations and indicate what other possible courses of action you also considered and why.

8 MISTAKEN INTERVIEWS

It has been said that the basic mistake made by most employers is to rely on the interview as the first and crucial stage in the recruitment and selection process. Why is this a 'mistake'? What should employers be doing?

ILLUSTRATIVE QUESTIONS

9 INEFFECTIVE COMMITTEE

You are a member of a committee which is ineffective. What factors would you consider in trying to understand the causes? What do you consider to be the characteristics of good committee work?

10 GROUP DISSATISFACTION

John Frost is having problems in managing his group, the members of which all express a variety of dissatisfactions. Basically, they say that he does not given them any leadership. John himself is very confident and takes many initiatives. He likes to get on with things and cannot understand why others are so slow and reactionary.

One of John's subordinates, Ken Marshall, is in his fifties. He has always worked in the same department, and is very disturbed at John's apparently arbitrary and risky decisions. Ian Prince, on the other hand, is very frustrated. He has a lot of ideas for change but John never has time to listen to them. The result is that Ian feels resentful and frustrated. A third subordinate, Frank Cadell, is frightened of John who is always in a hurry, does not appear to care whether Frank is there or not, never asks how he is getting on, and does not help to overcome his anxieties about whether he is doing his job properly.

Required

How would you advise John to change his behaviour?

11 MANAGEMENT ACTIVITIES

The process of management is often described as comprising planning, organising, directing and controlling. Describe each of these activities, and comment on their inter-relationship.

12 ENCOURAGING DELEGATION

What factors would influence your decision to delegate work to a subordinate? What are the major barriers to delegation?

13 OVERLOADED SUPERVISOR

One of your supervisors is consistently in trouble with his manager because his department always seems to be in a state of confusion. Work appears to be allocated on a haphazard basis; some people are overloaded, others have little to do. He does not produce information when required and he appears to be consistently harassed and preoccupied in trying to solve the latest crisis.

Required

What steps can be taken to help him?

14 LEADING ACCOUNTANT

Derek is a young branch accountant who, after completing his Associateship examinations recently, was transferred to a small old-established local branch.

At his first progress review with his superior, he was very confident and enthusiastic about numerous initiatives which he had already taken or was about to take. Derek expressed disappointment that his staff were so reactionary and unco-operative.

Enquiries by Derek's superior among the staff uncovered general dissatisfaction about Derek's leadership. The younger ones are frightened of him, and feel he has no interest in them. They say he is always in a hurry, and they have no idea of whether their work is up to his requirements or not.

The older ones, who have worked in the department for years, are very worried about his apparently arbitrary and risky decisions. Others are resentful and frustrated that Derek never bothers to listen to their ideas. Derek has been informed of these comments.

You are required to recommend the behaviour which Derek should adopt to improve the situation.

15 EFFECTIVE WORK TEAM

What are the characteristics of an effective work team? Describe briefly one training method by which an effective team can be developed.

16 BANKING STYLES

Although many banks offer similar services, they often adopt contrasting styles in their approach to business operations, organisation, staff and customers.

Required

How do you explain these differences of style? How can a bank change its style? What should it do and what methods should it use?

17 STRAINED WORK RELATIONSHIPS

X is a junior manager in his early forties who joined his bank at the age of sixteen. He sticks to a strict routine, arriving and leaving work punctually. He is married with two children at school. He has always worked in the functional section which he now manages and he is regarded as one of the branch's most experienced employees in his particular field. He is, however, not familiar with the latest developments in data processing and feels that he is being swamped by an excess of useless information. He claims that he is, in any case, aware of the information he needs, but his subordinates worry because they notice that he ignores information which does not agree with his opinions.

D is a young graduate who has recently passed her CIB Associateship. She works in the management information department. She has been promoted quickly to supervisor level, having joined the bank a few years ago straight from university. She is single and lives close to the bank and often works late because she loves computers and is fascinated by their potential. She is expert in computer language and has no time for 'stick-in-the-muds' who don't see the advantage of the information revolution. She frequently and fluently tells anyone willing to listen that the bank is old-fashioned and needs to be dragged into the 20th century. X hears this, disapproves but does not comment, and carries on in his usual way.

Although D and X are located in different offices in the same branch, their work requires them to co-operate regularly. Their relations are getting more and more strained and their work is suffering.

You are required:

(a) to identify and describe the barriers to communication between the two colleagues;
(b) to suggest how these barriers can be overcome.

18 BRANCH WORKFLOW

A recently appointed senior manager of a large city branch is concerned that the work of the branch does not flow smoothly.

His departmental heads are capable managers. The objectives which they set their departments are clear, challenging and generally achieved.

Nevertheless:

- A worrying number of customers have complained of delays when the work of more than one department is involved.

- Reports which require input from different departments are generally submitted close to deadlines and are sometimes late.

- There is an atmosphere of competitive rivalry (or even hostility) between departments.

- There is evidence of a number of breakdowns in communication between departments.

Required

(a) What are the possible causes of this lack of inter-departmental co-ordination?
(b) What steps could be taken to deal with this problem?

19 MANAGEMENT INFORMATION SYSTEM

'The mainspring of managerial success is an adequate and effective management information system: for appropriate and effective decision-making is dependent upon the timely provision of good quality information.'

Required

(a) Define 'management information system' (MIS).

(b) Show how developments in information technology have contributed to improvements in the quality of information in management information systems, illustrating by reference to any financial control system with which you are familiar.

ILLUSTRATIVE QUESTIONS

20 NEW TECHNOLOGY

'New technology will bring mainly problems for the bank manager'. Discuss.

21 ENRICHING JOBS

What do you understand by 'job enrichment' and what do you consider to be its main advantages and disadvantages.

22 OPPORTUNITIES AND THREATS

What are the major opportunities and threats which the banks are likely to face in the next five years?

23 OBJECTIVE SETTING

Why do organisations set objectives, and how do they go about achieving them?

24 MARKETING TO THE UNBANKED

About 40% of the adult population of the UK do not have a bank account. Which sections of the community come into this category? Why are they not customers of the banks, and what can be done to influence them to become customers?

25 STAFF STABILITY AND TURNOVER

What are the main factors which affect the rate of staff turnover? Why is staff stability important?

SUGGESTED SOLUTIONS

1 KEEPING TIME

(a) *Main problems*

(i) Reg's job has outgrown Reg: he is no longer able to cope with the workload or responsibility.

(ii) Reg is becoming incapable of making necessary decisions.

(iii) Reg is suffering himself - showing signs of stress, working long hours etc.

(iv) This problem is also affecting:

    (1) the manager, who has to take unnecessary decisions;
    (2) the staff, who are demoralised to the point of leaving; and
    (3) the performance of the bank.

(b) *Action*

The manager is in an awkward position.

(i) Reg has been with the branch for many years, and until recently has done a good job. The bank would wish to help him as much as possible; but

(ii) performance is suffering, and some action will have to be taken. If Reg really can't be helped to manage his new job, his future as supervisor at Makebridge should be reviewed.

A possible programme of action is outlined below.

(i) Consult with Reg. He may have been ignoring the decline in morale and performance, or attributing it to factors other than himself: it is only fair to tell him what you (the manager) take to be the situation. Reg should be encouraged to give his side of the story, ie to describe the problems as *he* sees them: there may be faults in the organisation or procedures in the bank to which he attributes the pressure on him, and which might usefully be reviewed. He may feel unable to delegate because of the poor quality of his staff etc.

(ii) Advise Reg. He may need advice, coaching or even off-the-job training in:

    (1) *planning*: how to set targets and standards, schedule and allocate tasks etc. - both for his staff and for himself;

    (2) *control*: how to ensure that targets are being met, how to follow up on the results of decisions etc;

    (3) *delegation*. Reg will have realised that he has become responsible for more people and more decisions, but may not have understood the principles or advantages of delegation. The manager should encourage him to delegate responsibility and should ensure that Reg doesn't feel that he will be regarded as shirking his responsibilities if he does delegate. If Reg continues to worry the manager with decisions he ought to take himself, the manager will have to be helpful and supportive - but firm: Reg will have to get used to shouldering responsibility.

      (iii) Monitor Reg's progress. The manager will have to check (without undermining Reg's authority with the section) that Reg is in fact delegating work. Regular appraisal information should be given to him, ie feedback on his performance, and on his section's performance, perhaps follow-up interviews to see how he feels about the situation etc. The performance and morale of his section may be the best barometer of how Reg is coping.

      (iv) Review the situation. After a reasonable time period, say six months, the standard of performance in Reg's section, and the symptoms of stress visible in Reg himself, should show some alteration - for good or bad. It might then be time to decide whether there is a continuing future for Reg in the Makebridge branch. If Reg is not going to be able to cope better, the best the manager can offer him might be a post in another, small branch - preferably still in Makebridge.

2   SCHOOL LEAVERS

Selection methods

(a)   There should be a labour turnover target within the framework of a manpower plan.

(b)   Job descriptions, but more importantly personnel specifications, should be prepared and studied by the interviewer (Mr. Hoskins).

(c)   The jobs should be advertised in such a way that the short-term as well as long-term career prospects of employees should be explained, together with the nature of the work recruits will be expected to do.

(d)   Applicants for a job should be asked to fill in an application form. The questions asked should:

      (i)   help the selector to decide whether the applicant is possibly suitable for the job;
      (ii) provide the interviewer with a basis for asking questions at the interview.

(e)   The interviews should be planned, and should last longer than ten minutes. They should enable not only the interviewer to assess the candidate, but the candidate to find out more about the job and assess the organisation. Candidates should be encouraged to talk at interviews and to answer questions.

(f)   Candidates need to be judged against the requirements for the job and the personnel specification.

Before going on to consider Mr. Hoskins's relations with local schools, it is worth considering his failure to recruit applicants who stay in the job. New recruits tend to leave quickly which suggests that the job they have taken is nothing like what they were led to expect. Clearly, the problem could be due to a combination of two factors.

(a)   The failure of applicants to understand what the job entails.
(b)   The failure of Mr Hoskins to select the right sort of applicant.

Misunderstanding by applicants can be put right by:

(a)   providing more information about jobs and career prospects in advertisements and brochures;

(b) asking applicants to explain why they are seeking a career in banking when they fill in an application form, so that obvious misunderstandings can be identified from what the applicant writes;

(c) making sure that the job is explained again at the interview;

(d) inviting candidates at interviews to put questions about the job, career prospects and the bank as an employer;

(e) better liaison with schools.

Failure of the interviewer to do his job properly can be put right in the following ways.

(a) Mr Hoskins's willingness to adopt the selection methods recommended above. If his judgement of people is suspect (which is quite possible) it might be suggested in particular that he gives candidates a score or rating out of a maximum number of points for each quality in the personnel specification. A scoring or rating system might help to clarify the interviewer's judgement by putting figures to opinions.

(b) If he considers himself unable to change his methods or opinions, he should be advised to delegate the job of interviewing and selection to a subordinate.

(c) He should try to find out more about potential applicants, by having a better liaison with local schools.

His attitude to local schools might be partially justified, but mere criticism is not constructive, and he should do something about the problem. Better careers literature about jobs in banking should be made available to schools careers offices and other people enquiring about jobs, and he should discuss his recruitment problems with these schools. However, he could promote a better liaison and communication with school teachers and school children by implementing any of a number of possible schemes, eg:

(a) inviting teachers and children to open evenings at the branch to see practical demonstrations of banking;

(b) sending staff (or going himself) to talk to schools, with the aid of films (if schools are agreeable to such visits);

(c) inviting schools to send groups of children to a training centre for a short course in banking, if this can be arranged with the training department of the bank;

(d) sending representatives of the bank to any careers conventions held by local schools;

(e) visiting local schools (and government) careers offices from time to time.

Mr Hoskins should be set a target of reducing the rate of staff turnover in his branch to levels comparable with those of other branches in the area.

3   KNOWLEDGE OF MOTIVATION

(a) The function of management is to manage people in order to get the best out of them, so that they work efficiently and effectively. To this end, managers should try to understand what motivates their subordinates, and to harness their efforts to the advantage of the organisation.

(b) It is important to put the importance of motivation into perspective, and a manager should be aware that by trying to improve the motivation of his staff, he will not necessarily achieve the improvements in performance that he is hoping for. This is because several factors affect performance. Suppose, for example, that an office manager is faced with an ever-increasing mountain of unfinished work in his section, and he needs to find some way of increasing the work rate in the section in order to keep up with the work flow. The solution to the problem might be obtaining extra staff, or introducing new equipment into the office to help out (eg office computers). The problem might also be resolved by a better organisation of work procedures carried out by existing staff with existing equipment.

(c) A manager needs to understand that the link between motivation and better performance is not a clear one, and that it might take time and patience before any benefits materialise. An individual might put more energy and enthusiasm into his work, but unless it is properly channelled by his superior, the extra energy might not be applied usefully. For example, an employee who is motivated to work better might spend a long time trying to raise the quality of his work to a level of 'perfection', with the result that his work rate might slow down. If his manager wants greater productivity, the employee would not be responding in the required way.

(d) Managers need to understand that motivation will only work if the following conditions are met.

   (i) The individual's greater *efforts* should have a significant effect on performance. It might be a waste of time, for example, trying to motivate an individual in a processing unit where the pace of working is dictated by the speed of machinery (although *some* efforts should be made to avoid hostile and negative attitudes amongst employees).

   (ii) Better performance should be rewarded - eg by more pay, by promotion, by some sort of official recognition or by an elevated status within the work group.

   (iii) The individual should value those rewards, and gets sufficient satisfaction out of them to continue his extra efforts in his work.

   A system of rewards should therefore be designed so as to give the employee a sense of achievement from his efforts and real satisfaction from those achievements.

(e) A knowledge of the theories of Herzberg might help managers to understand the effects of different policies for trying to provide employee satisfaction. If the theories of Herzberg are accepted, management must continually pay attention to improvements in 'hygiene' factors, such as pay, quality of supervision, job security, working conditions, and interpersonal relations, in order to prevent dissatisfaction at work. However, if employees are to be motivated to put more energy into their work managers must offer them something extra and different - ie 'motivator' factors such as challenging work, responsibility, and advancement and recognition. These are not easily offered and managers need to be aware of the size of the task they are undertaking if they try to motivate their subordinates.

(f) A knowledge of motivation is necessary for managers to plan the way they try to manage people and motivate them. Paying lip service to motivation without offering real incentives to employees will only result in failure. For example, if a manager says that he wants to encourage participation by subordinates in his decision-making responsibilities, or will delegate more of his authority to them, or will reward them for effort, he will only stand a chance of succeeding if his intentions are genuine. He must create a decision-making procedure which provides for participation, he should delegate authority freely without trying to keep looking over his subordinate's shoulder to see what he is doing, and he must be able to provide the rewards he has promised.

(g) A manager should be aware of the various ways in which motivation of employees might be achieved. These include:

(i) job design;
(ii) pay incentives;
(iii) participation in decision-making;
(iv) delegation of more authority to subordinates.

The motivation of an employee is likely to vary, however, according to different circumstances and situations. For example, he might respond to good leadership for a short while, but then fall back towards his previous levels when restrained by work group 'norms'. He might then have his interest revived by some challenging new work, or the incentive of a reward, only later to go off the boil again owing to fatigue or illness or worries about factors outside his work life (eg family problems).

(h) If motivation can improve performance, a manager should understand the signs of *poor* motivation and be able to measure them or monitor them. Some of the signs might be readily quantifiable (eg absenteeism, labour turnover, productivity) but some are more qualitative, and judgement will be necessary to measure them (eg the degree of trust and exchange of ideas, the willingness to offer constructive suggestions to others, an understanding of the organisation's objectives and the group's role in achieving targets etc).

(i) Knowing what employees expect from work might help the company in the development of:

(i) a pay structure accepted as fair by everyone in the organisation;

(ii) a policy for attracting new recruits to the organisation. For example, a bank should consider why new recruits might want to become employees of a bank, and emphasise these attractions;

(iii) management training or development programmes.

4 MERIT RATING

(a) Job evaluation is defined by the British Institute of Management as 'the process of analysing and assessing the content of jobs in order to place them in an acceptable rank order which can then be used as a basis for a remuneration system'. The definition shows both that it is a complex task and that its objective is to evaluate a pay structure whereby there are fair differentials, in terms of pay, between jobs. This should ensure that staff know they are being fairly treated, and so should improve their motivation. Because of the sensitivity of such an operation it is usual for job evaluation schemes to be introduced in consultation with employees, who should also usually participate in the analysis of tasks which is necessary.

It is clear that this company's job evaluation project has been carried out without the involvement of the staff, since C is merely 'informed' of his job value without any indication of what these values really indicate. The fact that 'specialist consultants' were used to design the scheme also suggests that internal staff were not involved, although in itself the use of specialist consultants for such a complex job is a good idea.

SUGGESTED SOLUTIONS

The fact that staff were not involved means that the scheme has a number of weaknesses.

(i)   No-one (not even, apparently, C's manager) understands that the objective of the scheme is to stimulate motivation by establishing fair play.

(ii) No-one was briefed on the task of the specialist consultants and so they may have got the value system wrong.

(iii) The fairness of the value system is not evident because the employees do not know how the particular values of their jobs compare with high or low evaluation, nor how each component of a job is weighted.

The method of job evaluation used, points rating, works by identifying the factors which make up a job (such as know-how in D's case) and allocating a number of points against each factor to give a weighting for the importance of that factor to the job. The job's points are then totalled to give a value for the job as a whole to the organisation, and the basic salary reflects this value. Each individual can then be given up to 15% more or 10% less than this salary, depending on his merit award.

The objective of the two schemes is to identify the differences between people holding the same job and to make the reward commensurate with their performance of the job. This should provide an incentive to people to perform well (since rewards tie in with performance) and allow a line manager to have authority over the rewards of his staff.

However, this objective cannot be met if staff do not understand the schemes and/or are not informed of the real meaning of the points awarded to the jobs they hold. Because C does not know the maximum value that could be awarded for each factor he does not know whether his job has been properly evaluated.

The merit rating scheme used is a fairly common one, so that the basic salary is seen as 'average' and people can be remunerated on the basis that their performance is above or below average. It works as an incentive scheme if the possible maximum and minimum are sufficiently different from the basic to reward effort fairly. This certainly appears to be the case here. The problem is that the merit rating is assessed rather subjectively by the managers in practice. Although ratings are awarded on performance in relation to previously set targets, because this is a new scheme the employees cannot have been warned of the significance of these targets in terms of pay and so the award on this basis now would not be fair. In addition, C's manager has proved unwilling to set measurable targets at all, instead relying on subjective and imprecise value-judgements.

To summarise, these two schemes are valuable in themselves but have not been introduced in consultation with employees nor with their understanding and commitment. The fact that there can be negative merit awards in fact suggests the opposite - that the schemes have been *imposed* by management. This lack of negotiation and involvement probably negates the objective of the schemes, which is to motivate staff by providing fair and objective pay structures.

(b) Job evaluation and merit rating, when introduced effectively, improve performance because staff are motivated to perform well given that their rewards are fairly based on their objectively evaluated performance. They are particularly useful where staff are motivated by recognition of their efforts and by money. But however much they are paid or praised, staff cannot perform well and develop unless they have the resources (finance, labour) and the training which their jobs require.

Because the job evaluation and merit rating schemes have apparently been introduced without consultation or explanation, it is unlikely that these good effects will be felt.

(i)   The imposition of the schemes without agreement will at best be met with bemusement and at worst with hostility and non-cooperation.

(ii)   Unless the schemes are properly explained and the staff trained to accept targets and identify 'factors' in their own jobs, they will be ineffective since employees will be confused. In addition, many (like C) will feel that they have no way of knowing whether their job has been properly evaluated or their rating assessed fairly. This feeling of lack of control will demoralise the staff and the schemes will be the objects of resentment.

(iii)   Targets couched in the terms used by C's manager are not useful and again produce confusion. Since staff do not know what to aim for they will be worried that they have no guarantee that they will not be downgraded, however hard they work.

Conclusion

Because the schemes provide no real measure of performance, staff are unlikely to perform better as a result of them and, given the conditions for resentment and hostility which their introduction will breed, performance is likely to deteriorate in some cases.

5   WASTED APPRAISAL

Apparent advantages of appraisal

The apparent (or, rather, 'potential') advantages of appraisal include its usefulness for:

(a)   evaluation, enabling the organisation to distribute rewards, promotions etc to best effect and with apparent fairness;

(b)   auditing (discovering the work potential, both present and future, of individuals and groups);

(c)   planning (collecting information about the utilisation of human resources that will aid corporate, manpower and operational planning);

(d)   identifying training needs (by exposing inadequacies in comparison to job requirements which could be remedied by training);

(e)   motivating staff (by providing standards and objectives, a framework for personal and career development, and the opportunity for formal reinforcement ie praise or censure);

(f)   developing staff (by setting improvement targets, identifying strengths and weaknesses, eliciting information about staff's career aspirations etc);

(g)   control (ie ensuring the effectiveness of management's deployment and handling of human resources by identifying and correcting shortfalls in plans; monitoring the effectiveness of organisational structures, systems, technology etc which may emerge from appraisal as the cause of appraisee's performance problems).

SUGGESTED SOLUTIONS

A waste of time?

Appraisals may in practice be a waste of time because of faults in the appraisal system, or simply because appraisals are *perceived* as a waste of time, since management commitment is vital to the effective conduct of appraisal. Problems may include the following.

(a) The objectives of the system may be unclear or even conflicting. A system used purely as a justification of pay and promotion decisions will focus on past performance, and be judgemental in nature; a system aimed at problem-solving and future improvement will be quite different. A single system is unlikely to achieve both objectives.

(b) Managers may be reluctant to perform their appraisal duties conscientiously.

    (i) 'Managers are uncomfortable when they are put in the position of playing God' (McGregor).

    (ii) Interviewers have difficulty handling the interpersonal aspects of negative feedback.

    (iii) The appraisers' own experience, and the culture of the organisation, indicates that appraisal is time-consuming, difficult and fruitless.

(c) Appraisees may be defensive and suspicious of the objectives of appraisal, especially if they perceive it to be a purely judgemental exercise.

(d) Criteria for assessment may vary from assessor to assessor, or within sub-units of the organisation. Perceived unfairness, lack of consistency, and uncertainty in the minds of assessors as to what they are supposed to be assessing, may result.

(e) Feedback on performance is an on-going process: formal appraisal may be perceived as superfluous 'window-dressing'.

(f) If there is no post-appraisal action in terms of training initiatives, increased responsibility, improvement of performance etc, a low opinion of the usefulness of appraisal will be perpetuated.

Making appraisal more worthwhile

Ways of making appraisal more worthwhile may include the following.

(a) A constructive approach should be taken towards the process. Maier *(The appraisal interview)* identifies three approaches to appraisal interviews: the 'tell and sell' method, the 'tell and listen' method and the 'problem solving' approach. These mark progressive stages in the move of the assessor from the dominant role of assessor and critic, through to a counselling and guiding role, where the appraisee is led to identify his problems and to commit himself to personal improvement. Maier, and research by the Behavioural Sciences Research Division of the Civil Service Department in 1973, concluded that appraisees had a more positive attitude to appraisal where the interviewer listened more, and where elements of self-assessment and self-direction were encouraged.

(b) The objectives and elements of the appraisal system should be clearly expressed and understood by all concerned. Appraisal criteria should be specific, consistent and relevant to the purposes of appraisal: credibility may be enhanced by moving away from subjective trait appraisal and towards results-oriented assessment.

(c) The appraisers should be trained in assessment and counselling techniques, given time to prepare and conduct appraisals, and encouraged by senior management to perceive appraisal as an important part of their responsibilities.

(d) The results of appraisal should be clearly stated. A jointly-agreed, concrete conclusion should emerge, ideally in the form of a written summary or statement. Agreed action on both sides should be implemented and monitored.

Any of the above measures might not only help to render the system itself more constructive, but might enhance its credibility, and the level of commitment from all parties on which its effectiveness depends.

6 TRAINING NEEDS

A 'training need' exists when a barrier, removable by training, is hindering the achievement of objectives, or will do so at some future time.

Training needs may arise because faults in the present systems and skill resources of the organisation are identified, or because environmental and organisational changes alter the requirements for performance and create gaps in present provisions.

Symptoms of problems (which may, or may not, be entirely solvable by training, but may in any case indicate a need for training as a contributory factor) include:

(a) high turnover among new recruits;
(b) reduced productivity, higher wastage or machine breakdowns;
(c) production bottlenecks and missed delivery deadlines;
(d) increased customer complaints.

Training needs largely arise from change, in the objectives of the organisation or in the factors affecting the achievement of those objectives. For example:

(a) entry into new markets or the introduction of new products/services;

(b) adoption of new production processes or work methods;

(c) technological innovation in the environment, to which the organisation must adapt in order to remain competitive;

(d) new legislation or regulation altering work processes and patterns, or requiring new knowledge or practices.

The adaptability of the workforce, the organisation's commitment to training and development as an on-going process, and the 'cultural' response to change within the organisation will influence the extent to which such changes create skill/competence gaps in the organisation's manpower resources. A discrepancy may develop between the workforce's competence and the organisation's new requirements, if training has not been pre-planned or if the workforce is slow to adapt.

SUGGESTED SOLUTIONS

Training needs analysis

A 'training needs analysis' should be systematically carried out, if the objectives of the training programme are to be clear and relevant. The analysis should itself have clear objectives and parameters, so initial study will have to be made of specific areas for investigation, and the commitment of management secured so that action will follow the analysis. Data will need to be collected with regard to:

(a) job requirements; and
(b) resources, ie the workforce's present capabilities.

Job requirements can be determined by:

(a) job analysis, identifying and recording in a job description the component elements of a job and the circumstances in which it is performed;

(b) skills analysis, for more skilled jobs;

(c) role analysis, for managerial and administrative jobs requiring a high degree of co-ordination and interaction with others;

(d) existing records, eg job specifications and descriptions, person specifications, the organisation chart (depicting roles and relationships) etc.

The present level of the workforce's competence (which includes not only skill and knowledge, but inclination/motivation as well) can be measured by testing, appraisal counselling, attitude surveys, results etc.

The information will then have to be interpreted. Where there is an identifiable gap between job requirements and current capability, there may still not be a case for training programmes. The solution to shortcomings in the capabilities and inclinations of employees may not be the provision of training, but a review of the work environment, systems and procedures, technology, industrial relations, leadership style, motivation and incentives etc.

Recommendations will be drawn up if training *is* indicated. Job requirements will indicate the objectives of the training programme, ie the 'terminal behaviour' of employees in the training system.

7   POP GROUP BANKER

The basic symptoms of the problem are as follows.

(a) Dixon has been with the city centre branch for about one year.

(b) Only one attendance record has been submitted by the college, showing a bad record of absenteeism. We are not aware that Dixon has yet taken an examination at the college, nor that he has been asked to explain his absenteeism yet.

(c) His time-keeping is poor, but we are not told that he has been warned about it yet.

(d) His work is only just good enough, but he has never been warned.

(e) His appearance is not good, perhaps because of his involvement with a pop group.

(f) His out-of-work interests are stronger than his work interests, which suggests poor motivation to work, and also that Dixon might not see banking as a long-term career.

The following matters must be considered.

(a) Why has Dixon behaved in the way he has done?

(i) His poor attendance at college, his poor work performance and his lateness might all be ascribed to poor attitude, poor effort and a lack of interest in banking work.

(ii) His poor attendance at college might be explained by his own unsuitability for college courses, or by his resentment of a bad course with bad tutors.

(iii) He might have a difficult personal relationship with his boss, which accounts for his lateness and poor motivation in his work.

(iv) His lateness might also be due to particular travelling difficulties.

(v) His appearance might be influenced by his pop group activities. Does the bank have a right to expect him to be tidier than he is already?

Dixon's reasons for his poor performance should be found out, but it is not clear whether finding out should be the job of the personnel manager or Dixon's supervisor.

(b) The supervisor's actions, or lack of them, are puzzling. Since Dixon's performance has been so bad, surely he ought to have been warned already about his attendance at college, his time-keeping, his appearance, and even his general attitude? If Dixon has not been warned, the poor supervision must be blamed for much of the problem and the actions taken about Dixon - and the supervisor - will be influenced by this factor.

(c) The college might not come out unscathed from the analysis. The personnel manager should ask why the poor attendance record of Dixon was not reported sooner.

(d) Dixon has only been with the branch for one year. Since his attitude seems to be all wrong, and his supervisor has perhaps not done all that he should, we might also ask whether Dixon was given proper introduction into the workings of the bank.

(i) Does he appreciate just how bad his performance and attitudes are, and that he has stepped over the mark?

(ii) Is he aware of the rules of discipline in the bank, and the consequences of disobeying them?

We should now turn our attention to possible solutions to the problem. As far as Dixon is concerned, we have the options of:

(a) immediate dismissal;
(b) a formal reprimand;
(c) an informal talking-to.

The reprimand or informal discussion would be given by the supervisor, personnel manager or other manager in authority (eg the branch manager himself). We would also consider whether Dixon should be allowed to continue with day release.

The role of the supervisor should also be considered. A reprimand to the supervisor would seem excessive, but at the very least, he ought to be asked to explain what he has done about Dixon and why, and his superior should discuss what he can do to improve his performance as a supervisor in future.

A recommended solution might be as follows.

(a) Dixon should be given a formal interview with the branch manager, at which a staff association or union representative is present. At the interview:

    (i)   the manager should set out the criticisms of Dixon's performance;

    (ii)   Dixon should be invited to reply to them;

    (iii)   if the answers are not sufficient to clear Dixon from blame, he should be told that he is being given a formal (oral) warning about his conduct, and what the consequences of failing to improve will be.

        In other words, the bank's formal disciplinary procedures should be set in motion;

    (iv)   Dixon might also be informed that if he fails to pass his college examinations at the first attempt, he will be barred from day release in the future.

(b) The branch manager should ask the personnel department to monitor Dixon's college records (perhaps by chasing for more frequent reports) and time-keeping.

(c) The branch manager should arrange for Dixon's supervisor to discuss his performance as a supervisor informally with his superior.

One alternative solution would be instant dismissal, but this is much too severe under the circumstances. Dixon would probably be able to appeal to an industrial tribunal with a justifiable claim of unfair dismissal.

Another possible solution is to place more of the blame on the supervisor, and advise the bank manager to have a meeting with him in which he should set out the criticisms of his poor supervision. The supervisor should then be instructed to deal with Dixon personally, and the future progress of both Dixon and the supervisor should be monitored closely. This approach is not recommended here because blaming the supervisor and not Dixon might encourage the supervisor to take out his own humiliation on Dixon and treat Dixon unfairly.

A further solution would be to ask the supervisor to have an informal discussion with Dixon. In view of the catalogue of Dixon's failings, however, this would seem to be an inadequate first step to dealing with the problem.

8   MISTAKEN INTERVIEWS

The objective of the recruitment and selection activity of an organisation is to get the right people for the jobs required by the tasks of the organisation, in the most efficient way possible. This will not be possible if the job itself is ill-defined (ie candidates are selected for the 'wrong' job) or if candidates are inefficiently assessed with reference to the job's requirements (ie the 'wrong' candidate is selected).

With this in mind, it is a 'mistake' to rely on the interview as the *first* stage in the process.

SUGGESTED SOLUTIONS

(a) The organisation must take very seriously the business of defining and describing the job itself, and the type of person required to perform it. A systematic approach to recruitment and selection must start with job analysis and description (or review of same). A person specification may also be useful preparation for certain general grades of job.

(b) Interviewing is a time-consuming and costly method of sifting through applicants who may be obviously unsuitable for the post. Pre-selection and screening can be achieved through:

    (i) the placing and content of the job advertisement (so that only potentially suitable people see it, and are able to exercise some self selection from the information given);

    (ii) the consideration of application forms, employment histories (CV) etc; or

    (iii) the use of employment agencies or recruitment consultants to short-list candidates for interview.

It is a 'mistake' to rely on the interview as a *crucial* stage in the process, because although it does allow a face-to-face encounter with the candidate, the opportunity to elicit information about him and some experience of his skills in communication and social relations, the technique is subject to severe limitations.

(a) Interviews are highly subjective. Interviewers may each have a different opinion of a single candidate. Even where they agree, they may be prone to errors of judgement or perception.

    (i) Perceptual selectivity. Interviewers may latch onto a single attribute of the interviewee and thereafter see only what they want or expect to see, by what is called 'the halo effect', or stereotyping.

    (ii) Ill-defined ideas of qualitative factors such as motivation, honesty or integrity and how they can be assessed.

    (iii) A tendency to influence the behaviour of the interviewee by 'contagious bias'. Candidates tend to want to please the interviewer and falsify their responses to give the interviewer the answer that he appears to want - especially if the interviewer phrases questions 'Don't you think ...?'

(b) They are not accurate predictors of how a person will perform in the job, and within the work group. The interview is a 'false' situation, and the candidate can often sustain a 'role play' for the duration of the exercise which he could not keep up in the real context of the job. The interview may give some indication of communication and human relations skills, but there is much else the organisation ought to want to know: the candidate's expertise, initiative, soundness of judgement, capacity to handle responsibility etc. (Even were all this information available, the candidate would not necessarily be suited to the particular systems, work group, culture and politics of the organisation.)

What should employers be doing?

As indicated in part above, the prospective employer should use interviews at a later stage of the recruitment and selection process, after suitable preparation and more cost-effective pre-screening:

(a) job analysis and description or review;
(b) careful preparation of a job advertisement for a limited audience and of limited appeal;

(c) the use of agencies, where appropriate, to carry out the initial screening;
(d) scrutiny of relevant items of information on job application forms and CVs; and
(e) short-listing of only the most potentially suitable candidates for interview.

The employer should also place less reliance on the value and validity of interviews as accurate predictors of future success in the organisation. Depending on the type of job, various other selection techniques may be suitable to confirm or assess suitability. Selection tests may be used (although, again, these are often only marginally more objective and accurate than interviews): aptitude tests or proficiency tests may be appropriate where the demonstration of a particular skill or ability is essential to the job, eg typing, numeracy etc. Intelligence testing and personality testing are more problematical. For more senior posts, or where leadership/human relations/communications/group problem solving skills are important, 'assessment centre' (group selection) techniques may be appropriate, combining tests, interviews and group problem simulation and discussion sessions.

Apart from any of these alternative methods, employers should look to make the interview process itself more efficient and effective. Interviewers should be educated and trained in objective assessment and interview technique. Time should be devoted to preparation for the interview, and facilities provided for the conduct of it in appropriate surroundings.

9 INEFFECTIVE COMMITTEE

The causes of an ineffective committee

(a) The purpose or objectives of the committee should be clear, and its authority and responsibility specified. A committee will be ineffective if it does not know what it is expected to do, or what powers it has to make decisions, and if other managers in the organisation do not know what its powers are. For example, a committee which has executive powers might only make recommendations or give advice. Equally ineffectively, a committee might fail to cover all the areas of its authority (ie overlook certain aspects of its work) or might spend time on aspects over which it has no authority (ie overstep the boundaries of its authority).

(b) The size of the committee might be too large for constructive action. The time taken by a committee to resolve a problem tends to increase in direct proportion to its size.

(c) Because a committee's work necessarily involves discussions between members, the preparation of agenda for meetings, and minutes of meetings, as well as the meetings themselves, committees are time-consuming and expensive. In some cases, managers might find that they are spending too much time on committee work and not enough time on their other executive tasks. The timing and length of committee meetings should therefore be considered closely.

(d) A particular problem might be that *routine* decisions entrusted to a committee are delayed unnecessarily by slow committee procedures. The nature of any routine decisions taken by the committee, and the effectiveness of those decisions, should therefore be considered.

(e) Since there is no individual responsibility for decisions made by a group in committee, there may be a tendency for committee decisions to invite ineffective compromises. Weak management can hide behind committee decisions. As in (iv) above, the committee's tendency to compromise should be considered as a cause of inefficiency.

(f) The ineffectiveness of the committee might be due to other organisational and procedural factors apart from those listed above.

(i) The committee might lack a nominated leader or chairperson.

(ii) The committee might lack an efficient secretary to prepare *minutes* of meetings and *agenda* for forthcoming meetings, to chase up action points arising in minutes, and to make sure that all committee members are well briefed about the matters on the agenda before a meeting begins.

Ineffective committee work can be caused by poor administration, with members not being sufficiently briefed before a meeting starts, or not being clear about action points agreed at a meeting for which they are personally responsible.

(g) It will also be necessary to consider the personality, skills and attitude of the committee's leader.

(i) The leader might lack sufficient knowledge of the task to lead the committee well.

(ii) The leader might be a stranger to other committee members, or disliked or mistrusted by them.

(iii) The leadership style adopted might fail to bring out satisfactory contributions from other committee members. For example the leader might:

(1) be unable to chair discussions effectively, and let them get out of hand or become irrelevant;

(2) be unable to draw all members into contributing to committee discussions - ie he might overlook more reticent members;

(3) be unable to bring committee discussions to a point where clear decisions can be made.

(h) The membership of the committee should also be considered carefully.

(i) There might be inadequate representation on the committee, so that enough management or technical skills (or departmental interests) are represented in the membership.

(ii) Proceedings of the committee might be dominated by one or two aggressive members who try to impose their views on others.

(iii) The membership might be apathetic, either through lack of interest, frustration at being unable to participate to the extent they would like, or a belief that their other executive work is more important.

(iv) The individual members might be unable to work together effectively possibly because of personality clashes, but also because of an inability to speak concisely and to the point, or to listen to what other people have to say.

(v) The members, without good leadership, might be unable to discuss problems in committee so as to arrive at constructive effective decisions.

The characteristics of good committee work

To a large extent, the characteristics of good committee work are the opposite of the factors contributing towards ineffective committee work, as described above. Briefly, these may be listed as follows.

(a) The objectives of the committee should be clear, and the authority of the committee should also be properly specified. The time scale for the committee's deliberations should be stated, and adhered to.

(b) There should be an efficient secretary (or secretariat) who makes sure that all members are given an agenda of meetings well in advance, together with some indication of what members might be expected to contribute to the meetings.

 This will enable members to have all the necessary information available if and when required in discussions. The secretary should also prepare and distribute minutes of meetings quickly and accurately, and should draw the attention of members to action points for which they are responsible.

(c) The decisions entrusted to the committee should only be those which will benefit from committee discussions; for example, routine decisions should not be entrusted to the committee.

(d) The committee should be capable of making clear and unambiguous decisions (and to avoid compromise decisions where these are inappropriate to the problem).

(e) The committee should have an able chairman, with personal qualities to co-ordinate and motivate members.

(f) The members of the committee should together combine all the required knowledge or skills to fulfil the committee's functions properly.

(g) The committee's meetings should allow free and open discussions, with all members participating fully (and interested in ensuring that effective decisions are reached).

(h) For complex deliberations, there should be sub-committees, to save unnecessary waste of time in discussions in full meeting.

10 GROUP DISSATISFACTION

John Frost's problem is one of leadership style. We do not know what the performance standards of his work group are, and so we do not know whether his group is achieving or exceeding its targets. However, in view of the dissatisfaction of his group members, it is likely that the group's performance is not good, in spite of the work done by John Frost personally.

We are told that John Frost is very confident and takes many initiatives, but does not understand why others resist his decisions. His style of leadership might be described as the 'tells' kind of leadership, or autocratic style, because he appears to take decisions himself without consulting his subordinates and then tells them what his decision is. His style of leadership might also be described in some ways as 'laissez-faire' because having taken decisions, he appears to leave his staff to get on with their work and shows no obvious interest in what they are doing.

The problems with his leadership style are evident in the dissatisfactions of the subordinates.

(a) Ken Marshall has been in the department a long time, and might be nearing retirement. He is upset by the radical approach of John Frost to the decisions he takes. Ken is obviously well used to established ways and resistant to change. John Frost is failing to explain his reasons and persuade Ken of the need for change.

SUGGESTED SOLUTIONS

(b) Ian Prince is frustrated because he is not allowed to participate in the decision-making processes. His opinions are not asked for, and his ideas are ignored, even though, unlike Ken Marshall, he does not object to change.

(c) Frank Cadell wants to do his job well and wants to be a well-liked subordinate, but he gets no personal interest or attention from John Frost, and he is intimidated by John Frost's distant and 'busy' manner.

The consequence of John Frost's poor supervision in each case is low morale, and probably poor performance, from his staff.

John Frost should be given advice on each individual subordinate's problem.

(a) *Ken Marshall.* Ken Marshall is quite probably too much stuck in his ways and resistant to changes for the better. On the other hand, he has had a lot of experience in the department, and some of his words of caution might not be inappropriate.

The problem in his case is probably a need for respect for his experience and security in the face of change. John Frost should explain the reasons for changes. Knowing why change is needed helps to reduce resistance to change. He should also explain how Ken will be affected personally by any changes, and how he can adapt to them. His specific responsibilities and targets as a result of any change should be spelled out clearly, and John Frost should try to convince Ken that he is capable of carrying out his new tasks well. If there are any risks that Ken can see in change, John Frost should be willing to discuss them. Ken Marshall's experience should be used constructively, whereas it is currently expressing itself negatively, in frustration and resistance to change.

(b) *Ian Prince.* In his case, John Frost should be much more prepared to listen to his subordinate's ideas for change. These ideas might not always be good ones but a task of supervision is to develop staff. This can be done by encouraging ideas and initiative, discussing them, and then explaining why they might or might not be good ones. A more consultative or participative style of leadership will almost certainly reduce Ian Prince's frustrations, and also help to develop his own skills and experience.

When Ian's ideas are accepted, he should be informed about the progress of implementing them, and their success or failure. He might be responsible for implementing the ideas himself, in which case feedback about his performance should be given to him, and John Frost should regularly counsel him about it.

(c) *Frank Cadell.* Frank Cadell needs closer supervision, in the sense that John Frost should spend more time with him. He should show an interest in him and his work. Frank needs more social contact, and to be reassured by praise for doing his job well. John Frost must be prepared to give these.

Conclusion

It is not easy for a manager to change his leadership style overnight, and the advice to John Frost should include suggestions for setting about making changes. Regular staff meetings would be one suggestion. It might also help him to make a record of the time he spends each day with each of his subordinates. John Frost should be counselled regularly by his boss as he tries to change. A formal review of his success in changing his style, and the effects of his new approach on group performance and attitudes, should be made after some months.

11   MANAGEMENT ACTIVITIES

(a)   *Planning* is involved with the establishment of objectives, and the strategies, policies, programmes and procedures for achieving them at all levels of the organisation. Long-term strategic planning occurs at the top level of management and is concerned primarily with objective setting; tactical planning is concerned with the means of achieving objectives through procedures and systems and the allocation of resources; operational planning is carried out at the lower levels of management, and is concerned with day-to-day decisions.

Planning is a function of all managers. It precedes all other management functions: an organisation must have an idea of its objectives and tactics before management can determine the organisational structures, leadership styles, resources and standards of performance necessary to achieve them. Plans are also mechanisms for the co-ordination of individual and group effort to a stated end.

(b)   According to Cole. 'If planning is considered as providing the route map for the journey, then *organising* is the means by which you arrive at your chosen destination'.

Organising is not the same as 'organisation' ie the actual grouping or network of relationships, but is the *process* whereby organisation is formed and put into action. Organising involves:

(i)   identifying, grouping and giving structure to the activities the organisation needs to perform in pursuit of its objectives (ie forming functions, departments etc);

(ii)   determining 'roles' which will be needed for the performance of those grouped activities (ie allocating responsibility for functional areas);

(iii)   delegating authority and establishing accountability for performance;

(iv)   devising systems, procedures and rules for efficient working.

In other words, organising is the putting in motion of purposeful activity, in order to put plans into effect.

(c)   *Directing* (sometimes known as 'commanding') involves giving instructions to subordinates to carry out tasks over which the manager has authority for decisions and responsibility for performance. Once the organisation has planned its activity and created structures and systems to accomplish them, the people must be mobilised to perform specific roles, functions and tasks. Information must be given to employees that will (a) enable them to perform their tasks, and (b) indicate the standard to which they must perform their tasks.

Some theorists have argued with Fayol's term 'commanding', suggesting that 'leading', 'persuading' and 'motivating' are more true to the interpersonal nature of management, and the manager's dependence on his subordinates for co-operation in fulfilling plans.

(d)   *Control* is the process which ties all the above together, establishes whether the organisation, leadership and co-ordination are contributing to fulfil effectively and efficiently the plans made - and indicates corrective action, or adjusted plans, if they are not. According to Fayol himself '...control consists in verifying whether everything occurs in conformity with the plan adopted, the instructions issued and the principles established. It has for its object to point out weaknesses and errors in order to rectify them and prevent recurrence. It operates on everything; things, people, actions'.

The basic control process or control cycle in management has six stages:

(i)   making a plan; deciding what to do and identifying the desired results. Without plans there can be no control;

(ii) recording the plan formally or informally, in writing or by other means, statistically or descriptively. The plan should incorporate standards of efficiency or targets of performance;

(iii) carrying out the plan, or having it carried out by subordinates; and measuring actual results achieved;

(iv) comparing actual results against the plans. This is sometimes referred to as the provision of 'feedback';

(v)   evaluating the comparison, and deciding whether further action is necessary to ensure the plan is achieved;

(vi) where corrective action is necessary, this should be implemented.

12   ENCOURAGING DELEGATION

(a) Factors influencing decision to delegate include the following.

(i)   The work load of the superior. There are physical and mental limitations to what one man can do.

(ii) Any specialised or technical knowledge which the subordinate might have, making him or her better-suited to handling certain tasks.

(iii) The nature of the decisions which are involved. Decisions have been analysed (by Drucker) as having four characteristics.

(1) The degree of *futurity* in the consequences of the decision. Decisions which either have a short-term effect or which can be reversed quickly are more suitable for delegation. In other words, where the cost of a wrong decision is high, authority should not be delegated.

(2) The *impact* of the decision on the work of other departments, sections or people. Decisions should not be delegated if they will seriously affect the work of another manager of equal status. These decisions should be made by their common superior, who acts as co-ordinator.

(3) The number of *qualitative* factors in the decision calling for the exercise of judgement by the manager. More complex qualitative factors in a decision would indicate the inadvisability of delegation.

(4) 'General rules' or 'guideline decisions' or 'policy decisions' should be made by more senior managers.

(iv) The skill, knowledge and attitudes of the subordinates will help to determine how much delegated authority they want to have and how much responsibility they are properly capable of undertaking.

(v) The management philosophy of the organisation may encourage or discourage delegation.

(vi) The geographical dispersion of subordinates and the rate of change in the environment. When subordinates are not in the same office or building, and the work is not readily formalised owing to the rate of change in the business environment, greater delegation should be provided by the organisation structure. On the other hand a rigid specification of organisation tasks (job structures) will restrict the boss's options about how much to delegate.

(vii) Work involving membership of committees should be handled by a manager with the status appropriate to the committee's membership.

(viii) Some work demands the attention of a senior manager (eg dealing with important customers or managers at a very senior level in the organisation).

(b) Major barriers to delegation include the following.

(i) The superior's lack of trust in the subordinate. He may consider the subordinate incapable of doing the work well enough.

(ii) The superior's wish to retain control over even the most straightforward tasks.

(iii) The superior's fear that the subordinate will do the work better than he could himself.

(iv) The lack of a good relationship and communication between superior and subordinate.

(v) A rigidly-defined task structure for the organisation. In association with this, concern for 'status' and 'seniority' might result in an insistence that work of a certain 'status' should be done by a manager of corresponding rank.

(vi) The reluctance of the subordinate to accept responsibility (perhaps for fear of the consequences of failure).

13 OVERLOADED SUPERVISOR

The problem concerns a supervisor's failure to plan adequately, control the activities of his staff, set targets and achieve results. There are a number of possible reasons for this situation.

(a) The supervisor has received little or no training in how to plan and control.

(b) The organisation has not adequately communicated its objectives to its employees. As a result, the supervisor does not know what is required of him and where the activities of his department fit into the overall corporate plan.

(c) The department may be short-staffed or the subordinates unable to do anything more than routine tasks.

(d) The supervisor may not be suited to leadership.

SUGGESTED SOLUTIONS

The following facts should be obtained.

(a) Details of the supervisor's background and performance ratings.

(b) Details of the activities of the department. One would need to know what it is required to produce when and the importance of its output relative to other departments.

(c) Details of the level and calibre of staff under the supervisor's control.

The supervisor should be given a counselling interview and asked to give his views of why his department is under-performing. He may point out that it is under-staffed (so deadlines cannot be met) or that some staff cannot be entrusted with difficult work (so that capable staff have to be overloaded). It may even be the case that he receives little or no guidance or encouragement from his superiors so that he ends up 'firefighting'.

Depending on the reasons identified for the failure of the department, the following remedies could be suggested.

(a) The supervisor could be sent for training on the importance of planning and control and the management techniques available.

(b) More and better staff.

(c) A revision of departmental duties so that its work becomes more manageable.

(d) Greater involvement from senior management, particularly as regards (i) explaining objectives and the role of the department within the overall plan and (ii) being available to give advice and encouragement.

(e) Transfer of the supervisor to a less demanding job.

If the principal reason for the supervisor's under-performance is indeed his inability to plan and control, a management by objectives (MBO) approach should be considered. Briefly, the supervisor will be informed of corporate and departmental objectives and the key result areas of the job identified. The supervisor will then be invited to set his own performance targets: achieving these should ensure that departmental goals are also achieved. In addition, the system for evaluating the supervisor's performance will be closely linked to the targets set by him. This should encourage the supervisor to plan the activities of the department efficiently and control them effectively, since this will help achieve the standards he has himself set.

Follow-up

A review of the situation after a few months would be made to see the department is now being run efficiently. If the same problems exist, further training or a transfer may prove necessary.

14 LEADING ACCOUNTANT

Derek's problem is one of leadership style. We do not know what the performance standards of his branch are, and so we do not know whether it is achieving or exceeding its targets. However, in view of the dissatisfaction of his subordinates, it is likely that the performance is not good, in spite of the work done by Derek personally.

SUGGESTED SOLUTIONS

We are told that Derek is very confident and takes many initiatives, but does not understand why others resist his decisions, dismissing them as reactionary and unco-operative. His style of leadership might be described as the 'tells' kind of leadership, or autocratic style, because he appears to take decisions himself without consulting his subordinates and then tells them what his decision is. His style of leadership might also be described in some ways as 'laissez-faire' because, having taken decisions, he appears to leave his staff to get on with their own work and shows no obvious interest in what they are doing.

The problems with his leadership style are evident in the dissatisfactions of the subordinates.

(a) The younger ones want to do their job well but get no personal interest or attention from Derek. They do not know whether they are doing well or badly nor by what standards they may be judged.

(b) Some people are frustrated because they are not allowed to participate in the decision-making process. Their opinions are not asked for, and their ideas are ignored.

(c) The older ones might have been in the branch a long time, and might be nearing retirement. They are upset by the radical approach of Derek to the decisions he takes. They are obviously well-used to established ways and resistant to change. Derek is failing to explain his reasons and persuade the older ones of the need for change.

The advice to Derek should be to urge him to recognise his supervisory responsibilities.

(a) He seems unaware of the problems his leadership style is causing. One measure that should be taken is to tell him that his performance will be judged on the achievements of his section as a whole, not just on his own personal efforts. If his subordinates are performing badly, he should be held responsible. It is his duty to improve this performance, and he should receive regular feedback about his section's results, for comparison against planning targets or standards.

(b) His attitude to his staff should change. He should not be in such a hurry nor so autocratic, because these leadership styles are unsuitable for his subordinates. In general terms, a more 'participative' or 'democratic' or 'consultative' style of leadership is needed.

(c) Derek is responsible for motivating and encouraging his staff, and he should give each of them individual attention, counselling and encouragement. Since supervision of staff is one of his responsibilities, he must find time to devote to this task, and he must not be too busy with other work to bother about his subordinates.

(d) He should also recognise the advantages of group attitudes and motivation. In addition to giving subordinates individual attention, he should also try to encourage a group identity and cohesiveness. Regular meetings in a group with his subordinates should be recommended to him.

Derek should tackle each of the specific worries of his staff.

(a) The younger ones require closer supervision, and Derek should spend more time with them. This will show that he takes an interest in them and also that he is not frightening. In addition, he should set clear standards for their work and, at regular appraisal sessions, let them know whether they are meeting these standards.

(b)   In the case of the ones who are resentful that Derek never listens to their ideas, Derek should be much more prepared to listen. Their ideas might not always be good ones, but a task of supervision is to develop staff. This can be done by encouraging ideas and initiatives, discussing them, and then explaining why they might or might not be good ones. A more consultative or participative style of leadership will almost certainly reduce their frustrations, and also help to develop his own skills and experience.

When an individual employee's ideas are accepted, he should be informed about the progress of implementing them, and about their success or failure. Staff might be made responsible for implementing the ideas themselves, in which case feedback about performance should be given to them, and Derek should regularly counsel them about it.

(c)   The older ones may be stuck in their ways and resistant to changes for the better. On the other hand, they have a lot of experience in the department and Derek should try to see the benefit of making use of that.

The problem is probably a need for respect for their experience and for security in the face of change. Derek should explain his reasons for changes. Knowing why change is needed helps to reduce resistance to it. He should also explain how the staff will be affected personally by any changes, and how they can adapt to them. Their specific responsibilities and targets as a result of any change should be spelled out clearly, and Derek should try to convince them that they are capable of carrying out new tasks well. If they do perceive risks in change then Derek should be willing to discuss them. The fact that they all feel the same way may be a case of 'group-think' but it may equally be that many heads are wiser than one and that he should take their point. Their experience should be used constructively, whereas currently it is being expressed negatively in frustration and resistance to change.

Their complaint that Derek makes apparently arbitrary decisions could be addressed by Derek adopting a more consistent style and *explaining* the processes which lead to a particular decision being taken.

Conclusion

It is not easy for a manager to change his leadership style overnight, and Derek should seek advice as to how to make changes. Regular staff meetings would be one suggestion. It might also help him to make a record of the time he spends each day with each of his subordinates.

Derek should be counselled regularly by his boss as he tries to change. A formal review of his success in changing his style, and the effects of his new approach on the branch's performance and attitudes, should be made after some months.

15   EFFECTIVE WORK TEAM

C B Handy in his book *Understanding organisations* describes a contingency approach to analysing group effectiveness. The factors involved are the 'givens', which are the group, the group's task and the group's environment, the 'intervening variables', which are group motivation, the style of leadership and processes and procedures, and the 'outcomes', which are the group's productivity and the satisfaction of group members. Characteristics of an effective work team can be identified in all of these variables.

The group itself should contain a suitable blend of the individual skills and abilities of its members, so that the group not only has enough personnel to do its job, and people with sufficient experience and skill, but also it should blend the individual members in an effective way. A project team, for example, probably needs a man of ideas, a man of drive and energy, a logical evaluator of suggestions, a man who can do the detailed, routine work and a 'conciliator' who can bring individuals to negotiate and settle their differences.

The group's task must be clearly defined, otherwise it cannot be effective in carrying it out. The group should also be given the resources to do its job properly and if necessary, it should have the authority to carry out certain actions which it considers necessary as part of its task.

If the task is a temporary one, the work group should be a temporary project team which will be disbanded when its job is done. If the task is a continuing one, the work group should be given a defined place and role in the formal organisation structure.

The group's environment refers to conditions of work. The characteristics of an effective work group in this respect are that members of the group should have ready contact with each other. An open plan office for the group might achieve this purpose. The group must also have easy and good contacts with other groups with which they work; inter-group conflicts will reduce the efficiency of every group involved.

The motivation of the group as a whole develops as a group norm. If motivation is good and positive, the group will try to be efficient and effective. Poor motivation will result in an ineffective group. It would not be true to say that participation by group members in decision-making is necessarily a characteristic of an effective group; however, participation, when it promotes a positive group motivation, will be a means toward group effectiveness.

The style of a group's leader also plays an influential role in determining group effectiveness. This style might be autocratic, democratic or laissez-faire. Likert distinguished between exploitive authoritative, benevolent authoritative, consultative authoritative and participative group management, and suggested that the latter type will promote a more effective group.

An effective work group will use well-designed processes and procedures. Characteristics of these might be a formally designed management information system, or the use of modelling and operational research techniques, a management by objectives system, up-to-date technology, or scientific management techniques etc. A formal group structure should not necessarily be rigid, but each member of the group should be aware of his own individual responsibilities and tasks.

The characteristics so far described should create outcomes which 'prove' the group's effectiveness. The effective group will be efficient in its work, if the work is continuous, or it will achieve its task, as defined in its terms of reference. At the same time, it should be expected that in a group which works well and accomplishes its tasks, the individual members will show a marked amount of job satisfaction.

Training can help to create an effective work group both by building up a group identity and also by showing other members how each individual thinks and reacts in various situation. Although group learning is not common in industry, it is used by various non-industrial organisations. 'T groups' is one name given to group training, in which a series of exercises are carried out. Each exercise will involve certain members of the group, and at the end of the exercise, other group members will be asked to comment on how the exercise was performed. These exercises and discussions enable individuals to understand how they react in a given situation and how these reactions appear to other people. This helps to develop an understanding of how members of a group inter-act and to suggest ways in which these interactions can be made to work more constructively.

16 BANKING STYLES

(a) *The external environment,* ie the economic situation, national culture and customs, the nature of the market and extent of competition, the technology available, customer tastes and requirements, the demography of the country (age distribution etc). The style of the bank will be different according to its awareness of, and response to, who its customers are, resources it has available, competitive pressures etc.

(b) *The task,* ie the nature of the business: retail or merchant banking, domestic or international, emphasis on particular market segments eg small business, corporate, 'relationship banking', or diversification.

(c) *The origins, history and life stage* of the bank. Its origins, nationality and age will influence its values and perhaps its flexibility in the face of environmental change. The life cycle of the bank may be in the mature or declining stage, or may have entered a new development stage with the advent of new technology.

(d) *Organisational structure* - ie the extent to which authority is delegated in the organisation, geographical dispersion, adaptability (eg to allow for the increasing role of middle-range management in selling of new services/financial products), the size of the bank and the number of levels in its hierarchy, the extent to which it is broken up into small work groups with manageable spans of control etc.

(e) *Organisational politics* - ie where the power and influence is centred, where formal communication structures are supplemented or replaced by informal ones, what status symbols are prized in the bank etc.

(f) *Policies and practices* - ie the way the bank carries out its functions and its obligations to staff, customers etc. Policies and practices will also embody the bank's *attitudes* and *values* eg to staff welfare, training and development, to customers, to risk and innovation, integrity in dealing etc.

(g) *Leadership style.* Leaders in any organisation stamp their personalities on the organisation style, both directly (through representing the organisation and creating/implementing the policies and practices of the bank) and indirectly, by influencing the morale and motivation of their subordinates, encouraging formality or informality, by 'selling' the values and beliefs of the organisation (or failing to do so) etc.

(h) *Visible artefacts* - the style of offices, dress 'rules', display of diplomas, 'trophies' etc.

Changing style

Changing the style of a bank is a long and complex process which requires:

(a) a vision for the new style and direction of the bank, a sense of 'mission', a set of guiding values;

(b) the selection, development and encouragement of leadership who are committed to, and able to communicate the vision. 'Bottom-up' changes in style face almost insuperable difficulties;

(c) a plan, detailing practical means of guiding the cultural change. These may include:

(i) new products or services;

(ii) new technology and ways of working;

(iii) a rethink of the environment (many banks are currently redesigning branches to create a new image - both for customers and staff);

(iv) selection, training and other procedures to ensure that management and staff are suitable or able to adapt;

(d) targets - and timescales where practical - for change, so that progress towards the vision is measurable. This is important so that with each step, change can be recognised and rewarded: with each step achieved, the whole vision looks more achievable;

(e) reinforcement, ie sanctions against those who resist change, rewarding those who embrace it; 'buy in or get/stay out';

(f) keeping the channels of communication open, so that feedback can be received, problems handled immediately etc.

17 STRAINED WORK RELATIONSHIPS

(a) The barriers to communication between D and X can be grouped into three main areas.

(i) *Differences in attitude arising from the many differences between them and their circumstances*

Attitudes are mental and neural states of readiness, developed through experience, which direct an individual's response to all objects and situations with which they are related: in less technical terms, they are 'standpoints' which pre-dispose individuals to act and react in certain ways. Attitudes can thus become barriers to communication because they encourage perceptual selectivity and distortion: people hear what they want to hear, filter out information that is inconsistent with their own views and are therefore able to stereotype other - different - individuals (eg D calling people like X 'stick in the muds').

The differences between D and X are many. There is a wide age gap, and differences in sex, marital status and life-style, work experience and education (X being superior in the first, D in the second). These things add up to their attitudes to life. In particular, one gets the impression that X is rather staid, likes routine, dislikes new developments, while X is young, free of family obligations, flexible in her work patterns, progressive and committed to the 'information revolution'. It is explicit in the scenario that each disapproves of the other's attitude.

(ii) *Problems in the communication process itself.* Both D and X are making mistakes in the way they communicate.

(1) X ignores information which does not agree with his opinions: He is a highly selective 'receiver', which will make it difficult for him to listen objectively to D.

(2) D is an expert in computer language, and is quite likely to use technical 'jargon' which X has no means of interpreting, and which may be perceived as a way of 'excluding' and rebuffing non-experts like X. The education/training gap between D and X will become a problem because of this.

(3) X fails to communicate openly when he recognises that a problem exists. He 'disapproves but does not comment': there is thus no meeting of the two points of view which might encourage attitude change, and both parties continue in their mutually exclusive way. (D on the other hand, is arguably *too* communicative, being rather free with her criticisms to all and sundry, without directly addressing the person concerned.)

(iii) *The organisational context.* Two aspects of this stand out.

(1) D is only a supervisor, while X is manager - but X has risen to this 'junior' management position over a period of twenty-five years or so. D's advancement has been much swifter. This may already cause some jealousy on X's part, but a greater problem looms: the cultural change advocated by individuals like D - and perhaps heralded by her selection and promotion - is threatening to the security (psychological and physical) of people like X, who may see themselves as too old to change and being ousted by young 'whizz kids'.

(2) D and X are geographically separated, despite the need for regular co-operation. One assumes, therefore, that they communicate by telephone or memo, which means that they have little opportunity to communicate informally, and that they cannot use non-verbal communication to clarify or confirm verbal signals. (If D was smiling when she spoke about 'stick in the muds', X might have interpreted her meaning differently.)

(b) *Steps to overcome these problems*

Some of the steps which should be taken to overcome these problems are unilateral, ie D and X individually will need to be educated, counselled etc to change their own attitudes. Other measures will need to be more co-operative, ie getting them together to work out problems.

Attitude change is much harder to achieve than behavioural change. It will be no good just telling X to get used to new technology and stop being jealous of D, or telling D to be more tolerant of X's resistance to IT.

Measures that could be taken include the following.

(i) X should be sent on a short training programme. He seems to be not *resistant* to new technology, but unfamiliar with the latest developments, and unconvinced of the need - since he claims to be aware of the information he requires. A training course emphasising the practical application to management of new technology, dealing with the latest developments, and teaching the basic vocabulary which X lacks may help to:

(1) improve his understanding of D's language;

(2) improve his attitude to IT - since he may find it more useful and less threatening;

(3) give him some common ground with D.

(ii) X should be individually counselled by his boss, perhaps as part of the appraisal process. He should be encouraged to identify his problems of communication with D as the source of his deteriorating work performance. (Attitude change is more likely to occur if he himself perceives the need for change.) He may be led to identify the nature of the particular problems themselves. It could then be explained to him that the organisation values his experience, ie he need not feel threatened by D - but that adaption to new technology is also desirable, and that the organisation wishes him to benefit from D's expertise.

(iii) D should similarly receive individual counselling and perhaps even discipline. She has been contemptuous of the organisation - and, by implication, of her senior colleagues like X - in a singularly unconstructive way. It not only undermines the authority of management among the junior staff, since D seems to have little discretion, but is offensive to individuals like X. If this is pointed out to D, while admitting that X's own attitude is undergoing review and that steps are being taken to encourage change in the organisation, she may realise that she has overstepped the mark. It may even have to be suggested to her that her further advancement in the company depends on her development of greater discretion and human relations skills. She may also simply need to be alerted to the fact that her use of computer language is making her an ineffective communicator.

(iv) D and X should, if necessary, participate in a joint problem-solving session, guided by a superior to both. Some of the resentment that has built up will simply have to be aired: X for example, has said nothing to D directly so far. A frank meeting of minds - controlled by the presence of an impartial and authoritative third party - will help them to understand each other's attitudes better, to clear up misconceptions, and perhaps to start a process of getting to know each other. They should be encouraged to commit themselves to this process, through being brought to realise that their work is suffering and that the organisation wishes the situation to change.

(v) D and X should be encouraged to meet face to face more often. If possible, their offices should be moved into closer proximity. If not, regular scheduled meetings should be instituted, for the briefings, reports etc required between them. It might also be possible to arrange that they both serve on the same committee or task force, or that they be appointed to co-operate in some 'extra-curricular' projects, eg organising staff entertainments etc so that they start to communicate informally.

18 BRANCH WORKFLOW

(a) *Possible causes of lack of co-ordination*

The problem is not with the management or objectives of the individual departments: we hear that *departmental* objectives are being achieved.

However, customer complaints indicate that the departments are not working together effectively. Input to joint departmental reports is uncontrolled. There is open conflict and communication breakdown.

Possible causes of the lack of co-ordination, strictly speaking, include the conflict and communication problems outlined. Taking them as *symptoms* of the whole malaise, however, possible causes of the situation might be the following.

(i) Poor communication systems and information flow in the organisation. It seems that there is inadequate co-ordination and control over the input and exchange of information between the departments. The preparation of reports seems to be fragmented and information is received late: it is not good quality information.

Problems with information flow may also explain delays in inter-departmental work. The branch is large, so a reporting and information system will have to be efficient in order to cope with the complexity of the organisation.

(ii) Conflict - issuing in competitive rivalry (which can be a healthy force, but in this case tends to 'hostility') may be the cause of communication breakdown even if the systems and procedures for communication are good. Such conflict may have arisen because of:

(1) competition for a share of the limited resources available within the branch;

(2) differences in goals, and ways of doing things;

(3) disputes about 'territory', the relative power and importance of each department;

(4) clashes of ideology, 'culture', specialisms etc;

(5) jealousy about differences in accommodation, rewards, career structure etc.

(iii) There may be personal hostility between departmental managers, restricting information flow and creating cultures which reflect the managers' feelings.

(iv) The timescale and objectives of the work of each department may be incompatible with those of others: some may be 'fire-fighting' with day to day concerns and have no patience for the long-term ('slow') tasks of others etc.

(v) We gather that each department has clear, challenging individual objectives: employees may be *so* committed to these that they regard inter-departmental work as irrelevant. Specialisation frequently causes lack of awareness or understanding of what goes on in other departments, and even a sub-unit culture that can become antagonistic rather than co-operative.

(vi) The branch is large, and banks are diversifying their activities: sheer fragmentation will make it difficult for departments to get a clear picture of their role and position in the organisation. 'Tunnel vision' may prevent them from being aware of the affect of their individual action on the bank as a whole.

(b) *Steps to deal with the problem*

Various steps could be taken to improve communication, reduce conflict, integrate tasks and enhance the organisational awareness of the departments.

(i) Design and implement information systems and communication procedures to encourage comprehensive communications between the individuals and departments on a regular, formal basis. House journals, notice boards etc should be used to promote a more 'global' culture ie 'we are one organisation'.

(ii) Interdepartmental meetings, committees, working parties etc may be used as the mechanism for bringing individuals together and enhancing their awareness of other departments' tasks, objectives etc.

(iii) Co-ordination must be built into planning from the earliest stages. All those affected by budgets, report and project requirements etc should be informed and involved in planning: deadlines, schedules, control systems, resource allocation etc should be planned across departmental boundaries, so that work-flow and timescales coincide.

(iv) Charles Handy suggested that liaison or co-ordinating positions might be developed or created to aid integration. The 'cross-over' point in the hierarchy - ie where departmental heads all report to the senior manager, in this case - is a good place to start: the one boss can co-ordinate departmental activities through the heads. A special liaison officer/ progress chaser might otherwise be appointed for particular projects or on a permanent basis, to ensure that tasks are being carried out and information flowing smoothly.

(v) The competitive element might be diverted from its present hostile course. If the departments can be 'switched on' to the objectives of the organisation as a whole, or to the completion of the tasks in hand, there may be constructive competition between the departments to raise standards, cut costs etc - but with an essentially co-operative atmosphere and sense of direction.

(vi) The organisation as a whole should try to develop and promote its 'culture' and objectives, so that all departments commit themselves to co-operative effort, and do not feel the need to develop sub-unit cultures and allegiances of their own.

19 MANAGEMENT INFORMATION SYSTEM

(a) A management information system (MIS) is a term used to refer to the system within an organisation for collecting and analysing data in order to provide information to managers to help them to carry out their management tasks.

The term 'MIS' therefore refers to such matters as what data is collected and analysed, and how, what files of data are kept, the content of information provided to managers, the frequency of providing it, in what form it is provided, when and to whom, its accuracy and reliability, and its purpose, and so on.

Managers need information to help them to make planning and control decisions, and so the MIS is a key element in management decision-making. Every organisation has an MIS, but some are more formally structured and better designed than others. The purpose of an MIS ought to be to provide suitable information to the managers who are responsible for taking decisions, at an appropriate time, so as to help managers to make good quality decisions.

(b) The features of computers and IT which might improve the quality of an MIS are as follows:

(i) Speed of data processing. Computers can process data more quickly than manual methods of data processing. In a system of budgetary control, for example, this means that regular variance reports for each control period can be made available to managers much sooner after the end of each control period. This will make the information more timely, and control action can be taken where appropriate with a minimum of delay.

(ii) Volume of data processing. Computers can process large volumes of data. This means, for example, that in a system of budgetary control the comparison of actual results against budget can be taken to greater depths of detail, or can be analysed in a greater number of ways. In some cases, microcomputers might make budgetary control feasible in situations when before it was impractical with limited staff resources.

Managers can therefore make planning and control decisions on the basis of more comprehensive information than before, and this ought to improve the quality of their decisions.

(iii) Accuracy of data processing. Computers should process data more accurately than manual methods of data processing. This is especially the case when computerised data capture methods are used; for example, card and badge transmission devices can be used to record labour times accurately for a production control and budgetary control system.

(iv) Computers can hold large volumes of data on file, and large databases can be built up. In a budgetary control system, for example, a database can be built up of sales trends and costs of resources, so that managers can if they wish draw on the data that has been built up to prepare revised budgets or forecasts.

(v) Computer technology has improved so that systems can provide for:

(1) speedy data transmission over long distances, so as to improve communications in the organisation that is geographically dispersed;

(2) multi-user access to common data files.

In a large company, multi-user access can improve financial control, by allowing management at different levels in the management hierarchy (eg at head office and in a branch) access to the same database files.

20 NEW TECHNOLOGY

The problems facing managers as a result of technological development are likely to centre on the following areas.

Customers

Banks become aware of their customers' requirements and adapt accordingly to provide the service expected of them. Increasingly, this adaptation takes the form of technological alterations and improvements eg autobanks. Although these changes should benefit the customer, the manager will find that there is a natural fear of the new, particularly when the human element is removed. Customers used to dealing with a friendly cashier will consider that something has been lost from the service they expect when they find that they have to deal with an impersonal cash dispenser. To the young, a modern efficient bank equipped with VDUs and word processors are a great improvement on the friendly corner bank with manual ledgers, but the old will fear that the service will become depersonalised along with the surroundings.

The bank manager must consider doing the following in order to overcome this problem:

(a) he should point out to his clients how much more efficient the service his bank can provide now it is equipped with modern technological devices;

(b) he should stress that change has been made only for the better, that is, change has not been made for change's sake;

(c) he should attempt to keep the personal touch as far as possible, eg friendly leaflets explaining the services available. To an extent technology can help keep the human element, for example the preparation on word processors of standard letters to which personal details can be added.

Commercial enterprises

One of the big modern developments to date is Electronic Funds Transfer Point at of Sale - EFTPOS. This is where a customer in, say, a shop pays for goods by having his bank account automatically debited by the cashier. To date, EFTPOS is not as far advanced in the UK as expected because of objections by the retailers who have to co-operate with the banks in installing the hardware. Some companies take the view that they are being expected to foot the bill for a system which is designed primarily to benefit the banks.

The manager should consider:

(a) pointing out to the retailers the likely demand there will be from the customer for such a service;

(b) explaining the benefits that will accrue to shops etc when customers have this facility, eg increased sales;

(c) pointing out the success EFTPOS has had on the Continent where it is much further advanced.

Employees

Employees fear technological change for two reasons: they are worried firstly that they are to become mere prisoners of the machine, and secondly they fear the loss of their jobs. Some reduction in staff numbers must of course be expected, and it will take some time before the situation resolves itself to see clearly what skills will be required of bank staff in the future. These factors may cause an increase in union militancy or, at the very least, a lack of co-operation amongst staff in helping implement and work with the new machines.

This situation will test the skill of the manager in handling people as he prepares to do the following:

(a) he should explain that technological innovations are designed to improve the service to the consumer and the efficiency of the bank, two aims which the staff should endorse;

(b) automation will reduce the need for staff to perform boring, mundane tasks, freeing them for more interesting work;

(c) full training will be given to staff working with the machine. This extension of their skills will make them more attractive employees on the labour market or, if they wished to stay in banking, possible candidates for promotion;

(d) the hoped for expansion in business as a result of technological developments should create exciting opportunities for all capable staff members.

21 ENRICHING JOBS

Job enrichment is the process of building into jobs a greater sense of meaning, challenge and potential for accomplishment. Since it involves a restructuring of the design of jobs, it should be planned, deliberate policy on the part of management to make greater use of the skills, knowledge and potential of subordinates by giving them greater scope for self-expression and therefore a greater motivation to work better.

The advantages of job enrichment are as follows.

(a) For the employee doing the job:

   (i) it provides more interesting and challenging work, with greater responsibilities for the job-holder and therefore less supervision;

   (ii) it gives the employee greater opportunities to learn more skills and gain more experience;

   (iii) it gives the employee a greater opportunity to see a purpose in the work he or she is doing;

   (iv) since employees are given more challenging work, they should expect greater rewards (higher pay, better opportunities for promotion etc);

   (v) employees are better motivated in their work, and if sufficient rewards for better results are offered, they will be likely to put in greater efforts to achieve success.

(b) For the organisation:

   (i) a better motivated work force is likely to work more efficiently and effectively towards achieving the goals of the organisation;

   (ii) since subordinates are given more freedom of action, superiors are given greater opportunities in turn to devote themselves to more challenging aspects of their management function;

   (iii) the work force as a whole will become more skilled and capable;

   (iv) better motivation might well reduce the rates of labour turnover, absenteeism, and accidents etc which can be costly for an organisation;

   (v) more challenging work with accompanying rewards might attract a better quality of applicants for job vacancies.

The disadvantages of job enrichment affect both employees and the organisation.

   (i) Unless the redesign of jobs to give job enrichment to employees is introduced throughout the organisation, some jobs in the organisation will have responsibilities taken away and given to subordinates, but no extra responsibilities added to replace those relinquished. This might adversely affect the motivation of those job-holders.

(ii) Employees might not want extra responsibilities or greater challenges. Some people feel more secure being told exactly what to do. Any attempt to enrich their jobs would not succeed in achieving the potential advantages of job enrichment, and would probably mean that the efficiency and effectiveness of the work force would decline.

(iii) Since there are likely to be some people in many junior grades who do not want extra responsibilities and challenges, and some who do want them, there will probably be problems of co-ordination and co-operation between the motivated and unmotivated employees if a job enrichment programme is implemented.

Those people trying to work harder might have their efforts frustrated by those who do not want to accept greater work responsibilities; and those 'wanting a quiet life' might be irritated by well-motivated colleagues pestering them to do more work than they want to.

(iv) Senior managers might therefore spend much of their time trying to supervise the job enrichment programme, which would defeat the main object of the exercise.

22 OPPORTUNITIES AND THREATS

(a) The environmental opportunities facing banks are economic, technological, social and cultural, and political and legal.

(i) *Economic*

(1) There might be opportunities for expansion into overseas markets, or for the development of banking services for international trade.

(2) There might be opportunities for further expansion into new markets related to banking, such as accountancy services, mortgage business and estate agency work, etc.

(3) If there are prospects for sound economic growth, there might be a growing market for (profitable) business borrowers, and a growth in personal savings.

(ii) *Technological.* The development of information technology provides banks with the potential to:

(1) offer more services to customers;

(2) offer quicker services (and perhaps more reliable services) such as automated teller machines and cash dispensers;

(3) achieve greater staff productivity;

(4) acquire better information about their position (eg their customer foreign exchange exposure) and their customers (eg who are the bank's best or most profitable customers) etc.

(iii) *Social and cultural*

(1) There might be a gradual progress towards more widespread acceptance of banking services amongst the population.

(2) The 'cashless society' is still a long way off, but it is probable that the use of cash will very gradually decline.

(iv) *Political and legal*

(1) There will be opportunities arising overseas from the continuing expansion of the EC and the changes which have taken place and are taking place, in what used to be the Iron Curtain countries.

(2) There might be political pressures for some form of legislation over the banking activities of non-banking organisations, should these develop significantly.

(b) Environmental threats may be considered under the same four headings.

(i) *Economic*

(1) There is the prospect of increasing competition to UK banks from foreign banks.

(2) There is the likelihood that building societies will try to continue to compete very actively for personal savings.

(3) Other firms might begin to compete in traditional banking markets.

(4) There might be the prospect of trade protectionism, which would depress international trade and affect international banking activities adversely.

(ii) *Technological.* The development of information poses threats as well as opportunities:

(1) Non-banking firms might start to offer banking services. This development is already occurring in the USA, and is seen in the UK too.

(2) 'Cash management systems' which are provided by banks to company customers will enable company treasurers to use their funds more profitably which will have an adverse effect on banks' profits.

(3) There might be considerable staff unrest and industrial relations problems as new technology is introduced, because jobs and careers will appear to be threatened.

(4) There might be adverse customer reactions to new automated services.

(5) The introduction of new technology might involve banks in considerable expense.

(iii) *Social and cultural*

(1) There is a possibility that competition for well-educated school-leavers and graduates will become more intense, in spite of high unemployment levels.

(2) Staff might expect more challenging jobs with less dull routine work content.

(3) There might be pressures for a shorter working week if other sectors of industry and commerce pioneer progress in this direction.

(iv) *Political and legal*

(1) There might be political uncertainty about the future of Britain in the EC, or the effect of single European market legislation.

(2) The uncertainty of the international political situation might threaten economic stability and international trade. There is a recognised threat that some countries might default on their debts to overseas / international banks.

(3) There is the continued threat of government intervention in the financial sector of the economy in order to regulate the national economy.

(c) Internal strengths of banks are as follows.

(i) Experience in the provision of banking services.

(ii) A good public image, based on the high integrity of individual banks and of London as a financial centre.

(iii) Banks should have sufficient funds to finance innovation (new services, or services with new technology) and diversification into new markets.

(iv) A reasonably good tradition of industrial relations.

(v) Well-trained staff, with appropriate qualifications.

(vi) The major clearing banks have a large (and valuable) network of domestic branch banks, many in prime sites in towns and cities.

(d) The weaknesses of banks are as follows.

(i) Many members of the public still mistrust banks and are not prepared to keep their money in a bank account.

(ii) Banks no longer have a particularly good public image of caring for the interests of people and society - unlike their competitors, the building societies.

(iii) Many bank employees are unwilling to accept new technology, and are insufficiently trained. Innate conservative traditions in banks create resistance to change.

(iv) It is questionable whether the traditional 'paternalistic' style of leadership by bank management is well-suited to motivating employees.

(v) Although there are opportunities for diversification and innovation, training in banks is no longer sufficient to provide suitably qualified experts. Consequently, recruitment of 'outsiders' will be increasingly necessary (eg of data processing specialists, accountants, and possibly other professional experts such as chartered surveyors, lawyers etc).

(vi) Banks have a bureaucratic structure which might be unsuitable to the dynamic business environment we could expect in the future.

23   OBJECTIVE SETTING

Organisations set objective to assist corporate planning which is the ongoing process of planning a business, ie:

(a)   identifying what business an organisation is in;

(b)   identifying what its objectives should be;

(c)   formulating strategic plans to achieve those objectives. The strategic planning period might be five or ten years, or even longer;

(d)   formulating budget plans within the longer-term corporate planning strategies and objectives;

(e)   formulating operating plans to carry out budget plans and day-to-day activities;

(f)   establishing policies, procedures and rules for the organisation.

In other words, it is the formulation of objectives at all levels of organisational activity.

The *reason why* corporate planning is carried out is that:

(a)   the organisation needs to look at the future, to identify its current direction, and how it may need to change direction to adapt to changes in the environment, ie it needs a sense of purpose, which takes into account possible threats and opportunities in the future; and

(b)   the organisation has to pursue its chosen objectives in an efficient manner, co-ordinating its many components and tasks into a directed effort. Planning provides a framework within which the minutiae of business resources can be integrated.

The strategic component

The strategic component of corporate planning may be divided into three basic stages.

(a)   *Identification of the corporate mission, or purpose:* ie 'What business are we in?' This is deceptively simple: in fact, it may necessitate a fundamental reappraisal of the organisation. The Hollywood film industry, for example, defined itself as being in the movie picture business, and adopted a strategy of competition with TV - with nearly disastrous results. Only after a redefinition of itself as being in the entertainment business did Hollywood realise the vast growth market for its products offered by TV and video.

(b)   *Setting objectives.* Corporate objectives are the broad targets to which the firm as a whole directs its efforts: they should be regularly refined as the environment changes, performance feedback is obtained etc. Objectives might be related to finance (eg profitability, return on capital employed), market position (eg market share, growth of sales), product development (eg quality level at a certain price, develop new range), technology, employment (eg to pay wages above industry average, to reduce labour turnover), organisation (eg to implement MBO, quality circles), or public responsibility (eg to support the local community, improve ecological controls).

These objectives enable management to direct the organisation towards its primary goal; they are the framework for strategies, tactics, budgets etc and the yardstick against which they are measured;

(c) *Strategic planning* - ie formulation of means to reach objectives - the organisational 'game plan'. This will involve identification of the purpose of organisational functions, the nature of the environment (threats, opportunities, stability etc) and the strengths and weaknesses of the organisation itself. The organisation will then be able to decide where its best options lie for fulfilling its objectives: if its objective is profitability, for example, it will still have much to decide about what markets or market segments to operate in, what processes to use, whether to be market-orientated, product-orientated, how resources are to be used etc. Strategic plans will still be in fairly general terms, but should be genuine, identifiable objectives against which actual performance can be measured.

The tactical component

Tactical planning is the next 'stratum' of planning, at functional/departmental level. It develops strategic plans in more detail, by considering the following.

(a) Which alternative courses of action, within the chosen strategy, the organisation should take. Detailed options will be sought, evaluated and selected, using modelling, forecasting, market research etc.

(b) How the resources of the organisation can be used effectively and efficiently in the accomplishment of strategic plans: eg how to allocate resources between different functional activities, how to price a new product etc.

(c) In the pursuit of effectiveness, what performance on budgetary targets should be set: ie, the basic aims, criteria and standards of control systems for operational activities.

(d) Formulation of policies - ie guidelines for response to a range of standard or recurrent eventualities. These guarantee a consistency of response, and save time on decision-making in routine situations.

The operational component

Operational planning is designed to ensure that specific tasks are carried out effectively and efficiently within the defined framework of strategic and tactical plans. Tactics 'harden' into detailed, quantified plans, including:

(a) procedures (ie a chronological sequence of actions required to perform a given task);

(b) rules (specific, definite courses of action that must be taken in a given situation);

(c) programmes (ie co-ordinated groups of plans, procedures, etc);

(d) budgets (ie formal statements of expected results, set out in numerical terms, and summarised in monetary values. Budgets are the 'nitty gritty' of corporate planning, used to allocate resources, set standards and timescales, and compare plan with actual performance).

496

24 MARKETING TO THE UNBANKED

(a) The sections of the community which, in general, do not have a bank account are:

    (i)   weekly wage earners (as distinct from monthly salary earners);

    (ii)   old people, especially pensioners;

    (iii) the unemployed;

    (iv) low income groups;

    (v)   people who rent council houses or flats;

    (vi) wives depending on money from their husbands and child allowance etc for their income;

    (vii) people who left school at the minimum age.

(b) The reason why they are not customers of the banks can perhaps be categorised as follows.

    (i)   They are used to receiving income in cash (wages, pensions, etc) and have the attitude that cash is 'real money', whereas a bank account involves giving money away to the bank and so never actually having it in their possession. A wage earner with a wage packet in his hands might feel 'rich', whereas a cheque book would not give him the same feeling of wealth.

    (ii)   Low income earners might wish to watch over their money and see it being spent. This attitude encourages a preference for holding cash rather than having a bank account.

    (iii) Some people, especially older people in working class communities, have an old fashioned approach to debt and consider it rather shameful to owe money. They would not want to have a bank loan or overdraft, and therefore cannot see any advantage in many services offered by banks. Since current accounts do not generally pay interest, they will see little value in letting banks have their money.

    (iv) It is widely known that there is a substantial 'black economy' where people earn income which is undisclosed to the Inland Revenue authorities. Payments for goods and services in the black economy are necessarily in cash, because transactions by cheque are more likely to be exposed to the Inland Revenue. Some people will therefore avoid bank accounts to preserve secrecy of earnings.

    (v)   Members of low income groups and some racial communities are brought up to mistrust people in the middle classes, and especially financial men. Bankers and accountants are regarded as people who make money out of the work and income of others, and for this reason are 'unfriendly' and not to be trusted.

    (vi) Arguably, there has been little encouragement from banks to persuade people to open a bank account. Opening hours are restricted, and there is a commonly-held belief that banks operate for their own convenience and not for the convenience of customers. In contrast, building societies or the Post Office (Giro) open longer hours and are equally (if not more) accessible to customers. In addition, building societies pay interest on share accounts. An individual with cash to save might be more inclined to put his money into a building society account than into a current account or even a deposit account at a bank. The reason is not just the interest rates offered by the building societies, it is also the 'friendly' and 'helpful' image which building societies have so successfully fostered over the years.

(vii) Uneducated people might feel that bank accounts, cheque books, credit cards etc are too confusing and complicated.

(c) To encourage these groups to become customers of banks, a number of options are open to banks.

(i) Banks should conduct market research into why particular groups of people do not have a bank account, and take steps to overcome the resistance.

(1) If the problem is the unfriendly image of banks, advertising campaigns might be developed which stress the helpful nature of a bank. Unfortunately, 'unfriendly' images must take many years to wipe clean, and the success of some recent campaigns in creating new customers for banking (rather than for a particular bank) has yet to be evaluated.

(2) If the problem is a dislike or mistrust of money men, education of the population is needed. Banking management should perhaps make serious efforts to provide information about banking services through schools (economics courses etc).

(3) If the problem is one of accessibility - ie opening hours which are inconvenient for customers wanting to withdraw cash - the current development of cash points by all the major clearing banks might eventually result in an increase in the number of bank customers.

(ii) Alternatively, banks might find that there is a need for social or economic change before customers are willing to have a bank account. Some aspects of social change cannot be influenced by the policy of banks, but in some respects banks can try to encourage social change to occur.

For example, if people will only open a bank account if they are wealthier, there will have to be an increase in total national wealth before lower income groups find it useful to have a bank account.

On the other hand there are other ways of increasing usage.

(1) Banks can encourage the expansion of credit cards as a means of payment for goods. It has been suggested that the UK will eventually follow the example of the USA, where consumers use credit cards rather than cash. If cash loses its status as 'real money' and 'plastic' money becomes more important, it is certain that more customers will want banking services. They will need a cheque book to settle their credit card bills. Banks are in a position to encourage the development of credit cards, and progress in this direction will probably be the most significant factor in the expansion of the number of customers with bank accounts.

(2) Companies usually consider it more convenient administratively and therefore cheaper, as well as more secure against error, to pay employees through a bank account instead of by cash. Most salary earners are expected to be willing to receive payment of their monthly salary direct into a bank account. In contrast, most wage earners are paid in cash. Since companies themselves will probably

prefer to pay them through the banking system, bank policy should be to encourage companies to persuade wage earners to accept payment in this way. The form of such encouragement might be the provision of an efficient (and cheap) service to companies, or advice on setting up such a system of payment, or help in 'selling' the system to the company's wage earners.

(3) If there is a preference to put earnings into a building society instead of into a bank, banks might choose to offer competitive interest rates to depositors, or even to pay interest on current accounts. This policy would probably only succeed in attracting new customers to banks if it is accompanied by one or more of the other 'enticements' listed above.

25 STAFF STABILITY AND TURNOVER

(a) The main factors influencing the rate of staff turnover are as follows.

(i) The 'climate' or 'culture' of the organisation. Organisations are mostly capable of classification into a bureaucracy (ie an organisation structure based on rules, regulations, job descriptions and a clearly-defined formal hierarchy of authority, responsibility and accountability) or an 'organic' structure, as defined by Burns and Stalker (ie an organisation that is more flexible in structure, where authority and responsibility are less rigidly defined, and there is much more scope for individuals to be creative and innovative, or to share in decision-making). An individual is likely to have a preference for one type of organisation over another (ie for a job with more or less responsibility for the same pay). When individuals decide that the organisation does not suit them, they will leave.

(ii) The age structure and 'culture' of the personnel. It would appear that there is a greater tendency for staff to leave an organisation if they:

(1) are young; or

(2) have been in their job for only a short time; or

(3) are approaching retirement age and would be pleased to accept early retirement if offered to them.

On the other hand, an organisation which recruits people at a young age (eg a bank) and keeps them for a few years will then probably find that labour turnover is low amongst these employees. Organisations which employ middle-aged women (eg women returning to work after their children have grown up) might experience a low staff turnover.

(iii) Pay and conditions of employment. Staff might leave for more money or for better conditions of employment. The extent to which an organisation can offer conditions to meet employees' expectations will determine the level of staff turnover. The conditions of employment will relate to:

(1) 'perks' in addition to basic pay (eg company cars, pension schemes);

(2) physical conditions at work - ie comfort, cleanliness, safety, noise levels, lighting etc;

(3)   the location of work. Labour turnover might be higher in some city centres than in smaller towns, owing to the time it takes to get to work and the high costs of travelling.

(iv)   The state of the national economy and the job market. Labour turnover is likely to fall substantially when it is difficult for would-be leavers to find alternative employment easily.

(v)   The nature of the work itself. Some jobs might be unpleasant to do, so that labour turnover will be high. Jobs which do not provide sufficient interest, incentive or challenge to employees might also lead to greater staff turnover. In other words, the structure and content of jobs might influence turnover rates.

(vi)   Leadership style. The style of leadership can vary from autocratic and disciplinarian to paternalistic to democratic to *laissez faire*. There is no one style of leadership which is necessarily better than others, but employees in a particular type of job might prefer one style to another. A sudden change of leadership style (eg from democratic or authoritarian) might unsettle the work force and lead to higher staff turnover.

(vii)   The strength of trade union influence. Employees might be able to channel their dissatisfaction and grievances through their trade unions, in which case they will be less likely to leave a job when they become annoyed or dissatisfied with aspects of their work. Where trade union representation is weak or non-existent, employees might have no alternative but to leave when they have a grievance.

(viii)   Social relationships at work. Where the 'informal' organisation is strong and employees enjoy their social relationships with other people at work, staff turnover is likely to be low.

(ix)   Training and career development opportunities. Staff turnover is likely to be higher in jobs or organisations where training is not provided, or where opportunities for promotion or career development are restricted. Ambitious employees will be forced to leave such jobs if they are to make a career for themselves.

(b) Stability of staff - ie a low staff turnover - is important for a number of reasons.

(i)   When turnover is high, the morale of the work force might be low. Motivation to achieve targets and performance efficiency will also be low. Poor morale will therefore reduce the efficiency of the organisation.

(ii)   When a trained employee leaves, the organisation loses his skill, training and experience. Employees might be considered 'human assets' and staff turnover represents the loss of valuable assets to the organisation.

(iii)   When staff leave, they must be replaced, and there will be additional costs of recruitment, introduction and training.

(iv)   New recruits will be less efficient than the more experienced people they have replaced, and there will be a temporary fall in efficiency and work quality until the new staff 'learn the ropes' in their job. When staff turnover is high, there will probably be a permanent reduction in general productivity levels and quality of output.

(v)   In jobs where employees have direct contact with customers, customer loyalty might depend on personal relationships with those individuals. When an employee leaves there will be a risk of the customer taking his business elsewhere.

(vi)   There may be a problem of continuity. When a new recruit takes over from a person who has left, he or she might have to carry on doing an unfinished task. He or she might have no information about what has been done so far or might have his or her own ideas about how the job should be done. The consequences might be a lack of continuity in the work (eg a much-publicised example in recent years has been the problem of continuity on social work, where the rate of staff turnover among social workers is high).

INDEX

FURTHER READING

For further question practice on CIB *Management*, BPP has published a companion Practice & Revision Kit. This contains a bank of questions, mostly drawn from past examinations. Fully worked suggested solutions are provided for all questions. The latest edition was published in January 1993 for the old syllabus *Management* Paper and you should note that it does not therefore reflect recent changes.

You may also wish to test your grasp of the subject by tackling short questions in multiple choice format. BPP publish the Password series of books, each of which incorporates over 300 multiple choice questions with solutions, comments and marking guides. The Password title relevant to this paper is *Organisation and Management*. This is priced at £6.95.

To order your Practice & Revision Kit and Password book, ring our credit card hotline on 0181-740 6808. Alternatively, send this page to our Freepost address or fax it to us on 0181-740 1184.

To: BPP Publishing Ltd, FREEPOST, London W12 8BR   **Tel: 0181-740 6808**
Fax: 0181-740 1184

Forenames (Mr / Ms): _____

Surname: _____

Address: _____

_____

Post code: _____   Date of exam (month/year): _____

Please send me the following books:	*Quantity*	*Price*	*Total*
Management in Banking Kit	....	£8.95	....
Password *Organisation and Management*	....	£6.95	....

Please include postage:

UK: £1.50 for first plus £0.50 for each extra book	....	....
Europe (inc ROI): £2.50 for first plus £1.00 for each extra book	....	....
Rest of the World: £4.00 for first plus £2.00 for each extra book	....	....

Total   ....

I enclose a cheque for £ _____ or charge to Access/Visa/Switch

Card number ☐☐☐☐☐☐☐☐☐☐☐☐☐☐☐☐☐☐☐

Start date (Switch only) _____ **Expiry date** _____ **Issue no. (Switch only)** _____

Signature _____

To order any further titles in the CIB range, please use the form overleaf.

ORDER FORM

Any books from our CIB range can be ordered by ringing our credit card hotline on 0181-740 6808. Alternatively, send this page to our Freepost address or fax it to us on 0181-740 1184. *Please note that the Practice & Revision Kits were published in 1993 for all the old syllabus papers and do not therefore reflect recent changes.*

To: BPP Publishing Ltd, FREEPOST, London W12 8BR   **Tel: 0181-740 6808**
Fax: 0181-740 1184

Forenames (Mr / Ms): _____

Surname: _____

Address: _____

_____

Post code: _____   Date of exam (month/year): _____

Please send me the following books:

	Price Text	Kit	Quantity Text	Kit	Total £
Certificate					
Business of Banking	13.95	-	....		....
Business Calculations	13.95	-	....		....
Business Communications	13.95	-	....		....
Economics and the Banks' Role in the Economy	13.95	-	....		....
Introduction to Accounting	13.95	-	....		....
Banking: the Legal Environment	13.95	-	....		....
Supervisory Skills	13.95	-	....		....
Banking Operations	13.95	-	....		....
Customer Services	13.95	-	....		....
Associateship - core					
The Monetary and Financial System	16.95	8.95	....	....	....
Law Relating to Banking Services	15.95	8.95	....	....	....
Accountancy	16.95	8.95	....	....	....
Management [Management]*	16.95	8.95	....	....	....
Associateship - options					
Investment (Text: FA95; Kit: FA92)	16.95	8.95	....	....	....
Branch Banking: Law and Practice	16.95	8.95	....	....	....
Lending	16.95	8.95	....	....	....
Management of Information Technology	16.95	-	....		....
International Trade Finance [Trade Finance, Payments & Services] *	16.95	8.95	....	....	....
Marketing of Financial Services [Marketing] *	16.95	8.95	....	....	....

Please include postage:

UK: Texts £2.50 for first plus £1.00 for each extra	....	....	....
Kits £1.50 for first plus £0.50 for each extra.	....	....	....
Europe (inc ROI): Texts £5.00 for first plus £4.00 for each extra	....	....	....
Kits £2.50 for first plus £1.00 for each extra.	....	....	....
Rest of the World: Texts £7.50 for first plus £5.00 for each extra	....	....	....
Kits £4.00 for first plus £2.00 for each extra.	....	....	....
Total			....

I enclose a cheque for £ _____ **or charge to Access/Visa/Switch**

Card number ☐☐☐☐ ☐☐☐☐ ☐☐☐☐ ☐☐☐☐ ☐☐☐☐

Start date (Switch only) _____ **Expiry date** _____ **Issue no. (Switch only)** _____

Signature _____   [* Name of old syllabus paper: Kit only]

REVIEW FORM - CIB: Management (10/95)

Name: _____

How have you used this Text?

Home study (book only)	☐	With 'correspondence' package	☐
On a course: college_____	☐	Other_____	

How did you obtain this Text?

From us by mail order	☐	From us by phone	☐
From a bookshop	☐	From your college	☐

Where did you hear about BPP Texts?

At bookshop	☐	Recommended by lecturer	☐
Recommended by friend	☐	Mailshot from BPP	☐
Advertisement in _____	☐	Other _____	

Have you used the companion Kit for this subject?   **Yes/No**

Your comments and suggestions would be appreciated on the following areas

Syllabus coverage

Illustrative questions

Errors (please specify, and refer to a page number)

Structure and presentation

Other

Please return to: BPP Publishing Ltd, FREEPOST, London W12 8BR